# Great Economic Thinkers from Antiquity to the Historical School

Bertram Schefold is renowned for his distinctive approach to the history of economic thought. This book brings together commentaries from his series *Klassiker der Nationalökonomie* (Classics of Economics), which have been translated into English for the first time. Schefold's choice of authors for the series, which he has edited since 1991, and his comments on the various re-edited works are proof of his highly original and thought-provoking interpretation of the history of economic thought. This seminal volume shows that study of the history of economic thought should be explored far beyond its most widely known figures.

This selection focuses on notable, but neglected writers, localizing the beginning of economic science not with Adam Smith, but with the moral question of usury and the good life in Antiquity. The volume takes a global perspective, with its coverage including the German Historical School, mercantilist Spain and Arab and Asian classics of economic thought.

This book will give the reader a far broader view of economics than has previously been available, and is written with the aim of achieving a universal history of the subject. The volume is suitable for those who are interested in and study history of economic thought as well as economic theory and philosophy.

**Bertram Schefold** is Professor of Economics at Johann Wolfgang Goethe-University, Frankfurt, Germany.

# Routledge Studies in the History of Economics

*For a full list of titles in this series, please visit www.routledge.com.*

# Great Economic Thinkers from Antiquity to the Historical School

Translations from the series *Klassiker der Nationalökonomie*

**Bertram Schefold**

Routledge
Taylor & Francis Group

LONDON AND NEW YORK

First published 2016
by Routledge

2 Park Square, Milton Park, Abingdon, Oxfordshire OX14 4RN
52 Vanderbilt Avenue, New York, NY 10017

*Routledge is an imprint of the Taylor & Francis Group, an informa business*

First issued in paperback 2019

*British Library Cataloguing in Publication Data*
A catalogue record for this book is available from the British Library

*Library of Congress Cataloging in Publication Data*
A catalog record for this book has been requested

ISBN: 978-0-415-43066-1 (hbk)
ISBN: 978-0-367-86443-9 (pbk)

Typeset in Times New Roman
by Taylor & Francis Books

# Contents

# Illustrations

## Figures

## Tables

# Preface

This book documents a large research project in the history of economic thought. It contains a planned, coherent and amended selection of my introductions to the commentary volumes of the *Klassiker der Nationalökonomie*, translated into English. As explained in more detail below (in the Introduction), the Klassiker series was composed of 100 facsimile editions of classical texts of economics, the facsimile being that of the first edition (in some cases, for texts older than the invention of printing, the facsimile was that of a manuscript). Each text was accompanied by a volume of commentaries, to which I usually had written an introduction. The focus is on the continental tradition, in a German perspective, but with a wide temporal and spatial horizon, going from antiquity to the twentieth century, and including not only European, but also Arab and East Asian authors; they were chosen according to criteria which also are explained in the Introduction below, together with the history of the edition of the Klassiker. The initiative to have the essays translated came from the late Mark Perlman who thought that these texts might provide an insight into currents which are alternatives to the Anglo-Saxon tradition. A selection had first been made by Volker Caspari; it was edited as 'Beiträge zur ökonomischen Dogmengeschichte. Ausgewählt und herausgegeben von Volker Caspari' (Schefold 2004a). Here, for the English version, the moderns (classical, neoclassical, Keynesian schools) are treated in a separate edition (forthcoming 2016); introductory and documentary material has been added. Thus the reader can form an opinion on the programme of the Klassiker-series as a whole (the complete list of the series is found in the Appendix). The series, to the extent that it resulted from my choices, but especially this selection of introductions, reflect my special interest in the modern revival of classical economic thought, which offers a rigorous theory of value, but is open with respect to historically changing influences on distribution, demand and employment. Where others have only mentioned the importance of social, political and historical factors on economic development, I have increasingly sought to integrate the economic with historical and cultural approaches and demonstrated that the same endeavour can be observed in the normative economics of antiquity and the Middle Ages, in the intensely political texts of mercantilism and cameralism, and that the historical schools (in the widest sense, including Marx) continued this tradition as an inter-disciplinary approach, combining economic, sociological, historical and legal considerations, even psychology and cultural studies. German ordoliberalism is an heir to this tradition, despite its rejection of historicism and its reliance on neoclassical modelling, especially in the case of Eucken. Neoclassical theory offers more partial insights, founded on more restrictive assumptions and models.

I first shrank away when Mark Perlman asked me to translate the essays, because of the time it would take, but also, because I felt that I was not up to the task. It is one thing to write, as I have often done, in a foreign language on matters of pure theory, where the vocabulary is given, and another on cultural matters. In these essays I felt free to use a more literary prose, since the Klassiker-series addressed a more general public. In the end, Mark Perlman provided a generous grant from the Earhardt-Foundation to pay for the translation.

The book thus has been translated not by myself, but by Staci von Boeckmann and Stephen Starck, with the exception of a few essays translated by Keith Tribe, who also revised all texts. My former assistants Sebastian Beck, Marion Hackenthal, Jan Hermann, Christian Klamer, Jens Reich, Susanne Rühle and Christian Schmidt each read some of the texts critically and helped to check the references, in particular providing the standard English versions or translations of texts quoted in German in the original work. Secretarial work was provided by Reinhild Spieß and Erna Jeganathan. In the end, I read and corrected the entire manuscript. I should like to thank the Earhardt-Foundation, the translators and my collaborators for all the efforts they have undertaken.

Languages are to the historian of economic thought as indispensible as mathematics to the theorist and statistics to the econometrician. I have insis-ted that occasionally a quote be left in the original language, to give colour to the wording; translations of these quotes can be found in the notes. In the German edition, by contrast, most quotes were given in the original language (Greek and Latin, English, French and Italian). But in the case of the Arab and East-Asian authors I had entirely to rely on translations.

To work on the Klassiker was delightful, and the tasks were manifold. Here it was a question of understanding the logic of an argument, or model, and to help to provide an analytical reconstruction. There it was a matter of clarifying the historical context, trying to learn about historical facts, about predecessors, about the intellectual atmosphere of the time. Occasionally, it became necessary to study an old historical manuscript. The facsimile published in the case of *De Moneta* by Oresme, for instance, was based on a beautiful, handwritten and illuminated manuscript; and this manuscript version, a century younger than the text, had to be compared to the modern printed editions of other manuscripts in Latin and French of the *De Moneta*; I was proud to find one significant emendation after five weeks of close reading. But the main pleasure did not consist in such detail; it arose from the slowly and steadily growing awareness of the immense riches and the variety of the ideas which make up the history of economic thought. The experience led me to hope that, as we multiply the economic problems of the modern word, we shall also be able to solve them. It would give me the greatest satisfaction, if I could convey the variety of these ideas in an ordered form to my readers, so as to share the fruits of discovery.

I was tempted to transform this book into a more complete collection of my essays in the history of economic thought, in particular by including more of the essays written for the Klassiker-series and by adding essays I wrote as introductions to another series, the economic texts in *Historia Scientiarum*, a collection of rare and neglected, but important works in the history of German science. A prime example is the *De Aerario* by Kaspar Klock of 1651, a comprehensive and voluminous work on taxation and finance which contains a description of virtually all the countries of the world with their natural resources, their history and customs and with their financial systems (Schefold 2009). Another example is the *Traité de la richesse des princes* by Ernst Ludwig Carl of 1722, a German cameralist who wrote in French and anticipated physiocratic ideas (Kunze and Schefold 2000). A third example is *Die Theorie der Nationalwirthschaft* by Georg von Buquoy, Count in Bohemia, who also wrote in German and was remarkable as a mathematical economist, with a formalization of the Smithian theory of value and a kind of qualitative input-output table, published 1815–1818 (Baloglou and Schefold 2005). In the end, I decided here to retain the focus on the Klassiker-series, for this project involved the collaboration of many eminent economists. My hope to have all the contents in the commentary volumes translated and published in English, as a collection or, as in German, together with the facsimile editions, could not be realized, no publisher being prepared to take the risk. This work then is a substitute, but I should like to remember the first editors Wolfram Engels, Herbert Hax, Friedrich A. von Hayek and Horst Claus Recktenwald, and to thank Karl-Dieter Grüske and Arnold Heertje who became co-editors later. A special thanks goes to Michael Tochtermann, the publisher from beginning to end.

Frankfurt am Main
April 2014
Bertram Schefold

# Introduction

## 1 From the history of economic analysis to a universal history of economic thought

Academic disciplines have surprisingly different histories, some extending over thousands of years, others only over a few decades. They all have institutional aspects – some disciplines originated in universities, others are rooted in the works of practitioners – but the principal interest almost always concerns the evolution of their contents. Teachers and students wish to know how the present state of knowledge has come about. Like their colleagues in other faculties, academic economists usually take pride in the history of their theory. They regard the analytical history of economics as a history of progress. The actual state of economics provides the measure of importance for earlier ideas, which, directly or indirectly, contributed to the achievement of the present state of the art. The endeavours of the past are interesting, but only to the extent that they help to explain how progress was made (Niehans 1990).

The analytical approach is primarily concerned with economic phenomena which occurred, or could have occurred, in all phases of human history. However, in subsequent approximations even pure theory makes assumptions about the existence of specific institutions which influence economic development such as the status of the worker, the form of the wage contract or the existence of futures markets. A relativist approach emphasizes such differences and tries to relate them to specific stages of economic evolution. Most economists probably are predominantly materialists, in that they ascribe a determining role to the level of technology, and accept only a moderate importance of cultural factors as autonomous forces shaping institutions and affecting behaviour. Marx (1974) was convinced that the perception which members of social strata have and the ideological conceptions used to express them can be derived from the economic context in which they find themselves.[1] He even thought that the real scientific task was to show how these conceptions necessarily arise as false appearances, and to confront them with a true picture of actual relationships, for example by proving that exploitation, not abstinence, explained profits. Revealing the inner contradictions of the system would provide insight into the nature of its inevitable future transformations. One opposite view is that market relationships are more efficient and will prevail, that distribution under capitalism can be fair, and that no major transformation of the fundamental economic structure is to be expected, while it is not denied that such fundamental changes had occurred in the past. All relativists thus admit that the perception of economic phenomena, hence all thinking about them, changes with historical conditions, even if such perceptions differ over causal relations. Progress remains important for the relativist position, in that ideas are considered characteristic of their time. And progress moves on different planes, as practical and theoretical knowledge in institutions and organizations, even as moral progress.

One objection to the materialist interpretation of history is that it does not leave room for the creative power of political, social and religious movements. Is it really possible to look only at the formal economic institutions if we want to understand the difference between, say, early imperial Rome and Medieval Italy, or Medieval North Africa (Maghreb)? Even if the economic historian may have much to say about such differences without discussing paganism, Christianity and Islam, this will be quite impossible for the historian of economic thought. The texts that we encounter here are not very interesting as pieces of rudimentary economic analyses, although in each case we would find evidence that people had understood some economic mechanisms, for instance, advantages of the division of labour. Such texts are also only of limited interest to the economist if they are read as expressions of their times (from the perspective of a relativist) – our perceptions are always limited by what we learn from others, from tradition, and they depend on where we find a field of action. The texts are really interesting only if we recognize a 'political' dimension and try to interpret them as expressions of the will to shape, to preserve or to change the world – and even the interpretation of economic and social reality by the philosopher serves that goal. The will to change can mean a wish to maintain an order, or to revert to an older one, and it can also mean what Marx intended: the transformation of the present for the sake of the realization of an ideal (which he regarded as inevitable).

Economic texts in particular are written in order to act on reality, or to make such action possible, or to demonstrate the fruitlessness of such action as planned by others. Often, external constraints are invoked to let a desired course of action appear as inevitable. We understand texts by identifying with the concerns of the authors and their contemporaries. We therefore must be ready to bear the tension between contrasting visions of the world; we must enter the hermeneutical circle of understanding the expressions in the text and recreate their vision, visions for whose realization the texts are written, and in turn the visions are interpreted to provide a better understanding of the expressions. We thus have to use texts and their concepts to reconstruct the meaning of the historical situation; historical research helps us to gain improved understanding of these concepts. There are many examples, but I may mention three which I have found challenging, and which are sufficiently simple for a short exposition.

The Epicurean Philodem, a contemporary of Cicero, lectured on the material preconditions for the good life of a philosopher. He explained that it was difficult for a philosopher to have the necessary leisure for thinking, if one had to work to make a living; the philosopher needed the benefit of a substantial legacy. But even if one had a fortune, one should not seek to increase it, but live on the revenue it could generate, by letting houses or slaves for morally unobjectionable purposes. Better than this was to own an estate, for landlords can gather in the countryside and engage in learned and pleasurable discussions. But, he concluded, it was best for the philosopher to live on the stipends paid to him by his students, provided his lectures were good and honest 'neither hair-splitting nor cantankerous' (Schefold 1999a). (The Epicurean advice to the modern academic thus is: Do not try to arouse interest by being overly sophisticated, critical and quarrelsome.)

The Medieval churchmen were opposed to such a philosophy of pleasure. With regard to income not earned by one's own work, in particular with regard to usury, their distinctions grew subtler towards the late middle Ages. Azpilcueta is my second example.[2] He recognized the legitimacy of taking interest if an opportunity cost existed. However, the opportunity cost had to be real in the sense that one was actually prevented from working with one's capital only because one had lent it. If a moneychanger lent some of his own capital and received interest, it was not usury as long as the moneychanger had to interrupt – and did interrupt – his activity of money-changing for lack of capital. But if he had enough capital left to continue his operations and did work, the opportunity cost could not be recognized, and interest-taking then was usury.

Ibn Khaldūn, the great Arab historian, philosopher and lawyer, who lived mainly in Northern Africa and met with Timur in 1401 at Damascus, wrote in his Muqqadima about the nomadic tribes of the desert who are able, because of their solidarity, to conquer towns which represent a more advanced culture.[3] Their chief becomes the ruler of the town and founds a dynasty. To begin with, so long as the modest lifestyle of the tribe is preserved, the rulers remain just, handicraft and agricultural work in the surroundings flourish, and the economy grows. As successive rulers learn to indulge in a more luxurious lifestyle, they feel compelled to raise more taxes, and the economic burden of a decadent and corrupt elite leads to their economic downfall. The town is ripe for a new assault by a fresh tribe who appears from the desert. The economy is thus subject to a cyclical movement, imposed by the logic of political, social and economic development; only knowledge will continue to increase, however spasmodically.

Economic ideas of this type may have some general meaning, but they impress us as coherent characterizations of a culturally and historically definite context. If there were nothing analogous with our lives we should not be impressed. We also feel, like the Epicureans, that the philosopher needs leisure, although it would be politically incorrect to take Philodem's stance explicitly. We also feel, like the scholastic, that unearned incomes are something of a problem, or that the theory of generations continues to hold and applies to ruling dynasties, hence, like the Arab historian, we accept fate and the up and down of just and unjust domination. But the general here is somewhat trivial, while the specific fascinates: historical realities which we glimpse, hoping to learn more. All three cases ask how economic arrangements serve to sustain or prevent certain forms of life; to this extent there is a political element. The difficulty lies in understanding the meaning of such texts, both as regards the concepts used and the aims for which they were written. This political element is most visible in the relationship between the economy and the state, hence in public finance, where there are enormous contrasts, like between the liturgy system of classical Athens and the modern system of compulsory taxation, each associated with different forms of democracy, but also with visibly different effects of expenditure on culture.[4]

We thus have moved from the conventional history of economic analysis to the history of economic ideas, embedded in cultural contexts, and ask how this field of investigation may be demarcated. None of the three texts we have mentioned was written as a contribution to economics as a discipline; they are pre-modern in that they were conceived at a time when an economic subsystem had not yet been separated from other subsystems of social activities. We recognize economic elements, using either the formal or the material definition of economics, hence two modern conceptions. We are therefore in danger of viewing, interpreting and indeed evaluating the history of economic thought teleologically, by asking, as in the history of economic analysis, which developments led to the formation of the modern view of an economic subsystem.

The temptation to place ourselves as the goal of all hitherto existing history will never be completely resisted, but there is another criterion to judge the value of past economic ideas which avoids this teleological perspective. We may ask whether the authors under consideration explain their own situation satisfactorily, especially the interaction between their economic problems and their socio-political life and goals as expressed in a religious or political programme. If this question is not sufficient to liberate us completely from the teleological perspective, since we tend to interpret programs and designs with reference to our situation, it will at least help us to gain an understanding, which is not dominated by the perspective of progress.

Caution with respect to the teleological perspective is also important because a history of economic ideas, as here broadly conceived, is necessarily a universal history, a world history by intention. Whether this universal history can actually be written depends on the texts which can be found. Economic problems in a rather concrete form may have been among the first on which man reflected, but among the latest to be formulated in specific treatises.

The teleological perspective is mistaken in principle because we cannot know whether the outcome, the modern world, was a necessary and inevitable development, or whether other historical paths would still have been possible at the time when early economic ideas were formulated. Without the industrial revolution in Europe there might have been no such event at all, or there might have been one elsewhere, in other conditions, with other outcomes. If the proto-capitalist development in Japan had overtaken that of Great Britain, early Japanese development would be regarded as the model for the path to modernization.[5]

The history of economic ideas that are not derived directly or indirectly from the Judeo-Hellenic tradition has only recently begun to be discussed at an international level, and a universal history has not yet emerged for this field. The idea of a world history in general is an old one. In Schiller's famous essay 'Was heißt und zu welchem Ende studiert man Universalgeschichte?' ['What is universal history, and for what purpose does one study it?'] (Schiller 2000), he thought it a philosophical endeavour to study the histories of different cultures, still believing however that the modern European world was to the less developed nations what adults are to children. It was only in the twentieth century that universal histories were written that emphasized the diversity of cultures, without recourse to an idea of linear progress which ordered them hierarchically and which emphasized the similarities between non-European cultures, like that of imperial China at the times of the Han dynasty and of imperial Rome. Toynbee (1976) was perhaps the most famous representative of a movement which endeavoured to overcome the Euro-centricity of general history.

No Toynbee has appeared so far in the history of economic thought. There are pragmatic reasons: the history of economic thought is not regarded as sufficiently interesting to warrant the effort necessary to overcome the language barriers, enhanced by the fact that it is often not sufficient to understand the modern language in order to read old texts.[6] But there is also the more sub-stantial reason that Euro-centricity imposes itself so easily for economists trained to study the economic problems of the modern world. This field of research therefore is open, and I only want to indicate that it might uncover a paradox: it could be that the economic thought of other cultures might reveal a better understanding of the integration of economic, social and political forces because those cultures remained more homogeneous in regard to their fundamental structures than the European tradition in which social control of the economic was less secure, so that the transition to the modern society was unhindered. We shall see in this book, for example, that Chinese economic thought was very much concerned with the degree to which trade should be controlled: ideologically, through the state, which acted as a proxy, and through stratification, which lent scholars a high rank. In fact, a certain reserve with respect to traders seems almost a general phenomenon among stratified pre-modern cultures.

The denunciation of usury is central only to the religions and schools of economic thought which are heir to the Judeo-Hellenic tradition, and the form of the denunciation signifies that the direct control of trade was weak. One often finds that the significance of the self-interpretation of pre-modern societies, as expressed in what we here class as their economic thought, is underestimated, because the texts seem imprecise, lack quantitative data and remain ideologically biased. It could be doubted whether our fundamental ideas are better, in view of the discrepancy between modern aspirations to provide for the future and actual outcomes. But how little we know about the economic past without such self-interpretations becomes clear if we compare our knowledge of societies for which we have only an archaeological record with others from which we have literary texts, examples of the former being early Meso-American cultures, examples of the latter the city-states of ancient Greece.

These self-interpretations differ in quality, as the examples show. Philodem is justly little known, for what he says about economic matters is hardly more than the expression of the attitude of the hedonistic philosopher. A more detailed rendering of Azpilcueta's treatises shows the work of a very sophisticated intellect who is able to conceptually organize complex economic problems (quantity theory, theories of the exchange rate), but there is no concern for broader questions of economic development; his only problem is that of separating legitimate from illegitimate forms of interest taking. In his integrated view of how the economy interacts with social and political forces Ibn Khaldūn is one of the greatest authors in the discipline of all times.

## 2  Classics of economic thought: a canon

We have discussed three approaches to the history of economic thought, termed positivistic, relativistic and political. They can be combined; the chapters of this book contain examples of all three. I have expressed my sympathy for relativism and for uncovering the political dimension in the economic discourse. The endeavour to work towards a universal history of economic thought was reflected in the Klassiker-series, but only in the small way of adding editions of three Eastern and Near-Eastern classics; Chayanov as a pioneer in the application of formal economic analysis to pre-capitalist forms of production was included in this group. It now must be explained how the broader canon of the series was created.

The series Klassiker der Nationalökonomie ('classics of economics') was begun in 1986, its first managing editor being Horst Recktenwald. I became his successor in 1991. 100 facsimile editions of classical texts were published, each accompanied by a volume of commentaries written by international specialists. The main volumes are facsimiles of the first edition, if one exists, of the corresponding works. In a few cases, an early manuscript was reproduced. In the beginning, the choice of the texts was not so difficult, since the most 'classic' among the classical texts had to be reproduced; the series predictably started with a reprint of the first edition of the *Wealth of Nations* by Adam Smith. But the choice grew more and more difficult as time went by and it became the tantalizing task of defining a canon for the history of economic thought, when it had been decided that the series would comprise neither more nor less than 100 volumes.

The canon that resulted (see Appendix) can be analysed according to different criteria. A simple one is languages; they were Greek, Latin, German, English, French, Italian, Spanish, Arabic, Chinese and Japanese, and translations were offered for the Greek, Arabic, Japanese and Chinese texts. The two Far Eastern classics were partially translated into German for the first time on this occasion, all translations being included in the corresponding commentary volumes. Russia was represented by one, Scandinavia by three works, which had first been written in German. Pinto, a Dutch Jew, wrote in French. In this way, it was possible to include works from countries, whose languages are little known in Germany. I spent some time looking for a Byzantine classic, without finding a satisfactory solution.

According to periods, one can distinguish the economic thought of Antiquity (Xenophon), of the Middle Ages (Thomas of Aquinas), Mercantilism (Serra and Petty) and Cameralism (Becher and Hörnigk), Physiocracy (Quesnay) and classical period (Smith, Ricardo), historical school (Roscher, Hildebrand, Schmoller) and institutionalism (Commons), neo-classicism (Böhm-Bawerk) and Keynesianism (Keynes), but the classics outside the European tradition do not easily fit into such categories.

We also wished to represent the sub-disciplines, therefore ethics (Aristotle, Berkeley and Max Weber), theory of prices (Cournot), theories of growth (Mill), monetary theory (Knies, Keynes), monetary policy (Bagehot), finance (Stein, Wicksell), agricultural economics (Chayanov), theory of games (von Neumann and Morgenstern), statistics (Süßmilch), technology (Babbage). Liberalism is widely represented in its different forms, beginning with ante-cedents in Antiquity (Cicero), with the great exponents of the classical period (Smith, Ricardo), of the neo-classics (Gossen, Jevons, Menger, Walras, Marschall) down to ordoliberalism (Müller-Armack, Röpke, Eucken), but early Socialism (Saint-Simon), German 'Katheder-Sozialismus' (Wagner) and Marxism (Marx, Hilferding) also were represented.

Histories of economic thought were included (Roscher). As for different forms of exposition, monographs dominated, but there are also dialogues (Xenophon, the Chinese classic), satirical expositions (Mandeville), collections of questions and answers (Berkeley), and several controversies. The German 'Münzstreit' documents the first debate about an economic problem which we have in the form of printed pamphlets, the collection of the corn-law pamphlets shows the origin of the theory of rent and of its early political applications, the debate on returns to scale in the Economic Journal shows how modern con-troversies take place in journals. Paul Samuelson, with his 'Foundations of Economic Analysis', was the only living contributor. This is not the place to present a full discussion of the canon. The choice clearly had to correspond to a multidimensional set of criteria, and problems like that of the availability of good editions and of marketability could not be ignored entirely.

In the end, three authors not belonging to the European tradition had been included, one being Ibn Khaldūn, whom we have mentioned. Three are few, if one considers world population or the availability of texts, but it was a pioneer effort in view of the fact that almost all books on the history of economic thought to this day remain centred around the European tradition.

## 3 Some remarks on the introductions to the Klassiker-series selected for this book

The historian of economic thought who turns from modern economics to pre-modern authors, prior to mercantilism, first looks in vain for systematic causal analysis and gets the impression that they uniformly condemned the profit motive and demanded instead a dedication to some form of communitarian spirit with reasonings which differ according to the philosophical foundations – socratics, hedonists, stoics, etc. Closer reading reveals that the various schools of philosophy also differed with regard to economic matters, although they shared some fairly common conceptions. Of all the texts of antiquity which have come down to us in more than fragmentary form, those by Xenophon are probably the closest to modern economic thought. They were widely read during the renaissance. On the one hand, they were probably quite influential for the formation of modern economic thought in two ways. His account of the interdependence between the division of labour and the size of the market influenced Adam Smith via his predecessors. Other insights may have influenced mercantilist and early classical authors in that he had his way of formulating the problem of returns, of diminishing returns in agriculture and of constant returns in handicraft production – the number of artisans adapts to demand in each branch. On the other hand, Xenophon belongs to the Socratic tradition, emphasized the duty to be dedicated to work, praised the life of the farmer and husbandry, and shared the idea that commercial activity might threaten the cohesion of the city; it was there, it was needed, but it was no noble pursuit.

This antagonism was famously described by Aristotle with his distinction between natural and chrematistic forms of acquisition, the former being the main basis for the life of the citizens of a democratic polis, the latter also being necessary for the state – what would Athens have been without maritime trade – but not to be recommended as an activity for the young Athenian attending his lectures. The second essay attempts to represent the Aristotelian position as the philosophical expression of an understanding of the Greek life form which in Athens was shaped by the archaic, even Homeric tradition, earlier expressed in the form of myth and poetry, now, in the last years of free Athenian democracy, in the form of logical discourse in the schools where the young men were educated.

Virtues are the ideals which are formulated in order to set goals for the process of education. Some can be taught, others are primarily gifts, which must be praised so as to promote the worthy. Some virtues like liberality have economic significance. They were discussed by all the schools. They placed different emphasis on different ideals. The cynics were for poverty, the Epicureans for comfort and the avoidance of pain, the peripatetics (Aristotle) for moderate wealth, the stoics for the recognition of one's true self-interest which consisted in one's submission to a preordained order of the world (this latter idea was to form the basic model for Adam Smith). The Roman orator, statesman and philosopher Cicero had studied the Greek philosophical schools in Athens and created his own synthesis, intent to lead to practical solutions. His *De officiis* was enormously influential in the renaissance, in an attempt to identify the rights and the duties of the honest citizen of the state.

If three works were to be chosen to represent antiquity, Xenophon, Aristotle and Cicero still seem to me to be the ideal choice (why I preferred Cicero to one of the agrarian writers is explained below). The main author to be chosen for the Middle Ages would have been Thomas of Aquinas, but he had been edited by Recktenwald. Azpilcueta was one of his greatest successors as far as the debate on usury is concerned, and he was chosen to represent authors of the Iberian peninsula – he was a Bask, called 'El Navarro' – and he was edited, paired with Ortiz, the first great mercantilist with a clear perspective of development. It may seem paradoxical that the chapter on mercantilism thus begins with an introduction to Azpilcueta and Ortiz, therefore with a discussion of scholastic economic thought. In my opinion, this could be justified not only in this individual constellation, but in principle, because the mercantilists owed more to the scholastics than they were ready to admit in references. I am convinced that the great Petty in particular owed much more to his Jesuit education than he would acknowledge in his writings, partly because he opposed the learned style of the scholastics with their many citations – modern thought should not derive from authority, he insisted – partly because of his puritan environment. In the end, to be honest, the pairing of Azpilcueta and Ortiz had more to do with the pragmatic consideration that the two Spanish pamphlets taken together might form a nice volume. Ortiz was theoretically far less sophisticated than Petty and not at the height of scholastic intelligence, but rich in his vision of developmental possibilities. He is paired with one of the sharp minds of the scholastic tradition.

Given that Aquinas had to be excluded, the first medieval author presented is Oresmius, the bishop of Orême, whose theory of money and coinage, rediscovered by Roscher in the nineteenth century, is an amazingly coherent theoretical text which induces much historical speculation about the rights and duties of a king and the requirements of a solid monetary system as the reader will see. Money was mainly based on coinage for 2,500 years, from the sixth century BC down to the nineteenth century, and these monetary systems were more complicated than modern fiat-money, because there was typically a circulation of gold, silver and copper alloys. The intrinsic value of the metals was variable, whether we think of their cost of production or their scarcity. It repeatedly happened that the precious metals became scarce so that there was a tendency towards a deflation in terms of gold and/or silver coins and simultaneously a tendency towards inflation in terms of the copper coins which were issued in excess by the princes in order to pay for their soldiers or servants. This could be corrected by devaluing the copper coins relative to the silver coins, as happened in Roman times (Diocletian) or in the nineteenth century (Goethe, as a minister, once was asked to give advice on such a monetary crisis in the dukedom of Weimar). Oresmius, however, was a fanatic adherent of the principle that each coin, be it of gold, of silver or of copper, circulate at its intrinsic value, and seigniorage only should reflect the cost of minting and, except in exceptional circumstances, should not be used to raise revenue for the prince.

The subsequent chapter is concerned with discussions about economic and primarily monetary matters during the Reformation, based on Saxon pamphlets of 1530 and 1531, the oldest discussion of problems of political economy in the form of printed pamphlets we know of. The controversy is little known outside Germany and may be of special interest to the Anglo-Saxon reader. One of the pamphleteers, the Catholic, advocated the circulation of silver coins, minted from Saxon silver, to be issued at the cost of production of the coins, believing that this would help the country to prosper and that it was good for Saxony to depend on the export of silver and silver coins for its trade with other German and European countries. His opponent, the Protestant, deplored the mercantilist policies of foreigners who exported luxury goods to Saxony in order to obtain Saxon silver. He accused England, Portugal, Venice of trying to rob Saxony of its wealth by selling unnecessary luxury goods which, the Protestant thought, was morally problematic and bad for domestic Saxon production by artisans and peasants. He hoped to hinder such trade by minting debased coins in limited quantity, so as to avoid inflation and render the export of such coins unprofitable. This approach represented a curious combination of conservative (the aversion against luxury imports) and progressive (the early identification of mercantilist policies) ideas. In this context, Konrad Peutinger is also discussed who professed strikingly modern conceptions about free competition (for the large merchants and against the policy of the guilds) and opposed his plea for free competition to the tendency of the German parliament (Reichstag) to decree laws against monopoly.

This chapter ends with a text on the greatest of the late scholastics, Lessius. With supreme clarity and intelligence, he represents the watershed between the Thomasian tradition of treating justice as the leading virtue, the main column of the political and social order, and the beginnings of an exact analysis of markets so as to find not only the just price of commodities, but also rules for the maintenance of competition in the face of the temptation to grant monopoly privileges and, above all, a rational treatment of money, capital and the rate of interest. As an observer of the stock exchange of Antwerp, the predecessor of Amsterdam and London, he accepted that there were opportunity costs for any lender able to invest his capital in stocks; insofar interest was licit. He recognized that the holding of cash balances was necessary for merchants and traders, hence he recognized a form of liquidity preference. The critique of usury was maintained in principle but in practice restricted to a denunciation of the small money lenders in the countryside who claimed excessive interest rates. Lessius formulates a number of principles of modern economics in his traditional language. One is thus tempted to say that modern economic theory, as developed in Europe, received one of its main stimuli from the prohibition of usury, combined with a scientific rationalism and the will to confront the realities of emergent capitalism. To explain profit became the principle task because profit taking had been denounced. In particular, interest was considered as unnatural in the Aristotelian tradition. This was a more specific accusation than the disdain of commerce so frequent among aristocracy all over the world. The example of Lessius shows that the scholastic prolongation of Aristotelian thought resulted in this remarkable turnaround. In the end, capitalism emerged as an order thought to be natural.

As already stated, the chapter of the mercantilists, who lived in the same period as Lessius, opens with the juxtaposition of Azpilcueta and Ortiz, an early Iberian scholastic and an early Spanish mercantilist. The other mercantilists discussed in this book form a very colourful and varied group. The Neapoletan Serra, with his remarkable insights about external and internal returns to scale, monetary circulation and the trade balance, was the first to identify economics as a special discipline, distinct from law or philosophy, but he failed to invent a name for it. Savary's treatise follows an established pattern as a text as on how the young are to be educated to take up jobs in commerce, but is unique in its worldwide success based on his position as an advisor to the government for the establishment of commercial law in France under Colbert; the spontaneous order created by the merchants became the principle of legislation through him. Hörnigk's book, similarly successful in the German speaking area, formulated the program for developing the Habsburg monarchy into a unified national state, based on a program of economic integration. Petty's political arithmetic represents the most remarkable attempt of the mercantilists to provide quantitative empirical foundations for their developmental programs. Justi was a pioneer in transforming cameralism into an academic discipline, advocating a schooling of the economic experts according to the industries in which they were to be employed (mining, commerce, etc.), so as to render development a systematic effort, with a rational build-up of infrastructure, organization of public finance and general education.

I see a great deal of continuity between German cameralism and the German historical school, as indicated in the preface above. Smithianism made economists in Germany aware that they shared his belief in the power of the market to let industrial enterprise flourish, but they thought that some governance by the state was necessary to bring growth about: that private education would not suffice, that nascent industry needed some support were ideas voiced not only by Friedrich List, but already by Sartorius, the very translator of Smith's Magnum opus. When the historical school actually formed around 1840, Hildebrand looked to the market for the solution of the social problem and criticized what he saw as utopian errors on the part of the communists, among whom Marx began to get a name. He identified rules and institutions which would help to set the power of the market free, like investment in education (universities), infrastructure (railroads) and credit for small business. His theory of stages was based on the advances made possible by the progress in the institutions of money and credit. Roscher is represented with two books, his Ansichten with essays containing a programmatic view of the researches to be undertaken by the historical school and some specific essays on economic crises, and his history of economics in Germany, learned and with notable discoveries, which tries to trace a lineage of German economic thought from the late Middle Ages to the nineteenth century. The existence of the historical school did not preclude more analytical approaches like that by von Mangoldt, whom Marshall regarded very highly as a precursor, almost like von Thünen. Another important theorist, even mathematical theorist, of economics was Launhardt, who was best known for the backward bending supply curve, which represented a rational explanation of what others considered a traditional attitude: to work less when wage rates rose, since fewer working hours then sufficed to meet given needs. The chapter contains an introduction to Knies' book on money. Knies, earlier among the founders of the historical school, had very famous pupils at the University of Heidelberg, among whom Böhm-Bawerk and Wieser, later prominent in the Austrian school. Knies was open for new theoretical ideas, and his book on money is not excessively historical. Wagner stood in a critical relationship to the historical school, and he tried to develop Ricardian theory. The chapter closes with a text on Max Weber and his Protestant Ethic. Schmoller had been edited by Recktenwald with a contribution of mine on Schmoller's theory (Schefold 1989c); he was the head of the younger historical school. Max Weber is not so easily situated. He held chairs in economics at Freiburg, Heidelberg and Munich, but wanted to teach sociology. His work was an outgrowth of the younger historical school; sometimes one speaks of the 'youngest historical school', to group him with Sombart, Simmel and others. He is most often presented in the perspective of his ultimately having become a founder of sociology, but it is of interest to trace his evolution as an economist.

After having presented prime examples of the history of specific advances of modern economic theory, we return to the general problems of the economic, social and political subsistence of society which, we now find, have been reflected upon, one way or the other, in all high cultures based on the formation of states. As mentioned in the preface, the paper on East Asian economic thought, longer than all others, is based on an abbreviated combination of two introductions to classics in the series, on the Chinese classic by Huan Kuan and the Japanese by Miura Baien, dating from the first century BC and the eighteenth century AD respectively. I have endeavoured to present these works in their historical contexts, emphasizing some continuities and discontinuities, in a way which no doubt cannot satisfy the specialist but will, I hope, interest the historian of economic thought and help to promote research which has been neglected in the West and seems on the whole little known among professional economists even in the East. Matters are different as far as the Arab author Ibn Khaldūn is concerned whose ingenious Muqqadima is now mentioned often, but there are other contributions to Near Eastern economic thought not only in the Arab world, for example, from the Ottoman empire. A chapter on this was in preparation, based on the thesis of a pupil of mine, but it has now not been included for reasons of space and because the thesis has been published in English (Ermis 2013).

I hope that this short guide will have helped the reader to set his priorities in studying the book.

## Notes

1 Marx himself is represented together with the moderns (classical, neoclassical and Keynesian schools) in another edition of essays on the history of economic thought (*Great Economic Thinkers*, second volume, forthcoming 2016).
2 Cf. 'Spanish economic thought at the dawn of the modern era', Chapter 3.
3 Cf. 'Ibn Khaldūn's socio-economic synthesis: rise and fall in economic development', Chapter 5.
4 The distinction between positivist, relativist and political approaches is discussed in greater detail in Schefold (2014a). For my view of the contrast between economic thought and behaviour in classical Athens and modernity, see Schefold (2013). An amazing variety of systems of public finance in the countries of the world of the seventeenth century was described by Kaspar Klock. Cf. Schefold (2009).
5 Max Weber was one of the authors who emphasized the specificity of modern capitalism as an outgrowth of a specific Western development. Important steps of this evolution were the separation of household and firm, such that a specific rationality of profit maximization could arise, different from the rationality of political capitalism of antiquity, and fostered by the Protestant ethic. He also endeavoured to show that the great cultures of the East were shaped by different ethical norms which prevented the emergence of modern capitalism. Recently, the California school of economic historians argues that, on the contrary, Western Europe, China, Japan and other areas had reached similar levels of development in the eighteenth century, and that the outbreak of the industrial revolution in England, not elsewhere, was due to contingent factors. Cf. Schefold (2014b).
6 For additional remarks on the importance of language skills for the history of economic thought; cf. Schefold (2002, pp. 131–134; 'Some Personal Observations and Conclusions').

# 1 Antiquity

## Xenophon's *Oikonomikos*: the beginnings of an economic science?

It might seem a *contradictio in adiecto* to call a work dealing with the *knowledge of household oeconomy* [Hauswirtschaftslehre] a 'classic of political economy' if we understand by political economy a knowledge of the market processes arising between households and businesses, with the household being only one party to this exchange. In antiquity, however, the household and economic enterprise typically coincide as ideal types. *Knowledge of household oeconomy* also seems to fall by the wayside when emphasis is placed on the political dimension of political economy. And if we understand economics to be a theory of rational action then the concept of rationality, which for modern economic theory is universal and autonomous, appears in the science of household oeconomy [Hauswirtschaftslehre] within the broad context of 'the good life', from antiquity through to the eighteenth century. The household is governed by a complex web of relations constituting a single unit, which can however be viewed from a variety of perspectives: in terms of emotions, of rights and duties, of the division of labour, and also with respect to pecuniary success.

Yet all the same, modern economics can be traced back to this older *knowledge of domestic economy*. The state oeconomy was initially a domestic economy writ large – the state was thought of as the king's household. Exchange between households was already the object of early analyses of the market and of money; state services were financed by wealthy households whose development was, in turn, fostered by state protection. Thus, household oeconomics continued even after gainful activity began to be pursued separately from the household, workers now living in their own homes and not in that of their master; and also after the economy began to be understood as an abstract, distinct dimension of social life. Although marginalized, *household oeconomics* still exists today. There are indeed interesting questions to address here, especially in development economics; for the shift from domestic to wage labour, the transition from subsistence wages to incomes increasing with the productivity of the economy, the shift in demand from necessities to luxury goods is in every case connected with qualitative changes in the household, such that macroeconomic development cannot take place without development at the microeconomic level.

Even those who consider mathematical approaches the ideal form of modern economics must recognize that *household oeconomics* remains a permanent component of the discipline of which it was once the most important element – and that modern economics derives directly from it. The oldest literature that deals specifically with the nature of the household is Xenophon's *Oikonomikos*: and in this sense it can be considered a genuine classic of political economy.

This is not the place to trace the complex history of the concept of 'economy'. One spoke in German as of *Hausväterliteratur*, a theory of domestic administration. It was also applied to the state's 'household' in the form of public finance. It was transferred to the political sphere (in the early modern sense of the term), once it was combined with an analysis of market processes (rooted originally in Aristotelian chrematistics) and employed in the evaluation of opportunities and risks for state economic policy in regard to distribution. This gave rise in turn to the political economy that academics sought to objectify in the last third of the nineteenth century, so that the term 'political' once again fell into disuse, on account of its connotation of partisan thought and antagonism toward scientific knowledge. Instead, the term 'economy' was used to refer to the sphere of activities itself, and 'economics' used to refer to the science.[1] The novelty of mercantilism in comparison with ancient and mediaeval traditions is evident in the works of an entire group of authors, among whom are Serra (1994 [1613]) and Petty (1992 [1690]).

While the household is central to the economic thought of antiquity, other factors were also taken into consideration, such as its relationship to forms of government, to state financing, to state-fostered prosperity, to the attitude toward work, and to the monetary system. It is Aristotle who shapes our image of ancient economic thought. How states deal with the economic tasks with which they are confronted depends, according to Aristotle, upon their constitutional structures. Above all, tyrants must legitimate their domination through the display of splendour and power; hence they levy heavier taxes. Work is more drudgery than a matter of fulfilment, yet there is respect for conscientious craft work, and the necessity, where possible, of integrating slaves into the family and offering them a future through the hope of manumission with a small sum of capital.

In these domains it seems possible to organize economic life in its entirety. This traditional perspective is not undermined, but instead reinforced, by tragic conflicts, the outcome of wars, political upheavals and lack of freedom. It is only in regard to money that Aristotle differs from this, believing that once money has become an aim in itself there are no limits to its acquisition. To see this in terms of risk, or the limits of abstinence, as did later authors, could not have been further from his mind; for there was no virtue in simple moneymaking. Virtue lay rather in the pleasure that the citizen of the polis took in generous philanthropy, not in the penny-pinching caution of the moneylender. Aristotle not only criticizes a monetary orientation in relation to usury, but also with regard to wage labour and even the production of goods for sale. Once the economy began to be understood as an independent sphere of social life, however, running as if according to its own natural laws, attempts were made to draw clearer boundaries, and legitimate a market economy which prohibited only crass forms of usury.[2]

Although Xenophon includes Socrates in his dialogue on household oeconomy and also claims to be himself Socratic, he not only lacks the philosophical acuity of an Aristotle, his writings also contain elements leading in an entirely different direction to that of Socratic asceticism. According to the age-old and never-fully-resolvable controversy between primitivist and modernist interpretations of antiquity, either the features of household oeconomy here predominated – extensive self-sufficiency, small units of production, hand work with customized production, moderate development of the monetary system and credit, chiefly in the form of interest-free loans to friends on a reciprocal basis – or alternatively early forms of banking and industrial production, with trade spanning the Mediterranean, as well as entrepreneurial activity. Modernists must however consider the Aristotelian call for the 'good life' in a household with limited needs, an ideology whose nostalgic character is apparent in the imminent decline of the city-state, and the development of the Hellenistic territorial empires which would later be inherited by Rome.[3]

There are also ambivalences in Xenophon's book, apparent from the variety of the interpretations to which it has been subject. Its subject-matter alone appears to support a primitivist argument. The book contains not only a straight-forward description of household oeconomics, but it also praises country life, repeatedly asserting that farming is so 'natural' that it needs no further comment. On the other hand, some elements, such as the advice that one could systematically earn money with the purchase and sale of farm property, support a more modernist position. In his *On Revenue*, also cited as *Poroi*, he speaks of wholesale trade, of state businesses and of rich individual entrepreneurs with hundreds of slaves.

Here we do not propose to settle questions of historical economic facts on the basis of a few texts. However, there is evidence of 'Xenophonic' economic thought, and it can be interpreted as such. And despite some similarities to formulations of the seventeenth and eighteenth century, its differences to early modern bourgeois thought can be identified clearly enough.

Xenophon had even less interest than Aristotle in creating abstract, absolutely binding principles. He was an experienced soldier and commander and, though his military character is apparent in his texts, his work offers young people well-meant advice which they are free to accept or reject. The economic instance does not appear here in the form of an automatic mechanism with its own laws; rather, it is presented as certain life experiences that can be had in the economic sphere and which are worth passing on. While it is possible, for instance, to earn money through farming, there is no talk of thus having to become a farmer. The dialogue relates to an inherited estate on which it would be worthwhile to live; one need only put it in order, treat the people fairly and give the property sufficient attention so that it might flourish rather than decline.

A love of the country life is taken for granted here, a love that we see throughout the literature of antiquity. One recalls Homer (1834, p. 294): how in his garden outside the city Laertes, the father of Odysseus, had the work done for him:

> Pass'd from the city to the distant plain, Where old Laertes' sweat manured the soil Bought by his wealth, and cultured by his toil. A shed ran round his house on every side, 'Neath which the labourers that his wants supplied Eat, sat, and slept: and there a faithful crone, An aged Sicilian tended him alone.
>
> He saw in that well labour'd grove his sire Lone digging round a plant in mean attire, Patch'd here and there, and on his legs were bound Patch'd leathern greaves to ward the briar's wound And gloves on either hand to guard the thorn, And on his brow a goatskin covering borne.

For the small farmer of Hesiod's *Works and Days*, however, the environment is more hostile (Schefold 1994b, pp. 204–08). We often encounter country life in the literature of late antiquity, but sometimes with an ironic inversion. In Horace's well-known 'Beatus ille qui procul negotiis…' we hear a beautiful poem concerning an idyllic country setting; not until the final lines, however, do we learn the identity of the orator:

> When the usurer Alfius had uttered this, on the very point of beginning the farmer's life, he called in all his funds upon the Ides – and on the Kalends seeks to put them out again.[4]

Already in Homer the country estate is outside the city. Laertes had retreated there, as wealthy Romans were wont to do. The study of philosophy was an ideal component of this lifestyle into late antiquity. A letter from Emperor Julian Apostata (Wright 1961, p. 79) offers a picturesque description of the country estate he is giving to his friend, an orator. From there, one could see the Bosporus and the city, now called Constantinople:

> but you will stand on smilax and thyme and fragrant herbage. Very peaceful it is to lie down there and glance into some book, and then, while resting one's eyes, it is very agreeable to gaze at the ships and the sea. When I was still hardly more than a boy I thought that this was the most delightful summer place, for it has, moreover, excellent springs and a charming bath and garden and trees. When I had grown to manhood I used to long for my old manner of life there and visited it often, and our meetings there did not lack talks about literature.

In his *Oikonomikos* Xenophon has no less than the great King of Persia declaim the pleasures of the connection between beautiful gardens and erudite conversation.

Any attempt to understand Xenophon's text in the context of an inherited intellectual tradition must also touch on philosophy and religion. Xenophon identifies himself as a student of Socrates, whereby the two most significant works of Xenophon's are his *Memorabilia* and *Symposium*. As in the text on household oeconomy, Socrates does not appear in Xenophon's other works as a wise teacher explaining the difficult questions of epistemology, of logic and mathematics, of political theory or of love, but rather as an inimitable, quick-witted, funny man-of-the-people always ready with a cunning response and able to give advice for any of life's situations, a figure who only occasionally lets show his deeper religious solemnity and moral rigor.

Though Xenophon identifies himself as Socrates' student, his own life did not follow the path of philosophy. In *Anabasis*, his record of a military expedition in Persia, he recounts an episode that for him seemed characteristic (*Anabasis* III.1.5–7). On Socrates' advice, Xenophon asked the oracle of Delphi to which god he must sacrifice if he were to take part in the expedition, and the oracle indicates certain sacrifices. When Socrates learned of this, he reproved Xenophon for not asking the god first if he should undertake the trip at all; since, however, he had already asked and received an answer, he must make the sacrifices and accompany the mercenaries. At the end of another and shorter piece (*Hipparchikos* – advice to a cavalry colonel), Xenophon responds to a hypothetical critic, wondering why Xenophon so often counsels to act in accordance with the gods, that this could not surprise anyone who had been in battle and looked danger in the face (IX.8).

Xenophon was a good, skilful and multi-faceted writer, who loved military adventure, who enjoyed country life as a respected and influential citizen (despite the crooked course of his political career), who took part in city culture, in discussions with wise teachers, in theatre and religious celebrations and who was guided to reflection on his life experience by his encounter with Socrates.

While this preamble might seem superfluous, it will I hope make it easier for readers to place Xenophon's *Oikonomikos*, but also increase their pleasure in reading it – for without such context, they could run the risk of seeing here only pedantic instructions for tidying up the kitchen or fertilizing the fields.

Xenophon's *Oikonomikos* is closely related to two other Socratic texts, *Memorabilia* and *Symposium*; it even begins, following the text handed down to us, with 'I once heard him discuss the subject of estate management in the following manner...' (*Oikonomikos* I.1); the dialogue starts *in medias res* without identifying the main speaker. Since one of Socrates' interlocutors, Kritobulos, also appears in *Memorabilia* and *Symposium*, it seems appropriate to briefly discuss these two texts.

We do not know who Socrates really was. According to Olof Gigon (1979, p. 4), this is one of the longest-standing problems in the history of the ancient world. There is a rich Socratic literature which has come down to us in fragments, and to which Xenophon makes reference. There is an older interpretation, which is preferred by the lay ancient philologists and which, specialists say, is gradually gaining ground against Gigon's scepticism. According to this perspective, Xenophon certainly tried to present a real, simple Socrates who shared his experience of life, defending Socrates' memory against attacks already contained in Attic comedies during Socrates' lifetime (in Aristophanes' *The Clouds*), which attacks contributed to the charges made against him and which even ultimately led to his death sentence. While we therefore have Plato to thank for the heights of artistic expression and philosophical depths in his portrait of Socrates, the historical Socrates may rather lie halfway between the Xenophonic and Platonic representations.

A broad cross-section of people receives advice from Socrates in *Memorabilia*. There is the youth, Glaukon, who, though not yet twenty, has already developed the ambition to participate in state affairs. While his relatives drag him from the speaker's podium, Socrates seeks at first to minimize the foolishness of his pretensions by praising the youth, congratulating him on his youthful drive, seeking to gain his attention. Proceeding question by question, however, he then makes clear to him how specialized is the knowledge required for participation in politics – for instance, with respect to the state's income and expenses, or its means of defence. So the young man becomes aware that in his efforts to establish a good reputation he could only, ultimately, make a fool of himself (*Memorabilia* III.6). In another place, Socrates says that by far the biggest fraud is the person who falsely claims to be capable of leading the government (*Memorabilia* I.7.5). He who seeks to relate knowledge to a proper life conduct is able to see wisdom (σοφία) in knowledge (ἐπιστήμη) but this – together with wisdom – has limits (*Memorabilia* IV.6.7), The notion, familiar from Platonic epistemology, that it is important to be aware of these limits appears repeatedly in *Memorabilia* in connection with the practical problem of state responsibility.

Private individuals should also avoid activities for which they are not suited (*Memorabilia* II.8.6); Socrates, however, offers a great deal of advice about how one can improve oneself in practice. For example, he advises a friend who was impoverished by war to set up with his relations a small textile manufacture in his house (*Memorabilia* II.7). To a Hetaira called Theodote he suggests how she can gain friends, influence and wealth, though in so doing he mischievously draws a comparison with his own efforts (*Memorabilia* III.11). He knows how to describe the essential goal of each craft occupation. The sculptor, he says, must give expression and shape to the emotions of the soul (*Memorabilia* III.10.8); the armourer, he suggests, should attend not to tight-fitting armour, but to that which does not hinder movement (*Memorabilia* III.10.15). At the same time, there are some surprising assessments of work and labour. A citizen impoverished by war performs physical labour, which Socrates considers undesirable since it leads only to premature exhaustion. He advises the person to seek a position as an overseer or harvester for a rich landowner – although that person would take on the subordinate position of farmhand (δουλεία) only with great reluctance – even (higher-ranking) slaves were often overseers (*Memorabilia* II.8.1–4).

All of these topics reappear in modified form in *Oikonomikos*; the comparisons deepening the understanding. In *Oikonomikos* friends are treated as possessions. The impression is created of hair-splitting differentiations. In *Memorabilia*, the complaint is made that those who do not stand out from others through their humanity cling too closely to the possession of objects, and cannot understand the benefits and comfort one finds in friendship; this message also appears in *Oikonomikos,* though conceptually more open and less clearly expressed.

We must also mention, finally, how Kritobulos, Socrates' first interlocutor in *Oikonomikos*, makes his appearance in *Memorabilia*. Kritobulos is young, more sensible than reckless, but hazarding love, and so Socrates gives him a warning (*Memorabilia* I.3.8–15). The insecure young man is also questioned about what kind of people one should seek out as friends, and how good and hard-working people can find friends with like qualities (*Memorabilia* II.6). In *Symposium*, we meet Kritobulos as a handsome, somewhat complacent young man who is in love, in one of Xenophon's masterfully sketched dialogues (Bruns 1961). In *Oikonomikos* Kritobulos has inherited his father's estate and now requires the advice of Socrates, as a kind of second father, to learn how he should manage it. While his character cannot be fully discerned in *Oikonomikos*, this seems to be a difficult but not impossible task.

We do not know whether Ischomachos, the second interlocutor in *Oikonomikos*, was a historical figure. The assumption seems to be that Ischomachos represents Xenophon himself, who reports his experiences with the estate in Skillos, including practicing his military equestrianism. Banned from Athens, he had been given the estate by the Spartans. No doubt *Oikonomikos* reflects his attempt to run it properly. The wife of Ischomachos, who is not named, seems lovable – married when very young to an older man. She must actually be Xenophon's wife, Philesia, as she is called in a modern introduction: "My dear, where is it?' asked her methodical husband; and Philesia, not knowing the answer, could only hang her head and blush. So she had to listen to a long homily on the beauty of *order* in the house, with illustrations drawn from the army and the navy.' It is comforting to know that now, in at least one house in Skillos, pots and spindles, sickle and spear lay, hung or stood in rank and order, as the editor comments (Xenophon 1979, p. XXVI).

Of the key texts of Xenophon to be compared with *Oikonomikos,* the most important, *Poroi*, has not yet been introduced.[5] It is a short, complex and much-discussed work in economic history and the history of economic thought; I will mention here only a few basic ideas. The starting point is Athens' increasingly difficult economic situation after the allied war in which Byzantium, Chios, Kos and Rhodes gained their independence (356 BC). Support had to be gained from Attica; the increasing population of the city could no longer seek their salvation in the payment of subsidies from the Imperium. The city had therefore to be fed from its own land and in the most just manner (*Poroi* I.1). Analogous questions are found in early modern texts in which the author, as Xenophon does here, seeks out the advantages of the location, such as climate, agriculture, coastal areas as well as export goods, in this case marble and silver. In this crisis situation Xenophon turns to the less respected classes. Non-citizens, whose economic contribution should, he recognizes, receive better treatment so that the tax which they paid might increase. More respect should also be shown to foreign merchants – for example, by invitations to the theatre and the provision of better accommodations, apartments and market halls (III.13). The intention of improving the supervision of ports, so that disputes could be settled quickly and fairly, also warrants mention (III.3).

The most important suggestion concerns the silver mines of Laurion, whose output at the time of Themistocles supported the fleet, which was currently besieging the Persians. Xenophon (1968, p. 207) considers – the reader will be reminded of a Marshallian analysis – that silver mining is different from other trades, increased production normally leading to a drop in sales for individual sellers until business becomes unprofitable and their number once again falls: 'An increase in the number of coppersmiths, for example, produces a fall in the price of copper work, and the coppersmiths retire from business. The same thing happens in the iron trade.' The demand for silver, on the contrary, is completely elastic: 'No one ever yet possessed so much silver as to want no more; if a man finds himself with a huge amount of it, he takes as much pleasure in burying the surplus as in using it' (ibid.).

Xenophon thus recognizes that the demand for silver relates not only to it being a raw material for luxury goods (even for this the demand is quite elastic), but that silver can also be hoarded as a treasure – a purpose for which, as Aristotle might have added, there is no limit. Silver serves mainly as raw material for money. Xenophon, however, lacks the conceptual precision needed to follow this train of thought to its conclusion. He does not even consider the consequences of a possible surplus of silver money; his economic thinking is briefly abstract, then immediately returns to the concrete. He discusses the economic success of large mining leaseholders, and how the state could share in their profit by acquiring the slaves necessary for the work and leasing them in large number (figures between 1,200 and 10,000 are named; *Poroi* IV.23–24). Gradually, this capital (as we would call it today) should increase. During times of war, slaves can be used to row ships. He expects considerable secondary effects from investment – smelting ovens are referred to as an example, plots of lands should increase in value – and so the city would not only increase its monetary riches, but would also be better prepared for war.

Prosperity acquired in this way requires peace, not war, however, and Athens is a centre for philosophy, art and trade (*Poroi* V.4). Xenophon makes several observations regarding strategic goals and the means of a new politics of economic expansion and deterrence, rather than military conquest. He concludes with memories of great festivals and the holy shrines of the Athenians, he mentions contributions made to priests, to the council, government officials and the cavalry and finally advises seeking the approval of the oracles at Dodona and Delphi, and making sacrifices to the gods.

This text, so rich in economic details of historical interest, not only offers important arguments for a modernistic interpretation of ancient economic life, but bears comparison with mercantilist and cameralistic models for the state promotion of economic activity aimed at improving national assertiveness. Xenophon's adherence to the social values of his era, Attic art and the Greek religion does not contradict such an argument, since mercantilist authors themselves believed in the force of powers beyond the market such as state absolutism and Christianity.

The call for state support of industry and trade is also reminiscent of mercantilism. For example, in one of Xenophon's earlier dialogues (*Hieron*), in which a rich tyrant, Hieron, complaining of his personal misfortune – he is never secure from enemies within – is advised by a wise poet and interlocutor to make himself agreeable to his people by using his wealth. One way of so doing is to distribute prizes, since rivalry (φιλονικία – craving for victory) everywhere leads to great fervour and more abundant production. This even happens in agriculture (*Hieron* XI.7), in which such rivalry – where it seems apparently that it is not profit-oriented economic competition that is at stake, but instead renown, perhaps even exclusively – appears otherwise to be absent. The tyrant should not accumulate private wealth, but through enriching the city become victorious in the most magnificent and splendid public contest (*Hieron* IX.7). He will then be not only be loved, but also be an object of admiration (*Hieron* XL.11).

Hieron as an ancient Sun King? Xenophon an ancient Colbert? We have seen elsewhere that Savary, encouraged by Colbert to outline French trading laws and trade practices, saw a great future for France's economic development if the bourgeoisie did not aspire to an aristocratic life style but, on the contrary, the aristocracy made their wealth available for bourgeois accumulation. The proposed model was not Molière's *Bourgeois gentilhomme* but a *Gentilhomme bourgeois.* [6] Ancient development went in a different direction, however. What was evidently lacking was the emancipation of a bourgeois class who maintained their ideal of thrift, honourable work and economic competition. The attitudes which characterize the dialogues testify to a different economic spirit. To the extent that historical analogies are valid and one is willing to attempt historical speculation, the ideal of the Greek citizen in relation to the economy does not correspond to that of the modern era bourgeois but rather – in respect of work and capital accumulation – to that of the old aristocracy. This is apparent even in the choice of words; the tyrant Hieron's display of wealth is, for Aristotle, the virtue of a citizen of the polis, promoting the general good through generous donations.[7]

Xenophon also wanted to pursue Athenian ideals into measures, defended in *Poroi*, promoting trade and production. If one thinks them through to the point where the interests of merchants would have been fully legitimated and where craft production would have assumed an early-industrial character, where the accumulation of slaves in a peaceful empire could no longer rely on conquest and would have led to the emancipation of labour – this would have undermined Xenophon's ideals and led Athens into a transition to a form of early capitalism. This was however a process which was nowhere and never completed in the ancient world.

The significance of the economic spirit and the conditions of social life for the Athenian form of economy can best be understood in *Oikonomikos* itself, to a summary of which we will now turn.

The text begins abruptly with the definition of arts according to subject, the art hence therefore of housekeeping through household oeconomy. But the question quickly arises as to where to draw the line. Possessions outside the house belonged, paradoxically, to the household. A wealthy Greek in Athens could own several estates which might conceptually be understood as one household. He had, so to speak, a portfolio of assets, and had to decide whether they could yield anything. In this sense the administration of the household can be delegated against the payment of a wage, and since this knowledge of household economy is transferable, the manager can increase the yield (I.4).

'Have not some men acquired enemies?' asks Socrates (I.6), and Kritobulos replies to this rather curious question that, naturally, it would be ridiculous to pay an enemy a wage as well. Socrates is subtly alluding to the higher meaning of friendship, while Kritobulos is thinking of an estate manager who gets his superior into difficulties. Why does he make this point? 'Because it seemed to us that a man's household was what in fact his property is' answers Socrates (I.7). Kritobulos then limits the concept of property to a 'good' (*agathon*) or, as Socrates says, a 'useful thing' (*ophelimon*).[8] In what follows, Socrates adopts Kritobulos' more restricted conception of utility so that he might engage him in dialogue, only occasionally referring to his own more ascetic lifestyle and stricter ethical standards.

One must know how to use goods if they are to serve their owner as goods; those who do not know how to make such use of them can sell them, if they know instead what they are selling them for. Now Kritobulos gets the feeling that money, too, should count only as a good, as a real possession, if one knows how to deal with it as such. Thus a person who spends his money on his lover (a hetaira) might thereby be plunged into disaster. On the other hand, by how much have the households of private individuals been augmented by war and by how much by tyrants (I.15)? Socrates makes playful use of irony here. Modern accounting also has similar problems to set limits when it comes to assess 'good will' or environmental circumstances. How should one estimate the value of land polluted to a degree which is unknown?

Kritobulos now arrives at his own problem: Some have the means and the knowledge to augment the household, and yet they do not manage to do so. Can that knowledge still be regarded as an asset? 'Are you starting a discussion about slaves with me, Critobulus?' retorts Socrates mischievously (I.17), because for him knowledge is an eminent good; it is characteristic of a lack of freedom if people are not able to live according to their knowledge. In Xenophon's text Socrates therefore describes the evil forces which can prevent people from reconciling insight and action, 'if at least you regard idleness and moral cowardice and negligence as vices' (I.19). Kritobulos objects that some who lack neither means nor knowledge, who try to work hard, still remain unsuccessful. Socrates mentions other vices, such as extravagance and ambition, through which these people may be prevented from achieving their goals. These are enemies. Enemies can, however, force people to become better by leading them to prudence (I.23).

In the second chapter Kritobulos confidently maintains that he himself 'has such passions ... pretty much under control...' (II.1); he clearly hopes that Socrates will finally reveal the secret of sound commerce. Socrates, however, keeps him on the edge of his seat a little longer, describing himself as rich and expressing pity for Kritobulos' poverty. It is easier to understand that Socrates, given his lack of need, is able to manage with little than it is to understand his diagnosis of Kritobulos' situation.[9]

The demands made on Kritobulos, on his lifestyle and his reputation, derive from social obligation; he needs the fellowship of friends. Our translator's expression ('benefactors') calls to mind the need for patronage in a society in which social standing is based on social rank; and we should not forget the dependents, the existence of a clientele, as with the Romans. Furthermore, the state requires the provision of services, such as the maintenance of horses for knights in war, the trierarchy (the personal financing of triremes) or the financing of a choir for the representation of a tragedy (the translator of the eighteenth century, not informed about this ancient institution) rendered this as the obligation 'to give a ball'.

> There was a general expectation that the wealthy would at every oppor-
> tunity make use their money for the good of the community; and this
> constrained them, in a manner no longer intelligible for us, to represent
> the ancient aristocratic ambition by stepping forward and displaying their
> own wealth through ostentatious generosity, if not sheer waste.
>
> (Meyer 1986, p. 30)

These services, originally voluntary in form, increasingly assumed the character of taxes after the Peloponnesian war.[10] While the ability to pay had to be considered, the estimation of wealth was difficult (the Athenians spoke critically of 'hidden' wealth, to which the extension of credit belonged).[11]

Kritobulos now becomes very subdued, and Socrates has achieved the most important goal: to bring the young man to composure. Socrates feigns modesty, declaring his inexperience in acquiring wealth, while Kritobulos asks him once again to reveal to him how he can more easily make a profit with his large fortune. In fact, Socrates' lifestyle would give no grounds to suspect he has any knowledge of how to do so. Socrates would like to withdraw from the conversation, however, Kritobulos, with justification, holds him to his word that the art of household management offers an example of transferable knowledge. At this critical moment, we learn that this discussion has taken place among friends, hence there are witnesses (III.18). Socrates has no choice but to concede that he obtained his knowledge from someone else; thus, he can instruct Kritobulos how to become a 'clever man of business' (II.18).

With that, the exposition is concluded. Socrates turns to an overview of the subject; then follows the central part of the dialogue, on which we can only comment briefly here, for lack of space.

The various concepts of orderly administration[12] are now examined: orientation to need, the proper use of resources, skilful leadership of people,[13] what is to be cultivated, and what is needed to do so. People learn through observation – naturally, not simply by watching, like those who go to the theatre just for the sake of the pleasure it gives them, but rather in the manner of those who go to learn the craft of the playwright. One has to come to terms with the knowledge gained in this way. Socrates elicits from Kritobulos – and *he* now recalls that it is a discussion among friends (III.12) – the admission that he trusts no one with his affairs as much as his wife, but that he hardly ever talks to her about such matters. Since it is, on the whole, woman's work to spend what men earn, the household cannot prosper if the two do not cooperate.

The subject then supposedly turns to agriculture. Socrates immediately dismisses the manual arts, which Montesquieu (1793, p. 63) explains as follows:

Il faut se mettre dans l'esprit que, dans les villes grecques, sourtout celles qui avoient pour principal objet la guerre, tous les traveaux et toutes les professions qui pouvoient conduire à gagner de l'argent, étoient regardés comme indignes d'un homme libre. 'La plupart des arts', dit Xenophon [in reference to *Memorabilia* II.8 – BS], 'corrompent le corps de ceux qui les exercent; ils obligent de s'asseoir à l'ombre, ou près de feu: on n'a de temps ni pour ses amis, ni pour la république'.[14]

Since Kritobulos is apparently too good not only for manual labour but also for agriculture, there then follow nice descriptions of how the emperor of Persia distinguished himself by addressing himself not only to the control of the army and the defence of the country, but at the same time, through another administrative hierarchy, cared for agriculture. He even worked in his own garden, the so-called 'Paradise'. Oriental despotism thus here appears in a more favourable light. Agriculture offers a sense of peace; it requires physical activity, which suits the free man; it lends ornamentation to altar and idol; it promotes diligence, bravery and neighbourliness; when it flourishes the other arts follow suit. The farmer must also work with servile labourers – reprimand them, reward them and give them hope, so that they do not run away.

In Chapter 6, Socrates recounts how he walked in the city, as Plato and others also report, so that he might speak with the people about their occupations, and how he came upon the wealthy Ischomachos who then, asked by Socrates, continues the teaching.

Ischomachos also complains about the liturgical payments that are demanded of him.[15] He tells first of the distribution of tasks within marriage, of special talents: the supervision of servants and the division of provisions. In Chapter 8, the topic is order, which for the Greeks – with their beautiful temples, pillared halls and narrow undrained lanes – must have been of especial value.[16] Xenophon mainly thinks of comparisons with the military sphere – one is reminded of the famous parade scene in *Anabasis* (I.2.13–18), where the Greek hoplites vigorously march in four closed ranks to such effect that their own allies from Asia Minor ran off in fear. He also describes in his writings on the Lacedamonians (XI.5–10), complicated shifts between marching and battle formations. The conception of order is also extended to menials servants and maids – the men's and women's quarters are separated by bolted doors (IX.5). The housekeeper is carefully selected and sworn to loyalty. The young woman will be taught to value a natural way of life and physical movement (X).

Socrates once again proclaims his lack of knowledge,[17] and asks Ischomachos about his own activities. Ischomachos reports that he takes care of administration personally, because with his wealth he can honour the gods and contribute to the enhancement of the city (XI.9). Socrates finds this good and proper – indeed, he and many poor people could find that quite admirable, but he wants to know more precisely what Ischomachos does; so he begins to ask him about the details of his daily routine. He supervises the fields, he replies, practices riding (XI.17)[18] and public speaking: the latter as mediator or supervisor, before the civil the court or in the army – and he tries to remain as truthful as possible (XI.25).

The informative twelfth chapter deals with the delegation of responsibility. We notice here similarities, but also considerable differences, in relation to modern conceptions. Estate supervisors are required because Ischomachos – like any citizen of the polis – has things to do in the city. Marx referred to this in connection with his theory of interest, since he believed that the payment of interest arose from a conflict over distribution between those who possessed capital funds and entrepreneurs; the former received interest payments (or, in a corporation, dividends), while the latter received an entrepreneurial wage, the total gain, proportionate to the general rate of profit, being divided in this way according to the macroeconomic balance of power between the two agents. What Schumpeter considers the decisive entrepreneurial activity here plays no role; Marx refers to Aristotle, who viewed the overseeing of slaves as not particularly difficult work and thought slave owners delegated this responsibility to particular administrative slaves, so that they might devote themselves to politics and philosophy.[19] Xenophon, however, deals with the problem of supervision and its delegation (thus including the problem of superintendence by the owner) quite differently and in more detail than did Aristotle and, later, Philodem.

Thus, it turns out that material incentives (reward and punishment) play an important role for Ischomachos, but in the extended family the character of personal relationship is prominent; on the other hand legal relationships are not sufficiently precise to settle proceedings solely through contracts. Loyalty,[20] industriousness and other characteristics are required, and are at least in part presented as virtues that can be taught. Apart from that it also depends on the remuneration (XII.16), praise (XII.15) and the example that is set, for in contrast to Aristotle, the head of the household is ultimately in charge of the household. In this regard he is equivalent to a teacher.[21] The education of subordinates is also the subject of Chapter 13; this is achieved not only through reward and punishment, as with household pets, but through the cultivation of understanding, especially in recognizing when work has been well done (XIII.11).

Chapter 14 is truly remarkable. In this chapter Ischomachos reports that he taught his servants the difference between mine and thine by telling them of the laws of Dracon, of Solon, even those of the great king. Here again it is not a matter of punishment. One cannot reward materially those who refrain from stealing, but they can be honoured for it; therefore, ultimately, the lover of honour (φιλότιμος) is contrasted with the lover of profit (φιλοκερδής) – and stealing makes poor profits (XIV.10).

In Chapter 15, farming is described as a noble art that can be learned – and far more easily than other arts. Craftsmen sought to keep their knowledge secret (during the middle ages guilds did in fact agree on trade secrets), but farmers everywhere freely let themselves be observed and were are open to questions (XV.12).

Agriculture is a science open to sensory impression, for one can see what a particular soil yields and can in future yield (XVI); this leads into a consideration of the technical details of cultivation in respect of laying fallow and sowing, to fertilizing and irrigating, all of which we must here pass over. At issue is protection against both flood and drought, weeds (XVII), harvesting, threshing and winnowing (XVIII), and, finally, the planting of fruits and vines (XIX). Even in viticulture the vine shows what must be done to nurture it.

Socrates appears to be familiar with most of these techniques; it is a question of recalling something that has already occurred (XVII.10). I might add here that, in contrast, Platonic recall is directed to the non-empirical. In Plato's *Menon* the slave 'remembers' a mathematical context, which just as in Xenephon he 'rediscovers' through questioning: how one, given a square, works out what would double its area (this is done by finding the diagonal of the first square).[22] For Xenophon, there is nothing metaphysical about recollection; it does however serve to elevate the object remembered: that agriculture is a natural, time-honored art, rooted in the conception of the good life.

Socrates maintained that 'questioning is a form of teaching' (XIX.15), and now in Chapter 20 he asks the question that Kritobulos most urgently wants answered, and which can now be more precisely stated: Why are there differences in wealth, *despite the fact* that agriculture is an art easily learned from experience? In response we hear once again the discomforting praise of hard work – a person gets into debt not by planting the vine incorrectly but by not planting it at all. In war, too, it is not so much lack of knowledge as negligence which is the problem: whether a soldier marches through enemy territory in the proper formation or leaves himself vulnerable. Xenophon here insistently repeats commonplaces, if with linguistic and stylistic ornamentation. One can more readily forgive him for this if one remembers that he actually has at his disposal what we might call interdisciplinary knowledge; and without such insistence, the Greek community – which enjoyed such freedom and tested so many new ideas, such a variety of art and life during the classical period – would have lost all education and civil order.

The diligence with which the individual must deal with the land must correspond to that of the overseer. And now comes an unexpected turn which reveals the moneyed capitalist behind the noble country gentleman – so suddenly that one asks with bated breath whether everything has just been a masquerade. Ischomachos admits that he had already learned from his father that well-cultivated estates were expensive, so that one earned very little through their acquisition; a large profit awaited one who purchased poorly cultivated estates, improved them and then sold them. And father and son had done this not only once, but had often been able to obtain a price many times higher after such improvement (XX.24). So are the modernists right?[23] We cannot tell from this passage how important such trade in agricultural property was. The textual context of such chrematistic behaviour, as Aristotle scornfully dubbed it, appears to be more a matter of shrewdness than an everyday matter, or at least not generally practiced.

How is it possible to make such a profit? Ischomachos says that his father was hardworking (X.26). At this explanation, Socrates remarks ironically that seafaring corn dealers also behave in this way and also love this kind of 'work'. Ischomachos has to laugh at this, his merchant temperament being exposed, and remarks that housebuilders also enjoy their work.

"'By Zeus," (said I with a curse of indignation) ... and I at least declare, Ischomachus, that on my oath that I believe you, that all men naturally love whatever they think will bring them profit' (XX.29) retorts Socrates. The tension between the two forms of living thus remains; it is not merely a masquerade – both are genuine.

Chapter 21 returns again to the topic of successful cooperation. An example are the triremes: in one, the exhausted oarsmen congratulate one another and are pleased that they have managed to return early to port; in the other, they are late, although not covered in sweat, but they hate each other and their overseer. Xenophon regards the charisma possessed by certain leaders and which creates such differences as most magnificent; it is not, as with so much in agriculture, something which can simply be learned: instead it is a talent, something divine.

There are a number of other writings on household oeconomics from antiquity which follow on from Xenophon. Aristotle includes a thorough discussion of the household in *Politics*; additionally, there are three shorter texts bearing his name, which are cited in the literature as *Oeconomica* I–III. *Oeconomica* III has come down to us only in a Latin translation from the Middle Ages and focuses on the division of labour in the household, and marital love – and the value of marital faithfulness is supported with fitting quotations from poems;

when both are friends to one another, they will benefit as a couple. Though the original text of *Oeconomica* III may stem from Aristotle himself, *Oeconomica* II most certainly does not; this later manuscript mainly assembles anecdotes on how the state can increase its revenues. What is remarkable in this piece is the differentiation of four kinds of 'economy': one for the royal court, for the provinces, for city-states and for private citizens. The term city-state is associated with the Greek expression 'political economy'. This word pair appears here for the first time, but without its full, modern meaning.

*Oeconomica* I focuses on household oeconomics in the Aristotelian sense; the text probably comes from the hand of Theophrast, Aristotles' successor. Since the system and content of this text derives from Aristotle and Xenophon, it will not be summarized here; however, there are original formulations such as, for example, 'dissimilarity of habits tends more than anything to destroy affection' (1344a18), in reference to married life. Or, referring to slaves, 'a slave's reward is his food' (1344b4). With regard to possessions, there should be more yielding than non-yielding assets; the increase of the house thus depends on productive investments (1344b29). When making use of resources, one must ensure that not everything is put at risk at the same time, but that risk is diversified. Regarding the supervision of possessions by the owner, the text cites the Libyan proverb that the best fertilizer is 'the landowner's footprints' (1345a5).[24] In Spartan houses,[25] everything has its place (1345b3); with possessions one should therefore keep to the Spartan and the Persian system, although Athenians do change their possessions more often, which also has its advantages (1344b33f.).

The writings of Philodemos[26] on household oeconomics have come down to us only in the form of a damaged copy found in Herculaneum. He writes as an Epicurean. As much as his text owes to Xenophon and, in particular, Theophrastus, his perspective differs from theirs because he believes that householding requires only as much attention as is necessary to ensure that no one starves. He therefore criticizes Xenophon and maintains that a philosopher should put more distance between himself and such matters (Philodemos 1857, p. 29). We will pass over the details and additional criticisms (of Hesiod as well, ibid., p. 31) and emphasize the main argument.

'It is exhausting and unfitting for a philosopher to get up earlier and go to bed later than servants' (ibid., p. 35). The philosopher should therefore pay absolute attention to his comfort; the simplicity of the Cynics is exaggerated and unnecessary. A happy, peaceful life which is free from worry is for the best. Such a life is not always attainable without work, if one is poor. Badly invested wealth can give rise to anxiety; but here, and in contrast to Aristotle, the problem is more a question of the improper use of resources than a problem of wealth in itself. A wise person will make use of his possessions for the sake of friendship; although in so doing possessions should not be depleted. Philodemos openly assumes the position of the rentier, for in the course of a working life one may be forced to do things unbecoming to a virtuous man. He would like therefore to remove the burden of earning money from the philosopher, but not the condition of being wealthy. For a fortune can at least be maintained without undue effort.

He adopts this perspective in assessing potential occupations. He excludes war, something which kept Xenophon so busy. Living from commerce is unseemly if slaves do the work, and discreditable if one does it oneself. Working in the fields is also very wearisome, but the possession of an estate 'is fitting for the noble' (ibid., p. 53). Here one has the best chance of meeting friends and living among respectable people. The renting of homes and of slaves (when the work is not objectionable) is also acceptable. 'But those are only things that come second and third in importance. The first and finest is to live from scholarly addresses (ἀπὸ λόγων φιλοσόφων) to a receptive audience, here one gains the most thankful reward (as was due to the greatest honour for Epicurus), that is, to live from decent, uncontroversial and, in a word, dispassionate addresses, for sophistries or disputatiousness are not one jot better than popular rivalries or hair-splitting' (ibid., p. 55).

What might the university teacher of today be able to add to this? More substantial instruction on the administration of wealth follows. Philodemos recommends the keeping of a variety of separate accounts, following the example of many Romans; this practice may have improved as yet under-developed accounting. The manuscript breaks off following some remarks on the way to deal with administrators and with risk.

Philodemos was a Greek contemporary of Cicero. We find in the Romans rigorous and serious thinking, in Christianity the final move is made to the veneration of work – Christ and his apostles were simple craftsmen. From this point on Christian teaching regarding household management developed, its influence reaching up to the eighteenth century.

Erich Egner (1985) concludes in his book, *Der Verlust der alten Ökonomik [The Loss of Ancient Oeconomics]*:

> The economic interests of acquisition have a … fundamentally different orientation from those related to the family household and provision for its maintenance. By their very nature, the acquisitive interests are determined quantitatively and monetarily; conversely, those of household main-tenance are by their own nature qualitative, aimed at concrete goods (or services) to meet need. Conceptions of acquisition and of maintenance correspond to this like two sides of the same coin.
>
> (ibid., pp. 218ff.).

Need is clearly not one fixed quantity; nor did the Greeks think so. One can, if one likes, call 'economists' those who treat the preferences of the individual as a given and determine the market balance which leads to a Pareto-optimal satisfaction of suppliers and consumers. But this fails to take into account why particular priorities are set in the meeting of need – the economist simply assumes that the agents in his model somehow have solved the problem. The norms we have set for our needs, for our concept of a well-maintained life, should take into account the possibilities of production, the quality of work and of the environment. Knowledge of acquisition and of maintenance belong together. The clear coexistence of different ways of life in the ancient world, and the household as a unity in production, distribution and consumption made it easier for ancient philosophers to think about things in this way. Hence the conceptions of subsistence, administration and maintenance will in future tend to return again and again to the classic writings on this subject, and especially to Xenophon (Richarz 1991).

## Aristotle: the classical thinker of ancient economic theory

Every science has its own particular history, which at the same time constitutes an element of the history of science in general. One of the deepest roots of this general history can be found in the works of Aristotle, one of the most important thinkers ever to have lived. His works ensured that the ancient sciences remained a formative force throughout the Middle Ages and into early modernity. Even the path along which modern disciplinary sciences developed can be traced back to ancient sources, and this is reflected in their individual histories. The Humanists, as Burckhardt formulates it, 'chiefly through their rediscovery of the results attained by antiquity, mark a new epoch, with which the modern period of the science in question begins with more or less distinctness' (Burckhardt 1944, p. 148).

Aristotle can certainly be counted among the classics of science as the embodiment of the systematic acquisition of knowledge, yet the degree to which Aristotle, or any Greek author for that matter, can be considered a progenitor of economic science is a matter of debate. Mathematics, not as a method of counting but as a science involving systematic proofs, originated with the Greeks. Astronomy, medicine, zoology, botany, jurisprudence, linguistics and natural theology – these all have their roots in Greek or ancient sources. However, one of the defining features of Greek economic thought is that it does not conceive the economy to be an independent object of knowledge, nor therefore as a specific discipline, but rather treats it as an integral part of political, societal and familial relationships shaped by practical concerns.

Hence we cannot expect to find among the ancients economic theory in the sense of a causal analysis of the pattern of autonomous economic processes founded upon on the distinctive economic rationality of human agents and functional relationships in the production of goods. The physics of the time simply lacked a developed theory of mechanics which might have served as a model for such thinking. Yet based on what we know of the ancient Greeks, pure scrutiny in the original sense of theory, or description without valuation, does not seem to have been regarded as an appropriate approach to economic issues. Modern science assumes that the objective of human economic activity can be equated with advantage, profit or utility, that it has no prescribed 'natural' objective. Instead, it considers evolution to be determined by chance and the struggle to survive. The ancients, by contrast, dealt with the problems of economics as an aspect of ethics, a wide-ranging philosophy of moral action, for which Aristotle assumed a natural framework.

Since every reflection upon appropriate economic activity must take into consideration extraneous events, it was possible for observations of economic regularities to be absorbed into ancient economic thought. It was for example soon noted that rivalry improved performance and that cultural creation required a division of labour. Whoever defines political economy in modern terms will only find in the Greeks fragmentary observations in philosophical reflections or literary accounts, some of which can be traced back to the ancient east. Such formulations may appear especially insightful, astute or poetic in their original sources, yet taken together they do not constitute a complete causal analysis. Many historians of economic thought have therefore preferred to begin the history of political economy in the era of Mercantilism, where the notion of a self-governing economic process first became accepted. In the Classical era, liberating markets from state restriction becomes a programme in which the application to economic processes of a causal analysis rooted in the natural sciences in the form of *Laissez-faire* was bolstered by the fact that it did seem to be effective.

However, the idea has never disappeared that economic thought should not only be directed to the limitation of state activities, but should lay down principles for just and fair economic action, for social responsibilities (in modern parlance) and for environmental protection. Contemporary economics and its neighbouring disciplines, such as political science and sociology, history and jurisprudence, converge over numerous questions, so that we could even talk of a partial restoration of the old unity of the 'State Sciences'. In this sense, Aristotle is not only a progenitor of modern economics from the perspective of a general history of the sciences, but also of political economy.

Although Aristotle occasionally discussed economic questions in other writings, *Politics* is without question the most important book for us. It includes not only the extremely significant differentiation between the 'natural' art of acquisition in meeting the needs of the household, and a Chrematistics oriented to the abstract accumulation of wealth; it also explores many later conceptions of the correct form of government and provides an analysis of the Greek systems of rule, both of which have left their mark on subsequent legislative systems. These systems of government grew out of the confrontation between democracy and more or less despotic tyrannies. While some states limited their power through constitutions and laws, others were subject to arbitrary government.

We would do well to remember that Aristotelian philosophy played an essential role in nineteenth century German political economy. Not only was the Historical School, and Schmoller in particular, strongly influenced by Aristotle – many of the Historical School turned their attention to him. He also exercised considerable influence on Menger in the Austrian School.[27] Young people of every generation have been fascinated by the force with which Aristotle's practical philosophy derived general maxims regarding proper conduct from elementary premises, at the same time verifying his conceptions by confronting them with his vision of urban life both in his own time and in Greek history. When in the nineteenth century the Historical School sought to establish rules for economic order founded upon Aristotelian precepts for social life in a (now national) community, and when the Historical School hoped to establish rules for structuring the economy in the context of advancing technological and civil development, they thought they could also measure Aristotle's values with their own. They rejected Aristotle's justification of slavery and had reservations about his approval of direct democracy.

Aristotelian economic thought is the culminating point of ancient economics to the extent of our knowledge of it. We know that practical instruction in economics must have existed in antiquity; Aristotle himself refers to it (*Pol.*, 1258b40), but no such texts have been preserved. Many of Plato's dialogues in the classical era refer to economic questions. Philosophically, they attain at least the same stature, stylistically they are superior to those of Aristotle; but the *Republic* and the *Laws* stand in stark critical contrast to Greek reality.[28] Xenophon's works are also quite significant.[29] For the rest, the earlier philosophical tradition of the classical and pre-classical periods has only come down to us in fragments so far as economic thought is concerned. And yet we can develop a truly comprehensive and coherent picture if we seek not so much an analytical understanding of abstract connections, but instead attempt to understand the economic mentality of the educated free citizens as expressed in the poetry of the time between Homer and the Classical period.[30]

Whoever looks in Aristotle and his predecessors for the beginnings of the study of economics will find, even with generous interpretation, only vague echoes of modern analyses of value, price, the division of labour, money, interest and the financing of state spending. But these same texts are rich sources if understood as descriptions of the conditions (life aims, customs, law, system of government) under which the danger of a break-up of the *polis* through autonomous, economic powers can be kept at bay. The art of domestic economy ('oeconomy') serves the good life of the citizen who wants to avoid the art of monetary acquisition ('chrematistics'), although, like slavery, it is indispensable. Modern theory is in contrast no longer primarily ethical, but oriented on the question of truth, whether action based on self-interest leads to the best possible supply of goods at a given cost.

In *Politics* Aristotle develops criteria by which life forms, occupations and careers can be evaluated with regard to their proximity to, or distance from, the ideal form of the self-sufficient and free citizen capable of knowledge and head of a household. Thus *Nicomachean Ethics* organizes forms of living according to the level of attainable happiness, the merchant's life being seen as very limited in these terms. The subordination of the economic to the political manifests itself here in the instruction on just exchange and reciprocity, where the spontaneous giving and providing of services for the state (liturgy) form the basis of communal life among free citizens.

The history of economic thought usually begins with Aristotle or his successors in the late Middle Ages. Yet, in a history of economic thought one stage farther removed we want to search for thinkers predating Aristotle himself, and show that his economic theory represents neither a new conception, nor a radical critique of tradition, but can be understood as a further development of economic conceptions already to be found in Homer. The latter have been preserved in archaic lyrics and – less explicitly – in classical drama, although one of the most important turning points in economic history takes place in the sixth century BC: the introduction of coins and a monetary economy with the rise of the merchant class.

It is widely acknowledged, even by the Greeks themselves, that Homer influenced the spiritual and intellectual world of the Greeks. Plato speaks of 'Homer's admirers saying that this is the poet who has educated Greece, that we should learn from him and follow this poet in the arrangement and conduct of our own lives' (Plato 2008, p. 328). Though philosophers, such as Plato, struggle against Homer's influence, it can be quantitatively verified: nearly half of the literary papyri discovered in the sands of Egypt are fragments of Homer transcriptions.

For the modern reader, the task of finding traces of economic events in Homer must at first seem hopeless, for the magic of the poems is founded on intricate plot structures and the closely entwined worlds of the gods and humans, so that first the earthly reality appears to be exceeded by the godly, then the godly world is felt to be in human proximity. A reasonable interpretation[31] suggests that the poems were recited to an aristocratic public in the eighth century BC, since the plot structure and the conception of a martial nobility establish which figures are central to the sagas, and which people or classes are marginal. Thus, in the *Iliad*, a common foot soldier takes part in the military assembly, but he never speaks and remains nameless. Against a backdrop of common soldiers the heroes stand out. The gods live in a heightened version of the world of the nobility. The army or people of a city honour champions and kings with gifts appropriate to their rank; conversely, the champions feel a duty to repay this honour by prevailing in battle. As in Plato's *Republic*, the martial order protects the city. Among the honours is a large share of war booty, gifts, prizes from games and also contributions in kind from the people. War and contributions are essential sources of princely acquisition, and only some is retained, the remainder being apportioned not only to family and clan, servant and maid, but also to the common people; gifts are also used to strengthen alliances with other nobility.

None of the ideas worked out in Greek economic philosophy is so clearly represented in the Homeric epics as the notion that the dream of the good life will be realized in an orderly and wealthy (but not ostentatious) household. In the *Odyssey*, for example, we see the mismanagement of the court in the absence of the king, contrasting with the well-ordered residences of the returned Nestor and Menelaus, and the extraordinary increased wealth of the Phaeacians. One of the great, unforgettable images in the *Iliad* is the behaviour of Hector toward his wife Andromache in the sixth Book: This man, who everywhere cares for his city and family, proves himself a hero – although at a disadvantage by comparison with the most important Greek heroes – in his continued struggle for his family, ignoring the dark premonition of his own downfall, the destruction of the city and the enslavement of its women.

The nobility is involved in domestic production. Thus Odysseus finds his father Laertes, dressed quite simply, with his gardeners, and the princess of the fabled Phaeacians, Nausicaa, goes with her maids to the stream to do the washing. The wealth of which one gladly boasts remains bound to the idea of an ideal, simple rural existence.

These differences, which philosophers would later bridge by introducing conceptual reconstructions, or abolish by imposing unilateral norms, are elaborated by Homer as contrasts which enhance his poetics. Alongside the image of the reduced but well-satisfied household, there are lists of dazzling wealth, for instance the enormous amount of gold, of cauldrons, basins, horses, women taken as booty, all of which Agamemnon promises Achilles to make up for an insult at the outset of the *Iliad* which is the basis for the Son of Peleus' rage. The wealth of the good life is realized on the landed estates of the nobility, while their material wealth comes from their deeds as warriors. Distinct different from later conceptions of peace based on natural rights, in Homer we see the violent confrontation between societies as a magnificently cruel fateful power; the differing powers of the gods with respect to each other is also determined by their physical force.

We only glimpse the work of production by servants and poor freemen in passing. It is said of Odysseus's household that 'twelve women laboured at these together, grinding the barley and wheat men thrive on' (Homer 1834).[32]

The craftsman is, however, a secret hero of Greek economic thought. This should be no surprise considering the artistic heights of Greek crafts; but this is not immediately obvious in the philosophical texts where the craftman's activities are superficially viewed as a less respectable form of work, preferably left to non-citizens and slaves. A fragment of a humorous poem has been handed down to us from the time of Homer about a certain Margites, who was a bungler, because he tried everything but could do nothing right. Margites is the opposite to Odysseus, who was inventive and appears as a hero experienced in all the arts, as warrior, defender, hunter, as the builder of a raft for his rescue, as well as the architect and builder of his own palace. In mythology, by contrast, the advantages of the division of labour in craftwork are linked to the goddess, Athena:

> She was first to teach the craftsmen of this earth how to make carriages and chariots with intricate patterns of bronze. And she taught lustrous works to soft-skinned maidens in their houses, placing skill in each one's mind.

> (Homer 1976)

This is the simple, ancient image of craft labour which is part of life and which decorates it. The origin of the division of labour derives from the various talents represented by the gods and goddesses of mythology. Thus Artemis is the goddess of the hunt, Hephaestus is the blacksmith – and to Hephaestus is ascribed the power to make automatons. He forged tripods with golden wheels which rolled to Mount Olympus by themselves. We will see the effect of this image on philosophical economic thought. The precision of craftwork serves for poetic comparison; Odysseus constructed his bed according to its blueprint. That also corresponds to the representation of the variety of artistic works of Hephaestus, the forger of weapons, who saw himself as a 'sooty monster'. Only concentration on the essential, the division of labour, can yield something exceptional which then earns praise: 'A good healer is worth a troop of other men' (Homer 1990, XI, verse 607, p. 313).

Our legal terms make a clear difference between the labour of free workers and of slaves, but considering work as a craft, we see how free citizens, even princes, work side by side with common people and slaves, particularly in the *Odyssey*, and it is not by accident that Odysseus' faithful slaves fight on the side of the returning king against the traitorous free people. In *The Iliad*, a poor woman is introduced in a poetic comparison: she weighs wool in order to earn a meagre income for herself and her children. This view from the palace of free labour performed for wages is rare in Homer. There also seem to be free day labourers who help with the harvesting, but these remain unclear. What predominates is the slaves, bound to the house, who enjoy in part a certain affluence, in some cases possess in turn other slaves, and are in any case paid with room and board.

Although the Rome in the time of the Caesars reminds us of the worst images of slaves in chains, of slave revolts and crucifixions, a patriarchal image of household slavery remained until late classical antiquity. It was significantly moderated by the slave's prospect of being freed and given a small amount to secure his existence; this considerably eased the lot of the slaves. Slavery was so much an element of the ancient conceptual world that rebel slaves thought not of eliminating the institution altogether, but only of the reversal of the power relations.

However, loss of freedom when one had led a secure, independent life was an appalling experience. Aristotle, who decreed in his will the freeing and provisioning of some of his slaves, cherished the notion that automated production, if it could exist, would make slavery unnecessary. We are amazed see in *The Iliad* the dream brought to fruition by the god Hephaestus: He possesses artificial virgins which he has made himself, the image of their living sisters, who assist him 'Intelligence fills their hearts, voice and strength their frames' (ibid. XVIII, verse 490, p. 481). The image of automation is thereby enhanced.

One of the worst horrors of war depicted in *The Iliad* was enslavement, which could happen even to captured nobility, like the sons of Priam. It was also quite clear that captured slave women could be taken as lovers; thus, the slave is even as a person less than the free person. How the contrast between two truths – that of the captivity and the human closeness to house slaves – can be expressed is, in Homer, a sign of his poetic stature. This conflict between a lack of justification and the economic necessity of slavery becomes a philosophical problem later in Aristotle; it remains unresolved, and this dilemma reflects his philosophical integrity. In the lamentations of Patroclus, in *The Iliad*, we see the ambivalence: Briseis, as Achilles' lover and sympathetic to his friends, is filled with real mourning for the fallen, though not the other maids around her, crying out of a sense of duty: 'Her voice rang out in tears and the women wailed in answer, grief for Patroclus calling for each woman's private sorrows' (ibid. XIX, verse 356, p. 498).

While defeated enemies are either killed or enslaved, warriors could be certain that survivors would be provided for by their own city, if the city remained free and the warriors would otherwise die.

The complexity of the bartering process is the strangest feature for the historian of economic thought reading through Homeric epics for economic phenomena. From ethnology, we know that in all primitive societies complex systems of reciprocity exist, whereby exchange follows certain obligatory forms, but can also takes place voluntarily out of the sheer pleasure of giving. Linguistic research has revealed deeper layers of an Indo-Germanic legacy in Homer. Emile Benveniste has shown that the concept for gift in Homer is shared in common with Indo-European institutions – that one German term for gift or present corresponds to an entire array of substantively varied Greek terms. On the other hand. Beneviste discusses trade in Homer as an occupation lacking a name (Benveniste 1969). In pre-monetary exchange there was also haggling if good was traded for good, as well as the generous gift which called forth another gift in response. Superficially both cases involve an exchange of objects. The social relations are however quite different.

First of all, in the Homeric epics we find a characteristic multiplicity of standards of value. In one case, a tripod costs 12 cows, and in another case, a slave is worth four cows. Apparently, there exists an interest in establishing such values; these and the hierarchies and equivalences connected with the awarding of prizes for games are not economically very plausible, but are ostensibly a source of fascination for the poet and his public. Despite a certain preference for cows as a standard of measure, there is no commodity that assumed the function of money. It is therefore easier to understand that Aristotle celebrates money as a practical invention, which naturally makes it necessary for him to call for everything in an exchange to be appraised – the charm of an older world, in which one does not know the exact value of something, is lost on Aristotle, though he is still a long way away from drawing up a quasi-mechanical law of exchange.

Under the keyword 'reciprocity', gifts which hosts and guests give each other are of prime importance. Normally, it is the host who gives the guest a gift, thus requiring the guest at some later date to entertain him or his descendants. Similarly, generous wedding gifts are also mentioned; they recall the bridal purchase, if the bride did not 'repay' the gift because the groom had fallen in war. Gifts are also exchanged in duels, in order to make their chivalrous character evident.

Heroes and princes placed special value on appropriate gifts and shares of plunder when they have broken a siege or gain a leading position – honour will be offended if the share does not accord with chivalry. Aristotle writes in the *Nicomachean Ethics* that gift givers should be of the same rank before and after the exchange, something that is better suited to the context of status relationships and gift-giving than to that of buying and selling. For Aristotle the point at issue is 'distributive justice'. The most important example of wounding someone's pride with an inadequate distribution of gifts is of course the conflict between Achilles, whose virtue consists in being the best soldier, and Agamemnon, who demands the largest share as the supreme leader of the Greek army. That Achilles' honorary share, namely Briseis, also Achilles' lover, should be ceded to a lesser soldier by a higher authority is the cause for Achilles' scorn, and for his almost-fatal (for the Greeks) refusal to continue fighting in the war.

The next level to be observed is the exchange of gifts between nobility and those dependent upon them. They can be interpreted as 'taxation' and 'redistribution', and there has been an attempt to reconstruct a Homeric political economy; however, for that we lack the necessary legal obligations and the regularity of trade partnerships. Hospitality, practiced by the princes, has a public function. In particular, they provide meals for the aristocracy, who appear to have a right to sit at the king's table. During wartime, the promise of plunder appears to take the place of soldier's pay. The way in which soldiers acquire their pay by repeatedly trading objects of plunder is illustrated in one place in *The Iliad* – according to Thucydides, without the bands of looters and the plundering the Greeks would have conquered Troy sooner. On the other hand, there are payments that the masses as well as the leaders have to raise for the community, which objectively replace taxes but which cannot be seen as such, since a fixed basis for measurement is lacking and the payment therefore appears voluntary, so long as it is not obtained under the threat of violence. Here, too, the comparison with the philosophical writings, in which the prospect for voluntary payments to the state becomes a precondition for the cohesiveness of the community. The way of thinking in which the exchange of gifts between free people has to be equivalent and is fixed by custom is thus carried over to the relations between the lower and higher ranks. It is even reflected in the relations between humans and gods, as can be seen in Homer and in later Greek religion. Sacrifices are made to the Gods so that they might provide a certain amount of protection; the prayer is sometimes heard, sometimes not.

Ultimately it is difficult to fit trade into this way of thinking. Wherever the merchant appears he is seen as the opposite to the warrior, as shown in verses in which Odysseus is challenged, that he is not a man who is very good at battle:

> More likely, I think, you are one who plies here and there in some big ship, a master of trading sailors; anxious over the cargo out, watchful

over the cargo home and his greedy gains; nothing about you speaks the athlete.

(Homer 1834, VIII, p. 88)

Despite anachronisms in the translation the sense is clear. The provocation works: Odysseus is angry and ready to do battle.

Mythology also entrusts the roguish god of thieves, Hermes, with the protection of trade. The oppositional attitude toward trade cannot be overlooked. On the other hand, I have not found a trace of hatred for usury in Homer, a sentiment that typically accompanies this attitude in later history and which appears as a convention in Aristotle. In pre-monetary societies the lending of an inheritance takes place – in fact gifts already create a kind of debt – but lending as a career is difficult to imagine before the introduction of money. The topic of usurers, therefore, is new, in Aristotle, relative to the Middle Ages. Thus Aristotle only wants to show why trade tends to lead to a destruction of 'the good life' – and that traders, philosophers or warriors each have different mentalities and ways of living (to put it Max Weber's terms, different economic spirits) is hard to dispute.

The spiritual influence of Homer upon Greek thought is probably the main reason for its unmistakable individuality. As Burckhardt writes in the introduction to his Greek cultural history, 'the great mythology, which flooded all of Greek thinking, seeing and feeling, is the real intellectual and mental 'Okeanos' of this world' (Burckhardt 2003); However,

> the beneficial stimulation of Homeric poetry which extended into related areas of intellectual life, such as all branches of poetry and fine arts, had ensured a mystical view of Homer in antiquity within areas of thought whose very structure lay beyond the bounds of the poet's work, a development which ultimately hindered the timely development and dissemination of knowledge and thought.
>
> (Strasburger 1972, p. 9)

This is true of moral concepts – thus Plato's opposition – but it is especially true of economic concepts. Homeric domestic economy thus became a 'societal model' for the Greeks and Romans (Strasburger 1976, p. 43). Looking back on a period of some 800 years 'there exists a uniformity of principles from the Odyssey to ... at least Columella', that is 'so unbelievably great as to enable us to make a general statement about antiquity' (ibid., p. 53). To this belongs the curious indecisiveness in the treatment of the slave, whose ambivalent position lies on the one hand in being viewed as a member of a large, paternalistic family; and on the other as something that can be simply sold off. Aristotle's philosophical definition of slaves as a 'speaking tool', and the humane manner in which he treated some of his slaves in his will: these stand in stark contradiction. The way in which contradictions are dealt with is characteristic for an artistic style as well as for the stylistic unity of a historical epic or an economic system. Without vision it cannot be understood.

Thus it is remarkable that the Homeric models, in varied form, can be found again in the poetry of the period between Homer and the Classical era. If we are here pursuing the 'history of economic thought at one remove' and look into the concepts of economic action which were critical for classical Greek philosophy, then we must turn next to Hesiod, whose *Work and Days* is often cited as a primary source because of the explicit references to the problem of estate management. Chronologically, Hesiod still belongs to the Homeric era; he is the first poet about whom we have personal information. However, he does not deal with the world of the wealthy nobility, but instead with the simple farmer, struggling hard for his daily bread, living and working where he was born, for whom war service, trading ventures, journeys by land and by ship are all terrible in their own way. Nonetheless, the bare farmhouse is similar to the Homeric princely court: here, too, husband, wife and family members work together. Before harvesting, all of them have hard work to do, and afterwards the field hands can stretch their legs and loosen the cows from their yokes (Hesiod 1914, verse 607).

Work is praised here; not to work is a disgrace, but 'shame sits next to poverty' (ibid., verse 319). Domestic economy, which was later often only referred to without further detail, is extensive in scope. It is not very structured, and is mixed up with rules relating to the time of year, offering ethnologists insight into the popular beliefs of the day, but this sounds like a call for pious action, as in the later Greek enlightenment and philosophical economics. Although Hesiod admits to having sailed only once on 'many-pegged ships', (ibid., verses 646–662) he advises setting out at the right moment, in order to return with a profit. Shipping trade is not however treated as an independent trading activity, but instead is connected with domestic production. Each trip is viewed as dangerous; it should only be risked at the best time of year and all one's possessions are never to be endangered on a single ship journey.

Thus a farmer remains connected to a village community in which neighbourly help and friendship are maintained through reciprocity. The neighbourhood provides protection in cases of poverty and robbery; one helps those willing to work if they are in need. Those who sit in the 'common hall' because they do not have enough food are often filled with 'forlorn hope', and the idle man (ἀεργὸς ἀνήρ) often tends toward wickedness (ibid., verses 497–500). It is advisable therefore to increase the household reserves. An entire catalogue of bourgeois virtues and of thrift is presented, but in an historically specific form, which now prohibits the old desire to plunder on the part of lords, and does not envisage the possible connection of bourgeois virtues to wholesale trade. The goal is not to increase great wealth, but instead maintain a modest prosperity.

Insights which the poet himself clearly considers important are presented in mythical form. Hence a good and a bad goddess of strife, Eris, is introduced to personify quarrelling and rivalry. While quarrelling dissolves the community, rivalry enhances production: 'And potter is angry with potter, and craftsman with craftsman...' (ibid., verses 24–25). Aristotle later understands the advantages of the division of labour, competition and private property in just this *agonistic* sense. On the other hand, he had no concept of competition in the sense of capital movements producing an equilibrium rate of profit.

Hesiod also perceives a sequence of eras in the old legends, which after initial extravagance in the world led to shortages, in which Zeus 'keep[s] hidden from men the means of life', (ibid., verses 42–53) so that such means would have to be produced through cultivation. The community threatens to dissolve under the pressure of a mythical decline of the human race, yet it faces a higher power: justice. It is not yet, as in later philosophy, based upon natural development – in Hesiod legal relationships are something unknown to animals – but nevertheless godly power and human insight work together when justice prevails; and then nature, too, is abundant.

In Homer's aristocratic world virtues are individual, while fate is the common principle which unites people. In the Aristotelian *polis*, virtues are formally structured in a teleological system through moral maxims and legal terms. It is only in *Wealth of Nations* that a balance of interests according to quasi-mechanistic controls comes into play.

Sweeping economic, political and societal changes divide the Homeric world from the classical epoch. Among these changes is the introduction of coins beginning, according to Herodotus, with the first minting in seventh century Lydia. 'It cannot be too much emphasized that coinage was never invented', Burns (1965) remarks, who along with many other writers views the introduction of coinage as a gradual development, which led from the establishment of certain goods as general equivalents in bartering to their standardization and legal set up, to the definition of weights and measures, to the formation of a standardized coinage in the Classical and Hellenistic period, and the emergence of a Mediterranean maritime trade based on the exchange of currencies and trading credit.

Only a very few passages have come down to us which contain explicit reflections on the character of this historical transformation of an economic system. However, economic institutions were created which entirely altered life. Alongside the old noble class there now stood rich merchants; property relations were altered with the possibility of mortgaging land and also one's own person in the form of debt slavery; and politically the demand for common legal conditions developed. Economic institutions were now unquestionably reflected politically. Cities had to decide whether they wanted to mint their own currency or to enter into unions with other cities and use the same currency. An important currency union arose for example between the Greek cities in Asia Minor at the time of the Persian war (ibid., p. 91). Reflection upon the political advantages of the identity established for a city through minting its own coins, with full awareness of the use of currency for the promotion of trade on the one hand and the risks of setting up a mint on the other, does not of course mean that the regularities in the circulation of money or the connection between the circulation of production and consumption were analytically recognized.

How little these early capitalist forms of exchange in an ancient society could facilitate the emergence of an economic rationality, or even give insight into the larger economic picture, is clear from pre-Socratic philosophy, and also from archaic didactic poems that began to problematize wealth, which was only considered legitimate in connection with a virtuous life. Sappho says that wealth without virtue is damaging,[33] and Pindar's fifth Pythic Ode begins with the connection of the 'far-reaching power' of wealth and virtue. In the ancient lyrics we also hear voices lamenting the demise of the ancient privileges of the nobility and their expulsion by new rulers, as well as calls for the creation of a popular assembly and respect for civil rights.

From the turmoil at the turn of the seventh and sixth centuries the figure of Solon, honoured equally as statesman, poet and philosopher, stands out. By taking a step toward the democratization of Athens he calmed the warring parties, renounced tyranny and in his laws and writings gave expression to a new sense of justice. He deplores that there is no limit fixed – by the gods – to human wealth, that greed cannot be satisfied. He also advises that one must become conscious of the inner value of a moderate life. There are warnings against the hybris involved in transgressing the law which gods protect. Finally, Solon's poems related in proud verses how he established laws to end debt slavery, to redeem mortgaged land, to guarantee return for exiles and to make possible cooperation between upper and lower classes – all of this without yielding to the temptation to gain power for himself.

Greek history is marked by the fact that a spiritual connection is maintained between the religious concepts of the earlier epoch and the time of the democratic emancipation of citizens and of philosophical enlightenment, despite some questioning, as expressed for instance in the confrontation between the Sophists and the Socratics. New topics emerged in the tragedies and comedies of the high and late classical periods which had to be reconciled with the ideas handed down to younger generations.

Examining the comedies of Aristophanes for insights into economic life yields truly amazing results, particularly with respect to money: Whether the state can put devalued currencies into circulation, whether harbour fees influence international trade, and so on. Local market activity springs to life in the bawdy realism of common people – naturally Aristophanes knows, as does everyone else, that prices have an effect on supply and demand. However, such economic insights appear only in individual observations, in exemplary sentences, or in short interludes. The main direction of the major plot follows unswervingly the traditional guidelines of economic ethics.

In connection with tragedy, it becomes even clearer that historical changes had little effect on the thinking here examined. The placing of the plot in a mythical past moderates the realities of material life. An examination of Euripides reveals the linkage of changes in political conceptions to the advance of democracy. The theme of the growth of human technical power can be attributed to economic thinking, and is endorsed by Aeschylus in *Prometheus* and by Sophocles (1912) in the brilliant chorus 'Many things cause terror and wonder' in *Antigone*, invoking the material power of humans over nature, their language, their political understanding and medicine – 'yet for death he hath found no cure'. The conclusion remains, however, that in the state only those who are faithful and honour the law of the gods flourish.

In view of this overwhelming evidence of an economic mentality which – appealing to traditional values, and also legitimated by all-pervasive religious thought – seeks to block the impact of increasing wealth on a free market, has been repeatedly questioned what sort of Greek economy might have existed that would allow for this interpretation without contradicting it. We cannot here recapitulate the controversy, begun by Bücher and Meyer and continued by modern historians of the ancient world, over primitivist and modernist interpretation. This involves the question of whether the Aristotelian concept of a predominantly agricultural economy with limited commodity markets, restricted markets for land, moderate slavery, little export trade and the barest access to credit corresponds to the reality in Athens at the end of the fourth century; or whether at some point a stage of development was achieved which can be compared to the early modern world. This alternative is probably a false one since it originates in a conception of stages that all historical economic forms go through a single line of development, from primitive to modern conditions. It further does not consider the possibility that other developmental paths could have opened out, and that in the ancient world unique forms perhaps came into being whose organizational structure clearly deviated from that of the early modern period. Thus the Renaissance could view the ancient world as a cultural model, although the Renaissance had already gone beyond antiquity's technical management of nature in certain decisive areas.

There are conspicuous peculiarities in the Athenian economic style which is itself a distinctive variety of the Greek *polis* economy and which is for example reflected in the speeches of Pericles. Here there belongs the distinctive political and cultural solidarity of which the Athenians could speak with pride, how their pre-eminence rested on the power of trade, their maritime system of alliances, how their citizens competed to distinguish themselves in politics, war and culture without ever losing sight of the welfare of their city, through whose existence they were able to realize themselves. Over-population could have led to the proletarianization of Greek cities; instead, there was emigration to colonies which in constitution and lifestyle replicated that of the mother cities. The equally unavoidable growth of the state could have been linked to bureaucratization – Aristotle speaks, in *Politics*, of the variety of state administration.

Instead there was an attempt to approach the real equality of citizens through privatization and their direct involvement. There were the liturgies, the contributions made by citizens beyond what was formally required – for the theatre, public festivals, support of wars. Goldsmith (1987) has attempted to estimate Attic national wealth during the time of Pericles. Quantifications are certainly questionable without systematic statistical bases, but he was astonished at what he found. Given the Athenian focus on a free market, and the distance established between Athens and the wealth of oriental despotisms, it turned out that more than half of Athenian wealth was in public hands, not as an expression of state centralization but as a means of participatory democracy, where citizens jointly administered a considerable income which came, for example, from marine alliances or silver mines. A large part of public possessions consisted of temples and religious icons. As Perikles said according to Plutarch, the employment effect of public buildings was familiar; but despite the Sophist movement there can be no doubt of the religious belief of the citizenry, for whom religious and every-day life remained closely connected.

> Every state is as we see a sort of partnership, and every partnership is formed with a view to some good, since all the actions of all mankind are done with a view to what they think to be good.

Thus begins Aristotles' *Politics*. Here we appear to be close to a utilitarian explanation of socio-political and even economic relationships, if we replace what humans view as 'good' with what they view as 'useful' and if a discussion followed as to how the community can survive if each individual considers as useful that which is useful to him. But Aristotle immediately turns away from the individual and toward the state when he asks what good the community is struggling to achieve, and it will turn out that he is not seeking a functional connection according to which independent individuals seek their own benefit. He is instead seeking to determine the content of the good so that it can guide the behaviour of the reasonable citizen, and only through it – through public spirit rather than individual interest – can community be preserved. And so he then turns to the art of domestic economy, with its division of fields respective to roles. In books 7 and 8, the topic is a proper education. It is evident just here that the old ideal virtues retain their validity.

As regards slavery, Aristotle held the often admired idea that it would become redundant once automatic machines took over production. We have seen that – far from seeing something in the future that still remains for us largely utopian – Aristotle in fact went back to Homeric concepts of godly powers, for it is precisely the superhuman art of Hephaestus that allows him to fabricate self-propelled three-wheeled chariots and artificial virgins. If Aristotle seeks to spare at least the Greeks from the inevitability of slavery he expresses a consciousness of the cultural unity of the Greek tribes; but it is still true that whoever is outside this extended community has, as a defeated survivor of battle, no right to freedom.

Aristotle divided acquisitive activity into domestic economy which produces what is necessary for the 'good life', and chrematistics, the art of personal enrichment. The 'good life' remains embedded in the state; and the primary goal for Aristotle in his *Politics* is to discover the appropriate constitution for a state and the proper education of citizens.

Thus the art of domestic economy and the external goods produced according to its rules do not appear in Aristotle as consumable goods which directly bestow utility, but are instead only a means to something higher, namely a way of life free citizens may choose. Like Aristotle in the *Nicomachean Ethics*, the citizen can devote himself to a theoretical life (which culminates in the philosophical point of view and is for Aristotle the happiest), to a practical political life, a life focused on the increase of pleasure or to a life of commerce (*Nic. Eth.*, 1095b18–1096a10). This last employs the chrematistic techniques of acquiring wealth and is treated by Aristotle as forced, compulsive (ὁ δὲ χρηματιστὴς βίαιός τίς ἐστιν, ibid., 1096a8).

Menger (1976, p. 286) wrote that 'The predominantly ethical standpoint from which the people of antiquity regarded human relationships is reflected in the views of ancient writers on the nature of utility and the nature of goods'. If we adopt Menger's division of goods into various kinds of goods – consumable goods with an immediate utility as the first order; goods of the second order as resources for producing goods of the first order; and finally goods of a still higher order which are resources used to produce resources of a lower order, and thus to indirectly become consumable goods – then it is apparent that the Aristotelian conception of goods as means for the attainment of higher level goods translates into Menger's conceptions.

Aristotle's critique of Platonic ideas separates him from a conception of the higher-order good as the idea of Being, the one, the absolute good. But he also believes: 'the paradigm of being that always is – be it the being of the divine … – remains the ultimate point of reference in treating the practical nature of human being' (Gadamer 1986, p. 172). He denotes the teleologic cause as the 'wherefore and the good' (*Met*, 983a31). Thus there remains a higher order, a good of so-to-speak zero order, which all others, the physical goods, including all consumable objects, replace in a hierarchy of resource relationships. This 'good' is not a case of a consumable object and certainly not a technical resource like goods of the second or higher orders as in Menger; instead it is a question of the spiritual foundation of a way of life through which a fortunate life, a Eudaemonia, is hoped for. Eudaemonia is the ultimately desired good (*Nic. Eth.*, 1097a31).

Traditional Greek conceptions of the good life are introduced and employed philosophically in the Aristotelian theory of the Eudaemonia with which *Nicomachean Ethics* begins. Aristotle sought to ground the art of domestic economy serving the good life in a human nature whose aim was the life of the state. For it would be tautology to represent the Eudaemonia abstractly as that for which we strive, whatever that might be (ὁμολογούμενόν τι, ibid., 1097b23). The necessity of reflection upon the good life establishes the precedence of theory over praxis.

However, even a spiritually-oriented life requires a material foundation. External goods are useful only insofar as they serve this goal. The useful is therefore a good that is not good in and of itself, but serves other goods – this is a definition of utility in Aristotelian philosophy (ibid., 1099b15). Aristotle is therefore to that extent not a utility-theoretician, since utility-relations do not arise of themselves, as happens in the modern postulate of a preference order for each subject; instead the internal hierarchy of goods is derived from higher principles. Since it is the nature of humans to create a politically – we could perhaps say 'culturally' – determined community, it is not so simple for them to determine the useful in the same way that, for example, we know the nutritional requirements of a particular animal. But it remains necessary because – as we say today – a human without cultural norms is not able to communicate, nor is even capable of living. Guidance by instinct alone is not enough, although a sensory psychology interpretation of 'utility' suggests this.

After the positive characterization of the good life, Aristotle also had to critically examine the thesis that the good or the useful was to be measured by an increase in pleasure, by intellectual or sensual pleasure. He devotes the tenth book of the *Nicomachean Ethics* to the refutation of hedonism. The result is that a life well-led is also satisfying. This comforting consequence is however secondary; satisfaction is the result, not the cause, nor the primary identifying characteristic of a proper orientation to life (ibid., 1099a8). It is true that pleasure and pain appear to be deeply rooted in the human psyche, so that according to Aristotle many desire the good – not least the increase in the pleasure from a reward is a means of education – but for Aristotle that only goes to show that pleasure is *one* good or can be, but is also frequently a source of harm. And since various things will be felt as pleasurable by various people, it has to be asked what might be viewed as a proper satisfaction.

Aristotle decides for the perception of the good as a standard, since virtue and goodness are the measure of all things (ibid., 1176a18). Humans develop themselves by realizing the highest human possibilities. Therefore pleasure is not an end for Aristotle, but only a means; it is a form of rest and relaxation so that one can regain energy for other endeavours (ibid., 1176b34). He once again turns to the evidence that complete happiness is connected with theoretical activities. For their realization, however, the state community and its economic foundation is required. Here at last the goal of economy activity is explained.

Aristotelian theory cannot be justly dubbed utilitarian, even if some of his conceptions can be further developed into, or reduced to, utility-theory. When he speaks of the sensible boundaries to the basic necessities of life, he is not talking about diminishing marginal utility which in the neoclassical household is associated with an increase in effort and the formation of an equilibrium. He is not talking about work and effort, after all, but about a proper life: he sees, so to speak, the entire bundle of goods which serve the good life, together with household and lands. Thus attachment to the established concept is at the very heart of Aristotelian economic thought; there are reasonable limits to household wealth. While the Stoic limitation of need on the part of wealthy Romans might seem hypocritical, the life of the Greek citizen – limited by common expenditures, and evidenced by an astounding spiritual and cultural orientation, occasionally regulated by a statute on luxury – should today be imagined as on the whole quite modest.[34]

After having outlined the philosophical orientation of this good life and elaborated it in terms of contemporary Greek reality, Aristotle turns to the question of how this is to be secured by the state and its policies. The great danger, always a threat to order in antiquity, was the destruction of city life by foreign or domestic wars. It did not lay hidden in changing economic circumstance, like endogenous economic crises, or at least there are no voices which express such concerns. The cause of war is generally thought to be greed; the constant concern of political philosophers was to find a constitutional balance, possibly in a reformed democracy. Education was of no less importance; one can read in Aristotle's *Politics* how even music belonged to political education, and that the choice of tonalities had a character-building effect.

But Aristotle discovered in Chrematistic yet another 'economic mischief-maker' (Salin). Aristotle's turn against usury corresponds to a widespread attitude in most traditional societies familiar with money. It occurs when money-lending is seen one-sidedly in connection with the exploitation of emergency situations such as bad harvests and the like, instead of in connection with an influx of capital into production. Aristotle differentiates between an abstract amassing of wealth, which as such knows no limits, and the concrete provision of the necessities for household production, whose limitation is inbuilt. When Aristotle speaks here of two different ways of using money, one focused on exchange and one serving abstract increase, and when he, at the same time, expresses surprise at the possibilities of value comparisons of concrete objects of wealth, his discussion bears traces of a pre-monetary perspective in which the existence of equivalences in the sense of relative prices in exchange was questionable, not only because one primarily provided for oneself and exchange with others involved multiple transactions, but also because, additionally, other equivalences were repeatedly established by the exchange of gifts. Philosophical unease with the process of abstraction whose underlying laws he does not know leads Aristotle not only to condemn the abstract amassing of wealth in chrematistics and the associated professions of trading and money-lending, but also a work relationship such as wage labour that can only be regulated by means of money.

This insight is however most sharply revealed at an earlier point: When Aristotle separates the use of a thing from its exchange value, he must also ask for what purpose the work is done. In household production, for example, a shoe is not made for the sake of trade, but so that it can be used (*Pol.*, 1257a13). That should be generally true, insofar as enterprises are understood as households that exchange their surplus products. Behind this looms the old Greek conception of craftwork whose effort is focused on the quality of the object, which is why the division of labour in Greek philosophy is based from the start on the improvement of quality, not the increase of quantity.

> For it is not the function of courage to produce wealth, but to inspire daring; nor is it the function of the military art nor of the medical art, but it belongs to the former to bring victory and to the latter to cause health.
>
> (ibid., 1258a11)

In his text Aristotle organized a variety of professions according to their proximity to natural activities, whose characteristics are limited or outlined; I have compiled Figure 1.1[35] from this.

According to this figure, even robbery is relatively natural, Aristotle explaining this through the existence of beasts of prey, but in fact only understandable when placed in the context of a tradition of the laws of war. The values he touches on here do not exhaust the definition of the good life. In practice he remained open to the chrematistic professions. He recommended a range of authors for various forms of acquisition, and also for chrematistics (*Pol.*, 1259a8). These would be ancient texts on economic management, of which we possess a few on agriculture from the time of imperial Rome. Aristotle is far from raising his condemnation of chrematistic acquisition to a dogma, as later happened. However, among his students – *Politics* is, after all, a set of lectures – he argued for a turn toward the philosophical life that he himself practised.

There has been a great deal of speculation over Aristotelian exchange theory offered as part of the theory of justice in *Nicomachean Ethics*. The theory of justice includes distributive justice, which has to take account of rank. In this case it is more appropriate to think of the old division of honorary gifts than of the context of modern conceptions of distributive justice in a system founded upon wage labour. Aristotle chose proportionality as a symbol for just division: That which must be distributed, for example the honorary gifts,

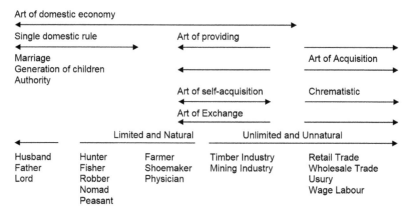

*Figure 1.1* Terms for chrematistics

Note: 'Professions' are partly hypothetical, ordered to the right and down according to reduction of self-sufficiency. With question marks: problematic insertion. The peasant provides for himself, the farmer exchanges surpluses.

must proportionate to the rank of the person. If the same proportion governs persons and things the distribution of goods does not alter rank. In fact, when A and B are the people to be honoured and C and D are the relevant gifts, the appropriate proportion is as follows:

$$A : B = C : D.$$

From that follows according to the intercept theorems:

$$A : B = (A + C) : (B + D).$$

After distribution proportionality remains.[36] With commutative justice, in contrast, a mean must be found. In a civil process, a judge, for example, finds a compromise; to symbolize that Aristotle introduces the arithmetic mean.

Finally, there is reciprocity (ἀντιπεπονθός), which is not always just: When an officer strikes a soldier the soldier cannot properly strike back (*Nic. Eth.*, 1132b29).

Aristotle differentiates between a contribution (μετάδοσις, 1133a2) and exchange (ἀντίδοσις, 1133a6). He states that contributions or donations keep the community united. The offering of contributions makes it clear that the community is free – subjects are encouraged to contribute. 'This is why they give a prominent place to the temple of the Graces – to promote the requital of services' (ibid., 1133a3).

The Charites (the Graces) are the goddesses of grace and gratitude; they are introduced because one should just as often spontaneously offer a contribution as respond to another with gratitude. This is the Homeric and even more ancient conception of an exchange of gifts surviving in the practice of the Liturgies, so long as they remained voluntary in the Greek city-state, a service of the citizen toward the community (*Pol.*, 1261a32). But also in *Politics* we find that reciprocity is said to maintain the city.

The exchange to which Aristotle turns, although his treatment is somewhat obscure, takes place between people who are different as such but who exchange equivalents (*Nic. Eth.*, 1133a18). The equality of different items is determined by money, which is why it was introduced, but which can also be neutralized (ibid., 1133a32). Aristotle is thinking here of coinage as a conventional means of exchange. He sees that there must be mutual needs in order for an exchange to take place; need 'holds everything together' (ibid., 1133a28).

But this explains only the qualitative preconditions of exchange; scarcely anybody today thinks that Aristotle assumed there to be a quantitative explanation for relative prices in terms of a kind of theory labour values, or of supply and demand. There is an interesting hypothesis that Aristotle, when he refers to proportions in connection with exchange, actually means a 'proportion of the proportions': that producers must be related to their product after an exchange as they were related to them beforehand. And so if A and B are people and C and D are their products:

$$(A : C) : (B : D) = (A : D) : (B : C),$$

which gives C = D, thus the equivalence of the exchanged gifts. Under these circumstances the rank order of a society, varying according to the form of society, is not altered by exchange.

It would lead us too far astray to describe here social strata and analyse the constitutions which Aristotle believed appropriate for various configurations of a city.[37] The guiding thought of his economic reflections seems to be a description of the conditions under which the respective forms of wealth acquisition, of distribution and of exchange do not disturb the order of the state. He distinguishes monarchy, aristocracy and constitutional democracy from their deviant forms, tyranny, oligarchy and democracy as the rule of the poor (*Pol.*, 1279a35–1279b10). In an ideal state citizens must also possess all civic virtues, and should therefore remain discharged from strenuous labour such as done by a peasant or craftworker (ibid., 1278a11). More realistic, however, is the to moderate class antagonisms and to choose democratic governmental forms; Aristotle calls for a stronger middle class to promote the balance of interests (ibid., 1308b30). An economic balancing of another kind takes place under tyrannies, when they repress the rich with taxes and thus hamper their chances of gaining followers, and at the same time employ the poor through public construction projects like the pyramids in Egypt or the temples built by Peisistratos (ibid., 1313b25). Solon also appears in Aristotle where he links measures of economic and political reform (ibid., 1273b36ff.).

From these somewhat arbitrarily selected examples it can be seen how Aristotle thought the political and economic orders were entwined. Wherever he senses that economic events have their own logic he seeks to direct them with political measures that allow him to uphold the principles of the good life for citizens. Citizens should strive to distance themselves from professions beneath their dignity; and the constitution should, as far as possible, not allow the occupants of such positions to become citizens. Although Aristotle is to a certain extent opposed to the way that economic theory finally turned out, he becomes one of its most important originators. His reflections on the exceptions and the limits of his system led, through the analysis of ecclesiastically permissible terms for the collection of interest, to an understanding of how interest developed and to the establishment of conceptions of a just wage and a just price, from which – much later – the concept of the 'natural' and finally of the 'normal' price developed. The obverse of this was the attempt of the Christian state to either make minorities (Jews) take up the undesirable jobs or – a utopian idea – to eliminate the real and necessary element of interest altogether.

But this critical turn would not come until the end of the middle ages and in early modernity. In antiquity, the systematic nature of Aristotle's economic thought stands out among the Hellenistic and Roman philosophers who followed him, insofar as we have any texts at all which even in the broadest sense refer to economics. For example: Theophrast, Aristotle's successor as head of his philosophy school, has left us images such as that of the miser who bends over to pick up the smallest coin and never allows any interest gained in money-lending to escape his clutches (Edmonds 1953, p. 66). This perspective does not, however, suggest an underlying theory. Or we find Teles, active around 240 BC, who catalogued edifying sayings about the constancy of a good character and the changeability of wealth, about the value of modesty and poverty (Nestle 1922, pp. 126–134). From Dikaiarch (around 310 BC), we have a very small fragment of a historical stages theory, which connects the concept of poverty of hunters and collectors with the conception of an original state of peace among them; war coming with the second stage (the nomads), followed by agriculture (ibid., p. 264). This theoretically important fragment too quickly becomes anecdotal. Ethical questions about economics are then dealt with systematically in other ways when, under the influence of Stoic philosophy, questions are raised about the appropriateness of certain actions. Thus, for instance, Cicero ponders whether problems should be made public when engaged in transactions. Must the seller of a house admit that an awful stench is rising from the cellar by announcing: 'Domum pestilentem vendo'? Naturally, says Cicero, honesty is not only morally correct but also necessary, otherwise one damages one's reputation (Klotz 1855, p. 95).

Aristotle also enjoyed the vivid example. But the anecdote functioned for him as proof of the theory, not as a narrative for which one needs to establish quite what might be meant. The reader is led by systematic thought that, even if it cannot or does not contain an economic model in the modern sense, for the most part derives from a philosophical structure whose consistency never fails to impress. Insofar as he touches on economic topics, he left behind a dual legacy: as witness to the economic thought of another epoch and, beyond mediations and reversals, as the father of modern theory. Here we have neither praised nor condemned the famous father, but rather questioned this lesser-known witness and, surprisingly, found that Aristotle represents not a one-sided late-classic perspective but – in the language of philosophers – a tradition that reaches back into the early period of the Greek legacy.

### Cicero's *De officiis*: the moral duties of mankind

*Roma aeterna* – Roman tradition is the ligament which binds Western culture together. This is the source of our thinking about law and the state; and both Greek culture and Christianity have come down to us through this tradition. We might therefore naturally expect to find a Roman among contributors to the history of economic theory. On the other hand, there is the well-known statement from Salin (1923, p. 4):

If economic relationships had the power to shape science and systems, if intellectual constructions were only the superstructure built upon material relations, or if they were necessarily linked to a specific economic or social situation, then Rome would have had to have provided the foundations for an economy theory of antiquity ... From Caesar to Trajan, the *Imperium Romanum* was in this regard a world economy ... like no era before or since; to a great degree an extensive economy of money and credit had replaced the old local forms based on exchange in kind, and all manifest 'sociological' prerequisites for a scientific economics were abundantly available.[38]

There were Roman texts which addressed economic questions, but no conscious, articulated system capable of representing the autonomous functioning of a complete and independent economic structure.

There are various explanations for this historical state of affairs. It could be that the best Roman economic texts have been lost. Yet if such texts had effectively expressed the idea of a self-regulating economy we can assume that this would be reflected in the historical record. What we do know, on the evidence among other things of the vast ruins and objects of daily use scattered throughout the former Roman empire and beyond, is that during this era productive forces warranting comparison with the Early Modern era and the onset of the Mercantile period were developed. Sixteenth and early seventeenth century authors testify to this; Serra, for example, reports that it was only in international trade between the old and the new world that the modern era really surpassed Antiquity.[39] Roman production and trade were sufficiently developed that oil lamps from a single establishment were sold all over the Mediterranean area, that Italian wine and olive oil reached all parts of Gaul and Britain, and that international trade reached as far as India and China.

One might argue that the absence of Roman economic theory could be attributed to the practical orientation of the Romans. But the Romans never tired of Greek philosophy and religious speculation. Thus the paradox in Salin's statement can also be attributed to the fact that a Roman market economy in its modern liberal form never emancipated itself from a political framework, so that real autonomy of the economy never became apparent; there was not even any effort to advance the significance of the economy.

According to Marx's followers, the ancient mode of production was based on the institution of slavery. Max Weber's alternative interpretation (Love 1990) follows on from the controversy between Bücher and Meyer over the 'primitive' character of economic forms in classical Greece (Finley 1973). Bücher claimed that the cultural achievements of the Greek city-states rested on a comparatively simple economic foundation, with trade only moderately developed. The rural household, integrated into the wider society by virtue of the participation of citizens in political life, formed the basic unit. Meyer sought to draw exact parallels with the developmental stages of the late middle ages, and therefore saw the economy of imperial Rome as related to the modern one. Since both sides in the dispute referred to real phenomena, it is only possible to reconcile the opposing interpretations if the ancient economy is understood not simply as a preliminary stage of our economy – lacking only this or that institution, and which had not yet achieved the technological breakthrough to industrial production – but is instead defined positively: the rationality of the citizen; the interlinking of the state and the economy – many of the supporting institutions were not simply different from those today, but reproduced themselves according to their own logic, a logic which Max Weber sought to establish.

According to Weber, means of production were available as in modern capitalism, but the form of the division of labour and hence the prospect of increased production differed from their equivalents in an industrial economy because of the use of slaves – the later emergence of industrial economy was related to the use of free wage labour assisted by machinery. Weber saw that there were limits to the division of labour in workshop-based production; he regarded the city more as a centre of consumption than of production; he emphasized the importance of tribute and distinguished rental payments from profits. Since slaves simultaneously represented a capital investment and performed labour, a great deal of capital was expended per unit of work. There was therefore little flexibility in the use of labour, it was hard to relate costs incurred to goods produced, and the institution of slavery hindered above all the use of material incentives. Different forms of acquisitive behaviour conformed to no one pure rationality, as in tax farming, small-scale usury and the sale of offices. Only the formation of a strong imperial power, supported by military expansion, could overcome local, particular interests. The imperial orientation did not help free entrepreneurs, who developed new products and methods of production and thus successfully developed their own markets; this imperial orientation instead benefited those economic agents who knew how to work the political system and pick up contracts. There was especial difficulty with the efficient use of slaves in agriculture, where a number of different activities had to be integrated. It was difficult to find constant employment through the year for slaves when various fruits, vegetables and field crops ripened in sequence – although during large harvests the slaves could be supplemented with free wage-labourers. In rural areas it remained especially difficult to keep track of production costs in the individual branches of production, and to focus efforts to improve production in the appropriate area. The supervision of estates was delegated to administrators, permitting an orientation to profit and the introduction of simple forms of accounting to be associated with forms of allocation that allowed rich citizens to live out ancient ideals without themselves having to be efficient businessmen. However, at the same time the market process did not improve productivity, as it does today. The concentration of wealth, the introduction of new consumer goods and the provisioning of a realm which stretched from the Atlantic to the Black and the Red Seas lead to other forms of change: The Romans were genial inventors when it came to giving clear expression to displays of power and pomp; their typical architectural style was imitated well into the twentieth century.

Given the small number of laws by comparison with today, and the restrictions of customs which affected all aspects of life – even the prosperity of the *beati possidentes* – made it hard for individuals to live their lives 'correctly', oriented to others but without neglecting one's own advantage. What favours could be done for the powerful, which duties were owed to the family, which means of control were to be used with regard to slaves, which forms of life led in such an environment to prestige, to outer and inner happiness?

What we call an economic ethic could barely be distinguished from the ethics related to the practical conduct of family life, but this must have played an important role. I have therefore chosen to discuss the Roman author Cicero, the humanist, whose work *De officiis* was of such momentous importance for the early modern era, and which has since been widely disseminated. This choice was also promoted by the recent debate on the influence of Stoicism upon Adam Smith (Vivenza 1999, pp. 97–126). In the past, this influence went unregarded, but its introduction has made it possible to expose the ancient roots of Smith's conception of order. Cicero may have associated himself more with the New Academy than with the Stoics, but Stoic thinking forms the basis for *De officiis* and has been diffused via this book since the late middle ages. The question posed by Cicero, how the useful and the virtuous can be combined, is *the* problem of an economic ethic.

Before we turn to *De officiis* some additional points can be made about the Roman state, its economy and Roman economic theory, extending Weber's remarks. 'Like virtually no other ancient society apart from Sparta, the Romans accepted a regime of moral standards set by the censor' (Demandt 1995, p. 390).

Cicero was a *homo novus* who found his way to the heights of the old society. Climbing the social ladder in Rome usually took several generations. The *servi*, who were without rights, had some prospect of being set free. The free non-citizens (*peregrini, provinciales*), bound by the same civil laws as citizens, could become *cives Romani* through civil or military service. The wealthy among these were the knights (*equites*); they were able to become a member of the nobility (*nobiles*), with a career in civil service. Cicero made his way to this last step, leading from the approximately 20,000 knights to the roughly 600 senatorial families, through promotion from one post to another until he reached the consulate, then becoming a leader of the senate. This was the supreme consultative institution which, while formally possessing some emergency rights, governed by virtue its *auctoritas*, since it was limited to making proposals. While not possessing any formal position in the senate, Cicero was able to use his eloquence and integrity to extend his influence, although at times subject to serious criticism.[40]

At all levels relations of dependency based upon personal bonds of loyalty (*fides*) played an essential role, a system of clientelage such as that of the former master towards a man whom he has freed and provided with some capital. The magistracy – the highest level of government officials – was not the executive body of the popular assembly but the holder of a delegated authority, possessing the freedom to make its own decisions. Since formal law allowed individuals far more discretion than did custom and expectations, a great deal turned on the personal behaviour of citizens, whatever the significance of the functions involved. They were constantly tempted to exceed their capacities and responsibilities, checked only by the threat of a loss of prestige. Cicero, opposing utility to virtue, often speaks of the influence of reputation at both philosophical and practical levels, each time endeavouring to prove that conflicts between the two are only apparent, and that real utility and real virtue coincide.

Formal laws represented a fixed but porous filter which in many respects left a great deal of discretion to the Roman state, while on the other hand the more malleable customs of Roman society, so closely enmeshed in daily life, today appear much more rigid and inflexible. We find a comparable contrast in the economy, where the market enjoyed an autonomy which has today been subordinated to the state; the Roman state largely (but not exclusively) financed itself on the one hand by tax farming, and on the other by auctioning or directly contracting-out state activities, such as the provisioning of the army, the construction of buildings and elements of the infrastructure. Hence a type of entrepreneur (*publicani*) came into existence, dependent on state contracts for survival. Highly-detailed regulation had to replace disputes over relevant moral standards and struggles over the reputation of participants (when the *publicani* were too arbitrary in their actions the reputation of the Roman official who had assigned the contract also suffered); and since the nineteenth century state administrations have sought to free themselves from this by privatization. For instance, during the Roman Republic the Postal Service was the object of a leasing arrangement. In individual provinces – in the wealthy East – it was the *publicani* who collected taxes which formed a major part of Rome's income, and it was the job of the Roman governor to determine the respective rights of agriculturalists and tax farmers; for the latter could enrich themselves if they dishonestly exceeded their authority. We know that Cicero intervened in such cases to ensure a fair settlement.[41]

For the inhabitants of Rome during Cicero's time the era must have seemed to be one of an unprecedented boom, in which ever larger amounts of the wealth of the known world poured into the city and was there further augmented – not to the immediate benefit of all, since the proletariat was in constant danger of decline, but to the benefit of the rich. However, the businesses of the rich and the building projects which they initiated maintained in turn an ever-increasing metropolitan population for whom 'bread and circuses' was a way of life.

This form of division between rich and poor does not merely express the contempt of the former for the latter, as it might seem to the modern reader; instead it related to a social order whose existence and basic characteristics were only exceptionally questioned by contemporaries, where the wealth of citizens and that of the state were much the same thing. For Cicero the contrast of rich and poor was as natural as that of upper and lower, or the elite and the masses (*locupletes – tenues, summi – infimi, optimates – multitudo*); the people could be ordered by wealth, social rank and age ('descriptus enim populus censu, ordinibus, aetatibus') (Mratschek-Halfmann 1993, p. 4).[42]

Mratschek-Halfmann writes (thinking especially of Cicero): 'While Stoicism and the nostalgic reverence for early Roman simplicity continued to praise poverty, in practice poverty was despised.' Some perspective on this accusation of a moral double-standard by this philosophical tradition – and morality would never be a problem if it were not constantly associated with a double standard – can be gained by a comparison with Ancient Greece. The difference between rich and poor citizens in classical Athens, where democratic forms were more strongly developed, was significantly less and could more easily be ameliorated – and this in a smaller area, with basically the same means of redistribution, employment and connections with overseas colonies. The cultural opposition between high and low also increased with the growth of Roman power, to the point where praising poverty seemed utterly hypocritical. The cultural upper class in the time of Caesar Augustus pursued refinement of a kind whose literary reflection we still enjoy, but a refinement in which the *plebs* took little part; the average Athenian citizen by contrast could and did attend performances of the tragedies of Aeschylos, Sophocles, and Euripides. There were exceptional cases of individuals overcoming poverty, and three from the time after Cicero can be named: the well-known Stoic philosopher Epictetes, a freed slave; the poet Horace, the son of a freed slave; and the shoemaker Vatinius, who went from having nothing to possessing a fortune which made him the richest man of his time (ibid., p. 213). Epictetes was finally able to boast of friendship with three emperors.

The wealth of the senators lay above all in large estates – most of them spread between several villas – together with a large house in Rome, in which politics, business and the enjoyment of life could be cultivated. Whoever lost this fortune quickly lost respect, posts and influence.

Understanding of the interconnection between economic, social and political hierarchies allows the Weberian thesis (that Rome can be typified as 'political capitalism') to be extended. The rich Roman citizen clearly had to play several roles: he was not only husband and father, but also the head of a large family, a patron, citizen, office holder and magistrate, and, in certain phases of life, also a warrior and an army commander. Whereas neo-classical theory clearly distinguishes between the economic action of a utility-maximizing household and a profit-maximizing businessman, we are here presented with an identity between house, enterprise, and political unit, where coherent action is only possible by virtue of the way in which these different functions are united in the same person. If the various subsystems of society were to be understood as essentially independent mechanisms with their own terms of reference this dispersion would lead to severe conflicts of role and interest; but instead the individual deploys a variety of criteria and principles to settle such conflicts of interest within his own person.

The counter-image is the unity of statesman and head of household, as advanced by Plato. Insofar as acquisition related to natural products, Aristotle considered the art of acquisition to be an organic element of householding (Schefold 1989a, pp. 15–55). For Cicero, as a Roman, the art of acquisition was not so systematically organized. *De officiis* presents the Roman citizen together with all his associated tasks, and Cicero proposes that philosophy be introduced so extensively into the practical world that those whom he has so educated are better able to arrive at decisions in concrete situations by conforming to custom (conceptions of virtue) and exploiting their talents, and in the act of uniting the two appearing as a complete person, worthy of respect.

The most important role conflict is not the one with which we are familiar from development economics, where when dealing with agriculture in poor countries a clear separation is made between households and economic activity. The techniques employed are often said not to be 'rational', i.e. selected according to the criterion of profit maximization; instead the organization of work and risk-taking are determined by traditional preferences, so that attempts at modernization are met with resistance which, while reducing the income of the producer, in their eyes increases the utility they draw from it. The clear conflict regarding economic factors was according to Cicero, who was moderately wealthy, but not extremely rich, something quite different: as an ambitious politician struggling for influence he had to impress his equals and those dependent upon him by entertaining them and giving them gifts; impressing them with his *liberalitas*, or generosity, which corresponds to Aristotle's concept of virtue. But Cicero, the social climber, also knew that he could not simply spend his way to the top and that a fortune has to be earned and secured. His philosophy ruled out the usual motivation of striving for profit, but he was also responsible for his family; thrift is therefore also required. We shall see how in this conflict he formulates the problem in such a way that the preservation and, at most, moderate increase of wealth is regarded as virtuous, while any regard for purely entrepreneurial action oriented to acquisition is entirely suppressed.

Due to the remoteness of Roman economic thought, little mention of its literary expression has made its way into writings in the history of economic thought. There was more interest during the nineteenth century than in the twentieth. Adolphe Blanqui (1860, vol. 1, pp. 74–110) deserves mention as a pioneer in France. In Germany, the first history of economic thought was written by Julius Kautz (1970 [1860]), who included detailed discussion devoted to the Roman authors. For the time being we will not examine Christian Rome in late antiquity, as our focus here is on Cicero.

Cicero is the only Roman to whom Kautz devotes an entire part of one chapter. Given his knowledge of all Cicero's works, he thought he had arrived at a 'rather clear and complete impression of his ideas and principles regarding political economy' (ibid., p. 80). A fortune was to be earned through prudence, hard work and the avoidance of luxury. Frugality is important, but so is the ethical use of wealth, that is, generosity. Kautz found citations which recognize the importance of work and the division of labour which, of course, sit alongside others which say that commerce and craft activity are unworthy of free men. In this way the values of ancient economy are reproduced; Cicero only 'mildly condemned' wholesale trade. Cicero recommends investing the profits earned in agriculture; he was opposed to the export of money and the charging of interest, and he noted various influences on prices, such as the size of the harvest, changes in consumption, and competition. There is little theory behind many useful observations, but the manner in which they are put together provides an impression of the special features of Roman economic thought.

Kautz, who moves on to deal with other authors, emphasizes the orientation of Roman economic policy toward the general good ('salus rei publicae suprema lex esto'; the welfare of the state shall be the highest law) (ibid., p. 179, own translation). The following citation by Cicero from the lawyer Paullus shows quite clearly how money emerged as a commodity form that could simplify exchange processes, the varying amounts of this commodity given in exchange equalling the price of other goods.

> Origo emendi vendendique a permutationibus coepit; olim enim non ita erat nummus, neque aliud merx aliud pretium vocabatur, sed unusquisque secundum necessitatem temporum ac rerum utilibus inutilia permutabat, quando plerumque evenit, ut quod alteri superest, alteri desit. Sed quia non semper nec facile concurrebat ut cum tu haberes quod ego desider- arem invicem ego haberem quod tu accipere velles: electa est materia cuius publica ac perpetua aestimatio difficultatibus permutationem aequalitate quantitatis subveniret; eaque materia forma publica percussa, usum dominiumque non tam ex substantia praebet quam ex quantitate, nec ultro merx utrumque sed alterum pretium vocatur.
>
> (ibid., p. 173)

Translation:

> The origin of purchase and sale is derived from exchanges, for formerly money was not known, and there was no name for merchandise or the price of anything, but every one, in accordance with the requirements of the time and circumstances exchanged articles which were useless to him for other things which he needed; for it often happens that what one has a superabundance of, another lacks. But, for the reason that it did not always or readily happen that when you had what I wanted, or, on the other hand that I had what you were willing to take, a substance was selected whose public and perpetual value, by its uniformity as a medium of exchange, overcame the difficulties arising from barter, and this sub- stance, having been coined by public authority, represented use and ownership, not so much on account of the material itself as by its value, and both articles were no longer designated merchandise, but one of them was called the price of the other.
>
> (Cicero 1932, vol. V, p. 3)[43]

The clarity of this definition of money is a result of an effort to solve the legal problem of differentiating between purchase and exchange. In Chapter 3.23 of *Institutions* in Emperor Justinian's (circa AD 500) *Corpus iuris civilis*, there is a comparison between the acquisition of things by means of barter and their purchase by money; the exchange contract which leads to a *permutatio*, is different from one which results in a *venditio* (Behrends, Knütel, Kupisch and Seiler 1999, p. 191).

Hence the definition of the just price finds its starting point in Roman law. In the same chapter of *Institutions* (ibid., p. 189). it states that no sale is possible without a price, and that the price must also be a definite price (otherwise the exchange contract is open to challenge): 'nulla emptio sine pretio esse potest sed et certum pretium esse debet'. The agreed price (*certum pretium*) later becomes the just price (*iustum pretium*) where an elevated price charged by the seller cannot be questioned by the purchaser. In *Corpus iuris* there are already signs of the conception that costs for raw materials and labour must here play an important role, since for instance a distinction is such that a contract of sale exists when someone orders a ring from a jeweller who makes it with his own gold, while there is a service contract when the jeweller makes a ring from gold that belongs to the purchaser. This already points to way to the development of an early-modern labour theory of value, although this path is not yet taken. In the example here the value of the ring would be determined by the amount of work which went into the production of the gold, plus the work of the jeweller.

The contribution of Roman writers in regard to agriculture is well-known; the works of Cato, Varro and Columella in particular have survived. The elder Cato, who lived at the time of the Punic Wars and was sceptical of Greek influences, commended husbandmen and small farmers as the foundation of military prowess, and developed very precise concepts of well-found agricultural enterprise requiring adequate capitalization, communication between farm and outside world, and decisive labour management. Varro divided agricultural enterprise into its various activities and raises the question to which activities investment should be profitably directed. To manage the farm workers he recommends the employment of foremen who, given a degree of education, should have a basic literacy and be hard-working, competent and older than the workers they direct (Varro 1996, p. 188). He further recommends providing them with livestock together with female partners, so that they might be more securely attached to the estate. He understood the purpose of the division of labour not only to lie in proper employment of labour by day or by season, but also to be a means of ensuring control over slaves, who were in themselves a form of property, making up an important part of the capital invested. He therefore considered that it was better in unhealthy areas – for example areas where malaria is common – to work with day labourers rather than with slaves.

Among the writers on agrarian subjects Columella (1981–1983) has the most to say. Writing during the imperial period he criticized those who possessed wealth but who spurned just that form of employment which was ethically unblemished ('quod omne crimine caret') and who, rather than learn techniques of cultivation, appoint their best slaves to be estate managers and generally develop their spirit and character through agricultural activity, instead devoted themselves to the urban pleasures of feasting and bathing. Columella also has a good deal to say about leadership. He maintains that an illiterate person can also be a suitable leader if he knows how to lead and has a good memory. An owner himself must know how to motivate his people and to assess the abilities of the workers so that, for example, he might be capable of judging how and when to profit from viticulture, be able to form groups of workers who work harmoniously together, where an individual will not be punished for a failure on the part of the group. We cannot go into detail on the above points, but Columella's examples of precise planning are famous, when for instance he proposes that for an estate of a given size a particular relationship between draught animals, ploughs and day labourers is necessary so that for the planting and harvesting of various crops there is a suitable number of workers available. If what he here describes is sketched out in tabular form the resemblance to linear programming is striking (Columella 1981, p. 655).[44] His comparison of the costs and yield from viticulture, including interest charges (but not compound interest) has also been cited (ibid., vol. 3, Chapter 3). The estimated yield is then compared with the annual interest yielded from an equivalent financial investment, and from this it is determined whether investment in viticulture is profitable. In the history of business administration Varro's treatment of daily work has been seen as a very early example of a work schedule, noting that not all magnitudes increase in proportion to the cultivated area, so that it is important to pay attention to the relation of the parts to the whole. Schneider (1981, p. 86) has called Columella's analysis of viticulture the first attempt to formulate an investment appraisal, or to calculate efficiency.

Whoever looks for any similarly impressive macroeconomic insights in Roman writers will be disappointed. The most striking and comprehensible economic intervention of the Roman era is Diocletian's price edict of AD 301, a law valid for the entire empire and which was, at least in the East, in many different locations carved in stone, so that by collecting together fragments from more than one hundred sites it is possible to reconstruct price lists for hundreds of commodities and services.[45] Such price regulations appear to have already existed before Diocletian, becoming even more common later, during the transition to the Byzantine era: 'In fact, a permanent price policy which does seem to have also been supported by the army, sought to secure production and tax revenue, and above all an occupation structure based upon social standing' (Lauffer 1971, p. 5). It was for instance decreed that a mason or a carpenter should receive double the daily wage of a camel or mule driver, a painter who simply painted walls three times the wage, while a painter who painted images on walls received six times the daily wage of a camel driver (Giacchero 1971, pp. 276ff.). Transport by land was much more expensive than by ship. Wine from good areas was five times more expensive than vinegar (ibid., pp. 272ff.).

However, the rationale behind the edict was far removed from principles that would be required for an economic, or especially monetary, policy aimed at the stabilization of monetary value; the inflationary pressures that it seeks to counter were attributed only to usury: 'For who is so dulled and devoid of human feeling that he cannot recognize, does not notice that, with regard to goods sold in trade or circulating daily between cities, there has arisen such arbitrariness in price that rampant greed can be checked neither by the broad range of products available nor by the ample stocks remaining from previous harvests?' (Freis 1984, pp. 240ff.). The 'arbitrariness of price' (*licentia pretiorum*) and 'rampant greed' (*effrenata libido rapiendi*) (Giacchero 1971, p.135) referred to here is however merely the moralistic expression of the infuriation of an administration able to meet its needs only by ever-increasing expenditure, seeking its salvation in comprehensive supervision and control. Cicero's text *On Duties* on the other hand, which we here treat as representative of Roman economic thought, deals for the most part with the responsibility of the individual citizen.

We here insert a few words on the Cicero edition, which was used for the facsimile edition of the *Klassiker der Nationalökonomie*. It may well be the first printed text of classical antiquity.[46] In 1465, two editions of *De officiis* were published: the one used in the series, published by Fust and Schöffer in Mainz, which is possibly somewhat older, and another brought out by Sweynheym and Pannartz in the monastery of Subiaco. Lactantius and Cicero's *De oratore* seem also to have been printed in Subiaco later the same year. In any case, the text reproduced in the series is the first in which Greek words were printed with Greek letters (Cicero 1961b, p. XV).

The beautiful print mimics the Medieval style of handwriting, leaving room for book lovers to have chapter initials added by calligraphers in the contemporary style.

The Cicero edition from Fust and Schöffer includes some additions which correspond to the Humanist era: poems in new Latin and, bound with it, Cicero's text *Paradoxa Stoicorum*. Cicero had composed this in early 46 BC. It is a philosophical text, with a rhetorical resonance:

> The truculent tone betrays Cicero's frustration and anger at ingratitude, decline in prestige, being forced to live on the sufferance of what he regards as the wrong side, which has won the civil war; whereas, in a better world, he and his fellow citizens would be enjoying the ideal state of *On the Republic* and *On the Laws*.
>
> (MacKendrick 1989, p. 32)

The energy with which the Stoic fundamentals are here exposed, and the manner in which their radical formulation is set against contemporary decline extends and amplifies *De officiis*, which sought to re-establish the principles of the just and good life.

For example, if we leaf back ten pages from the end of the book, we find a rather casually set Greek heading:

ὅτι μόνος πλούσιος

which is translated into Latin in the Fust and Schöffer edition, as:

Quod solus sapiens dives.

There then follows Cicero's text on this paradox, which runs in English:

Only the wise man is rich.

To illustrate the point of the *Paradox* we can briefly summarize Cicero's explanation of this statement, providing some insight into his economic thought. A rich person is someone who is content with his possessions. A poor person is someone who is tempted into wickedness by money; for while the treasure chest may be full, the spirit can be null and void. Cicero alludes to the rich man Crassus, who had claimed that no person could be rich who could not maintain a private army. A criminal use of accumulated wealth is here evident: provinces will be ruined and politicians put under pressure. The rich person who accumulates debt is more dependent than the humble person who gets by on his own income. Even Cicero (who owned more than half a dozen villas and a house on the Palatine!) admits that perhaps he consumes more than he should. 'Sed quid ego de me loquor, qui morum ac temporum vitio aliquantum etiam ipse fortasse in huius saeculi errore verser?' (Cicero 1953, p. 50).[47] It is thus the lifestyle and not the *census* that determines real income, for only the virtuous person is really rich (MacKendrick 1989, pp. 90ff.).

The new Latin verses which frame and supplement the *Paradoxa* and form the conclusion to the book, are not important poems in themselves but express well the humanistic endeavor to improve contemporary life through the revival of the old. There are twelve epitaphs (*Versus XII sapientum*) and a poem by Flaccus: *De vita(e) humana(e) brevitate*.

Cicero, who was born in Arpinum on 3 January 106 BC and murdered near Gaëta on 7 December 43 BC, spent his school years until 82 BC in Rome; he studied in Greece and Asia Minor from 79 to 77 BC and gained a wide-ranging philosophical and legal education. His rhetorical talents enabled him to move from the rank of knight to a career in the senate: he was *Qaestor* in 75, *Aedil* in 69, *Praetor* in 66 and, despite the reluctance of the nobility, *Consul* in 63 BC. Since the trial of Verres (70), he was regarded as Rome's prime orator. His political career ended with Caesar, whose politics of violence he rejected. In 59 he went into exile in Greece. In 57, he joined the triumvirate and was *Proconsul* in Cilicia in 51. He attempted to mediate between Pompeius and Caesar, and found the latter's victory in the civil war to be the greater evil.

After Caesar's victory he sought in vain to persuade Caesar to restore the old order. When his daughter Tullia died in 45 BC he sank into depression. Caesar treated him with respect, but Cicero's hatred of the absolute ruler knew no bounds and he welcomed his assassination. He now once more played a leading role in the senate, until the second triumvirate of Antony, Lepidus and Octavian proscribed him – 200 senators, among them Cicero, together with 2000 knights were victims of this persecution. During this final phase of his life, fleeing his pursuers, moving between his villas, Cicero nevertheless remained active, philosophizing and writing (Andresen 1965, col. 627ff.).

As an orator and philosopher, Cicero followed classical models. As a philosopher, he was closest to the younger Academy. Demosthenes is considered to be his model as an orator. The extensive amount and contemporary significance of speeches and letters that have survived have become important sources for the study of history. The surviving letters 'make Cicero the best-known person of antiquity' (ibid., col. 632). As a philosopher, Cicero is also close to the Stoics, as a person even closer to the Epicureans, although they were his scholarly opponents. Thus *De officiis* has various Greek sources and deals at the same time with Roman tradition, although the first two of the three books are, by Cicero's own account, based on the Stoic Panaitios of Rhodes (ca. 180 until 110 BC) who had already written for a Graecophile circle of Roman readers, making use of classical texts from the fourth century BC.

Plutarch's portrait of Cicero (his biography is paired with Demosthenes) reported many anecdotes about him, two of which can be noted here. The first takes place following Cicero's courageous public stand against Sulla, whom he avoided by fleeing to Greece. When as a student he gave his first assigned speech before his teacher, Apollonius, his teacher is said to have

> desired Cicero to declaim in Greek; and he readily complied, because he thought by that means his faults might the better be corrected. When he ended his declamation, the rest were astonished at his performance, and strove which should praise he was speaking; and when he had done, he sat a long time thoughtful and silent. At last, observing the uneasiness it gave his pupil, he said – 'As for you, Cicero, I praise and admire you, but I am concerned for the fate of Greece. She had nothing left her but the glory of eloquence and erudition, and you are carrying that too to Rome'.
>
> (Plutarch 1841, p. 98)

Concerning Cicero's flight at the end of his life, Plutarch tells how he finally went to the lake at Gaëta, where he owned a small estate that had served him as a summer resort. As the murderers closed in, his slaves carried him in a curtained litter through covered arcades from the villa down to the lake. A student who hung back is said to have betrayed him. His pursuers hurried after the litter, which was stopped and set down. Cicero's head and hands were cut off; they were brought to Rome where Antony had them nailed to the podium. Many years later Octavius sought reconciliation with Cicero's family.

We will now examine the structure of *De officiis*, although the editors complain of its lack of order. The book is throughout addressed to Cicero's son Marcus, who was then studying in Athens. He was thus receiving moral and philosophical instruction from his father, together with examples from Roman history, Cicero also regaling his son with personal memories of his beginnings and the high points of his career, references which were not always pleasant for the son.

The son has to be able to speak Greek as well as he can speak Latin, and oratory and philosophy complemented each other. The use of philosophy consists in its recognition of duties: 'Nulla enim vitae pars ... vacare officio potest' (I.4; 'For no phase of life ... can be without its moral duty').[48]

Honor (*honestas*) consists of the pursuit of duty, and its negligence leads into baseness and disgrace (*turpitudo*).

In place of a formal definition of duties as right and proper action, we find a differentiation between correct and an only probably correct duty. This follows Panaitios in determining whether an act is morally correct, whether it leads to pleasure or comfort, to wealth or power, or whether there is a contradiction between the honourable and the useful. Cicero wanted to build on Panaitios in particular because he understood these terms to be relative and not only absolutes, seeking through comparison the better and more useful in each.

Humans are distinguished from animals by their ability to differentiate and deliberately shape their own future. In particular, man seeks truth and dominance; both arise from the natural instinct for self-preservation. It is furthermore possible to distinguish the four (cardinal) virtues from which the honourable arises: truth (*perspicientia veri*), justice (*tribuendo suum cuique*), bravery and magnanimity (*magnitudo animi*), and modesty (*modestia et temperantia*). These concepts (I.15) are deployed by turn to lend emphasis to their different aspects; thus, theoretical wisdom (*sapienta*) is commonly differentiated from practical intelligence (*prudentia*).

The practical Roman rejects a life that loses itself in pure science, for virtue shines in action: 'Virtutis enim laus omnis in actione consistit' (I.19; 'For the whole glory of virtue is in activity').

Since humans are born social creatures, the maintenance of order depends on justice (*iustitia*) and charity (*beneficentia*), which are also connected with generosity (*liberalitas*). This introduces the idea of the economic, starting from a theory of possession. Property is not natural, but arises from long-standing possession following victory, a law, a contract, a trade, an exchange, a purchase and reallocation (I.21). The right to property and the obligations and duties of men are conjoined, especially the duty of avoiding doing something unjust, not forgetting extending protection against injustice done to others. Greed is often a cause of injustice. Wealth, sought after to meet basic necessities, to quench enjoyment or satisfy ambition leads to an insatiable desire for money. While efforts to improve a family's property are not to be criticized, injustice must always be avoided in the process. 'Nec vero rei familiaris amplificatio nemini nocens vituperanda est, sed fugienda semper iniuria est' (I.25; 'Still, I do not mean to find fault with the accumulation of property, provided it hurts nobody, but unjust acquisition is always to be avoided').

The most recent example of a ruthless transgression of the boundaries of justice is Caesar's *principatum* (I.26). It is always great minds who are led into temptation.

Duties change with circumstance; it can be wrong to hold fast to a formal obligation, and Cicero expresses that in a proverb: 'Summum ius summa iniuria' (I.41; 'More law, less justice').

After a thorough discussion of martial law there follows a consideration of justice with respect to slaves and workers. Here Cicero avoids the issue of whether slavery is justified (the Stoics refuse to justify it on the grounds that it is a natural phenomenon); he limits himself to commenting that slaves should also be fairly paid for their work (I.41).

Nothing suits human nature ('nihil ... naturae hominis accomodatius') better than charity (I.42; 'Nothing appeals more to the best in human nature'). The beneficiary should not thereby be harmed (as for example with flattery), it cannot exceed our means, and it must respect the dignity (*pro dignitate*) of the beneficiary. Hence one cannot do as Caesar did, and steal from others in order to give presents to friends. Indeed, modern politicians are quite fond of being generous with other people's money. *Liberalitas* should also not be accompanied by ostentation ('ab ostentationem magis quam a voluntate') (I.44; 'ambition to make a show of being open-handed'). We should do more for the more virtuous, and the most for those who love us; no duty is more necessary than showing thanks.

When exchanging presents, should one seek to exceed the gift of another? Cicero refers to a verse from Hesiod (2007, p. 12): 'Take fair measure from your neighbour and pay him back fairly with the same measure, or better, if you can; so that if you are in need afterwards, you may find him sure.'

Cicero is in favour of an augmented exchange of presents *maiore mensura* and says that one should at the same time 'imitate those fertile fields which yield far more than they have received?' (I.48).

The physiocratic analogy is thus applied to the exchange of presents, and not to production. On the other hand, the exchange of presents is voluntary, and they are not owed to a bad person.

Human society is united by race, nation, language, community, but finds its most intimate expression in the family, which is the foundation of the state: 'id autem est principium urbis' (I.54; 'And this is the foundation of civil government').

Pre-eminent is friendship based on morality and the community of good manners. When it comes to duty, however, the fatherland comes first.

Following these closely-related considerations regarding justice follows the praise of the greatest virtue – bravery – for which Cicero sets limits:

arrogance, bravery without justice and fighting for one's selfish aims all count as evils, not virtues. And as an *odiosum* he finds that generosity easily turns into a hunger for power (I.64). He himself feels – and says as much – to be on slippery ground and seeks a path from martial to civil courage. An independent life can be led among the elite or, if one retreats from such a life, in the countryside, like many philosophers. Whoever has political talent should however put himself forward. Freedom is no less important than war and:

Cedant arma togae, concedat laurea laudi

(I.77)

Yield, ye arms, to the toga; to civic praises, ye laurels

– this hexameter should remind one of Cicero's suppression of the Catilinian conspiracy. Was it not like this while Cicero ruled as consul? And did he not earn more fame by saving the peace than others gain through waging war?[49] Following on from this Cicero introduces many examples from Roman history in which the courageous become equable, even polite.

This relates organically to the fourth virtue, moderation, which is often in the Christian symbol system portrayed as a modest girl pouring a little wine from a small jug into a very large bowl. Cicero, on the other hand, is interested in the appropriate, the πρέπον, which he renders in the Roman language as *decorum*. This characteristic strength shows itself in self-control, in refined humour, in the control of sensuality; one difficulty with this virtue is that it is needed by the young when however one is not yet sufficiently mature to decide on a life-path that corresponds to one's own talents (Heracles at the crossroads) (Cicero 1961b, book I, 118).

Humans live under the sway of *natura* and *fortuna*. If a career is poorly chosen, because an individual chose contrary to his own nature or talent, or his luck changed, a gradual transition is called for, and it has to be demonstrated that a change was made for goods reasons ('ut id bono consilio fecisse videamur', I.121; 'that we have done so with good reason'). Following this there is a very detailed description in which *decorum* is linked to age; there is, however, also a characterization of *decorum* according to rank, an approach which is closer to our main topic: the enumeration of *officia, magistratum, privatorum* and *peregrinorum* (the non-citizens) for the three groups of free and legal equals. The government must represent the state, preserve its honour and dignity, enforce the law, ensure all citizens enjoy their constitutionally guaranteed rights, and each representative must remember his sworn duty. Citizens should live together as equals, neither servile nor rebellious, and strive for peace and honour within the state. Non-citizens should pursue their own affairs but involve themselves in a state which was not theirs. Hence all should conform to rules and behave predictably.

*Decorum* is also apparent in physical movement, in aesthetics, in custom, in language and eloquence. Since Cicero deals elsewhere with rhetoric, public speaking, there then follows a wonderful treatment of private speaking: about the ethical way of conducting good conversation and arranging hospitality.

Life is ultimately like a good speech: everything fits together and each action is related to the place and context in which it takes place. If unsure what might be suitable, then ask someone with experience. Unexpectedly the examination also touches on economic matters, since it turns out that one should avoid occupations that arouse hatred (like a customs agent or a usurer), or in which one carries out unworthy, troublesome and uninventive work, or where one loses oneself in wrangling over petty trade, let alone occupations such as that of showmen and jugglers (I.150). Greater *prudentia* – and with greater virtue, more prestige – is associated with medicine, architecture and teaching. Nothing, however, comes near to agriculture, nothing is healthier, sweeter or more worthy of free people (I.151).

The gradations that we here find remain linked to the ancient tradition in written sources that reach back to Homer: they express essentially the same values. In poetry, such gradations are praised in the representation of the heroic life; in Aristotelian philosophy they are by contrast theoretically founded upon an attempt to differentiate 'natural' and 'artificial' employments (Schefold 1992a, pp. 13–89). Here they are embedded, as a *decorum*, in a doctrine regarding good behaviour which the author cannot express without reservation either in himself or the reader, for the celebrated *agri cultura* has for a long time been more a matter of the possession of a villa than of tilling fields with one's own hands. But Cicero makes emphatic reference to the elder Cato (I.151).

Virtues have ultimately to be weighed one against the other. Cicero attempts to set priorities according to societal relationships, for people's duties arise *ex communitate*, not only *ex cognitione*. Naturally, society cannot be made an absolute, cannot be raised over every *moderatio*; there are actions that are so universally repulsive that they cannot even be permitted for the sake of saving the fatherland. He thereby distinguishes himself once more from violent humanity.

The subject of the second book is the useful. This *utile* is not fundamentally opposed to *honestum*, but apparent contradictions between the two frequently arise. Much concerning the rootedness of individuals in a society is here recapitulated in modified form; ultimately it is established that it is part of the nature of virtue to reconcile hearts and incorporate them into its goals: 'proprium hoc statuo esse virtutis, conciliare animos hominum et ad usus suos adiungere' (II.17; 'I set it down as the peculiar function of virtue to win the hearts of men and to attach them to one's own service').

Gift-giving is initially dealt with in terms of utility. People give to someone (and thereby create a bond) out of charity, honour, trust, respect (fear of the person receiving their gift), out of selfishness (they hope to gain something from the receiver) or because they expect to later receive payment for it. Cicero describes here the integration of society through favours which must be granted, which cannot be extorted by violence and which should not in any case be exclusively motivated by economic and material incentives (II.21).

In discussing motive he emphasizes how wise it would be of the Romans to be charitable with those who have been beaten in battle when it comes to their assimilation into the *imperium* (II.27). From his Roman perspective a conquest which does not end in annihilation seems to be a merciful gift. He speaks of friendship as a useful relationship and of the consequences of fame, of how to gain goodwill and trust. To put it in modern terms, a striving after fame integrates economy and society. If we translate *gloria* with 'reputation' and *fides* with the simple word 'trust' we obtain two contemporary parallels terms which are often used by modern Institutionalism to demonstrate how business relationships can be stabilized.

Cicero adds to this that durable admiration attaches only to those worthy of it (II.36). Cicero despises inactive, lazy and indifferent people, and so through such positive and negative characterization he approaches the definition of *viri boni*, a condition immune to the temptations of sensuality or money (II.38). Genuine renown can be won only by those who properly fulfil their duties (II.43) and actually are just what they seem to be (II.44). Here the study turns from the useful back to virtuous. Once again, generosity plays an important role, which is naturally limited by the fact that the more people one helps financially in the present, the fewer can be so helped in the future (II.53). One should therefore also provide support through action. Caution is called for when the objectives are doubtful, like public games and banquets; on the other hand the suspicion of miserliness must also be avoided. Cicero takes pride in his ability to achieve high office with little expenditure of money, and he recommends contributing to tangible and material ends such as the construction of city walls, ports and aqueducts.

Cicero does not hide the fact that such giving is related to the giver's self-interest, but this is not the sole motive: *vir bonus* is admired for real *benevolentia*. He cannot be a *vir bonus* if he is not credible, and he will not be credible if it is not true. Here the philosopher goes beyond the economists' boundary, for the latter only ask what the apparent preferences of the individuals are, not how these preferences are formed internally. In this sense, Cicero argues, it could be advantageous to occasionally give way and not pursue one's own interests: 'Est enim non modo liberale paulum non numquam de suo iure decedere, sed interdum etim fructuosum' (II.64; 'For it is not only generous occasionally to abate a little of one's rightful claims, but it is sometimes even advantageous'). Ultimately he writes, in an almost paradoxical reversal of self-interest, 'To be able to practice liberality, without at the same time losing all our wealth, is indeed the greatest enjoyment of wealth' (II.64).

In a play on words that is difficult to translate he also suggests that in a pecuniary exchange the partners separate without any further obligation, while, if favour is granted and thanks are shown, fellowship remains (II.69). The rich and powerful do not therefore want to feel obliged by the services performed by those dependent upon them, and even think them someone a favour in accepting a service, whereas a man of modest means relates the services he receives to his own person and considers the services that he can himself provide to be negligible.

The state can also do good deeds, but its primary duty is to secure property. Against the speech of the people's advocate, Philippus, who dared to exclaim that in Rome there were only two thousand wealthy citizens, Cicero says: 'That is a highly dangerous speech: its aim is equality of property. Can there be a greater pestilence than this?'.[50]

The state should ensure that it manages without forced contributions from the citizens, and in so doing must look far ahead. But of greatest importance is that its officials are not suspected of taking bribes.

The state will be undermined by those who seek popularity by confiscating possessions or remit debts. All legal equality will thereby be abrogated. Saying this, Cicero does not really believe for a moment that the remission of debts would be that popular since he acutely observes that the beneficiaries would, from fear of being thought insolvent, hide their relief, while those creditors who lost out would air their complaints. And so debtors, even when numerous, have no more influence than creditors (II.79). Cicero affirms that agitation for the remission of debts was never greater than during the period of his consulate, yet he managed to ensure that payments would be fulfilled, which then did happen. Perhaps Cicero managed in this case to prevent a financial panic through decisive action, for if he had not done so creditors would have become completely insolvent.[51] In support of this interpretation it can be said that Cicero might wish to use those measures employed to secure the interests of the creditors (details of which measures he does not elaborate) as an illustration of the statement: 'Nec enim ulla res vehementius rem publicam continet quam fides' – 'for nothing binds the state more firmly together than trust' (II.84). This sentence is no doubt intended primarily in the sense of moral trust, but it can also refer to the economic relationship of trust between creditors and debtors.

Finally, the second book is also concerned with the comparison of utilities. A rhetorically effective example is the quote from the elder Cato, who placed the greatest value on well-conducted stock rearing, followed by other forms of agriculture activity, and who equated the charging of interest with murder and manslaughter. The link to the previous point shows clearly enough that such a traditional attitude in respect of usury does not mean that Cicero was unaware of the necessity for monetary affairs in the city; only that in the life of his stratum and in the determination of policy it should play no very great role.

The third book deals with contrasts and contradictions between the useful and the honourable which are regarded as only apparent. Here we may concentrate on the interpretation of a few principles and illustrations.

Cicero never demands that people should sacrifice their own legitimate interests: 'Nec tamen nostrae nobis utiliates omittendae sunt aliisque tradendae' (III.42; 'And yet we are not required to sacrifice our own interests and surrender to others').

Chrysipp expresses this with his usual skill: When someone enters a competition, he must compete as hard as he can, but he cannot trick someone in order to win. A follower of Smith would here emphasize the advantages of regulated competition in achieving economic efficiency, but Cicero does not go beyond stating the principle of the need for rules of play in any competition. Such rules can become confused, especially through friendship, and Cicero seeks to establish the essential priorities: One cannot place the useful, like honour, before friendship; but on the other hand one is bound to tell the truth under oath, even with regard to friends. It is especially difficult to find the proper balance of such values in relationships between states.

Often one comes upon an example in which the useful appears to contradict the honourable. In the following examples, which are quite well-known, one can find a surprising parallel to the modern economy (III.50ff.).

In a magnificent literary passage, Cicero writes of a travelling merchant from Alexandria arriving in a ship heavily laden with wheat in Rhodes, where there is great hunger. The merchant knows that there are more ships with the same cargo on their way, and that with their arrival the price of wheat will fall to a normal level, though at the moment he can sell his cargo at a greatly inflated price. Should he sell his cargo at these prices, and keep his knowledge of the prospects of a rapid improvement in the food supply to himself?

Cicero has two Stoic teachers appear: Diogenes from Babylon, 'great and serious', and Antipater, his student, 'a very acute man' (III.51). Antipater is against any secrecy, while Diogenes, on the contrary, thinks the merchant has to reveal only as much as the law requires. In fact today it is only the qualities of the goods which are regulated, not the market conditions.

Cicero has the two discuss the problem of quality with regard to purchase of a villa, the present owner knowing it to be poorly built and unhealthy: the rooms smell and it is infested. Antipater insists on disclosure, while Diogenes says that it is not forbidden to present the sale as that of a beautiful, well-built house; if the purchaser can himself ascertain the condition of the house then fraud is impossible: 'Ubi enim iudicium emptoris est, ibi fraus venditoris quae potest esse?' (III.55; 'For where the purchaser may exercise his own judgment, what fraud can there be on the part of the vendor?').

According to modern law at least Diogenes here contradicts himself, insofar as any hidden defects in the house must be noted. On the other hand, the purchaser must inspect the house. Both of our philosophers dispute the position of the Stoic: Which obligation follows from the nature of man as a social animal? Diogenes seeks to make the requirement that all must be revealed appear ridiculous and argues that it places the institution of private ownership in question ('num ista societas talis est, ut nihil suum cuiusque sit?', III.53; 'that those bonds of fellowship are such that there is no such thing as private property?'). Indeed, ownership without power of disposal, and thus without special knowledge of the objects possessed is hard to imagine, and, in the case of the seafaring merchant, the issue is not the defects in a particular good, as in the case of the villa, but in the market relations and knowledge of them – and it cannot be demanded of him that he reveal his knowledge.

Nevertheless, Cicero takes the side of Antipater. He says that in this situation concealment is not the behaviour of a simple, just and good person, but that of a fraudulent and wicked man, a scoundrel, and he even multiplies the terms of abuse. Then he comes to the point: 'Haec tot et alia plura nonne inutile est vitiorum subire nomina?' (III.57) – 'Is it not inexpedient to subject oneself to all these terms of reproach and many more besides?'.

The social judgment which the Romans apparently dared to so strongly articulate, despite *decorum*, ensured that the subject making the decision aligned the good and the useful. Whoever is not honest with customers will gain a bad reputation and will thereby lose custom. In modern theory the same argument is removed even further from moral grounds, when we talk of asymmetrical information (the seafaring merchant knows, the people of Rhodes do not) and realize that it can be of advantage to offer information, since a person can gain a reputation in this way. The rational analysis of decision-making situations, assisted by game theory and the examination of conclusions through experimental economics often uncovers differences which one can then attempt to relate back to individual psychological and social factors.

Cicero discusses many other cases. Custom is not necessarily more harsh and rigorous than civil law, but Natural law is; civil law should not contradict custom (III.69). Good should be done for its own sake, but Cicero's fallback position remains that no advantage can outweigh the loss of a good name (III.82). In politics, too, fair dealing is also appropriate. In Cicero's examples justice is interpreted in terms of its advantage for the Republic. He would have preferred not hold the *publicani* too strictly to the contracts they had signed, rather than to deprive them of the associated rank of Knight and so drive them into Caesar's camp (III.88).

We conclude our summary at this point, because further consideration of the balancing of virtue and the useful are of less importance for our question. Naturally courage gains from support good reputation or fame. The discussion of moderation provides Cicero with the opportunity of polemicizing against the Epicurians. In the end he takes leave of his son and expresses the hope of seeing him once again, but that was not to happen.

The later fame of this book was great, and its influence on the emergence of political economy was important, since the path to knowledge of the ancients led through Cicero. It is arguable whether Cicero was right to base possession on anything other than natural right, and also to so strongly defend ownership in a time of such inequality. Stoic concepts, passed down by Cicero, form the basis of the liberal systems of Quesnay and Smith (Kraus 2000). Smith cites Cicero often, especially in his *Theory of Moral Sentiments* and in the *Lectures on Jurisprudence*. But the explicit references are related mainly to specific observations from Cicero upon which Smith draws as illustrations, whereas the influence of broader Ciceronian ideas on Smith are not attested by the latter; they cannot therefore be assumed to exist without thorough examination.

## Notes

1 The latter differentiation is not always made in German speaking countries. For more on the history of the concept see the entry 'Wirtschaft' in Brunner, Conze and Koselleck (1992, pp. 511–94). On the historical economic developments leading to the rise of political economy see Bürgin (1993).

2 For a more detailed exposition of this argument see Schefold (1994a). It can also be shown that the positions taken up by Plato and Aristotle are rooted in an older, literary tradition. See Schefold (1994b, pp. 158–248) and 'Aristotle: the classical thinker of ancient economic theory', Chapter 1. On the significance of images of virtue [Tugendbilder] see Schefold (1998a, pp. 235–56).

3 The origin of the debate was the Bücher-Meyer controversy. The primitivist position can be ascribed to Finley (1973); the modernist to Rostovtzeff (1972). For more on opposing interpretations of the credit system in fifth and fourth century Athens see Millet (1991) and Cohen (1992).

4 Horace, The Odes and *Epodes 2*, p. 369.

5 I base my argument primarily on Xenophon (1982).

6 Cf. 'Jacques Savary's "Parfait négociant": the organization of markets by merchants and the state', Chapter 3.

7 *Hieron* (XI.8) speaks of μεγαλοπρεπεστάτῳ … ἀγωνίσματι. On μεγαλοπρεπεία as a virtue in Aristotle with economic connotions, cf. Schefold (1998a).

8 Marchant (Xenophon 1979: 365) translates the latter as 'profitable to its owner', putting profit and use together. Pareto introduced into modern political economy the Greek word as *ofelimità* or ophelimity (the power to satisfy an individual desire) to replace the value-laden use of the term 'utility' by a more neutral foreign term.

9 Five mines, the putative value of Socrates' possessions (II.3), are equivalent to the payment of about two years' wages to a construction worker and the cost of an ordinary house; the cost of a Triere was estimated about 12 times that figure (one talent or 60 mines). Fifty mines appear to have been viewed as a large sum for building a house. If Kritobulos had 500 mines, then he was in fact quite rich.

10 But the letters of Libanios in the time of Julian still cite the Greek tradition of donating and offering thanks on occasions such as public performances and the construction of new buildings. Cf. Libanios (1980, pp. 76ff., 99ff.).

11 Conversely, in *Symposium* the newly impoverished (once wealthy) Charmides felt liberated from his previous duties and freed from public opinion; he recalled: 'then I paid tribute to the state, now the state pays tribute to me by maintaining me' (Xenophon 2002, p. 169).

12 One could speak of efficient administration, but this term allows one to easily overlook the connection of order with tradition.

13 In his work, *Hellenika* (III.3.6), Xenophon reports the hate of the helots for the class of masters in Sparta, in the context of describing a conspiracy (III.3.4–11). Cf. Brockmeyer (1987).

14 English translation see Montesquieu (1777, pp. 48–49): 'It is observable, that, in the cities of Greece, especially those whose principal object was war, all lucrative arts and professions were considered as unworthy of a freeman. "Most arts (says Xenophon) corrupt and enervate the bodies of those that exercise them; they oblige them to fit under a shade or near the fire. They can find no leisure either for their friends or for the republic."'

15 Ischomachos reports that they εἰς ἀντίδοσιν καλῶνται him (VII.3) and they also requested an exchange of fortunes. In a fortune exchange, a person who was supposed to make a Liturgical payment could go to court and demand an exchange of fortunes from someone who withheld performance of a Liturgy, but was probably richer; if the suit was successful, each took over the other's house. By threatening such a suit, the less wealthy person could force the richer to make a donation (cf. II.6).

16 The practicality of order, however, is not lent as much emphasis as we find in Savary for whom 'l'ordre est l'âme du commerce' [order is the soul of commerce], cf. 'Savary', Chapter 3.

17 The play on weighing the winds (ἀερομετρεῖ⊠; XI.3) comes from Aristophanes' *Clouds* (II.2.5), where Socrates rises into the air.

18 One is reminded of Xenophon's text on the skill of horseback riding.

19 On Marxist theories of interest and their relation to Aristotle, cf. Schefold (1998b, pp. 127–144).

20 εὔνοια (XII.5).

21 διδάσκαλος (XII.18).

22 'For Plato, the existence of mathematics is tantamount to proof of the existence of an immortal soul. For since the postulates of this science cannot be acquired through experience, they must inhere in the soul, and their discovery is in truth a recollection' (Speiser 1925, p. 24).

23 Cf. the review of Baloglou and Peukert (1996, pp. 499–503) and Salin (1967, p. 16).

24 Similar to Xenophon, *Oikonomikos* (XII.20).

25 Like Xenophon's in Skillos.

26 On fragments from other Hellenistic writings on household economy, cf. Baloglou (1998, pp. 105–146).

27 Cf. Priddat (1991) and Smith (1990).

28 Cf. Schefold (1989a, pp. 19–55).

29 Xenophon, *Vorschläge zur Beschaffung von Geldmitteln oder über die Staatseinkünfte* (1982); *Oeconomicus* and *Memorabilia* (1979); see 'Xenophon's *Oikonomikos*: the beginnings of an economic science?', Chapter 1.

30 This interpretation is based on my essay 'Spiegelungen des antiken Wirtschafts-denkens in der griechischen Dichtung' (Schefold 1992a, pp. 13ff.). English Trans-lation 'Reflections of ancient economic thought in Greek poetry, Greek economic thought as a problem of historical dogma' in Schefold (1997: 99–145).

31 I thank H. Patzer for valuable assistance and suggestions, especially in the interpretation of Homer.

32 Additional indications on Homer passages only summarized here can be found in Schefold (1994b) in particular places.

33 Cf. on text critique Schefold (1992a) among others.

34 A classical description of the material basis of Greek life is still Büchsenschütz (1962).

35 Cf. Schefold (1989a, p. 43).

36 How far this way of thinking is from modern quantitative analysis is clear in that here the people and their honorary gifts are added symbolically.

37 The origin and internal cohesion of the Greek *Polis* have been newly described by Sakellariou (1989). He places especial value on the intensity and variety of shared living in religious and cultural associations which goes far beyond the cohesion of a medieval city state or a modern nation.

38 In the revised fifth edition of this work this passage is unchanged, except that Trajan has been replaced by Marcus Aurelius, who ruled 60 years later (Salin 1967, p. 19).

39 'In questo solo li moderni han superato gl'antichi', cited in Schefold (1994c). Cf. 'Antonio Serra: the founder of economic theory?', Chapter 3.

40 A surviving *invectiva* (diatribe) attributed to Sallust accuses Cicero of just about every evil act of which Cicero in his speeches accuses his own opponents.

41 Cf. in this regard Badian (1997).

42 English translation in Cicero (1961a, III.44, p. 512): 'the people are divided according to wealth, rank and age...'.

43 *Pandects*, book 18.1.

44 Related to Columella, Book II, Chapter 12.

45  Cf. Lauffer (1971) and Giacchero (1971).
46  Information from Dr Bettina Wagner of the Bayerische Staatsbibliothek.
47  English translation in Cicero (1960, p. 301): 'But why do I talk about myself, who owning to the fault of our habits and of the times am possibly even myself somewhat involved in the present generation's error?'.
48  We refer to and cite from Miller's edition (Cicero 1961b).
49  It is quite impossible to synthesise the very many references which centuries of Cicero scholarship have found for almost every excerpt from *De officiis*, this excerpt included. Cf. Dyck (1996, pp. 208ff.).
50  Philippus' immediate demand was focused only on the distribution of grain. Cf. Dyck (1996, p. 464).
51  Dyck (1996, p. 477) alludes to the possibility that the state made money available at a low rate of interest.

# 2 Middle Ages and scholasticism

### Nicholas Oresme: monetary theory in the late medieval era

Nicholas Oresme, one of the greatest figures in the scholastic tradition, a high priest and advisor to the French king, gave the Aristotelian monetary theory of the Medieval era its most compelling form. Since the time of its rediscovery in the 1860s – Roscher (1863, pp. 305–318) in Germany made scholars aware of the text's importance and Wolowski (1864) in France edited and commented on the text – his *Tractatus de origine et natura, iure & mutationibus monetarum* has attracted controversy in the history of economic thought, concerning not only the interpretation of the text but also questions of priority. The text therefore provided an important impulse for the analysis of the economic sub-stance of Medieval theology and late-Medieval jurisprudence and, ultimately, raises questions of general interest for the history of economics.

Oresme, who was commissioned by the king to produce French translations of Aristotle's *Politics* and *Nicomachean Ethics* among others, and who was aware of the difficulty of expressing scientific concepts in modern language, also produced a French edition of his *Tractatus*. Though altered by later additions, this edition provides assistance in construing some of the less clear passages of the earlier Latin version.

Oresme's clear presentation and his linear argumentation make a strong impression, but if read in isolation it can mislead. There are complex inter-pretative issues and historical connections, while the wealth of Oresme's scientific knowledge is too easily overlooked.

In the following sections, I will attempt to provide a brief overview of the historical context, of Oresme the man and his other scientific activities, as well as a history of the text and its interpretation. My own interpretation follows in conclusion.

Modern states only exceptionally finance themselves by printing money. John Maynard Keynes' *Tract on Monetary Reform* offered a brilliant analysis of the great inflation of 1923, in particular comparing Russia and Germany: 'by printing paper money … a government can … secure the command over resources – resources just as real as those obtained by taxation. The method is condemned, but its efficacy, up to a point, must be admitted' (Keynes 1971

[1923], p. 37). It might seem that financing state expenditure through the creation of money would only be possible where there is a paper currency, as described for example by Goethe in *Faust* Part II, where Mephistopheles' invention of paper money replaces the alchemical project of the artificial production of gold (Binswanger 1985). When precious metals circulate as money the state has to devote not inconsiderable resources to the acquisition and stamping of bullion which then circulates as coin. An inflation involving paper money easily turns into hyperinflation and quickly escalates, making a currency reform unavoidable. Medieval rulers on the other hand, even entire dynasties, financed themselves for centuries by reminting the currency. And yet the system neither collapsed, as with modern hyperinflation, nor was seignorage negligibly small, as with the stamping of gold under the gold standard.

At times when the conditions for general and just taxation barely existed, the debasement of currency out of sheer necessity may have appeared unavoidable; it did finance warfare but was considered immoral. Florence minted the *fiorino* with a stable gold content and Dante, conscious of this stability, ranked King Philip the Fair of France, who was killed in 1314 chasing a wild boar, among the most malicious rulers of Europe on account of his currency debasement. At the Last Judgement this group will be even further removed from Christ than the pagans:

> Li si vedrà il duol che sovra senna
> induce, falseggiando la moneta,
> quel che morrà di colpo di contenna.
>
> (Dante, *Paradiso* XIX, pp. 119–20)

> [There shall be read the woe, that he doth work
> With his adulterate money on the Seine,
> Who by the tusk will perish.]
>
> (Dante 1867)

France suffered terrible catastrophes during Oresme's lifetime, yet the foundation for centralization was laid. In 1356 the promulgation in Germany of the Golden Bull provided for the election of the Emperor by the electors [Kurfuersten]. It consolidated their territorial position, weakening thereby the Imperial idea, while also reducing papal influence. In northern Italy the *signori* fought for supremacy in the cities. True, wealth was greater there than in the realm of the Neapolitan kings, and the Republic of Venice claimed to be the greatest power in the Mediterranean area, but its focus was to the east. The Pope was held captive in Avignon. Though shaken by the Hundred Years War and, like the rest of Europe, afflicted by the Black Death of 1348 and in following years, France developed into a western European territorial state and expanded. The foundation was laid for a sense of national unity and absolutism. Likewise the basis was created for central administration, with a treasury, chancellor's office and Supreme Court; Philip IV the Fair was considered to be the ruler with the most extensive powers.[1]

On occasions, French kings depended upon the Estates General and their predecessors, the Estate Assemblies, but none of the kings devolved any powers to these assemblies, nor were the assemblies able to develop what were potential parliamentary powers. From his republican perspective Sismondi was dismissive of such acquiescence to tyranny: Of Philip the Fair he writes, 'the three orders are rivals only in the servility and abasement which they show in their obedience to the tyrant' (Simonde de Sismondi 1839, p. 421). Sismondi was an admirer of the feudal system, but expressed regret that in the course of the century the most important of the King's vassals lost power. He considered Charles V to be a cunning monarch – superstitious, taking advice from astrologers but lurking in his palace like a spider, seeking to draw his enemies into his web – and Charles replaced the vassals with his relatives, increasing his control over the country (ibid., p. 497).

The political history of France and its dynastic background provide an important context for understanding Oresme's historical allusions in the *Tractatus*. After Philip IV (the Fair) there came Louis X and then his brother Philip V, Louis' daughter being denied succession according to Salic law. Charles IV, the youngest brother of Louis X, succeeded Philip V, and then Edward III of England, son of Isabella who was sister to Louis X, claimed the French throne. However the estates favoured of Philip VI of Valois, Philip the Fair's nephew. In the war which followed the English foot soldiers armed with long-bows prevailed, and their horsemen laid waste to the rest of France. At the Battle of Poitiers the English, led by the Black Prince, captured John the Good; he was the son of Philip VI, a knightly figure but misguided and as a monarch during his rule from 1350 to 1364 very greedy. The Dauphin, the later Charles V, was able to persuade the Estates General to overturn the concessions his captured father had made to the English while also avoiding open battle when the Black Prince once again invaded France. He succeeded in reducing the ransom demanded by the English somewhat, although it was never paid in full – a very important episode for the *Tractatus*. When John was released from captivity and returned to France one of the royal hostages, serving as a guarantor for the payment of the ransom, fled. John the Good, outraged by this dishonourable action, gave himself up to the English and died in London in 1364.

The Dauphin now assumed the throne as Charles V. He was not thought to be a knightly figure and was physically weak, far too well-educated for a prince; he valued order and representation, was hard-working and, despite his penchant for astrology, enlightened, also very cunning. As one of the most successful kings of France – he is called 'the Wise' – he made his country the leading European power once again. It is said that he was raised by Oresme just as Alexander the Great was raised by Aristotle, but today this is considered a legend; in the five volumes *Histoire de Charles V* (Delachenal 1927–1931), Oresme is only mentioned five times.[2] However, there are good reasons to think that Oresme had an important influence on Charles V apart from monetary matters. Oresme – this much is certain – was significantly supported by his king, well-rewarded for his translations of Aristotle and released from his teaching duties. While it may be surprising to see Aristotle's *Politics*, a work related to Greek city-states, employed in the French late medieval era, Oresme's translation was plainly conceived as the basis for a related programme of prudent rule (Babbitt 1985).

Despite the devastation visited upon the people of Western Europe in the fourteenth century the arts and spiritual life flourished, and the use of the vernacular language spread (Duby 1981, pp. 191–194). The decline of feudal privileges was matched by an increase in taxation. In France devaluation of the currency 'could be exploited by a strong monarchy to break down the power of the landed nobility who were in financial difficulties' (Dopsch 1968, p. 194, my transl.). Payments were now fixed in money and 'the conversion of payments of interest and services in kind to a monetary payment often occurred at the request of debtors, for whom there was economic advantage in fixed interest rates because of the constant debasement of the currency' (ibid., p. 183, my transl.).

The financial system itself was in upheaval. Nineteenth-century economists considered the frequency of payment in kind during the early medieval era to represent a return to the barter system. Written agreements allowed for the payment of debt with coins of a particular denomination or through the delivery of particular goods; these documents also show mixed payments composed, for example, of a horse, a certain amount of grain and some coins. In such exchanges, coin served as a good and as a form of payment, but not as a general standard of value and equivalent, so that it did not take the form of money in all of its functions. Cipolla cites examples of this practice into the sixteenth century; in the year 836 CE, a dependent of the monastery at St. Gallen was obliged to make annual payments as follows: '3 maldros sive 6 denarios vel precium 6 denariorum in ferramentis, qualecumque ex his tribus facilius inveniri possimus' (ibid., p. 138; Cipolla 1956, p. 8). The promise involved payment in sacks of grain, silver coins, iron implements, 'whichever of the three we might most readily find', because, in fact, there were often shortages of coins, from time to time in different regions. Precious metals were siphoned off into coin hoards and burial sites, turned into jewellery and transformed into palace and church treasures. Since production remained inelastic, the annual supply amounted to only a small fraction of the available mass of precious metal as a whole and the transaction costs of its use as money appeared high. Thus people often made do with other means of payment, i.e. barter.

From the fifth to the seventh century Byzantine gold coins played the role of an international means of payment. Later Arabic coins assumed this function, but in the middle of the thirteenth century these were then superseded by gold coins from Italian city-states (initially those from Florence). By the fourteenth century, coin had long been the predominant method of payment – even in the countryside (Spufford 1988, pp. 334ff.). However, small coins quickly lost value by comparison with gold. Since gold was available in Florence in sufficient purity and stamped into coins at a constant weight, and the volume of Florentine export trade was also high enough to acquire enough gold for the mint, the florin became the standard by which currency debasement might be measured – and this is still the case for retrospective comparisons. Somewhat later the Venetian ducat played a similar role, since it remained essentially stable from the first minting in 1284 until the end of the Venetian republic (Cipolla 1956, p. 23).

Trust in the purity of the metal (weight was easier to check) played a large role. Economically weak cities sustained a constant loss of precious metals due to an adverse balance of payments, necessarily limiting exports of capital and imports. Three hundred years after Oresme this problem would become a topic for Serra, writing in Naples, who was the first to recognize the connection between (in modern parlance) the real terms of foreign trade and monetary factors. Lacking a macroeconomic vocabulary, he explained this in the language of a lawyer schooled in Aristotle, with the help of distinctive case studies (Schefold 1994c).[3] Oresme does not appear to have recognized that a strong currency and vigorous foreign trade are mutually reinforcing.

In the Medieval era, internationally-accepted coins made of precious metals had to be of high unit value on symbolic grounds but also, practically, to save on transaction costs. Providing the correct change for large coins was a significant problem. In the nineteenth century, low-value small coins were minted whose convertibility was guaranteed; this coinage had to be sufficiently scarce so that the purchasing power of an amount of small change, corresponding nominally to the gold coin, possessed the same purchasing power. According to the older doctrine, full-value gold but also silver coins were supposed to circulate together, and only for smaller units would alloys of low value money be introduced. This bimetallism led to the difficulty that the local government had either to adjust the exchange ratio between gold and silver coins far too frequently to match the prevailing purchasing power, or had to accept that overvalued coins disappeared from the market. Bimetallism did not last. It was a typical practice in the Medieval era – also for the Florentines – to mint a great deal of undervalued small coin, especially through the admixture of copper. When the dues owed by peasants were nominally fixed as a certain amount of cash the devaluation of the small coins must have appeared to them to be as an advantage. It was different in the city, where daily wages were fixed. In Florence, the Popular Party which came to power in 1378 wanted to limit the inflation of small coin; they were even prepared to bring about a real deflation by the withdrawal of small coin from circulation and melting it down, so as to increase real wages; but this failed due to resistance from the party of the nobility, and their subsequent victory (Cipolla 1956, pp. 35ff.).

Everywhere in the medieval era fiduciary money was used alongside real money, highlighting any change in value and serving to provide larger sums with a consistent unit of value. This development can however best be seen not in money but instead in the exchange rate of the florin, documented in Figures 2.1 and 2.2 (Spufford 1988, pp. 296–297).

Figures 2.1 and 2.2 show the change in value of florins and ducats in twelve currencies between 1252 and 1500. Florence and Venice are included because

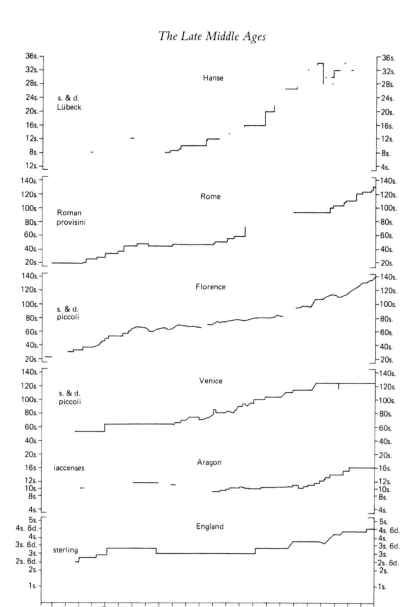

*Figure 2.1* Change in value of florins and ducats in 12 currencies 1252–1500
Source: Spufford (1988, pp. 296–297).

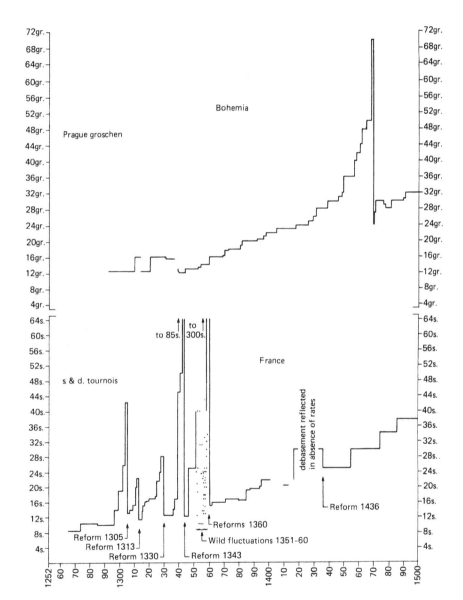

*Figure 2.2* Change in value of florins and ducats in 12 currencies 1252–1500
Source: Spufford (1988, pp. 296–297).

in both cities small coins were devalued with regard to the florin or the ducat. This development was particularly dramatic in France, especially in the two decades before 1360; afterwards there was a stabilization. France does not however represent the most extreme case of west European inflation. From 1300 to 1400, a debasement of about factor 2.2 took place, while the corresponding factor for Castile amounted to 11.4. Naturally there were forceful complaints. In 1354, the abbot of Saint Rémy in Reims explained that the monastery was impoverished 'on account of the little money that we have long received' (ibid., p. 300).

We should now seek to differentiate between the ways in which individuals and groups in society experienced the significant event of devaluation of the currency (a problem of the history of economic thinking), how individuals sought to deal with this in a scholarly manner (the problem of the history of ideas), how positions and interests were politically represented (which we must class with political or economic history) and what kind of counter-factual activities might have been in the interests of the participants. Although this last question lies on the boundaries of possible scientific investigation, it is the one which is from the contemporary perspective most important. Some authors have emphatically argued that the policy of sound money presented by Oresme was in the interest of the overwhelming majority of the population, although it appears to have been experienced differently by many groups of the population, and not a few historians have been influenced by this fact.

Currency debasement was hotly debated in the representative assemblies of many countries. Edward II was put under pressure by parliament and did not risk a currency devaluation. Cities wrung out of the Duke of Brabant the promise that he would not depreciate the currency without their consent. In the kingdom of Aragon, neighbouring the Kingdom of Castile in which inflation was rife, the currency remained stable for the most part, since the king swore to the legislative assembly that he would not alter the currency.[4] Gradual devaluation from simple wear and tear has to be distinguished from a sudden devaluation which was a substitute for taxation and which in many years made up more than half of the French crown's income (Spufford 1988, pp. 312 and 316). The monetary outcomes varied greatly. A moderate devaluation by Edward III in England produced £1,827 gross, and after deductions around £800. A devaluation introduced by Philip VI in France at about the same time brought, in terms of the exchange rate of that time, almost 100 times more net (ibid., p. 317).

The circulation of money was further disrupted by illegal practices. Clipping ('Kippen') cutting the edge of the money that was left in circulation in order to acquire some metal, and 'Wippen', the withdrawal of coins that were clearly heavier than the average coin so that they could be melted down (the official mints were not in a position to precisely maintain the appropriate weight for individual coins), were forbidden, but virtually uncontrollable practices. There were also local counterfeiting operations (in which even the official mints participated) and finally foreign coins were copied and illegally introduced into circulation. Since it was commonly believed in the medieval era that punishment should fit the crime, counterfeiters who were captured were usually themselves 'melted', i.e. executed in boiling water. For rulers a covert debasement was more profitable than an open one, since in the latter case there existed the threat of immediate compensatory price increases. The disadvantage to these disruptions in the currency systems were, put in modern terms: uncertainty in the fulfilment of contracts, significant changes in the general prices of goods, increased interest and interruptions in foreign trade. Once a currency has been devalued its restoration to a strong currency was associated, then as now, with high costs and problems of adaptation (Sraffa 1993 [1920], p. 17).[5]

Who was the author who turned to such questions in the middle of the Hundred Year's War? *Nicole Oresme*, whose name was also expressed in its Latin form as Oresmius, following his signature, was born in Caen in 1320, in the region of Normandy. His name first appears on a list of the Collège de Navarre, on which he was entered 29 November 1348, as a member of the 'Norman nation'. He must have come from modest, quite possibly even rural origins, because the Collège de Navarre was for young people who could not pay for their education themselves. He probably took a doctorate in theology and in 1356 was the headmaster of the Collège. The future Charles V, still Dauphin at this time, sent him to Rouen in 1360; there he was supposed to negotiate with the city for their contribution to the ransom for King John, then held captive in England. In 1362, he became canon of the cathedral in Rouen and, in February 1363, of the Sainte Chapelle in Paris. In 1363, he was part of a legation to the papal court in Avignon. On Christmas he delivered a sermon, in the Pope's presence, opposing the centralising policy of the church.

In Paris, Oresme was acquainted with French Humanists in contact with Petrarch, and with musicians and poets. He conceived his activity as a translator to be one of the transmissions of cultural values: the Latin legacy must be translated into the French language in the same way that the Greek legacy had been translated into the Roman language. He once declared that he felt more certain of the presentation of scientific matters in Latin. The philosopher Buridan, twenty years older and university rector, was his colleague. Buridan's influence on Oresme can be seen in his work; Buridan also cited Oresme.[6] We do not know how Oresme managed to gain this position in the court and begin a career in the church, a career which appears to have served the interests of the king more than those of the Pope. One document designates him as secretary to the king; clearly, he received considerable support from the king for his translation of Aristotle, and he was Bishop of Lisieux from 1377 until his death on 11 July 1382, but he appears to have spent most of his time in the capital.

Alongside the *Tractatus* and the translations of Aristotle there are several critical commentaries on Aristotle in Latin (on *Meteorologica, De sensu et sensato, De anima, De generatione et corruptione, Physica* and on Euclid). He wrote texts on mathematics, physics and astronomy, opposing astrology and fortune telling, and finally there is evidence of over 100 sermons and other religious texts, all of which demonstrate a critical spirit and awareness of the problems of the time. His career was that of an 'intellectual' (Gautier-Dalche 1988).

The variety of works Oresme produced seems to represent the ancient project of a universal science; yet individual pieces – the *Tractatus*, for example – suggest an effort to differentiate the disciplines from one another. Duns Scotus had at the beginning of the century argued that reason was not enough to prove the truth of creeds. The nominalism of Ockham held the singular to be real, and universals to be syntheses of the human spirit, which in turn named them. Clearly Oresme had to associate himself with the church's rejection of Ockham's philosophy, yet he was deeply influenced by these ideas (ibid., p. 11).

Oresme's fame in the natural sciences is so great that historians of science might, as with Copernicus and Locke, be surprised to discover that historians of economics are familiar with his reputation. He has been praised as possibly the best mathematician of his epoch (Molland 1988, p. 14) and his *De proportionibus proportionum* is the 'by far most abstract and venturesome piece of mathematical thinking in the period from Greek antiquity to the seventeenth century' (ibid.).[7] The basic ideas of this text are so brilliant that we shall outline it briefly. Natural numbers $A$, $B$, $C$, $D$ for Oresme stand in an irrational proportion of proportions, if no natural numbers $p$, $q$ can be found such that

$$A/B = \left(C/D\right)^{p/q}.$$

If $B = D = 1$, then $A = 2$ *and* $B = 4$ are in a 'rational' relationship, because

$$2/1 = \left(4/1\right)^{1/2} \text{ or } 2 = \sqrt{4}.$$

Oresme constructed a system of calculating rules, verbally formulated, which naturally sound much simpler in modern style and include statements like $a^{n/m} = (a^n)^{1/m}$. He suggests applications to arithmetic, geometry and musical compositions (Youschkevitsch 1988, pp. 115ff.). The application for probabilistic calculations is quite remarkable. By way of introduction he considers whether the number of stars is a cubic number. He believes this to be unlikely, since there are fewer cubic numbers than other numbers.[8]

Underlying these curious reflections is an attempt to discredit astrology. Similar to the way in which cubic numbers are 'unlikely', 'rational' proportions prove to be 'unlikely', and the above-defined 'irrational' prove 'likely'. Thus it is also 'unlikely', he goes on, that the revolutions and speeds of heavenly bodies are in a rational proportion to each other. For that reason, the constellations of planets in the sky do not repeat themselves. Oresme concludes from this fact that astrologers themselves cannot derive prognoses from experience – constellations are always novel – unless a deterministic relationship exists between the pre-determined movement of the planets and the phenomena of human life. However, Oresme argues that freedom itself undermines any notion of predictability in the events of a human life. Oresme's procedure does in fact seem quite modern from the standpoint of chaos theory, where the starting points of processes are often unpredictable because of imprecision in the determination of preconditions for deterministic processes; and also if exact knowledge of preconditions is precluded by the probabilities of quantum mechanics, placing in doubt the individual prognosis.[9]

We have yet to mention that Oresme's cosmological conceptions are of special interest for their critique of Aristotle. He also considered the motions of constantly acceleration masses, and sketched diagrams for this. He discovered the average speed which is equivalent to that of a constantly accelerating mass between two points using a form of infinitesimal method. His proof is comparable to Galileo's, which was itself first published between 1632 and 1638. He also observed infinite rows and knew, for example, that $\frac{1}{2} + \frac{3}{8} + \frac{1}{4} + \frac{3}{16} + \frac{1}{8} + \frac{3}{32} + ... = \frac{7}{4}$ was valid (Youschkevitsch 1988, p. 119). However, it is not only in the history of the natural sciences that Oresme is said to have been ahead of his century.

> How great ... was my amazement at finding here in the fourteenth century a theory of coinage which is from the standpoint of nineteenth-century knowledge entirely correct; and expressed with a brevity, specificity, clarity and simplicity of language that says more than anything else about the mastery of the author. This is all so far removed from what we tend to think of as the financial barbarism of the middle ages that one might be tempted to think it a forgery, if only the slightest objective ground of such a suspicion were present; and if its excellence were not almost equally as remarkable in the sixteenth century, when the document was printed, as in the fourteenth.

This is how Roscher (1863, p. 306, my transl.) introduces the 'well-polished diamond of the purest water' which he immediately recognized, 'despite the dust', while studying the history of German political economy for the Munich Academy. In an introduction to the French and Latin editions of his book Wolowski (1864, p. 9) responded: 'The name and the works of Nicole Oresme are not in any respect alien to us, but the paper by M. Roscher has fully revealed their importance.' While Roscher presented a thoughtful summary of the work still worth reading, Wolowski interpreted it historically: France was divided, the treasury empty, the towns besieged, bands of soldiers laid waste the country, the plague and famine returned, and a ransom for the king had to be raised. A pale man appeared, too weak to use a sword but capable of negotiating with a strong will, enlightened, decisive: Charles V, the Wise, organized the state, reformed the army and also the currency. The style was that of the empire of Napoléon III, if we are to make sense of Oresme's achievement in the context of national restoration. We have already seen that the endorsement of Roscher and Wolowski also had an echo in Britain: 'The whole exposition is so clear that it might have proceeded from the pen of Adam Smith, and so correct that it would not have been disowned by any member of the Political Economy Club', declared the *Edinburgh Review* (Bridrey 1906, pp. 4 sq). Later studies in France and Germany did however moderate Oresme's claim to originality (especially Endemann 1863). The *Palgrave Dictionary* warned that it was necessary to wait until the Canonists were better known. Roscher (1863, p. 316) had already sensed their influence. Kaulla believed that in Buridan he had found Oresme's teacher (Bridrey 1906, p. 9), until Bridrey attempted to prove quite the opposite: Buridan's reliance on Oresme.

This struggle for precedence is in itself of little importance. Precursors to nearly all the importance ideas from Adam Smith have been found, sources he found unnecessary to cite, and yet his work remains the pre-eminent synthesis. But there is a point to understanding the most important steps in the debate over Oresme, for these arguments are important aids to interpretation, even if they contain mistaken conclusions about the textual history which had among other things repercussions for the German translation.

Bridrey attempts to prove in his wide-ranging book of over 700 pages that Oresme's text does not represent a later clarification of the monetary policy of Charles V, but was instead written earlier and guided this policy. He observed that the printings of the sixteenth and later centuries, before Wolowski's text, were about three chapters shorter than the Latin manuscripts and that the French translation, ascribed to Oresme, is certainly more recent than the Latin text. He then assumed that the shorter version of the printing was based on an earlier Latin version of the text now lost; the more complete Latin version was written later to reflect the political development of France that had taken place in the meantime, and the same thing could be said of brief additions to the even later French translation. Edgar Schorer, the German translator, adopted Bridrey's theory and attempted to reconstruct both versions and set them side-by-side in his Latin-German edition of the work (Oresme 1937). Schorer does not appear to have noticed that the existence of two different Latin versions had already been the subject of definitive criticism in 1909 (Landry 1909). More recent authors like Spufford also adopted Bridrey's thesis uncritically, while Johnson's (1956) authoritative edition of the Latin text summarily dismisses it.[10] At the risk of straining the patience of the reader, I will here recapitulate the most important arguments. Despite the conclusions of modern scholarship, they remain of interest, and they also clarify the significance of Schorer's translation.

We will spare ourselves the enumeration of manuscripts and printings, thoroughly discussed by Bridrey and more briefly discussed by Johnson in his introduction, where he also introduces newly discovered material. Wolowski explained the difference between the shorter printed edition and the longer manuscript by reference to a copy of the manuscript which has since been lost, used for the first printing and in which two pages were missing. Bridrey objected that it would be very strange if two omissions of this kind had not affected the comprehensibility of the text. Moreover, he believed that what he took to be two distinct versions could also be differentiated on the basis of content. We know that Oresme repeatedly revised his works; there were similar insertions in revisions of his commentary on Aristotle's *Politics* (Bridrey 1906, p. 39). The first 'supplement' to the *Tractatus* was rather scholastic and reflected the increasing influence of Aristotle. The second was, however, more interesting. While in the first version Oresme uncompromisingly rejected recoinage, the second version – and in that version, in the second 'supplement' – argued differently, granting this right to society (*communitas* – ie., the representatives of the estates), while still categorically denying it to the ruler. The political event that prompted Oresme to change his ideas was the capture of King John, mentioned in the supplement, and the exorbitant ransom demanded. Up to this point the *Tractatus* had been given a late date because on the title page Oresme as author appears in his role as Bishop. Bridrey then suggested the evidence of his post as bishop should be seen as an editorial addition. He consequently assumed that the first edition came out before the capture of King John in the Battle of Poitiers on 9 September 1356, and the second edition afterwards. In 1355 the Estates-General had imposed the salt tax, criticized by Oresme in the *Tractatus*, on the whole of France. The English took the captured king from a besieged Bordeaux to England in 1357, and in 1358 the Estates-General agreed to a devaluation; the composition of the long version could therefore be assumed to have taken place between 1357 and 1358.

More light is thrown on Oresme's achievement when Bridrey attempts to reconstruct the thesis opposing the position developed in the *Tractatus*. It can be found in the prologue to the work and, in our manuscript, it is indicated briefly and significantly through the placement of this opposing thesis in the first lines in the miniature, which adorns the manuscript. In the Middle Age monetary matters were considered entirely a matter for the ruler. This was firstly symbolic, for Thomas Aquinas states: 'Ex numismata majestas domini relucet. Numisma est ornamentum regis et regni, et cujuslibet regiminis, quia in eo representatur imago domini regis' (ibid., p. 108).[11] The coinage not only reflects the majesty of the ruler, but also that the coin is the sole prerogative of the king; he can exploit it as he wishes. In 1346, Philip VI of Valois proclaimed:

> Nous ne pouvons croire que aucun puisse, ne doive faire doute, que à Nous seul á Notre Majesté royal, n'appartiengne seulement et pour le tout, en nostre royaume, le mestier, le fait, la provision e toute l'ordonnance de monnoyes, et de faire monnoier telles monnoyes, et donner tel cours, pour tel prix comme il nous plaist, et bon nous semble pour le bien et prouffit de Nous, de nostre royaume et de nos subgiez, et en usant de nostre droict.
>
> (ibid., p. 118)[12]

Accordingly, the ruler possessed the right to mint, could stamp money as he wished and set an exchange rate that suited him and which was to his profit (where the exchange rate was related to money already in circulation or to money of account). As Aquinas recognized, all French kings had made use of this right, even if he expected moderation on the part of the ruler in exercising this right.[13] The ruler can dispose of the right to coin as he wishes: he can sell it, give it away or make it over to a vassal; and one could ask, along with Bridrey, whether any other solution was even conceivable in the feudal era, for kings were generally quite incapable of collecting taxes and were essentially reduced to the income they derived from their own lands (ibid., p. 135 and 142). Difficulties during the transitional period of the fourteenth century were apparent not only in respect of money but also in respect of taxation, especially in the setbacks experienced in attempts to extend it.

Bridrey then gathered together the indications which proved the influence of Oresme on monetary policy. In 1356, King John published still another ordinance which imposed the same legal claim as that cited for Philip VI in 1346. But formulations appeared in subsequent decrees preparing the way for the monetary reform of 1360 which were similar to those in the *Tractatus*. Thus, Bridrey finally proposed that there had been a kind of virtuous conspiracy on the part of the professors at the Sorbonne – Buridan and Oresme together – for the public good and the good of money, which the Estates-General finally agreed to. And yet he had to confess that he could nowhere prove Oresme's direct influence (ibid., p. 509).

Bridrey contends that the reform was not simply successfully carried out once, but was systematically continued throughout the reign of Charles V (with the exception of minor modifications which are here unimportant). Nonetheless, it was a failure in that it was loathed by the people because they hated the new taxes; poverty prevailed and the population shrank. But even the factual accuracy of this claim is contested and, so far as the economy did slowly develop, the continuation of warfare might also have been responsible for it. A reluctance to establish new taxes can however be read in the *Tractatus* itself.

Landry already argued that Bridrey's conclusions regarding the economic results of Charles V's reform were faulty, while at the same time he thought Bridrey's ideas in respect of a 'feudal monetary theory' were interesting, if exaggerated (Landry 1909, p. 146). He resolutely rejected the idea that there were two versions of the text. He called attention to the fact that the 'supplements' were approximately the same length, and between them one piece remaining in the short version was approximately double the length, so that one could think of two lost pages, separated by two pages in the hand-written manuscript from which the print was made. He points out that the long version contained cross-references between chapters which were consistent and correct, but which appear inconsistent in the short version, despite attempted revisions on the part of the editor. He also points out how odd it was that Oresme was supposed to have produced the long version through two insertions each of which were placed in the middle of a sentence, and he showed that these two sentences, where the insertions are said to have taken place in the shorter version, do not at all appear to be grammatically correct or to make sense in the context but are instead garbled; the impression of distortion, however, disappeared in the long version. Other differences between the short and the long version he attempted to trace back to later efforts to revise the text by the editor of the printed version (ibid., p. 156).

Landry also dealt with many of Bridrey's textual arguments. He suggested that the short version might perhaps be better expressed because of its greater brevity; but it should not therefore be regarded as a revolutionary youthful work, as Bridrey supposed. In fact, following Landry, one could argue that the long version was more revolutionary because it conceded to the Estates-General the right to devalue the currency, which was otherwise the prerogative of the king. But Landry concluded that Bridrey overlooked the fact that even Chapter VIII of the short version already includes comments on the precedence of the community: 'Ex quo patet, quod nunquam debet fieri mutacio monetarum, nisi forsan emineret necessitas, aut euidens utilitas pro tota communitate' (Johnson 1956, p. 13).[14]

Schorer translates as follows: 'From which is clear that reminting should never be done, unless out of extreme necessity or for the obvious advantage to all owners of money.' The term 'communitas' here is however apparently the same as in the concluding chapters, where it stands for the community of people represented by the Estates General. The decision on whether such a depreciation may be carried out is based on its value for the community. Granting to the community the decision whether to depreciate or not is an obvious step.

It is clear from Landry's reference to the capture of the king that the *Tractatus* must have been written after the Battle of Poitiers, thus after 1356. Are we dealing with a pamphlet preparing the way for, or afterwards defending, the monetary reform of 1360?

A formulation at the beginning of Chapter XVII appears to be more retrospective, or to use a political category, a justification. Schorer's translation reproduces it in his 'seventeenth chapter' as follows: 'Many [depreciations – BS] have lately been seen to occur (breui tempore nuper transacto) in the kingdom of the Franks' (Johnson 1956, Ch. XIX, p. 30). The 'transacto' seems to express the hope that these depreciations are now over. And could a ruler's devaluation be compared with counterfeiting (Chapter XIX) as long as King John, who repeatedly instigated depreciations, still reigned? In this light Oresme would not have been a man of action but one who experienced the period between 1356 and 1360. Naturally, a later dating of the *Tractatus* does not rule out an early position as adviser for Oresme. If perhaps the text was not composed before 1360 then not long afterwards, otherwise the reference to the Estates-General would no longer have been relevant.

Our focus is now closing in on the work. Schorer allowed himself a loose translation, since his edition confronts the Latin with the German text. The interpretation implicit in his translation must be rejected today, insofar as it underscores Bridrey's thesis. Schorer often achieves fine formulations, but his antiquated expressions should not obscure the fact that his choice of words involves technical modernizations which at times make an understanding of the historical context more difficult. Thus, for 'princeps' he often writes 'the State', instead of simply translating it as 'the ruler', and runs into difficulties where there are references to the law of royal succession. At times he translates 'monetary mutation' ('mutationes monetae') directly; sometimes however he translates it as 'devaluation' or 'debasement'. The problem of minting good money that can be found in Oresme he takes to be a current issue; in the introduction to his edition of the text and translation of Oresme he criticizes 'neomercantilism', of which he says: 'Its characteristic form is the destruction of the international, free money market by depreciation, originating in Great Britain' (Oresme 1937, p. 3, my transl.). Schorer published his introduction in 1937. In the happier political situation we have today historical parallels with Oresme's work are still of interest.

The grammar and syntax of the Latin language was dealt with more freely in the medieval era than in antiquity. The recurrent accumulation of mistakes on the part of the writer and the frequent use of abbreviations make reconstruction of the original text more difficult. It occasionally happens that the more corruptions a manuscript has the more elaborate the script and design is; however the splendid *manuscript*, adorned with a miniature, reproduced as a luxurious facsimile reproduced in the series *Klassiker der Nationalökonomie* and referred to here was produced for Louis de Bruges and is very good, 'right two or three times where all the rest are wrong' (Johnson 1956, p. XV). In 1484 a similar *printing* was produced in Cologne, adding it to the *Opera Johannis Gerson*, while the first *printing* of the 'short version', in which two pages were not included, appeared in 1511 in Paris. Only one copy of this Kees edition appears to exist today, in the *Bibliotheque Nationale* in Paris. Unfortunately, despite its defects, it became the model for all later printed editions before Wolowski.

Oresme begins with the Aristotelian theory of exchange, based on a concept of a division of labour (shepherds and farmers are mentioned), and products are exchanged for labour ('de labore ... pro pane').[15] Money appears to be an instrument of exchange, an artificial development which can arouse a desire for wealth. The citation of Ovid involves the doctrine concerning the artificial accumulation of wealth, Aristotle's *chrematistic*, which is unlimited.[16] Oresme discussed this topic extensively in the commentaries included in his Aristotle translation – he created the term 'pécuniative' for it. However, the use of money is, in itself, a good thing ('de per se bonus'). Here, only key elements in Aristotle's theory of money are discussed which are necessary for a discussion of the minting of money. In particular, Oresme avoids the consideration of just exchange in Aristotle which would later in the medieval period become the crystallizing point of value theory (Schefold 1994a, pp. 113–157). His commentaries on passages dealing with just exchange in the *Nicomachean Ethics* offer little insight, especially by comparison with Buridan.[17]

The fact that small amounts of precious metals could be exchanged for larger amounts of other goods is introduced as an argument in favour of its use as monetary material. Providentially gold and silver remain scarce and cannot be artificially produced ('neque possint per alkimiam leuiter fieri', *De Moneta*, Ch. II).[18] Apparently, here money is both a commodity and valuable in itself. Oresme's thoughts on pure exchange are enough to determine this – 'Barter is enough. Oresme prefigures what one could call the Smithian tradition of political economy, the thesis that money is no more than a veil' (Arena 1988, p. 198, my transl.). The situation changes when money is no longer neutral but is deliberately accumulated for itself; yet Oresme raises the problem of *chrematistics* here, only to put it aside.

The issue for Oresme is the use of money as a measure of value – hence the emphasis that it should have as high a degree of purity as possible in order to be reliable (see the comment in our manuscript on the use of precious metals for the production for jewellery when gold is not pure but mixed). Alloys are certainly necessary for the production of small coin, but suspect ('omnis talis mixtio de se suspecta', Ch. III).[19] The fourth chapter teaches that monetary denominations involve weight but also the purity of the metals – a principle that comes from time-honoured authorities ('per sapientes illius temporis prudenter provisum est', Ch. IV).[20] This saves on transaction costs ('tediosum erat ... crebro ad trutinam recurrere') and must be guaranteed by public authorities – 'impressio fieret per unam personam publicam', as the miniature of the manuscript expresses it. The design should make it impossible to forge ('contrafaciendum difficilis', Ch. V);[21] imitation is not only a crime but, should the occasion arise, a ground for war. The main point in these considerations is the authenticity of money as a measure – a quality theory of money, as it were.

Whom does money belong to? According to Oresme, to the ruler. Is not the image of the ruler on the coin proof of that, and had not Jesus said, in this regard: 'Render unto Caesar that which is Caesar's'? According to Oresme the image of the ruler is not a symbolic claim to possession, but instead denotes his commitment to ensuring the quality of the coins (Chapter V). Chapter VI emphasizes the right of possession accorded to individuals by God, and not just by the ruler. This train of thought supports Bridrey's thesis that Oresme criticizes a prevailing 'feudal monetary theory' in which the ruler treats finance as his own domain.

Currency debasement is however not only related to the exigencies of the ruler and his need for representation, but also on the supposed need for an improved money supply: 'Les causes qui nous meuvent á faire de tells monnoies sont pour que notre dit people qui était et est en grande souffreté e pauvreté de monnoie ... puisse plus abondamment et plantureusement, et plus tost, estre rempli de monnoies nouvelles et coursables...' (cited in Menjot 1988, p. 182).[22] As we saw, a local shortage of money in medieval circumstances was not unusual and led to the demand that more money be put into circulation. Conspicuous shortages in means of payment appear in modern circumstances above all during periods of hyperinflation, such that for example government agencies do not have the means to pay increasing public sector salaries and print more money to do so. The Reichsbank proudly claimed in 1923 that it had maintained the ability to pay government officials, though this amounted to no more than an admission that they had passed up an opportunity to combat inflation. Oresme was by contrast of the opinion that the money supply in a well-ordered system of metallic money is achieved by an appropriate level of seignorage and appropriate compensation for the precious metal used through market forces. Let us turn our attention now to Oresme's justification for his argument, long before the merging of macro- and micro-economic aspects of monetary theory, against the idea that currency debasement was necessary to finance the ruler and to supply the people with money.

The first and most important step consists in the determination of minting costs and seignorage, dealt with in Chapter VII and which is entitled:

> Ad cuius expensas fabricanda sit moneta
> At whose cost money should be minted.[23]

A dealer in precious metals who takes his wares to a state mint, or to a licensed mint farmed to a private monopolist, will receive fewer coins for a particular amount of metal than will eventually be stamped from it. The difference will cover the costs of stamping the coin:

> pro labore et necessariis ad monetandum
> for labour and the necessaries of minting.

The seignorage must be sufficiently large that the cost of minting is always covered, Oresme argues, so that the mints never have to close down, and the seignorage which goes to the ruler should be no larger than the temporary rent that arises if the coining costs occasionally fall. High profits could have negative consequences, as one might appreciate.

Yet the potential harm of high seignorage is not so obvious, as can be readily seen by adapting the problem to a modern model. Digressing for a moment, suppose we assume a circulating currency of pure silver in a closed economy; $p_I$ is the price per pound of silver for industrial use to be paid in silver coins and $p_M$ is the price to be paid in silver coins received by the mint for a pound of silver. If $z$ is the number of standard coins which will be coined from a pound of silver, we can write $z = k + g$ where $k$ is the minting cost[24] for a pound of silver and $g$ the seignorage. When $p_M < p_I$, no silver will be brought to the mint; there is a deflationary tendency and $p_I$ falls. Above all, the seignorage represents an incentive to mint silver, so that $p_M$ increases and the two prices converge. If on the other hand $p_M$ is greater than $p_I$, silver will be withdrawn from industrial uses, brought to the mint, and demand will cause $p_I$ to increase, which contributes to a general inflationary tendency by virtue of the scarcity, expressed by $p_M$, of silver available for minting and therefore also for circulation.

The example of a pure paper money currency proves that such a system can function even when the 'seignorage' exceeds coining costs many times over, i.e. $g/k$ is large, because the purchasing power of a one pound bank note is many times higher than that of a pound of unprinted or even printed paper, except in times of extreme inflation. Essential preconditions for the circulation of paper money are of course that counterfeiting will be prevented and the amount of paper money in circulation will be restricted.

Under the conditions of a stationary economy and a constant rate of circulation, the price level remains constant only when the amount of money is kept constant. While the level of 'seignorage' might seem quite extraordinary with an increasing amount of money, it collapses to nothing under constant conditions because no additional money may be brought into circulation. The bank must on the contrary supply additional money on demand when old notes are presented for exchange, or if it decides to replace all the existing circulating notes. Only in a growing economy does the 'seignorage' from additional money pose no danger to the stability of the value of money, and can be used to cover the costs of wear and tear suffered by coinage in daily circulation.

In the long run yet another condition presents itself for a silver currency: $p_M = p_I = c$ must hold, where $c$ represents the normal costs for the production of a pound of silver measured in the number of silver coins needed. If rivalry between nations leads to a situation where the public only accepts the currency of countries where the seignorage is negligible, the conditions for an international precious metals standard are given; then $p_M = p_I = c = k - d$, with $g = 0$ and $k = p_M + d$ holds. The entire cost of minting is divided between the cost of the metal and the technical costs of minting $d$. One can speak of nominalism if it is thought that a positive seignorage is a possibility, and the price level could remain above the level corresponding to the production costs of money, i.e. the extraction costs of the metal and the actual minting costs; and also of bullionism, if an equality is thought to exist between them. It has long been disputed whether in latter case the production costs of metal for coins can actually regulate the price level. One objection is that the annual increase in the amount of precious metal is small in relationship to the amount of money in circulation and the amount of metal used by industry, so that in any case the production costs could only prevail in the long run. On the other hand, the production costs themselves are variable, due to technical advances in the extraction of precious metals and the diminishing returns that has to be assumed for specific mines and the given level of technology. Some nineteenth-century adherents of bullionism like David Ricardo thought that these tendencies were of secondary importance, and that they could therefore be ignored.[25]

And so in the Medieval era we are not only far removed from this model because people did not think of the causal connection in this way, but also because the abstraction conceals important complications. For example, use of the bill of exchange as a substitute for money had begun to spread from Italy (something Oresme does not mention), barter frequently recurred, there would have been much counterfeit money and so forth. Nonetheless, our equation $z = p_M + d + g$ does appear in Oresme insofar as he considers, in Chapter VI, how from one Mark of silver $z = 62$ solidi can be minted, such that, if $d + g = 2$ solidi can be deducted for stamping costs, the one Mark silver can be reimbursed with $p_M = 60$. The Mark therefore weighs as much as 62 coins but is only represented by 60. Hence when Oresme in the following chapter turns to consider the change of coinage conducted by rulers discussion of the consequences indirectly leads to formulations which represent early elements of currency theory.

We need to be clear in extending our model that a larger seignorage can only be realized in stationary systems through reminting. Beginning with a stationary system with stable prices and silver production with constant yields, we can suppose that a ruler who wants to exploit an existing seignorage (that is, $g = k - p_M - d > 0$) buys silver on the open market, mints this and puts it into circulation through the demands of his Court, spending on warfare, buildings and the like. If the economy does not expand nominal prices, including the costs of silver metal $p_M$, will begin to rise so that seignorage will tend to disappear. Under these circumstances the quantity equation is not only tautological, it can also be interpreted causally as a quantity theory: the price level depends on the amount of circulating money; with a constant $z, p_M, p_I$ and $d$ increase. However, $p_M$ can only for a short time at most rise above $z - d$, because with a boom in silver metal fostered by speculative hoarding silver coins will be melted down and withdrawn from circulation.[26] In any case, the ruler can make no further profit from the system without reminting.

As long as $z$, which here represents the number of coins that can be stamped from a pound of silver and at the same time represents the weight of individual coins, does not change, and where $g = 0$, a new balance is achieved with $z = p_M + d = c + d$, whereby the law of the circulation of bullion holds: if the state now attempts to mint additional silver and put it in circulation, the purchasing power of silver will fall further and silver coins will again be removed from circulation as coins are melted down and silver is hoarded; 'industrial' usage will then increase. Given $c$, the price level will be stabilized in the long run. The quantity equation is still valid, but we must here decide on the amount of money that can circulate on the basis of the price of goods determined by real conditions, including the price of money as a product, hence the relation between the general price level and the production costs of coins (metal plus minting costs); and not – as in the quantity theory – proceed in the opposite direction and infer the quantity of money from prices. I would like to call this principle the Law of Circulation.[27]

As so often happens, apparently mutually exclusive economic theories have their own validity under historically different circumstances. We found above a nominalistic position coupled with positive seignorage. It may be surprising that these appear to be historically connected to the names of philosophical realists like Plato and Thomas Aquinas who took ideas and universals to be real, while the bullionist position associated with zero seignorage is advanced by Oresme, who is considered a Nominalist philosopher. Besides the name, however, philosophical and economic Nominalism have nothing in common. In Aristotelian monetary theory both positions are adopted: metallism, insofar as for Aristotle money arises from exchange, pieces of precious metals facilitating exchanges because of the convenience. Precious metal is then stamped (he does not mention under whose authority and at what cost) to give the quantity. His Nominalistic position is reflected in the designation of money as a cleverly-invented instrument, denominated as a standard ('nomisma'), which makes it necessary to value all commodities. This can be determined separately from its circulation.[28] He thus appears to have seen in part that, depending on circumstance, both positions are admissible.

So far we have only discussed monometallic circulation, having only mentioned bimetallism and trimetallism in connection with our historical discussion of coinage in the Medieval era. Oresme examined a trimetallist circulation of gold, silver and alloys, and in so doing called for a full-valued gold and silver money, and even full-valued token coins of copper alloy. This metallist principle was faced with the fact that rulers gained their seignorage even from reminting their bullion currency, and cities like Florence often devalued at least small coin.

By comparing coinage with legislation in Chapter VIII Oresme recognizes its systematic character. Certain salaries and annual rents ('pensiones et … redditus annuales'; 'pensions and yearly rents') are nominally fixed, so that money cannot be altered without coming into conflict with the law. Unnecessary modifications to the law create popular turmoil ('murmur in populo'; 'murmuring among the people'). Even if the aristocracy should have felt their interests in a strong currency more keenly than other social classes, Oresme is anxious not to appear to be their defender, but rather someone formulating a common interest. Changes of currency can affect appearance and shape, the proportion between various (especially gold and silver) coins, their value and designation (this is relevant in the relationship between the coins), quantity or weight and, finally, the material substance. He asks when and for whom, how and why such alterations could possibly be justified.

There is no essential change when, as still happens today, the image of a new head of state appears on a coin; this does not invalidate the old coinage or essentially change the character of the new coins. New money and the demonetization of the old coin ('cum prohibicione cursus antique'; 'and demonetising the old') is permissible if excessive counterfeiting requires the replacement of the coin, or if the existing money is too worn. In these circumstances new money which can be distinguished from the old money must be put in circulation ('si … antiqua moneta esset uetustate nimia impeiorata uel in pondere diminuta'; 'if … the old money was too much injured by age or reduced in weight'). Since Oresme does not wish to allow any real seignorage, the replacement has to be made in such a way that the weight of the new coins of a particular denomination are the nearly same as the old, so that melting down the old coins brings only a marginal profit. The new coins must therefore be a little lighter than the average weight of the old coins, which due to wear and tear are in turn lighter than when they were minted.

In Chapter X, Oresme explains that the value relationship of gold and silver must follow natural conditions in production and consumption: 'ista proporcio debet sequi naturalem habitudinem auri ad argentum in preciositate'.

It is a matter of relative scarcity: if less gold is discovered than hitherto then it must become more expensive in comparison with silver. The ruler could arbitrarily determine the bimetallist relationship and buy his people's gold cheaply with silver, then raise the gold price and bring it back into circulation at his profit. This kind of procedure is compared by Oresme with the fixing of prices at which the ruler purchases the grain of the country in order to arbitrarily increase the price, and then re-sell it. If the counter-thesis is that the state possesses a monopoly on coins, as it does for example on salt ('monopolium seu gabella salis'; 'monopoly or gabelle of salt') and can thus set a monopoly price, Oresme responds that all such monopolies are unjust. This is a thoroughly modern, anti-mercantilistic remark of lasting relevance if one thinks of the unrest caused by the salt tax in France up until the French Revolution;[29] perhaps however also a very conservative remark, for what was left for the ruler – without seignorage and commodity taxes in the Medieval era – except for tariffs and income from his domains? Direct taxes, which caused Charles V so much trouble? Here a comparison with the story of Joseph in Egypt lends the text a particular pathos.

In the section on the denomination of coins, or their division into larger and smaller units, Oresme betrays his love as a mathematician for medieval numerology by citing Cassiodor. If a solidus is divided into 6,000 dinars then this symbolizes the 6,000 years of the existence of the world. The number 6 is privileged as a perfect number in the system. The time-honoured system of monetary denomination deserves to be preserved. The thrust of the argument is clearly only that denominations should not be altered because rent payments are nominally fixed, and so uncertainty over contracts would arise.

Oresme considers altering the weight of coins (Chapter XII) particularly deceitful and criminal. The ruler misappropriates foreign currency: 'princeps per hunc modum sibi posset acquirere pecuniam alienam' ('the prince can in this way get possession of other people's money'). And he cannot alter the weight for gain without such deception and theft; he receives high-quality coins and covertly makes coins of a lesser weight [30] for his own use.

Chapter XIII explores changes in the alloys, a factor which Oresme from the very beginning restricts to coins of inferior value, since those of a higher value should be of pure metal. This is for reasons of transparency, while with coins of inferior value the risk associated with the use of alloys may be taken (cf. Chapter III). This shows very clearly that Oresme required full value for small coin made of alloys as well as those made of silver and copper ('black money'), thus diverging from the prevailing convention in states with full-value gold money but inferior small coins (as in Florence). If silver becomes scarce it is permissible, he writes, to put less silver into the alloy. The reverse is also the case: if silver becomes plentiful, more should be put in the coin: 'si haberetur de argento habundanter plus quam ante, tunc plus de eo deberet poni in illa mixtione' ('if silver were more abundant than before, the quantity of silver in the mixture should be raised').

The integrity of the coin will only be guaranteed if in this case exchange, which is difficult for the public to supervise, is done with especial care. While the community has the right to do so, the ruler never does: 'mixtionis mutatio facienda est per communitatem ad maiorem securitatem habendam ... nunquam potest hoc licere principi' ('such a change in proportion should be made by the community, for greater safety ... never by the prince'). It is only this recourse to the community that guarantees transparency. Combinations of changes to the coinage (for example of weight and of materials) are even more dubious (Chapter XIV).

Oresme believes that the main reason for altering coins was to realize a seignorage; all other reasons he considered excuses. He did not see that the use of low-value money saved on the extraction costs of precious metals. It would be of interest to learn more about how the gain was appropriated. He does not tell us, for it seemed quite obvious to him. It would also be of great interest to know what other reasons for currency debasement there might be and how Oresme would have criticized them. But he says nothing about them, and only wants to prove that seignorage is unjust (Chapter XV).

Let us look at the argument for the generation of seignorage in a simplified case in the monometallistic system already discussed (reduction of the weight, Chapter XII). From a pound of silver instead of $z$ units of coins now $z'$ are coined, with $z' > z$. At the old equilibrium the range of seignorage has been reduced to zero, thus $z = p_M + d$. We assume at this point that the old coins will remain a legal means of payment, at least for a transition period; we also want to show that the ruler is tempted to cheat even then. If he manages to introduce the new coins without much fuss, so that the nominal prices remain unchanged (as a rule inflation is to some degree ultimately anticipated), $p_M$ and $d$ do not at first change; there is a seignorage, therefore, of $g = z' - (p_M + d) = z' - z$. The ruler pays with new money. The silver value of the old coins will be higher than that of the new; if this is noticed the old coins will be hoarded and a silver shortage will occur. In order to overcome this, the mint must be prepared to purchase silver at a higher price $p'_M$, through which seignorage is reduced; the silver shortage disappears however when the increase is great enough to make the melting down of the present silver coins profitable. When the old coins are not heavily worn $z$ of them weigh a pound. A pound of the old silver coins has, according to the exchange rate fixed by the ruler, the purchasing power of $z'$ new ones. In order for the melting of the old coins to be profitable at least $p'_M = z$ must hold and the seignorage for new coins is reduced by the adjusted $d$ to $z' - p'_M - d = z' - z - d = z' - p_M - 2d$: the nominal seignorage from a pound of silver is equal to the nominal coined amount of money, reduced by the earlier nominal pound price for silver and the doubled minting costs, since the silver recoined is also stamped twice. Silver will also be offered from the hoards if $p'_M > p_I$. The silver supply is reduced with increasing prices and increasing $p_I$. The silver scarcity of the mints is thus easier to eliminate, the less inflation is anticipated, i.e. the better it manages to deceive the public regarding the amount of debasement taking place and regarding the future state of affairs. The more quickly it is noticed that the old coins are worn-out, so that $z''$, with $z < z'' < z'$, weigh a pound, the faster the silver price will increase to $p''_M \geq z''$. Thus the analytical argument leads, independent of any argument about distribution (it could be that this form of taxation was allowed to rulers on the grounds of financing necessary expenditures), to a moral argument: in order to be more successful, the ruler *had* to commit fraud. Oresme concentrates his critique directly on this point. Behind this critique there is an understanding for the context; we do not know how much of it came from intuition, whether it was based on experience, or how much it came from mathematical analysis.

To begin with: the ruler takes what does not belong to him. The assertion that it is for the public good is the typical pretext of tyrants ('sicut solent mentiri tyranni'; 'the tyrant's usual lie'). We must speak of tyrants here because if the ruler appears once as justified in financing himself in this way then he will do it again and again. If he repeatedly devalues the currency he acquires almost all the wealth of his subjects and makes them dependent, like slaves (Chapter XV). Indeed, it is the very essence of inflation taxation that it is much more difficult to fix a limit to it than for public taxation or a tribute, which may reflect a power relationship but because of its transparency is not so despotic. That is in any case how they thought at the time.

The issue of repeated devaluations raises the problem of the indeterminacy of the boundary of such wealth acquisition, representing an analogy with the critique of *chrematistic* wealth accumulation that can be found in Aristotle. Oresme also discusses by a comparison with Aristotle's criticism of usury (Chapter XVI): in conformity with his monetary theory he calls interest unnatural, because here money generates money. The profit from altering coins is however even worse than usury, because the ruler cheats with false monetary denominations and, moreover, by controlling the rate of exchange employs coercion, while in an open contractual relationship the debtor voluntarily agreed to pay interest to the creditor.[31] It is thus forcible robbery as well as fraudulent misappropriation ('violenta predacio vel exaccio frau-dulenta'; 'violent plundering or fraudulent extortion'). Bad practices may be permitted, when necessity requires them, but altering the currency ruins the country, as is proven by the decline of the Roman Empire; and, indeed, late antiquity suffered from inflation.[32]

The final part of the *Tractatus* is perhaps the most interesting, because it gives a political slant to the economic and moral arguments. Through deva-luation the ruler harms himself, for through his deception he suffers a loss of honour, acting like the kind of counterfeiter whom he punishes with 'turpissima morte', and claims that his base actions are in fact good. By devaluing their money he dishonours his ancestors, acts tyrannically and loses prestige. This stance is a political one because it seeks to form an alliance against the alteration of money, and to that end gathers arguments important for every party (Chapter XIX).

It must therefore be shown that the community as a whole will be harmed, not only by the burden of the covert tribute that will be paid – no levy of taxation can be more general or strict, Oresme claims – but there will also be a loss to the national treasury, because gold and silver will be exported. In comparison with Gresham's Law this is a challenging passage, and it explicitly formulates one of the economic processes whose understanding appears to be taken for granted by Oresme, but which otherwise remain implicit:

> aurum et argentum propter tales mutationes…minorantur in regno, quia nonobstante custodia deferuntur ad extra, ubi carius allocantur. Homines enim libencius conantur suam monetam portare ad loca, ubi eam credunt magis valere.
>
> such alterations and debasements diminish the amount of gold and silver in the realm, since these metals, despite any embargo, are carried abroad, where they command a higher value. For men try to take their money to the places where they believe it to be worth most.
>
> (Johnson 1956, p. 32)

We saw that with monetary debasement, the more the ruler earned, the less he paid for precious metal; therefore – so Oresme appears to think – it disappears from the market. He then points to the problem that would become the title of Serra's treatise: in countries where there are no rich deposits of precious metals the ruler who mints bad money cannot obtain enough precious metal for the production of good money: 'ubi non exuberaret materia monetabilis in mineris … princeps non habaret, unde facere posset sufficienter de bona moneta' ('unless the material is abundant in mines … the prince would at last be unable to coin enough good money').

What Oresme is expressing here, in his French-tinged Latin, is a description of the situation: the country devaluing money lacks precious metals. Why is the ruler, or the country, not in a position to pay more for precious metal? We would say: the ruler receives too little or spends too much. In respect of the country, Serra went beyond this by determining that the flow of precious metals was due to the deficit in the balance of payments, not to the devaluation. The deficit in the case of Naples had structural causes and led to manipulation of the exchange rates. Oresme does not consider that devaluation could even contribute to an improvement in the balance of trade. In any case, a ruler who purchases silver at home for his silver coins, because the silver coins have a stronger purchasing power than the metal they are composed of, cannot do this abroad when the value of the coins there is only fixed according to their weight. In a realm without mines, in receipt of no subsidies, precious metals only increase when a trade surplus is achieved with other commodities. Oresme does not appear to have seen this. He does not so much formulate an early version of Gresham's Law – he understands its substance, as is evident from his condemnation of the money changer – as sketch a theory, not completely overcome until Serra, according to which the lack of precious metal is due to the poor exchange rate, instead of the reverse: the trade deficit leads to a lack of precious metal. In any case, he points out that traders avoid states in which the currency is in chaos. He thus identifies one of the cumulative results of economic ruin. And in a cumulative process, the causes and effects are not longer easy to differentiate. Thus he falls back on the principle of good money, which corresponds to the later development of economic thought.

Those who naturally accumulate wealth by pursuing honourable and constructive employment, and Oresme counts church functionaries, judges, soldiers, farmers, merchants, craftsmen and others in this group, will be harmed by monetary transformations, while the money changer makes a profit. Whether this inflationary process affects all moneychangers advantageously to approximately the same degree remains an open question. Oresme does not attempt to prove it (Chapter XXI), but instead presents a much more interesting argument: if the ruler does not announce the time and form of the alteration in advance ('quando princeps non facit prescire populo tempus et modum future mutacionis monete'; 'when the prince does not announce beforehand the date and the scheme of the alteration'), then the money dealers, taking advantage of superior knowledge, can very quickly become rich by purchasing with bad money and selling for good money ('emunt ... pro moneta debili ... postea vendunt pro forti'; 'the buy ... with the weak money ... they sell again for the sound') – speculative trading that Oresme considers reprehensible in itself, while according to modern standards it is the one-sided preferential treatment of one class by the state which would have to be criticized. The counterfeiter, he adds, then have an easier time since many people do not really know any longer what genuine money looks like.

In Chapter XXII the community is given the right to carry out monetary transformations on their own, since money belongs to everyone. If this were the sole argument, then we might like Bridrey wonder about the turn in the discussion. The example taken (here the requirement for the ransom money occurs which was so important for the dating of the *Tractatus*) is a predicament in which the ruler is indeed absent, so that others must decide; according to Oresme's legal thinking the Estates-General, although he does not say so in so many words. But cannot a ruler also be faced with a predicament which justifies taking advantage of inflationary taxation which Oresme surprisingly and correctly specifies? No one can escape this tax, and it can be collected with low costs and few personnel. Oresme seeks to anticipate potential criticism by predicting the argument of his opponents and considering when the ruler might possibly be justified in altering the currency. The Pope, church or emperor, or even the community, could entrust the ruler with the right to devalue, and in any case the ruler should have an income which accords with his royal majesty's standing. Does it not disgrace the king to take this right away?

For many of these questions there is a quick answer (Chapter XXIV): The Pope cannot allow evil to be done, while the emperor cannot give a king a right that the emperor himself does not possess.[33] The community, however, cannot confer a right on the ruler that he will inevitably misuse. Misuse is possible when the seignorage is not limited. In the language of our model: $g > 0$ is admitted, if $g$ is a certain (i.e. predictable and known) and definite size: 'debet esse certe et determinate quantitatis' ('it must be fixed and limited in amount').

Seignorage may not come from the despicable practice of monetary mutation ('ex detestabilibus mutationibus'; 'from the detestable changes'). Oresme apparently possesses a remarkable insight into economic relations if he knows that a fixed levy can at the best only ensure the ruler a limited income (theoretically it arises in the first place through the annual coining of additional money for the maintenance of a growing economy); a larger seignorage is achieved from unannounced devaluations.

That only the community and not the ruler may devalue does not at all follow from the universality of the possession of money. In a skilfully written chapter (XXV) employing many fine citations, Oresme brings out into the open a deeper motive for his writing. What the ruler and what the community may do with the monetary system is only a part of the more general question concerning the exclusion and inclusion of power in a Christian realm. Worrying that the monarch could become absolute, rulers of the principalities admonished him to put the common good first. Oresme cites Cassiodor:

> Disciplina imperandi est amare quod multis expedit.
> The art of ruling is to love what benefits the many.

Science and art are examined through similes. A tyrannical state is like a body, one part of which swells up, which draws energy from other parts of the body, and which then finally dies. The well-ordered state is like the harmony of a chorus of many voices; the tyrant however produces dissonance. Above all: the well-ordered state survives, as examples from antiquity demonstrate. The breadth of Oresme's education is evident, and it is no wonder that Roscher was so enthusiastic about his writing.

Chapter XXVI returns to a formal, almost scholastic form of rhetoric in order to prove that through monetary disorder the ruler loses honour and inheritance, since he ruins the realm and is despotic. But the generosity of the French Kings will not be transformed into tyranny, nor will the Gallic people learn to be submissive: 'Neque enim regum Francie generosa propago tyranizare didicit, nec seruiliter subici populus Gallicus consuevit' ('For neither has the noble offspring of the French kings learned to be tyrannous, nor the people of Gaul to be servile').

Who would have expected this appeal to nationalism[34], apparently sensing the tensions that would mark the following centuries? Humble and yet proud, the author finally offers his work to those with insight and prudence ('prudentes') for their intellectual enrichment.

The main points of criticism in the *Tractatus* – that the alteration of money undermines its value as a measure of value and that the ruler, in the process, takes something which does not belong to him – are not in and of themselves remarkable, but rather in the way in which they are presented. Two minor arguments are especially powerfully developed: the accusation of deception, and the political classification of the economic role of the ruler.

The ruler deceives his people on many fronts. He pays in devalued coins but he receives taxes in older (un-devalued) coins. He admits that people are deceived about the metallic content of the currency. He promotes speculation, and indeed the mints were even instructed in 1351: 'Be sure to keep this so privy that none might suspect it...' (Menjot 1988, p. 184).

When Oresme concedes at most the right to devalue to the community, he claims on the one hand the consent of those to be taxed, a theme which played such a large role in the history of the English parliament. On the other hand, he demanded that – and this is specifically for monetary transformations – that an otherwise excluded public be constituted. An overt devaluation is different from a covert one, because when everyone has the same information they all have the same chance to orient themselves to new economic conditions. The circle of those who can protect themselves by anticipating a loss of assets expands – which certainly reduces the gains to be made from the operation. Oresme rejects the applicability to the monetary system of the tradition which concedes to the government the right to conduct policy covertly on behalf of everyone.[35]

Whatever weight he attaches to deception, it will become clear that he interprets a transformation of the monetary system decided upon and announced by the community as an especially fair form of taxation, whereas covert devaluation falsifies the measure of value, and the ruler sows mistrust where he should instead inspire trust. Whoever believes we have come a long way from such ideas should remember how currencies on fixed exchange rates were suddenly devalued without warning to achieve their effect, and that an emphatic official assurance that the exchange rate will not be changed should often be seen as the signal that it is about to change.[36]

Should it be demanded that the ruler identify himself with the common good? Buridan went down this route,[37] and Oresme was not far from the idea when he cited Cassiodor's requirement that an element of being a good ruler involved loving what benefited many. What is essential in his solution is however something else, namely the separation of powers. It is certainly the ruler who makes gold into money by guaranteeing the denomination with his image. However, in contrast with Buridan, Oresme deprives the ruler of the right to carry out devaluations on his own initiative – and even those above the ruler, the Pope and the emperor could not do this or permit it. Instead this function is assigned to the community.

Now, the community cannot prevent the ruler from invoking the vested right to alter the money – there is no constitution, he is in command of an army that would transform into a standing army – and the ruler's authority is so obvious that Oresme is not even prepared to state such things. However, he knows that – at least in temperate climates ('maxime in regione temperata et remota seruili barbaria' – Chapter XXV; 'especially in a temperate climate, far from slavish barbarism') – politics and economics are so mutually restricted that the ruler harms himself and the monarchy by altering money. For that a special logic of institutions must be developed: the ruler who devalues once will do it again; by ruining the economy he will put himself in the position of having to act despotically, and through that he will – after he has almost destroyed the economic foundation of his realm – wipe out entirely the legitimacy of the monarchy which keeps it together.

Oresme was only distantly aware of the liberal ruse of reason, that markets regulate themselves; and it was not his goal to replace the moral duty of individuals to society with an invitation to act according to personal interest. However, thanks to the limits set upon legitimate rulers, the citizens' rights of possession are recognized and their infringement by the ruler prevented. As a reminder of the duty of loyalty this thought is rooted in the past; as an anticipation of an unwritten constitution regarding the separation of powers, it points far into the future. With this synthesis, Oresme created a work which in his century had no equal.

## Economy and money in the age of reformation

Germany's economic literature is as variable as its external history. Following the decline brought about by the Thirty Year's War, an epoch began during which German Cameralism produced numerous low grade books on the administration of princely domains and the improvement of agriculture, but only a few works were printed which can be seen as forerunners of modern economic theory.[38]

Not many historians of economic thought know that in the sixteenth century, during the time of Humanism and the Reformation, a new economic concept was making its way into print. This new thinking mirrored the impetus which seized Germany's south in particular during the Age of Discovery. Roscher, who published so much on the early history of the German national economy (Roscher 1992 [1874] and Roscher 1861a), also called attention to the three pamphlets (Lotz 1893)[39] we will examine below. These documents may constitute the earliest example of a controversy on economic questions carried out in printed pamphlets.

Before Roscher taught us to appreciate these currency pamphlets as embryonic versions of political economy they were cited as a source for the history of money and, in particular, coins.[40] Roscher, to whom we already owe the rediscovery of Nicholas Oresme (Oresmius 1995), saw the chief merit of these texts on coins in determining the principles according to which good money should be minted, for which Oresme – admittedly primarily employing ethical arguments – had already called. This position takes the Albertinian side in the debate. Saxony had been divided for dynastic reasons: the Albertinians, who demanded that the silver content be maintained at its current level, ruled one (Catholic) fraction, while the Ernestinians, who championed a reduction of the silver content, ruled the other (Protestant) faction. The dispute was unavoidable as both sides used the same currency, and the ruling houses found themselves united by common ownership interests in the silver mines. It ended with a temporary rupture – for reasons similar to those advanced by sceptics of the European currency union as possible grounds for a future collapse.

If it were only a question of maintaining or modifying the coinage the few extant copies would have remained half-forgotten on the shelves of libraries and archives. Roscher, however, recognized that they contained early formulations of mercantilist theories. Today we can see in their efforts to establish some theoretical foundation the outlines of classical perspectives, apart from their attention to vital political and economic questions of the Reformation era. Opinions are expressed, disputed, rejected and taken up again on the causes and effects of domestic and international trade, the advantages of stable monetary value and the effect that debasements had on employment, the benefits of competition and the danger of monopolies, the hoped-for or imagined economic improvement due to the politics of guilds or through governmental direction. In the exchange between the two anonymous speakers – we do not even know what positions they held, or where they acquired their knowledge of facts and connections – the passions of the era also resonate: which faith is to be professed; how farmers, manual labourers and nobility would manage to get along with one another; whether one has to be amenable to the storm of novelties introduced by trading companies; how one might exploit the easily exportable wealth of the country, the silver; and how one could reconcile one's own gain with that of the community.

The arguments, laid-out in the language of Luther, can therefore be read as a debate about the approach to modern economic challenges. They appear more multifaceted than the nearly contemporaneous monetary texts of Copernicus (1965, 1978).

The centre of economic development in early sixteenth century Germany lay in the south, where cities like Augsburg and Ulm maintained business connections with Venice and Antwerp, domestic industry (weaving) developed, and, in the case of individual goods, the first links for a future network of international trade were made. Saxony, which would only later be transformed into an industrialized region, had little to offer apart from its exports of silver. The currency pamphlets address a conflict that always arises for countries rich in raw materials: Should they simply enjoy their wealth as long as it lasts, or should they promote the development of an economic structure through regulatory measures which would in future make other exports possible?

The economic forms of the early modern era are closer to those of today than to those of the ancient world or the high medieval period. The philosophical, legal and theological considerations that had once intimately connected to economic deliberations were shed like an old skin. In many places, both authors seek to convince their readers of their sincerity in matters of faith, but connections between faith and economic goals play only a diminishing role.

In what follows, I will attempt to contextualize the Saxon currency pamphlets within the history of ideas by examining other texts in German regions in the sixteenth century, shedding light on contemporary approaches to particularly controversial questions: Peutinger on the role of trading companies and the so-called monopoly, Fronsperger on self-interest as the driving force of economic trade, Luther on attempts during the Reformation to revive connections between the economy and the Christian notion of a pious life in society. I will then summarize the currency pamphlets, focusing on these three dimensions.

The legal and politico-economic argument regarding so-called monopolies was the 'first political-economic debate in our history that provoked the attention of all ranks and classes of people, forcing them to make their desires known' (Bog 1967, pp. VII-VIII, my transl.). Astonishment at the rise of large bourgeois dynasties, doubt about whether the accumulation of wealth had been honest, admiration for entrepreneurial achievements and fear of impoverishment, either absolutely or in comparison with successful people, still resonate today. Richard Ehrenberg's (1963) description of the economic power of the Fuggers became a classic of economic history and was translated into many languages. The late nineteenth century saw a relationship between the era of the Fuggers and the formation of commercial dynasties in its own time, and Ehrenberg (1925) followed up with a popular science version in which he drew parallels to the Rothschilds and the Krupps.

The Fuggers, to elaborate the case in point, were important merchants in business relations with Venice, who then became involved in mining operations and managed up- and downstream businesses comprising a part of the silver extraction process. The shifting of trade routes from Venice to Lisbon and Antwerp complicated wholesale trade, and, in turn, they expanded the use of credit and determined the choice of emperor in 1519. These new trade routes made it possible for Charles V of Habsburg to triumph over François I. Step by step, the Fuggers slowly rose into the aristocracy (a handicap to business), becoming the objects of both renown and hatred.

But a monopoly in the strict sense never materialized: with silver and fustian, never; with copper[41] and pepper only temporarily. During periods of falling prices, attempts were made to restrict production. The king of Portugal enjoyed a monopoly on the pepper trade, which he exploited to support the costs associated with maintaining his colonies. Farther down the distribution chain, however, trading companies competed in the pepper market.

The Fuggers actively sponsored the arts and sciences and made donations to the poor; the latter is still in evidence today in the buildings constructed for the needy in Augsburg. Since that time, the Fugger Myth has become an independent object of historical examination (Burkhardt 1996). New economic phenomenon placed in question traditions such as restrictions on the size of a company, the setting of prices by the guilds, and the ecclesiastical contempt for usury. Political action was taken against trading companies, and they became a focus of negotiations at the Reichstag in Cologne in 1512. At the Reichstag in Nuremberg in 1522–23 an attempt was made to place limits on the capital of trading companies. The Imperial Court ruled against several Augsburg trading companies, on suspicion of a monopoly, while the emperor on the other hand sought to protect his lender. Several expert opinions were written, among which those of Conrad Peutinger (Bauer 1954), the Augsburg town clerk, stand out. While these opinions have aroused the interest of historians, they should also be considered by the history of economic thought on account of their clarity and keenness of argumentation. Let us now turn now to an examination of some excerpts from these texts.

From among many, we have selected in particular the final and most comprehensive of Peutinger's memoranda from the year 1530, which can be seen as a refutation of the 'Memorandum on account of the monopolies' (ibid., p. 16, my transl.)[42] from the Monopoly Committee of the Augsburg Reichstag.

In 1523 Peutinger had already argued against Guild regulations which limited the number of apprentices and journeymen and thereby robbed the better and harder working craftsmen of opportunities for further development.

> Et exempla quottidie habemus, quod si inter artifices conventum est, quod unus habeat nisi tot famulos, vel hoc tantum in suo artificio exerceat, in ista quidem conventione meliori artifici et qui bene suum artificium curat, prodigalitatem fugit, parsimoniam amat, semper obstat egens, pauper, prodigus, nihil curans et decoctor.
>
> (ibid., p. 4)[43]

The realization of God's will would be hindered, together with luck ('fortuna') and better output. The traditional organization is not that decreed by God; instead, the goal is, as he then said, 'In sum, every man should be free in buying, selling, allotting work or taking it on' (ibid., p. 13, my transl.).

The opposing position was formulated in the 'Memorandum on account of the monopolies' (ibid., p. 16). Accusations were there made against the companies – against cartel-building, if you will: 'maintenance of the association especially for selling ... encouraging the buyer or seller to give nothing to anyone to sell, or that he should not so give, for that is all counter to the common good, harmful and disadvantageous' (ibid., p. 17, my transl.).[44]

According to the Memorandum, Roman law and the decisions of the Cologne Reichstag, as well as Emperor Maximilian, argued against the construction of such monopolies. The king of Portugal's pepper monopoly was said to give rise to arrangements with companies that allowed prices to increase – though not all at once, so that it would not be easily noticed (ibid., p. 18). The companies were made responsible for the export of precious metals which supported the import of useless luxury goods; they took control of the metal trade and even sold to unbelievers. Ultimately their business activities also included traditional commercial areas such as cattle and grain and 'as a result the poor people were ruined by the rich companies and sellers' (ibid., p. 19, my transl.). Countermeasures such as prohibitions and size limitations were supposed to act as a corrective (ibid., p. 20ff.).

In Peutinger's careful answer, which examines the accusation in detail, the arrangements are disputed primarily on the grounds of their implausibility.

The king of Portugal, it is true, has his pepper monopoly, but he sells to many (ibid., pp. 29ff.), and Peutinger points to competitors selling substitutes: 'similes species aromatum eciam in magna quantitate urbi Venetiarum et aliis emporiis apportari solent' (ibid., p. 30).[45] Selling at high prices is not necessarily a sign of a monopoly, but instead a merchant's right. The price increase cannot be attributed to merchants, because it derives from the power of the Portuguese king as sole vendor, from harvest fluctuations, and, furthermore, from the general tendency of prices to increase which cannot originate from companies alone since it reflects a general tendency in all goods (ibid., p. 31).

In mining, too, the existence of so many mines makes eliminating competition impossible ('pluribus diversis societatibus eciam simul coniunctis impossibile esset, has mineras et metalla omnia in unam manum deportare vel constringere', ibid., p. 33).[46] He adds that even if prices in mining were driven up by a cartel, there would be one advantage: as a generous offering from God, the mines would be better maintained (ibid., p. 33). (Monopolies impede the conditions of static efficiency, according to Pareto's criteria, but they can be more efficient than competition if profits from the monopoly are invested in the improvement of production technology.)

The export of precious metals is bolstered by the division of labour among those countries involved in global trade ('licet una provincia alteram naturali quodam instinctu alat et eidem subvenit', ibid., p. 34).[47] The companies do not make people poor and have on the contrary made many rich. Thanks to their size, they alone can develop far-off countries (ibid., p. 35), and if the merchants wanted to deal with Antwerp individually, goods would become more expensive.

The companies are accused of being selfish (he cites the German word: 'aigennutzig handtierungen'), but trading in one's own interest ('proprium commodum quaerere', ibid., p. 37)[48] is not forbidden, and if merchants expose not only their goods and their assets but also themselves to the physical hardship and dangers of travel, then the idle and sedentary will benefit as well. The pursuit of self-interest is closely tied, it seems, to public interests.

A monopoly, if there was one, would have to be prohibited, but in the spice and ore trade no such monopoly existed. A size limitation on trading companies is not possible, because if one were imposed these companies would move abroad. Additionally, forbidding a person who has acquired wealth, by the grace of God, to increase acquisition of honour and right (in harmony with God) through diligence, work and achievement and to prevent him from improving conditions for himself and his family is unthinkable. Therefore, the attempt to limit the size of companies is 'contra non solum privatam, sed eciam contra omnem publicam utilitatem et ideo maius monopolium induceret quam forte hactenus est auditum' (ibid., p. 38).[49]

Introducing tariffs (price fixing) is impossible because price fluctuations are unavoidable with crops, and production must decrease if prices are set which fail to cover costs. Forbidding trade would only lead to others taking it over. He concludes by recommending cities and traders to the emperor and assuring the emperor of his obedience.

The interests of the cities of the realm were, nevertheless, not identical (ibid., issue 2, p. 154). The cities of the Hanseatic league relied on the old privileges, while Ulm and Frankfurt feared competition from Augsburg. Thus, Peutinger felt forced to address his opponents' arguments and to present them with their conditions. He is chiefly interested, however, in defending private enterprise, which he perceives as something ordained by God and which can only be limited within the framework of honour and law.

This resolute position, comparable to later arguments for free trade based on natural law, makes Peutinger appear to be an important forerunner. He constructs his technical arguments astutely by asserting that there was no monopoly at all in Germany, thus establishing the qualification that only a literal monopoly, and not merely imperfect competition, would be objectionable. He acknowledges only the King of Portugal's monopoly. Höffner remarks, in disagreement:

We saw, however, that foreign trade led to further monopolies, with a particular preference for the princely monopoly. Conrad Peutinger says nothing of that even though he was well aware, for example, of the Fuggers' attempts to monopolize the copper trade (Höffner 1941, p. 59).

Peutinger apparently saw the dynamic of market processes, which repeatedly, if temporarily, remedied emergent imperfections and concentrations of power – and when the dynamics of the national market did not suffice, he cited international competition. Accordingly, he thinks in terms of gradations of wealth distribution rather than a polarization of capital owners and dependants. In the concluding chapter of volume 1 of *Capital*, where he considers so-called 'primitive accumulation', Marx connects the beginnings of capitalist development with the separation of the proletariat from a class of proprietors; the proletariat was formed by driving out independent agricultural labourers – since capital had passed beyond the threshold to where sufficient capital was available to purchase the means of production and to use this to 'exploit' foreign labour – through violence and plundering, especially in regions outside of Europe. Peutinger's entrepreneurs obtained their earliest fortunes through diligence and their own work, due to courageous trade and, at a higher level, through international commerce and the mines, while the credit system is hardly mentioned in his analysis. Sombart again took up the Marxian question and theorized the initial creation of wealth through the accumulation of land rents. Strieder (1935) later shows that in Augsburg the fortunes of wealthy families and patricians derived primarily from trade, which often resulted from activities connected with the guilds, and developed gradually. Thereafter, merchants and traders acquired the capital for the expansion of their businesses largely unaided and without changing their professional positions. Though such phenomena are otherwise of little interest to Humanists, within the framework of a legal analysis of monopoly, Peutinger defined the development and specific transitional social position of the early modern bourgeoisie, its economic functions and position in the state.

Authors of the Mercantile period emergent in the sixteenth century, quite often merchants themselves, sought to demonstrate above all that they were not undermining society but, on the contrary, serving the good of the princes as well as the community. The further argument that pursuing self-interest might also serve the interest of the whole, as has been put forth in modern economics since Mandeville and Smith, would not be made until some time later. While there are echoes of the idea in Peutinger's text, they are not developed in detail. The ancient Stoics had already introduced the idea – at first without a connection to the economy – but Christianity and the Medieval era called for devotion to God and those close to one, so that serving one's own self-interest was seen as contrary to the general good.

Thus we should be surprised, though it is characteristic of the force and direction of German economic development in the sixteenth century, that in Frankfurt am Main in 1564 a little book was published that praised self-interest as Mandeville (1990 [1714]) would later dare to do in 1714 (his text was printed in book form exactly 150 years later). The text is headed by the rhyme:

> I am called self-interest
> Well-known to high and low classes
> But not as evil as people make me
> If you look at things fairly
> To many much good comes through me
> But no praise is devoted to me.
>             (Fronsperger 1564, my transl.)[50]

The woodcut on the title page displays a cheerful, carousing man in the open countryside, his hair wind-blown, in one hand a duck and in the other a knuckle of pork. He sits on a hill with a bottle of wine and bread at his feet with 'Everything is mine' written on his abdomen.

A society of ranks consists of those who rule and those who serve – at least that is how it represents itself. It is written that common good guides the individual. Those above must provide the conditions which allow those below to produce food for all. The various members of society are dependent upon one another like the organs of a living being, as in the analogy of the Roman Menenius Agrippa, who depicted the patrician as the stomach, the plebeians as the arms and legs of the body of the people. It thus came as a great surprise when, in 1985, during a presentation in the Bavarian Academy of Science, a text was referred to which 'upon closer examination proved to be nothing less than an anticipation of what Mandeville had written at the dawn of the eighteenth century' (Schulze 1987, p. 20, my transl.). In place of the concept of social relations, established by norms, entered one based on individual self-interest.

A citizen of Ulm, Fronsperger reports in the foreword that for years he had discussed with a well-known friend, one Doctor Oswald Gut, who was the Margrave Chancellor, that the important thing was not public welfare but rather self-interest. Gut had planned to write a book on the concept of self-interest. In the end, however, he requested that Fronsperger complete the text. We know that Gut was made a noble by Charles V in 1530 and that in the following year Margrave Ernst named him chancellor; he died in 1554. Fronsperger had written books about warfare and on practical questions of urban economics; according to Schulze (ibid., pp. 26–7); however, these books can best be characterized as compilations.

Given our lack of information about the author's background, we can only comment upon the text itself. It begins in an amusing, even ironic way with the remark that people praise the comfortable and criticize the uncomfortable, and do not praise self-interest even though they have lived according to it since the time of Adam. Self-interest (which speaks in the first person) is, instead, the object of complaint, 'as if I were someone who ruined land / a destroyer of all good policy / honour / customs / harmony / peace...' (Fronsperger 1564, p. 2, left, my transl.). Children's verse is rhymed with it: 'the gospel would not be so difficult / were there no self-interest' (ibid., p. 2, right, my transl.); yet the world could not exist without it.

As proof, the reader is led through the unveiling of an array of self-deceptions. People believe they can bear the truth but have to learn that flattery often maintains the peace. Erasmus had already revealed how distorted the world can be with his praise of folly: 'As the Goddess Folly ... by the highly educated, surpassing eloquent man / Erasmus from Rotterdam / is thus praised and caressed for this / that one now considers / and believes / that she creates for human beings not a little understanding and utility' (ibid., p. 9, left, my transl.) – however, Self-interest believes that the praise bestowed upon Folly is really owed to him.

As might be expected from a political book of the old school, the series of illustrations starts off with marriage, which is entered into not for the common good but out of inborn lust. The same is true of friendship – and life without friendship would be like the earth without the sun. Then after having attributed to self-interest, much which others may have attributed love, the text goes on more easily to examine the supply of goods – what farmer would toil away for the public welfare? – as well as skilled labour and merchants. An occasional deed for the common good does not violate the basic rule. Clergymen and the regents, in the end, seek their offices out of self-interest but not, as Erasmus claimed, out of folly. Do people want to tend sheep for their own sake (as is demanded by the teachings of the ancient and Christian world)?

Self-interest counters: 'I cannot know / whether Christ, the saviour of the world, was the only good shepherd / but such things will be sought for vainly in human beings' (ibid., p. 22, my transl.).

The suggestion is that God created the world like a single 'policey', thus in the form of a single state; this idea can be found in Cicero where it represents a development of natural law ('from natural light', ibid., p. 26, left, my transl.). God has organized the world in such a way that each country needs the other and, similarly with people, as Bryson wrote: People depend upon one another, forged together like links in a chain. Obviously, this explanation focuses on how good arises from self-interest, in a return to the Stoic tradition upon which, as we know today, Smith's theory would be based 200 years later. Thus God created the individual for the good of others, and the resources of the world are there for all – but not, as the rabble believes, neither for forced distribution nor for common possession. Instead, 'through inequality and struggling opposites appears the greatest equality / and the sweetest harmony and unity / which no tongue can speak of or fully praise enough / no heart can sufficiently admire / as in an organ are many and various pipes / short and long / big and small / none of which is like the other in tone / but from such unequal voices come the sweetest harmonies of music' (ibid., p. 29, my transl.). And so we arrive with Fronsperger at the musical analogy of harmony. He ventures to offer a stoic interpretation of Christian doctrine: Humans should consider themselves the administrators of the goods with which God has entrusted them. No one really knows the common good, but they certainly know self-interest, and therefore self-interest in person goes so far as to assure, 'if there is common good on earth / or can be / then it has its ... origin / thus / that I want to be rightly named his father / etc.' (ibid., p. 38, left, my transl.).

Later, in a daring turn, God is praised thanks to self-interest, for people want to partake in eternal life; meanwhile, the author renounces every criminal misuse of self-interest with the example of Chrysippus: for self-interest should be pursued like the runner who may strive to pass the opponent, but who is forbidden to obstruct the rival by pushing him or blocking his path. Finally, self-interest preserves wealth. In the story of Lazarus, the rich person is not damned because he possessed so much, but because he failed to share of his abundance.

Thus, Fronsperger's conceptual world arises from the confluence of antique and Biblical influences: 'one should work and create as if we could live forever / and seek reconciliation with God / as if we had to die at once' (ibid., p. 45, right, my transl.). While Mandeville unsettles his readers with cynical undertones, Fronsperger seeks to gratify them with humour and edify them with worldly erudition and the piety of certain salvation.

It has been proven that not only Fronsperger but also Mandeville was dependent on Erasmus, and it has further been suggested that it was the term 'self-love' (*philautia*) developed in *Praise of Folly* which opened the way for establishing self-interest as the general impulse for trade (Schulze 1987, p. 23).

Naturally, Erasmus' amusing irony resists a simple reductive reading. He demonstrates without doubt that folly (understood as narrow-mindedness) is an essential condition of all human production. Folly, for instance, thinks of authors:

> The whole tribe of them are deeply in my debt ... They change, they interline, they erase something and put it back in, they rewrite the whole thing, after rephrasing a passage they show it to their friends and after all they closet up the manuscript for nine years but without ever satisfying themselves – and this for an empty reward of praise from a mere handful of critics ... All this grief they gladly accept as the price of having their work appreciated by a couple of blear-eyed experts.
>
> (Rotterdam 1989)

In accordance with the facts, or perhaps simply to lend his literary venture the appearance of exaggerated seriousness, in his dedication to Thomas More Erasmus reports that he wrote the text on a trip from Italy to England: 'ne totum hoc tempus, quo equo fuit insidendum, αμουσοις et illiteratis fabulis tereretur' (Rotterdam 1780).[51]

The Humanist Movement, which recognized Erasmus as one of the most learned and wittiest minds, tended to remain somewhat distant from practical life. Even so, the Mirror of Princes *Institutio Principis Christiani*, published by Erasmus in Basel in 1516, also contained future-oriented notions such as the idea that all people were naturally free, and that the initiation and implementation of servitude and serfdom was against nature. While Erasmus recognized diligence and work, the tradition of the Medieval critique held greater sway in his assessment of merchant activities (Autorenkollektiv 1977, pp. 64ff.).

As the Reformation, for which Erasmus helped prepare the way (if unintentionally), spread across Germany and Europe and people were faced with the most difficult matters of conscience, the confrontational force turned not only against the church's dominance but also against economic phenomena that were felt to be abusive. Protestantism sought to overcome these powers, which had been criticized but not overcome by Catholicism. Here we refer to several passages from Luther's (Luther 1987 [1524], 1962) *Sermon on Trade and Usury.*

This is not the place to explore Luther's other engagements with questions of economics, and accordingly to examine his polemic against usury and excessive profits, or his praise of work, of fair payment and of pricing based upon the measurement of the effort expended in producing the product. What interests us here is the issue of monopolies, mentioned briefly:

> On the trading companies I ought to say a good deal, but the whole subject is such a bottomless pit of avarice and wrongdoing that there is nothing in it that can be discussed with a good conscience ... monopolies? Even the temporal laws of the heathen forbid them as openly

harmful to the whole world ... This year they raise the price of ginger, next year that of saffron.

(Sheet D III from the original, Luther 1962)

The polemic not only takes up popular anger at the new entrepreneurship, but also their annoyance at the outflow of precious metals and the consumption of luxury goods, then seen as unnecessary:

God has cast us Germans off to such an extent that we have to fling our gold and silver into foreign lands and make the whole world rich, while we ourselves remain beggars. England would have less gold if Germany let her keep her cloth; the king of Portugal would have less if we let him keep his spices ... Frankfort is the gold and silver drain through which everything that springs and grows – or is minted or coined – here, flows out of Germany.

(Sheet A II-III from the original)

People wanted to act just as passionately as Luther preached. Young, energetic people became the theorists of the Reformation. 'From the very beginning, Luther's following was primarily one thing – young' (Schöffler 1936, p. 33, my transl.). The professors around Luther were under thirty at the time of their appointment; about half of the 2500 inhabitants of Wittenberg were students, and these young people saw themselves standing up to the old prelates in the Catholic hierarchy.

Roscher, who considered Luther the most important German in history, compiled In his examination of Reformation economics some astonishing demands from the 'Wild Pamphlets' in the era before the Peasants' War. Eberlin von Günzburg called for a government hierarchy in which no post was inheritable, all office-holders were salaried, and compulsory education was universal; in 1524 Thomas Müntzer preached in front of the Ernestinian prince at the Allstedt castle:

The source of usury, of thievery and robbery are our princes and lords, claiming all creatures as their property ... thus they mistreat exploit the poor farmer, the craftsman ... so he then attacks the lowest and for that he must hang ... The lords themselves turn the poor man into an enemy.

(Roscher 1992 [1874], pp. 84ff., 89, my transl.)

In 1534, the Anabaptists in Münster then demanded a return to common property, following the example of the apostles.

This is the spiritual environment in which Roscher places his description of the three currency pamphlets, which he includes among 'the strangest monuments to the older economic doctrine'; the two Albertinian pamphlets are written in 'such a pure, clear, objective and yet powerful, beautiful German such as might only have been expected from a contemporary of Luther or

Hutten'. Roscher praises the Ernestinian because his pamphlet contains 'the basic ideas of the so-called Mercantile system' a century before Thomas Mun (ibid., pp. 103ff., my transl.). Müller-Armack confirms this judgment in his *Genealogie der Wirtschaftsstile* [Genealogy of Economic Styles], where he writes: 'the first text justifying the mercantilist world policy, the Ernestinian polemic pamphlets from 1530, already derives the necessity of an undervalued domestic currency from the goal of developmental assistance' (Müller-Armack 1944, p. 83, my transl.).

Finally, to more fully set the scene for the situation in Germany in 1530, when the first of the currency pamphlets appeared, we must also take note of contemporary political developments. Returning to Germany from Italy at the height of his power, Charles V attempted to deal with the Reformation – initially without threats. At the Reichstag, taking place in Augsburg with great pomp, he summoned the Protestant leaders and attempted to convince them to renounce preaching. Margrave Georg von Brandenburg replied: 'My lord, before I would forsake God's word, I would rather kneel down right here and have my head cut off.' Ranke, whose narration we now take up, continues:

> the emperor, who wanted only to use mild words and was benevolent by nature, was himself shocked by the option presented to him by someone other than himself. 'My dear prince,' he responded to the margrave in broken lower-German, 'no head off'.
>
> (Ranke 1933, p. 149, my transl.)

The Protestants had hoped that the emperor would act as arbitrator; he found himself forced, however, to speak for the Catholic majority. That the Protestant princes held fast, despite his growing harshness, was mainly due to Johann von Sachsen, of whom Ranke (1933, pp. 161ff., my transl.) writes:

> he was not born for pleasures and worldly desires; discomforts which could not be avoided affected him all-too-deeply and tortured him more than the enjoyment of mild pleasures brought. [...] From Luther's first appearance, he dedicated himself to Luther's doctrines; his disposition which was naturally serious and deeply religious was gradually pervaded by them. [...] After the peasants' war, the ideas of the Reaction arose to the most violent; as much as they were recommended to him by his worldly-wise cousin who was practiced in business, Johann did not allow himself to be overwhelmed [...] In all of this, Luther now had great influence upon him. [...] Thus following Johann the protest then occurred which gave the entire party its name and worldly position.

However, the Reichstag became expensive for Johann von Sachsen: 'we have high costs here, had to borrow about 12,000 gulden: his imperial majesty did not address a single word to us', he wrote on 28 July (Charles V arrived in

Augsburg on 15 June). 'Luther declared that had this prince wavered, then none of his councillors would have remained true' (ibid., pp. 163ff., my transl.). Had there been no threat from Turkey, perhaps the emperor would have promptly used force. These few suggestions will have to suffice in order to illustrate how the Ernestinian stood courageously and radically on the side of the new religious issues and at the same time neglected the economic foundations of his rule, while his Catholic Albertinian cousin, already in government a long time, clung to the conventions of the time.

I would now like to examine the history of Saxony immediate preceding the currency dispute. The following overview is based on the account from Lotz and Klotzsch.[52]

Because of generally low tax revenues even the Saxon princes had to resort to currency debasement as a source of income in the first half of the fifteenth century; in the second half, there were efforts at reform. When Saxony was divided, an action undertaken for dynastic reasons in 1485, a decision was made to leave the mines in common property, to make common use of them and to settle accounts annually. The Electoral incumbent, the Ernestinian Friedrich the Wise who lived until 1525, and his Albertinian cousin, Duke Georg, worked together to create a stable monetary policy. In 1525, John (Johann) the Constant replaced Friedrich the Wise. As we saw, he supported the Protestant faith, while the Albertinian Duke George remained Catholic. Count Albrecht von Mansfeld, who participated in the Saxon monetary union, suggested raising the price of silver and combining that with a currency devaluation. One reason for this was that coins were melted down because of their high silver content and coins of weaker foreign currencies were put into circulation in their stead (the good coins became rare in domestic circulation – conforming to Gresham's law).

At first, both parts of Saxony favoured the reform; however, in 1526 Duke Georg spoke out against it. It is uncertain whether the duke did so for commercial reasons or if religious differences also played a role here. Klotzsch believes that Duke Georg felt bound by his oath to his subjects not to devalue the currency. 'In the meantime he yielded to the suggestions, repeatedly made by the Elector, for joint consideration in person, which was held in the city of Zeitz, Monday after Valentini in 1526, at which the subject was defended and disputed but nothing decided. Duke George steadily maintained the grounds for his opposition and both princes separated from each other, but not without concealed displeasure' (Klotzsch 1779, pp. 250ff., my transl.). The Elector, however, did not let up.

Now after Duke George had convinced himself over time that his sustained opposition would only be a vain attempt to halt what he could not entirely prevent, he finally tacitly conceded the demands of the Elector for a separation of the coinage (ibid., p. 251, my transl.).

The two princes closed their common mint in Schneeberg and for several years shared the silver mined *in natura*, from which they each minted their own coins. This led to the currency pamphlets, in the first of which the partisan of Albertinian Duke Georg 'spoke very loudly against a reduction of the coin' (ibid., p. 252, my transl.).

The result was that both parties minted coins separately, each with their own name and coat of arms. Duke George finally found himself more or less compelled to submit to a currency devaluation. A meeting of the state assembly was called and in 1534 John's successor, Johann Friedrich, called for a return to common minting. 'And at the beginning of 1534 new common coinage, bearing the images of both princes and their coats of arms, appeared' (ibid., pp. 259ff., my transl.). In the end the opponents of currency debasement enjoyed only a partial success. Later, the Albertinian Moritz wrested the Electoral incumbency from the Ernestinians and in 1549 issued currency regulations which did not rescind the debasement of the coinage but in certain respects simplified a complicated system.[53]

The history of currency in Saxony should not be viewed in isolation, since it is so closely related to the development of coinage within the German realm, where repeated attempts were made to standardize the currency system. Yet, the princes refused to allow their treasuries to be plundered, for they ensured income and expressed their sovereignty through the circulation of coins bearing their coat of arms and images. Coin debasement was not merely the result of repeated depreciations intended to increase revenues, but was something that could not be entirely avoided since the coins themselves wear out in circulation, even when they were not illegally shaved or ground down.[54] The inflation in the sixteenth century, generally explained with reference to the importing of precious metals from the Americas,[55] had already begun in the previous century; for Munich, Augsburg and Frankfurt the beginning is dated between 1460 and 1470. The introduction of precious metals from the New World is not mentioned in the currency pamphlets of 1530–31. Cleary then, the importing of precious metals cannot have been the sole cause of the inflation; along with currency depreciation, various factors having to do with cost and demand come into play,[56] many of which are addressed in the currency pamphlets.

With his opening words, the Albertinian author of the first currency pamphlet, 'Common Voices', makes his purpose clear. Since the Biblical Fall, the order of the state has been such that

subjects should be obedient to the authorities in all things honourable and proper which are not against God. On the other hand the government's duty, for their salvation, is also to seek only the useful and the best for their subjects (Lotz 1893, p. 3, my transl.).[57]

The authorities should keep their subjects on the path of virtue; subjects are to remain obedient and support the authorities in any way possible so that they can be well governed. Under such a regimen both sides prosper. One can see in Saxony, Thuringia and Meissen what fine cathedrals, hospitals and residences have been built. General welfare was enhanced by this. 'That of others has also substantially improved – as can be seen in the buildings of many places' (p. 5, my transl.).

The Albertinian does not claim that a sound legal system and the development of free enterprise has made this growth possible, although he could hardly have recommended any other measures if he thought in such modern terms; he expresses himself differently. God has given the land rulers more concerned with the general good than with their own, who do not forgo expenditures to keep peace and who – we now come to our topic – mint genuinely good coins. Specifically, a great deal is spent on the mines, 'whose sinking and maintenance is [not] possible without significant expense' (p. 7, my transl.).[58] From them there derives increased prosperity, since the population increases and sales of goods and, in turn, the income of the nobility, the citizenry, craftsmen and farmers. The causal connection made here is quite simply this: increasing income opportunities and growing population are mutually reinforcing, while at the same time the improved circulation of money eases trade.

'For where there are many people goods are put forward' (p. 7, my transl.). Thus the population, employment and volume of production expand. Quality of life improves. Technical progress, in the sense of an increase in productivity, however, is not addressed.

Unfortunately, the economic prosperity had been met with the question of 'whether it was good to have good but few coins in the country' (p. 7, my transl.). What follows is a very clear summary of the opposition party's arguments, which maintain that too much silver is exported and that taxes are too high for difficult times. Furthermore, the amount of silver from which 8¼ Guldens is currently stamped should in the future be used to stamp 10 Guldens. This would amount to a profit of 1¾ Gulden for the lords, thus more than a tax, and would continue to provide a yield as long as the mines remained open. The (depreciated) coins would remain in the country, few luxury goods would be imported, and even basic foodstuffs would become cheaper. Silver, however, would become more expensive and hence of better value.

The opposing argument from the Albertinian writer begins with a contention that a modern reader, too, will find it easiest to go along with: a critique of the view that seignorage is a good and long-term form of taxation. Taxes are too high as long as prices remain unchanged, but it has to be remembered 'that the value of coins, like all goods made of metal … is measured precisely in what the coins themselves contain in silver and metal…' (p. 11, my transl.).

This writer is therefore a metallist; the value of coins is based on their metal content so that in the event of a reduction, the cash price of all goods must increase. He does not take into consideration that, according to the quantity theory, the purchasing power of coins as money could be higher than their metal value, just as the purchasing power of a bank note is higher than that of the paper it is printed on. We will see later that, following a reduction in metal content, the Ernestinian writer resolutely demands that the money supply not be allowed to swell and that 'over-minting' be avoided. To that extent, the position adopted by the Ernestinian is based on an idea rooted in quantity theory.

The metallist viewpoint is more convincing in foreign trade, where the currencies of numerous principalities and coins of every age are traded. The Albertinian notes ironically that no one abroad wants the debased coin. In fact, he cannot purchase anything with them abroad as long as the bearer in the domestic market receives more for their nominal value than they are worth abroad, where they are traditionally valued according to their metal content. It will be difficult for the Ernestinian to respond to this point, since he lacks our modern experience of exchanging bank notes, outside a country, under normal conditions at stable rates which are based on the balance of trade, purchasing power parity and other factors – moreover, he has even less access to theories that might explain this phenomenon.

We, however, can understand why coins abroad were valued according to their metal content. Their value was not less because they could be melted down, and at the same time not higher because the greater purchasing power they enjoyed at home was not recognized abroad because otherwise little could be exported. The Saxons' most important export product (on this point the opponents agree) was silver itself, and their currency would have increased in value with decreased silver content only if the export situation had improved.

Both authors did to some extent understand this relationship. The Ernestinian did not seek to increase exports so much as to curb imports, since imports appeared to consist primarily of luxury goods which he thought reprehensible. His assessment confuses economic questions with socio-political objectives, both of which touch on religious positions. The Albertinian seeks to keep separate out the arguments; he promises no moral improvement from economic measures, and goes so far as to claim:

> one would still not be rid of luxury in one's own country. Rather than give up their extravagance, some would prefer to send to Venice for it; of course he would have to spend money and assume the risk of transporting something across land that was once brought to his door free of charge.
>
> (p. 13, my transl.)

If traders no longer import spices, spice lovers will go themselves to Venice and buy them! With regard to the sale of basic goods, their procurement always depends on the quality of the money: 'Whether bread, beer and all other goods are delivered depends on the coins [used as payment]; the salesman cannot be fooled' (p. 13, my transl.).

Clearly, then, reducing the silver content of the coins in no way led to lower prices, as the Ernestinian assumed.

The basic metallistic position seems to indicate a classical theory of value, which sets prices based on production conditions in the long run, ignoring subjective influences. Indeed, it is said of the merchant that he 'focuses on the natural value of the coins, which they have based on the silver content, and not according to their chance valuation' (p. 15, my transl.).

The Albertinian treats his assertion – that the purchasing power of silver coins must be estimated according to the value of the silver contained in them – as an axiom, hence as a statement which is a presupposition of all others and is itself not rigorously established, but is instead plausible. The axiom appears plausible to him especially when applied to foreign countries, for if full-valued silver coins from foreign mints circulated then a lower-valued Saxon Gulden would not be their equal. Perhaps we should say that the purchasing power of coins could not go much beyond their silver value in a world in which the state was still weak, because otherwise there would be a dangerous increase in attempts to produce counterfeit coins. He believes that an overvalued exchange rate could only prevail if it were accepted by all other countries, which he thinks to be as unlikely as all peoples agreeing on one language, a set of customs and the same religion.

Thus he states that 'the face value of the coined silver cannot be increased, unless it occurs in all nations' (p. 15, my transl.).

To maintain a higher seignorage the Ernestinian plan stipulates that the mines must surrender their silver at the same nominal price as before. When the Albertinian writes in this respect that:

> if the mine owners are paid for the silver with the same number of coins as previously and nevertheless have it stamped into coins of higher face value and put in circulation ... [this] contradicts all holy and natural rights,
>
> (pp. 17ff., my transl.)

he appears to justify metallism as a God-given, natural law just as we saw with Oresme. But the sentence continues 'because the mine owners have often invested much money in the mines' (p. 19, my transl.), pointing to the production costs of silver which, as he later suggests, must increase with the ensuing, seemingly unavoidable, inflation due to coin depreciation. To that extent this line of reasoning confirms that metallism anticipates a cost of production theory. The legal structures of mining operations were such that some stakeholders lived in distant cities (fraudulent sales of shares relating to mines in poor condition were already occurring). The warning that at least some stakeholders would withdraw from mining construction if profitability sank because of inflation is reasonable enough. Mine owners would have to produce greater amounts of silver in the future in order to be able to purchase a specified amount of other goods.

During the course of the sixteenth century many European mines became unprofitable not only because of the debasement of coin within the country, which is what is complained of here, but also because of competition from the New World in silver production. As a result not only coins but silver itself declined in purchasing power. Both phenomena therefore occurred when the number and content of coins minted in given amounts of silver did not change. The American mines ultimately had lower production costs.

The Albertinian author now moves on to examine the effects of inflation on the various social classes, and states once more that the authorities have an obligation to provide welfare in this regard. He points to cities such as Prague and Regensburg, impoverished 'by wicked inferior coins' (p. 21, my transl.). Poverty assumes a curious form – in old houses whose iron work (nails and brackets) is more valuable than the house itself.

Then follows an apt description, no surprise to us, of the effect of inflation on loans and rents, there being unavoidable conflict between debtors and creditors. He concludes: 'the inferior coins will have destroyed trade, reduced customs and transit fees, made mining more difficult and one has discontent hanging from one's throat, hence life and soul may perish' (p. 23, my transl.).

The disruption of social peace opens the way for sinfulness. Merchants can be included among the beneficiaries of inflation, as Oresme had already remarked, for their superior market knowledge allows them to make a profit in the exchange of money. The Albertinian points out, however, that these merchants are also for the most part moneylenders, so that as creditors they might potentially lose far more than they could gain by changing money, since the total of the outstanding loans far exceeds the amount of cash in hand.

After this surprisingly progressive assessment, the author goes on to settle accounts with those who are resentful, and those who would prefer not to see Jews in the country, 'so they can run the usury business themselves. Those are wicked people' (p. 25, my transl.).

The text concludes, as it began, with an appeal to the Lord for wealth and salvation.

The deliberate and thoughtful remarks of the Catholic Albertinian – well-organized and focused on progress within a given framework – are followed by the many strikingly original criticisms of the Protestant Ernestinian: assessments which are longer, often sharper, sometimes contradictory, and just as often looking toward a desired future as to a golden past. The title is meant to provide reassurance that the author is also well-intentioned and submissive, but it is immediately followed by a warning: the author of the opposing text is like a wolf who recommends to sheep that they graze near the forest. He represents the merchants' interests. These people and their partners are pursuing their own advantage not that of the public welfare. Full of outrage, the Ernestinian adds: 'For this the people use God's holy word as a cloak for their offensive usury' (p. 29, my transl.).

Finally the author accuses the Albertinian, who of all people is so concerned with order, of agitation. Instead, he says, discussion should take place calmly. If the prince is asked to set the silver price to the merchants' advantage, why not also request – the writer asks ironically – that he dictate to the merchants the maximum price for goods and so prevent their raising their prices? (p. 31) Which is preferable: 50 or 60 rich merchants in a city at the cost of the impoverishment of the rest of the population, or the well-being of the majority?

The Ernestinian links the already emergent inflationary tendency to price increases and profit-taking on the part of merchants, because declining competition results from increasing concentration. Rising demand for luxury items plays into the merchants' hands. This demand could however be controlled, and if the acquisition of luxuries were made more difficult, it would by no means lead to consumers travelling abroad to purchase these luxury items themselves, as was suggested by the Albertinian with his example involving Venice. Lotz (1893, pp. 30ff., my transl.) talks here of 'suggestions regarding trade policy and protective tariffs in which we find a police spirit hostile to luxury combined with a confusion of money and wealth, this last being mistakenly considered characteristic of all earlier mercantilists'. Nonetheless, the Ernestinian is correct with regard to the Albertinian when he argues that debasement reduces imports and makes it more difficult to meet the demand for luxury goods.

After this skirmish the author points out that the arguments had already been exchanged at the meeting in 1526 mentioned above, that the various imperial orders had expressed themselves on this subject, and the Ernestinian therefore doubts whether the merchants are able to present a well-founded memorandum. Although the Ernestinian appears to share the prejudice of the experienced administrator regarding uneducated merchants and expresses himself in strong, not to say incendiary, language, he emphasizes the most important thing here: economic issues should be discussed and settled in objective terms. And then he attempts to do just that.

Currency depreciation would not be solely advantageous for the lord, since increased seignorage would be off-set by losses of income from interest payments. That depreciation might not be purely advantageous for the prince could also be seen in lower revenues from toll which could be anticipated as a result of reduced imports. Losses suffered by proprietors and wagoners must be accepted in view of their wealth. There remained, in any case, the regional trade of essential goods. 'These are all absolutely necessary goods without which no one could live at home or abroad' (p. 39, my transl.).

Naturally therefore the intention is by no means to eliminate all trade or industry. The reader cannot help but think of Luther's sermons on a modest lifestyle, in which profit and trade are allowed to play at most a modest role. They were then considered a venial sin. The administrator's position becomes clear when the text mentions that the various revenues from toll roads have been estimated; he desires an appropriate policy (p. 37) here: to see rigorous taxation of, and legislation against, luxury.

The author now broaches what appear to be the most important subjects to him. After complaining about the amount of silver that had been produced and exported, he asks what the country has gained from it. It will hardly be argued that in the years immediately following the Peasants' War the general population was thriving. If readers see only the confusion of (lost) money and (lost) wealth in the Ernestinians remarks, then they have failed to appreciate the then-pressing question of whether wealth might not have been better distributed.

Anyone demanding change must first prove that the current situation is unsatisfactory. Employing numerous examples, the Ernestinian shows that, despite payment in full-value coins, prices have increased – for the last 25 years rather than just the previous three or four. As we have seen, recent work in economic history lends support to the view that inflation did not result from monetary factors alone, but had already begun in the previous century. The conclusion argues that the good coins generated no advantage, which naturally remains unproven, since inflation would certainly have been greater with continuing currency reductions, as the Albertinian will not fail to point out in his response.

Silver was supposedly overvalued because it had been melted down on account of it being cheaper to obtain silver in this way than by buying silver bullion. Lotz, who may not have thought of the possibility of an over-issue of silver coins, suggests that the lords' silver monopoly led to an inflated price for silver ore (ibid., pp. 45ff.). The Ernestinian, in contrast, speaks of a 'surplus of such overvalued coins' (p. 47, my transl.). In order to understand this argument, which is almost technically irrefutable and can also be found in Copernicus, one has to imagine that merchants and traders extracted the good coins and left bad or – occasionally – foreign coins to circulate among the population, a practice which leads the Ernestinian writer to make the comparison: The working horses who plough the land will get the least of the oats that are grown (since the oats are reserved for riding horses).

In short: the rich, foreign lands Italy, France, Lower Burgundy, as well as England, etc., primarily set up their trade in such a way that they send their goods to foreign lands in order to acquire wealth, i.e. money, for it (p. 47, my transl.).

The Ernestinian acutely grasps the mercantilist policy of export-oriented countries which lacked access to mines for the production of precious metals at that time indispensable for the circulation of goods. The formulation that one has to sacrifice wealth (namely, money) in exchange for luxury goods appears to rest on a naïve conflation of wealth and money; but, as the context makes clear, the author wants to draw attention to the fact that the export of silver and the import of luxury goods benefits only a few: the mine owners and those dependent on them, and those who become rich enough to import luxury goods. There is little profitable employment here for traders and arable farmers. These people suffer from an overvalued currency.

A situation arises in which hundreds perhaps become rich, the princes, though, and the little people suffer losses. The number of the latter, however, praise be to God, amounts to more than one hundred thousand. Without all this, they would all have been able to live much better (p. 47, my transl.).

Theory shows that by exploiting their comparative advantages two countries improve their position in international trade; however, these advantages are not necessarily of benefit to all. And if productivity increases due to technical advances in only one country, then the relative position of the other will deteriorate in the long run. In the Ernestinian's view, moreover, trade relations will be troubled by what appears to be a paradoxical connection of the over-issuance of coins to a high silver content.

In later arguments we come across an interesting attempt to uncover the dubious practices of wholesale merchants in competition. They stockpile high-quality products and sell inferior products to smaller merchants. When the smaller merchants attempt to bring these inferior goods to the customers, representatives of the wholesalers appear with the higher-quality products and oust the smaller merchants from the market. 'A number of monopolies' (p. 53, my transl.) have claimed that this has happened; the practice was such 'that the small merchant cannot prevail against them', (p. 55, my transl.) and thus the sellers find themselves in a position to raise their prices further.

Most importantly, coinage must be determined by the price of silver. On the other hand, mine owners should receive less than if they sold their silver on the open market. Since, thus far, silver has been purchased at market price, the measure is appropriate and does not represent a danger, unless 'God bestows upon us new, rich mines' (p. 57, my transl.).

Just this happened. The European mines were faced with more competitive American silver production.

In this paragraph the author seeks to present his measures as very moderate, and he again points out that at present good, middle-sized Saxonian coins are being melted down, minted abroad at reduced costs, and then reimported. This practice must be stopped. The large coins, on the other hand, remain in circulation but with a premium that impedes their being melted down. The Ernestinian does not deny the legitimacy of the premium; for him, however, it is evidence that the monetary system must be reorganized. What is necessary is 'a proper limitation, a change and reorganization ... according to the correct price and the value of silver' (p. 63, my transl.).

Nevertheless an over-issue of coins is not a proper response to the increased silver price. 'It is, however, not at all our opinion that one should recklessly over-issue coins and devalue silver money' (p. 65, my transl.).

The Ernestinian wants, accordingly, to have an undervalued coin minted and to keep it scarce in circulation. In line with this interpretation, he not only understands, with Copernicus, that a glut of money leads to inflation, but also that a careful issuance of even undervalued coins can be consistent with stable prices. In so doing, however, he considers it necessary to fight price inflation due to imperfect competition. This connection of ideas goes far beyond the conception, emerging later in the sixteenth century, of a quantitative relationship between money supply and prices.

Our Ernestinian is at much more of a loss (but not at a loss for words) when forced to explain what the mines should do in a period of deteriorating profitability. He speaks of the poor miners who open shafts and dig for ore, of the merchants who then purchase a share of the mine and of the good administration which the business requires. When people approach the prince with ever more demands, the Ernestinian believes it is 'mutiny', like the rebellious peasants who had said 'we want to be free and owe no obligation' (p. 69, my transl.).

The mine owners should therefore accept reduced profits but obediently invest all the same. Finally he returns to the mercantilist *leitmotiv*. Countries with extensive trade and industry, like the Netherlands, northern Italy, England and France, are called rich. If these countries are rich because of trade, why would anyone wish to limit the expansion of trade in Saxony? The first, simple, and astonishing answer for us goes as follows: wealth is money and Saxony already has access to this wealth. It is in danger of losing this wealth through trade. For:

> The kingdoms, lands and islands mentioned have set up their industry, their trade, their policy and their working lives in all kinds of ways to bring goods from their own countries or foreign lands, in masses, to we Germans, Hungary and Bohemia, but to keep the money themselves. As a result, they will become rich and prosperous.
>
> (p. 75, my transl.)

These statements constitute a clear and unambiguous expression of mercantilist doctrine, according to which a favourable balance of trade in countries poor in precious metals first allows the importation of precious metals, without which, under the prevailing conditions, money circulation and trade between markets is impossible. The difference is that the doctrine of a favourable balance of trade is not presented from the point of view of countries needing to import precious metals, as in the famous English mercantilists, but instead from that of the exporters of precious metals. Why, however, is the outflow of precious metals unacceptable to him, as long as merchandise is purchased with it?

The Ernestinian gets lost here in gloomy omens: the country, excepting individual privileged traders, will become poor. There is no sketch of a contrasting picture – at least in a direct form, since it can always be read implicitly – of how independent industrialization might be better achieved without the export of precious metals. Such was the doctrine of Ortiz[59], in Spain, some 30 years later. Various reasons may have prompted the Ernestinian not to pursue such ideas himself. Perhaps he was too conservative, or perhaps he was not clever enough to formulate the goal of developing a broad economic base in a conceptually clear manner. Probably the contemporary situation was decisive: reformers were preaching the simple, modest life. The Ernestinian wants nothing more and nothing less than a decent livelihood, according to the old customs, for the majority of the population, without the disruption brought about by new needs and new products, higher prices and the declining purchasing power of income, and without waking feelings of envy through the emergence of new social groups. A few hundred people in the lands of the princes of Saxony are amply provided for. However: despite 'God's kind gift of the mines and the great fertility of the land' (p. 75, my transl.) we have 'thoughtlessly … imprudently … decline of the land and of the common people' (p. 75, my transl.).

In contrast it would be righteous and cheap to make, by the grace of God, many thousands 'rich through farming and honest trade' (p. 75, my transl.). It is not necessary to summarize the remaining attacks on wholesale trade. After praising farmers repeatedly, the author finally goes on to express his sympathy for small business. He does not hope to instruct his opponents but, instead, discerning third parties: 'answer the fools ... for the good of others' (p. 79, my transl.).

As a Protestant, he connects the citation from the Book of Proverbs with the indication that he too has read the Holy Bible. None may conclude without a profession of faith.

The first edition of the third pamphlet, the Albertinian's response, was originally published in 1531. Since this edition has been lost, a reprint followed, based on the 1548 edition. The existence of numerous printings provides evidence of a lively discussion. The Albertinian ardently defends himself against the accusations leveled at him, addressing his opponent as an acquaintance. He cannot accept the accusation that he has misused God's word. He responds that it has become normal to take advantage of the appearance of divine language in making an argument or to claim that this or that position is 'against God' (p. 85, my transl.). The counterpart should instead be able to prove his faith with better fruit – from the Catholic point of view, proof of belief in God is demonstrated in good works.

No important new arguments come into play, although individual minor arguments possess historical interest. For instance, the Albertinian responds to the Ernestinian's assertion that the princes had no prevailing self-interest in the reduction of silver content with a reference to the negotiations in Zeitz, where the advantages for the princes were no secret. The deciding question of whether the advantages outweighed the disadvantages for the princes goes, as one might have expected, unanswered. Even the farmers spoke out for the retention of good coins, he points out. The hardships resulting from a reduction of mine profitability would affect many people – workers, farmers, and craftsmen, too. Thus, the Albertinian clearly hopes that silver exports will finally lead to an expansion of the economic base. He resolves the numerous misunderstandings between himself and his opponent on the subject of inflation in part by methodically addressing each individual argument put forth by the Ernestinian. He warns against a downward spiral in which the reduction of the silver content of coins and the increase in the value of silver in the coins repeatedly mutually reinforce one another. 'The face-value of silver was increased in this manner so often and so high that in the end the coins became mere copper' (p. 105, my transl.).

If the Ernestinian opposes luxury, then he should simply enact laws against luxury and not devalue the currency because of it – the Albertinian, too, agrees with the rejection of 'new-fangled clothing ... and the similarly superfluous extravagant pieces' (p. 107, my transl.) while the lavish listing of such fashion items might make the reader think of Holbein portraits displaying the great beauty of such goods. However, the Albertinian critique comes across as significantly more moderate – people will simply never change.

That the price of goods has increased, despite the policy of good coinage, is somewhat grudgingly admitted: 'some spices have become somewhat more expensive' (p. 109, my transl.).

He then proceeds to introduce his non-financial explanations for inflation. Spices have become more expensive due to the shifting of trade routes to Portugal and the increase in the amount of spices in demand – arguments which are not very convincing, since the new trade routes were sought out due to competition, and the increased amounts should have contributed to lower prices thanks to economies of scale in transport. Waste is denounced: 'when a man has once or four times blown on a jacket, a cap, a hat, a pair of trousers, a jerkin, a pair of shoes, then we already throw it away' (p. 111, my transl.).

Inflation arises due to the wastefulness of society in the sixteenth century! Here the modern reader, influenced by modern theory, is more likely to point to 'over-minting', about which the Ernestinian warned, but which the Albertinian does not address. The Albertinian's best argument is to emphasize that if money is already devalued in a good minting, how much worse it must be with a bad minting! He points out that while silver may, indeed, be more likely to remain in the country with bad mintings, it remains in the hands of the princes not the people. Saxony had very little to export apart from silver. The Albertinian fails to realize, here, that this point is precisely the problem the Ernestinian is struggling to articulate. Among the urgent questions of industrialization, however, it remains conceptually unclear. The second text from the Albertinian ends as his first one began, with a reference to good order and to the authorities who bear responsibility for maintaining it.

We are going to risk a summary in modern words, aware of the risks that arise when one judges from atop the shoulders of later economists.

The reserved Albertinian starts out from the axiom that the purchasing power of silver coins is based on the value of the metal content. His suggestions about the determination of prices refer immediately to production costs. This is the classical position that will later be developed by Smith, that the amount of money in circulation will be determined endogenously. Whoever takes prices, the velocity of circulation and transaction volume as a given must arrive at an adjustment of the money supply. Coins minted in too large quantities are melted; much of that silver flows abroad. For the Albertinian this appears harmless. He proves himself an economic liberal in advocating the export of silver as a product as an equivalent for imports, and he hopes for a strong increase in employment as a result of both silver production and imports. As a believer in orderly general economic conditions, he comes out in favor of ensuring this usually self-regulating process with a stable currency system.

The effusive Ernestinian is both old-fashioned and modern at once. He views inflation as a result of market power, on the one hand, and, on the other, explains it with the quantity theory of money. While he does not say, as Keynes later would about the gold standard, that silver money is a 'barbarous relic', he would like to reduce its emission in order to reach a controlled rate of forced exchange that lies significantly above the value of the metal. With this he pursues various objectives: a fiscal one that benefits the prince, one relating to employment (because he expects a debasement compared with the outside) and a moral one (luxury imports will be more difficult to acquire). He accepts the disruption of legal relations between creditors and debtors; the curtailing of exports of the mercantilist English, French, Dutch, Italians, and Portuguese gives him satisfaction. He regards the blow to import merchants as a defence of Protestant values. Not wanting to put an export economy in place, he instead aims for the slow, organic growth of a self-sufficient, aboriginal domestic economy of farmers and craftsmen, in a state governed by a prince who is supported by government officials. The reader takes notice of unsettling gestures toward state intervention, which applied reasonably have become 'natural', as well a hints of an attitude which would later contain and even misdirect German development.

Despite such misgivings, whoever reads the currency pamphlets in the original, with even moderate attention, will be left with the impression of having confronted a serious debate led with great personal engagement, religious and patriotic zeal, as well as a sense of responsibility. While reading the translation can be an aid to interpretation, it weakens the overall impression of the debate which itself derives from the struggle of these authors to find a new language with which to understand economic events. With respect to Peutinger's and Fronsperger's texts, above all, we obtain a new perspective on the origins of economic theory in Germany, which has only very weakly been reflected in German texts on the History of Economic Theory and was almost nonexistent in international histories. At the same time, it deepens our understanding of one of the most important chapters in European history: the Age of Reformation.

## Leonard Lessius: from the practical virtue of justice to economic theory

Leonard Lessius is known to historians of economic thought as a leading economic thinker of the late Scholastic era. He is virtually unknown to any other public, or if known, then as a theologian (Kasper 1997, col. 852–853) and member of the Jesuit Order (Dictionnaire de Spiritualité 1976, col. 709–720) who, as a result of his devout lifestyle, earned a reputation as a saint (Enciclopedia Cattolica 1951, col. 1203–1205), though efforts to obtain his beatification were unsuccessful. Lessius assumes a unique position in scholastic literature, for while he upholds the traditional principle that loans must be granted freely, his discussion of the conditions which justify the charging of interest in trade and commerce can be seen as an anticipation of the modern understanding of the determination of the payment of interest. He was familiar with the Antwerp money market, and also appears to have been familiar with trading practices, since he has a more precise economic understanding than his contemporaries of price determination, monopolies, and of economic institutions as they relate to the conduct of trade. His book, *De iustitia et iure*, is not an simply an isolated phenomenon; it is part of a wider literature, from which however it stands out clearly. The Scholastics often studied economic questions. Lessius continued, above all, the work of the authors of the Salamanca School, who are represented in this volume by Azpilcueta and Ortiz.[60]

Lessius was certainly not the last person to discuss the legitimacy of market-based economic institutions from a Catholic perspective, for this debate continues to the present day, as we shall see. Moreover, modern Catholic social theory, which has also been taken up by Protestants (Müller-Armack 1999 [1947]), is plainly a source for our contemporary understanding of the Social Market Economy.

Much of this literature remains unknown to us. Representatives of various disciplines dealt with it in detail during the mid-nineteenth century. Endemann's text of 1874, *Studien in der romanisch-kanonistischen Wirtschafts- und Rechtslehre bis gegen Ende des siebzehnten Jahrhunderts* [Studies of Romanic-Canonistic Economic and Legal Doctrine to the End of the Seventeenth Century] (Endemann 1874, 1883), is still cited internationally, despite its critical bent. Individual scholastic authors in the early Renaissance like St. Bernhard of Siena (Hünermann 1939) and Antony of Florence (Ilgner 1904) are systematically reviewed by Endemann. Following the Second World War, however, German historians of economic thought appear to have lost interest in the subject. Edgar Salin (1967) is the only scholar to have devoted any space to the late Middle Ages in his *Geschichte der wirtschaftspolitischen Ideen von Platon bis zur Gegenwart* [History of Economic Ideas from Plato to the Present]. Lengthy monographs on Scholastic thought were published – but not in Germany; contributions by Noonan (1957) and especially on Lessius (Raymond de Roover 1955) deserve mention here. It seems that in Germany we need to reconnect our work to a tradition of scholarship to which leading thinkers of the Historical School like Schmoller (1860) and Roscher (1992 [1874]) contributed.

More recently, Louis Baeck (1994) has reminded us of the breadth and underlying coherence of the Scholastic tradition by presenting Jewish, Greek, Roman, Arabic and Christian writings as a unitary Mediterranean heritage. Naturally, there were also discontinuities. Noonan (1957, p. 14) drew attention to the fact that the early Christian critique of usury denounced it as a form of avarice, while the Scholastics later considered it to be a violation of the virtue of justice. We have to thank Langholm (1992) for a monumental study of the thinking of theologians and lawyers at the University of Paris. By observing the daily work of trade and commerce the School of Salamanca was led to make distinctions which can be seen as contributions to economic analysis, moving beyond moral-theological judgments and politico-economic calculation. They are familiar with the quantity theory of money (Grice-Hutchinson 1995). Gordon (1975) subtitled his book, *Economic Analysis before Adam Smith, 'Hesiod to Lessius'*. He places *De iustitia et iure* at the peak of a line of development that, although it had not yet reached its end, inspired no further works of equal importance. Mercantilism broke with the Scholastic focus on the problems of just price, interest and the formation of monopolies, shifting the central issue to the development of the economy as a whole.

We will develop this opposition between Scholasticism and Mercantilism later with reference to Azpilcueta and Ortiz.[61] Lessius can in this perspective be compared with Serra (1994 [1613]),[62] who while active at the same time as Lessius asked very different questions. Lessius approaches the just and virtuous man of affairs in a friendly and encouraging manner, judging people on grounds other than economic success. Serra on the other hand admires the commercial dedication and skilled manipulation of markets in Venice, while lamenting the backwardness and the misguided economic policies of Naples. Lessius' man of affairs answers to his conscience, while for Serra he acquires wealth and power for himself and the entire country. In Lessius the connections between people, in the marketplace and in contracts are morally determined, and public welfare is measured in terms of morality. Serra gives free reign to the passions, to the love of pomp and to assertiveness, so long as this remains within the limits of legal restrictions and serves the will of the prince. Lessius examines monetary exchange so that he might advise the future confessor when to take steps against usury. Serra examines problems in the balance of payments, the successes of export trade and the transfer of income so that he might formulate a currency policy favourable to growth. For him, monetary transactions are permissible as long as deficits do not lead to interventions that could, in turn, restrict production and thus the generation of wealth. The theologian Lessius explores the details of monetary transactions, but only so that he might determine the difference between just and unjust practices. Both, however, employ the casuistic method. Lessius continues in the Scholastic tradition, while the lawyer Serra seeks to express new ideas with the old language. Serra anticipates development economics, while Lessius anticipates economic ethics. They are marked out from their contemporaries by their more precise identification of regularities, such that Serra grasps the connection between growth and increasing economies of scale, while Lessius discovers liquidity preference as a determinant of the rate of interest. In turn, their stance with regard to the times in which they lived differed. Although we do not know anything directly about his person, Serra appears to be a scientific revolutionary who in one short pamphlet points to new horizons, amazed by the internal logic of the economy and, like Galilei, discovering a form of mechanics. His perspective reaches beyond an absolutist Naples dependent upon Spain to the free and dynamic republic of Venice. Lessius, writing in a Netherlands ruled by Spain and Austria and shaken by civil war and religious division, looks inward and seeks conciliatory formulas which both strengthen old beliefs and bind the new economy to them.

Charles van Sull's (1930) comprehensive biography of Lessius has been criticised as hagiography because it was written in support of a fellow-Jesuit's beatification (Beutels 1987, p. 13); but it is in fact a very lucid account of a life, portraying a youth constrained by poverty, the struggle for a secure place within a religious order and in science, the terror of religious upheavals and the turmoil of independence, and finally, an old age spent in tireless activity, despite serious illness.

Lessius (Leys before his name was Latinized) was born on 1 October 1554, in Brecht, a small city in Brabant, not far from Antwerp and on the border between modern-day Belgium and the Netherlands. He was from a family of farmers and craftsmen. At five he lost his father; and his mother died a few weeks after her remarriage in 1560. Along with his three sisters, Leonard was looked after by relatives. Early on he showed an inclination for reading and prayer. Though at nine he was supposed to be apprenticed to a cooper, with some effort he managed to obtain permission to attend school. A priest taught him Latin, his talent became obvious and, in competition with an older boy, he managed to win a scholarship to study at the University of Leuven at the age of 13. He thus avoided the fate planned for him because of his aptitude for mathematics: to send him to Antwerp to study commercial sciences. At university, the most important subjects included Humanist studies, philosophy, and the reading of Aristotle. Besides the lectures there were also debates in Latin, sometimes becoming a vehicle for wit, but never for coarseness.

Lessius headed the list in his final exam and was duly celebrated as the best in the university. To the great regret of the professors, he turned down the purely academic career now open to him and announced his decision to enter the then still-young Jesuit Order as a novice. On 20th July 1572, the head of the Order for the province proudly announced to the Jesuit general – Lessius was not at the time even 18 years old: 'Admisimus primum universitatis istius, adolescentem Brechtanum 17 annorum, optimis corporis et animi dotibus praeditum' (Sull 1930, p. 26).[63]

Entry into this order, which at that time had barely existed for 30 years and already had more than 80 martyrs, should be understood as a religious and a political statement, and also as a renunciation to any individual and independent claim to shape history.

We should remember here that the northern and southern parts of the Netherlands – the inheritance from the house of Burgundy which went to the Habsburgs – represented the most flourishing industrial districts in mid-sixteenth century Europe. From its taxes Charles V received seven times as much revenue as the silver from America. Rotterdam and Antwerp were important centres of trade, and the Antwerp bourse was a centre of European monetary affairs. From a strategic point of view France was bounded by the Netherlands to the north and Spain to the south. Here the religious wars of the Reformation era assumed a particularly horrific form. In 1566 Philip II handed over the task of pacification to the 'Iron Duke', Alba; in 1568, as the youthful Lenaert Leys entered university, Egmont was executed. The battle for Dutch independence continued from this year until the Peace of Westphalia in 1648, when Spain finally recognized the new republic in the north.

Lessius had hardly concluded his conversion when in 1572 the Protestants threatened Brabant and marched against Leuven. The clerics changed into civilian clothes and fled. Lessius managed to reach Lille on foot, and then St. Omer. In 1574, after much study and several spiritual retreats the novice finally became a monk. He was appointed to a post in philosophy at the Jesuit College in Douai. So at the age of 20 he was already a professor. His studies expanded – he learned Greek, theology and medicine. As the Geuzen forced him to flee a second time, this time from Douai, he succumbed to an infection which would affect him for the rest of his life. He was ordained as a priest in 1580, and in 1583 he received permission to study in Rome at the Collegium Romanum. Bellarmin taught there; Lessius also met Suarez. From 1585 until 1601 he taught theology in Leuven (Türks 1951). He now began to teach not from Peter of Lombardy's *Sententiae*, as was usual, but from Thomas Aquinas' *Summa Theologica*. [64] The lectures were very successful, and his *De iustitia et iure* developed from them. Jesuit students of the college as well as students from the university attended his lectures. But as a result of this tensions developed: Lessius became involved in a conflict with Baius, a theologian from the University. On the question of predestination, Baius took a position that was close to Calvin, while Lessius opposed him: the free individual can by striving to avoid sin obtain mercy, or fail to do so (Sull 1930, pp. 91ff.).

Lessius acquired a great reputation among his contemporaries as a writer. His varied literary writing was remarkable for its simple and clear form of expression. His power of judgment was of such renown that many disputes and cases in which there was reasonable doubt were put to him. Archduke Albert is said to have put *De iustitia et iure* on a level with the sword of Austria: the former gave him decrees, while the latter enforced them (Chamberlain 1939, pp. 133–155). In 1601 Lessius was relieved of his teaching duties; but he remained productive and worked until shortly before his death in 1623. Popular veneration and new Latin poetry praising him[65] helped keep his reputation alive.

Before looking at the works themselves, we should familiarize ourselves with some elements of Antwerp's economic history and the questions arising from them. Antwerp's best years had been around 1500, about a hundred years before Lessius' book appeared. After the discovery of the sailing route around Africa, India and southern Germany were linked through Portugal and Antwerp, to the disadvantage of Venetian Mediterranean trade. Antwerp shared the textile trade with England, as well as textile processing. In the years leading up to the middle of the century the spice trade weakened, while trade with England expanded. The growth of Antwerp's money market was connected, among other things, with the European politics of Charles V: limitation to the emperor's sphere of influence of the 'international' area in which funds could be raised separates this period from conditions in the preceding late-medieval period, when the trade in goods was more confined, but monetary dealings were more extensive. It is also a period quite distinct from the absolutist phase of the seventeenth century, when politics was in effect nationalized.[66]

Decline after the mid-century was due, in part, to politics; it was however also related to agricultural stagnation in Brabant.[67] Above all, it was a result of religious wars and wars of independence. Before Alba's arrival, Antwerp had been a centre of religious agitation. The Anabaptists lived in poverty; the Calvinists had just come to power in England; the Lutherans were influential in German principalities – all of these factions had their preachers. The volatility of the masses led to iconoclasm:

The contemptuous prosperity of the enemy religion offends their poverty; the pomp of their temples scorns their exiled beliefs; every cross upon the highway, every saintly image they encounter is a triumphant memorial to their defeat, and they must all be torn down by their avenging hands (Schiller 1880, pp. 2–3).

Subsequent campaigns devastated the surrounding countryside. Wolf packs roamed the fields.

A hesitant recovery came only in the years following 1590, and the Antwerp money market gained new significance, especially as a market for Spanish government bonds. Industrial recovery remained weaker (Wee 1963, vol. 1, pp. 281ff.). But the city's monetary institutions cannot be considered modern. An atmosphere of speculation prevailed. Betting and lotteries were mingled with serious financial transactions. Nonetheless, Antwerp's specific contribution lay in the development of an independent bourse (ibid., p. 368).

Observation of the bourse was the empirical background which marked Lessius out from Spanish Scholastics such as Azpilcueta, who was familiar only with currency and money markets as advanced institutions. The significance of the bourse became even more plain when it was compared with the sluggishness of industrial development.

From the standpoint of traditional Catholics the new bourses must have seemed like a usurers' convention. Calvin proved less strict (Nelson 1969, p. 73). Prejudice toward the behaviour of both denominations regarding the economy led Schiller to state that: 'In short: the Roman Catholic religion will, on the whole, be found more adapted to a nation of artists, the Protestant more fitted to a nation of merchants' (Schiller 1877, p. 380). To this extent Max Weber's (1976) important idea that Protestantism prepared the ground for the spread of the capitalist spirit has deep roots. Economic historians have in part confirmed, in part questioned this thesis, given the similarities and differences in the development of the Netherlands in the Catholic south and the Protestant north. From the perspective of the history of economic thought it has been both confirmed and challenged through the texts of the reformers and the Scholastics, among whose works Lessius' stands out.

*De iustitia et iure* never presents itself as a manual for economy, law or ecclesiastical law, but instead as a work about virtue. Yet, virtue is a term with which we associate only vague ideas. Philosophy of science assigns it no especial place. In a work which led to a tentative renewal of virtue as a concept, a renewal which today is apparent in the notion of 'communitarianism', Alisdair MacIntyre suggests that the state of our current conception of virtue is as unreliable as our knowledge of physical theory would be if left to journalists who talked about elementary particles and the like without having any real understanding of modern physics. Only a few intellectuals are today familiar with the older system of virtues. The decline of values is often attributed to the market or the media, and not without reason. Yet the state has certainly also contributed to the decline of a sense of duty through the bureaucratic displacement of the importance of family and neighbourhood in social life.

On the other hand, one can speak of a 'Market in Virtue' (Baurmann 1996) where new norms are developed, when market agents realize that their standing, and hence their prospects for economic advancement, depend upon their proving themselves to be trustworthy.

Lessius no doubt saw contemporary warfare as partly a decline in virtue, and as partly a clash over the proper virtues – for even heretics had virtues which they sought to promote. What was urgently needed was a new common understanding of how to live together. Spain was inclined to rely simply on force. In Goethe's *Egmont* Alba argues that, according to received wisdom, peace within and among states can only be ensured by strict laws and foreign troops, while Egmont, representing the native nobleman, invokes a new sense of citizenship. Following some initial moderate attempts to reach a settlement, they say:

> Alba: The tumult has been stilled, and each man seems to have been charmed back within the confines of obedience. But does it not depend on the caprice of each, not to abandon them? ... Where is the guarantee that they will be faithful and submissive in the future? Their good will is all the security we have. Egmont: And is a people's good will not the safest, the noblest security?
>
> (Goethe 1984, pp. 76–77)

As one of the original Jesuits Lessius was certainly no stranger to discipline and obedience, let alone their foe. But order should not only be achieved through violence, but also promoted by charity and a sense of duty, Goethe's Egmont summarizing this as 'popular goodwill'. We will therefore attempt to consider Lessius' book not only in terms of its contribution to economic theory, but also take seriously the broader ethical questions of virtue concerning the life of the individual in society, and the transcendence of this life through Christian belief.

The layout of the first few pages suggests such a reading. On the elaborately decorated frontispiece the sign of the Jesuit Order (a cross with the letters IHS) is superimposed upon a sun of truth, supplemented by the heart and the three nails from the cross as symbolic of the order. The coat of arms is held by the Apostle Peter, holding the key which opens the gate to heaven, and the Apostle Paul, holding a sword representing militant faith. They are flanked by the virtues of bravery (armed) and moderation (moderation pours from a small pitcher into a shallow dish, suggesting restraint by reference to moderation in the consumption of wine). The lower coat of arms with a golden fleece refers to rule by the Habsburg dynasty, and the individual parts of the coat of arms indicate the individual branches of the dynasty. Left of the title we find the virtue of prudence or practical wisdom (*prudentia*), with a mirror (looking at a mirror signifies self-knowledge – Socrates called on his students to look at themselves in a mirror) and a snake, at once a symbol of intelligence and of sin which had to be suppressed. On the right of the title is justice with her scales, a sword symbolizing her power. The complete title (*De iustitia et iure caeterisque virtutibus cardinalibus libri IV*) is a reminder that while justice may indeed be central, it is not the only cardinal virtue which will figure in the work. Combined with the subtitle, which places the text as a commentary on Aquinas's *Summa*, Lessius places the work firmly in a recognisable tradition.

The dedication which follows, to Regent Archduke Albert of Austria, expresses the purpose of the book: according to Aristotle, the goal of law is the improvement of citizens. Everything flows from the head (the princes) into the body of society; therefore, virtues must first of all be instilled in princes. In the foreword the author instructs the reader. The foreword is headed by an engraving evoking the symbols of the Passion and the mysteries of the Cross, referring again to the Order. Here the author instructs the reader that the greater part of the text, on justice, dates back to notes dictated some eleven or twelve years earlier which have been revised and in part expanded through discussion of the other three cardinal virtues. Initially he had not wanted to publish this text, its subject having already been dealt with by so many others. But he had been persuaded otherwise and now sees its primary merit in its more systematic organization of material than that of Aquinas. He develops his principles governing the division of his material, assures the reader that he had wanted to be brief – although the discourse on justice is much longer than the others – and strives to be exemplary both *ad usum* (in 'practice') as well as *ad speculationem* (in 'theory'). He has limited the number of proofs and examples and striven for clarity. 'Sententiam veriorem in singulis indagare, et omni ope firmare studui, allata, qantum licuit, ratione aliqua fundamentali; insinuata tamen sententiae diversae probabilitate, si quam forte habere videbatur' (Lessius 1605, 'Praetfatio ad lectorem').[68]

Lessius thus declares his allegiance to epistemological moderation and an inductive approach. He seeks here to formulate the truer statement – not the absolutely *true*, because there can be no certainty when dealing with the matters raised here – and he seeks this truer statement in details, using every possible aid, once a foundation has been prepared, if such is possible. But this does not exclude the possibility that another statement might seem more valid. A thesis thought to be valid will therefore be compared with an opposing thesis that has a degree of probability; knowledge of these is advantageous, and as a rule necessary, in making conscientious decisions (*in foro conscientiae*). The work, divided as it is into books, sections, chapters and 'Dubitationes' (doubts), consistently states potential objections which are then often followed by responses to these objections, so that readers are led dialectically from prejudice to critique and finally to their own decision. This mode of presentation is more like a didactic philosophical discussion than conclusions from first principles modelled on a mathematical, natural-scientific method.

A further introductory section ('Brevis explicatio') describes the place taken by virtues among human capacities. He assigns them to the highest rank, to intellect and will. Virtue is the perfection of the thinking being (*natura rationalis*) that focuses on the true and the good. The intellect is perfect when certain of truth in all things, as far as granted by divine right (*quantum fas est*). The will is perfect when it cleaves to the good and honourable (*honestum bonum*). The perfection of imagination (*facultas imaginatrix*), drives (*appetitus inferior*) and the power of asserting oneself (*potentia executiva*) depend upon the perfection of these other abilities. Thus it is not drives that determine the mind, as in psychoanalysis, but instead intellect that determines drives, insofar as a being approaches perfection. Although drives contain habits furthering virtue, such that habits also appear to be virtues, it is more likely (*probabilius*) that they are only the shadow (*adumbrationes*) of virtues. In these lower abilities there is no freedom, and their exercise only deserves praise insofar as they conform to the movement of the intellect and the will.

There are two different kinds of virtues: those of the intellect and those of the will. Those of the intellect centre on truth; those of the will on the honourable, the proper (τὸ πρέπον, ibid., Explicatio, 4). Conditional virtues (*secundum quid virtutes*), like theoretical wisdom (*sapientia*), science (*scientia*) and art (*ars*) make it possible to do (think, know, create) something good, without however necessarily producing a moral good, while the absolute virtues, such as practical wisdom (*prudentia*) and faith (*fides*), only lead to the doing of good works when the work is, at the same time, a good work in itself. Lessius further (ibid., Explicatio, 7). differentiates between theological virtues – faith, hope, love (*charitas*) – and moral virtues, among which four are considered cardinal. These are the subject of the book: caution or practical wisdom (*prudentia*), justice (*iustitia*), bravery or strength (*fortitudo*), moderation or level-headedness (*temperantia*). They are all ordered by theoretical wisdom (*sapientia*, ibid., Explicatio, 9), which is itself only a conditional virtue, for I can be aware of a system of virtues without adhering to it.

Along the way to the culmination of the text, the book on justice and law where there are passages of interest to economists, there is only one other section which repays attention: the book on *prudentia*, consisting of only two chapters. It is the first cardinal virtue since its exercise provides guidance to the others. Lessius wants to derive *prudentia* (practical or life wisdom), from farsightedness (*porro videndo*, ibid., 1.1.1. [first book, first chapter, first numbered paragraph]); in Greek, it is φρόνησις. This cardinal virtue serves as a guide to ethical action. Following definitions from Augustine and Aristotle, Lessius offers his own: 'Prudentia est virtus intellectus, qua in quovis negotio occurrente novimus quid honestum sit, quid turpe' (ibid., 1.1.1). I translate this as: 'Foresight is the spiritual virtue through which we know on every occasion what is honourable and what is disgraceful.'

Lessius breaks down this definition and thoroughly explains each element. While we cannot here examine his analysis, we should keep in mind the fact that his formulation, in contrast to those of his predecessors, already clearly carries the prospect of its practical application in economic life.

He immediately confronts an objection to his claim that he is capable of determining what is virtuous in concrete cases. The objection is as follows: 'Philosophi dicunt, de rebus singularibus non esse scientiam' (ibid., 1.1.3).

'Philosophers argue that no science can be built on singular events', yet we can make our own judgement about individual cases in respect of existence and quality: and this is based upon universal rules that can be observed in such cases (ibid., 1.1.4).

Lessius particularly emphasizes that where there is uncertainty *prudentia* provides guidance on just and proper action before action takes place, but that nonetheless *prudentia* is certain in respect of the will to avoid sin. This certainty of good intention is not superseded if doubt or regret arises after the act – when it turns out to have been wrong (ibid., 1.1.5). Essential to our understanding of *prudentia* is that it guides individual actions; *prudentia* is not abstract knowledge about what is appropriate or inappropriate. Lessius differentiates it from other virtues, like *sapientia* (ibid., 2.1.13), which is purely observational by nature and which focuses, ultimately, on the Divine.

He differentiates between doing (*facere*, ποιεῖν) and acting (*agere*, πράττειν). Doing has only a temporary effect on the outside world, while acting is immanent: a person will become either good or bad by his action. Foresight makes activity honourable, while art (a virtue of doing) lends form (*forma*) to the creation (ibid., 1.1.14). *Prudentia* can make proper assessments, judge reliably, provide precise instructions (ibid., 1.1.17). Every sin directs itself against *prudentia*, but not every sin is a result of *imprudentia*, a lack of foresight, because sin can also be triggered by desire (ibid., 1.1.16). (We will omit here a discussion of the exaggeration and understatement to which one may fall prey through lack of foresight.) Lessius concludes with the warning from the Sermon on the Mount that people should not allow themselves to be overwhelmed by earthly woes: 'Therefore take no thought, saying, What shall we eat? or, What shall we drink? or, Wherewithal shall we be clothed?' (Matthew. 6.31). But, he would not be Lessius if he did not add a quote from the Old Testament: 'Go to the ant, thou sluggard; consider her ways, and be wise' (Proverbs 6.6).

What ever one might think about this doctrine of virtue, it forms a system which, as MacIntyre argues, is different from our confused modern notions of virtue. It developed out of two millennia of Platonic and Aristotelian ethics, and is saturated with Christian ideas.[69] Foresight (φρόνησις) in Aristotle carries no transcendental implication and rather suggests a heathen joyfulness and earthiness. It grows within the individual through experience. A young man does not have it, even if he is considered a good mathematician (*Nicomachean Ethics*, 1142a14). 'Now it is held to be the mark of a prudent man to be able to deliberate well about what is good and advantageous for himself ..., but what is advantageous as a means to the good life in general' (ibid., 1140a). and this characteristic, he goes on to say, is especially present in politicians and economists: 'εἶναι δὲ τοιούτους ἡγούμεθα τοὺς οἰκονομικοὺς καὶ τοὺς πολιτικούς' (ibid., 1140b11).[70] Can we rely on that?

To begin with, the virtue of justice is defined as general (symmetrically with the application of other virtues); as a special virtue of the will to do right and to give each his own; and finally, as lawful justice oriented to the common good (*bonum commune*). Lessius believes it plausible (*probabile*) that legal justice is equivalent to patriotism or loyalty to one's nation (*pietas patriae*, Lessius 1605, 2.1.12), but considers the notion that they are different to be more true: lawful justice indicates the responsibility of the part to the whole, while love of one's country arises from what we receive from our country (ibid., 2.1.14). Finally there is also the Aristotelian view, according to which lawful justice means obedience to existing law (ibid., 2.1.15–19). Particular justice is subdivided, following the Aristotelian model, into distributive and commutative justice. Deviating from an accepted interpretation, Lessius does not consider wage hierarchies to be an expression of distributive justice, but of commutative justice. For different wage levels are appropriate for various kinds of work; they should not correspond to arbitrarily prescribed ranks.

Law also appears to have a variety of meanings: as what is just, as statute law, and as lawful force. Law is also further differentiated into natural law and positive law, and the latter is split into human and divine. Divine law consists of the old and the new (specifically according to the Old and New Testaments), while human law is divided into law of nations, ecclesiastical law and civil law. Positive law arises from the free will of God or humans, and natural law from the nature of the thing itself.

After the two introductory chapters in the first section of the second book, four chapters follow on the right of ownership, and these are of direct interest to economists. Among other things, Lessius here develops a concept of capital and its use, the viability of which is tested in argument over the payment of interest. The conceptions of virtue and the law which we have considered in detail appear to be of lesser interest here, but remain important for the explanation of institutions and the judgment of deviation from norms, or perhaps even for their justification.

Lessius in particular here explains disposition over an object through rulership and ownership (*dominium*), usufruct (*usus fructus*), use (*usus*) and possession (*possessio*). *Dominium* refers to the power of disposition over an object. A question, still relevant today, arises: 'Dices: Dominium videtur quid prius Iure' (ibid., 2.3.10; 'You will say: *dominium* appears to pre-exist the law').

To which the answer: 'Respondeo: Perfecta ratio dominii non est prior Iure & potestate disponendi de re; sed hanc essentialiter includit' (ibid., 2.3.11).[71]

According to the materialist conception, not only advocated by Marxists, power and the law are rooted in the material conditions of economic reproduction. Technical development up until the industrial revolution engendered capitalist forms of production and a judiciary system appropriate to these forms. According to the Social Rights school of thought – a branch of Institutionalism[72] to which Commons (1995) is very close – property rights define the economic system; diverse systems can moreover exist at the same technical level. Lessius implies that the complete concept of the power of disposition does materially include political power and, as he later states, also the law. Factual and legal power of disposal must coincide; however, he does not here indicate which is prior, and from what it derives. Expressed platonically, the idea of *dominium* formulated here does not have to be unconditionally valid in any given individual concrete case, if for instance a new right of possession conflicts with a traditional one. *Dominium* will not however fundamentally be questioned. In its fullest form, it consists in God's dominion over the world (Lessius 1605: 2.3.1). Among humans, *dominium* is normally obtained through a document of title or transfer of ownership (ibid., 2.3.12).

'Usufruct' lies at the heart of concept of capital, which Lessius has yet to develop: 'Est ius rebus alienis utendi fruendi, salva rerum substantia' (ibid., 2.3.17). Usufruct is the therefore right to use something belonging to someone else as long as its stock or extent is maintained. The elements of this definition are explained in detail and illuminated with examples. A person can have usufruct in the wool of sheep, or fellable trees in a forest, but in the case of fruit-bearing trees usufruct relates not to the timber but to the fruit. On the other hand, due to 'natural dignity' usufruct is not permitted with respect to the children of a maid (ibid., 2.3.17). The real difficulty, however, lies in explaining the 'salva rerum substantia' 'grex est aeternus; sed singula capita seorsim pereunt' (ibid., 2.3.18).

The herd persists, while each individual member dies. Buildings must be maintained. Lessius holds fast to the idea that the stock of things in a changing world can, in principle, be unambiguously determined. Later Böhm-Bawerk,[73] developing the work of Scholastic authors, would argue that at least the relative price could change, so that not only capital could alter its real form, but also its monetary form, specifically, its value. The model of intertemporal exchange introduced by Böhm-Bawerk does not depend on the ability to define a permanent capital stock in terms of object and value.

*Dominium* exists only for conscious beings ('soli naturae rationali dominium competat', Lessius 1605, 2.4.1), hence for God, angels and humans. Factual possession in good faith leads to *dominium* in the sense of lawful property, if it remains unchallenged (ibid., 2.3.52). Limits are here set. For example, man is not the owner, but only the guardians of his life (ibid., 2.4.57), Lessius also citing pagan philosophy on this point – although the attitude toward suicide in the ancient world was a matter of dispute.

But what is the origin of the first seizure and division of property? We are still far removed from Locke's proposal that the right of ownership is founded upon labour (Schefold 1993). Division takes place by negotiation, lottery or violence. That ownership itself was allowed is certain ('est certo tenendum', Lessius 1605: 2.5.2). Arguing against those heretics who erroneously believe that like among the apostles, everything must be communally owned, Lessius defends private property for, as Aristotle said, men tend to take better care of their own property, otherwise there would be continual war. Moreover, the original state of common ownership in Paradise was annulled by the Fall. Lessius considers the rule of private property, which we examined above with regard to the term *dominium*, to be right and proper. But the division of property occurred neither according to divine law (with the exception of the assignment of the Holy Land to Israel, it was not the subject of divine revelation), nor according to natural law (because in nature everything remains in common), but according to law of nations (*ius gentium*, ibid., 2.5.7–9). Division was necessary because it is a part of the human condition to love oneself and neglect the other, and that each is a wretched (*miser*) victim of his own greed and ambition.

Legal concepts do however differ from one another in detail. Throughout the book, ecclesiastical law is opposed to civil law, sometimes sharply differentiated, but more often in the attempt to establish agreement. Roman law (*ius Caesareum*) offers a standard of comparison, but is not valid for all peoples. Good order can be take many forms.

And so slavery is generally considered to be lawful, although in particular cases the conventions vary. Lessius does for instance wish to grant slaves the right to run away when they are treated unfairly, or are forced to commit sins (ibid., 2.5.11–17 and 2.5.18–19). Slavery derives first of all from the law of war and arises from a natural sympathy for the defeated enemy, who is made a slave rather than killed ('ex naturali quandam commiseratione'). Christians, however, do not enslave one another.

Finally, considerable space is devoted to the duty to return property that has been illegally acquired, especially through theft. Restitution (*restitutio*) for Lessius includes compensation (*damni compensation*, ibid., 2.17.15). The reason for this is revealed in later chapters: The confessor should lead the sinner to feel regret and lead him back to the path of righteousness. However, as long as there is no restitution, the thief continues in sin (ibid., 2.12.11). This detailed discussion of *restitutio* in impermissible transactions, and his distinction of usury from acceptable rates of interest, can be understood in terms of Lessius' conceptions of property, capital, sin and remorse.

Throughout the second section of the second book the legal concepts developed in the first section are applied to wrongful actions. Of economic interest are for example considerations of the order in which the various debts of an insolvent defaulter should be repaid to creditors.

The third section, on contracts, begins with the differentiation between contracts with particular titles (*contractus nominatus*), like a contract of sale, and undefined contracts (*contractus innominatus*). Mere agreement (*contractus nudus*) is also compared with a formal contract (*contractus vestitus*). The first binds only the conscience (*obligatio in foro conscientiae*), while a formal contract is also binding according to civil law (ibid., 2.12.12–18).

Lessius deals chiefly with civil law, supplementing it with the additional obligations arising from religiously-founded decisions of conscience. Ethical considerations regarding the role of justice for a god-fearing life are displaced in favour of a discussion of a broad and painstaking treatment of formal law. In the ancient doctrine of virtues, for example, spontaneity of giving and reciprocity play a role as the essential basis of civic life; generosity and magnanimity are, for Aristotle (Schefold 1992a, 1998a), virtues of the citizen possessing public spirit. Reciprocity is therefore one of the central concepts of justice in *Nicomachean Ethics*. In Lessius, it plays no independent role. All the same, he distinguishes a voluntary gift inspiring gratitude from that which is received due to legal title (Lessius 1605, 2.18.14). For him, alms for the poor are more important. Charity, from which alms-giving derives, is however a cardinal virtue in its own right. We can therefore expect no thorough treatment of *charitas* by Lessius in this book or – which would be of interest for economists – the problem of poverty in general. Instead, we find only subsidiary questions related to social welfare, such as: whoever has obtained a gift by pretence of impoverishment must return it, if the donor is still known, or must otherwise pass it on to the poor.

A long Chapter 20 is devoted to lending (*mutuum*) and usury (*usura*). *Mutuum* is the transfer of a thing of definite quantity which the recipient has to return in like kind and quality. He not only includes consumption goods such as wine or wheat as objects of *mutuum*, but also money and precious metals which he does not view as goods for consumption, in contrast to Azpilcueta, whom he cites here as 'Navarrus'. On the other hand, it is no *mutuum* when a person lends an ox with the proviso that a different one may be given back in return, because oxen are so different from one another; this is a *contractus innominatus*, comparable with handing over a small sack of coins when another small sack of coins will be expected in return – without counting the contents. If on the other hand restitution is expected in the form of a different item, then it is not a *mutuum* but a *permutatio*, an exchange (ibid., 2.20.3–5).

Usury (*usura*) is now defined as gain arising directly from a contract (*immediate, ex vi pacti mutuationis*) to lend (*mutuum*). Profit (*lucrum*) is here understood as a surplus ('acquisition of some thing') calculable in money with respect to capital, and which is as such gratuitous (which finds no justification outside the terms of the *mutuum*): 'Lucrum vocatur acquisitio rei supra sortem pecunia aestimabilis, & alias indebitae' (ibid., 2.20.18).[74] Why then is usury prohibited, a circumstance that Lessius presumes? Only by the positive law of God and of men? Divine prohibition comes from *Old Testament* scripture and from *Luke* 6.35 ('mutuum date nihil inde sperantes'), while the prohibition of Canon Law rests on a number of decrees. Usury is also unjust in terms of natural law. Here Lessius cites traditional arguments: The same thing (the money the borrower receives) is 'sold' for two prices: the first price is the return of the capital, the second is the interest charged. Moreover, he does not admit the argument that it is the use of capital which is sold, for this use consists in spending the borrowed sum or in the consumption of goods by the borrower; thus it is not the use of capital which must be paid for, but rather the money spent which must be replaced. If it were objected that usury cannot be against nature, since it would otherwise be prohibited by civil law, it would still have to be conceded that imperial legislation did not generally authorize usury. Even with maritime loans, in which the creditor assumes the risk, interest is limited to 12 per cent, and in other cases Lessius names significantly lower legal maxima for interest rates (ibid., 2.20.31–34).

Remarkably, Lessius counts not only helpfulness and charity but also self-interest among motives for *mutuum*. It is a *mutuum* without *usura* if I lend so that someone views me favourably, or to build a client base during an election, for such advantages cannot be estimated in money. Lessius even believes it is permissible for a *mutuum* to be granted for the sake of friendship, because it is hoped that it might later provide pecuniary benefit (ibid., 2.20.40). Difficult cases for one's conscience involve issues such as whether I may loan money in order to receive a pardon for a punishment, or to obtain an official position (Azpilcueta argued in the latter case that the fruits of the office must not yield more than the effort it cost in acquiring the position) (ibid., 2.20.47–63).

Slowly and progressively, following these concessions in drawing moral boundaries, reasons for the charging of interest itself are admitted: 'Notandum est, damnum emergens et lucrum cessans communiter vocari interesse' (ibid., 2.20.68). It is therefore maintained that damages arising and profit foregone should be called in general *interesse*. A *damnum emergens*, an injury, arises first of all when the debtor falls behind in payments ('in mora est'); we remember that even Plato, in the *Nomoi*, allows for interest when there is a delay in payment. Cases of injury arising before the due date are much more difficult to assess.

More interesting are the considerations related to the loss of gain. Money – 'est enim veluti semen foecundem lucri per industriam' (ibid., 2.20.80) – is like a fertile seed of profit from hard work; whoever gives his money away robs himself of this hidden gain: 'dum illud (mutuum – BS) das, simul das fructum in eo latentem' (ibid., 2.20.80). Here he alludes to the thesis that will later be explored more closely, that capital can be productive. His predecessors from Thomas Aquinas to Azpilcueta, by contrast, would have ascribed any existing permissible gain to a factor of production, such as work or effort. Lessius states more precisely that whoever lends money offers not only the money itself but also the hope of profit, and such hopes can be estimated as a price: 'haec spes est pretio aestimabilis' (ibid., 2.20.80).[75] He quite explicitly states that the hope of gain should not be thought any less important than the fear of being affected by an injury. This is justified by the thought experiment that whoever is forced to lend money is clearly entitled to compensation corresponding to the expected gain foregone. This experiment is not merely hypothetical, since merchants were put under pressure to lend money to princes or to the state (ibid., 2.20.81). When Aquinas objects that a person cannot sell future profits ('non potes vendere id, quod nondum habes'), Lessius answers correctly, courageously and decisively that in fact the expectation of profit is worth less than the profit itself, if realized; Aquinas' argument thus does not rule out the inclusion in the contract of provision for compensation in case of losses arising from the failure of gains to match expectations. As Gordon (1975) explains, this shift to subjective evaluation is one of the most significant innovations through which Lessius shifts from the justification for interest to explanation of different interest rates (ibid., 2.20.82).

Finally, lending my tools is similar to my lending money. Underlying this argument is the idea that capital goods can be valued not only according to costs but also according to expected returns. But of course the notion that the equivalence of both values is a condition for equilibrium still lies far in the distance.

Azpilcueta made a condition of the applicability of the argument regarding gains foregone that a creditor expecting payment of interest must abstain, for the duration of the loan, from that economic activity the gain foregone of which justified the demand for interest. Insofar as Lessius admits the productivity of capital, he would not actually have to worry about the lender abstaining from alternative activities, since the same capital cannot be invested twice. Azpilcueta, who in this context links profit to work, has by contrast to require that the creditor does not devote his working time to alternative activities, since he invokes this abstention for justifying compensation for profit forgone. Lessius does however adopt Azpilcueta's argument in a modified form (ibid., 2.20.85);[76] extending it by consideration of the different potential hardships that might be associated with alternative activity.

The supplementary charge added to a loan can be derived from three kinds of alternative gainful objectives. First, through 'emptio rei frugiferae, ut census, agri, domus' (ibid., 2.20.86). Given reasonable investment, farmland and buildings can bring a profit; and so any reference to foregone profits here appears unproblematic. *Census* means something like a bond: the purchase of a periodic payment at constant rates. With a perennial bond, the purchase of such paper is not thought to amount to the taking out of a loan, because there is no repayment. This would remove any suspicion that the *census*, as traditionally understood, was really a loan. Lessius examines this form of contract elsewhere. The juxtaposition of these three possibilities here avoids a question much debated in arguments over usury, a question to which Lessius turns later: whether or not participation in the ownership of a building or farmland is usurious where a right to a regular income is thereby gained, if the purchaser of this stream of income does not participate in the trouble and risk of the enterprise, but is instead more like a sleeping partner.

Lessius's second condition is also interesting. Older Scholastics argued that the creditor, having lent, should not have access to idle money any more, since its existence demonstrated that the creditor could simultaneously support the debtor with a *mutuum* free of charge and could make profit in some alternative activity. Lessius qualifies this condition by pointing out that idle money is necessary for, in modern parlance, transaction and precautionary cash balances.[77] These examples remind us of the transaction costs and risks of profit-yielding investments at that time, when even savings for old age were held in the form of 'idle money'.

Thus it is also *lucrum cessans* if I take money to be lent not from a current alternative possibility, but from a future possibility. It was for this reason that merchants were able to claim for opportunity costs incurred when they kept funds in reserve funds in anticipation of having to make forced loans to the state:

> Haec ratione excusari videntur mercatores, qui praescientes Regem petiturum, pecuniam suam a negotiatione subducunt, ... ut ingentes summas

paratas habeant: non enim id faciunt sine magno lucri detrimento; & alia ratio non suppetit ad tantam vim numeratae pecuniae simul repraesentandam.

(ibid., 2.20.86)[78]

Third, the foregone profit argument can be valid when no particular economic alternative exists, for if I may set money aside so that I might if necessary be able to make loans to princes, then I can also do this for other citizens. Lessius responds as follows to the objection that the latter case is more uncertain and unsure: 'Etsi nulla particularis mutatio seorsim sit causa; tamen omnes collectim sumptae sunt causa totius lucri cessantis' (ibid., 2.20.91) – 'Even if no particular bill of transaction is the cause alone (of the foregone profit), taken together they are the cause of the entire foregone profit.'

Lessius thus supports his position with a macroeconomic argument. In brief, it is a question of the '*expected* gain, after the deduction of estimated physical effort and costs' (ibid., 2.20.95, italics mine).

But then some doubt is introduced. Might such reasoning, where one merchant invokes the gains made by other, anonymous merchants, serve to conceal usury? On the other hand, he admits that he would not dare to force restitution in such a situation. In any case, to decide this one has either to wait and see what an alternative deal would have brought, where someone charged with deciding on the legality of interest charges observes a merchant who actually carries out such a business and makes a profit – this would be an *ex post* observation – or else the contracting parties must simply agree *ex ante* about the *spes lucri*.

Later *dubitationes* are dedicated, among other subjects, to risk (*ratio periculi sortis*). Lessius considers the charge for risk justified when the risk really exists and is a burden for the lender. He opposes Azpilcuetas' uncertainty on this issue together with Gregory IX's statement in 'Naviganti'[79] without, it seems to me, being able to resolve satisfactorily the contradiction between his own assessment and that of the Pope.

There is an important and very interesting *dubitatio* in which he asks whether a charge for *carentia pecuniae* may be demanded due to a lack of money or, in modern parlance, a shortage of money – or in even more modern terms, because of liquidity preference (Lessius 1605, 2.20.119). Money functions in support of trade, and the lack of it signifies a loss which can be measured in money. Merchants will determine, through mutual agreement, the price of liquidity foregone (*carentia pecuniae*) appropriate to the common good (*bonum commune*). When a general lack of money exists in the present (*cum plurimi pecunia praesenti egent*) no one will offer interest-free loans (*gratis mutuare*), partially because of the risk (*periculi sortis*), partially because the money is necessary for exchange.

We appear here to be verging on an analysis of the setting of interest rates through supply and demand, but the market process is not actually described.

Lessius speaks of the setting of the interest rate by experienced merchants. Since this amounts to an expression of the good will of good citizens, it seems to him that the custom and practice of the Antwerp bourse ('usus Bursae seu Peristylii Antverpiensis') – where the merchants gather together daily and agree on a limited interest rate in accordance with a maximum rate of interest prescribed by Charles V – is excusable ('consuetudo ... excusabilis'). However, he immediately shows signs of doubt again; 'the merchants' should 'not be given such free rein' (ibid., 2.20.124–26).

Lessius has now considerably distanced himself from the medieval concept of an isolated, bilateral credit-debtor relationship. It is clear to him that in the bourse the greatest variety of causes determine liquidity preference on the one hand, and expectations of gain on the other; however, the path from this observation to models of the quantitative calculation of interest is long and winding, and we cannot suggest that its end is in sight.

Lessius goes on to deal among other things, with the problem of whether the object of a loan must be returned in the same quality and amount in which it was given if a change in prices has intervened. An exact ruling is not here possible, due to the incompleteness of the accepted contracts (ibid., 2.20.144).

Finally, how are usurers to be punished? Not through fines, corporal punishment or imprisonment, but instead by making the guilty aware of their status as outsiders: while under civil law the usurer loses his status as citizen, the church also excludes him from the community of believers, graded according to the level of guilt – by refusing them communion, confession, or Christian burial.

The book contains much more, even in our selection. In a weighty *dubitatio*, the *montes pietatis* – publicly-supported pawn brokers, or those who extend credit to the poor – are defended, because they displace small usurers with their extremely high interest rates. ('sublatis usurariis, qui ubique dominantur, & plebem exhauriunt', ibid., 2.20.194).[80] We are reminded here of Hildebrand,[81] who expected social progress for the poor to result from modern developed credit systems. Lessius discusses the money exchange and the discounting of bills – the latter in connection with, among other things, the Frankfurt Trade Fair (Lessius 1605, 2.23.53).

Purchase and contract lead to a consideration of just prices, which can be established for the general good by public authorities, or based on communal estimation ('communi hominum aestimatione', ibid., 2.21.7). This is in line with his statements about interest. He also believes the valuation of luxury goods to be far from arbitrary, being instead determined by communal estimation. In the face of an uncertain future, expectations of all free markets will influence the estimations of buyers and sellers, but because they are uncertain, the contracting parties will not be required to publicize their information – although Cicero in a famous passage in *De officiis* offers an opposing opinion (ibid., 2.21.39–40). Lessius (ibid., 2.21.144) understands monopolies in a more generally sense than modern usage; they are an expression of market power (the monopolists can set prices).[82]

In his discussion of the *census*, which Luther termed *Zinskauf*, 'interest purchase', Lessius speaks – without compromising his theory of usury – of a general preference for the present, almost in the nature of a Böhm-Bawerk: 'pluris communi hominum aestimatione censetur valere pecunia praesens...' (ibid., 2.22.30).[83] Here it is not a question of comparing money available with money that is spatially distant (the received theory of exchange contended that the money which is spatially nearer had greater value), but instead it is a question of temporal proximity.

Lessius also justifies the triple contract, consisting of the capital contribution by a partner in a business, the insurance of this capital, and a regular payment to this depositor, so that such a partner is silent; the legality of the entire agreement depends on the silent partner waiving a portion of the uncertain expected profit in exchange for a lower, fixed payment; such contracts are to the advantage, for example, of widows and orphans, who can thus invest their money (ibid., 2.25.22–32).[84]

Lessius was successful: 'Peu d'ouvrages connurent un succès plus éclatant et plus mérité' (Collin 1925, p. 247).[85] Twenty editions of *De iustitia et iure* appeared between 1605 and 1734. In modern textbooks Scholasticism admittedly plays only a secondary role. As de Roover remarks, we know of Thomas Aquinas and several other authors from the late Middle Ages, yet the economic analysis of the Scholastics flourished in the sixteenth and seventeenth centuries, influencing economic theory of the second half of the eighteenth century (authors such as Galiani and Condillac), which theory in turn forms the basis of modern economics. De Roover (1955, p. 187 and 173) even suggests: 'There was basically nothing wrong with the scholastic theory on value and price. It rested on utility and scarcity, and Adam Smith did not improve upon it.'

Noonan (1957, p. 5) maintains that scholastic thinkers were the intellectual leaders of the whole of Europe for centuries, their influence reaching well beyond the Reformation. While the economic doctrines of the late Middle Ages were not consistent, particularly on the question of usury, they were entirely successful; entrepreneurs were placed under pressure to invest productively, rather than behave as money lenders (ibid., pp. 194 sq). But in the modern era Lessius could be seen as 'the theologian whose views on usury most decidedly mark the arrival of a new era' (ibid., p. 222). He would have really felt at home in the modern financial world. 'Careful, perceptive, boldly logical, modest, and sure of himself, Lessius is a master of scholastic economic analysis' (ibid., p. 222). Accordingly, use of the argument of *carentia pecuniae* is said to have first gained prominence in his writings. Lessius is said to go great lengths to justify all professional money lending. No significant authority before him had allowed business people to claim gains foregone if they lacked a plan to invest in trade or agriculture. Lessius for the first time justified the general participation of individuals in money lending, with its potential for profit, provided there were competitive conditions; it was 'a momentous, if logical, step' (ibid., p. 263).

Lessius can thus be seen as a liberator from the constraints of older dogma and as an unprejudiced theoretician. But we have seen that he clearly denounced certain forms of usury (specifically that practised by small moneylenders); he has some reservations with respect to large moneylenders; and we must also remember that his book is really about virtue. It was written for future priests and monks, not future lawyers and merchants. While it is true that he considers each case from the viewpoints of differing legal systems, his thought turns upon Canon and Roman law. In the final analysis, however, he speaks as a theologian. Ecclesiastical law originates in the principle of volition, whereas Roman law works from the principle of explanation. A civil judge who has to settle a dispute must determine which kind of contract was actually made. The priest on the other hand, hoping to lead the sinner on to the path of righteousness, asks: why did you do that? Hence according to Lessius, usury 'requiritur ut mutuator intenderit mutuarium ex vi pacti mutuationis obligare' (Lessius 1605, 2.20.19). In order for it to be considered usury, therefore, 'it is necessary that the lender *intentionally* [italics mine] bind the borrower by force of contract'. But why should a usurious contract weigh heavier on the conscience than any other contract, where both sides voluntarily enter into a binding agreement? What is behind this struggle over the question of usury, and this hesitation in the justification of modern, capitalist forms of commerce? Did this hesitancy in easing restrictions on usury spring from a wish to maintain an older communal ethic, or was there instead an intellectual reluctance to face down a legacy of misunderstanding over the nature of money and interest?

Brants (1912) has already associated the development of Lessius' thinking with the Reformation. Calvinism permitted the use of money in credit relations, and thus made it possible for financial speculation to assume a hitherto unprecedented scale. Lessius sought conscientiously to familiarize himself with the new economic mechanisms. Yet economic and political concerns remained subordinate to the higher aims of God. According to Brants, it was part of the natural order of things for Lessius that what seemed autonomous at a lower level proved from a higher level to have another purpose. The task of the virtue *prudentia* was therefore to pursue the well-being of the individual, the family or the political community according to relevant natural logic, while however being constantly oriented to the good (ibid., p. 77).

Of course, according to Weber the contribution of Protestantism goes further. It is true that Weber in no way suggests that Protestantism brought about capitalism. Nor does he deny the reverse that economic development had an impact on religious thought. However, he believed that Calvinism fostered the formation of a capitalist economic disposition by substituting predestination for the free will and good works which Catholics were convinced would bring people closer to salvation. Hence, election through grace can be observed in this life, and commercial success is an expression of a higher blessing. When at the University of Leuven Lessius was confronted with a similar tendency, advocated by Baius, he opposed it (Sull 1930, Ch. 10).

In his famous and controversial book about the idea of usury, Nelson (1969) notes that Weber's (1976) essays on the spirit of Protestantism describes only one chronologically and spatially specific transition in the entire history of the human development of rationality from traditional thinking and tribal behaviour to modern capitalistic calculation. This has two sides: the doctrine of efficiency in the enterprise, and an orientation to the consumer in the household, both of which are connected by a vocational ethic oriented to work. Nelson believes that in this general development one aspect, the evolution in thinking about usury, mirrors a universal historical tendency. He seeks to develop Weber's sketch of a universal-historical vision of the evolution of rationality into a kind of longitudinal analysis examining changes in the attitude toward usury, while Weber himself uses more detailed, cross-sectional analysis to expose the formation of a new economic mentality in the Reformation. Citing remarks and writings on usury from Biblical, canonical and patristic sources, as well as from those composed during the Reformation, Nelson seeks to trace a path from a supposed origin in a Jewish tribal brotherhood, which clearly differentiates itself from alien peoples, to a modern society of contract that can in principle be global in its reach. Weber's thesis in a narrower sense, regarding Protestantism, is maintained by Nelson's analysis of Reformation writers, where the two historical perspectives intersect.

The two most important Old Testament passages, which form the starting-point of the investigation, are certainly these two:

> Thou shalt not lend upon usury to thy brother; usury of money, usury of victuals, usury of any thing that is lent upon usury: Unto a stranger thou mayest lend upon usury; but unto thy brother thou shalt not lend upon usury: that the Lord thy God may bless thee in all that thou settest thine hand to in the land whither thou goest to possess it.
>
> (Deuteronomy 23, 19–20)

Alongside the distinction between members and outsiders comes the duty to support those of your own people closest to you. 'And if thy brother be waxen poor, and fallen in decay with thee; then thou shalt relieve him: yea, though he be a stranger, or a sojourner; that he may live with thee' (Leviticus 25, 35).[86]

For the Early Fathers of the Church (Ambrosius) usury is a weapon to be used against enemies; this principle was practiced during the Crusades until finally usury began to be seen as a general sin in the time of Albertus Magnus. Everywhere the spirit of the Reformation led to fraternities which sought to renounce usury entirely, but the leaders of the Reformation – Luther hesitatingly, Melancthon and Zwingli more clearly, Bucer decisively – gradually supported a more liberal view. The actual revaluer of all values was however Calvin, who did away with the idea that peoples were alien to each other, generally sanctioned the charging of moderate rates of interest and decreed generosity toward the poor. The price of this transition to a more inclusive society has however been emergence of a greater distance between individuals.

However, scholastic justification for the prohibition of usury bears no recognizable connection to the changes in social attitude implied by Nelson. Let us look back to an older author and follow Antoninus of Florence.[87] Money can be lent either as *mutuum* or *capitale*. Capital should serve the production and sale of goods. Whoever invests money in a commercial enterprise in this way can share in any profit. Usury occurs when a surcharge is demanded for the loan of money or things which goes beyond restoring that portion which has been used, since when a consumption good is consumed (which is itself the entire purpose of the loan) it is used up. The good is thus actually sold for consumption, and the price consists in the return of the same amount and quality of goods. This therefore presupposes that money is understood in the Aristotelian sense only as a means of exchange (where its use is in being spent) and, further, that the handing over of a consumption good is bought by the promise of its eventual return. If neoclassical theory had introduced the possibility that consumption goods can in general have at different times different prices, that for example 100 kilos of wheat at the beginning of the year may be exchanged for 110 kilos at the end of the year, the term *mutuum* would have disappeared. But late-Scholastic literature, and Lessius, only has the beginnings of such dating of prices and amounts, and this did not lead to the elimination of the concept of usury. More important for the argument is therefore the discovery of other functions for money. Money could be capital not only in respect of loans made as a social contract, but also for alternative uses mentioned as opportunities by the lender (foregone profit or, the costs arising from delayed payment). Finally Lessius even broke through the barrier posed by the conception of money as means of exchange: when there was a complete scarcity of means of exchange *carentia pecuniae* was a basis for charging interest. The reasoning underlying the prohibition of usury, prevailing from the high point of Scholasticism until Lessius, seems therefore to be solely concerned with the logic of money, capital and interest; and there is no trace of the change in social attitude claimed by Nelson.

Had then the church first rejected monetary dealings altogether, then later gradually changed its position and relaxed its intolerance, having recognized the practical constraints – or from the Church's perspective, thanks to an improved understanding of natural rights? A modern Catholic theologian does not see it this way (Collin 1925, p. 256) because the church still today advocates charitable free loaning of consumption goods; on the other hand, it has always permitted compensation for creditors. Lessius is said to be a pastmaster at discovering such 'extrinsic' grounds for charging interest; but he is also thought by Collin to have been the first to justify interest on intrinsic grounds compatible with contemporary theory, introducing the concept of 'productive capital' (money as 'semen fecundum lucri', ibid., p. 258). Brants proposed a similar argument, seeing in Lessius a precursor of the Encyclica *Rerum Novarum*. De Roover (1969, p. 3) maintains that this entire approach is an anachronism; the church's new stance was shaped by its confrontation with the socio-economic problems of the nineteenth century. In response to Collin it might be possible to argue that the Scholastic discussion of the *mutuum* did not see it merely as neighbourly assistance offered out of a sense of charity. Otherwise the centuries of discussion and scrutiny of various forms of loans would have been superfluous.

Let us consider this ourselves. During the Middle Ages, when economic conditions were quite different from those prevailing today, the extension of interest-free credit, replacing money as a means of exchange, must have been quite normal, especially if *mutuum* was worthy of such frequent discussion and so was something more than a halfway house between the giving of alms freely and providing consumer credit under usurious conditions, for which the interest rate just happened to be zero per cent.

Once we remember that monetary transactions in the Middle Ages depended on the relatively irregular circulation of metal coins, of which there were often local shortages at certain times, so that people often temporarily reverted to barter, it becomes plain that small amounts of credit to compensate for shortages of coin would have constantly occurred.[88] The rich farmer, whose barn was full after the harvest, might temporarily lack the cash to buy nails from a merchant, especially when at the same time the shepherd who buys his grain has no coins either. If in the ensuing bartering the goods to be exchanged do not match mutual needs then credit is required, which would in the short-term doubtless be interest-free, for the very irregularity of the process meant that no general money market existed, although to satisfy basic needs exchanges had to occur. Of course, not everybody was wealthy, and there thus emerged a social division between the so-called 'usurers', who systematically lent money during times of scarcity but only at high interest rates, and the large mass of others, who transacted their business with weaker participants in the market and accepted an occasional delay in payment with greater or lesser generosity. Later, as coins circulated more steadily because of the convergence of economic regions, the need for this kind of transaction credit decreased, and usurers who had become rich from the poor were confronted with commercial creditors. If this historical-economic interpretation is accurate, then it explains why Lessius, who makes quite clear the extremes of usury between village and the Antwerp bourse, remains remarkable vague when it comes to giving an example of when a *mutuum* should be offered without interest rather than as alms; hence a *mutuum* in which the money lent was actually supposed to be employed as a consumption good, as a medium of exchange. Other forms of *mutuum* survived, but an important form had become rare.

We could also make it easier for ourselves by abjuring any hypotheses regarding economic history and take the concept of interest-free loans to be pure dogma. The conflict over 'Naviganti', the decree of Gregory IX's noted above, provides grounds for this. Coulton (1921) assumes there to be an unbridgeable discrepancy between historical reality and ecclesiastical tradition. He cites the following text:

> The man who lends a certain sum of money to another who is under-taking a sea-voyage or about to visit a fair, on the terms that he takes the

risk upon himself, and is to receive anything beyond his bare capital – that man is to be adjudged a usurer.

(ibid., p. 71)

The text appears to us illogical, for whoever assumes a risk also has a right to a risk premium. Indeed, generations of Scholastics contested this point, once risk (*periculum sortis*) was recognized as a basis for the charging of interest. An older tradition simply forbade the charging of interest outright – in any case, Coulton assumes that Gregory IX had originally intended to have the sentence end with the words 'is not to be adjudged a usurer', but at the last moment crossed out the 'not' out of respect for older traditions, without however altering the apparently paradoxical formulation.

While Coulton believes the doctrine of usury to be ideology and regards the endless debate over the text from 'Naviganti' as the outcome of Papal improvisation, there are those who defend the doctrine as theory. Schumpeter (1972, p. 105) argues that the Scholastics were 'in this respect much superior to nine-tenths of the interest analysts in the nineteenth century'; he recognized the real logical problems with the theory of interest. He suggested that they perceived interest primarily as a monetary phenomenon, which was in itself no great achievement. They cited various reasons for positive interest rates, none of which, however, would have been sufficient to show that interest rates were necessarily positive in general. The sole justification for positive interest in capitalist production is according to Schumpeter entrepreneurial profit, and the chief contribution of Scholasticism consisted in recognizing this. In other words, Schumpeter found in the Scholastics the principal elements of his own theory of interest! These elements can be easily identified: the monetary character of interest, the development of positive interest as a part of (for Schumpeter, dynamic) entrepreneurial profit, and the disappearance of interest (for Schumpeter, in a long-run stationary state), if there were no particular factor such as a positive rate of time preference (which hypothesis Schumpeter does not think worthy of consideration) that brought about a positive rate of interest.[89]Schumpeter (1972, p. 104) concludes, surprisingly, that the three-fold contract does is insufficient to avoid accusation of usury, for a sleeping business partner either has an alternative opportunity of earning interest, in which case a contractual arrangement was unnecessary; or, if he lost no profits, then he was only entitled to interest of more than 0 per cent if he actively participated in the business.

Now the Scholastics denied that there was any moral justification for positive interest, apart from in an ever-extending number of numerous special cases. Schumpeter, in contrast, wanted to show that competition eradicated interest. The interconnection of ideas which appear quite different, but which Schumpeter correctly recognizes to be related, derives from the fact that under competition the rates of profit equalize. The objective, modern theorist holds to this result (that the rate of interest is homogeneous). The theologian on the other hand considers the perceptions of individual merchants, who justify charging interest by reference to the fact that everybody else does.

Lessius points beyond Schumpeter to Keynes insofar as he presupposes the relatively general acceptance of a preference for liquidity. As has however been seen above, this has more to do with the motivation of transactions and regards precaution than speculation in a strict sense, if we may employ such terms here. Clearly, liquidity preference can only be expressed where there is access to a money market. In the absence of such a market, there is only mutual lending – I help you today, and you help me tomorrow – in a simple agrarian or early town economy lacking in means of circulation and threatened with a relapse into barter.

In our interpretation, Schumpeter understands the prohibition of usury as an ethical expression of an analytical insight: that interest on secure investments under competitive conditions – excepting an existing preference for the present, or a preference for liquidity which is theoretically just as coincidental – tends to zero in the long run, and that the payment of interest can only arise from constantly renewed, although temporary, entrepreneurial profit. While this conclusion may be of interest for the history of economic analysis, it reveals nothing about the origin and social importance of the idea. Let us look once again at how the usury debate can be viewed as a phenomenon in the history of mentalities. Our starting point has been Nelson's thesis, which we found lacked confirmation. Noonan (1957, p. 401) emphatically rejects Nelson's thesis:

> On charity and brotherhood there is no significant development reflected in eight hundred years of scholastic opinion. [...] Usury theory is modified, but it is modified in response to changes in economic conditions or as a result of more thorough investigation of the rational demands of justice. Its modification reflects no transvaluation of values...

Fanfani (1933, p. 151) refers however to a change in economic spirit. He defines this in a manner similar to Spiethoff, Sombart or, later, Müller-Armack: 'Per spirito economico intendiamo quel complesso atteggiamento interiore, cosciente o meno, per cui un uomo di fronte agli affari agisce in un determinato modo.'[90] Modern European man treats wealth as a means of satisfying one's own needs, while pre-modern man viewed it as a means of attaining eternal life. The former is ultimately hedonic, while for the latter the life forms and the means for their development are structured by a theocentric system. Hence he will seek to use permissible means instead of usury – and if he continued to practice usury he would not be a modern capitalist, but a remorseful person (ibid., pp. 158ff.). However, in the fifteenth century 'the neighbour ceased to be a brother and assumed the form of a competitor' (ibid., pp. 162ff.). Fanfani seeks to demonstrate the stages of this development, early forms of capitalism developing first in Italy. However, the principal families soon retired to their country estates and a spirit which had barely been aroused in Italy quickly dwindled.

The strengthening of capitalist spirit, attributed in particular to Calvinism's adherence to the idea that proof of self in work was a sign of divine predestination, found other support during the Reformation. Luther rejected the monastic life and so increased the value of worldly occupation, although work had already been accorded a higher status in the early years of Christianity than it had in antiquity. But there is at least in part a close relationship between Reformation ideas and those of the late Scholastics. Höffner (1941, p. 156) openly claimed that: 'we have established that the Calvinist economic ethic of the seventeenth century went no further than writers of the later Spanish scholastic period had'. In some polemical commentary on the subject by authors plainly more interested in the impact which they might have on the present rather than historical accuracy, it is ultimately claimed that it was the Jesuits who paved the way for this new capitalist spirit, or at any rate, that they played no lesser part than adherents of the Reformation; the contending parties often invoke Lessius as witness to this process (Brodrick 1934).

Even as early as Endemann we can detect a premonition of the coming *Kulturkampf*, from the Protestant camp in this case. He warned of the 'influence which restoration of the doctrine of usury would necessarily have on the shaping of law, specifically the law of transport and trade' (Endemann 1883, p. 421). Knoll outlined the internal conflict within the Catholic Church, comparing the doctrines of the Dominicans with those of the Jesuits. He describes the favourable attitude toward interest on the part of the Jesuits as a 'dogma of the order'. Referring to Lessius and other authors who had contributed to such arguments he states that:

> If the Dominicans adhered to a (conservative) social 'ideal' in respect of the prohibition of interest and hence believed themselves to be loyally serving the Church in this way, the Jesuits by contrast abandoned this 'ideal' and embraced (capitalist) reality, sanctioning the charging of interest, believing this to be the quickest and most certain way of achieving the aims of the church.
>
> (Knoll 1933, p. 137)

The controversy would continue into the twentieth century; the last important advocate introduced by Knoll is Oswald von Nell-Breuning, who taught both at the Jesuit College and at the University of Frankfurt. To effect a reconciliation between ancient and modern economic theory he began from credit, and not from the altered nature of money. Credit is generally understood to imply the economic involvement of the creditor in the affairs of the debtor, a relationship in which the creditor gets a 'legal claim' over the latter. But the Dominican tradition is also said to persist (ibid., pp. 188ff.).

Having taken stock of Lessius' basic positions, it is easy to find evidence which makes clear his developed understanding (by comparison with the older Christian tradition, or that of Antiquity) of the capitalist world and its political importance beyond his often-discussed analytical insights into the functions of markets and institutions. Thanks to new forms of lending, the individual usurer is already practically obsolete. His punishment is traditional:

expulsion from the community. Merchants and traders are not ultimately to be governed by the authority of church or state, but by natural authority where it is a matter of creating institutions for monetary exchange and price formation, or even when it is a matter of evaluating acceptable and unacceptable behaviour. At the very beginning of the book, *prudentia* is a virtue in the conduct of trade, and it is even somewhat disturbing to note that Lessius is occasionally prepared to subordinate relationships between people to *prudentia*.

In comparing the Catholic and Protestant positions in the south and north of the Netherlands I am in no position to weight the relative significance of Jesuit and Calvinist doctrine for our discussion of usury; and certainly not on the basis of this very brief introduction. One thing is certain, however: that it would be a regrettably short-sighted on the part of the history of economic thought if recognition of Lessius's achievement were limited to his indisputably great merit in theoretical analysis.

There is not one paragraph in the book that allows one to forget that in tumultuous times Lessius constantly fixed his attention on the concrete detail of economic affairs, seeking to assure both himself and his readers that decisions were always made with regard for higher ends. The goal most clearly evident in his doctrine of virtue is the improvement of humanity, so that people might come together in a life which theologians would describe as more pleasing to God. Perhaps it is not therefore simply anachronistic to close by saying that Lessius sought an irenic formula, as did Müller-Armack.

## Notes

1 Cf. Myers (1976, pp. 563–618).
2 Mostly supported by Bridrey's hypothesis, criticized below.
3 'Antonio Serra: the founder of economic theory?', Chapter 3.
4 Naturally, minor devaluations had to be introduced every 60 years or so to take account of the wearing out of the circulating currency. If such devaluations were not carried out then an excessive difference in weight between the old and new coins would develop, and new coins would be removed from circulation because of their higher metal content. The official mint had to cover the costs of stamping and could involve a profit for the crown if the money was inferior, such that from about 100g-silver 105 coins could be minted, 100 coins then corresponding to the value of 100g of silver (cf. entry 'Münzwesen' in Conrad 1910, p. 818). Whoever has 100g of silver will therefore receive from the mint as many coins as corresponds to the market value of the silver, namely 100 coins. The mint retains five of those minted; they cover their costs in this way and also pay a tax, or – if the mint belong to the king – the profit from minting (seignorage) goes to him, as an expression of the not-yet-absolute royal monopoly on minting in fourteenth century France. When in time the coins suffer a loss of weight and the silver price increases, so that now 103 coins are required in order to purchase 100g of silver, a depreciation is necessary, in which – given an unchanged mintage – 100 old coins will be used to stamp 108 new ones. These are then just as heavy as the worn, old coins, so that both can circulate together. If those in power wish to provide an incentive for bringing the old coins to the mint for melting down, they can declare them void; and/or if a somewhat stronger devaluation is required, the old and new coins can be declared nominally the same, though the silver content of the older coins is

higher, so that for the money-changers it is worth collecting them and having them melted down (Spooner 1972, pp. 105ff.).

5  E. Fournial's book *Histoire monétaire de l'occident médiéval* [A Monetary History of the West in the Medieval Era] (1970) contains abundant details on finance and the altering of coins in France, from the internal organization of mints (p. 14), to their supervision by the crown (p. 16), to the independent minting by barons (p. 148), to the money reform of 1360 (p. 158) and also such details as the techniques of the counterfeiters as well as their punishment (p. 17).

6  Cf. Dupuy (1989, p. 40).

7  In Struik (1967) Oresme was declared the most important clerical mathematician of the Middle Ages.

8  "Numerus stellarum est cubicus.' Dicimus enim quod possibile est, non tamen probabile aut opinabile aut verisimile, cum tales numeri multo sint aliis pauciores.' Cited in Hugonnard-Roche (1988, p. 157).

9  Cf. Meusnier (1988, pp. 165ff.).

10  Spufford (1988, p. 300) cites Oresme from Johnson and then refers to Bridrey's theory at second hand.

11  'The majesty of the lord is reflected in the coin. The coin is an ornament of the king and the kingdom and of any dominion, for the image of the lord, the king, is represented in it.' (My transl.)

12  'We cannot believe that anyone is able to doubt that to ourselves alone and our Royal Majesty there belongs solely and entirely in our kingdom the ministry, the deed, the provision and everything relating to monies, and to make money as money, and to put it into circulation at what price is pleasing to us, for the good and for the profit of ourselves, our kingdom and our subjects, according to our law.' (My transl.)
   'In qua quidem etsi liceat jus suum exigere in cudendo numisma, moderatus tamen esse debet princeps quicunque, sive in mutando, sive in diminuendo pondus vel metallum.' Aquinas, cited in Bridrey (1906, p. 126).

13  'In qua quidem etsi liceat jus suum exigere in cudendo numisma, moderatus tamen esse debet princeps quicunque, sive in mutando, sive in diminuendo pondus vel metallum.' Aquinas, cited in Bridrey (1906, p. 126).

14  Schorer's Latin text (Oresme 1937) corresponds with this, except that there is 'forte' instead of 'forsan' (in our manuscript 'forsitan'); moreover, Schorer repeats the 'forte' in front of 'euidens'. Johnson's (1956, p. 13) English translation: 'From which it is clear that a change in money should never be made, unless perhaps under eminent necessity or for obvious advantage of the whole economy.'

15  Oresme defends the right of property ownership (for the individual as well as the church) and the acquisition of goods through work; he objects to begging and the class of beggars (Babbitt 1985, pp. 121–25).

16  Cf. the excerpts from Oresme's translation of *Politics* in Dupuy (1989, p. 93).

17  Cf. the corresponding excerpts in Dupuy (1989); for Oresme, pp. 117ff., for Buridan, pp. 153ff.

18  I am citing the Latin from Johnson (1956) and the corresponding chapter division in the long version; Johnson's English translation (ibid., p. 6): 'that they cannot well be made by alchemy'.

19  'The reason is that all such mixture is naturally suspect...' (Johnson 1956, p. 8).

20  'it was wisely ordained by the sages of that time...' (Johnson 1956, p. 8).

21  'was tiresome constantly to resort to the scales...'; 'should be made by one or more public persons'; 'difficult to engrave or counterfeit' (Johnson 1956, pp. 8–10).

22  Fournial (1970, p. 95) does not believe that such reasons – at least when referring to the first third of the fourteenth century – are merely an excuse; the deeper causes of debasement arose from the necessity of harmonizing the legal exchange rate of the money with the market value of precious metals. 'The things which move us to

make such money are for our people which was and is in great suffering and shortage of money ... which will soon be more abundant and flourishing if supplied with new and useable money.'

23 Schorer (1937) translates: 'For what purpose do we create money?'. (My transl.)

24 Costs here already include the achievable normal profit of the mint under given competitive conditions.

25 Senior (1920) is an account of bullionism still well worth reading, including variable production costs and the influence of demand for precious metals for industrial uses, providing empirical evidence from the history of Mexican silver mines.

26 Rather more than 35 years ago a boom in silver metal forced the Swiss National Bank to replace circulating silver coins containing a high concentration of silver with identically designed coins of a copper-nickel alloy, because silver coins were being taken to foreign countries by the truck-load and melted down (Iklé 1970, p. 41).

27 There is also a Law of Circulation that holds for Keynesian theory, insofar as transaction volumes are determined by effective demand and the nominal amount of money is given; so that when the price level derives from a money wage level determined by pay negotiations, increased by an average mark-up, the interest rate is so set that exactly enough money circulates as a means of transaction as is necessary for a given velocity of circulation for transaction purposes, while the remaining money is held by those who expect a fall in the price of bonds and therefore do not invest in them. For Keynes, speculative holdings function as a buffer in a similar way to that of industrial demand for silver in the model described above. What I here call the Law of Circulation is discussed by Marx in Chapter 3 of the first volume of *Capital*. Cf. Marx (1909, p. 135). However, Marx fails to discuss the cost of minting coins and seignorage, leading to a radicalization of the bullionist position. He does not differentiate between the purchasing power of the metal concentration of the coin and the coin as a physical coin in respect of new coins because he does not want to admit that money created by the state is distinguished from that in a natural exchange economy by its purchasing power and its nature as a 'general equivalent'. He also denies therefore the possibility which today is a reality: a capitalist world in which not a commodity, gold as a precious metal, functions as 'global money', gold does not serve as a 'world money' but where the currencies of the principle commercial countries are held as reserves.

28 The Nominalistic interpretation is suggested in the *Nicomachean Ethics*: Money appears as a means and a measure (1113a20), it leads to the valuation of everything (1133b15), it is not natural but created, and can be altered: νόμισμα ... οὐ φύσει ἀλλὰ νόμῳ ἐστί, καὶ ἐφ' ἡμῖν μεταβαλεῖν καὶ ποιῆσαι ἄχρηστον (1133a31). In *Politics*, by contrast, stamping determines the weight: ὁ γὰρ χαρακτὴρ ἐτέθη τοῦ ποσοῦ σημεῖον (1257a42), where minting costs – as is so often the case with bullionists later – are not discussed. Plato was more clearly than Aristotle a Nominalist, but also offered a compromise: low-value token money for use within the *polis* and full-value money – or in any case money made from precious metal – in circulation between city states. Cf. Baloglou (1994, p. 184).

29 'The tax on salt, otherwise called *les gabelles* ... how to suppress the sad thoughts which this tax prompts. A harvest which the gift of providence sends cheaply to one part of the citizenry is sold dearly to all the others...' (Lough 1969, p. 210f.). Probably for reasons of conscience – like a remorseful usurer, who was promised mercy if he returned the interest – Charles V on his death bed waived important taxes that placed his successor – or his guardian because the *Dauphin* was a child – in a predicament. Under Charles VI, they were reintroduced 'with timidity and clumsiness, covertly, as if it were a bad move' (Delachenal 1927, vol. 5, p. 412).

30 In the French translation: 'de petit ou moindre poix'. In our manuscript: 'tempore mutilato pondere' (Chapter XII). What is here under consideration is not money worn-out over time, because wear-and-tear justifies devaluation (Chapter IX).

Correct: 'parvo sive mutilato?' Johnson's (1956) Latin text follows ours and other manuscripts; he then translates: 'of short weight'.

31  The above argument from Oresme on the contemptibility of changing currencies is based on a well-known modification in the medieval reception of Aristotle which, in the Aristotelian treatment of retail trade (καπηλική), due to an error in the translation, reads as a disparagement of converting money ('campsoria') (Dupuy 1989, p. 45). In a commentary on Aristotle's *Politics* Oresme transforms minor usury (όβολοστατική) into money changing (ibid., p. 111). Oresme does not need to go into the extensive Scholastic attempt to compile criteria which might differentiate usurious from non-usurious contracts because this would represent a digression from his topic. Lessines' (1864) *De usuris* can be cited as an example of a thorough argument in this regard; in it the chief characteristic of the usurer is defined as profiting from the passing of time ('causa temporis', p. 419). The author wants to show, among other things, that the sale of a fixed income, in a lease, for several years does not signify usury [except in a contract that offends charity or is based on profit rather than the necessities of life ('ad utilitatem vitae humanae')], although the purchase price of the income is below the total sum of the income. He provides two reasons: 'vendentis liberalitas' – freedom of contract, i.e. the seller could freely give away the income, even gratis – and fair trade, which is given due to the inferior quality of goods in the future ('res futurae per tempora non sunt tantae aestimationis sicut eaedem collectae in instanti'). Now, a modern economist would also argue similarly in the case of simple borrowing. Aegidius in fact sees usury especially in such contracts which in some way are unequal, e.g. with regard to risk. The variety of cases is conceded by Oresme in his commentaries on Aristotle's *Politics* without discussion (ibid., p. 114); his core argument against usury is that the creditor gives the debtor a sum of money which now belongs to the person and, according to the nature of money, will be further spent and thus cannot be returned. With the allocation of an object for use there can only be a replacement (p. 113) or, perhaps, compensation (p. 114). It is not, however, usury. In *Tractatus* (Chapter XX), he describes certain loans as a work of Christian charity, which would become more rare in times of inflation. Langholm (1992) discussed the writing of Aegidius which is more differentiated.

32  The citation from Cassiodor included by Oresme refers once again to an alteration of the currency, under which at first the noble beneficiaries of fixed annuities suffered, so that even this provides a certain support for the interpretation of Oresme's text as primarily motivated by the interests of the upper classes.

33  The effort of the French throne to maintain a necessary distance between the Papacy and the Empire is echoed here. Oresme preached accordingly in Avignon; when Emperor Charles IV visited King Charles V in Paris in 1377, the latter sent a black horse to meet the Emperor, since it was customary for the Emperor to enter his own cities on a white horse (Delachenal 1927–1931, vol. 5, p. 77).

34  'It is possible to piece together a conception of national sovereignty from … Oresme, although we find no puissance souveraine but pre-eminence of the royal or national government, not nationalism but national sentiment' Babbitt (1985, p. 67f.).

35  Cf. Moss (1995).

36  This might also seem reminiscent of the discussion of 'dirty floating' – cf. Schefold (1972, p. 86f.) – of which Kaldor was then the sole proponent, arguing that the Central Bank was best able to function in the interests of the country by keeping their intentions secret.

37  Cf. Lapidus (1997).

38  For example, the important J.J. Becher (1668) *Politischer Discurs*; P.W. von Hörnigk (1684) *Oesterreich über alles*; and J.H.G. von Justi (1756) *Grundsätze der Policey-Wissenschaft* all appeared in the series *Klassiker der Nationalökonomie*.

Moreover, I owe a debt of gratitude to Dr Karl Kunze for suggesting the repub-lication of the rare volumes of E.L. Carl's (2000 [1722–1723]) *Traité de la richesse des princes et de leurs états et des moyens simples et naturels pour y parvenir.*

39 Lotz reproduces the text in a beautiful and powerful but today no longer easy-to-understand German of the era of Luther; he added a translation, which is at the same time an interpretation. This classic work was reprinted by Stadermann (1999), accompanied by his own introduction, as well as the one from Lotz, and in a modern version so that the modern reader, if necessary, can refer to this translation.

40 Cf. Klotzsch (1779, pp. 250–54).

41 In the appendix to his first volume, Ehrenberg (1896, pp. 417–20) published two contracts for large Augsburg trading companies on the formation of a syndicate for copper trade.

42 The German original reads: 'Ratslag der monopolia halb'.

43 'And we have examples every day that, if it is agreed among artisans not to have more than a certain number of journeymen or that only that many should work in a work-shop, by this convention the needy, poor, lavish, negligent and bankrupt will stand in the way of the better artisan who works with care and avoids prodigality.' (My transl.)

44 The last sentence reads in the original German: 'alles dem gmaynen nutz zu unwiderpringlichen nachtail unnd schaden'.

45 'For it is customary to bring similar kinds of spices in great quantity to the city of the Venetians and to other parts.' (My transl.)

46 'It would be impossible for the many and diverse societies to bring and force in one hand these ores and metals, even if they were tied together.' (My transl.)

47 'It is possible that one region nourishes the other on account of a kind of natural incentive and comes to its support.' (My transl.)

48 'Seeking one's own advantage'. (My transl.)

49 'not only against private, but also against all public utility and it would perhaps lead to a greater monopoly than has been heard of so far.' (My transl.)

50 The German original reads: 'Der Eigen Nutzen bin ich genannt / Hoch und nidren Stenden wol bekañt. Doch nicht so böß als man mich macht / Wo man die Sachen recht betracht. Manchem vil guts durch mich beschicht / Hergegn man mir kein lob vergicht.'

51 First sentence: 'that not the whole time I had to spend sitting on the horse be wasted with artless and uncultured stories.' (My transl.)

52 Lotz's introduction was reprinted by Stadermann (1999, pp. 59–67).

53 A compilation of the various currency systems, with lists of coins, their weights and standards, combined with an explanation of the high points of currency history, tables of coins and maps of the Albertinian and Ernestinian lands can be found in Haupt (1974).

54 Cf. 'Nicholas Oresme: monetary instruction in the late medieval era', Chapter 2.

55 Cf. 'Spanish economic thought at the dawn of the modern era', Chapter 3.

56 Cf. Braudel and Spooner (1967), esp. p. 401.

57 Page references in the *Münzschriften* will be included in the following citations without further information.

58 The word in brackets is not in the text. Mines, however, are not to be opened and kept running without high expenditures.

59 Cf. 'Spanish economic thought', Chapter 3.

60 Cf. 'Spanish economic thought', Chapter 3.

61 Cf. 'Spanish economic thought', Chapter 3.

62 Cf. 'Antonio Serra: the founder of economic theory?', Chapter 3.

63 'We have admitted the best of this University, a young man from Brecht, seventeen year old, with excellent gifts of body and soul.' (My transl.)

64 Cf. Aquin (1991).

65 Some examples are printed in an appendix to Sull's book (Sull 1930, pp. 340ff.).

66 'An intermediate state between full internationalism and full nationalization of high finance, a situation where financial powers that might in most countries have belonged to foreign countries were forced to take sides in the struggle for political power – this is characteristic of the age of the Fuggers' (Ehrenberg 1896, vol. 1, p. 412, my transl.).

67 For this and the following point, cf.: Wee (1963, vol. 1, p. 209).

68 'I strived to trace down the truer proposition among the several [formulations] and to strengthen it by [every possible] mean, with an added fundamental reason, if one presented itself, revealed, however, through the probability of another proposition, if one strongly seemed to impose itself.' (My transl.)

69 Cicero also represents an important step in the development and his *De officiis* is also published in the collection *Klassiker der Nationalökonomie.*

70 English translation by Rackham (Aristotle 1990, p. 339): 'and that is our conception of an expert in Domestic Economy or Political Science'.

71 'I answer: the complete foundation of domination is not prior to justice and the power of disposition, but it is essential that it includes it.' (My transl.)

72 On the Social Right School cf. Diehl (1941).

73 Cf. Schefold (1991, 1994e).

74 'Gain is called the acquisition of a thing beyond what is possessed, estimable in money and not due otherwise.' (My transl.)

75 'This hope can be estimated by means of a price.' (My transl.)

76 'Buying of a fruit-bearing object, like a bond, fields or houses.' (My transl.)

77 He cites family support, a dowry for the daughter, for the comfort of old age, and protection from danger.

78 'One can see how by this reasoning merchants are excused, who, foreseeing the king's demands, withdraw their money from a business opportunity ... in order to have enormous sums ready; for they do this not without great damage to their profit, and no other mean suffices for making simultaneously available such a mass of cash.' (My transl.)

79 Cf. 'Spanish economic thought', Chapter 3.

80 '[There will be betterment, once] usurers have been eliminated, who dominate everywhere and exploit the people.' (My transl.)

81 Cf. 'Bruno Hildebrand: the historical perspective of a liberal economist', Chapter 4.

82 On Lessius' numerous observations on inadequate competition, cf. also Roover (1951). Market power is rejected, but exceptions, hinted at because of great advantages, are allowed – then a charge should be applied (Lessius 1605, 2.21.148).

83 'Present money is thought to be valued more by the general estimation of men.' (My transl.) A general theory of interest is certainly not presented. Lessius approves of the lowest price for *census* without making clear its connection with high interest rates (ibid., 2.22.45). There is an anticipation of Gossen's first law in the insight that the possession of a given coin is more important for the poor than for the rich (ibid., 2.23.50).

84 It is essential that good will exists and presumes that the profit comes from a proper source (ibid., 2.22.62). The payment of interest on bank deposits can also be justified when such contracts and intentions exist, despite the citation of Azpilcuetas' contrasting opinion (ibid., 2.23.75).

85 'Few works had more shining and more merited success.' (My transl.)

86 Cf. additionally: Exodus 22, 24 and Deuteronomy 24, 10–11.

87 From Ilgner (1904, pp. 115–121).

88 On the frequent relapse from a money to a barter economy cf. Dopsch (1968).

89 On Schumpeter's claim that in long-term equilibrium interest rates must tend to zero, cf. Samuelson (1966, 1977).

90 'By economic spirit we mean that complex attitude, conscious or not, by which a man, confronted with business, acts in a determined fashion.' (My transl.)

# 3   Mercantilism

## Spanish economic thought at the dawn of the modern era

In the sixteenth century Spain was the world power. From that time there remain memories of great discoveries, of Spanish theatre and the art of the *siglo d'oro*, as well as of the language which is still spoken in former colonies. However, very few who are not specialists know of Spanish economics, although the modern era is thought to have begun with Columbus' crossing of the Atlantic and the resulting shift in trade routes which led to the formation of a world economy. Economic thought and activity seems to have remained bound fast within the framework of a rigid Catholicism inherited from the medieval era: severe rejection of usury, loyalty to noble ideals, charity in dealing with poverty. But there was no unleashing of an independent economic rationality as a driving force, and no economic freedom facilitating economic development as known elsewhere since the eighteenth century. Nevertheless, the opposing impulses of spiritual self-assertion in Counter Reformation and the unheard-of territorial expansion due to trade, war and conquest led to quite remarkable economic reflections. At a time when globalization seems to be breaking down remaining local economic and cultural connections, consideration of an epoch characterized by a renewed and intense religious experience and attempts of strengthening the embedding of the economy deserves special attention.

The Spanish Scholastics in Spain produced their most important work only around 1550, connecting church and law in a manner elsewhere in Europe already in decline (Grice-Hutchinson 1952, p. 40). In the 1530s Vitoria was already attempting to adapt law to the needs of the Spanish empire. Soto wrote a famous treatise about aid to the poor while Spain starved in the 1540s, and also in 1553 his *De iustitia et iure* – a text that would be read for the next 200 years – on monetary questions. Diego de Covarrubias, a student of Azpilcueta, was known in Italy as a specialist in Roman law. Grice-Hutchinson has described the development of the purchasing power theory of exchange rates as the most original achievement of this group; it can be attributed primarily to Azpilcueta. Larraz Lopez (1943), who was the first to direct attention to the connections between the economists of the School of

Salamanca, describes their thinking roughly as follows (ibid., pp. 67ff.): Xeno-phon observed in the *Poroi* [1] that the value of goods ultimately decreased when more was produced, although this was not true of silver, which as money and also as jewellery always found buyers. Aristotle, by contrast, viewed money as a commodity and Thomas Aquinas, considering its value, already referred to the money supply. Antoninus of Florence recognized that hoarding diminished when more goods could be purchased for the same coin, and Copernicus' quantity theory of money, dating from 1619, was even more precisely formulated.

It is impossible to determine a clear beginning to the quantity theory of money, and Azpilcueta does not lay claim to being the originator – in contrast to Jean Bodin, to whom the discovery of quantity theory is sometimes falsely ascribed. On the contrary, the phenomenon of the varying valuation of money in different countries and the resulting trade in currencies by means of letters of credit was for him so familiar that he was able to formulate an astute and illuminating representation of purchasing power parities: the amount of precious metal in circulation in a country determines its purchasing power, and precious metals gravitate to wherever their purchasing power is greatest.

In the colonies price increases first became apparent with the exploitation of the newly-discovered mines. For example, Popescu[2] refers to a Juan de Matienzo, who was born in Valladolid in 1520, who had a law license and lived in America from 1561 onward. He stated: 'Panis eiusdem naturae est in Hispania et apud Indios, sed maiori hic pretio venditur quam in Hispania, propter indigentiam et argenti aurique abundantiam, quae causae augendi pretium' (Popescu 1986, p. 168).[3] Azpilcueta had formulated his ideas before Matienzo left for America; and we cannot prove that his insights concerning quantity theory were based on news from overseas experiences abroad, but such a conclusion seems plausible.

In Catholic Europe and in Latin America the economic thought of the Spanish late-Scholastics and especially of the School of Salamanca was influ-ential until well into the Mercantile period. In Latin America its influence was felt into the late eighteenth and early nineteenth centuries. Popescu (1986, p. 190) writes of Azpilcueta: 'El 'Manual de Confesores' era uno de los libros predilectos de las bibliotecas públicas y particulares de todas las provincias de las Indias.'[4]

The original severity of the prohibition of usury weakened over time, however. If the argument concerning profit (*lucrum cessans*) is admitted, such prohibitions could hardly be sustained. The loss attributed to lenders if they did not themselves use their money could only be judged according to the duration of the loan. One distinguished, following Aristotle, between the prime and usual use of money in exchange, and a secondary, commercial use (termed *chrematistic* by Aristotle). As soon as the second included lending, the payment of interest had to appear acceptable. Azpilcueta is, as we shall see, familiar with the argument. He defended himself against it by conceding the validity of the argument from *lucrum cessans* only on the forcefully repeated of the condition that, so long as the money was loaned out, the lender interrupted the activities from which he could have earned a profit from the use of his own money. But one can hardly imagine such an interruption in monetary transactions where various exchangeable capitals are traded (Tortajada 1992, p. 78).

By contrast the two other justifications for charging interest, *damnum emergens* and *periculum sortis*, caused fewer difficulties: if a loss (*damnum*) occurs, it must be compensated and if someone offers insurance and takes on a risk, then this person can demand a premium for the service. The issue here, it was felt, is actually that of costs. *Lucrum cessans* was more difficult: what appeared to be *chrematistic*, profit for the sake of profit, remained prohibited. But it was not *chrematistic* if a lender could plainly have made a return from his own work and money but did not because his money had been placed as a loan. This potential remuneration for services potentially rendered was called profit foregone, and a charge (an *interesse*) could only be demanded where this profit had truly been foregone. Pure profit, a component of a price which could not be traced back to the cost of materials and labour, to specific and concrete costs, was not considered acceptable. If, while taking confession, a priest learned from a merchant that insurance was only a sham, or that *lucrum cessans* was only pretended since the lender actually continued to work and therefore had not lost anything through lending the money, the penitent was supposed to be threatened with a flaming sword, and the restitution of the unjust interest had to be required. Those who belatedly regretted their actions had to make a bequest to the church in penance. While Azpilcueta sought to do justice to the growing complexity of trade he remained merciless towards pure usury.

Further pursuit of the logic of the *lucrums cessans* principle leads close to the labour theory of value. One can simply admit that lenders must somehow reduce their business because, until they receive repayment, they have access to less capital: then the rug is pulled out from under any further charges of usury. Or one can state more precisely what was meant by a business-reduction in order to justify an extra charge: not only a reduction of the capital investment but apparently also a reduction of the labour expended on the part of the lender. Thus, labour would appear as the 'value creating' element. One can understand, finally, why Böhm-Bawerk's capital theory arose from a connection of the critique of Scholasticism and Marx.

Between the church, whose prohibition against usury had grown out of an age-old prejudice of archaic societies against trade, and the arising mercantilism that would open the gates for trade wide, there exists for us, in retrospect, a large substantive opposition, but they meet in Spain. Azpilcueta[5] published the primary version of his *Commentario* in 1556; the text from Ortiz (Instituto de España 1970), first published after the Second World War but already known in manuscript form, dates from 1558.

The texts are stylistically different: the educated dialectician Azpilcueta with his complicated explanations facing Ortiz, very clearly writing from his own experience, who cannot even construct proper sentences but instead writes almost without punctuation, as he might have spoken, with parts of sentences linked only by an 'and'. Yet there are commonalities, not only in the Counter-Reformational zeal which inspired both, but in the economic situation: 'A spectre haunted Europe in the Mercantilist period: the fear of ending up like Spain: rich in gold, poor in production, and with a frighteningly unfavourable balance of trade' (Perotta 1993, p. 18).

Ortiz can be called the first European mercantilist, according to Perotta. He is, though early, not guilty of a fetishization of precious metals, the flow of which out of the country he struggles against, instead, he suggests that the country should attempt, by means of its own production, to substitute for the imports which are streaming in due to the export of precious metals. It is all too common to associate the mainstream of Mercantilism with England and, especially, with Mun (1989 [1664]), who was confronted with the problem that much of the Spanish precious metal, acquired by England through trade, was flowing from London to India by means of the purchase of luxury goods. Serra's (1994 [1613]) analysis of balance of payments was older and subtler. Analytically, Ortiz does not come close to Serra, who carefully differentiates the components of the current account balance on a case-by-case basis and provides reasons for the materialization of an outflow of precious metals, despite a positive balance of trade, and deliberates on how such a problem can be fought. Ortiz thinks in simpler categories, but likewise has his eye on the same problem: how the outflow of precious metals can be offset by the strengthening of production. In so doing, he shows, though not always intentionally, the political and social – alongside the economic – obstacles which stand in the way of such a reform.

Ecclesiastical tradition and the dawn of Mercantilism confront each other particularly in concerns about the increasing impoverishment of those without work, who were engaged in activities such as begging or vagabonding and spread insecurity. The church retained the duty to provide for the poor through the giving of alms and hesitated to centralize the support. In the fifteenth century, St. Antoninus of Florence differentiated between acceptable and unacceptable activities (usury was included among the latter); he also accepted work for speculation. However, the differentiation between productive and unproductive work is not yet touched upon, which will be introduced by Ortiz – still without an appropriate term, however – in 1558, when he wants to see idlers, beggars, soldiers transformed into servants in active, craft work, thus producing commodities (Perotta 1988).

Ortiz's conviction that the country was threatened with decline might seem even more astonishing given that the rise of Spain, as a nation, had not happened in the distant past. Machiavelli was an admirer of Ferdinand of Aragon who, thanks to his marriage to Isabella of Castile, had laid the foundation. In the chapter that deals with how the prince should adorn himself in order to be thought majestic, Machiavelli writes:

> Nessuna cosa fa tanto stimare uno principe, quanto fanno le grande imprese e dare di sé rari esempli. Noi abbiamo ne' nostri tempi Ferrando di Aragonia, presente re di Spagna. Costui si può chiamare quasi principe

nuovo, perché d'uno re debole è diventato per fama e per gloria el primo re de' Cristiani; e, se considerate le azioni sua (sic), le troverrete tutte grandissime e qualcuna estraordinaria.

(Machiavelli 1971, p. 108ff.)

Nothing enables a ruler to gain more prestige than undertaking great campaigns and performing unusual deeds. In our times Ferdinand of Aragon, the present King of Spain is a notable example. He might almost be called a new ruler because, from being a weak king, he has become the most famous and glorious king in Christendom. And if his achievements are examined, they will be found to be very remarkable, and some of them quite extraordinary (Machiavelli 1996, p. 76).

Ferdinand thus became the first King of Christendom, and Machiavelli lists among his greatest feats the attack on Granada which laid the groundwork for the country, the inclusion of the Castilian nobility in the hostile action, the cleverness with which he made the church the financial source for the long war, and the devout cruelty with which he plundered and drove out the Marranos, consequently even the converted Jews and Moors. He also listed the attack on Africa and the initiatives against Italy and France – though Columbus is not mentioned even once.

Our authors therefore only emerged one or two generations after those credited with Spain's initial ascension. Charles V, who was born in 1500, inherited Spain in 1516, and was elected German emperor in 1519, put the future development of Spain as a nation in doubt with his vision of a universal Christian kingdom even if Spain was to become the core country of his worldwide possessions. Since he failed to unite Germany and could not conquer France, the idea of a realm was not realized. But when Philip II, his son, obtained Spain and then later, after his abdication, his brother Ferdinand became emperor, Spain was no longer an isolated possession: to be precise, Philip possessed the Spanish Netherlands, southern Italy, and the colonies. However, the nation state idea had become accepted: Ortiz appears to view the Spanish possessions in Europe, outside of the Iberian Peninsula, as foreign countries, while insisting on sovereignty over the colonies. He sympathizes with the duty to persecute Moslems and heretics, thinking thereby of preserving the purity of Spain as a nation and of the Spanish faith. Accordingly, he does not perceive the extent and importance of the new trading empire. Jakob Fugger financed Charles V's election; Anton Fugger possessed important licenses in the Spanish colonies; later, Charles' activities were financed by German, Flemish and Italian (specifically Genoese) merchants.[6] Ortiz recognizes the problems with Spanish state finances (Philip had been king since 1556 and was at war with France); however, he does not present them in their international context.

At the time Ortiz is writing, the Jesuits are already powerful (Loyola died in 1556) and the Council of Trent is meeting, but the great epoch of Spanish literature and art has only just begun (El Greco was born in 1541, Cervantes in 1547). At the same time, *Lazarillo de Tormes*, the Spanish picaresque novel, quite appropriate to Ortiz, was published in 1554: it is the story of an orphan boy who first serves a blind beggar, then a stingy clergyman, a poor nobleman, a cunning dealer in indulgences and others; he learns to go hungry, to beg, to pray and dissemble, to swindle and to be a rogue (Rausse n.d.).

It is hardly doing justice to Azpilcueta and Ortiz, if attention is drawn only to the advance of theory each achieved, like the use of quantity theory by the former and the recommendation of import substitution by the latter. They teach us to better understand the values of their time and because of that they are themselves historical sources as much as the information found in their texts. They seek new compromises in the tension between the economic development of opposing traditions and the requirements of economic self-assertion. The emergence of an early-capitalist type of entrepreneur on the world market and the international cooperation of financiers was naturally for the most part unknown to them; the latent opportunities for development were, as a rule, first clear in hindsight. Nonetheless, we can and should attempt to seriously address the patterns of thought appearing in the texts and to demonstrate their cultural importance. Then usury is not, even for the church – specifically in its own businesses – an ancient relic, for which it can find reasons to excuse. It is, instead, the phenomenon upon which the attempt to connect the economy with charity tragically fails. Reciprocity is broken for the benefit of the selfish pursuit of profit, which turns out to be the actual problem, and the economic terms developed by the ancient writers prove to be suitable for understanding a world which appears to push usury to the side as a recurring exception, as a never entirely-avoidable mortal sin of humans (Clavero 1996).

The economic historical facts comprising the background for the works explored here are known in general, but the details and their explanation remain a source of controversy. Hamilton (1971), the pioneer of research on the Price Revolution in Spain, argues that inflation in the sixteenth century was more conspicuous in Spain than elsewhere in Europe and that, within Spain, it stood out particularly early and conspicuously in Andalusia. Gold and silver poured into the port at Sevilla, Spain (which could be reached by ship at high tide, although it was located 80 km inland), first from the West Indies, then from Mexico, finally from Columbia and Peru. The crown monitored the transport of this gold and silver and thus safeguarded its share. Throughout the sixteenth century, the amounts imported increased, as Figure 3.1 shows.

A very steep increase in the import of precious metals is noticeable until 1600; afterward there is a decline in these imports and in trade as a whole. Hamilton now constructs a price index, based on the purchasing prices of the administration for equipping the fleet. With this index, he established that price levels almost quintupled between 1510 and 1600, and the price level increase and the precious metals import curves coincided with the trend; the later fall in prices, however, did not correspond with the decline in imports.

Hamilton (1971, p. 179), thus, emphasizes that prices increased faster in Andalusia than elsewhere in Europe, but a glance at a depiction of the change in prices in Europe in general shows that it was a continental phenomenon. On Figure 3.2 and 3.3 the price changes are entered in logarithmic scale, from

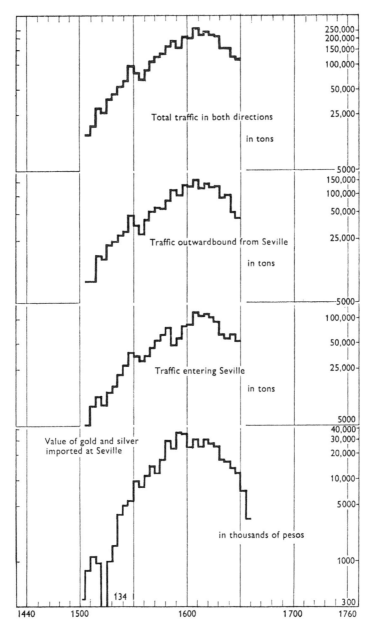

250,000
200,000
150,000
100,000

50,000

25,000

Total traffic in both directions

in tons

5000
150,000
100,000

50,000

25,000

Traffic outwardbound from Seville

in tons

5000
100,000

50,000

25,000

Traffic entering Seville

in tons

5000
40,000
30,000
20,000

10,000

5000

Value of gold and silver
imported at Seville

in thousands of pesos

1000

134

300
1440    1500              1600              1700   1760

*Figure 3.1* Trade with America in the Port of Sevilla (according to H. and P. Chaunu);
gold and silver imports (according to E. J. Hamilton)
Note: each darkened area shows the range of the maximum and minimum prices observed here.
Source: taken from the essay by Braudel and Spooner (1967, p. 485).

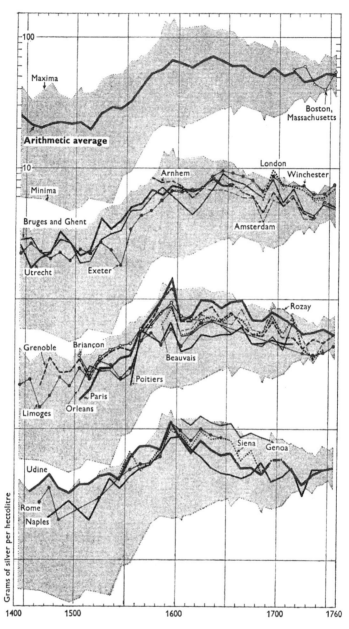

*Figure 3.2* The price of wheat in grams silver per hectolitre of wheat; 10-year average
Note: each darkened area shows the range of the maximum and minimum prices observed here.
Source: ibid. [Figure 3.1], pp. 470–71.

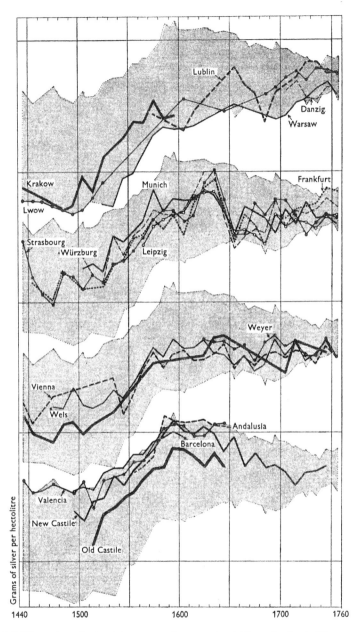

*Figure 3.3* The price of wheat in grams silver per hectolitre of wheat; 10-year average
Note: each darkened area shows the range of the maximum and minimum prices observed here.
Source: ibid. [Figure 3.1], pp. 470–71.

1400 to 1760, for a European average and then successively for cities in England, the Netherlands, France, Italy, Poland and the Baltic States, Germany, Austria and, finally, of interest to us here, Spain. The darkened area indicates the extremes of the average prices observed.

All over Europe in the seventeenth century, there is a conspicuous upward trend in prices. The gradual integration into a European grain market can be seen in the narrowing of the darkened area (it is also, in part, a result of the logarithmic scale). Local famines could therefore be avoided from the eighteenth century onward (Braudel and Spooner 1967, p. 396). Some extremes are related to politics, thus the increase in the price of bread during the siege of Paris in the 1590s. It is clear now that the price increase in Spain in the seventeenth century actually did move at higher levels, with an especially steep price increase in Andalusia, and only Old Castile, rich in grains, shows a movement closer to that of the European average.

The quantity theory explanation of inflation must at least be modified by a range of factors. Production costs for American silver were less than those of European and fell due to advances in mining technology. The volume of transactions increased with economic growth – which can hardly be quantified for the period under examination – and circulation rates changed because bills of exchange and government bonds served as monetary substitutes (Villar 1984, pp. 64ff.). The clearing of bills could not make the transport of precious metal unnecessary, but it could substantially reduce it. There was an attempt to halt the flow of gold and silver out of Spain through prohibitions (before 1551 and after the peace with France in 1559) (ibid., p. 138), but much escaped through smuggling, as our authors note; the Spanish crown had often already mortgaged its share of the precious metal import before it arrived – this then went immediately across the borders (ibid., p. 135) – and export permits were also granted ('licencias de saca', ibid., p. 139).

Domestic price increases did not necessarily have to outrun foreign ones; not only did prices increase, but there were also influences on economic activity, which were reflected particularly in a structural shift: skilled production either moved or in any case grew at a slower rate than was the case for important trading partners (especially France). The wealth of the conquistadores is still visible in the old Spanish cities; merchants also became rich; the lower ranks of the nobility and the skilled labourer classes, on the other hand, became impoverished. In Europe at this time, real wages appears to have tended to fall (Azpilcueta Navarro 1978, pp. 38–43).

In general, the importance of American precious metals should not, in pure quantitative terms, be overestimated. In an attempt to work out this figure, the entire amount of American precious metal, brought over by Spain between 1500 and 1650, in both gold and silver, amounted to about half of the assets already on-hand in Europe around 1500 (ibid., pp. 49–51). And the Castilian crown did not become as rich as might be expected: the entire annual income in the first half of the sixteenth century, estimated in silver, was a good ten times lower than that of France (we are not speaking here of

Charles V's entire realm, whose resources, added together, were well beyond those of France) (ibid., p. 37).[7]

Our brief historical overview shows how difficult it is to know the historical background of texts such as those from Azpilcueta and Ortiz which are so distant from the standards of the mid-European modernity. I am compelled here to work at the limits of my competence.

After his studies in philosophy, theology and law, Martín de Azpilcueta (1492–1586) first taught in French Toulouse. As a result of the popularity of his public lectures, he was offered a position in Paris, and then, as of 1524, at the University of Salamanca. In 1528, he gave a carefully worded public lecture, in the presence of Emperor Charles V, in which he insisted on the sovereignty of the people, based on natural law.[8] In 1538, he was sent to the University of Coimbra in Portugal; in 1548, he gave yet another famous lecture, about peace and the relationship between non-believers and Christians. He returned home to Spain in 1555 and was later active in the Court of Philip II. He was active in Rome in 1567 as an advisor to Popes Pius V, Gregory XII and Sixtus V and was a universal spirit, consulted by courts in Paris, Madrid and Lisbon; his warning to moderate nationalism earned him a charge of anti-Spanish, pro-French convictions. In his self-defense, he showed himself devoted to his homeland in Navarra, 'under the peaks of the Pyranees, where the Celtic Basques separate from the Celtic Iberians' (Azpilcueta Navarro 1965, p. XLI). Considered in the context of his century, Azpilcueta was tolerant and could show a great deal of worldly experience, from his travels and his international activities, which connected with a genuine interest in economic events, as was already evident in his instruction in Toulouse.

We now turn to the text.[9] A citation from *De usuris* by Gregory IX provides an introduction: 'Naviganti, vel eunti ad nundinas certam mutuans pecuniae quantitatem, eo quod suscepit in se periculum, recepturus aliquid ultra sortem, usurarius est censendus.' I translate: 'Whoever lends a shipper or a traveller to a fair a certain amount of money, so long that he has taken over the risk: if he receives more than the sum lent, then he is to be judged as a usurer.'

The scholars of an earlier time would have attributed: '... recepturus ... quod suscepit ...', the meaning of which could be summarized as follows: '*Whoever receives interest, because he insures* [10], *commits usury.*'

In contrast, scholars more recently (and thus even Azpilcueta himself in Salamanca in 1530) would have attributed: '... mutuans ... quod ...', which we could summarize as follows: '*Whoever lends, because he insures and receives interest, commits usury.*'

This second interpretation Azpilcueta now thought, absurd for the entire Christian world knows that insurance costs something (§ 1). He has additional arguments against this new interpretation; from the very beginning, it is grammatically wrong – if it were right, then it would have had to be '... ut susciperet ...' (§ 2). According to the second interpretation, it deals with a loan in which the lender assumes the risk for the loss of capital during a journey.

Azpilcueta, therefore, advocates a return to the first interpretation which he, however, changes in what is now seen as a deciding minor point; he emphasizes that it is not written 'usurarius est' but 'usurarius est censendus', which results in the following interpretation: '*Whoever receives interest, because he insures, is to be regarded as a usurer.*' Only God can truly know[11] whether the lender has a claim to the extra charge to cover the costs of a real risk or if the discussion of insurance is a pretext to be able to justify charging interest on a loan in what is actually a safe enterprise. In order to respond to the danger that every loan will include an interest charge under the pretext of a risk, Gregory recommended that the church, even in cases of loans to shippers, start from the premise that usury is intended. Civil law ('derecho civil'), on the other hand, views the requirement for an extra charge upon the repayment of a sea loan, due to such risks as shipwreck or piracy, as permissible (§ 3).

The critical consequence for the church results during confession ('si el penitente confiessa', § 6). Before confession, a sea or transport loan with an agreed-upon charge added to the repayment is suspected of being usurious. When in confession it is explained that the surcharge only covers insurance costs at the usual rates,[12] there is nothing to object to. If the charge was higher, however, the confessor must advise the penitent to pay back the portion of the charge that goes beyond what is permissable. This requirement arises from canonical law; Azpilcueta, whose text had its origin in an appendix in a book aimed at confessors, does not explore this issue from the perspective of civil law.

Azpilcueta admits that Gregory IX's statement 'goes too far' ('este texto es exorbitante', § 6), because he suspects guilt where perhaps there is none. It is therefore to be qualified rather than extended. It is not to be applied to guarantors or insurers in the usual sense (without lending). However, it turns out that the ecclesiastical prohibition must be directed not only against loans to the needy ('a los necessitados que lo toman para se mantener') but also to the rich (§ 7).

After an initial glance at the forms of bills of exchange, which we can omit here, Azpilcueta develops his monetary theory, at first in Aristotelian direction differentiating between barter and monetary exchange. In exchanges, money serves as a means of purchasing (price) and as a measure; however, we can also observe the exchange of money for money, partially because of its denomination, partially because of the various values in different countries, which gives rise to an art of dealing in moneys ('arte de tratar en dineros', § 11).

Many have earned a lot by mixing coins in barrels with olives or in casks with the wine and bringing furtively them to Flanders or France, where they were worth much more, and returning with goods ('que valian alla poco y aca mucho' § 11). He considers such money dealings on the one hand unnatural because, referring to Aristotle, there appears to be no other goal than profit ('que es un fin sin fin' § 11).

On the other hand, according to Thomas Aquinas, a moderate profit is permissible, if the merchant lives on this and the money market is also not unnatural. The ability of money to purchase other money is a derivative function, like the sale of shoes is a function derived from shoes, whose primary function consists in protecting feet. Here he touches on the root Aristotelian differentiation between natural and unnatural accumulation of wealth (Schefold 1994a, p. 134). Wealth can even be demonstrated with money – it can be sewn on clothes as jewellery, for personal pleasure and, above all, used to purchase products. The same value, corresponding to the debt, not the same coins, is to be given back. Thus, Azpilcueta provides money more space for permissible use than Aristotle does; it will all the more become more difficult for him to exclude usury.

Böhm-Bawerk would have objected that the lender of money never regained what he gave away because relative prices change, so that he understood the loaning of money as an intertemporal exchange in which the sum to be paid back, including interest, was determined by some arbitrary standard – usually as a nominal sum. Azpilcueta allows the exchange of money as long as it is a question of equivalents. He also has nothing against the exchange of money on-hand for the promise of a payment, because a surcharge can be included for spatial distance. With regard to the prohibition against usury, however, there can be no interest charge for the passage of time ('por razon de tiempo, y por esperar', § 14).

Thus the permissibility of the profession of exchanging currencies is tainted with doubt. Reasons why it might be allowed include the paying of wages for a work effort (for example for the exchange of foreign currencies), the requirement to serve the need of the state to borrow, as well as lost profit: whoever lent money can no longer trade with it; he must therefore really interrupt his money dealings when the loan takes place.[13] Public support of the pawnshops (the 'montes pietatis') served the poor: interest as a wage payment for surveillance by the pawnbroker is allowable but not as a compensation for time elapsed. An analogy should make this way of thinking understandable: judges, priests, and witnesses receive nothing for their fair verdicts, for the sacraments, or for their statements but are paid for their efforts. If, on the contrary, they were paid for the case, that would amount to taking bribes. Like law, time is not negotiable. What follows is a fascinating explanation with opposing arguments and a resolution: exchange as the loaning of money may be permissible before God, without government authorization, but it must be monitored, due to the danger of abuse as usury – in the sense of the introductory citation from Gregory IX; thus, it is advisable to place the exchange of money under governmental supervision (§ 18), while the exchange involving money in a narrower sense (exchanges of various currencies) remains permissible if the profit is moderate and it is done fairly (§ 20).

The letter of exchange, through which money – not actual money, however – is transferred from one country to another, is also generally considered allowable: 'es un traspasso virtual de dinero, por el qual quien quiere para otra tierra, dalo en esta' (§ 21).[14]

This money transfer service must be paid for fairly, according to the distance and risk (§ 28), but it provides many possibilities for the concealment of interest payments.[15] When a nobleman in Spain, in return for money, draws on a bill of exchange from Venice, where he has absolutely no credit, and this bill is then sent back to Spain, where the money changer presents it to the nobleman who pays it, it is a case of usury because the nobleman will pay more than he initially received; as far as that goes, the money changer gave the nobleman a usurious loan, if both knew from the outset that the bill of exchange would be returned (the nobleman swindled, we would say in any case, if he pretended to have credit). If business is carried out in such a way that it can get around the prohibition on usury, Azpilcueta even speaks of double-usury, because the money changer first left the money with the nobleman and actually the money changer owes a surcharge to the nobleman for the effort it took to safeguard the money, according to Azpilcueta's interpretation (§ 25). If, in contrast, the money is really physically transferred, then the charging of transport costs is without question permissible ('cambio por traspasso real', § 31), as long as the state does not forbid the transport of precious metals and equivalents are exchanged. In summary: surcharges are allowed for exchanges taking place over distances but not for those taking place over time. Due to the similarity of the effect, it is difficult to differentiate between the two; a smaller sum now and available in this place is offset by a larger amount of money, which is supposed to be paid later and in another place. The higher costs of spatial transfers in the sixteenth century were suited to concealing charges for temporal transfers.

The principles now known are repeated in 'cambio por interese' (§ 34): income lost by a money changer through lending may be compensated for with a surcharge, if the money changer actually reduced business during the period of the loan. Azpilcueta interpreted bank deposits ('cambio por guarda', § 36) solely as the transfer of money for safekeeping so that the depositor owed a fee rather than the bank (the money changer), for instance, owing interest! Both sides are in the wrong, if the bank does not charge for the safekeeping, because it wants to invest the money, for then the bank is committing usury and the depositor embezzles the fee (§ 40).

The following excerpts have theoretical importance for international money exchanges: 'la dificultad está en declarar, como se puede ganar por comutación de dinero, dando su justo valor'[16] (§ 43). How can the value of coins deviate from their face value? External reasons could be decisive, such as different metal alloys, assay value, the quality of the minting, and weight differences; furthermore, they could circulate in other countries, be subject to depreciation, there is a comparison between coins from different times, coin shortages, and that one kind of money might realistically be available while another is not. In Azpilcueta's examination of these eight reasons, the problem of the limiting of usury re-emerges. The value of money can change over time, depending on how much is available ('abundancia', § 46), but when none of the eight reasons comes into play then money retains its value and surcharges are not allowable (§ 47). On the other hand, someone who lends a hundred in gold has the right – if this gold receives a revaluation upward relative to silver and the lender is to be paid back in silver – to a premium (§ 48), thus to more than a hundred.

Considering the disputes among historians of economic doctrines about who should be designated as the author of the first written record of the quantity theory, it might come as a surprise to read how Azpilcueta presents its origin:

> dezimos … que haze subir, o baxar el dinero, que es de aver gran falta y necessidad o copia del, vale mas donde o quando ay gran falta del, que donde ay anbundancia, como lo tiene Calderino, Laurencio Rodolpho, y Sylvestro, con quien Caietano y Soto conquerdan. […] este es el comun concepto de quasi todos los buenos y malos de toda la Christiandad, y por esso parece boz de Dios y de la naturaleza.
>
> (§ 51)[17]

The basis of quantity theory appears here to be natural law, because the good and the evil have the same opinion. It is not new, but instead a commonplace known to the whole of Christendom. Azpilcueta then determines that all goods become more expensive, when there are fewer of them and there is more money and that with a surplus of money labour costs increase as well. A remarkable Latin citation, according to which money apparently has the same purchasing power everywhere, while it is available in one place for lesser in another place for greater usury ('aliis locis facilius … usuris inveniuntur, aliis … gravioribus…', § 52), does not lead him to the consideration that interest on money could also be dependent on its amount, but instead to the terminological problem of how money could have different prices in the first place. These differing prices are not to be understood as Platonic ideas, which multiply indefinitely; instead, under closer regulation of conditions, it is determined that one Ducat, at a particular time and place is worth so much, and in another time and place is worth such and such a price. And money is not necessarily only the price of a product; a use derived from money could also consist in the fact that it becomes a product itself during money exchanges (§ 55).[18] He opposes imaginary fiat money, which was often used in the late Middle Ages, because it leads to unfair loans and provides the occasion for borrowing (§ 56), and seeks to explain abstractly what it means when a market assessment of certain coins deviates from the legally-determined exchange rates (§ 58). He expresses the pious hope that the value of money will not increase due to unacceptable, usurious demand – when it increases at the fairs, it could be legitimate, because a higher demand for turnover exists there (§ 59).

What follows are clearly expressed and impressive considerations for showing that the international exchange rate is principally determined by purchasing power (§ 61). Since money changing is often transacted by means of a letter of credit, another principle, discussed earlier, also has to be considered:

the transport of money must be paid for and, necessarily, future money is worth less than present money (§ 62). The reasons for rate differences could cumulate or compensate. Azpilcueta now attempts to penetrate the increased complexity of transactions in order to differentiate between legitimate and usurious ones. He concludes (§ 80) by repeating the observation that a payment moratorium in return for interest should be considered usurious, because he had only permitted such interest charges in cases where the lender (money changer) interrupted his business (§ 34).

Without a doubt, this is an astute and original economic analysis, even if it is not carried out for purposes which motivate modern economists. However, as now concerns the question of primacy in quantity theory, the following formulation from Nicholas Copernicus from 1526 appears to me not only substantially older but also much more concise:

> Iusta autem et equa monet(a)e (a)estimatio est, quando paulo minus auri vel argenti continet qauam pro ipsa ematur, utpote quantum pro expensis dumtaxat monetariorum oportuerit deduci ... Vilescit h(a)ec ut plurimum propter nimiam multitudinem, utpote si tanta argenti copia in monetam transierit, quoadusque argenti massa ab hominibus magis quam moneta desideretur. Periit nempe hoc modo dignitas monet(a)e, quando per ipsam tantum argenti non licet emere quantum ipsa pecunia continet senciaturque profectus eliquando argentum in monet(a)e destructionem. Cuius remedium est non amplius monetam cudere donec se ipsam co(a) eqaverit reddaturque c[h]arior argento.
>
> (Copernicus 1978, pp. 48ff.)

My translation should suffice as commentary:

> The appraisal value of a coin is fair and appropriate when it contains a little less gold or silver than what can be purchased with it: it will only have been necessary for the minter to deduct something for the costs ... It usually depreciates as a result of the too large amount, when specifically a large amount of silver is turned into money, such that silver as a material is more in demand than the coins. Thus, however, the coins have lost their worth; if the amount of silver that can be purchased is less than that contained in the coin itself and an advantage is perceived in the melting down of the silver to destroy the coins. The remedy for this consists in not minting any more coins until their value is equal to the denomination, and they are once again more expensive than silver.

The money supply theory explanation for inflation is different from the late Middle Age explanation, which started from coin depreciation resulting from coin debasement (Oresme 1995)[19]; this in turn points to a determination of the value of money via the production costs of the precious metals. If these viewpoints are combined, there is a reversal of causality.

Let us also observe, like Azpilcueta, two countries and set up the Fisher Quantity Equation for them:

$$M_i V_i = P_i T; \; i = 1, 2$$

The resulting equation, based on quantity theory and assuming a constant rate of velocity of circulation and transaction volume, is Azpilcueta's Purchasing Power Parity theory of exchange rates:

$$\frac{P_1}{P_2} = \frac{T_2 M_1 V_1}{T_1 M_2 V_2} = C \frac{M_1}{M_2}; \; i = 1, 2. \; c \; const.$$

where the exchange rate of coins is based on the price of goods.[20] $M_1$ and $M_2$ are the amounts of silver in circulation. Now, there can be varying profits on printing (influenced by the government) in each country, which influences the exchange rate of the coins. The velocity of circulation may change in the conditions specified by Azpilcueta, as a result of the use of trade bills and other substitutes for money but possibly also due to the hoarding of silver. In the long term, the silver price itself is linked to production costs, and the silver exchange rate between the two countries depends on the transportation costs. It could be objected that the production costs themselves, as a result of the irregular productivity of different mines, represent a variable, but the discovery of American silver could also be interpreted as savings in production costs which led to the closing of European mines. If production costs are examined, the opposite conclusion can be drawn: a given price relationship with a given transaction volume and given velocity of circulation determines the money supply, which is endogenous, as in Marxian (Marx 1970, pp. 159–198) and in post-Keynesian approaches (Kaldor 1983, pp. 31–41).

Azpilcueta's fascinating and many-sided use of quantity theory, therefore, do not cover the entire range of exchange relationships which should be taken into consideration in the analysis of inflation problems. We will now see that Ortiz, as a founder of Mercantilism, assessed things differently: he thought that Spain was misappropriating the precious metals which were streaming in and strangling its own industry with imports, which made goods more expensive, just as today in a developing country the discovery and exploitation of oil resources can lead to an inflationary, fictitious prosperity, though an inflation-free growth of home production and income can be achieved with better economic policies and entrepreneurial activities.

Ortiz (Instituto de España 1970)[21] was a high-ranking Spanish government official, who was active in the military as well as the navy, as an advisor to the court and in various Spanish and north African cities. He wrote the *Memorial* in Burgos; the text, however, reveals a certain knowledge of other countries – and, in any case, a reference is made to a visit to Venice (ibid., MP 67).

We are essentially dependent upon the text itself, if we want to construct a portrait of Ortiz the man. He professes his catholic, monarchist and patriotic beliefs not only in the introductory and concluding chapters of his book, which are written with baroque pathos. Experiences are reflected in civil and military administration, knowledge of various Spanish provinces, including the northwest ones, and the reading of ancient writers who are cited as witnesses for Spain's natural wealth and the virtues of its Iberian inhabitants even before the Roman era. Ancient statesmanship and Christian faith were supposed unite in order to expand the Spanish hegemony, established by Charles V, to help the country achieve prosperity (ibid., MP 7v, 8).[22] The memoir is aimed at the 31-year-old King Philip II, who at that point had been ruling for two years. It requests that he first dedicate himself to his nation, before taking care of his more distant possessions.

On the first pages (as of MS 9), the main ideas are grouped together which mercantilistic and Cameralistic texts would repeat again and again into the nineteenth century: the balance of trade improves and there are income effects when raw materials are not exported, processed in foreign countries and then re-imported but are transformed into finished products in the country itself. Above all, human capital required for this – the handicrafts, for Ortiz – must be organized, educated and their political and social standing raised. As with later ones, this weighting of production stands in a certain opposition to the desire to reduce new fashions and luxuries, since the demand for luxury items will be met by foreign countries. His suggestion, prohibiting the import of processed materials and the export of raw materials for four years, in order to induce the changeover to a new economic structure through shock therapy, anticipates the suggestions of the Cameralist Hörnigk[23] in 1684, for example. This radical protectionism would later be moderately continued in the form of customs policies (MS 13). The middle-classes, upon which production rested, was supposed to grow; even the children of the upper classes and the knights should learn 'letras, artes o oficios mecánicos' (MS 10) – provincials and freight transporters were excluded. The mass of unproductive people disheartened him, and he includes students and writers as well as soldiers and immigrants in this group; if there were enough skilled labour jobs, the vagabonds and packs of thieves would disappear:

> Ya el dia de hoy es tan grande la holgura y perdición de España que caulquiera persona de calquiera estado o condición que sea no sabe otro oficio ni negocio sine ir a Salamanca o a la guerra de Italia o a las Indias o ser Escribano o Procurado y todo en daño de la república: lo otro que estando la gente toda ocupada en sus oficios, no habrá los ladrones, salteadores, vagabundos y perdidos que hay en el reino que con ir a Italia a las Indias la cantidad de gente que ha ido y de cada dia vá al presente ni caben en el reino ni en las cárceles...
>
> (MS 14)[24]

Ortiz risks a quantitative estimation of the gains which, having resulted, should be employed, partially to secure protection, partially for various tasks internally, in Italy, and in the colonies; at the same time, the prices of goods should sink because import costs would be avoided. On the side of state income, he wants to simplify the tax system; he wants to abolish the personal taxes for skilled labourers and farmers, who are to this extent to be equated with the nobility, and to balance or even increase the regular income of the state through indirect taxes and tax farming.

Following that are suggestions for the promotion of production in individual sectors, like hemp cultivation in standing waters – for the improvement of the watering system in general. Altered legal provisions also go with this; for example, land laying fallow should be allowed to be built on, even by those who do not own it. Water judges are to be elected. Women should use spinning wheels rather than spin by hand. And he deals with the printing of books in detail, where he is now also in favour of an import prohibition, on censorship grounds; on the other hand, he introduces a privilege allocation in order to ensure the publishers' rights on their books, with a time limitation however so that no monopoly comes into being. One could speak of a regulatory system for a young national industry.

With honey and wax, he also sees opportunities for import substitution: bee populations should not be decimated by the felling of trees with wild honey but instead beekeeping operations should be run; producers thus should, we could say, plan enterprise rationally.

Next, he suggests a plan for regional policy action to ensure the provision of grains in northwest Spain, which is important for fleet activities against the north and which is dependent upon French imports of grains. A state commercial agent should be charged with the necessary deliveries. Ortiz is thinking of a form of financing through new government bonds – which he here considers as good, for a change – with yearly repayments from the profits which the supplier makes and, thus, also yearly interest payments. A second financing scheme is added to this – after consultation with theologians – that on the surface hides the interest payment through dividing the profits between the crown and the supplier, though in carrying it out concretely, it appears somewhat similar to the first (MS 25v–26v, 28–28v). It is a government scientific project, constructed according to existing models. This project appears especially important to Ortiz for strategic reasons, due to the war with France and in order to remedy an economic nuisance: the province is currently subsidized with payments which are leading to an outflow of precious metals due to imports from France.

To greatly simplify matters, Ortiz has the following scheme in mind: until now, Spain has ruled the colonies with its soldiers and received gold for that; with this gold it imports goods from France so that only a few productive occupations remain in the country. A productive Spain must, on the contrary, export its goods to neighbour countries as well as to its colonies in the future.

Ortiz also blamed bureaucracy – or the business sidelines of administrators – for the price increases, though on the other hand he can only have meant that a more efficient organization of production would result in a reduction of costs. The intermediary trade, too, he believes is driving prices up; his solution consists once again, first of all, in prohibitions and governmental initiatives, but he also has competitive elements in view when perhaps through trade restrictions the farmers receive an incentive to keep more of their own cattle, 'con lo cual muchos se darán a criar ganados y no puede ser menos si no que han de bajar de los precios en que están' (MS 33),[25] whereby the price of meat would have to go down.

In his plans for the rationalization of trade, he keeps in mind that people should be led from unproductive to productive activities.[26] He provides numerous other suggestions for industrial improvements; thus, he suggests equipping canals with lock chambers.

Three decades before the Spanish Armada sailed for England, Ortiz called for an arming for the sea, especially to secure the Mediterranean from the Turkish, and in doing so attempts to show that he knows the material by going into great detail in his suggestions. He considers additional improvements to the tax system. It would be good if kings had access to great wealth, because they would not then be tempted to confiscate church property – he is thinking of Henry VIII of England – or to raise taxes. And the tax yield would most likely increase through the policy stressing industrialization and import substitution:

> està claramente conocido que con estar todo la república ocupada en sus tratos y oficios y con crecer el valor de lo que sale del Reino en tanta cantidad y los tratos dél siendo labrado [,] lo que saliere no puede ser menos sino que [–] sino daño de la común [–], antes en gran aumento suyo, crecerá el encabezamiento … al doble…
>
> (MS 47v)[27]

In addition, a rationalization of the sale of offices goes with this, a standardization of measure, and the introduction of industry inspections.

Ortiz wants to hand over the brassage to the king, in any case for the minting of token coins; he recommends concentrating the salt trade in the hands of the crown, but he warns against the draconian operation of a salt monopoly. He reveals himself astonishingly conservative with regard to bills of transaction which he suspected wholesale of usury – there is no sign of Azpilcueta's fine differentiation in this man of action and simple convictions. So far as they are not punished according to law, the rights of bill brokers as citizens should be limited.

Finally, he promotes, following the Venetian example, erecting communal storehouses in the communities; they would operate a countercyclical grain business, paid for by the state, in order to cushion price fluctuations. The discussion of whether the state should be involved here or whether the storage of grain to carry over during years of bad harvests should be left to private speculators was a lively one well into the eighteenth century; those in favour of government assistance, at various times, in this particular case include such different authors as Boisguilbert, Galiani, Steuart and Bentham (Hutchison 1988, pp. 113ff.).

Ortiz has become a classic only in recent years, later than Azpilcueta, because even historians of economic doctrines like Schumpeter had no precise notion of the beginnings of Spanish economic theory. The research is continuing, and it might be that some important texts, among the tens of thousands which were written during the Mercantilist period, will come to light. On the whole, they seem to confirm that just these manuscripts are marked by characteristics of the epoch and the nation. In any case, Azpilcueta and Ortiz represent two sides of Spanish economic thought in the early modern period with the dark lustre of religious strictness and the demands dictated by the culture which surrounded them.

### Antonio Serra: the founder of economic theory?

The works of Scaruffi and Davanzati represent the dawn of a science whose first traces supposedly appeared in Naples. Here a new philosophy had arisen whose removal from the wider cultural world served only to highlight its originality. This was the birthplace of Bruno, Campanella, Vico, Genovesi, and also of Antonio Serra, who became the originator of economic thinking. He was born in Cosenza and was imprisoned in a dungeon for many years. He endured the torments of his prison with a steadfastness redolent of Antiquity, observing the suffering of his fatherland, and seeking a remedy for such suffering. In this way he came to understand the general and common causes of the greatness and wealth of states. He sought the origins of wealth in the states of his time: of Genoa, Florence and Venice. He formed his own doctrine from their history and then set it down in a book. However, this book remained almost unknown to his contemporaries and was later forgotten. When it was later rediscovered others either showed no interest, or else sought to deny him the credit for being the original founder of this science. This relates not to Say, who at least partially acknowledges Serra's merit, but to McCulloch. His history of political economy gives precedence to British writers, and assumes from the title of Serra's book that it dealt only with coinage, hence diminishing the consolation Italy might find in the fame of its great men. Galiani judged Serra aright. But Serra's work has to be read for itself if its rich context is to be properly appreciated (Pecchio 1971 [1840], pp. 414–15).

This is the representative judgment of an Italian regarding Serra in the period before national unification, a judgement which was then adopted by the Frenchman, Auguste Blanqui. Serra's *A Short Treatise on the Causes which Cause Realms to Abound in Gold and Silver where there are No Mines* was also for Friedrich List (1909, p. III.XXVIII.7) 'the earliest work written especially about Political Economy in Italy'. While Serra had mines as sources of precious metals highest come first, he treated agriculture, manufacturing, trade and shipping as the main sources of national wealth. He placed particular emphasis on manufacturing as the basis for extensive trade relations, on industry, and on the importance of secure legislation for economic development. List considered Serra's treatment of politics better than that of those classical writers who dismissed him. Serra recognized civil liberty to be the ultimate precondition for prosperity.

Serra's text was indeed revolutionary. Not only his temporal precedence over the early texts of English mercantilism has to be acknowledged, but also his qualitative superiority must be conceded. It is only during the epoch of Locke and Petty that writers emerge whose analyses are definitely more far-reaching.[28]

Eugen Dühring, not usually well-disposed toward mercantilism, wrote: 'We could look upon Serra's book and its very characteristic title as a kind of inscription over the entrance to the more recent prehistory of economics.' Serra did not challenge the mercantile system; however, his book did not contain mere idle prattle.

> On the contrary, it is possible to study right here in these short texts how all main branches of economic activity are subordinated to the ruling idea of obtaining metal and are viewed only in relation to this object. Of course, it can also be seen that the crude imputations made recently by writers belonging to the mercantilist camp are the kind of nonsense that even children can see through, and in making such imputations such writers have entirely marginalized themselves wherever education and common sense prevailed.
>
> (Dühring 1900, p. 32, my transl.)

With regard to Italy in the first half of the nineteenth century, Romani (1993, p. 202) writes: 'Except for Francesco Ferrara, all the writers of the age believed that the first real economist had been an Italian – Antonio Serra – while there was no doubt that several eighteenth-century Italians had been among the best economists of all time.'

Modern histories of economic thought devote for example significantly more space to Mun than to Serra, if the latter is mentioned at all.[29] Arthur Eli Monroe's (1945) *Early Economic Thought*, containing excerpts from Serra's work in English translation, naturally creates an entirely different impression. The book examines 16 authors from Aristotle and Xenophon to Turgot and Justi. Between Bodin and Cantillon, four authors of the mercantile period are placed together: Serra, Mun, Petty and Hörnigk.

Schumpeter's assessment is deserving of special attention also in the case of Serra. He acknowledges the analytical character of the work, even if it represents only a 'quasi-system', and not a finished system. Decades before others, Serra had understood how the abundance of goods depended upon a number of other factors such as natural resources and the development of industry and trade – so that if the economic process functioned properly, then the monetary system would look after itself (Schumpeter 1972, pp. 195, 354). Schumpeter attributes the discovery of the law of increasing returns in manufacturing to

Serra (ibid., p. 258), and praises Serra's analysis of the reasons for Naples' adverse balance of trade, with its emphasis on invisibles in the balance of payments.

Of course, in one important respect historians of economics are correct in neglecting Serra and favouring others: Serra made so little impact on his contemporaries that hardly any references to his works have survived. He and his works were quickly forgotten until their praise by Galiani brought them back to public attention, and Custodi made them available by giving them a prominent place in his collection of Italian classics of political economy. The original edition of *Breve Trattato* is extraordinarily rare. Since so few examples have been preserved, the influence that Serra's ideas exerted when they were still relatively new can never have been great. He was rediscovered long after the development of theory had moved on. A work, however, is not a classic simply because of its own intrinsic value, but also as a result of the influence it had, and the theoretical trends and schools that derived from it.

And so the work was lost, and we know nothing of the author. The interpretation of the text is greatly hampered by historical distance, a difficult language (Serra loves long sentences), a complex historical background and a terminology which is not entirely precise. As a prisoner, Serra hoped to gain the attention of the viceroy. He used words of praise, refrained from open critical expression and withheld all concrete suggestions, hoping that after his release he might be allowed to present them in person. Thus we do not really know the specific details of the economic policy he suggested – or even how far he knew what he really wanted.

Anyone whose idea of the early modern era is linked to the clear proportions of Renaissance architecture could well be shocked by the wild, gloomy or intimidating forms used in Italian Baroque ait. Bold new speculations collide with old beliefs, the best astronomers are also astrologers, science relies on empiricism yet designs speculative systems. In 1613, the date given to Serra's *Trattato*, Galilei also published his book on sunspots. In 1616 Campanella published his *Apologia di Galileo* (Campanella 1968). Nineteenth-century scholars thought they could identify Serra as a participant in Campanella's revolutionary activities. We do not know whether Serra was prosecuted for a political offence or if he was charged with a crime – counterfeiting has been suggested. What is certain, however, is that we must think of Serra as exposed to the external turmoil and the spiritual passions of the era in which he lived. In his lifetime Giordano Bruno, for many years a Naples monk, was burnt at the stake on the *Campo dei Fiori* in Rome – in 1600, after seven years of imprisonment. Bruno lent poetic expression to the fervour with which he held to his philosophical beliefs:

> Cieco error, tempo avaro, ria fortuna
> sord'invidia, vil rabbia, inquo zelo
> crudo cor, empio ingegno, strano ardire
> non basteranno a farmi l'aria bruna,

non mi porranno avanti gli occhi il velo
non faran mai che il mio bel sol non mire.

Bruno's verses (Goetz 1953, p. 196)[30] speak of the passion with which a contemporary of the period in which the modern natural sciences were developing could hold on to a truth which was in part proven, and in part simply intuited. This was also true of Galilei. Serra was not on the same historical level as Bruno, and could not prove the most fundamental elements of his theses since he had no access to statistical material on payment flows. In the greater part of his work he generally creates the impression of serious argumentation in the style of a lawyer, supported with long years of experience as a merchant. But we can also see here a search for a mid-point between scepticism and dogmatism in his conception of truth. Hence he estimates not only Naples' trade balance and its money supply, but also its particular advantage. The construction of the book is calculated to foster the impression in the viceroy's court that he is the advisor they had been seeking, who can lead them out of their economic predicament.

Thus at stake is not only science but also conjecture, not only explanation but also a desperate attempt to stand out. In the foreword, in the introductory poems, in remarks scattered throughout the text, even in the ornamentation, the book develops rhetorical forms unknown to modern economic texts. It is only secondarily a question of how far the author uses them so as to conform to the spirit of the times, and how far he truly believes in them; such ambiguity is a particular characteristic of people from this era. On opening the book we must therefore ignore neither the coat of arms, nor the dedication, not even the poetical expressions accompanying it; we must pay attention to the author's demand to be heard, and to his expressions of loyalty, praise, and criticism.

La Maraviglia – the book begins with wonder and astonishment, employing a *topos* of the time which we can also find in Bruno. One wonders about great things purposefully, like our Lord, or out of ignorance. When ignorance is combined with evil, it produces wickedness; but to wonder is in itself good. Thanks to wonder the intellect can identify causes; it finds a way to truth through philosophy. Serra's pathetic expression of astonishment concerns not the supernatural, but something considered by the cultural elite until very recently as quite prosaic: an economic question, more exactly the contrast between different Italian states, some of which appear to be poor in precious metals while others appear to be rich in them, although there is a mine in only one of them.

So we do not now know whether this amazing example of epistemological theory is an expression of real astonishment and a real scientific desire to understand, addressing a profane object with almost religious fervour and which thus represents an epoch-making step toward secularization; or whether Serra merely wanted to employ a convenient figure of speech. In what follows we cannot determine just how much genuine respect he has for the viceroy. We read that he calls him a prince among philosophers and a philosopher among princes who has deservedly been charged by His Catholic Majesty with a most important duty, specifically to establish respect for the law, to let wealth prosper, and to keep the peace.

The poverty of Naples' position is expressed by a shortage of money, excessive debt and a high crime rate. Serra expresses the hope that this little book, offered to the viceroy from the dungeon of Vicaria by his most devoted servant, will be handed over in like manner to the poor widow contributing her mite.

Following that dedication, there are Latin couplets and an Italian sonnet in honour of Serra expressed appropriately enough in the words of a doctor, since the author seeks to compare his reform proposals with a medicinal cure. The conclusion of the Latin verse is quite beautiful: what wouldn't Serra be able to see – someone who even in prison can gather so much knowledge – if he lived in freedom rather than beneath the arches of a dungeon. The sonnet conjures up the use he could make of himself if he were freed from his chains.

In *Proemio*, Serra (1613, pp. 3–4) explains the character of the science to which he aspires. The art of governing – the knowledge of just governing – is as difficult as medicine: 'la scientia in se non hà mezzo certo di conoscere la verità, ne in quella si procede con demonstratione, ma solo con enthimemati, & argumenti topici…'.[31]

Serra, therefore, is not thinking of a deductive science based on a mathematical model, which like economic theory – tentatively since Petty, decisively since Ricardo, and also in the mathematical form since Cournot – begins which fixed but hypothetical assumptions in order to *prove*, but instead one which *convinces* through rhetorically logical forms ('enthimemati'),[32] and reference to general concepts ('loci communes', today degraded to 'commonplaces'[33]), based on plausible assumptions. Rhetoric does not here simply seek to persuade; it does not involve sophistry, let alone demagoguery; Serra instead confesses that he must rely upon intuitive arguments, just as the Historical School and Institutionalism would later, trends which have more than simply methodical features in common with the *Breve Trattato*. Serra also employs induction, known in rhetoric as the use of paradigms, especially in the comparison of various Italian states.

Serra does not want to write about policy or the art of governing in general (for that he refers to the ancient Greek philosophers); or about justice and injustice (for that he refers to the Roman legal tradition); he is instead concerned only with the cause of the shortage of money. Monetary wealth is important for public welfare, and especially for princes.

Serra places good government and the law above all else when talking of the dangers of strife and war, of biblical examples, and of the exemplary legal order provided by Justinian. Here he is certainly at least in part speaking for himself. For we should not only think here of Platonic and Aristotelian doctrine concerning the connection between law and the state, but also on the problem of arriving at a verdict within the framework of legal rights. To this effect, he quotes a verse from a sonnet by Petrarch (1966, p. 161, Sonnet LXIII):[34]

Or questo è quel che più ch'altro n'attrista;
che perfetti guidicii son sì rari
e d'altrui colpa altrui biasmo s'acquista.

If we may also apply this citation to Serra himself, then he is suggesting that the guilt of another has been attributed to him. He in any case expresses sadness over the weakness of human powers of judgment.

For Serra, a systematic scientific approach is not precluded by visual argument and the use of historical forms of explanation. On the contrary, one has the impression that for him at least a comprehensive differentiation between cases (which has led to accusations of dryness, boredom and casuistry) becomes the touchstone of his procedural logic. His book is a critique of a certain de Santis, who had suggested supervision and control of exchange rates. However, since this involves only one idea it cannot be a scientific approach – so says 'the philosopher' (Aristotle).

In the first part of his book Serra wants to discuss the general causes of a plentiful supply of money by comparing the Italian cities one with another; in the second part he criticizes de Santis' explanation; and in the third part he puts forward some suggested 'cures'. In all three parts we can see him striving for clearly-ordered thinking: in the first in respect of the factors of economic growth; in the second according to the modes of monetary transfer; and in the third according to the degree of radicality of proposals for economic reform.

Serra does not limit himself to an abstract explanation of the disadvantages of a scarcity of money. Perhaps he sensed that he lacked the theoretical concepts for that, while the resulting economic disadvantages and the need for action on the part of the government were obvious. The outflow of precious metals led to insufficient reserves for the circulation of token coins, paper money and deposit money, and bills became a substitute for money. In view of high private indebtedness among citizens, to which Serra alludes in his introduction, the danger of a financial crisis was also apparent. The government's solvency abroad was also in doubt, and it was repeatedly forced to take out foreign loans. Because Serra sees a connection with manifestations of crisis in the economy, it follows from this that he here also deals with public safety, which could be indirectly endangered by the outflow of precious metals.

On the following two pages Serra makes a differentiation for which he has, quite rightly, received the greatest praise: a differentiation between the comparative advantages accruing to a country from its natural resources, and those deriving from its political organization. These advantages, which Serra views as 'cause accidentali' in the Aristotelian tradition, consist in part of 'accidenti proprii', a country's own attendant circumstances. These might include the natural fertility of the land, such as those possessed by Naples in respect to the production of oil and wine, and the geographical location in regard to trade (for which Venice was favourably situated). A direct origin of an abundance of precious metals would be the existence of a gold or silver mine. Save one exception there are however no such mines in Italy, so Serra's discussion is limited to indirect causes of wealth.

Among these indirect causes are the 'accidenti communi', general causes which each state can in principle acquire. Serra lists first the amount of artificial products, the quantity of manufactured goods (in contrast to natural products resulting from the wealth of the land); then the qualities of the people (human capital, if you like); third wholesale trade; and fourth the foresight of those governing.

The advantage in the production of manufactured goods is independence of the weather. Above all, these goods can be reproduced limitlessly and even 'con minor proportione di spesa'. This brief phrase suggests the hypothesis of increasing returns, which are directly compared with decreasing agricultural returns with the help of a numerical example.

An additional advantage of manufactured products is that they are less perishable. The development of commerce not only facilitates transport between East and West (of the Mediterranean, we can assume) but also from one hemisphere to the other, in which case the imperishability of goods is a necessity.

'In questo solo li moderni han superato gl'antichi' – the only real advance with respect to Antiquity lay in the discovery of the New World. In the 'querelle des anciens et des modernes', Serra generally appears to be an advocate of the former. Ultimately more money can be made from manufactured products than from agricultural products. He does not attempt to explain this; he does not even define what he means by enhanced earnings – perhaps a rate of profit, calculated after subtracting the element of rent in agriculture? He recognizes, however, the potential variety of handicrafts and manufactured goods as a special feature of this 'second' sector, a variety which he contrasts with the quantitative surplus of agricultural products. The advantages in the production of luxury goods, deriving from the ease with which new markets can be opened both at home and abroad, is here touched on, but not made explicit.

The qualities of men and women consist in their activity, hard work and inventiveness; they are the basis for entrepreneurial initiative in foreign trade, in which Genoa excels but Naples lags behind. There is great clarity in Serra's presentation of this argument in terms of economic geographically, as with his application of these terms to the importance of wholesale trade as the third independent cause of wealth. Hence his theoretical considerations are not developed conceptually, but instead suggested by a succession of images.

But one can find scattered analytical insights:

> gioua la quantità dell'arteficij … il cui accidente causa concorso grand-
> issimo di gente, non solo à rispetto dell'arteficij, che in tal caso à quello si
> attribueria la causa, ma à rispetto del concorso di questi doi accidenti
> insieme, che l'vno somministra forza all'altro, che il concorso grande, che
> vi è à rispetto del trafico, & la ragione del sito cresce per la quantità

dell'arteficij, & la quantità dell'arteficij cresce per il concorso grande del trafico, che per il concorso predetto diuenta maggiore.

(Serra 1613, p. 18)[35]

Serra describes here a cumulative effect: the growth of the market (as a assembly of men and women) and the increase in the amount of goods for sale are mutually reinforcing. In Naples, whose marketplaces have no importance beyond the immediate region, the disadvantages of an unfavourable commercial location unfortunately also proves self-reinforcing.

If we turn finally to the treatment of government activity as a factor which should create comparative advantages for economic development, we find Serra to be far removed from a casual and optimistic attitude in respect of intervention. Different strata of the population react by no means uniformly to the same stimulus, making it difficult to govern by the use of incentives alone. Above all, the prince must not allow his own passions to divert him from his chosen path.

Sixtus V, who brought order to the papal states and whose legacy was the augmentation of the Treasury in the Castel Sant'Angelo, was considered by Serra to be the model for strong and effective policy. As modern historians report, Sixtus V ruled from 1585 until 1590 and not only reformed the state finances, confronted criminal excess, streamlined administration, and constructed useful buildings, but also refrained from commenting on theological questions. Ranke (1848, p. 17) however writes: 'In doing this, we cannot fail to remark the extraordinary fact, that the inexorable justice exercised by this pontiff, the rigid system of finance that he established, and the close exactitude of his domestic economy, were accompanied by the most inexplicable disposition to political plans of fantastic extravagance.' The Pope's political projects do not concern us here. There was an economic dimension to his cherished wish to conquer Egypt and re-establish the ancient canal system linking the Red Sea with the Mediterranean. Serra's evident preference for this Pope is an expression of the linking of two goals quite typical for him: a stable state and entrepreneurial economic policy.

Serra now turns to a thorough comparison of Naples and Venice. How is it possible that Naples, despite the high volume of its agricultural exports (Venice by contrast having to import foodstuffs), is in a much worse financial situation? Whoever brings silver (through bills of transaction, see below) from Venice to Naples gains 5 per cent. Naples therefore appears to be forced to pay a premium for the import of silver; the export of silver was prohibited. Why are Naples' tax revenues insufficient, and why is there no accumulation of monetary wealth, as in Venice? For Serra an important factor is Venice's old and tested government institutions, while in the Neapolitan monarchy a new king is experimenting with new laws – and this is all the more true of the viceroy. Whether Serra was favourable to the more democratic nature of the Republic of Venice is an open question. Whoever has learned from Schumpeter to recognize the instability of modern democracy resulting from the movement of voters from one political party to another will certainly be taken aback by Serra's explanation that the stability of Venice rests on the distribution of offices. What interests him is the question of how governmental wisdom and administrative experience can be transferred from one set of responsible officials to another, between overlapping generations as it were.

Serra's analysis of the balance of trade results in a surplus; the deficit in the balance of payments is caused by way in which aliens in the realm (among the aliens of which the Catholic majesty can also be included) transfer their income abroad. Serra regrets that this income is not reinvested or at least spent in the country, but for this the country offers too few opportunities. He also regrets that home-produced goods do not substitute for imports, but for this there is too little entrepreneurial activity.

It is not easy to follow the critical arguments with which Serra levels at de Santis to prove that the exchange rate cannot be treated as the cause of the scarcity of money, but that both must be related to underlying circumstances. Serra argues that if it were only a question of the exchange rate, the silver which left the country would finally have to flow back into it. The involvement of his argument is a consequence of the complexity of his differentiation of cases relating to the possible forms of transfer.

Exchange transactions, which are at stake here, begin with a so-called 'promissory note' which is used to move money to other countries. A promissory note is purchased by making a deposit with a local dealer ('campsor', 'banchiere'). By presenting the promissory note to a banker in a foreign city who has a business relationship with the dealer a trader is paid out in local currency to the value of the promissory note, whose original cost had included a surcharge for service and costs. Later, bills of trade were developed which merchants issued without the mediation of dealers, whereby Merchant A pays Merchant B for a delivery with a note which B can redeem with Merchant C, because A has credit with C. The final balance is secured by clearing. Comprehensive legislation regarding bills of exchange first came into being in the seventeenth century.[36]

For Serra, a higher exchange rate means that, disregarding the transaction costs related to discounts, commissions and transport, a bill costs a greater amount of silver in Naples than would be received, for example, in Venice. It might be thought (by de Santis) that an export surplus, for example in trade with Venice, would not lead to the import of silver into Naples, because the profits from exports that would be brought back would be worth more in silver in Naples than in Venice. Therefore a bill expressed made out in a specific weight of silver which was available in Venice would only be exchanged for a larger amount of silver in Naples (or, in view of the shortage of silver, for a substitute such as a deposit, which would represent this silver), instead of bringing the Venetian silver itself to Naples. The argument gets complicated because local coinage of varying alloy represents precious metals, silver circulating domestically in Naples whereas outside Naples gold was the principle monetary form.

Serra believed that one gained through accepting bills drawn on foreign silver, linking it to the idea of a balance of trade surplus. But all bills must finally be honoured through mutual clearing. To the modern reader is quite plain that an export surplus in Naples, in aggregate, must be balanced by a surplus of bills denominated in overseas precious metals which can only be redeemed by a transfer of bullion, so long as the remaining items in the current account are balanced. One would also anticipate that the exchange rate would alter in favour of Naples. If the transfer of bullion does not take place there must be a deficit somewhere else in the current account balance.

Serra does not seek to prove this by aggregation, but instead opts for the differentiation of cases. He considers what the exporter will do with his bill of exchange, according to whether he is a resident or a foreigner. If a resident, he will not always be happy to deal in bills, and if an export surplus exists he would in the end import silver; here an infinite regress is to be avoided, where residents ceaselessly trade these bills among themselves. However, the return flow does not happen, because – the second case – there are foreigners resident who transfer income abroad. That is the basic position; everything else is quite secondary and generated by the task of criticism.

For example: thirty years earlier there was a surplus of money; thus, the opposite argument is to be followed, 'essendoci l'esperienza maestra della cose, alla quale cede ogni potentissima ragione' (Serra 1613, p. 60).[37]

Even then the rate of exchange was not the cause of disequilibrium in one country, so that a low exchange rate did not bring about a monetary surplus; and in this case de Santis himself admitted this to be true: 'egli medesimo lo confessa, mentre assegna la causa di venirui denari in Regno alla robba, che si estrahe' (ibid., p. 61).[38]

Serra then turns to an examination of the change in the exchange rate, including the trade in coinage. In this way he raises the issue of the exchange of gold for silver, which leads him to differentiate between the use of a coin as money and as an object of trade: 'mai il scudo in Napoli è corso per moneta, ma per mercantia' (ibid., p. 72).[39]

Even in these comments Serra shows that within the framework of transactions involving bills of exchange there are opportunities to gain from the transfer of bullion to Naples. He then turns to the export of money by foreigners in Naples: even when this is done without the transfer of cash, sooner or later this result in a corresponding outflow of cash.

De Santis' economic policy is finally taken to absurdity. His aim of improving the situation by controlling the exchange rate, can certainly not be achieved because the existence of free trade in the rest of Italy would undermine Naples' protective measures. Economically, Naples is more dependent on the rest of Italy than the other way around (this is Serra's analysis of the situation). To be entirely consistent, de Santis should have called for a general prohibition on bills of exchange, since he believed the rest of Italy to be dependent upon Naples' agricultural exports: and for this the silver would have to be introduced.

None of these measures would however have been just or practical. It is true that the public interest does in principle prevail over the private. The government sometimes sets the maximum prices for food – as even in modern agricultural policy. But since de Santis' measures are based on false assumptions they have to be rejected; one needs to hold fast to freedom of contract, and especially the freedom of transactions in money and bills of exchange.

In his own era, which dreamed of great projects and left behind monumental buildings, Serra's 'cure' for overcoming Naples' economic emergency must have seemed timid. His 'cures' are discussed in the third part of the book. Even in medicine, knowing the causes of an illness does not mean one is able to cure them. Serra begins once again with a critique. The cures already attempted are: a prohibition on the export of money, and especially of bullion; a maximum price for the exchange of foreign currency; and permitting a revaluation of foreign money which is then supposed to circulate in the domestic market. It is also suggested that undervalued money be put in circulation.

The export prohibition is a disadvantage, because if imports are necessary they have to be paid for in cash, while if the money is invested abroad it will later flow back with profits. It is clear here that the Mercantilist tone of the book derives from the author's initial problematic. If Serra had really thought along Mercantilist lines, something that the title of his book has led many to argue, then at this point he would have treated import restrictions as a good thing. But he is against them. The damage that would follow from any attempt to introduce them would consist in a fall in the volume of trade. The Venetians limited only the outflow of foreign money so that foreign coins might be melted down and turned into Venetian coins. Of greater use would only have been to obstruct the transfer of income abroad by resident foreigners who lacked the opportunity to reinvest their profits domestically. But even this suggestion seems impractical, as Serra argues elsewhere.

The circulation of foreign coins involves among other things a danger that foreign princes will debase the coins for their own profit. Here Serra feels compelled to explain why even moderately inflationary state finances must be condemned: not because they would bring trade to a standstill, but from considerations of fairness, and because it would endanger foreign trade. There are no objections to the minting of small amounts of tokens of little value as small change; that happens all the time. The 'monete grosse' should however be a prime alloy. A city holds its own in the rivalry of nations through the minting of valuable, not worthless, coins.

Serra's discussion of inflation remains entirely limited to the horizon of Italian experiences. The secular inflation of the 'long' sixteenth century, brought about by the discovery of the New World, plays no role in his thinking. For this reason, and because he has no theory of value, the chapter in which he discusses the correct proportions of silver and gold, a matter of the value of precious metals, seems much weaker.

Since it would be neither practical nor fair to approach directly the causes he identifies for the scarcity of precious metals, by expropriating the income of alien residents or by prohibiting the export of this income, 'cures' other than those so far discussed must be found: 'leuando ... il defetto de gl'accidenti communi, con introdur in Regno gl'arteficij' (ibid., p. 132);[40] hence, in modern terms, through a process of industrialization, beginning with import substitution.

How is this to be brought about? If 'il padrone lo comanda' he will reveal it: 'con reforma grandissima, & beneficio vniuersale del Regno, & della Maestà Cattolica' (ibid., p. 133).[41]

Those factors of economic development open to change presented in the first chapter must be made subject to further alteration so as to compensate for unavoidable disadvantages, 'al quale non si può reparare direttamente: mà indirettamente' (ibid., p. 140).[42]

Ultimately it is a matter of skilful government, and with this ends what Serra calls his 'little work' ('operina') – the great work of reform itself remains to be done. The index which follows can in part be read as a collection of key points in alphabetical order.[43]

The idea that the comparative advantages brought about by economic policies are of greater importance for a nation than those naturally occurring is once more today especially relevant. Serra's thinking is located on a watershed between an older European tradition and modernity. He invokes the ancients not only so that he might comply with contemporary notions of style, but also to show that his political ideas are influenced by Plato and Aristotle. His dependence on tradition is even more apparent in his use of logic and casuistry. This gets him a long way – a fact which we might note – but he wishes to remain part of this transition, unlike Galilei, who seeks to supersede it.

This is in sharp contrast to his empiricism, and his belief in the possibility of moulding the economic order on the basis of a political order which defends freedom of contract, promotes private initiative and opens the way for industrial progress. Ancient and medieval economic ethics, as well as those of Humanism, are completely replaced by a new way of thinking, but which is expressed in the old verbal forms. Centuries would have to pass before an analytical language would be found adequate to this new thinking. Even later economists were not in a position to formulate this new language by themselves; instead, again and again they had to borrow from natural sciences which simplified their subject by experiment: first through the idea of mechanical causality, then through mathematical instruments, and today through the model of evolution.

Insofar as modern economics defines itself by its methods, Serra cannot be treated as its founder. His analysis of payments and commerce rises above previous accounts (e.g. Davanzati) only in virtuosity, and in his original treatment of the balance of payments. However, in the determination of those private and state interests which direct political-economic activities (and should so direct them), as well as in the understanding of those factors underlying the competitive strength of a nation, he seems so astonishingly modern that we should even be inclined to treat him as the founder of our economy, if only his work had been known, read and accepted.

## Jacques Savary's *Parfait négociant*: the organization of markets by merchants and the state

The best ancient and medieval texts that make reference to economics escape the modern differentiation between political economy and business economics. Aristotle at first was concerned with the art of acquisition for the household, where he deals not with independent management but rather with the provision of resources for 'the good life', serving the cultural and spiritual (philosophical) life of people in city-states. He was part of an even older tradition, when on the one hand he champions private property and, on the other, fears the growing autonomy of economic activity.[44] Even during his time there were texts that explored sources of income for particular branches of industry. Only fragments of these texts have survived from the classical era; Aristotle bears witness to their existence. From the Romans, we have genuine monographs on agriculture, especially Columella's *De re rustica*, a book that, alongside extensive advice on farming, addresses certain principles of enterprise management.

Texts on the situation in trade and enterprise, specifically on the character of guilds and manufacturers, have been published since the early modern era, beginning in Italy. Eduard Weber, in *Literaturgeschichte der Handelsbetriebslehre* [A History of Literature on Trading] (1914), mentions Pacioli, the author of the oldest printed text on double-entry accounting, and Cotrugli, who in 1458 wrote the manuscript *Della mercatura e del mercante perfetto* for the archive of the trading house; it was first printed in Venice in 1573. He provides a thorough discussion of the book *Il Negotiante* by Peri, published in 1638 and containing most of the building blocks of the emerging so-called 'science of commerce' [Handlungswissenschaft]. Trading practices are described, especially by comparing the most important cities involved in trade. Bills of transaction are explained, as well as trade and payments between fairs. He maintains the connection with late medieval literature on proper ethical behaviour, on the prohibition of usury, the legal use of interest payments, and on their specific use in business transactions (Meuvret 1971, p. 245). Gerard Malynes (1622) is an important representative of writers of this type in England: he defends the use of bills of transaction as developed among the traders against doctrinaire legal provisions (ibid., p. 245).

Savary's book stands out among the founding texts in the science of commerce: its comprehensive structure, its thorough treatment of all topics, the astonishing impact it had for at least a century as evidenced by new editions, reprintings and translations, as well as the close connection between his book and French commercial legislation, upon which it had enormous influence.

Savary's book must have been used in general commercial practice in France. His official duties allowed him to collect a huge amount of material (Leitherer 1961, p. 53). Weber says that Savary's 'rules and tips' are still valid, that even 'today' – before the First World War – no 'practical work of commercial science can be compared to his' (Weber 1914, p. 22). Commercial legislation of that era, very much influenced by Savary, also had a lasting impact: Bellanger (1856) in his essay on Savary and his book considered as a lawyer that the greater part of this legislation still had legal force, despite subsequent Napoleonic legislation. Savary's detailed description of the merchant world in the Baroque era, from the description of goods to instructions for apprentices, dealers and masters, on the establishment of trading corporations, on money transactions and company management, his descriptions of countries, his insight into the psychology of foreign peoples, their societies and legal structures, all of this also makes his book one of the most important and on the whole, it appears, trustworthy sources of economic history. Thus although it retains no theoretical value, it assumes a special place in the history of economics.[45]

Naturally, the sheer quantity of material can frighten off the modern reader. Cameralist science[46], which is related in character to commercial science, was similarly oriented toward questions of practical economic organization, considering questions such as how the wealth of a country and its princes might be increased through the improvement of agriculture, mining, trade, and industry, through the promotion of commerce and the introduction of an appropriate system of taxation. Using these terms of reference, systematic perspectives for organizing material could be developed with less difficulty, or in any case earlier than in commercial science. In the (actually Mercantilist) literature roughly contemporary with Savary we can detect in the work of authors like Petty[47] traces of modern macroeconomics, attempting not only to determine the employment effects of government expenditures, but even to quantify these effects.

Savary's organizing principles distance him from modern business administration and especially from economic theory, drawing him closer instead to economic education, of which he is a neglected forerunner.[48] Specifically, Savary follows the training of a young man who enters a business as an apprentice, then becomes a journeyman and finally becomes a master craftsman. At each step of the way, the appropriate material is presented and, in addition to the actual educational material, he didactically conveys concepts of the proper organization of household and business. 'Savary's "genetic" division remained unsurpassed and was not improved upon for approximately three-quarters of a century' (Leitherer 1961, p. 59, my transl.). Ludovici later introduced a differentiation between primary and secondary mercantile sciences. Savary retained a connection to economic ethics, which remained a general concern in literature about business administration well into the nineteenth century. The numerous topics Savary deals with could occasion a wealth of observations – however, only a small number of them would be of any importance from the point of view of modern science. Two topics are worthy of special attention: Savary's contribution to the theory of business administration, in the modern sense, and the importance of his book for economics as an articulation of Colbertism. In the dedication of the book, Savary makes it immediately clear that he is indebted to Colbert for generous patronage and prestige; on the other hand, it is hard to imagine Colbert's system without his contribution.

Martin Luther's *Sermon on Trade and Usury* identifies the usurer as the greatest human enemy and denies merchants the right to sell exclusively for their own self-interest:

> Because your selling is an act performed in respect of your neighbour, it should rather be so governed by law and conscience that you do it without harm and injury to him, your concern being directed more toward doing him no injury than toward gaining profit for yourself.
>
> (Luther 1962)

The merchant's activities are thus acceptable only when prudently conducted for small profits. In contrast, at the end of Thomas Mun's work *England's Treasure by Forraign Trade* [49], great tribute is paid to foreign trade:

> Behold then the true form and worth of forraign Trade, which is, The great Revenue of the King, The honour of the Kingdom, The Noble profession of the Merchant, The School of our Arts, The supply of our wants, The employment of our poor, The improvement of our Lands, The Nurcery of our Mariners, The Walls of the Kingdom, The means of our Treasure, The Sinnews of our wars, The terror of our enemies.
>
> (Mun 1954 [1664], p. 209)

Savary himself moves between these two poles. On the one hand, he identifies with the merchant career, is convinced of its national importance, and seeks to endow it with more recognition. The dedication of his book to Colbert is an expression of the mercantilist nature of these thoughts on trade policy:

> But what makes me think so well of you is that you have so inspired a love of commerce, and so favoured merchants in the new undertakings which you have designed and happily executed that my book is already awaited with impatience. It becomes every day more useful, since you have made known to our nation the disgrace suffered by its idleness in enriching foreigners to our great loss, and since you have taught the French through experience that they are capable of all things, more than any other nation of the world.
>
> (Savary 1675, dedication, my transl.)

On the other hand, Savary remains keen to portray his activities as ethical. This occurs not only in passages where he attempts to develop his discussion of the dividing line between charging interest and usury – especially in respect of bills – but it is also apparent in the pedagogical organization of the book and the intention of the book as a whole, which he summarizes in the 'Conclusion' to the book as follows:

> I hope that God will bless my work, that young people will draw advantage from it, and that the public will receive from it utility, that is what I hope

with a passion; for my one goal in undertaking this work is to lead young people during their time as a merchant onto just and reasoned paths, so that persons of probity are able to profit from all the examples with which I have dealt in all the places in which I have thought necessary to place them, and which are there well placed, either by embracing the good, or avoiding the bad.

(ibid., Livre second, p. 324, my transl.)

Savary is still a long way from understanding the economy in general as a self-regulating system guided by interests. As Hirschman put it, noting Smith's well-known dictum, we cannot expect our supper from the good will of the butcher, the brewer or the baker, but from the self-interest of each:

Smith fairly bubbles over here with excitement about the possibility of discarding moral discourse and exhortation, thanks to the discovery of a social mechanism that, if properly unshackled, is far less demanding of human nature and therefore infinitely more reliable.

(Hirschman 1981, p. 296)

Savary returns again and again to moral values – not because he expects to obtain his bread from the goodwill of the baker, but because he sees business everywhere endangered by shoddy work, attempted fraud, blackmail and legal loopholes, and because those at a disadvantage are particularly in need of support and assistance. Both private companies and the wider economy must be protected by, and developed according to, civil virtues: only then can the pursuit of interests lead to an increase in the number of goods. The conflict between an ethical imperative and a legal framework, on the one hand, and the pursuit of profit, on the other, does not occur where competition functions according to specific rules, but rather where merchants and officials disagree over the interpretation of laws which are broken.

It is well-known that Mercantilism has been variously interpreted (Minchinton 1969). According to Schmoller, the principal task of the era was to unite the national economic space, to adopt the necessary framework of state regulation, and in so doing supersede and replace the existing urban and regional regulatory frameworks. Savary was placed within this process, developing in France through the sixteenth, seventeenth and eighteenth centuries, without however achieving its goal before the French Revolution – for instance, it did not succeed in abolishing the guild system. Without fully grasping the historical forces involved Savary seeks appropriate compromises, borrowing from Colbert's policies. These policies are marked by international political rivalry and the French pursuit of hegemony, to which economics is subordinated. The importance of the economy for the strength of a nation and for economic competition itself leads not only rulers but also merchants to seek economic measures which could increase the might of a nation. The debate over the appropriate intermediate goals (Is a trade surplus to be pursued or should employment be maximized? Can free trade be beneficial?) is accompanied by arguments about suitable measures.

The reader will find numerous passages in which Savary engages in debate, in modern terms, at the level of macroeconomics and industrial policy. Savary does not take up the extremes of the discussion – free trade or protectionism, deregulation or reregulation – as abstract aims, instead he moves between them, considering emergent concrete problems of business management. There can be no doubt that in detailing the workings of French commercial laws, comparing the trading conditions between states, and investigating related social developments he is also considering the broader power-political objectives. It is especially clear to him that social divisions are an impediment to the civil economy, because aristocratic representation requires a great deal of money and human energy.

In his assessment of legislation, the actions of his fellow Frenchmen, and in the formulation of reforms, Savary made compromises. As a merchant, he championed private economic interests, and yet repeatedly seeks state support for these private interests. Elements of his own biography stand in contrast to the maxims he includes in his book. As we will see, he regrets the tendency of rich French merchants to join the nobility – and yet he ended up serving the throne. He advises young merchants to seek safety in a wealthy marriage – he himself obtained business and social advantages through his marriage yet afterwards suffered losses. These contradictions prevented neither his book nor himself from becoming objects of admiration. With unfaltering powers of judgment he repeatedly found solutions which at first surprised, then convinced and satisfied his contemporaries. In order to better understand the interplay of personal, social and state principles found in his work, we now turn to their linkage in his life.

The most thorough biography of Savary is found in Bellanger (1856, pp. 199ff.), who reconstructed it from the forewords to various editions of Savary's books, also taking account of additions to the text as well as comments made by Savary's sons in their own books. Hauser (1925, p. 2) and other twentieth-century writers have not got significant additional information in French archives.[50]

Jacques Savary was born in Doué, Anjou, 22 September 1622. Although the family was originally part of the nobility, he was forced to follow his father, who died prematurely, into business life. The mother had brought up both of her sons in Paris. The older chose an ecclesiastical career, while the younger, Jacques, encouraged by his uncle who had become rich as a merchant and also by another relative employed in royal service, worked first for a lawyer and acquired legal knowledge. This was of benefit for his later work, subsequently joining a business as a trainee and journeyman, until he himself finally became active as an entrepreneur in the wholesale trade. His wedding to Cathérine Thomas, daughter of one of the richest merchants in Paris, also allied him with noble office holders. Before long he was said to have become very wealthy.

As Bellanger doubtlessly correctly remarks, wealth was only a means and not an end, since only membership of the nobility assured independence and wealth in the long term. In the works of Savary and his sons there are many references to the difficulties faced by citizens who wanted to enter the nobility, although it was the policy of Louis XIII and Louis XIV to ennoble wholesale merchants and factory owners. In the discussion of corporate law in *Parfait négociant*, Savary himself underscores how advantageous it would be for France's economic development if the nobility, for its part, did not scorn to put its capital at the disposal of limited partnership companies.

Savary entered the finance and customs administration under Minister Fouquet but was almost ruined when the minister fell from favour. He then became an attorney for the Duke of Mantua and acquired additional experience in commercial affairs and legal matters. He enjoyed a reputation as 'an enlightened arbiter of great integrity' (Bellanger 1856, p. 204, my transl.).

Through a rather strange incident Savary now came to the attention of the court. The king held out the prospect of a considerable pension for each family father with twelve or more living children – and Savary, with 15 children in 17 years of marriage, was not only among the first who applied, but he was also given the task of examining the applications. Since the number of applicants proved to be quite high, the project fell by the wayside. Savary, however, was back in favour and obtained an ecclesiastical office for one of his sons. He now seized the opportunity to be of service by writing two reports: one on trade abuses which had caused a wave of bankruptcies, and another on a reorganization of commercial law, both of which were presented to Minister Colbert in 1670.

In the very first edition of his work Savary describes how a committee came to prepare the 'Ordonnance' of 1673, a committee whose most active member appears to have been Savary himself, with Pussort as their president, how the king took part in their work, and the committee's activity finally led to the suggestion that he write an introductory book for young merchants:

> As M. Pussort who there presides permits us to make overtures regarding matters which we will find to be useful, and necessary to the conduct of commerce, to be put in order, that gave me occasion to work on my own account and to apply myself vigorously to sight and read all of the ordinances concerning commerce and the matters which it entails, and to absorb all the matters that have passed through my hands, where there has been abuse, especially concerning letters of respite, and the statements of general defence prevailing for merchants, contrary to their creditors, of exchange and usury conducted in commerce, on which matters I drafted memoranda which were well received. Finally the regulatory project drafted by M. De Gomont having been thoroughly examined, the report being made to His Majesty in Council, who took the trouble to make some remarks for its revision, M. De Bellinzany, sires André le Vieux, Robert Poquelin and myself were again heard before the Council for Reform;

and on this last occasion some of the gentlemen who were members, after the rising of the Council, set me to work on several works on the subject of commerce which could be of use to young people wishing to enter the mercantile profession. I have thought it necessary to here give this small detail so that it can be seen that the majority of the matters dealt with in this book are drawn from my own experience, and to show that I had in mind in particular the Ordinance of the month of March 1673 which I have applied to the articles as well as the older ordinances, in those places I have found it necessary.

(Savary 1675, Préface, my transl.)

The 'Ordonnance' is now occasionally called the 'Code Savary'; the book was published two years later. It was a pan-European success, with eight French editions, some of which were printed in Paris and some in Lyon between 1675 and 1721, first by Savary himself and later by his sons; in the eighteenth century a number of further editions were published. A German translation was published in Geneva in 1676, a Dutch edition was published in Amsterdam in 1683, and English and Italian translations followed. Even during his lifetime he was cited in courts; his decisions 'were placed to some degree alongside laws … he became a consulting advocate, the oracle of commerce' (*Vie de Savary*, by his son, in the 1721 edition, cited in Bellanger 1856, pp. 207ff., my transl.) – this offers proof of the special authority with which Savary was regarded in France.

The second edition in 1679, which Savary revised himself, was expanded by the addition of a section on trade with the Levant. His reports on trade appeared in 1688, entitled *Parères, ou Avis et conseils sur les plus importantes matières de commerce.*

Following Colbert's death in 1683 Savary was given a government position, together with several of his sons, three of whom were employed as 'Inspecteurs de manufactures' among other things (Vignolo 1929). It is said that after the death of his wife, a source of profound sorrow, he was afflicted with a painful illness, although he continued to work until he died in 1690. Of his 17 children, 11 survived him. Many of them were later well-known as authors, in particular Jacques Savary des Bruslons, who achieved renown by editing the important *Dictionnaire universel de commerce* (1723). His brother Philémon-Louis, a priest, completed the publication of the *Dictionnaire* and wrote the biography of his father, included in the eighth edition of *Parfait négociant.*

When we read Savary's book we notice again and again the care and rigour of a teacher who, in a world threatened by the fluctuations of trade, fraudulent machinations, political caprice and personal bad luck, seeks to mark out a path to honourable and secure prosperity. The book was published in the midst of the war between France and Holland, which was only one of many conflicts the country was involved in under Louis XIV. Savary's children focussed their attentions on gaining government and ecclesiastical office rather than on independent entrepreneurial activity.[51] The sons' *Dictionnaire de commerce* represented a continuation of the economic work of their father. Jacques Savary des Bruslons had collected all available books on trade in France since 1686; around 1700, the archives were opened to him and he and his brothers began a systematic study of trade institutions. Here Philémon's educational background led to the inclusion of historical sources. In the eighteenth century, there were increasing calls for a systematic understanding of the multifaceted nature of the science: the *Dictionnaire* became a model of a genre that lay claim to applying the universality and precision of the Encyclopedists to commerce, and to the inclusion of this knowledge in the emerging field of political economy.[52]

The elder Savary never made such a far-reaching claim. His traditionalism in questions of business ethics had thoroughly practical consequences in his recommendations, for example with regard to the use of bills of exchange, and the unassuming sincerity of his advice. The casual mixing of original, second- and even third-hand sources makes him seem unscholarly, yet they provide a broad and thorough grounding in contemporary legal and economic issues, for instance in the question of exchange rates. 'It is certainly not a simple 'practical guide'; but neither is it an encyclopedia' as Meuvret (1971, p. 250) summarizes the nature of the text.

Jacob Burckhardt, in his lectures on the era of Revolution, was merciless in condemning the absolutism of Savary's time, although Burckhardt himself was the opposite of a modernist (Ziegler 1974, pp. 39ff.).

> The absolutist state now asserted its raw power over its own people and Europe, untrustworthy and inflexible, placing its own rights above all others. The king himself continually buildt new temples ... the government demonstrated to the people its terrible omniscience by violating every judicial, epistolary, and personal secret ... by its harassment in the supervision of industry, where the king prescribed how this or that kind of silk had to be weaved, so that all the advantage of commerce was lost ... He knew very well that his land was quite close to starvation, but this did not worry him; instead he spent 1500 million. This is not too high an estimate since Versailles alone cost 600 million – how these people built, and how they were betrayed! ... He gave the order to turn the Palatinate into a desert, so that there might be wasteland between Germany and France ... In politics, his breach of promises undertaken became the rule ... Louis XIV is a terrible scoundrel and all the reflections from Racine and Molière fail to place this greatest of all scoundrels in a better light.

The sale of government offices was common. The nobility made up the higher officials and military officers and administered the provinces, but had lost all sovereign power in France. Burckhardt went even further: 'The high nobility were entirely in the king's hands. Louis XIV knew how to trap them in that great corrupt institution, Versailles. The nobility could there make themselves so comfortable that they gradually became completely dependent upon the court' (ibid., p. 41, my transl.).

The privileges of the middle and lower nobility in the countryside were insufficient to ensure their old independence, and would become an object of hatred during the Revolution. The Third Estate found their way into positions of secular and ecclesiastical administration, seeking its way into the nobility. By centralizing its power the crown based itself upon this tendency, the Savary family providing a typical example.

Meanwhile, the aristocracy sought to demonstrate its nobility through its distinct way of life. The nobleman carried the sword, he was ready to serve in the army, in higher government and in the church; but he rejected the career of merchant or manufacturer. Colbert may have sought to organize France along more bourgeois lines, but: 'it is contrary to the spirit of the monarchy that the nobility concerns itself with commerce', as Montesquieu said in 1748; the driving force of the monarchy was instead honour:

> La nature de *l'honneur* est de demander des préférences et des distinctions ... L'ambition est pernicieuse dans une république. Ella a de bons effets dans la monarchie; elle donne vie à ce gouvernement; et on y a cet avantage, qu'elle n'est pas dangereuse, parce qu'elle y peut être sans cesse réprimée.
> (Montesquieu 1793, vol. 2, p. 143; vol. 1, p. 41, Livre XX, 22 or III, 7)[53]

If the king and his ministers fostered and regulated an economy for which society had little regard, they did so primarily so that they could better live off it and not have the members of their own stratum work in it, other than perhaps by investing their capital; even Savary had no illusions about that. He is the embodiment and harbinger of the necessity that trade must first help and organize itself so that the state might then lend legal support and definition the most important trade practices.

Savary probably did not even see that it was possible to create a theoretical discourse of political economy. He not only lacked the general humanistic education of his time, which he in any case thought rather a disadvantage for merchants, we also find in him no sign of the abstraction common to natural science later sought by Ricardo, who was initially a practical man but then became a self-taught scholar-scientist of the first order. There is hardly a trace in Savary of the major intellectual events of the time linked to names such as Descartes, Leibniz and Newton (*qui omne genus humanum ingenio superavit*).[54] But he helped create spontaneous market order. The Hayekian expression 'spontaneous' is here justified in part by its suggestion that the role of the state remains secondary. First, the market organizes itself, and then its order is consolidated by the state and secured against violations like fraud. On the other hand, applied to someone like Savary the concept of 'spontaneity' obscures the merit of the conscious realization of this order, its detailed formulation, hence making it fit for application. Naturally Savary did not act alone, although the success of the book shows that his action had considerable effect.

'Knowledge of commodities', *Warenkunde*, is today a neglected subject, but offers an example of self-organization. Even the economics classics spoke only of the use-value of goods as a scientific and social determination, without giving any thought to how this 'use-value' came about. To discuss a particular 'use-value' not only must the mass and weight be defined – a troublesome conversion if different weights and measures are used in every city – but it must also be aligned with the prevailing ways of living. Savary's almost loving description of raw materials and finished products carries on for many pages; as in antiquity, this typification by place, region and country of origin coveys to the reader sheer variety of preindustrial handicraft products. However, without a degree of homogeneity in the goods, at least in the sense of stan-dards according to which individual products can be assessed, there can be no meaningful comparison of goods, and thus no competition. To this extent the use-value has to be established before any idea of price competition and of a 'fair' or 'normal' price can be developed.[55] Savary dealt with *Warenkunde* extensively, but without reflecting on its economic importance; it is introduced by the argument that the merchants have need of it, and he then demonstrates how the state takes up the task of standardization and refines it.

Another example: the emergence of the bill of exchange is related to the history of merchants struggling with the inflation of currencies by free-spending princes. The princes, driven by requirements of war or luxury, yielded to the ever-present temptation to debase the coin in order to expand the purchasing power of their treasuries. With bills of exchange, merchants could deal in terms of the more stable currencies, or even create their own artificial currency.[56] In any case, the bill of exchange represents an instrument of payment that allows individual merchants to delay payment with state coin, or almost entirely avoid it if a clearing system for bills of exchange has been established. Although Savary seeks to outline a history of bills of exchange in his book, he does little in the way of illuminating their relationship to any theory of exchange – however much emphasis is lent to the importance of bills of exchange, as we shall see. Instead, he introduces the use made of bills, describes methods of clearing, and is most interesting where he suggests means for the prevention of abuse. Here regulations can substantially reduce losses.

We have already seen that Savary sought the formation of companies on a more secure basis through government assistance, and that he agreed with the Colbertian policy which tried to involve the nobility more closely in overseas trade. In comparison with other mercantilist authors, more marked statist features appear when he discusses projects for trading companies which, like the 'Compagnie du Nord' (supposedly responsible for trade with Russia), come into being through government initiative. The era gave rise to the pro-jectors who are ridiculed in Swift's *Gulliver's Travels*; many entrepreneurial plans were forged to profit from trade with the colonies.[57] One such example is the Suez Canal project.[58]

He ultimately expresses the thought that there is opportunity for rich merchants to invest their capital in manufacture, and he thus begins to consider, like most of the mercantilist authors, the importance of production, though without analyzing the organization of the division of labour.

Savary sketched the idea of the creation of spontaneous order at the institutional level, from a practical standpoint and hence one-dimensional, although very thorough since it takes account of all aspects of business; but he does move to the level of ideas when referring to all the interests which could be an issue for merchants. He discusses family life and the individual career, religion, customs and law. He does not here refer to the Puritan hope for salvation, the effect of which, in leading a practical life, Max Weber viewed as an element in the construction of capitalist economic action.[59] But a certain asceticism in the standard of living and moral rigour are unmistakably thought to be essential for business success, sobriety and objectivity, discipline and organization are supposed to ease the progress from apprentice to assistant to master, and that such reserve curbs adventurous entrepreneurial spirit in overseas trade and the development of projects to a greater extent than with other mercantilist authors.

Savary's simple rectitude and legal powers of judgement obviously contrast with contemporary practices, often barely distinct from corruption. Whatever traces of a resulting double standard there might be in Savary, they are insignificant. His critique of contemporary circumstances naturally stops short of the French authorities, to whom he often shows to be quite devoted. Compare, for instance, his assessment of Colbert's economic achievement with the murky image sketched by many historians of the minister as leader of a financial and aristocratic clique which amassed both wealth and position.[60]

We learn to live with the contradictions of the present; while those of the past are a constant source of astonishment.

As a guide to the contemporary French economy of his time, Savary's book might be thorough, but it is not complete. He himself admits that he does not systematically consider guilds. The guilds and crafts had developed spontaneously and were then in France, once more by Colbert, subjected to regulation.[61] Wholesalers were naturally independent and were frequently involved in disputes with the guilds. Savary entirely supports the regulation of the careers of apprentices and journeymen by corporate bodies, but capital requirements, the number of employees, and the opening up of world market to the wholesale trade, these all burst traditional bounds. He also calls for comprehensive accounting and supervision of the wholesale trade, and in this regard expresses his admiration for the geographical scope of Dutch trade and its banks. Savary is witness and advocate for many technical commercial improvements. In order to reduce the number of insolvencies in times of upheaval, the 1673 'Ordonnance' and his book place a special weight upon the correct way of dealing with postponement of payments, and the differentiation between simple and fraudulent bankruptcy – the latter was legally punishable by death, even if the punishment was in practice almost never carried out (Sée 1925, p. 104).

Savary proves a faithful defender of the Colbertian mercantile system. The minister himself said in 1665: 'All commerce consists in easing the import of goods which are used in manufactures within the realm, placing charges on imported manufactures, and relieving the right of export for goods manufactured within the realm' (ibid., p. 106, my transl.).

Assessment of Colbert's policies would remain controversial even if they had not led to France's involvement in wars with its neighbours. Savary shares the mercantilist conviction that, as shown in trade with the West Indies, international trade conducted by trading companies functions better where goods are exchanged for goods or goods for money, trade with the north by contrast being less beneficial since in many cases goods have to be purchased with money.

Colbertian protectionism not only privileged trading companies and created trading contracts, but it also founded and promoted manufactures, some of which involved the king's workshops. Others were established by the king with the right to bear the coat of arms of the crown; however, most were simply private, although privileged, manufactories which competed with guild handicrafts in certain branches. Colbert knew that privileging had its price: 'The privileges of manufactures ... always limit commerce and public liberty' (ibid., p. 34, my transl.). It was the early years of capitalism, and discipline in manufacturing industry was extraordinarily strict. Savary's references to the rules necessary for manufacturing concern more than honour and punctuality. The new standards, created independent of the guilds, had to be maintained: thus we also touch in his book on technical production as a counterpart to his *Warenkunde*.

Finally, Savary proves to be an economic geographer who, when referring to national characteristics, may at first appear to have in mind only national character, but who proves to have an eye for historical connections, and seeks to learn about the economic institutions of other countries. To that degree, perhaps, he is closer to Historical Economics than to theoretical economics, insofar as he makes any statement beyond the confines of the economics of the individual enterprise. If we adopt Spiethoff's terminology, we could say that Savary characterizes the economic forms of the countries he examines as different economic styles, in that foreign trade opens up a perspective on the economy as a whole. His descriptions seem alien and strange. Commonplaces and prejudice are mixed up with original observations; sometimes we have occasions to be surprised by the constancy of historical types in the past three centuries, less often with their mutability. The mentalities of peoples are not however interesting as a curiosity but as determining factors for economic development or, more directly, in the possibility they open of market development.

The value of his descriptions as sources varies. His book can be read as a complete commentary on the 'Ordonnance' of 1673, which was in part reproduced in the 1807 'Code de Commerce'. Savary des Breslons performed a greater service in collecting the remaining elements of commercial law (Bellanger 1856, p. 216).

Signs of a comparative acknowledgement of Savary's influence can also be found in Seyffert (1956, col. 1000) and in Penndorf (1925, pp. 7–19). Savary has been frequently cited as a source, especially in Sombart (1987), Braudel (1979), and in the *Histoire économique et sociale de la France* (Braudel and La Bruce 1970). For Sée as well Savary plays an important role as a source, while Meuvret (1971, pp. 248ff.) judges him more sceptically in this regard. Heckscher (1931) occasionally refers to him in his important work on Mercantilism. Here I can only claim Savary's value as a source; to judge his actual value as a source would be the task of an economic historian.

We now turn to selected excerpts from Savary's book. He must have felt himself that the volume of material might scare readers away, and therefore at the very beginning he explained his principle of division, provided an overview of the work in the second chapter, and did the same in the detailed table of contents. Ludovici, the first German author in commercial science at all comparable to Savary, argues in his foreword in regard to Savary and those who came after him, 'However, if one reads through these books, one will perhaps quickly discover that they are not formulated ... into a systematic framework' (Ludovici 1932, pp. 4ff., my transl.). Savary begins his book with observations upon the benefits of trade, arising from the providential, unequal distribution of foodstuffs among people which leads to their trading with each other – an idea, Hauser (1925, p. 6) points out, that prefigures the thought of Jean Bodin.

Savary's pedagogical approach leads him to inquire after the talents children must have in order to be suitable for a career in commerce. A variety of talents is required: from being naturally pleasant and engaging to possessing intelligence and powers of judgement. Children should not be forced into a career against their inclinations; these tendencies have to be recognized beforehand. Their ambition must be awakened:

> en leur donnant des exemples des Negocians qui n'avaient aucune chose quand ils se sont mis dans le Commerce, qui nean moins y ont amassé de grands biens, par le moyen desquels ils ont poussé leurs enfants jusques dans les plus hautes diguitez de la Robbe...
>
> (Savary 1697, A I 4, 33; IV)[62]

The parents must already have taught their children accounting and languages and, in addition, history, since that increases the powers of judgement. In contrast, Latin, philosophy, and rhetoric are useless, since in these courses of study children acquire an aristocratic disdain for business, incline to other careers, and, if they still turn out to be merchants, will become wasteful and fall prey to a seductive hope: that 'a good marriage will pay for everything' (ibid., A I 4, 35; IV, my transl.).

Savary names the trades upon which a decision has to be made, such as that of commodity traders, whose members do not work – that is, they are not allowed to work productively, as the Classical Economists will later say, since they only buy and sell goods, but do not produce them. However, from among their ranks there emerge long-distance traders who acquire great wealth. The apprentices who submit to masters are under his control: therefore the articles of apprenticeship must be very carefully drawn up. It might be thought that Savary's ideas are here determined by guild tradition, insisting that the apprenticeship period be worked without interruption, or that the master only be replaced in emergencies. But he also refers to typical guild abuses, since he warns parents, who are masters themselves, not to declare their children to the masters in advance. His reasons are based upon the necessity of a thorough education, which is supposed to guarantee business success later.

We might smile at Savary's advice that the apprentice and the master go to church together, and when he instructs the apprentice to maintain as healthy a respect for his instructor as he would for his father: sociologically, this is all about ensuring a certain status. Discretion and truthfulness are important, since they are the foundations of a reputation, 'so necessary for merchants, and without which they will never make their fortune' (ibid., A II 2, 50; VII, my transl.). Thus, Savary is a relatively 'modern' author. He supports moral arguments and educational goals with Utilitarian arguments and knows the economic consequences of social distinction. In Italy and England the nobility are active in business; in France, however, trade is not only socially unacceptable, but the training for it is also poor.

The apprentice should know how to measure correctly and should use a rule honestly. On the other hand, Savary has little to tell him about price policy. The notion of a fair price does not arise here; it is enough to know that competition in luxury items permits higher surcharges than on goods of daily use, so that under favourable circumstances it is possible to make considerable profits on expensive fashion items. But it is also possible to lose money if the merchant keeps hold of the goods. The master must be capable of broad discrimination:

No-one should be favoured, whether by price, by choice of commodity, nor should good measure be given without permission of their masters; for it is not for them to give what does not belong to them (ibid., A II 2, 51; VII, my transl.).

Exam questions are now put to the apprentice which touch on the conversion of various weights and measures. There is certainly more to memorize than to calculate. The variety of measurements can be attributed to medieval decentralization. Savary makes it known that Colbertian administration will also affect this area. An appendix to the second edition of the book explains why the king is particularly interested in the administration of the cloth trade: 'the King derives considerable sums from it' (ibid., A II 10, 86, my transl.), hence the monitoring of manufacturing which now extends to the measure and quality of cloth production in order to maintain its 'reputation'. The king believes that by taking these steps in time of war he can prevent a decline in production.

Savary then moves on to journeymen, an important section of the training in which there is a great deal to be learned and which cannot even be omitted by children of masters. Now proper conduct with other merchants will be learned, since it is important to learn how business works in other cities and learn from its successes. Following that is a chapter of particular historical interest on the use of bills of exchange, at which journeymen must be very skilled.

It is certain that there is nothing more useful to the State and to the public than the use of letters of credit and bills of exchange. But it is also important to be in agreement that there is nothing more dangerous than this commerce, which produces more usury and bankruptcy, when bankers, traders and merchants practice it with covetousness and impudence (ibid., A III 3, 104f.; XIX, my transl.).

The function of bills of exchange is first defined in terms of the problem of transportation, without mentioning the increase in social purchasing power which they facilitate. Instead, 'not being obliged to always hold their money in idle accounts without making any profit' (ibid., A III 3, 106; XIX, my transl.) – therein lies the advantage of this means of payment for individual merchants. Savary does not ask why money, when it does not lay 'idle', may accrue interest. We find, instead, a thorough explanation of the law regulating the bill of exchange, with a precise commentary on the corresponding regulations from 1673, with a discussion of all forms of bills of exchange and promissory notes and commercial usage regarding their use, as well as all regulations to be taken into account in case of insolvency on the part of someone involved in a related transaction. Young people engaged in trade have a pressing reason to know this material thoroughly:

> There is no invention nor subtlety that bankers and merchants who trade with money do not discover to avoid loss when bankruptcies looms, taking no account of nor dealing justly with interested parties, if only they get paid.
>
> (ibid., A III 6, 159; XXII, my transl.)

If one has once has got into difficulties when trading with promissory notes it is easy to fall into the hands of usurers, against whom Savary vigorously polemicizes: 'One cannot decry the bloodsuckers too loudly' (ibid., A III 7, 179; XXIII, my transl.) – luckily, however, the 'bloodsuckers' earn little, since they often loan money to insolvent people by mistake. Savary, full of resentment here for 'the Jews and the usurers', does not acknowledge that high interest rates also correspond to a particular level of risk.

Savary differentiates between the additional costs arising in dealings with foreign countries due to exchange rates, and those which come from the cheapening effect of discounts resulting from premature payments. His considerations on the exchange rate, where he allows for the effects of differences between individual countries in the valuation of precious metals, seem especially noteworthy to me (ibid., A III 1, 1; XXVII). His treatment of discounts, which mathematically amounts to the benefit of the rule of three, is on the other hand more naive (ibid., A III 13, 237; XXIX).

According to Meuvret (1971, p. 249), Savary's work reflects a particularly important development which had emerged in the early seventeenth century. Money transactions and bills of transactions had moved from fairs to banks and, in particular, to the stock exchange in Amsterdam. Savary, however, provides yet another good description of the impression that bills of exchange had left behind at the fairs:

> It is an admirable thing to see the manner in which the bankers and merchants of Lyon make acceptances, and their mutual payments in bills of exchange which they draw up and which they can use all over Europe; in two or three hours it will pay a million livres, without spending a sou; since it is surprising enough to those who do not know how such payments are made, it will not be irrelevant to recount it here.
>
> (Savary 1697, A III 12, 229; XXVIII, my transl.)

A brief description of the surprisingly simple technique of exchange clearing follows this account.

In subsequent chapters – in the second edition it is the fourth book of the first part – Savary turns to the master. Full legal capacity is attained at the age of 25, and Savary also generally recommends that people first make themselves independent at this age. He spends some time on the reasons why an earlier beginning might appear to be sensible, such as the take-over of a business through inheritance, and he discusses the provisions then in force. This book attracts the attention of the modern reader because of its consideration of accounting regulations; in this place, a few suggestions should suffice.[63] Savary does not start *in medias res*, but instead explains first how stores or businesses should be organized. He tries to impress upon the young master the maxim 'l'ordre est l'âme du commerce' (Savary 1697, 1697A IV 4, 245; XXXIII),[64] and then broaches the subject of how goods should be stored and presented, which business location is most advantageous – we gain, thereby, further insight into the living and working situation of Parisian trade in the seventeenth century. One must imagine dark alleys without display windows, one remembers Dutch still-lives, and then one can understand why Savary devotes so much time to how each product must be displayed in the proper light – one article in the morning, another in the afternoon and still another in the evenings. Beautiful women, he observes, also obscure their faces with veils.

Savary now takes up how the books are to be kept. He mentions here that fraudulent bankruptcy is punishable with death; merchants must therefore be cautious (ibid., A IV 4, 249; XXXIII). Ordinances on the division of books, on the dating of entries, on rendering it illegible and on audit by the authorities now conform to the law. 'Such legal provisions were also sporadically decreed even earlier, but with the *Ordonnance* (from 1673) they were for the first time valid for a large, self-contained economic sector' (Vehn 1929, p. 345, my transl.). With the establishment of bookkeeping came the need to foreground the monitoring and regulation of the business, its employees, as well as the derivation of net income. So that no mistake be made about profit, the valuation of the inventory should not be too high. With this suggestion Savary for the first time introduced the 'lowest-valuation principle' (ibid., p. 250).

The book closes with additional considerations of careful business conduct reminiscent of Molière's account of how the honest citizen can be tormented by the extravagance of the nobility (Molière, *Le bourgeois gentilhomme*, Act 3, Scene 4). Retail traders should not allow themselves to be seduced by the 'flattery and sweet words' of the great Lords, granting them credit without a definite prospect of repayment, and they should beware of all women who buy expensive clothes on credit, in order to sell them and gamble the money away while their husbands baulk at payment (Savary 1697, A IV 7, 301; XXXVI, and A IV 8, 308; XXXVII). The historical mindset suggested here offers a foil for Savary's principles: the relaxed and wasteful life of the upper class, which makes the strictness of organization he seeks all the more necessary and understandable.

The second part of the book (according to the structure of the second edition) opens up the broad horizon of foreign trade associated with the discovery, conquest and exploitation of distant lands. Savary differentiates between three kinds of companies: a so-called collective society in which several partners combine under their own names, which are stated publicly with rights that mirror the civil rights of the given civil society; a limited partnership in which some partners enter only as investors, while others assume management positions; and an 'anonymous' company, which is something different from a corporation with unnamed owners but is instead an alliance established with a contractual agreement for limited goals – the anonymity consists in the fact that the company, as such, has no name.

The above differentiation is presented in the form of advice given to young merchants. Whoever wants to found a company must be clear about the goals and must not be mistaken about the people with whom they join forces. Among the formalities which have to be observed at this stage is the accurate valuation of capital introduced in the form of property and goods, so that it is possible to make a fair division of the proceeds – or the assets in case of the dissolution of the company – in proportion to the capital contributed. Collective societies and limited partnerships should be established before a notary.

Savary believes limited partnerships to be the most profitable form of company structure because – before the development of the joint stock company – they represent an opportunity for investors to put money into manufacture or trade without being merchants themselves. Wealth is thereby mobilized which would otherwise lie idly in a chest. It enables hard-working entrepreneurs to realize their goals even if they possess very little capital, and along with this there are also prospects for employment, a point frequently proclaimed by

Mercantilists: 'artisans of all sorts of manufactures are very well employed and from that fact they can more easily support their families'.

Together with these general economic benefits, there are some for the princes, whose incomes will increase through surcharges ('denier') on goods – i.e. indirect taxes: 'the more manufactures in their state, and the more that commerce is there flourishing, the greater their revenues, by means of the surcharges imposed on goods and which flow into and out of their kingdoms and states' (both quotes ibid., B I 1, 15; XL, my transl.).

He wants to persuade the nobility to participate in such limited partnerships because such activities are not dishonourable: the nobility do not themselves have to be involved in business but simply reap the profits; additionally, the wholesale trade should not be considered dishonourable, because Louis XIII even enacted an 'Ordonnance' in 1627 according to which wholesalers could become members of the aristocracy. If it is permissible for refined people to trade while on distant voyages, then silent partnership has to be permissible. Consequently he points to the Italian nobility as a model, especially in Genoa, Venice and Florence, where aristocrats own galleys which sail the seas for them. And: 'In England the commerce is of such integrity that the highest aristocracy trade in wool and livestock, while gentlemen consider that such activity renders them less noble, whatever they might have in common with merchants, even with farmers' (ibid., B I 1, 16; XL, my transl.) – the sons even accept apprenticeship to masters so that they might learn their trade. Here, Savary's ideal is not the 'bourgeois gentilhomme', but instead the 'gentilhomme bourgeois'!

Naturally participation in limited partnerships turns out to be not quite so simple because responsibilities can also be allocated differently, because a certain amount of attention to the business is crucial, and it is necessary to take precautions, particularly for later dissolutions, especially in case of bankruptcy. Savary recommends that silent partners agree to a lower liability in exchange for a lower share in profits.

He includes among 'anonymous companies' several which are in our eyes quite different cases: a simple one, like an agreement in writing between a merchant who sails into the port of Marseille on his ship and another merchant resident in Paris, so that they might dispose of the goods jointly in the Paris market. Also included are however what we would today call restrictive trading agreements: 'the most powerful merchants make up anonymous societies ... which ... having bought from smaller merchants in the countryside can take their goods to fairs and markets and charge what they like.' This is actually a monopoly, established in opposition to the public good, which defies the rules of the marketplace: 'which reverses the economy of commerce' (both quotes ibid., B I 1, 23; XL, my transl.).

Such monopolies are at odds with good practice – they are still not yet forbidden, apparently; but they could be circumvented at the fair for example if a more competitive trade develops alongside the fair. Savary probably notices the irony that it was just this moderately competitive trade which bypassed the fairs, which was not formally permitted. Incidentally, he mentions that even 'persons of quality' participate in such businesses – and if they condescend to monopolistic practices, then why not to participation in a limited partnership?

From the models of various articles of incorporation, which are cited and discussed in the following chapter, we learn not only many details about business life, a cash fund held in common, communal welfare for poor people and the advisability of separating off the family of the partner; we also learn how responsibilities are to be managed, in particular on the part of merchants who have to deal independently of each other while on their voyages. Savary throughout puts value on rendering regulations compatible with incentives, and on monitoring the various kinds of risks for participants, but he is also convinced that, ultimately, in the absence of mutual trust, it is better not to set up a company since not everything can be exhaustively regulated.

Savary describes the excellence of wholesale trade with a certain pride. He now suggests that retail trade is somewhat servile, while the wholesale trade has something respectable and noble about it.

Forming a company is practically obligatory in the wholesale trade, because it requires a lot of capital in the form of advances to workers – the putting-out trade is probably meant here – as a result of warehousing, because retailers must be offered credit, and finally because buying and selling usually has to be supervised in different places, which a partnership does best by dividing the task among the partners.

The partners should be friends, but they and their families should not live in the same buildings, so as to avoid casual occasions for arguments about business. The most important task is cash management. Advice is offered about how to avoid keeping too much cash in hand yet remaining solvent, and how to deal with bad debts; during a temporary stagnation in trade the wholesaler should not drive retailers into undeserved ruin. Double-entry bookkeeping is urgently recommended, and he emphasizes that correspondence must be kept up: the 'Ordonnance' prescribes it, but it has always been good practice.

In the following chapters he discusses purchasing from manufactories, the manufactures themselves and finally the sale of products. When wholesalers purchase from manufactories they have to distinguish between a price increase due to an increase in the price of materials and one due to the scarcity of the manufactured product itself. Price increases in raw materials are usually slow and permanent, while the scarcity of particular manufactured products is often temporary, and therefore different kinds of advice about purchasing are to be given at any given moment. This relatively interesting analytical examination is illustrated by examples of a successful and an unsuccessful speculation. Savary adds that during economic slumps one must purchase from small producers, because they are forced to offer good prices given that they cannot wait for better times (ibid., B I 5, 78ff.; XLIV).

In the following chapter about the organisation of manufactories, modern readers will probably expect something different to what it actually delivers, given the title. Savary describes the perspective of a merchant who wants to enter into manufacturing, but does not go into the details of production. Characteristically, it is first asked whether foreign production methods should be copied, or if entrepreneurs should try their own. Imitation appears easier than it really is. There can be supply problems and location problems: Savary suggests that producers abroad enjoy an advantage from positive externalities which the isolated imitator lacks. He illustrates, if you like, Marshall's theory of positive external effects, which is today referred to in terms of 'industrial districts'. Knowledge is tied to locality, and is passed on if many firms in the same place and branch compete over quality and sales, and a certain exchange of knowledge takes place between firms because they recruit the best workers who themselves occasionally move between firms. This may be reminiscent of the newer theories of growth, which has drawn to our attention the fact that only a little of the advantage of innovation accrues to innovator, while the largest part goes to the imitators. Imitation is only difficult when craft secrets are faithfully protected. It may be that the imitation does not work if craftsmen cannot be enticed away from the place where the subject is really understood. Savary, who addresses these connections without presenting them systematically, recognizes the importance of labour costs as an issue of location whose difference he traces back to subsistence costs: 'in Paris workers are paid more because the cost of living is there greater than in the provinces' (ibid., B I 6, 85; XLV, my transl.).

Or should a person attempt to invent something? Savary's examples tend to point to small inventions in the textile branch, like a new fashion or a new way of organizing work. He reports how he himself invented gold brocade which sold very well at first, but which then proved to be insufficiently durable. He shares neither the inventive powers nor the technical interest of a Babbage, who, however, also belongs to the industrial revolution (Schefold 1992b).

'L'Ordre est l'ame d'une Manufacture', (Savary 1697, B I 7, 89; XLVI)[65] – with this statement, Savary begins the chapter on the organization of manufacturing. The merchant who acquires a manufacturing enterprise must at the very least know enough about production that he knows how to supervise and correct his workers. Those whose working methods cannot be changed have to be dismissed. From production, though, he soon turns back to sales and supervisory problems: how goods are to be sealed with lead because of inland customs duties, and how to protect against potential attempts at fraud on the part of workers which could lead to losses in volume or quality.

Finally, sales: Whoever wants to sell manufactured goods *en gros* must know the terms of retail trade, and especially the creditworthiness of the buyer, the owners of small shops. The new standpoint now introduced is that of supraregional trade. Savary believes that businesses remain largely dependent upon fairs. The alternative would be to sell on commission, which Savary repeatedly warns against: 'whoever works on commission quickly goes to pot' (ibid., B I 8, 104; XLVII, my transl.).

Readers will obtain a very dubious notion of the contemporary ethics related to payment when they read of the difficulties dealers encounter in trying to call in debts – usually there is no alternative to undertaking this unpleasant business personally. A progressive element of the 'Ordonnance' is that in such supraregional transactions the place of jurisdiction can now be agreed in the contract, whereas previously only that of the defaulter was legally binding.

Next comes an important section on colonial and international trade, with a great deal of information and consideration of particular countries, only a small part of which can be cited. Savary already treats pricing from the viewpoint of supply and demand, without including a notion of normal costs; 'goods and exchanges rise and fall in price according to scarcity or abundance' (ibid., B II 2, 112; XLVIII, my transl.). In the discussion of trade relations with the Dutch this perspective is now turned toward the conditions for merchants who act as intermediaries in trade between Netherlands and France. At irregular intervals, the fleet from East India brings large amounts of goods to the market in Amsterdam, each time fundamentally altering the composition of supply and demand. It is therefore almost indispensable that one of the partners bases himself in Amsterdam if they want to obtain good trading terms.

Most of the trade with the Netherlands takes place via shipping. Savary describes a new Parisian insurance association whose business exceeds that of the insurance business of the French ports. Amsterdam is naturally even better positioned. In various places, the superiority of Dutch trade is clear, despite the French war with the Netherlands. Savary remains silent on the political-economic goals of this war.[66]

While the Dutch are viewed as superior and clever but in general fair partners, Savary believes trade with England is manifestly unfair:

> There is no nation in Europe where the French find greater difficulty in trading or where they are worse treated than in England, and there is no-one which receives and deals more favourably with the English than the French.
>
> (Savary 1697, B II 3, 117; XLVIII, my transl.)

Savary thus considers France to be liberal, with low customs charges, and Great Britain to be protectionist, with its pronounced discrimination against foreign merchants – he would have been very surprised to learn that the British would become the advocates of global free trade. Savary's list of the ways in which England discriminates is long, and is expanded with reports on fraudulent British corporations, whose victims are said to be honest Frenchmen.

In the second edition Savary's section on Italian trade includes an interesting addition on the Bank of Venice, in which it is explained how a government bank can do more than exchange clearing since they are in permanent operation, they have lower transaction costs, they have access to government capital and the sum of deposits far exceeds the cash reserve:

> By this means the Republic of Venice, without enjoying freedom of commerce, became mistress of the money of its population, and without being obliged to resort to extraordinary impositions to sustain the war which had long been waged against the Turks ... The same fund supported something imaginary, but seeming real since it had the same value: it had money when it wanted.
>
> (ibid., B II 4, 126; XLVIII, my transl.)

Double-entry bookkeeping and bills of exchange were learned from Italy and nobody in the world is better organized than the merchants of Genoa, Venice and Florence. '... for that which is so admirable is that merchants of other states in Europe are taught to keep their books by double-entry. It is the Italians who have taught us the business of exchange' (ibid., B II 4, 135; XLVIII, my transl.). Savary admires the ingenuity of Italian merchants and the loving care with which they conduct their virtuoso affairs. If they think a trading partner is threatened with bankruptcy, they redouble their kindness and withdraw their money before they let the partner collapse entirely.

Spanish trade, once the best in the Europe, is thought by Savary to be in decline; one has to wait a long time for payments. It is protected by monopolies. For example, the Spanish king had reserved trade with the Spanish West Indies for the Spanish and threatened death to every foreigner who attempted to dispute this.

The section on the above-mentioned northern trades contains information on cities in the Hanseatic League that might be of especial interest to German readers.[67] Savary's information on Trade with Russia has been thoroughly covered by Marperger (1705, pp. 70ff.).

This northern trade with Russia was best conducted via Archangelsk; Savary considers the merchants of the interior to be unreliable and stubborn. Of course, French ships have only six weeks available for trading, with the journey from France to the North Sea in May and the return trip in October. Savary, however, sees comparatively large advantages from this trade, and so this provides him once more with an opportunity of making a comparison with Holland. Certainly the Dutch have the advantage that their sailors make smaller demands, that they can offer better insurance against storms and piracy, and, above all, their trade is better endowed with capital. In France, then, capital is repeatedly withdrawn from trade when merchants enter into public service, while capital in Holland is concentrated in merchant families and inherited. The only possibility for France would consist in establishing larger companies. The French problem remains: the state should strengthen capitalist development by direct intervention and civic institutions wherever social trends weaken it.[68]

The hopes for commercial policy that the patriot Savary has for his country lead him now into a strange deviation, though it is characteristic of the time.

He presents an early-modern History of Discovery, mixing fact and fiction in particular when writing of the beginning, in order to make the claim that the French were the first to set foot in the New Worlds. His report on the emergence of the great trading companies is of scholarly interest, especially when he compares Holland, which relied more on private initiative, and France, where the Crown was more deeply involved. The French enjoyed their greatest success in the West Indies (Haiti), and he sees potential for the development of French possessions in Canada.

This, unfortunately, leads to a consideration of the slave trade between West Africa and the West Indies. Savary feels it necessary to justify this trade: 'The trade seems inhuman to those who do not know that these poor people worship idols' (ibid., B II 10, 206; LIV). The slaves endure an even more brutal slavery in Africa; now they are taught the correct beliefs. Savary demands that they be well-fed during transport, so that none starve. As soon as they are on board, the ships should immediately set sail: 'The reason for this is that slaves have such great love for their country that they despair at leaving it forever, such that they to a great extent die of sadness' (ibid., B II 10, 206; LIV, my transl.).[69] Once the ship weighed anchor, the slaves calmed down. Music should be played aboard the ship, perhaps a violin, in order to amuse them, and if they could forget their unhappiness in dancing they would arrive in a healthier condition and be easier to sell.

The text concludes with at least indirect opposition to the slave trade; the other horrors of colonization are not even considered. Savary is still two generations away from Voltaire and the era of the Enlightenment. When we judge him, we should remember that even today contact between western civilization and primitive tribes usually leads to the demise of these civilizations and the dying-out of their members, while we comfort ourselves with the promise of greater material development for these people.

In the following chapters, Savary turns to professions which function as intermediaries in trade. Among these are factors and correspondents and, as we already saw above, Savary recommends particular care in dealing with them. They are, however, often indispensable, and he now attempts to show that a fair reconciliation of interests between client and agent is possible by making a comparison between teacher and student. Factors who think only of the clients will ruin themselves, while agents who only act in their own interests will forfeit the basis of the contract (Savary 1697, B III 2, 216; LVI). Banks are also dealt with in this context. He considers small banks which are usually in foreign hands. Savary recommends putting greater trust in resident merchants who provide ancillary banking functions, since they also possess goods as security. With foreign banks, by contrast, it is all too usual for them to flee with their customers' deposits.

Savary next explores the functions of bill traders and brokers, who play different roles in cities where there is general commercial freedom and in those with guilds, to which case brokers must adapt by joining the guilds. He explains the restrictions to which brokers are subject; specifically, they may not work on their own account. They bear great responsibility, since the creditworthiness of many depends upon their discretion. This section creates a strong impression of the variety of functions intermediaries perform in trade, from the organization which the merchants create to the regulations at various levels between city and state. Adam Smith dismisses the activities of merchants as unproductive because the services they provide continually expand and because the labour theory of value came into prominence. Savary knows that merchants reveal needs and opportunities for meeting such needs, that they are therefore holders of information.

In the final group of chapters the text culminates in an exploration of legal relationships and the appropriate response to insolvency and bankruptcy. He introduces this analysis as follows:

> Once more a merchant should be very skilful, so attached to his trade that he keeps his affairs in good order, that he has many gifts, that he has such application and prudence with which he can conduct his affairs, but if all that is not accompanied by good fortune he has no certainty of success.
>
> (ibid., B IV 1, 275; LXII, my transl.)

Shakespeare's *The Merchant of Venice* dramatizes what Fortuna, in the guise of the ups and downs of the maritime trade and credit, can mean for the merchant. Savary introduces a literary *topos* of the time[70] to separate wheat from chaff, the fraudulent bankruptcy from the law-abiding merchant who is a victim of bad luck. It is difficult and 'thorny' material, as he describes it. Merchants who are threatened with insolvency due to losses on the part of a debtor should at first act as if nothing is wrong, until they manage to obtain an overview of the real business situation and are in a position to decide whether they will take advantage of loans from friends, whether they must ask for deferred payment – which will, however, tarnish their reputation – or if they will go straight into bankruptcy.

We do not wish to go any further into the suffering of Savary's unhappy apostle – because here Savary is also writing as a pedagogue. How is equality under the law among creditors to be established where people of rank demand preferential treatment? How is the separation of property between spouses to be carried out? What are the duties of those entering bankruptcy? Savary tells of exemplary cases, for instance, public and exemplary punishment for fraudulent bankruptcy. These are punishments which we believe to be limited to the medieval era, but which are quite common in the early modern era.

But we cannot any longer follow the drama of the merchant, liable for himself and all his assets, in all his legal entanglements. The typical counterpart to severe punishments for the swindler is the ceremonial rehabilitation of the law-abiding merchant's reputation, granted by royal authority and thus absolute. This merchant has managed to pay-off his debts and is allowed a new beginning: 'il n' y a que le Prince seul qui puisse effacer la tache' (Savary 1697, B IV 5, 354; LXVI).[71] Just as none of Shakespeare's historical dramas ends without the restoration of the monarch, thus assuring the continuity of legitimacy, Savary's text[72] ends with the restoration of honour, 'Honour being the dearest thing in the world, after our salvation' (ibid., B IV 5, 354; LXVI, my transl.).

Savary writes as a child of his time; whoever really wants to read the entire text only to find traces of theories and ideas which anticipate our own has a dark and difficult task ahead. But the text itself proves surprisingly fresh, when the various elements are read in historical context. In the antiquated French we hear the voice of a merchant who after a long and varied business career, through disputes and political manoeuvring, has acquired experience and powers of judgment, access to the court which provided entrée to people of the same standing and connections to the world, and who has always, firmly and with dedication if also often naively, championed his own business affairs. Thus understood, despite their undeniable length, his pages speak to us in a livelier fashion than later textbooks, while at the same time they report in the language of commercial science advances during the mercantile period which will be decisive for later historical developments. Seventeenth-century philosophy produced more important ethics than his paternalistic maxims, the literature of the time had more exciting travel descriptions, and the encyclopedic claims of Savary's collection of laws was surpassed by his sons. However, reading it we can see why his merchant handbook, as a guide to practice in all fields of trade and their legal framework, containing reflections upon the political-economic requirements of growth, would be such a success.

Colbertism, with which Savary associated himself, is viewed sceptically. If he had been asked, he would certainly have expressed agreement with the principle, 'As much freedom as possible, as much regulation as necessary'. He strongly criticizes the trade restrictions of other countries (England). With regard to institutions in his own country, however, he raised fewer objections, and he appears to have sided with Absolutism.

Colbert's efforts to create an integrated French economic space could not overcome the many local and regional regulations, and even strengthened the guilds (Heckscher 1931, pp. 118–200).[73] Savary adapted himself to this reality just, as he wrapped himself in the social expectations of his environment: through very moderate criticism. The call for economic freedom in France reached the ministerial level only with Turgot. Trade, however, shattered corporate restrictions, although it also generated disputes and cartels. In the end, it was uncontrollable international rivalry and the French Revolution which brought about economic freedom. Savary could not foresee this development. However, he contributed to it as few others did with the success of his book, with the associated legislation, and the consequent strengthening of trade.

### Philipp Wilhelm von Hörnigk: 'Austria above all, if she only so wishes'

Hörnigk's striking title makes clear from the very beginning that we are dealing with an economic text carried along by patriotic passion. But if there were nothing more to it than this, it would naturally be forgotten today. Austria was faced with an external military threat to its survival, and Hörnigk wanted to strengthen Austrian finances as quickly as possible. His political vision was also focused on the role of the Austro-Hungarian state as a territorial unit and future power, sustained by the internal development of economic productive powers in a way that no one else had predicted or knew how to explain. The accuracy of the study is due to detailed knowledge of the means, the resources, the technical and political possibilities of achieving the goal of nation-building.

The political element in Hörnigk was given the more emphasis by historians of economic thought, the more relevant they thought his message. Roscher wrote in his *Geschichte der National-Oekonomik in Deutschland* [*History of Economics in Germany*], drafted during the Franco-Prussian war:

> This book is written under the fresh impression of the terrible events which beset Germany and Austria, in particular, from east and west between 1680 and 1684. I need note only the part of Louis XIV in the construction of the Reunion Chambers in 1680, the conquest of Strasbourg and Casale in 1681, the French invasion in the Spanish Netherlands in 1683, the capture of Luxembourg and Trier in 1684: each of these was as disgraceful as the contemporary siege of Vienna by the Turks was dreadful.
>
> (Roscher 1992 [1874], p. 290, my transl.)

Roscher even argues that 'a world dominion by Louis XIV was a greater threat than that of a hundred years earlier by Philip II, perhaps even a greater threat than that by Napoleon at the beginning of our century' (ibid., p. 267, my transl.). And, he continues, it is well-known with what

> claims to superiority Louis XIV's century made regarding art, poetry, science; how much it impressed the entire world and was considered a model not merely because of its courtly splendour but also with the deliberate establishment of a complete civil administration.
>
> (ibid., pp. 267–68, my transl.)

The challenge of the French was first dealt with in literature of the 1680s, and Hörnigk belongs there. The variety of German attempts to come to terms with this was still the object of irony in Goethe – in his *Faust* we read: 'A German hates a Frenchman sure enough – But has a true affection for his wine' (Goethe 1950, p.107). In the end, a dangerous prejudice was formed.

August Oncken's political classification of Cameralism begins with Charles V's government as a 'turning point in German history' and the anarchy of a realm divided along religious lines. In the sixteenth century the pamphlets on coinage are of particular interest, for example 'The dispute over coinage in the years around 1530' – probably the oldest economic controversy in Europe carried out in printed pamphlets – 'in which the two princely houses in

Saxony ... battled it out' (Oncken 1922, my transl.).[74] Among other issues, Oncken explores the problematic outflow of precious metals resulting from the import of luxury goods, a factor which also plays such an important role in Hörnigk's book. Following the destruction of the Thirty Years War in the first half of the seventeenth century, there was a need for guidance among government officials in the principalities [Landesfürstentümer] on the reconstruction of regions laid waste: to increase population, to promote production in the city and the countryside, to take advantage of each principality's natural resources – agriculture, lands, mines – and to establish an orderly state budget with manageable forms of taxation. Hörnigk also pursued this goal, but with a special urgency imposed by the state of emergency with regard to foreign policy, and in view of the already existing mismanagement.

Hörnigk was not an officer but a government official serving princely and ecclesiastical clients. The servant hid behind his works to such an extent that he published many texts under pseudonyms, bearing only his initials, or even anonymously. On the other hand, 'Beginning in 1684, Hörnigk's main work, *Oesterreich über alles*, was the most frequently reprinted economic publication in the German-language territories for a century' (Brauleke 1978, pp. 92ff., my transl.) and is said to have been at the time one of the most widely-read publications in the kingdom. Becher was constantly assumed to be the author (Oncken 1922, p. 230). Thus, the book became famous, but the writer did not. In the common literature about Hörnigk, about half of the information about his birth and death dates, his place of birth, the editions of the book, and the like, is erroneous;[75] and the biography, upon which we base our information today, contains no less than 34 different spellings of his name (Brauleke 1978, pp. 60ff.).[76]

Philipp Wilhelm von Hörnigk was born in Frankfurt am Main on 23 January 1640. His father was a professor and later a rector at the University of Mainz. The son Philipp Wilhelm enrolled there as a student in 1654. The Cameralist, mathematician, doctor and chemist Johann Joachim Becher was a student of the father and married Philipp Wilhelm's sister, Maria Veronika, in 1662.

It is easy to detect Becher's strong influence in Hörnigk's manuscripts. In 1660, Hörnigk was a student at the University of Ingolstadt. In 1665, he came in contact with Becher again, this time in Vienna. Hörnigk then appears to have accompanied the imperial envoy de Royas on a trip to Spain and on further journeys in Germany and to Sweden. In Vienna, Hörnigk (Hassinger 1951, pp. 174ff.) assisted Becher in the composition of his Cameralist masterpiece *Politischer Discurs* [Political Discourse] (1990 [1668]); he was in contact with the imperial court librarian Peter Lambeck – a connection which is said to have deepened his humanistic education – and as Royas' secretary he was familiar with the political and economic problems of the era. In 1668, Royas, who had in the meantime been named bishop, assigned Hörnigk the management of the royal [landesfürstlichen] parish St. Martin zu Hartberg, which Hörnigk held until 1676, apparently to the satisfaction of the bishop, and with great dedication to administrative tasks.

Hörnigk's administrative activities in the municipal parish can be verified by some records (Posch 1953). 'Ihro gestreng Herr' [Your mighty Lordship] (ibid., p. 350), as the young governor was addressed, was of great service in compiling a collection of documents about local history. There were occasional tensions with residents, which apparently arose from the fact that Hörnigk had to collect dues which were not spent in the parish because they were passed on to Royas, who spent them.

His first publication, a translation from the Spanish of the life of Sister Margareta of the Holy Cross, appeared as morality text [Tugendspiegel] (ibid., p. 351) of the time. During this period, Hörnigk also undertook journeys on imperial commission. In 1673, he travelled to Silesia, Northern Moravia, parts of Bohemia and Austria in order to gather trade statistics, which Becher then used in a memorandum about the commercial potential of the Hereditary Lands [Erblande]. This must constitute the source of the detailed economic knowledge which is so impressive in *Oesterreich über alles*.

Hörnigk further assisted Becher on a journey of inspection across Germany when he was commissioned to supervise the execution of an imperial edict banning the import of French goods. Hörnigk then accompanied Royas to Rome, travelling later to the courts of German sovereigns on a mission to reunify the church.

In 1680, Hörnigk entered the service of Count Johann Philipp von Lamberg, who as a special envoy of the Great Elector [Großer Kurfürst] was supposed to conclude an alliance between the emperor and Kurbrandenburg against France. Hörnigk, corresponding with Leibniz at this time, first expressed his thoughts on a suitable allied policy on the part of the imperial sovereigns to deal with the French threat (in 1681 the Free Imperial City of Strasburg was annexed). Frantic diplomatic efforts followed in order to provide Vienna support against the Turks.

In 1684, Hörnigk was named imperial secretary. That same year saw the swift publication of his book focusing on the new political situation: maintaining a balance with France and pushing back the Turks. Hörnigk moved back to Passau in 1689 and became an archivist there, while Lamberg was elected prince-bishop of Passau. He now began to write a great deal and he also produced new editions of his great work; but from our perspective closer examination of these activities is of less importance. He died in 1714. The death record of the Cathedral Rectory St. Stephan noted his death, listed the offices he held and characterized him as follows:

> Hic Francofurti ad moenum natus, et Moguntae in juventute educatus, uti fuit in vitâ Vir pius prudens sobrius castus et sapiens, iustus et misericors praesertim erga pauperes pupillos et oppressos, cuius longissimam seriem texêre non est opus...
>
> (Brauleke 1978, p. 39)[77]

It has been suggested that Hörnigk's importance has nothing to do with *Oesterreich über alles*, but instead with his so-called *Francopolita* manuscripts (ibid., pp. 81ff.). These three political pamphlets of 1682 (Gerstenberg 1930, pp. 820ff.), written on commission from Count Lamberg, made a careful case against attempting to defeat the French; as a result of that and their expressiveness they stand out from other pamphlets. The diplomats of the electorate of Brandenburg determined on a course of appeasement with France. Hörnigk wanted the German empire to be recognized as a legitimate descendent of the old French kingdom of Charles the Great; he favoured a moderate monarchy, and if the Germans collectively pulled together, 'the general welfare and the freedom of the fatherland will be well-served' (ibid., p. 827). Hörnigk's *Privilegien* [Privileges] manuscript, published in 1688, appears today equally a product of its time, arguing in support of the prerogatives of the House of Habsburg. His later treatises, found in various libraries in handwritten form, have an abstract scientific and historic character (Brauleke 1978, pp. 110–13 and Gerstenberg 1930, pp. 855–58). To the extent that this can be shown on the basis of excerpts from the few books available to us, these texts, and the correspondence with Leibniz in particular, generally confirm that Hörnigk is one of the few important authors in the German-speaking territories at the end of the seventeenth century who worked toward a cultural revival, following the decline wrought by the Thirty Years War. He wanted to inspire capable political bodies to a spirit of assertiveness.

It is surprising that a book like this, which over the course of a century went through so many editions, was prompted initially by a situation specific to that time: a war on two fronts which would have been so much easier to prosecute with a larger economy – if they had had one million talers more, they could have closed the route to Vienna for the Turks, Hörnigk (1708, pp. 6ff.) says. Throughout the kingdom, there is hardly a sovereign aware of the importance of economic questions and therefore ready to tackle the core problem of a new commercial policy – which is what the real economy of the country is, as opposed to the cameral economy of the ruler's territories. The imperial Hereditary Lands represent the most suitable economic space (ibid., pp. 4ff.). A restriction on imports is supposed to provide the means for introducing the new policy:

> One abstains for a very few years from manufactured silk, wool, and linen effects / as well as the so-called French goods / and in a state of extreme need and the danger of complete decline enjoys oneself with that / which God and Nature have so generously and adequately supplied.
>
> (ibid., p. 8, my transl.)

They should thus 'do penance for their pride' and 'in return keep the pestilential French fashion goods in their homeland' (ibid., p. 9, my transl.) – that is, until the local merchants have learned to imitate them! The Romans have already demonstrated that commercial production can be increased in the midst of a war, and that they create wealth like a Peruvian silver mine. This is also well-known, but the difficulty is – and here Hörnigk argues just like his brother-in-law Becher – that many merchants only sell imported goods: they buy manufactured products abroad and sell them at home, and the only equivalent acceptable in a foreign country, precious metals, disappears abroad. This complaint is made, it seems, in every century almost all over the world. Luther (1987 [1524]), too, as Hörnigk reminds the reader, has already made the same argument. The Japanese even made it in the Tokugawa era: Japan was artificially closed off to world trade but enjoyed a small, limited and controlled trade with Holland through a single, licensed factory. Since the Dutch had more interesting European goods on offer for which there was a demand in Japan than Japan was able to export to Europe via the Dutch, the resulting deficit had to be made up for by exports of precious metals from Japan. Arai Hakuseki (1657–1725) remarked that in something more than a hundred years Japan must have lost about a quarter of its gold and three-quarters of the silver in circulation. As a result, internal circulation, dependent upon precious metals, became much more difficult and demand fell off. The Japanese did not propose, for example, to promote exports, but sought to control and restrict the export trade (Morris-Suzuki 1989, pp. 22ff.).[78]

Hörnigk did not imagine that Austria could isolate itself over the long-term in the way that the Japanese had sealed off their distant island. Similar to List's protective tariffs, what he wanted was a temporary closure to enable the establishment of promising industries, especially textiles. Naturally, for this, the sovereigns must first of all actually condescend to devote their attention to economic issues. The author reminds the reader of models, like Maximilian of Bavaria, who were willing to do this:

> Also haben sich auch die beruehmtesten Helden / und die kluegsten Regenten dies seculi nicht geschaemet / Augen und Haende auf ihre Lands-Oeconomie, und in specie denen Manufacturen zu halten. Aber es gehoeren in gewissen Faellen und Umstaenden gleichsam Helden-Gemuether dazu / fast nicht weniger / als vor den Spitzen eines Kriegsheers zu stehen.
>
> (Hörnigk 1708, p. 17)[79]

Hörnigk sees nations gripped by a competition for wealth in which the country farthest ahead is the one which is the most developed; wealth and power have to be understood as '*Relativo*' (ibid., p. 20). The goods which are currently successful on the European market were unknown a few decades ago, and now 'through the cunning of the French, nearly everything is going to ruin' (ibid., p. 22, my transl.). Naturally, Hörnigk places achieving far-reaching autarky above success in exporting – a priority that can hardly be justified on purely economic terms and should even be, as in the ancient world, only understood as an example of power politics: in every war, an economically open land lacks critical imports and the export market collapses. He sees that manufacturing countries are richer than those well-provided with raw materials. The latter, however, are more independent.

Thus he arrives at his nine general rules for a national economy. The fundamental ideas may derive from Becher, but they became so widely disseminated by Hörnigk that, on the hundredth anniversary (1784) of his book, the editor of a new edition declared 'that Austria owes the greatest part of its prosperity to this book' (Brauleke 1978, p. 98, my transl.). It is a question of the utter exploitation of natural resources, even to the point where an efficient return on investment is no longer realized – of the domestic working-up of raw materials, and of the increase of population and its education. We also find here the appeal, characteristic of the Mercantile era, to combat idleness in any way possible.

These first three rules of the principles of production are followed by an additional three that may be understood as principles regarding circulation: gold and silver should remain in domestic circulation, thus, if at all possible, neither hoarded nor exported. If they are used for luxury items, then only for those produced inland. With regard to foreign trade, as far as imports are still necessary, direct exchange for products can help avoid purchases with precious metals.

The final three rules concern foreign trade: raw materials from abroad must be processed domestically (it is, therefore, a matter of creating domestic value). Exports should be sent to even the most distant regions, so far as the possibilities for export production allow. Finally, Hörnigk ends up insisting that domestic goods be purchased even if their price is twice that of imported goods.

Hörnigk (1708, p. 32) claimed that his rules were so obviously reasonable that they hardly required substantiation. The question arises, therefore, of what the economic circumstances might have been to make to experienced administrator seem right what in part radically contradicts principles of economic administration and modern liberal economics.

There were, although we hardly observe this happening today, frequent failures in the money supply due to the limitations of the credit system; hence continuous and uninterrupted circulation of coins appeared to be an indisputable precondition for prosperity. In the absence of more flexible substitutes for money, the outflow of precious metals caused crises both locally and regionally. Taking this and the backwardness of Austrian industry into consideration, and remembering the consequences of the wars, the lack of training and the resigned attitude of the population, it is certainly easier to understand why Hörnigk took such a drastic approach and was able to convince his readers. The uninterrupted circulation of cash was a necessary condition for continuous demand. In a state expanding in land, population and economic power, import substitution was supposed to increase job opportunities due to regional divisions of labour. In contrast, a decided orientation toward exports would, due to the dangers of the international situation, not generate stable prospects for development. The shock-therapy of a sudden prohibition on imports should promote the economic integration of the Habsburg empire, which could be united under absolutism but which had been weakened by linguistic, cultural and administrative differences, through legal fiefdoms and geographic fragmentation. The success recorded in the eighteenth century demonstrates how correct this vision essentially was; excessive formulations, whether rhetorical or due to a lack of economic insight, even the overrating of protectionism, are by comparison of little importance.

Hörnigk does his best to strengthen his analysis with detailed descriptions of economic conditions. Whoever has a sense for historical detail will read with pleasure his descriptions of the potential for agricultural development, and his (partly) implausible hope for the production of ore and precious stones. Having a wide-ranging and baroque knowledge of merchandise (*Warenkunde*), he does not fail to point out all the wonders brought by foreign trade with the Orient and the West, with the North and even more so with the South. He obstinately insists on the availability of substitutes: all kinds of food and clothing are actually available locally, smoked sea-fish on the other hand is unhealthy, spiced tea is unnatural, domestic wool is more useful than imported silk, and so on.

Then he reasons with the reader about the social conditions for the mobilization of the workforce. How can it be that the mountain farmers are richer than those labourers who work on the plain? Are they more industrious and the others lazy oafs, because nature forces the former to work? Is it not possible to make everyone work? Are the Hereditary Lands lacking in the understanding necessary for the construction of manufactures? The '*esprit brillant*' consists only 'in an untamed delicacy [Fürbrüchigkeit] of speech', not in an 'especial brightness of reason' (ibid., p. 54, my transl.). Even the hated French king – according to an anecdote – was forced to recognize the mechanical skill of the Nuremburg artisans – and artillery and printing are German inventions, are they not? Thus, growth can, in modern terms, be based upon endogenous technical progress, right?

After Hörnigk has described the natural and human wealth of the Hereditary Lands, he gets ready to illustrate each of his rules. The reader can discover here which of the various lines of agricultural and craft innovation preceded the Industrial Revolution and prepared the way for it. The draining of swamps, the clearing of forests, the introduction of agricultural products like potatoes, tomatoes, tobacco, of the mulberry tree for sericulture, and many others are mentioned, but what is most decisive is how the raw materials will be processed. Why always somewhere else and not in Austria? 'And anyhow do not we, like others, have brains / eyes / hands?' (ibid., p. 71, my transl.). As a result the author constantly reels between the contradictory poles of posing as the advocate of tradition and the enlightened advocate of economic development in Germany, a position which would long be a source of torment: the goal consists of successfully imitating and surpassing foreign production, but this production is actually ironically dismissed for its frivolity: 'the French wigs better befit German heads / than German hair itself' (ibid., p. 77, my transl.). Here finally is a quantitative estimation, of the kind found in *Political Arithmetick*, for which Hörnigk's contemporary William Petty (1992 [1690])[80] was renowned. Assuming a particular value-added per capita (thus, to echo Marx, a certain rate of surplus value), he estimates the profit earned by a successful Dutch city from handicrafts (Hörnigk 1708, pp. 79ff.). Attempts to quantify appear throughout the book, but only here is a serious calculation attempted which, if further developed, could have provided a starting point for a discussion of some theoretical depth.

Hörnigk now feels that an almost unbridgeable gap exists between the economic goals he proposes and actual practice in the land. He relies firstly on a change of consciousness, not on communicating with individual political figures:

> Yes, the happy Turkish plight / Austria's blessed havoc / desired flight from Vienna / when you provide the occasion / that eyes are finally opened / and lends a hand / and by your / so to say sacrifice of a part of the cargo / the absolutely dilapidated / ship of the Hereditary lands which will soon be succumbing to the tempest / will be saved from the brutal storm and collapse and be rescued!
>
> (ibid., pp. 86–7, my transl.)

Naturally, however, the realization of this policy can only be expected from monarchs. 'Yes, I say / our salvation must derive from the princes of our people / without them the community can do little' (ibid., p. 87). His polemic against the insecurity of the merchants shows how little trust he has for the spontaneous activities of entrepreneurs. It is the usual view that manufactures must be initiated through the granting of privileges. 'But these ways are in my opinion uncertain / boring / and to our German humour unfailingly petty at the start' (ibid., p. 100, my transl.). The rich who could invest money will not. Therefore, he recommends shock therapy in which import substitution comes not at the beginning but at the end; the prohibition of the import of foreign luxury goods is supposed to serve as the catalyst. His vision of the implementation of this project is certainly far too simple:

> Paper and ink / some decrees on tolls and passes / instructing a number of officials / establishment of inspections and customs / and compulsory and merciless punishment of the first or others / who are caught with stinking fish.
>
> (ibid., p. 102, my transl.)

This statement is followed by troubled praise of the deterrent effect of draconian punishments. In a countermove, so to speak, he expresses the hope that very few years might suffice to generate a rush of production that would in turn make at least the extreme form of protectionism superfluous.

The questionable nature of the therapy does not reduce our interest in Hörnigk's diagnosis. It forces him at least in the many pages that follow, written in a clear and elegant prose, to deal with polemic and counterargument. But we will here leave these to one side. He provides insight into the court's motives, mobilizes voices against lazy workers (are the people 'accustomed to laying around like wretches?', ibid., p. 122, my transl.), and cites Grotius and the law of nations in order to justify protectionism. Back in the ancient world, according to Strabo, it was allowed: 'importare merces quasdam licet, quasdam non item' (ibid., p. 129).[81] He does not however limit himself to the legal position. He also estimates potential countermeasures from foreign governments, and at the same time provides insight into the contemporary system of alliances, and the importance of dynastic relationships between the ruling houses. He considers seemingly modern support measures, such as the subsidy of banks, and wishes to allow the guilds no control over the manufactures. Like Savary (1993 [1675]),[82] he would like to see an improvement of the merchant class in society in order to inspire them with entrepreneurial pride. Even the scientific treatment of business techniques and the improvement of infrastructure (expansion of inland shipping) are part of his programme (Hörnigk 1708, p. 170). It is impossible to deny the comprehensive character of his conception of autarky.

From the conclusion of the book it is not difficult to gather that Hörnigk is anything but certain of success for his book: 'Odio, an amore dignus videbor?' (ibid., p. 194).[83] He had been very rough in his treatment of a running sore.

The title of the book survived the longest, and became a well-known saying. It was first modified to 'Teutschland über alles' [Germany above all] in 1798, and thus made its way into Hoffmann von Fallersleben's 'Deutschlandlied' [German National Anthem] in 1841.

Among the effects of the book was that after the wars in Germany Hörnigk – even if less than other Cameralists – helped awaken a hitherto slumbering interest in the technical aspects of manufactures and business (Troitsch 1966, p. 22). His strength lay in the field of administration. Though he did not come from Austria, he formulated policies for the Habsburg state because its 'large size and position of power … appeared to put it in the best position for commercial and economic policy in a grand style' (Facius 1959, pp. 23ff., my transl.). Herbert Knittler, in his overview of 'Die Donaumonarchie [The Danube Monarchy] 1648–1848' (1993), has described the rise of Austria-Hungary, and again and again in this text we come across conceptions consistent with those of Hörnigk.

Several facts on that subject: The Hereditary Lands in the second half of the seventeenth century consisted of territories under Austrian control, Bohemian territories and that part of Hungary not under Ottoman control, in all an area of about 100,000 km$^2$. In 1795, following the third partitioning of Poland, the Habsburg Monarchy had grown to an area of over 640,000 km$^2$; 'after Russia it was the second largest nation in Europe based on surface area' (ibid., p. 887, my transl.). The low point in population growth was not reached, regionally, until around 1680; after that a large population increase began (the first half of the eighteenth century ca. 10 million people, at the beginning of the nineteenth century over 30 million people, ibid., p. 890).

The increase is a result not only of quantitative economic growth but also of a qualitative transformation – as it were, a systematic transformation on the Cameralist model. The financial administration was centralized in a series of reforms. Income came from the dominions and state monopolies, and also from contributions; although income from the dominions had shrunk since the sixteenth century and in order to compensate for this the state monopolies (salt, mining, customs) and other monopolies (the tobacco monopoly) and indirect taxes increased. Contributions were based primarily on direct taxes on land and buildings. The state may have been chronically indebted; however, banking institutions which provided debt-servicing on improved terms gained in importance over the course of the eighteenth century. Time and again coins had to be devalued and precious metal content reduced. A more stable currency was finally achieved in the middle of the eighteenth century – and the Maria-Theresia-Taler dominated as a means of payment in the Levant trade.

Cameralism was an expression and medium in efforts toward reform and centralization during this phase of absolutist state-building. However, the suggestions of the Cameralists Becher, Hörnigk, and Schröder were only gradually implemented.

> The fundamental causes of this delay include scepticism about the court [Hofstellen], political considerations, a shortage of money, as well as wars. An array of plans and ideas only gained acceptance in the second, high-mercantilist period. It began with Maria Theresa's accession to the throne and, from approximately the time of the co-regency of Joseph II (1765), continued into the late-mercantilist period.
>
> (ibid., p. 901, my transl.)

The introduction of manufacturing and the creation of independent industrial textile processing also took place in the middle of the eighteenth century (ibid., p. 907). Attempts at increasing exports included the establishment of trading companies and the promotion of Mediterranean ports (first quarter of the eighteenth century), but production for the domestic market predominated (ibid., pp. 909ff.). Thus the connection between history of economic thought and economic history is especially close with respect to Cameralism, although this is not to suggest that the texts of the Cameralists were an immediate, significant influence on reality. However, they at least provided a decisive written form for the ideas for projects which were in the air.

There was possibly greater awareness on the part of historians of economic thought of the Cameralists in the first half of the twentieth century than in the second; works by Tautscher (1947), Sommer (1920), and Zielenziger (1966 [1914]) rank among the standards. The shift in values following the Second World War that led to this change is an expression not only of an adjustment in general historical consciousness but also of a larger, modern interest in liberalism and its traditions. Each generation chooses its own models.

Today, the unification of Europe could once again provide the occasion for a more intensive consideration of Cameralism, because there can be no doubt that its influence persists; and it must be understood as an expression, even as a determining factor for the various peculiarities of economic styles and administrative practices in European countries. Most modern economists, however, remain unconscious of the connection between the tradition of economic and political practices with those of economic thought. In addition, the dominance of the English language in the economic sciences has contributed to the superficial impression that Mercantilism was on the whole an English phenomenon. The continental traditions, therefore, remain to be explored; in any case, they require re-interpretation. Before we complain too loudly that international literature takes too little notice of the German-language inheritance, we should however also consider how little is known here in Germany about Italian, Spanish, and Polish economic thought, or of that of other countries, of any time, where there was a lively exchange of ideas among European writers and intellectuals – we should recall the long journeys Hörnigk undertook. There still remains much to study about the multifaceted character of early modern economic literature.[84]

## William Petty's *Political Arithmetick*

William Petty is one of the most colourful, adventurous and, one could well say, brilliant personalities in the history of economic thought. His bold and, for their time, astonishingly apt assessments, his theoretically sharp but practical conclusions, his visionary recommendations and perspective upon the future do, however, also occasionally culminate in suggestions that are alarmingly all but totalitarian. In *An Essay in Political Arithmetick Concerning Ireland (A Treatise of Ireland*, 1687, in *EW*, vol. 2, pp. 545ff.),[85] he attempts to show that the ordered resettlement of a million people from Ireland to England, leaving behind 300,000 who are supposed to raise cattle and produce milk, could be advantageous for the English crown and for the welfare of the kingdom as a whole. In a thoroughgoing cost-benefit analysis he calculates that the costs, including those for goods left behind, the ships and the resettlement, would finally be compensated by the advantage of gainful employment. At least he declares that it is not necessary to assert the right of the conqueror, since the removal of the population could also improve the well-being of those being resettled.

In the same spirit he estimated and compared the population size of world cities based on analyses of the number of people who died in hospitals (ibid., pp. 499ff. and pp. 519ff.), or calculated what today would be called the national product and national assets by estimating the size of the population multiplied by per capita wages, which sum is then multiplied by the product of the surface area of the country and its average return per unit of area. He then capitalizes the incomes (*EW*, vol. 1, p. 267).

The motivation for this kind of calculation is, firstly, the resolve to support a new scientific understanding, borrowed from natural science, based on

'Number, Weight, or Measure' (*Preface*, ibid., p. 244); and secondly, the desire to further the power and influence of the sovereign. At the same time, when developing economic and financial concepts, he always kept in mind the strengthening of social cohesion and military defence.

The period in which Petty was writing was not yet the age of the great syntheses in political national economy. Petty's multifaceted texts, some of which were published during his lifetime and others that first came to light posthumously, can sometimes be perplexing because of the contradictory statements they contain. The essential features of his thought do however stand out clearly. In this essay on Petty's *Political Arithmetick*, a work characteristic of his writing and incorporating his basic ideas, I will expand upon some of his ideas – aware of the risk of historical generalizations – and confirm that he is one of the precursors of the classic authors of what Adam Smith called the Mercantile System. In view of the time that now separates us from him, there is no need for artificial consideration when we are forced to describe the dark side of his century, something which is also visible in his life.

Petty, born in 1623 of humble origins, went to sea at 13 but was set ashore in France after an accident. In a Jesuit college in Caen, he studied Latin, Greek and French as well as mathematics and astronomy. After returning to England, he served in the navy but returned to the continent at the age of 20, primarily to study medicine. We next find him, at age 27, a professor in Oxford and somewhat later in London, but in 1652 he gave up medicine and became a surveyor in Ireland.

It was the time of the English Revolution and the Civil War that would finally lead to Oliver Cromwell's Protectorate. The political change appears to have been conducive to Petty's brief career as a scholar of medicine. Writing of the breaking of Irish resistance, Churchill referred to the 'Cromwellian brutality' with which the Puritan Republicans committed 'savage crimes' that only recurred in the twentieth century, on a larger scale:

> By an uncompleted process of terror, by an iniquitous land settlement, by the virtual proscription of the Catholic religion, he [Cromwell] … cut new gulfs between the nations and the creeds. The consequences of Cromwell's rule in Ireland have distressed and at times distracted English politics down even to the present day.
>
> (Churchill 1974 [1956], pp. 231ff.)

According to Petty's own estimations, more than a half million people were killed in Ireland in the fighting and by mass executions, but especially through famines and epidemics that came with the war.

The survey commission which Petty was able to secure for himself was an important project for the mapping of Ireland. A cadastral survey was to be made, which would then become the basis for turning over the largest part of Ireland to English landowners. Petty managed to profit from the distribution process and became an important landowner himself. Here he began to take a position on the question of the movement of populations ('transplantations'), which were important for pacification and land use. Over a thousand people took part in the surveying project led by Petty.

From that point on, Petty divided his time between London and Ireland. Land redistribution led to many unpleasant lawsuits, but they did not hinder his various technical-scientific activities. He presented himself as an inventor and co-founder of the 'Royal Society', an organization that promoted the new natural science knowledge and whose foundation was connected with the towering figure of Newton. He became politically active once more; his writings were influential, even if high political office was denied him. Petty enjoyed a happy family life. The difficulties that he at first had with the Restoration of 1660 gradually faded. In his papers he is clearly in favour of freedom of conscience and religious tolerance, but he constantly calls for strong government, avoiding considerations of legitimacy and the detail of division of powers within the state.

It is said of his method that:

> The author shows a marked tendency to keep in view the practical aspect of questions and to found his reasoning on observation and on facts gained through his own experience, rather than on those methods of deductive reasoning which were pursued by the economists of a later school. In this respect Petty's methods are far more suggestive of Adam Smith than of Ricardo; and they bring him into touch with the economists of the present day, such as … Marshall.

This is how Petty was interpreted by his entry in the old *Palgrave* in 1899 (Fitzmaurice 1899, p. 100). The comparison made by Fitzmaurice with Marshall should make clear that Petty was treated at this time neither as a statistician nor as a pure theorist, but instead as an applied economist; collecting figures, extrapolating from them, constructing contexts and seeking theoretical forms of expression.

It must be said that this scientific approach was still quite new. It might be true that Francis Bacon had done away with the old Aristotelian scientific view that theory was derived from first principles, placing it above the practical and useful applied sciences. However, although Newton's mechanics offered both a useful and a theoretical science, it only becomes clear in the late eighteenth and early nineteenth centuries how this could be of obvious practical use, in ballistics, or the static calculations for wide-span bridges. In fact precise ballistic calculations made in the early eighteenth century had no practical outcome since it was not then possible to machine the barrels of cannons sufficiently exactly, and the gunpowder employed could not be produced sufficiently consistently; the precision offered by theoretical calculation remained therefore theoretical and without practical military application. In the Renaissance, a century before Petty, the doctrine of proportions had resulted in a connection between mathematics and arts such as architecture, which had hitherto been treated as craft practices. Ideal relationships like the golden mean, which were thought to exist in nature, became a principal in construction. But the value of practical sciences and the possibility of reinforcing them with theoretical principles was still something that had to be fought for in Petty's time. This explains his constant need to defend his method, as he does in his foreword to *Political Arithmetick* where he describes his method as 'not yet very usual'.

There are personal and individual traits in the application of Petty's method. From my own experience his efforts appear to be most closely related to scenario calculation in the analysis of energy utilization (Meyer-Abich and Schefold 1981, p. 162), since such estimations are made on the basis of uncertain numerical data. These concern for example the contribution worldwide of firewood to power supply, the price of oil in twenty years, or the climate effect for future generations. A small number of different energy policies would lead to different outcomes, which are then in turn assessed politically and provided with outlines for their implementation. Some policies tend more strongly toward technical solutions, while others place greater trust in desired social changes, such as an increasing interest in the avoidance of wasting energy. For Petty, estimations, extrapolations, and judgments connect outcomes and political influences in a similar fashion. From these he quickly arrives at conclusions which identify economic regularities and place them at the service of state action, relying for this more on administrative and technical means than on social change and ethical standards; although he is also capable of making insightful sociological observations.

We habitually attribute the obvious differences between the development of European and North American civilization and the more traditional non-European cultures which lagged behind in the nineteenth century to the economic transformation of the mercantile period. In this period European states were successively united into principalities and territorial states which were increasingly subjected to the standardized legislation of the absolutist state. A process of growth began which drove nations, by virtue of their political rivalry, to reorganize their economic institutions as a way of securing their power bases. Immanuel Wallerstein goes so far as to speculate that a united Europe in the sixteenth century – he is thinking of the results of a particular successful outcome of Charles V's imperial policy – could well have obstructed the forces of progress, so that an Industrial Revolution might not even have taken place. China and other countries could have reached a technical stage comparable or perhaps even greater than that of the European nations in the sixteenth century; but in that case imperial policy suppressed the use of new technologies for factories, and restricted the opening and development of the empire through trade (Wallerstein 1974). This thought, however theoretical and different from historical fact it may be, still illustrates the questions we have to ask when examining the period of transformation between the dawn of the modern era, initiated by the discovery of the New World, and the development of industrial capitalism. What are the specific stages in the transition from feudal production, with predominantly local market relationships, to the development of ever-larger markets for goods? How did the national labour market establish itself where previously the connection of guild and social background prevailed? How did landed property change and, above all, how did the development of manufacture and industrial production come about?

Petty's book *Political Arithmetick* can be considered among the best witnesses of these changes. If the initial expression of mercantilist thought is that trading policy must be directed to the increase of gold and silver in the royal treasury, we also find this idea expressed in *Political Arithmetick*. However, the notion that there has to be a surplus on the balance of trade, so that through sales of English manufactured goods Spanish silver flows into the country, is so common in his work that it is quite conventional, more or less a literary topos. What is important is how he focuses his attention on the generation of the general conditions conducive to this goal, and considers other goals to be at least equally important – in modern terms economic growth, raised productivity, infrastructural development, employment policy, defence (for conquest is not really his intention).

We can demonstrate this with a few examples. In the *Treatise of Taxes and Contributions* (*EW*, vol. 1, pp. 1–97), Petty writes that export duties should not be so high that a competitive disadvantage develops with the exports of rival nations (ibid., Ch. 6, pp. 54–61). On the other hand, import duties should be high enough that imports are then more expensive than competing domestic products. These duties should be higher on luxury goods in particular, whose consumption should be restricted. However, all customs duties should remain low enough that they do not promote smuggling. Petty knows, incidentally, that a surplus on the balance of trade does not lead to a surplus in the balance of payments if the corresponding balance on transfers is negative, a thought which he naturally does not formulate in so many words. Instead, he illustrates it with the example of Ireland, where English landlords resident in Britain transfer their rents out of the country, impoverishing the unhappy island despite its surplus of export goods (ibid., p. 46).

Thus the balance of trade argument is not for him the only decisive point of view. The possibilities of intervention through duties are limited and, in itself, a positive balance of trade is not a sufficient condition for an inflow of foreign gold. Duties are not even Petty's preferred form of state financing. Instead, he tends to favour expenditure taxes, slanted more to luxury goods than the necessities of life. He naturally thinks of raising taxes in the form of duties and indirect taxes, but it is certainly appropriate to use the expression 'expenditure tax' here since he contrasts them with the notion of an income tax (*EW*, vol. 1, p. 271). As regards distribution, he makes it a requirement that the distribution of wealth be unaltered by taxation. He has no ambition to modify social structure through taxation.[86]

He defines the value of the money by the bullion content of coins (*EW*, vol. 2, pp. 437–48); and so the value of money changes just like that of other goods. Nevertheless, he recognizes in *Political Arithmetick* the trade-promoting effect of expanding the money supply through credit provided by banks (*EW*, vol. 1,

p. 265). Petty provides a clear illustration of the velocity of circulation of money, a concept which is for him very concrete. He imagines that craftsmen and workers are paid weekly, and that the richer have on average a slower turnover of cash in hand, related to the idea of the motivation for holding cash balances. The circulation of money between wages and necessary goods is however originally determined by custom. In any case, the amount of money is therefore no longer the measure of the wealth of a country: for two countries with the same money supply, if money circulates faster in one country than the other, then that country clearly enjoys a higher turnover of goods (*EW*, vol. 1, p. 113).

With regard to the level of the interest rate, Petty observes one condition for equilibrium: the interest rate of a secure investment cannot be lower than the net yield of an investment in land ownership. A theory of interest cannot be derived from this because the value of the land is itself dependent upon the capitalization of the yield through the interest rate. Petty's theory of interest is not entirely consistent since his value theory is likewise undeveloped. Keynes attributes to him a monetary determination of the interest rate: the money supply does not affect the price level(since the relative prices of gold and goods are determined by costs); thus the interest rate falls with the increasing circulation of money, and the holding of cash balances becomes a factor (Keynes 1967, p. 342).

We now return to Petty's treatment of the labour theory of value. His famous pronouncement about wealth, that 'labour is its father and the earth its mother' (*EW*, vol. 1, p. 68),[87] has old roots and can be interpreted only in hindsight as anticipating the labour theory of value developed by the classical school.

I find Petty's thoughts on the productive contribution of labour particularly interesting and characteristic. In his *Treatise of Taxes and Contributions* of 1662 he writes about a job creation scheme as follows:

> In the next place it will be asked, who shall pay these men? I answer, every body; for if there be 1000 men in a Territory, and if 100 of these can raise necessary food and raiment for the whole 1000. If 200 more make as much commodities, as other Nations will give either their commodities or money for, and if 400 more be employed in the ornaments, pleasure, and magnificence of the whole; if there be 200 Governours, Divines, Lawyers, Physicians, Merchants, and Retailers, making in all 900 the question is, since there is food enough for this supernumerary 100 also, how they should come by it? whether by begging, or by stealing; or whether they shall suffer themselves to starve, finding no fruit of their begging, or being taken in their stealing to put to death another way? Or whether they sahll [shall] be given away to another Nation that will take them? I think 'tis plain, they ought neither to be starved, nor hanged, nor given away; now if they beg, they may pine for hunger to day, and be gorged and glutted to morrow, which will occasion Diseases and evil habits, the same may be

said of stealing; moreover, perhaps they may get either by begging or stealing more than will suffice them, which will for ever after indispose them to labour, even upon the greatest occasion which may suddenly and unexpectedly [happen].

(*EW,* vol. 1, p. 30)

This encapsulates one of Petty's main concerns. The economy is subdivided into sectors which make very different contributions to the welfare 'of the whole'. Agriculture, manufacture, and export (to the extent that such activity contributes to the procurement of necessary goods) support a weighty super-structure which is itself ambiguous. On the one hand the intrinsic goal of the economic and social body appears to be the development of wealth, luxury and knowledge. On the other hand, however, Petty sees an involvement here with activity which is insufficiently productive. For example, he repeatedly condemns superfluous lawyers and priests, and proposes practical means whereby the number of people thus employed could be reduced to a reasonable number.

'The whole' is sustained by simple labour which has to be available for production; therefore Petty reiterates the notion that the productive potential of a country has to be strengthened by an active population policy, even including plans for the introduction of foreigners. He is thus engaged with the problem of how sufficient workers can be made available for long-term growth.

There is, however, also the constant problem that not all workers find employment, and the poor have to be cared for. The alternatives offered by traditional employment policies are quite openly identified by Petty: the suppression of the tendency toward crime in those living in poverty, emigration, the provision of mercenaries, and begging. If Petty presents an employment policy, this is not out of humanitarian motives, but instead for the sake of social control and the maintenance of a preparedness to work. He continues:

For all these Reasons, it will be certainly the safer way to afford them the superfluity which would otherwise be lost and wasted, or wantonly spent: Or in case there be no overplus, then 'tis fit to retrench a little from the delicacy of others feeding in quantity or quality; few men spending less than double of what might suffice them as to the bare necessities of nature. Now as to the work of these supernumeraries, let it be without expence of Foreign Commodities, and then 'tis no matter if it be employed to build a useless Pyramid upon Salisbury Plain, bring the Stones at Stonehenge to Tower Hill, or the like; [f]or at worst this would keep their minds to discipline and obedience, and their bodies to a patience of more profitable labours when need shall require it.

(ibid., p. 31)

The example of the pyramid was taken up by Keynes (1967 [1936], pp. 129–31), although in expressing his admiration he wonders why such employment policy measures for the most part made use of such absurd suggestions. Gold mines created no real utility, Keynes said, and suggested that it would be the same if the central bank stuffed banknotes into bottles, deposited them in old mines, had the mines filled and then invited the public to dig out the money so that work might be created. Do we really have to stoop to creating utterly *meaningless* work? There is however one argument against an employment policy targeting *meaningful work*: it reduces the number of investment opportunities for private entrepreneurs. A more appropriate economic policy seeks to promote growth through the creation of a suitable economic framework which would pre-empt any such dilemma between useful or useless work.

However the employment situation in developed countries may be assessed today, Petty speaks to us as an economist during a transition period in which the conditions for a functional employment market – with standard working hours and intensity, with training and with a guarantee of mobility despite social security – still had to be established. For a long time to come, the local parish remained responsible for the care of the poor and indigent, so that leaving home to seek a good wage but not necessarily long-term employment elsewhere was risky. Differences in economic organization between countries and eras are related to variations in the approach to unemployment. Petty's suggestions no longer appear cynical when they are compared to the real, contemporary alternatives he mentions.

The degree to which Petty should be included among the founders of Classic Economics will remain controversial. Why labour would for him become a measure of wealth can be seen in his vision of the production process. The division of labour into different sectors is for Petty also an indicator of the value produced in these sectors. He writes:

> Suppose a man could with his own hands plant a certain scope of Land with Corn, that is, could Digg, or Plough, Harrow, Weed, Reap, Carry home, Tresh, and Winnow so much as the Husbandry of this Land requires; and had withal Seed wherewith to sowe the same. I say, that when this man hath subducted his seed out of the proceed of his Harvest, and also, what himself hath both eaten and given to others in exchange for Clothes, and other Natural necessaries; that the remainder of Corn is the natural and true Rent of the Land for that year; and the medium of seven years, or rather of so many years as makes up the Cycle, within which Dearths and Plenties make their revolution, doth give the ordinary Rent of Land in Corn.
>
> (*EW*, vol. 1, p. 43)

Here we can see the emergence of abstractions which would later be so fruitful for the Physiocrats and Ricardian thought, solving the problem of valuation in the calculating costs and returns by reduction to one agricultural good, in which the product and the means of production are homogeneous. Later this procedure, with the additional precondition that corn be interpreted as the basic commodity, would serve to determine the rate of profit. Ricardo's successors followed the master in the formulation of 'corn models', or one-sector models, in which capital and return were expressed as amounts of corn.[88] At the time for Petty, isolating the surplus itself was enough.

Immediately following that, he goes a step further:

> But a further, though collateral question may be, how much English money this Corn or Rent is worth? I answer, so much as the money, which another single man can save, within the same time, over and above his expence, if he imployed himself wholly to produce and make it; viz. Let another man go travel into a Countrey where is Silver, there Dig it, Refine it, bring it to the same place where the other man planted his Corn; Coyne it, etc. the same person, all the while of his working for Silver, gathering also food for his necessary livelihood, and procuring himself covering, etc. I say, the Silver of the one, must be esteemed of equal value with the Corn of the other: the one being perhaps twenty Ounces and the other twenty Bushels. From whence it follows, that the price of a Bushel of this Corn to be an Ounce of Silver.
>
> (*EW*, vol. 1, p. 43)

Here an additional and more abstract step is taken in the determination of relative prices: all the various activities which are necessary for the production of silver, and in particular provision for the workers, are treated like a vertical, integrated process – one could talk here of a Sraffian subsystem[89] – so that all the necessary functions for the production of silver are reduced to the labour time of a single individual. The product of the labour time of the silver producer is worth the same as the product of the corn producer – including the costs of auxiliary products, says Petty – when both have worked the same amount of time. This is the labour theory of value theory in practically its rawest form. Petty may speak of complications that will arise from various risks, but it escapes him entirely how profit would be taken into account, how a uniform rate of profit or interest on capital can be assumed – in short, he is quite literally still centuries away from the issues that would later become objects of discussion.

Nonetheless, we find in him indications of the solution to one of the problems of the objective theory of value which was later neglected by classical economics. It is *one* question how the prices of goods are formed according to conditions of supply and demand, if one assumes uniform prices for these goods on account of their homogeneity and the similarity of production processes in each industry. The debates about value theory in the nineteenth and twentieth century turned on this question. It is a quite *different* question, however, regarding the basis upon which we could even assume homogeneous products, without which it makes no sense to speak of uniform prices. In local markets, even in individual exchanges, there does not have to be any such homogeneity. Thus even today in developing countries it can be observed how, without use of a pair of scales, fruit is sold by the piece, not according to weight or number but individual merits: one is perhaps better looking and smells better and is therefore more valuable than another, which is perhaps larger. Closely connected to the question of the homogeneity of the products – the uniformity of corn, apples, or iron, for example – is the question of how the various transactions in market segments are coordinated into an entire market.

For the subjective theory of value two physically different goods – like two different metal alloys – are considered the same when all buyers treat them as perfect substitutes. The Classical theory of value proceeded from the objective characteristics of goods, but strictly speaking only elementary particles are strictly indistinguishable as are, consequently, molecules strictly of the same composition. Solid bodies, crystals, are indistinguishable if they display strictly the same order of all the identical molecules – obviously too strict a requirement for uniformity in the economy, where two sacks of rice for all practical economic purposes could be considered equivalents, even when the grains maintain a certain individuality and their number only coincides approximately.

Petty deals with this issue in his 'Dialogue of Diamonds' (*EW*, vol. 2, pp. 624–30).[90] His answer is really quite simple: the diamond trade is run by special diamonds dealers, who maintain contact with one another around world – he provides an example how a change in the price of diamonds in Persia (because prices have increased perhaps due to a local celebration) also influences the London market. The traffic among the dealers does not however simply involve prices, which every economist discusses, but primarily the quality of diamonds, in which weight, appearance, cut, colouring and so forth are taken into consideration. Petty quickly runs through an explanation of certain rules, such as secondary characteristics (for example, colour) which can modify the basic price defined first of all by type and weight. In order for such pricing rules to be discussed, however, the commodity must have been described with its characteristics. For Petty, this is done between the merchants involved who form an association with its own organizational structures. Modern neoclassicism seeks the explanation for this in savings in transport, on transaction costs.

Here it must be remembered that seventeenth-century literature is rich in texts on the commercial knowledge of commodities (*Warenkunde*), in which merchants describe the characteristics of good Flemish cloth, French brocades, German embroidery, and so on. In the Classical era classical economics the collective work of describing goods was normally taken as a given, without further consideration, when they spoke of the 'use value' of these goods as a social determination. The associated institutions do have a long history, including the definition of weights and measures, regulations regarding the calibration of scales and weights, as well as agreements about standards of quality, all of which are preconditions for the price to be negotiated on the basis of a well-defined, fixed use-value; price fluctuations are then expressions of changes in the supply and demand relationship. In the Medieval era by contrast, it was often the case instead that the price was set and fluctuations – perhaps in the weight of the bread or the composition of the flour – were permitted if the wheat or rye harvest turned out better or worse than anticipated.

Violent shifts in politics, the economy and the thinking of his era are reflected in Petty's work and lend it a special fascination. Petty's social and political rise occurred during the era of Cromwell; but in Chapter 9 of *Political Arithmetick*, according to Hull probably drafted in 1676 and published in 1690, he writes of the fortunate *Restoration*, which had been preceded by the *Usurpation*. In Chapter 10, he looks forward to the time when the King's subjects trade on a global scale; through 'unity, industry, and obedience' (*EW*, vol. 1, p. 313), this goal is achievable and, in point of fact, the English later came quite close to it.

Chapter 1 of *Political Arithmetick* begins by pointing out the importance of increasing the productivity of land and labourers; the productivity of the latter is rooted in the use of talent, tools, and mechanization. A nation can realize its potential productivity as a result of location and historically-obtained advantages, but above all from an astute governance of institutions. The comparisons and assessment of countries that Petty presents are not an end in themselves, but instead serve the goal of keeping England's growth potential firmly in view. Here his particular attention to the proper allocation of labour reappears. He recognizes something like external economies of scale in the increase of population density, brought about by better communication and defence; but also because manufacturing is more profitable than agriculture, and trade is more profitable than manufacturing, both of which require spatial concentration.

Petty calls farmers, sailors, soldiers, craftsmen and merchants the real foundations of the state, while all the other great occupations have grown out of the weaknesses and mismanagement of the state. He values the exercise of these professions higher on the basis of their financial reward. This consideration appears to anticipate marginal productivity theory, though he would otherwise explain wage-levels to be determined by the level of subsistence, in a rather classic Malthusian manner. Petty's era is not yet ready for the rigour of Ricardian abstractions; they also run counter to his practical bent. Therefore, he is also undogmatic in his concept of wealth, and in a quite mercantilist step defines the acquisition of imperishable items of wealth – silver, gold, and jewels – as the ultimate effect of trade; he would also, however, consider other goods as wealth.

It is worth noting that in contrast with the Dutch, Petty does not discuss freedom of conscience as a value in itself, but instead as a means of promoting trade with sober and industrious people. This also avoids the costs imposed upon a larger community of believers by an excessive number of priests. It is always the minorities who most strongly advocate trade – even in France, where the Huguenots are the largest traders.

An awareness of the importance of institutional data is apparent when Petty refers to the clear control of property rights in Holland by a land registry, and to their banking system which by advancing credit on the basis of given gold reserves permits a larger volume of trade. He praises the cleverness with which the Dutch take advantage of the international division of labour by performing the most lucrative occupations themselves, and assesses in a remarkable passage how England's wealth could increase if it wanted to follow the same principle.

The second chapter, where questions of public finance are dealt with, studies the effects of tax incentives, which should mainly be used to counter luxury expenditure. Petty does not worry for a moment that such considerations might contradict liberal principles. On the payment side he tends to be strict, and denounces the crown's exaggerated displays of pomp – something that could perhaps be criticized with more justification with regard to France, and in any case with less risk than in England. The greatest resource of a country, however, is the 'improvement of natural knowledge'. Among the numerous and interesting remarks in passing is also the observation that people work less when bread is abundant and cheap, contrary to modern-day thinking. As in traditional societies, people tend to work only as long as is necessary to achieve a normal standard of living; afterwards, they can devote themselves to extended leisure time. This appears wasteful to Petty, even damaging, especially if increased leisure leads to habitual drunkenness.

By means of the naval policy explored in Chapter 3, Petty comes in Chapter 4 to one of his favourite questions, expressed here with some wit: how wealth might be increased – again it is a question of the resettlement of the Irish to England – by means of population concentration. Accordingly, he turns in Chapter 5 to the problem of the dissipation of power in Britain's colonies; he advocates promoting the core countries of Great Britain at the cost of the existing colonies and colonial expansion, which from the perspective of the later political unification of England and Scotland (1707) may well be interpreted as farsighted.

He then seeks to prove that England's power and wealth have increased over the previous forty years, and in so doing he significantly extends the notion of wealth; it is related to its impact upon income and property, also to the enlargement of the fleet, the increase in the use of coal, the development of coins, displays of pomp, and, last but not least, he mentions tripling the king's income. This increase in wealth will permit, assuming domestic peace, the defences to be secured.

The eighth chapter returns to employment policy, which is here primarily focused on hidden underemployment. A reallocation of functions to more productive occupations has to be achieved. An essential concern is import substitution which, however, should not simply be done because the surplus on the balance of trade is an idée fixe, but instead because Petty is, in modern terms, aiming at a restructuring favourable to industries with higher net added value. This demonstrates to the government how applied economics can increase its reach.

For decades, 'neo-mercantilism' was a catchword with the negative connotation of excesses governmental employment policies, guided investment, or protectionist practices. When we read Petty today and are led not only by antiquarian interests but also modern ones, we will certainly be even less inclined to doubt his liberal achievements, which were combined with a critique of Mercantilism. The modern task of returning Eastern Europe to a market economy is in some ways analogous to the liberation from mercantilist control propagated by Adam Smith, and realized in the age of the Industrial Revolution. From a sense of historical fairness, on the other hand, it should be noted that Liberalism was sometimes inclined to undervalue the interventions of the preceding era in order to underscore its own achievements, and in any case to prevent an increase in the density of interventions. Petty cannot be judged an interventionist, since he first wanted to establish important conditions for liberty, such as freedom of thought or of mobility. He was exemplary in showing the framework needed for trade to thrive, as well as in the determination of rights of ownership or his discussion of banking. More than anything else, he fascinates us with the audacity of his political and economic considerations which remain unmatched today, instructive in their clarity.

## Justi's *Grundsätze der Policey-Wissenschaft* (1756) [Principles of the Science of Police]: happiness and economics

*Policey-Wissenschaft* ('Police Science') – a remarkable title in a collection of essays on the history of economic thought. This is followed by a second peculiarity: Johann Heinrich Gottlob von Justi, without a doubt one of the most important European authors during the Mercantile period, is here called a classic of Cameralism, although he made a distinction between the *Policey-Wissenschaft* and Cameralism as two separate disciplines among the Sciences of the State. He primarily understood *Policey-Wissenschaft* to be the economic policy of a state directed to the promotion of general welfare, while his use of Cameralism would today be translated as 'Public Finance'. The continued use of the term 'Cameralism' as the generic term for the German literature, particularly in the seventeenth and eighteenth centuries, justifies our classification of Justi among economists. At first it was concerned with the prince's household, but later expanded its inquiry to the entire economic body of thought generated by middle-European conditions as they existed in the epoch immediately preceding the Industrial Revolution.

Seventeenth-century Germany, and even the eighteenth century before the time of Goethe, seems much more remote to us than seventeenth- and eighteenth-century France, Italy or England. Its language and conceptual world were greatly affected by the onset of Idealism; while the living material world of Goethe's *Dichtung und Wahrheit* today seems relatively familiar to us, everything older seems at first quite alien. In any case, authors like Justi express themselves in phrases which are unusual today, phrases which often do not immediately correspond to any modern terminology. Moreover, they frequently refer to other economic forms and always imply a different perspective upon the relationship between economy, state, and society, a relationship in which Liberalism only hesitantly took its place.

A literature dealing with house and field similar to the English 'husbandry literature' existed in sixteenth-century Germany and was referred to generically as *Hausväterliteratur.* This was Aristotelian in inspiration, concerned with domestic economy and agriculture, extending into the 'oeconomy' of princely households and the 'state oeconomy'.[91] The problems of commerce and trade, at first viewed critically in the medieval tradition, were gradually dealt with in terms of concepts such as *Commercien.* A science of commerce[92] emerged providing instruction in the nature of commodities (*Warenkunde*), the principles of management, accounting, and the advantages associated with the formal creation of companies. The great questions of the Mercantile period focused on the economy as a whole – foreign trade, finance, employment, political power and national integration[93] – issues with which Cameralism could deal, but at the cost of the terminological confusion endemic to Cameralist doctrine. Basic terms such as 'politics' and 'police', 'oeconomy', and 'household', 'economy', 'trade', 'commerce' and 'cameralistic affairs' lost 'all solidity' (Burkhardt 1972, p. 569). Looking back, there seems to have been no compelling reason for 'economics' to eventually become the generic term for economic sciences, whether we look to earlier meanings of the word or to conceptual history.

Louise Sommer interpreted Mercantilism with Schmoller as

> the literary counterpart of an economic policy that would have to be adopted by those in power to accelerate the nation-building process, and whose implementation would create the existential basis for large, consolidated economic agencies.
>
> (Sommer 1967 [1920], p. 40, my transl.)

Justi also did great service in connecting general economic questions to those related to the economy of the state, ordering them according to their ultimate political aims. By separating *Policey-Wissenschaft* from the other Cameralist disciplines he oriented economic policy to the improvement of welfare for all. He put forward a notion of the welfare of society, of the wealth and the power of the state, and of a flourishing economy which steered between on the one hand the self-centred promotion of princely wealth, ('Plusmacherei' as he derisively called it),[94] and a focus on the advancement of individual welfare, to which Liberalism later tended. For economic reasons he saw these elements as interdependent, while being convinced that this objective originated in the nature of the state as such.

In modern terms, this conception of happiness would be something like a social welfare function, whose independent variables are not merely goods but also institutions, including laws, customs, even the kindness and mercy of the government, thus something not readily grasped by formal theory.

Justi's general economic conceptions were buttressed by strong theoretical hypotheses which can easily be missed since they are only minimally worked-out and, in places, can hardly withstand rigorous criticism. However, they clearly testify to the effort of a restless intellectual – driven back and forth, vacillating between nations and social orders – to offer orientation to the conflicting social forces unleashed by the growing political and economic powers mixed into the ferment of Enlightenment.

The goal is clear:

> A nation ... is ... a society of people who inhabit a considerable part of the surface of our globe, united together for the ultimate goal of their mutual happiness and, to that end, have subordinated themselves to a higher authority.
>
> (Justi 1977 [1762], p. 3, my transl.)

Justi's primary goal as a Cameralist is not only to increase the prince's wealth, for pursuit of this latter end as an end in itself can also be very dangerous, since it is at odds with economic logic:

> A profiteer (*Plusmacher*) is a false Cameralist who seeks to increase the income of the state and to raise money for the prince without taking into consideration the welfare of the common wealth and of the subjects, or the just yield and use of objects, thus yielding income. [...] The righteous Cameralist indeed makes an effort to increase the state's income, but in a way that is not disadvantageous for the welfare of the common good, without oppressing the subjects.
>
> (Justi 1970 [1764], pp. 410–11, my transl.)

Justi provides numerous examples of how 'profiteers' endanger the economy; an especially typical and recurring one is the creation of conditions of imperfect competition when princes or their governmental organizations grant privileges or even monopolies to entire economic branches. It was not therefore the liberal Adam Smith who was the first to condemn such practices (for example, ibid., p. 436).

At times Justi expressed his concerns with passion:

> Oh! That the unspeakable kindness of eternal providence would fill those, who rule from their thrones, with fervent longing and a serious resolve to use the current blessed time of peace for nothing other than wise measures intended for the happiness of those people, to whom this very providence has entrusted them, and which demands that they look to the welfare of their people, for which they will be held to account. This happiness of peoples has been the sole wish of my life; and it is only this which has guided my quill during so many lonely midnight hours.
>
> (ibid., p. 537, my transl.)

Justi remains single-minded in his 'ultimate purpose', which provides the source for his general 'principles'. He then deduces his 'fundamental rules', from which all particular doctrines follow (Sommer 1967 [1920], p. 181 and Justi 1782, preface to the first edition, no page number [p. 8, para. 2]). Justi's intention, therefore, is to proceed rationally and deductively. One of the features which makes his era seem so foreign to us is that Rationalism frequently breaks on the lack of formal development of formal method, and on the substantive intertwining of disciplines. Likewise, it was necessary to yield to social conventions, and occasionally Enlightenment thought almost turns into superstition, as illustrated by the fact, occasionally cited, that Justi himself had hopes for alchemy, and once even claimed success in making gold (Frensdorff 1970 [1903], p. 149).

In Germany the economic sciences were already academic disciplines at the beginning of the eighteenth century, in France only towards the end of the century, and in England even later. Following the examples of Prussia, Hesse, and Sweden, in 1752 Maria Theresia commanded that lectures on Cameralistic science be given at the Theresianum in Vienna. Justi, who was not ultimately appointed, developed a programme of lectures in a report for the Empress, dealing with all the sciences serving state and economy, but proposed that the basic principles of public finance and Cameralism (in the narrower sense) be first presented. To follow this there were to be more specialized lectures and practicals in public finance, *Policey-Wissenschaft*, commerce and manufacturing, economy and the art of domestic economy in city and countryside, together with special lectures on the science of mining. The course was supposed to take three years in all and, starting off from the same basic theoretical principles, offer the audience a degree of specialization. When in 1763 the post was finally established with Joseph von Sonnenfels as incumbent, Justi's works were used by Sonnenfels while he prepared his own textbook.[95]

Justi's programme was notable for its derivation from first principles, its broadly inclusive system, and its connection to practical affairs, as is appropriate for the establishment of a special discipline at a university. *Policey-Wissenschaft* is logically prior to Cameral Science strictly speaking, for the former must sow where the latter will then reap (Justi 1782, preface to the first edition, no page number [p. 4, para. 2]). In so doing, Justi remained very self-confident with regard to the economic literature in Western Europe: 'Although the English and the French have worked over various parts of police, this science still lacks an orderly and coherent theoretical structure' (ibid. [p. 7, para. 2], my transl.).

'Justi, a German writer of much ability but also of bad morals and therefore a moving, strange fate', it says in the *Historisch-Literarischen Handbuch berühmter und denkwürdiger Personen* [Historical-Literary Handbook of Famous and Memorable People] published in 1797. Justi's military adventures, unhappy love affairs, failed attempts at other sciences like mineralogy, as well as his unfortunate end in prison – these are all vividly represented. He was a man of lively genius and enterprising spirit who was never content; he was a shrewd Cameralist, known for his writings – whether he should have written so much is another question (Hirsching 1796, pp. 163–65).

Today, Justi's scientific versatility is increasingly recognized, but there is still much to do with regard to the representation of his development as a whole and its interrelations. Moreover, the accusations Justi then faced appear now to be signs of a lack of scientific insight:

> The thematic breadth and volume of his writing extended to geology, physics, chemistry, military science, technology, and demography; he even produced stories, a novel, and a biography, alongside works on political science, business management, history, private law, moral philosophy, and theology. However, his working method made scholarly work more difficult.
>
> (Dreitzel 1987, pp. 160–61, my transl.)

M. Obert, who has called Justi 'possibly the most advanced political thinker of the second half of the eighteenth century' (Obert 1992, p. 312, my transl.), has sought to complete Justi's biography and bibliography, though the frame of reference for Obert's work is German constitutional law. Justi is presented here as an active critic of the monarchy and an opponent of despotism, who believed that government authority came from the people and should be so organized that freedom of the people means the freedom from exposure to governmental coercion in pursuit of illegal ends. Thus the means of achieving communal happiness must be related to circumstance and condition (ibid., pp. 297–312).

Superficially, Justi's *Policey-Wissenschaft* appears to block interpretation which turns on bourgeois freedom, since the term 'happiness' is so clearly focused on the 'happiness' of a whole. However, *Policey-Wissenschaft* is limited with regard to politics in general on the one hand with respect to Cameralism in the narrower sense, and public finance on the other, so as to undermine an identification of the totality with the prince's sovereign interests. This stands out above all in the idea of the interdependence of individual branches of the economy which require an appropriate structure for their development. State enterprises are rejected, and guild privileges cannot be reduced for sake of the state's fiscal advantages. Not only should every person be granted his own space to provide his subsistence, but Justi also sees 'happiness' – with certain moral restrictions – increasing in step with the luxury enjoyed by the citizens.[96]

And so if we want to understand Justi properly, we time and time again have to come back to the question of what is actually meant by 'happiness'. I want to go back a little farther here.[97] An intellectual root for the concept of happiness can be found in the Aristotelian notion *eudaimonia*. At the beginning of *The Nicomachean Ethics* (1095a 14–23), Aristotle holds that all politics is aimed either at a good or at happiness; the difficulty, however, is to determine this substantively. Is it passion, or the life of politicians and philosophers, or is it the acquisition of wealth? This last is certainly not the case, because wealth exists for the sake of another good.[98]

Aristotle finally gave preference to the contemplative life, and maintained that the amount of commodities required for such a life, and which therefore had to be acquired, was limited.[99] Politics serves to bring about a human community in which a life so oriented can develop. The modification of the term 'happiness' in later ancient philosophy, its transcendence by Christianity, the obligation of worldly success during the Reformation do not belong here. Through natural law, 'the term happiness regained its unrestricted profane meaning and thereby acquired its (modern) significance as a determining purpose of the state' (Engelhardt 1981, p. 41, my transl.). When Justi defines 'happiness' as the goal of the state, he attaches himself to Enlightenment secularization and confers upon rulers an obligation to assist in the increase in the well-being of his subjects rather than advancing his own power-interests. In so doing the concept of *laissez-faire* begins to take shape, although such a concept is still not available; it becomes increasingly plain that state intervention can be damaging. Sonnenfels (cited in Engelhardt 1981, p. 47) says that Justi was the only one who traced the science of the state, with all its branches, back to a *general principle*: the 'promotion of general happiness' (my transl.).

Happiness, however, is also a communal experience; it is not just a property of individuals and individual economic action, but also has supra-individual, social and political aspects. Justi finds himself poised in an unclear position between two philosophically and historically clear and comprehensible references: in Aristotle, wealth acquisition serves a form of life determined substantively; for Utilitarianism, it is a means of maximizing a utility which cannot be substantively determined. For Justi, it apparently means that wealth should be accumulated in different forms: both as population as well as things, substantively as well as a means of cultural representation, and indeed under the reciprocal restrictions established by custom and social forces, through the interests of individuals and that of state powers. Due to the multiplicity of objectives, theory in the modern sense of optimality is hardly possible, but critical observation of the changing relations of politics, economics, and society results in important maxims which form the objects of Justi's instruction.

Here the requirements of the modern state are clearly in the foreground. With surprising clarity – considering the modern crises of surplus population and of the environment – he places cultivation of land and the increase of population at the top of the list of the state's economic tasks, connected to an infrastructural programme and some instructions relating to international trade, state finance and a real or supposed need for guidance in individual branches of the economy. Only then does he finally provide the conditions: internal and external security, thus the preservation of peace, individual freedoms, above all legal security and freedom from repression. On this basis, citizens can attain happiness based upon sufficient wealth and security.

The gaining of happiness is not yet instilled in individuals as it would be later: 'I thought … each person must himself begin and at first create his own happiness, from which then in the end the happiness of all would unfailingly emerge', Goethe said to Eckermann on 20 October 1830 during a discussion of the St. Simonians. When Eckermann objects that the state should at least provide the infrastructure, the minister agrees and assures him he is aware of more tasks of this kind. He was also aware of a number of dangers that had to be avoided; however:

> we want to leave some evils unmentioned, so that something remains for humanity through which it can develop its powers further. For the time being my leading doctrine is as follows: the father take care of his house, the craftsman of his customers, the clergy of mutual love, and the police do not disturb harmony.
>
> (Goethe 1976, pp. 752f., my transl.)

If Justi had not dared to adopt such a liberal position, and his *Policey-Wissenschaft* had not dealt with the way in which external security might be secured and how the power of the state should be directed to the quiet unfolding of an individual's happiness – if however the state retains further organizational tasks then this is not mere opportunism, since Justi had often enough put his authorial independence on the line. In the era of Idealism the state's claim that it, too, could promote happiness would have been denounced as a potential source of despotism. According to Justi, the state not only had educational tasks, which he deals with concretely in his book citing school and university; it also enjoyed powers to limit freedom, since he considered protectionist economic policy to be necessary, while the legitimation of rulers in pursuing the path to happiness is not doubted. There is no question that one of the tasks of the state is the promotion of culture, for example through the construction of opera houses, which he advocates in *Policey-Wissenschaft*, not so much from idealist motives as with the argument that they promote immigration and reduce the emigration of the economically-active population.

It would not only be interesting but also necessary to the proof of my thesis to show that Justi's notions of appropriate economic policy were not only guided by abstract systematic considerations, but were also developed from his observations of current political and economic institutions, together with his experience of governmental and social developments. In the following I will cite several examples, chosen from *Policey-Wissenschaft*, in their order of appearance.

Justi favours in effect economic autarky, based on the cultivation one's own soil. Is it not possible to live for the most part from trade like the Maltese on their cliffs or the Dutch between their dykes?

> But such a people have no real internal strength and are always dependent upon their neighbours.
>
> (Justi 1782, p. 24, my transl.)

Justi is convinced that the relative decline in Holland's prosperity can be traced back to the lack of an agrarian basis, a thought reminiscent of his near contemporaries, the Physiocrats.

Justi also recognizes the weakness of the market economy's capacity for self-regulation. In any case, I interpret his forestry policy in this way, when he writes: 'Wood is spared when the neighbours squander their own, and when one can see that eventually they will have to buy from us' (ibid., p. 26, my transl.). It is not the individual forester who predicts this, but the state, and it could easily be established how much this idea related to practice.

He provides many examples of infrastructural tasks, such as the draining of swamps where he carries out precise cost-benefit analyses, estimating interest yields on investments (ibid., p. 28) in the construction of canals and dams.

He decisively rejects unnecessary burdens of country people: 'labour services' (ibid., p. 38, my transl.) should be abolished and transformed into 'direct payments' ['Dienstgeld']. Unreasonable imposition of 'services' is disadvantageous. The farmer 'completes his services as poorly as possible; and he cannot be made to work better without great effort because in such things thousands of excuses and objections can be made' (ibid., p. 38, my transl.).

In a similar vein he writes, 'Nothing is so badly utilized as common pastures' (ibid., p. 40, my transl.). Here it becomes clear that Justi sees forced labour as a characteristic violation of, in modern terms, the Pareto-Optimum: labour intensity on the farmland is higher than on the lands of the lords (or communal land, where above all care and attention is lacking). In an analogy with privatization, if this service were abolished, the same labour population could produce more. On the other hand, however, he also does not sketch out the institution of a pure tenancy system, and does not dare to argue in favour of the complete abolition of communal land.

It is not by accident that *Policey-Wissenschaft* appears to speak out most openly for a liberalization of institutions where the impact of international competition is felt. The threat of emigration is countered with a call for mild government, legal security, and religious tolerance. And here all the cumulative effects of the spatial concentration of economic activity become visible:

> The more people live together, the greater the consumption is of all goods and the more lively the circulation is. [...] Manufacturers enlarge foreign commerce and, on the other hand, commerce enlarges manufacturers. Indeed, that is the proper touchstone for deciding whether a means to the welfare of the state is good. For all means must correspond with one another and support one another. The state is a whole; and all means have a single goal: happiness.
>
> (ibid., pp. 79–80, my transl.)

The cumulative effects of concentration are therefore another observational fact serving to confirm Justi's view as a whole.

The state only has to remain moderate and take reasonable steps. He criticizes the 12-child-edict of Louis XIV which was supposed to provide a special reward to parents with twelve or more children – the Savary family was among this group. For Justi, this programme constitutes a mere show of good government and exaggeration. 'If the state seriously wants to do something here, then six living children are enough of a burden for a father and sufficient for the state, for a reward to be received' (ibid., p. 89, my transl.). He naturally means here that the state pays the father something. Following that are further considerations for increasing population size, as well as improving morality and health.

If international trade offers the strongest argument for the liberalization of certain institutions, it provides, alternatively, an occasion for immoderate planning. According to Justi, manufacture and factories are the primary cause of a flourishing food supply; the government must be able to judge what can be produced in the country and thereby ensure, specifically through taxation or even prohibition, that raw materials are not exported, on which additional domestic processing could be carried out. He attempts to supply examples of how the state must obtain materials in order to create statistical records (ibid., p. 137). Many references show that Justi oriented himself to Colbertism, some 80 years after the time of the great minister who adopted an economic policy of catching-up, insofar he anticipates List. If he speaks of the freedom of trading ('Commercien') as the merchant's soul, again and again international trade provides occasions for exceptions to this freedom (ibid., p. 176).

Justi's sympathies lie with small- and middle-sized enterprises, even if he also sees the advantages of large trading companies (ibid., pp. 178, 182); the notion that people can become rich in some other way than through 'Commercien' must be nipped in the bud. The honour – he means the nobility – should not withdraw money from trade; and England, where the merchant is as respected as the aristocrat, is praised (ibid., p. 198).

Justi finally deals concretely with administration and police, in the more modern sense, and in the end arrives at a strange conclusion:

> Da der Endzweck der Policey auf die Erhaltung und Vermehrung des Staats in seiner innerlichen Verfassung gerichtet ist; so siehet man leicht, daß alle diejenigen Bedienten des Staats, welche den besonderen Oeconomien des Landes und der Cammern vorgesetzet sind, zugleich auch die ihre Oeconomien betreffenden Policey-Angelegenheiten mit zu besorgen haben müssen.
>
> (ibid., p. 392)[100]

Ultimately the conclusion is that economic policy, the legal-economic frame of reference, management and legal surveillance have to be organized sector by sector. Mining has its own set of laws, a particular form of administration, a particular jurisdiction and police, and the same goes for forestry and other related central government administrations or other affiliated sectors. Such was Cameralistic reality, and some of its traces have remained visible up to the present day.

At first glance Cameralism, and Justi as perhaps its most important representative, appears somewhat obsolete and superseded. Upon closer inspection, however, we arrive at a better understanding of its unique ambivalence, and, finally, at a surprisingly new perspective upon our own time.

### The connection between theory, history and policy in James Steuart's *Principles*

How the rivalry between James Steuart and Adam Smith should be assessed, and how and why Smith prevailed is a familiar question in the history of economic thought. Adam Smith's ultimate triumph and his higher profile are unquestionable, yet past judgments have markedly fluctuated between the disparaging classification of Steuart as the last of all Mercantilists, and the claim that his writings are among the most important of all time. His works were not only published before *Wealth of Nations*, so that in writing this book Smith could learn from Steuart, but even after 1776 his works retained their importance. They anticipated population theory, the theory of effective demand and of employment, the theory of development, and the relationship between political power and economic law.

Vickers (1970) wrote of a Steuart Renaissance. In contrast, more than a hundred years ago in Germany Feilbogen (1889, pp. 218ff.) wrote:

> A few decades ago it was still the fashion to almost worship Adam Smith. [...] In Germany at the moment the opposite opinion is reigning. 'Smithianism' is considered wrong and finished; Smith himself is supposed to have said almost nothing that could not already be found in his predecessors.
>
> (My transl.)

In order then to help restore Smith to his rightful place, Steuart's contribution was relativized: Feilbogen was startled by Steuart's radical suggestions, sometimes attributing them to the spirit of the age, and sometimes to authorial extravagance. Today we see that Steuart's consideration of public assistance for the poor, or of a general sales tax have become reality. Walter Eltis (1986), who was also disturbed by Steuart's ideas about the welfare state, did not consider them absurd but instead measured them against modern practice, comparing Steuart's proposal to stockpile grain against a possible harvest failure and to moderate price fluctuations with the agrarian policy of the European Union.

Steuart is a strong critic of extreme positions taken by Mercantilists, such as confusing the influx of gold with a general increase in wealth. Alongside his conclusion that demand for luxury goods spurs growth we also find his praise for the Spartan lifestyle. His interpretation of the freedom of the individual as only developing within a legal framework is connected with the notion that, ultimately, economic laws also restrict the arbitrary power of government. Varying assessments finally come together to form a coherent picture once Steuart is also taken seriously as a thinker on the subject of historical development, who sees human society passing through various economic developmental stages involving differing economic conditions.

It is therefore difficult to arrive at a balanced assessment of Steuart's originality, and the following can only suggest how this might be done.

Steuart had a complex personality, influenced by the scientific and political ideals of the pre-Revolutionary era, but with a tendency toward metaphysical speculation and even to superstition. Chamley (1965, p. 149) described him as follows:

> Admirer of Newton and of Frederick the Great, surrounded by quietist influences but a *bon viveur* and having as associates men of little scruple, concerned with religious apologetics and theorist of political economy, a character of some spontaneity but accustomed to dissimulation, Steuart reflected in his personality the ambiguities of the century.
>
> (My transl.)

Steuart was a Scottish patriot and an outstanding representative of the Scottish Enlightenment which for a few decades made Edinburgh and Glasgow centres of a European culture. It has often been pointed out that his forced Continental residence and travels during his long years of exile provided opportunities for comparisons which most British economists did not have. The transfer of political power to London following the sealing of the unification of Great Britain in 1707 also brought with it the danger that Scotland might fall behind in economic development – Adam Smith pointed to this problem in the case of the Scottish Highlands. Steuart was aware of the negative impact of English rule over Ireland, agricultural rents flowing out of the country to be consumed by large landholders in London. He had enough examples of how cities, regions and countries could lag behind in development in comparison to others; he often points out historical examples of this, from Phoenician cities in the ancient world to Italian cities in the modern era. This historical perspective did not lead him to trust the balancing powers of market forces in the way that Smith did, and explains his interest in developmental policy.

It should be added that he understood the differences between the economic lives of various peoples to be an expression of the 'spirit of a people', in the same way as the Historical School and Max Weber in particular later spoke of an 'economic spirit':

> The spirit of a people is formed upon a set of received opinions relative to three objects: morals, government, and manners; these once generally adopted by any society, confirmed by law and constant habit, and never

called in question, form the basis of all laws, regulate the form of every government, and determine what is commonly called the customs of a country.

(Steuart 1770, Book 1, Ch. II, or *Works*, vol. 1, p. 10)[101]

Steuart's decision to proceed from the 'spirit of a people' reflects the keen awareness of the economic rivalry of nations which was a distinguishing mark of the mercantile period. However, we find many examples in Steuart's work that attitudes toward work, readiness to save money, and the tendency to invest might be specific not only to a population but also to an epoch, that they will be determined by institutions just as they determine institutions. Above all, Steuart is a theorist of stages. We are not here concerned with the notion of a necessary sequence of stages since this is not at the forefront of Steuart's interests, but instead in the specific internal logic attributed to specific economic stages and their own institutions. Steuart's repeated reference to slavery as the counter-image of modern economics forms based on free labour and free trade represents an example. In general, population growth requires that an agricultural surplus be produced which will be consumed by a working class producing manufactured goods. The question is, however, who they are working for: by force for an upper class, or in exchange for services provided by free labour. Only in the latter case is growth based on an increase in needs of the workers themselves: 'Men were then forced to labour because they were slaves to others; men are now forced to labour because they are slaves to their own wants' (ibid., Book 1, Ch. VII or *Works*, vol. 1, p. 52). Steuart systematically elaborated the various forms of dependence. Slaves are at one extreme, dependent upon the master for their lives; children depend on their parents for their entire room and board; peasants depend for their means of labour on the feudal lords; and workers depend for their income on the purchase of their efforts – their 'industry' as it was called in the eighteenth century. Thus Steuart attempts to reflect on the sociological requirements of dependence, and their effect on the underlying economic organizational framework and property relations. Whether or not this is economic determinism is an open question.[102] The emphasis on national characteristics, the praise given to model legislation, above all the interest in economic forms, indicates that Steuart viewed history and future development as open.

The majority of commentators on Steuart's works have focused on historical and, in particular, politico-developmental aspects. But his works also include an essential analytical contribution which prepared the way for classical thinking on growth and prices. If the structure of Steuart's theoretical concepts appears less firmly established than that of Smith, let alone of Ricardo, he still arrived at a theory of effective demand before they did, encapsulating the Keynesian elements of mercantilist doctrine and pointing to developments beyond the classical and neo-classical era into the twentieth century.

As already suggested, at the base of Steuart's thought is the notion of a two-sector model. He assumes a previous societal condition in which no agricultural surplus was produced, and the population lived from hunting and gathering. He noted that various agricultural techniques could then provide higher yields, enabling the production of an agricultural surplus. The amount of the surplus depended upon fertility and climate, and on the industriousness of the population. Given an exchange economy, those not involved in agriculture produce superfluous or luxury goods. He approaches this historically, from the emergence of handicrafts; Steuart knows, naturally, that such luxury goods could also become necessities. Money, which mediates exchange, will soon itself become a necessity; he pointed out that the introduction of money increased the demand for luxury goods. In a moneyless exchange economy only a few goods could circulate; money rendered variety possible.

Smith's distinction of market prices and natural prices does not appear in Steuart. He therefore often speaks of how supply and demand regulate prices, and that goods are subjectively valued. Here he usually starts from changing market relations. In Chapter 2 he successively develops concepts of demand, of progress from exchange to commerce, and the determination of prices under competition conditions. This line of thought leads to natural prices.

In the reconstruction of the analytical structure, one should not be distracted by Steuart's frequent references to international trade. Historical insights and economic concepts are woven together. Essentially, however, he focuses on the various forms competition can take, sometimes perceiving the effect stronger on the supply side, sometimes on that of demand. In Chapter 4 of Book 2 we finally find out what commodity value is when both parties have an effect on its determination. He differentiates between the *real value* of commodities and the *profit upon alienation*.

In order to calculate the real value, it is first necessary to know the amount of working time required to produce an item, using the average time required as the point of reference. Second, the 'subsistence level', hence the real wages, of the worker must be known. As with most of the Classical and pre-Classical writers, this real wage is a specified amount, which depends upon a particular subsistence need on the part of the worker, and is subject to certain modifications due to changes in local prices. Third, it is necessary to know the price of raw materials and costs for using the working tools. To that extent the determination of the real value amounts to a somewhat more rudimentary theory of labour value – rudimentary simply because the notion of embodied labour is lacking.

Steuart now assumes that prices must in any case cover real value. If a higher price can be obtained there will be a 'profit upon alienation'. 'This', he writes, 'will ever be in proportion to demand, and therefore will fluctuate according to circumstances' (Steuart 1770, Book 2, ch. IV or *Works*, vol. 1, p. 245). At the very beginning of *Theories of Surplus Value* Marx (1983, p. 348) accused Steuart of not sufficiently clarifying the source of this profit: 'Before the Physiocrats, surplus-value – that is, profit in the form of profit – was explained purely from *exchange*, the sale of the commodity above its value. Sir James Steuart on the whole did not get beyond this restricted view; he

must rather be regarded as the man who reproduced it in scientific form.'
However, Marx now also points out that Steuart (1770, Book 2, Ch. VIII or
*Works*, vol. 1, p. 275) differentiates between positive profit and relative profit:

> *Positive profit*, implies no loss to anybody; it results from an augmenta-
> tion of labour, industry, or ingenuity, and has the effect of swelling or
> augmenting the public good. ... *Relative profit* is what implies a loss to
> somebody; it marks a vibration of the balance of wealth between parties,
> but implies no addition to the general stock.

Profit comes therefore either from an increase in labour or from redistribution.
Like Ricardo and Marx, Steuart could have directed his attention first of all
to an economy with a given volume of production and considered how the net
output was to be divided between profits and wages. He could have analysed
this distribution from the product side or, like Marx, in terms of the labour
theory of value. Classical authors treated the growth process as follows: surplus
product is in part invested, demand increases and the quantity produced
increases, and finally production methods also change.

However, what I see as Steuart's individual and characteristic achievement
is that by allowing profit to be determined by demand, without the long
detour in which value is determined by given production structure, he indicates a direct connection between the theory of effective demand and profit
levels, and between effective demand and employment, prefiguring Keynesian
considerations.

Let us begin with Steuart's concepts of supply and demand in an individual
economy. These concepts should not be treated as curves, but rather as points
in a diagram showing price and quantity; and in fact Steuart at first viewed the
quantity as a given. Demand is 'high' therefore when the price is high. In this
way a higher profit would be obtained for a given quantity, even a 'profit upon
alienation'. On the other hand, Steuart says that demand is 'high' when a
greater quantity can be sold at a given price. Furthermore, he asserts demand is
'strong' when there is powerful competition on the demand side. He clarifies this
with examples. There is hunger in a port and ships arrive with provisions. The
inhabitants of the port fight over the corn, and the price increases until they
have no more money. Steuart then makes the assumption that the merchants
would not dare to charge the highest price imaginable; instead, out of sympathy,
or due to intervention from the state, they would sell at a low price, despite
the strongest competition imaginable on the demand side.

Steuart's terms simultaneously represent less and more than the point of
intersection of a supply-curve with a demand-curve: less, because the complexity
of the functional dependence of supply and demand with given preferences is
not expressed; more, because it provides access to the observation of dynamic
adaptive processes.[103]

Prices which represent the sum of the real value and the sales profit could
then be calculated as follows:[104] a homogeneous agricultural product, corn,

and a handicraft or manufactured product $l$ (a luxury good) are produced. The corn price is $p_k$, the price of the luxury good is $p_l$ and $w$ is the real wage (an amount of corn per unit of labour). The entire amount of corn produced is $q$, the amount of corn received by the workers is $q_s$, the amount of labour in the corn sector is $n_k$, so that $w = q_s/n_k$. Steuart rarely takes account of variations of the average return due to a given technology, and so we assume fixed production coefficients and constant economies of scale. Hence $m_k = q/n_k$ is the production coefficient which provides the per capita production of corn and $v_k$ is the sales profit accrued per unit of corn production. Accordingly, $x$ is the quantity of luxury goods produced, $n_l$ is labour employed in the luxury goods sector, $m_l = x/n_l$ is the production coefficient for the luxury good production, $v_l$ is the profit obtained per unit of output, and $q_x$ is the amount of corn consumed by workers in the luxury goods sector.

Therefore we get the following price equations:

$$p_k m_k = p_k w + v_k m_k$$
$$p_l m_l = p_k w + v_l m_l$$

If we take the production coefficients and the real wages to be given, then the price including profit upon alienation is calculable if the unit profits $v_k$ and $v_l$ are given. These calculate to:

$$v_k = p_k(q - q_s)/q$$
$$v_l = (x p_l - q_x p_k)/x$$

We have ignored costs related to the means of labour here. The equations express an interesting thought with regard to the setting of prices if we take Steuart's monetary ideas into consideration. Meanwhile we see that prices increase with profits. Steuart now had a quite clear idea of the quantity equation, which he, however, did not interpret only according to quantity theory.

Let us assume, in addition, that a country has access to a certain amount of precious metals which circulates as coins at a certain velocity of circulation. Let us next assume that the prices which include a certain sales profit are already set and that, given the transaction volume, an equilibrium exists between the quantity of money available for circulation and that which is required for circulation.

Now what happens if more bullion coinage (or paper money, about which Steuart writes in detail) flows in? According to David Hume, prices must increase. Steuart, however, asks if prices might already be determined by supply and demand. This implies that the profit upon alienation would not change, thinking back to our price equations with fixed production coefficients. Steuart assumes that imbalances in the money market disappear when surpluses of precious metals (i.e. gold) are removed from circulation and hoarded. The mechanism which produces this effect can be a temporary price increase which would allow the purchasing power of gold money to sink. Whoever now thinks that the purchasing power of gold coins no longer approximates their value will, at the prospect of increased purchasing power in the future, remove them from circulation and in any case choose not to spend gold coins. The opposite can also be said, that in this situation gold jewellery, turned into goods, will become cheaper. Viewed in this way, there is also an incentive to remove gold from circulation. Prices therefore again have a tendency to fall, because on the one hand circulation slows down (gold money is hoarded) and on the other hand the money supply is again reduced (gold is transformed into jewellery).[105] Unfortunately, we cannot here explore Steuart's interesting views on paper money, credit, and banks.[106]

However, it is just as possible that fluctuations in the money supply have consequences for production levels, and, as a consequence, on employment rates. Steuart emphasizes, much more clearly than the later Classic writers did, that his system does not require full employment and therefore the well-intentioned statesman, assumed by Steuart, must put into effect measures to ensure full-employment. Akhtar (1978, p. 66) expanded the price equations with quantity equations and showed that the product of complete employment $n = n_k + n_l$ and an average profit percentage $v$ is proportional to the assets in precious metals $E$, at a given velocity of circulation:[107]

$$nv = cE.$$

An increase in precious metals can raise prices and profits, or the employment rate.

The similarity to Keynesian employment theory has been discussed by many writers. Chamley has compiled a wealth of citations which are supposed to verify the affinity between Keynesian theory and Steuart's ideas. Low interest rates are the soul of trade, credit stimulates consumption and demand in industry, luxury requires economic growth, demand increases with the shifting of wealth from the nobility to entrepreneurs and, especially noteworthy, Steuart explicitly employs the expression 'full employment', by which he means the full employment of each and every worker. He means by this not only work has to be created for workers, but also that during all available working hours' idleness is to be reduced as much as possible.

The question has therefore been raised of whether there is an actual and direct line of influence on Keynes, leading from Steuart and passing through Malthus.[108] The answer is probably 'no'. However, Sen (1947, p. 35) believes:

> had not the brilliance of Adam Smith and the laissez-faire spirit of the 19. century combined to throw him [Steuart] into oblivion, it is quite possible that the school of thought which Malthus and List and Keynes took such a long time to build up might have been more rapidly developed.

Steuart was read in the years after the Second World War because of the desire to implement the Keynesian programme. Today he is read because of admiration for the way in which he foresaw the possibilities of intervention, interventions that have since proven ambivalent.

Steuart's preference for reading ancient and modern natural science bore strange fruit, such as an attempt to reconstruct the chronology of the Greek kings going back to Homeric times (*Works*, vol. 6).

An astronomical argument (moving back the beginning of spring due to the procession of the earth's axis) and a statistical one (the average length of the reign of European monarchs), etymological reasoning and a critique of the sources of Greek mythology were brought together to support a correction of the dating of the Trojan War suggested by Newton. Steuart often appears naïve when dealing with Greek fables, yet it is apparent just how fascinated he was in his youth by the darkness of history, reaching back in his studies almost to Genesis.

It was said that in later life 'With metaphysics Sir James now amused himself' (*Works*, vol. 6, p. 385).[109] According to the ideas of contemporary physics the universe was determined by laws: 'It is agreed ... that God governs the universe by fixed and determined laws; the absolute perfection of which he has from all eternity foreseen' (ibid., p. 90).

Their reason is the condition of freedom: 'That the Government of God is despotic, I do not deny; but the essential quality of this despotism is reason, and reason is the fundamental principle of liberty' (ibid., p. 85).

Steuart's *Principles* (1770, Book 2, Ch. XV) includes a controversial elegy to Sparta and Lycurgus' legislation. Steuart shows here that he is impressed by the power of education and the consistency of laws. He was convinced that freedom meant, above all, freedom from despotism and therefore saw the Spartans, with their public symposia and their warlike competitions, not as a symbol of totalitarianism but, difficult as it may be for us to understand this, as a symbol of personal development. Indeed, within the framework of a society bound by traditions with aristocratic virtues for individuals, there was at the same time full equality for the free before the law. The comparison of the lifestyle of the Athenians with that of the Spartans, frequently invoked since the Renaissance, therefore found an original formulation in Steuart.

What apparently impressed him is that a legislator appeared to have succeeded in influencing the life and the economic spirit of a state for centuries. More contemporary applications by Steuart of these basic notions involve the influencing of behaviours related to work and saving. Steuart himself is clear that self-interest must be set free for this to happen. Thus, the intensity of work is dependent upon wages:

> Set a man to labour at so much a day, he will go on at a regular rate, and never seek to improve his method: let him be hired by the piece, he will find a thousand expedients to extend his industry.

The incentives for increasing labour productivity are, however, to be selected according to institution: 'Why was a *peculium* given to slaves, but to engage them to become dexterous?' (ibid., Book 2, Ch. VII, or *Works*, vol. 1, p. 258). The 'peculium' was the financial 'tool' given to emancipated slaves so that they might support themselves independently.

The societal vision and the educational goal, the analytical apparatus and economic interventions based upon it, finally the treatment of international trade and how a nation should benefit from it – these are all combined if we understand Steuart's system as an attempt to create a general theory of the origins of accumulation: 'For this reason the "Principles" always had some degree of theoretical significance in places where primitive accumulation was in progress' (Kobayashi 1967, p. 8).

Since Adam Smith, 'original accumulation' has referred to the complex of tasks which result when a nation at a preindustrial, feudal, or semi-feudal stage is to carry out the social and economic transformation which leads to capital accumulation and, finally, to industrialization. The contradiction between Steuart's interventionism and his liberal conception of a state guided by laws, which with increasing economic complexity placed ever larger restrictions upon arbitrary rule, is resolved if we place him in this historical context.

Among traditional societies, the Spartan society is to some extent free – Steuart even takes trouble to collect evidence that the slaves in Sparta, the Helots, had more freedom than slaves of other Greek city-states. Naturally, however, Steuart feels that Spartan customs are brutal – Enlightenment reason will create space for further development.

Economic want does not however seem to disappear spontaneously. This explains his emphasis on population theory. The transformation ejects large numbers of families from the countryside and drives them into new centres of production. Where growth has not yet gained a firm footing or is stagnating unemployment is acute; but population growth is also fostered where new employment opportunities are concentrated. Therefore the deep sigh: 'I think it is absurd to wish for new inhabitants, without first knowing how to employ the old' (Steuart 1770, Book 1, Ch. XI, or *Works*, vol. 1, p. 78). During the transformation, employment will be influenced in a more conspicuous fashion than before, or after: by fluctuations in effective demand which must be regulated, opening the road to a more liberal economic system.

The most visible sign of progress is mechanization. This also seems two-edged, but Steuart is in favour of it. He is already discussing the effects the intro-duction of machines will have on increasing employment, although he could not have had in mind heavy industry based on steam power. Montesquieu wondered whether the introduction of water-powered mills might not displace workers. But who would dare to abolish the plough? Since Steuart cannot precisely determine how technological unemployment will be resolved he invokes his ideal statesman. The weakness of Steuart's theoretical analysis may be regrettable here; Ricardo was the first to take the decisive step toward the understanding of lay-offs and their compensation. It is probably easier, however, to do justice to the historical problem by acknowledging that Steuart wishes to manage the transformation and ease the consequences, rather than removing his ideas from their context and comparing them with modern interventionism.[110]

The chapters on the results of economic growth once it actually occurs are quite interesting (and also historically instructive, since they touch on attitudes). Prices increase, workers find more employment, and owners enjoy greater profits, while landowners complain about a lack of agricultural workers and experience some loss in purchasing power. Above all, however, whoever only maintains their wealth rather than increases it, will lose in economic influence and social prestige relative to the rising classes. Steuart recognizes that rising countries are immediately threatened by competing countries which imitate them. The advanced growth of industry will create so much employment that the domestic food supply may no longer be sufficient. That Steuart did not regard planning as an ideal, for his own time, can be seen in an example: He shows how even the best regent in this situation could not centrally organize corn imports. The Dutch, in contrast, serve as a model, since trade decentralized and regulated the exchange of Dutch manufactured goods against foreign grains (ibid., Book 2, Ch. IX).

The historically knowledgable Steuart did not hide the fact that the transformation process would also cause old cultures to disappear, and the process of creative destruction, as Schumpeter called the process by which entrepreneurial activity was diffused, not only produces the new but first pulls down the old. Steuart describes, for example, how the traders of a developed country make contact with traditional societies, through gift-giving seek to awaken the need for new products, and the pricing policies they then pursue in response to various conditions of competition so that they might in return negotiate good prices for the products of the 'primitives', for example furs. The effect on the 'under-developed' nations is not central to Steuart's analysis, but he shows that quite different developmental prospects are open to them, depending on whether they now have their own agricultural production, they retreat from this, or they seek their stabilization in trade relations (ibid., Book 2, Ch. IV).

Steuart questions finally how the spread of trade affects the form of the state, and which form of the state is particularly favourable to trade. Regardless of his political past, he concludes that republics have been the most successful in international trade – he is thinking in particular of cities like Venice and countries like the Netherlands. Monarchies, however, encourage demand for luxury items and are thus advantageous to domestic trade. The kingdom changes, too, because with the rise of trade the decline of the feudal lords begins (ibid., Book 2, Ch. XV). Steuart suggests the historical tendency leading to the development of the liberal state.

However, Steuart was historically too multifaceted, and his questions too tightly bound up with the ambivalence of a transitional and transformational epoch to fashion his book resolutely for, or even against, a liberal programme. In contrast to other authors Anderson and Tollison (1984, p. 466) argue that his relativist position enjoyed considerable literary success from the very beginning, which success was not immediately, but only gradually, overshadowed by the publication of Smith's *Wealth of Nations*. However that may be, the historical recognition his work has achieved and the influence it has exerted contribute to its historical status. It is true that Steuart must be ranked behind Smith; but Smith and many others stand on his shoulders. *Principles* includes much that was absorbed and more clearly formulated in the Classical era. However, it also includes much that the Classical era lost, and which, whether positively or negatively, we are today once more finding topical. Focussing on the first two books of the *Principles*, I have tried to emphasize the issues of employment and development policies, neglecting to some extent Steuart's treatment of money. Especially in the way he connects theory, history and policy, Steuart seems almost unique.

In his commentary on Justi, Tribe (1993) points out that Steuart's viewpoint, especially with regard to the state, can be traced back to his study of Cameralist literature in Germany. Thus Steuart is, through the influences which he absorbed as well as the impulses which he passed on, of especial importance for German political and economic science.

## Notes

1 B. Schefold, 'Xenophon's *Oikonomikos*: the beginnings of an economic science?', Chapter 1.
2 Bodin claims himself that he called attention to the increase in the amount of gold and silver as reasons for inflation (which he distinguishes from debasement). Cf. Bodin (1945, p. 127).
3 'Bread is of the same nature in Spain and with the Indians, but it is sold there for a higher price than in Spain because of need and because of the abundance of silver and gold which are the causes of the raising of the price.' (My transl.)
4 'The *Manual of confessors* was one of the most sought-after books in public and private libraries in all the provinces of the Indies.'
5 Azpilcueta Navarro (1556, pp. 48–104). Modern critical edition: Azpilcueta Navarro (1965). French trans.: Azpilcueta Navarro (1978).
6 The following letter is cited as an example of how much the emperor depended on the traders; it is quoted in the picturesque German of the time.
   'Karl, von Gots gnaden Romischer Keiser, zu allen zeitn merer des reichs etc.
   Edler, lieber getrewer. Wir geben dir gnediger meynung zuerkennen, das wir in willens sein, mit verleichung des almechtigen in kurtzentagen von hie zuverrucken und unsere reise auf Augburg zunemen und in deiner behausung daselbst einzukern, haben auch derhalben unsern hausfurier daselbsthin abgefertigt, wie du von ime vernemen wirdest; und ist demnach unser gnedig begern an dich, du wöllest uns dieselb deine behausung öffnen und die zimmer und gemach, die gemelter unser furier zu unser gelegenheit und notturft begern wirdet und du mit fueg entbern kanst, guetwillig einreumen und volgen und dich dieser wirtschaft nit verdrießen lassen. Das wellen wir uns bey dir genzlich versechen und in gnaden erkennen.

Geben in unser and das reichs statt Nurmberg, am 12. tag des monats July, anno etc. im 47., unseres kaisertumbs in 27.

Ad mandatum Caes. Et Cath. Mt^{is} propr. Carolus

J. Obernburger

Dem edlen unserm rat und des reichs lieben getrewen Antoni Fuggern.'

The letter from Emperor Charles V to Anton Fugger, dated 12 July 1547, is printed in Kirch (1915, p. 283). A portrait of the Fuggers as the owners of one of the first financial empires was drawn for a broader audience in the slender volume from Ehrenberg (1925).

7    The comparison is documented only for certain years.

8    The thesis is as follows: 'Il reino no es del rey, sino de las communidad, y la misma potestad, por derecho natural, es de la communidad y no del rey; por esta causea no puede la communidad abdicar totalmente de su poder' (Azpilcueta Navarro 1965, p. XVI). 'The kingdom does not belong to the king, but to the community, and the corresponding power belongs by natural right to the community and not to the king; the community can for this reason not give up its power completely.' (My transl.)

9    We cite him in the following according to the numbering of the subsections, which are used in the edition from Salamanca (Azpilcueta Navarro 1556) and in the critical edition from Ullastres (Azpilcueta Navarro 1965), among others, in the French translation by M. and B. Gazier (Azpilcueta Navarro 1978), as well as in the partial German translation which was produced for the *Klassiker der Nationalökonomie* edition (Azpilcueta Navarro and Ortiz 1998).

10    Cf. also the translation of the same passage in Lessius, present edition, p. XXX. More fully: 'insures' here means: 'because he assumes the risk associated with the lending of his capital and he wants to be compensated'. 'To insure' ('assegurar', § 1) is spoken of, as if the lender insures the borrower – this, in any case, is how we would understand it today according to modern meaning. We would say that the lender insures his own capital. However, according to the old understanding, the money lent must be given back, like a borrowed piece of furniture. If the borrower does not guarantee repayment with the rest of his possessions, the lender bears the loss in the case of damage and an extra charge which he demands for this actually assumes the character of an insurance premium, because the borrower pays the money back only if it survives the journey without any damage. In contrast, if the borrower provides an unlimited guarantee and, because he is otherwise rich enough, has the capacity in the case of a loss to replace the money lost, then he bears the risk; interest then could only be justified with the argument from *lucrum cessans*, so that according to Azpilcueta's understanding usury must be suspected if the lender does not reduce his business activities until the loan is repaid.

11    Probably because the contracts were incomplete – in a complete contract, according to our interpretation, it would have to be specified who bore which risk.

12    Additionally, according to our interpretation, the questions about security and liability must be explained.

13    It is not enough, here, for Azpilcueta, that whoever loans money will have less capital available for business activities.

14    'It is a virtual transfer of money, by which, who claims it in another country, given it in this.' (My transl.)

15    'The variety of exhibition and payment locations (*distancia locorum*) were largely under the influence of the canonical prohibition against interest beginning in the fourteenth century' (Jacobi 1955, p. 7, my transl.).

16    'The challenge is to explain how it is possible to gain from exchanging money, if one pays the just value for it.' (My transl.)

17    'We say that money must rise or fall when there is great lack or need, or when there is a lot of it. It values more when or where there is a lack than where it is

abundant. This is maintained by Calderino, Laurencio Rodolpho and Sylvestrol, with whom Caietano and Soto are of the same opinion. [...] This is a common conception of almost all the good and the bad of the whole of Christendom, and it therefore seems both from God and from nature.' (My transl.)

18  However, even Marx thought that interest as the price of money (as he expressed it) was an irrational expression, see Schefold (1998b).

19  Oresme (1995) and 'Nicholas Oresme: monetary theory in the late medieval era', Chapter 2.

20  Cf. Bernholz (1992, p. 261).

21  I am citing the text following the *Memorial* according to the pagination of the facsimile manuscript (manuscript page), which is also provided in the printed edition (Instituto de España 1970) and in the abridged translation in the *Klassiker der Nationalökonomie* edition (Azpilcueta Navarro and Ortiz 1998) each of which are given in the margins.

22  7v means the back side of seventh page, with 7 the front.

23  Cf. 'Philipp Wilhelm von Hörnigk: 'Austria above all, if she only so wishes'', Chapter 3.

24  'Already today the inertia and decadence of Spain are such that any person, of whatever region or condition it maybe, will not find an employment or business without going to Salamanca or to the Italian war or to the Indies or being an official or administrator and all to the damage of the state. On the other hand, if all are busy in their trades, there will not be the thieves, robbers, vagabonds and lost people who are in the kingdom. With going to Italy and to the Indies, the quantity of people, who did go and leave every day, have neither room in the prisons.' (My transl.)

25  'whereupon many will dedicate themselves to elevating cattle an inevitably they will find themselves compelled to lower prices.' (My transl.)

26  Kaldor followed a similar strategy with his 'selective employment tax'; he thought Great Britain was suffering from a surplus of old fashioned and out-of-date services. See also Schefold (1983).

27  'It is clearly known that with the whole state occupied its trade and artisan activities and with the growth of the value of what leaves the Kingdom in such great quantity and with the traded goods being manufactured, it cannot fail that, with its preceding increase, the tax revenue will grow to the double, without damaging the community.' (My transl.)

28  For comparison: McCulloch (1954).

29  Cf. e.g.: Spiegel (1971), on Serra (ibid., p. 694), on Mun (pp. 106–18). In a similar fashion: Hutchison (1988, pp. 19–20).

30  From a sonnet of Bruno's in *Italienische Gedichte* (Goetz 1953, p. 196). A rough translation of the German version, on p. 197, is as follows: Whether blindness, unfaithful luck, / heart-hardening poisonous envy and venom / and dullness will still celebrate their triumph today – / they will never drive me back into delusion: / its hate-consumed venom is unable / to mask the beautiful light of truth.

31  See the English translation in Serra (2011, p. 100): 'that science in itself has no certain means of arriving at the truth, and [4] proceeds not by logical proof, but by enthymemes and topical arguments'.

32  'ἐνθύμημα' is a rhetorical syllogism, that is, it is drawn from probable premises and is therefore not a strictly demonstrative proof" (Aristotle 1982, from the translator's 'glossary', p. 475). The enthymeme in rhetoric corresponds to the syllogism in dialectic (ibid., *Rhet.* I.2.8., 1856b). A maxim like: 'There is no man among us all is free' will become an enthymeme through explanation: 'There is no man who is really free, for he is the slave of wealth or fortune.' (Example taken from ibid., *Rhet.* II.21.2.) By the way, a good talk will be made worse through long enthymemes, thus through long, unnecessarily complicated explanations (ibid., II.22.3).

33  'τόπος ... literally, a place to look for a store of something, and the store itself; a heading or department containing a number of rhetorical arguments of the same kind.' The τόπος are of two kinds: Κοινοὶ τόποι, the commonplace which belongs to all rhetoric and specifically, e.g. to ethics or politics ('glossary', ibid., p. 482). An especially simple commonplace can come into being in which all natural preconditions are met, for instance: 'if the sky is cloudy, it will probably rain' (example ibid., *Rhet.* II.19.24). The *topos* of forensic prosecution sounds more bold: 'ἐι ἐδύνατο καὶ ἐβούλετο, πέπραχεν' – 'That if a man was able and wished to do a thing, he has done it' (ibid., *Rhet.* II.19.18), which, modified, forms the basis of revealed preference: 'Who could and did it also wanted it.'

34  In Serra (1613, p. 5); English translation, see Petrarch (n.d.):
    'Now that is what saddens us more than anything,
    that perfect judgement is so rare,
    and we are blamed for another's fault.'

35  Serra (2011, p. 108): 'Venice is also helped by its multiplicity of manufacturing activities, an accident which attracts a large number of people to the city. Here the determining factor is not the multiplicity of manufacturing activities alone, for if that were the case we would have to attribute the cause to that accident, but a combination of two accidents, each of which lends force to the other. For the number of people attracted by the extensive trade and the geographical position is increased still further by the number of businesses, and the number of businesses is increased by the extensive trade, which is itself increased by the number of people who come to the city.'

36  In a territorial city, at first through an 'Ordonnance' from Colbert in 1673. Thoroughly discussed by Savary (1993 [1675], esp. pp. 125ff.).

37  Serra (2011, p. 129): 'experience is the mistress of all things, and all arguments, however powerful, must yield to her.'

38  Serra (2011, p. 129): 'De Santis himself implicitly admits this, when he states that the cause of money coming into the Kingdom is the exportation of goods.'

39  Serra (2011, p. 134): 'nor has the scudo ever circulated in Naples as money, but only in trade.'

40  Serra (2011, p. 164): 'to remove ... the lack of the common accidents – and to introduce manufacturing activities into the Kingdom.'

41  Serra (2011, p. 165): 'If you so command, my Lord...'; 'a total transformation, to the great benefit of the Kingdom and his Catholic Majesty.'

42  Serra (2011, p. 168): 'which cannot be compensated for directly, but only indirectly.'

43  Serra remarks there, for example: 'Prezzo delle cose è in potere dell'uso' (Serra 1613, p. 146). He is referring to the relative price of gold and silver (ibid., p. 126) which the prince is forced to fix through the minting of gold and silver coins. The consideration of 'potere dell'uso' appears then to mean a consideration of purchasing power (or even purchasing power parity?). In any case, Serra rejects adherence to the ancient price relationships of gold and silver.

44  Cf. 'Aristotle: the classical thinker of ancient economic theory', Chapter 1.

45  Cf. Seÿffert (1957).

46  For example, Becher (1990 [1668]).

47  Cf. 'William Petty's *Political Arithmetick*', Chapter 3.

48  Economic pedagogy used to place great value on a broad, general education based on the Humanities, while Savary advises the young merchant against the study of the *artes liberales*, as we will see below. Economics pedagogy endeavours to counter the accusation of the narrowing of commercial thought. The utilitarian limitation certainly did not make the rapprochement between the middle class and the aristocracy any easier (something Savary desired), and Savary suggests that it even made his work more difficult, speaking of the deficiencies in his training

which he discovered in the writing of his book. I thank my colleague Ernst Wurdack for pointing this out.

49  Cf. Recktenwald (1989).

50  Cf. also Michaud (1969, pp. 105ff.)

51  The careers of the seven sons are noted in Bellanger (1856, p. 209).

52  Cf. Perrot (1992). Perrot spent much time with Morellet's project.

53  'The nature of *honour* is to demand preferences and distinctions ... Ambition is pernicious in a republic. It has some beneficial effects in a monarchy; it enlivens its government; and there is the advantage that it is without danger, for it can be unceasingly suppressed.' (My transl.)

54  The inscription on the base of his statue in the vestibule of the chapel of Trinity College in Cambridge ('who surpassed all mankind by his genius').

55  Cf. 'William Petty's *Political Arithmetick*', Chapter 3.

56  Cf. Stamm (1982, pp. 56–65).

57  *Gulliver's Travels* was first published in 1726 (amended 1735), officially *Travels into Several Remote Nations of the World, in Four Parts. By Lemuel Gulliver, First a Surgeon, and then a Captain of several Ships*, by Jonathan Swift.

58  Dealt with in an appendix on trade in the Levant, included in the second and later editions. Savary is apparently unfamiliar with historical sources on ancient freshwater canals (between what is today Suez and Cairo), which linked the Red Sea with the Nile and the Mediterranean; but he does present anecdotes regarding ancient attempts to construct canals. Leibniz, who supported the plan, is not mentioned. However, Savary correctly refers to the contemporary comparative standard, and praises the 'Canal du Midi', north of the Pyrenees, connecting the Atlantic and the Mediterranean via Toulouse: 'Il n'appartenoit qu'à nôtre grand Monarque d'executer une telle entreprise malgré les obstacles presque insurmontables, & avec un dépense que lui seul étoit capable de faire, & de sacrifier au bien de ses sujets' (Savary 1697, part 2, p. 473). A project which had already been discussed by François I and Leonardo da Vinci in 1516, this canal was built between 1666 and 1681 and is still in use today. Over 200 km long and containing numerous locks, it passes across aquaducts and even a through tunnel. It was the first modern canal, a wonder of its time, and a classic example of the infrastructure policies of Absolutism, just as the Suez Canal would later be an example of Imperialism (cf. Hadfield 1968, pp. 167–69).

59  Cf. 'Max Weber's *Protestant Ethic* as an inquiry into economics', Chapter 4.

60  Cf. Dessert (1984).

61  Cf. on this for the following: Sée (1925). In articles in Diderot and d'Alembert's *Encyclopédie* the ossification of the guilds is attacked.

62  The following quotations and orthography are taken from the 4th edn, Lyon, 1697, which – like the second edition – is divided into two parts, these two parts into books and the books into chapters; chapter numbering begins anew in each book. By contrast the first edition numbered the chapters from beginning to end. In my footnotes, A and B signify the first or second part of the book, the first Roman numerals refer to the number of the book, the first Arabic numbers refer to the chapter numbers and the second Arabic to the page number. The final Roman numeral refers to the corresponding chapter number in the first edition, which naturally does not correspond word-for-word with the fourth edition, and does not include certain additions. '[I]n giving them examples of merchants who have nothing when they enter trade, but who nonetheless have there accumulated great wealth, by means of which they have propelled their children to the highest office in the state...' (my transl.).

63  Cf. Schneider (1993) and the essay by Vehn (1929).

64  'Order is the soul of commerce' (my transl.).

65  'Order is the soul of a manufactory' (my transl.).

66  'While Louis XIV policy might have brought the smaller Netherlands to the edge of the abyss, it was England, not France, that profited from it' (Baasch 1927, p. 322, my transl.).
67  Hauser (1925, p. 18) verified Savary's statements on trade with the Baltic states; they proved accurate.
68  Cf. in particular Savary (1697, B II 8, 183; LII).
69  Savary is correct that in precolonial inner-Africa cruel conditions, for the most part independent of European influence, predominated in the slave trade. Cf. Peukert (1978, pp. 216–55), who seeks to refute the thesis that the character of the slave trade within Africa was fundamentally determined by export conditions.
70  Cf. Reichert (1985, pp. 48ff.).
71  'only the ruler can make this annulment' (my transl.).
72  With the exception of additions, mentioned above, in later editions.
73  On the assessment of Colbertism, cf. the positive evaluation from Born (1989, pp. 96–113).
74  Cf. 'Economy and money in the age of reformation', Chapter 2.
75  Unusual statistical information about this is in Brauleke (1978, p. 122ff.).
76  The biographical information which follows is for the most part taken from this book.
77  'He was born in Frankfurt (Main) and in his youth educated at Mainz; he then was in his life a pious, forward-looking, level headed, chaste and knowledgeable man, just and pitiful towards poor and affected orphans, whose very long list cannot be enumerated.'
78  Cf. 'Asian classics in a Western collection of the history of economic thought', Chapter 5.
79  'Thus even the most famous heroes / and the cleverest regents of this century have not felt ashamed / of keeping eyes and hands on their state economy and of keeping the manufacture in particular. However, in certain cases and situations it is the task of, in a manner of speaking, heroic natures / to do almost nothing less / than stand before a warrior's blade.' (My transl.)
80  Cf. 'William Petty's *Political Arithmetick*', Chapter 3.
81  'It is licit to import some commodities, others not.' (My transl.)
82  Cf. 'Jacques Savary's *Parfait négociant*: the organization of markets by merchants and the state', Chapter 3.
83  'Shall I look worthy of hatred or of love?'. (My transl.)
84  To offer only one example: Ernest Lluch (1996) follows the cross-connections between the Spanish writers associated with Mercantilism and those associated with Cameralism – a connection that naturally touches on the Habsburg reign over both countries and over the end effected by the War of the Spanish Succession. He shows, additionally, that history of economic theory had until now overlooked this connection.
85  I cite from *The Economic Writings of Sir William Petty* (Petty 1963 [1899], henceforth: *EW*), edited by Hull.
86  Cf. Roncaglia (1977, p. 63).
87  See also Marx (1887). Marx, who was a great admirer of Petty, cites him in this volume alone about 20 times.
88  Cf. Skourtos (1991).
89  According to the interpretation suggested by Roncaglia (1977, p. 89).
90  Interpreted by Roncaglia (1977, pp. 102ff.).
91  Cf. Burkhardt (1972, p. 560).
92  Cf. Savary (1993 [1675]).
93  Cf. Petty (1992 [1690]).
94  Cf. Justi (1970 [1764], p. 436). 'Profiteer'.

95   Cf. Stieda (1906, pp. 32–34).
96   Cf. Maier (1966, pp. 218–29).
97   Cf. for the following, esp. Engelhardt (1981).
98   Aristotle, *Eth. Nic.*, 1096a 7–8: ὁ πλοῦτος δῆλον ὅτι οὐ τὸ ζητούμενον ἀγαθόν. χρήσιμον γὰρ αλλου χάριν.
99   Cf. also Aristotle (1988).
100  'Since the goal of police is directed to the maintenance and increase of the entire internal wealth of the state; it can be easily seen that the servants of the state who are in charge of the particular oeconomies of the land and the chamber, have at the same time to manage police affairs affecting their own oeconomies.' (My transl.)
101  Steuart's *An Inquiry into the Principles of Political Oeconomy* (1770) is here cited from *The Works, Political, Metaphysical & Chronological of Sir James Steuart* (1967 [1805], henceforth: *Works*). In order to ease the comparison between different editions, in the following I cite first Steuart's division into book and chapter and then, when it makes sense, the volume of the 1805 edition and the page number.
102  Cf. Skinner (1962).
103  Cf. on this point Steuart (1770, Book 2, Ch. VI, VII and VIII).
104  Cf. Akhtar (1978).
105  Cf. on this point also Eltis (1986, p. 50) with reference to Steuart.
106  Cf. for this Sen (1947).
107  I am referring to a simplification of Akhtar's comparison here.
108  Cf. Chamley (1962); Lambert (1963); Chamley (1963).
109  According to a biography, written in the spirit of Utilitarianism and included in the 1805 edition of his *Works*.
110  Cf. Steuart (1770, Book 1, Ch. XIX).

# 4 Historical School, old and young

## Bruno Hildebrand: the historical perspective of a liberal economist

1848! It was the year of democratic revolution in Europe[1], and Bruno Hildebrand was himself a delegate to the popular assembly which met in Paul's Church, Frankfurt. He was among those who, in the aftermath of the failed German revolution, emigrated to Switzerland and put themselves at the service of the new federal state. Switzerland was the only country to have achieved its revolutionary goal, becoming independent not only *de facto* but also *de iure* two hundred years earlier in the Peace of Westphalia. Fifty years earlier it had been jolted out of its established order by Napoleonic conquest and occupation, being forced into the reviled, centralized state of the Helvetican Republic. After the congress of Vienna restoration of the old order was only partially completed. During this period popular movements in the Swiss cantons experimented with various forms of republican rule. In 1848 they established a new balance between popular sovereignty and representative democracy, between a centralized state and federalism.

Hildebrand was politically liberal, in the sense of advocating liberal political institutions and a constitutional state. He was also liberal in his rejection of communist, socialist and utopian cooperative tendencies, confronting them without prejudice and with personal courage. Later, he came to terms with the German constitution to such an extent that in 1861 he accepted an appointment to the University of Jena.

In view of common prejudices, it may seem paradoxical that Hildebrand, as a liberal, was not only close to the Historical School of Economics but is also usually named as one of its three co-founders, alongside Roscher and Knies. Indeed, he remained more determinedly faithful to the historical method than did Roscher and Knies. Hildebrand's critique of English classical economy was not merely limited to Ricardo and his school, but also extended to Adam Smith. In this he was not alone: for example Knies, or later Karl Bücher, also had marked liberal attitudes as people and as political activists. In Hildebrand's case it is especially clear that this liberality was rooted in his person, and revealed through his activities.

According to the ancient meaning of the word, liberality is the embodiment of the exceptional qualities of the free-born, whose noble character is revealed in contact with friends, in business activities, and in political action. *Liberalitas* can be traced back to *eleutheria* in Aristotle (*Nic. Eth.* II.7.4 and *Eud. Eth.* III.3.2); those virtues which, derived from freedom, like other Aristotelian virtues, establish a balance: generosity is a mid-point between waste on the one hand, and tight-fistedness on the other. Cicero, of whom Hildebrand thought a great deal, adds to this that *liberalitas* must be just, and it is unacceptable for it to appear as vanity (*De off.* I.14). Cicero characteristically added that an occasional, spontaneous gift is not only 'liberal' but profitable as well (because gifts may also be expected in return); but it is also necessary to be economical, without appearing to be mean.[2]

There was a long way to go before finally arriving at the modern political and even economic term *liberalism*; during this journey, the procedural rules of liberal contact between people stood – were even more clearly marked – while the old notions of virtue became blurred. They have not, however, disappeared entirely. We might think that it is liberal when the state intervenes in the event of a market failure for the benefit of the injured parties, and that if this intervention did not occur it would betray liberal tenets. In a sense the starting point presented by the forerunners to the Historical School in the first third of the nineteenth century amounted to this. Economists from the Ricardian school promoted free trade (although Ricardo himself, as a member of parliament, allowed exceptions), while List in Central Europe, which remained economically backward, sought protection for infant industries, and in so doing believed himself to be pursuing the contemporary form of the bourgeois ideal.

Hildebrand already recognized the importance of early industrial development – he would be actively involved in the construction of railways – but he was concerned with social distributional problems as well as with social cohesion. These concerns appeared to him to be old moral problems: whether free-market development furthered the progress of morals, bringing with it such values as punctuality, honesty and increased trust, a belief common in the early eighteenth century and a conviction shared by the young Adam Smith; or whether by contrast it undermined the traditional legacy of values. Modern institutional economics argues that an economy based on trust functions better than one continually in need of legal safeguards, but it does not follow that people interested solely in the maximization of utility will not also turn to illegal means if they believe this will go undetected, or when legal safeguards are not in place (Baurmann 1996). In order to develop the will to consistent and habitually virtuous activity, market participants must think beyond immediate utility, must clearly see that the honesty and reliability which they value in their trading partners is also something their trading partners value in them. Their reputation and influence therefore grows when they at least awaken the impression of strength of character. Among mature and experienced people the only person able to inspire a sense of moral uprightness is the one who *is* morally upright. They must know the meaning of virtuous activity, and have to be in a position to internalize the associated norms – in extreme cases, when it comes to oppression, putting their lives at risk.

The Historical School would repeatedly state that exchange depends upon people who treat each other responsibly based on an awareness of their mutual dependence, a recognition that their undertaking depends upon each individual personality, and thus on conscientiousness and the desire to appear reliable. In *Theory of Moral Sentiments*, Adam Smith describes the development of a kind of moral equilibrium in society, based on the fact that we have a conscience and that we wish to appear conscientious in the eyes of others. In *Grundriß*, Schmoller (1900–1904) had sought to show the importance of action guided by norms for economic development. The examination of ethics as a condition and result of economic transformation reached a high point in the work of Max Weber, who criticized the Historical School in order to better use what it had achieved for his own ends, particularly to highlight the manner in which legal regulation accompanied rationalization.

Although Hildebrand cast doubt on the idea that spontaneous moral improvement followed from the extension of the free market, he was convinced, as was Schmoller later, that it was possible to unite moral and cultural progress with technical and economic progress.[3] This optimism is also reflected in his theory of stages, which unites the concept of a chronological progression of various existing transaction forms (exchange – money – credit) with the appropriate legal relationships secured by the state, as well as the development of moral concepts (i.e. security of credit and the growth of trust). To the extent that progress is important this involves a theory of stages, though Hildebrand knew as well as anyone that stages are interconnected, that they overlap, and that occasionally older forms return so that, with regard to the connection of allocation and institutions, reference could also be made to systems. And just as the theory of stages already points toward system theory, an examination of the link with social morals already suggests the conception of 'style' (Schefold (1994d, 1995) that would later be developed. Stage theories are not popular today. However, what does the omnipresent talk of 'globalization' suggest if not the suspicion that a new stage of development has been reached via advances in telecommunications and the emergence of a new world economic order after the downfall of communism?[4]

The evident awareness on the part of members of the Historical School that different economic forms existed simultaneously has been traced back to their familiarity with the contrast between an industrialized England and backward countries on the European Continent. The deep, thorough and diverse knowledge of history which characterized many members of the Historical School went far beyond that, and is an expression of nineteenth century culture and education in the best sense of these words. At the same time, a prominent role was played by an intimate knowledge of ancient literature acquired through years of schooling and which then continued in private reading. No translation – and no comparison of translations – can replace the experience of struggling with the original language, and it can be shown that, as with Karl Bücher, Hildebrand's study of ancient thought exerted a significant influence upon him.

Hildebrand was known not only in Germany but was also recognized abroad as a co-founder of the Historical School. The School itself was a European rather than merely a German phenomenon – a fact that can be easily verified, but which has sunk to an even greater level of oblivion than the school's best-known and longest-lasting name, the German Historical School.

Born on 6 March 1812 in Naumburg, Bruno Hildebrand displayed a 'rare independence and energy'. He determined:

> to achieve the goals he had set himself on paths he had chosen. He showed signs of this early on in life when, as a young boy of 14 and without his parents' knowledge, he took an examination for a vacant place in Schulpforta. He was successful, and thus chose for himself the direction his future life would take, based on a classical education.
>
> (Conrad 1878, p. II, my transl.)

The *Gymnasium* in Schulpforta had been established during the Reformation as a prince's state school by Duke Moritz von Sachsen; in 1815, it became a Prussian school. Instruction in the ancient languages had been and remained its foundation. Klopstock, Fichte, Ranke, and Nietzsche would number among the famous students who attended this institution, which was a model of thoroughness. Hildebrand left Schulpforta in 1832, at the age of 20, and went to Leipzig, where he initially studied theology at the behest of his parents, and later philosophy, languages, and history. He earned a doctoral degree in history in 1836 and also immediately qualified to give lectures at the university. He earned his living as a teacher in a *Gymnasium*, was named associate professor in 1839, and finally, once he had begun to lecture in the field, he was appointed to Marburg as full professor for the *Staatswissenschaften* in 1841.

We know little from Conrad's obituary (ibid., p. III) about Hildebrand's extensive studies in shifting fields of interest during these years; it seems that for Hildebrand digesting the material, making it his own, was more important to him than publication. He is said to have had high standards for publications, and to have advised students against publishing anything unless they were completely satisfied with it, or anything which they might later regret (ibid., p. XI).

His extraordinary talent for organization and his heavy involvement in politics prevented him from realizing more ambitious academic plans. He was not driven by ambition, but rather by a passion for the subject. He must have embodied the image of an older liberality by communicating openly and in a friendly fashion with many people, elevating conversations to an intellectual level in an unforced way, unreservedly and without self-promoting vanity.

In 1845 he became vice-chancellor at the University of Marburg, and in 1848 he represented Marburg in the Paul's Church assembly in Frankfurt.

Then from 1849–1850 he represented the city of Bockenheim in the Hessian parliament. As an academic he was involved in many quarrels with his superiors concerning trivial issues but which implied more serious political questions (Should students be allowed to sing on the streets at night? Were they singing insurrectionary songs? Should professors be allowed to meet in academic groups open to the public, or to read foreign newspapers?) (Grünberg 1925). As a delegate at Pauls Church, he was among those:

> who took the bourgeois revolution seriously, who stood up for the sovereignty of the national assembly as a body for producing a constitution for the German people, who declared themselves in favour of moving the parliament to Stuttgart, and voted for the election of the imperial regent as well as the motion for the compulsory implementation of the imperial constitution.
>
> (ibid., p. 453, my transl.)

As a representative of the city of Bockenheim in the Hessian parliament, he introduced a motion to deny the government's unconstitutional request for additional financial expenditure – and as a result was dismissed from his position following disciplinary proceedings. He only managed to avoid arrest by flight.

In Zurich he was supported by friends, was given a professorship in political science, and later obtained honorary citizenship. In 1856 he was called to Bern, where he created the Swiss Office of Statistics. He returned to Germany in 1861 and became a professor in Jena, where he founded the journal *Jahrbücher für Nationalökonomie und Statistik* [Yearbook for Economy and Statistics] (1862). The statistical office of the united Thuringian states (1864) can also be traced back to him. He died in Jena on 29 January 1878.

His areas of interest spanned political science and the humanities. He never lost interest in the economics of Antiquity. He is even said to have produced in his last few months a text on financial theory in classical antiquity, which was at the time of his death almost ready for the printers (Conrad 1878, p. IX). On the other hand, he was time and again active organizationally: he was involved in setting up a fund for widows (in Marburg and Jena), a savings and loan bank in Bern, and in the establishment of railways – in Zurich the Nordostbahn, in Bern the Ostwestbahn, and in Jena the Saalebahn (ibid., p. III).

The political sympathies of the young Hildebrand are of particular interest with respect to his major work of 1848, *Die Nationalökonomie der Gegenwart und Zukunft* [The Economics of the Present and the Future]. An 1846 letter about a visit to a 'Deutscher Communistenclub' in London, written by Hildebrand and published by Grünberg, sheds light on his sympathies. Hildebrand was taken there by Karl Schapper, who was among the leaders of the 'Bildungsverein deutscher Arbeiter' [Educational Association of German Workers], as the communist club actually called itself.[5] During Hildebrand's visit to the London labour group questions of international policy were raised, the Christian religion was criticized, and the possibility of a so-called women's community as well as the emancipation of women was discussed. In this atmosphere, approaching midnight, Hildebrand took Schapper to task for his animosity toward liberalism; the political domination of the 'Geldliberalen' [moneyed liberals] had been a specific object of attack. The development of the credit system would become a central feature of Hildebrand's lifework.

Hildebrand recognized that Germans played a particularly important role in the European Communist movement – he mentioned Schapper in London, A. Becker in Switzerland, Marks (*sic!*) and Engels in Belgium, as well as Schuster in Paris. They were political refugees, whom he characterized as follows:

> These people, who were exiled for political reasons, were the most authentic proletarians, combining a wealth of physical and mental strength with a complete lack of means and capital and who therefore never rose above their fight for their existence. [...] They had all studied at German universities, had grown up under philosophical influences, possessed a natural disposition toward speculation and thus grasped the new world of ideas with all the more energy. [...] What was more natural than that their patriotic desires and ideals transformed into cosmopolitan [desires and ideals]? [...] To my great joy, the German refugees have led communism to recognize science. Material life should only be a means to spiritual life. The communist constitution should as it were simultaneously replace the slavery of antiquity and free all humanity from material labour or, rather, from its burden.
>
> (cited in Grünberg 1925, pp. 458ff., my transl.).

Hildebrand's characterization of the fate of these immigrants is particularly pertinent to the material situation and intellectual attitude of Marx – whom he did not even meet in London – and his interpretation of the communist goal as the creation of a society able to live out the ideals of spiritual development and friendship, like the Greek citizen, without however being burdened with the evil of slavery. He expressed in this historically unusual but appropriate formulation the idea of a utopia free from alienation. The left Ricardians, by contrast, formulated their critique with reference to the doctrine of labour value. For example, Hodgskin's well-known early explanation of exploitation, which Marx would later take up, should be remembered: 'Fixed capital does not derive its utility from previous, but from present labour; and does not bring its owner a profit because it has been stored-up, but because it is a means of obtaining command over labour' (Hodgskin 1969, p. 55). What is meant, in Marx's sense, is that the capitalist aims for profit because he possesses the means of production. It should follow therefore, if Marx is right, that the worker will be freed from exploitation when the means of production are handed over to the workers. Although Hildebrand had recognized the impossibility and the danger of the communist utopia, he found a way of his own to express their basic thoughts: by means of historical analogy.

Before we consider Hildebrand's main work, let us first turn to a few shorter texts. His 1845 Latin *Rektoratsrede*, dealing with the economic doctrines of Xenophon and Aristotle (Hildebrand 1845), is certainly not read very often. It constitutes, however, a particularly important record of the influence of the study of the ancient world upon the development of the Historical School.

The short pamphlet, written in long sentences, begins with the assurance, or rather, the conviction, that the common idea that the ancient world had no conception of economics was without foundation. Boeckh and a good half dozen authors who followed him had produced the evidence. While many still sought to discover individual references to their own modern theories in the ancients in isolated places, the state of modern economics, he maintains, requires more precise and subtle knowledge of the history of economic doctrine in the ancient world. Criticism of Smithian doctrine, which had by then spread across the whole of Europe, is justified, he maintains, for it rationalizes every selfish decision by the profit motive: this undermines honesty and leads to conflict between individuals. 'In the ancient world, the private economic sphere was moderated by public administration and was directed for the benefit of the entire community' – '*antiquis temporibus oeconomia privata per publicam auctoritatem temperata dirigebatur ad commoda civitatis universae*' (ibid., p. 3, my transl.) – a confusing formulation since Hildebrand has in mind neither a planned economy nor Keynesian interventionism. Rather, he is more concerned with mutual reinforcement of state law and private morals, when he says further of the ancient world: '*quas honestatis leges sequebatur civitas, easdem civium studia ac negotia sequebantur*' (ibid.).[6] And, in contrast to this, he points to the growing number of grievances in that year – which was indeed a year beset by crises. Complaints about poverty and unemployment, the dependence of industry upon monetary capital, and demands from factory owners for subsidies are reported in classical language. He considers as a moral duty the implementation of a social policy, through which the nineteenth century later alleviated the horror of early industrialization, and which was supported not only by the state but also by private and cooperative initiatives[7] – think of Hildebrand's fund for widows.

The Rector's speech does not however pursue any particular economic programme, but instead establishes Hildebrand's interest in the economic doctrines of Xenophon and Aristotle, with the simple advice that economics should follow its neighbouring disciplines (apparently the Historical School of Law (which preceded that of economics) is meant), and the thought of the ancient world should be united with that of the modern: '*quam secuta antiquitas est ratio quasi coalescat cum ea quam nos sequi consuevimus....*' (ibid., p. 4).[8] He thus goes on to reconstruct the doctrines of individual ancient writers. Socrates directed the attention of philosophers toward ethics, politics and economics, and '*oeconomia*' is given no less weight than the doctrines '*quae ad mores et ad rem publicam spectant*' (ibid., p. 4).[9] This is demonstrated with reference to a text from Philodem, discovered some two decades earlier in the Herculaneum, in which the Xenophontic economy is discussed in detail, criticized, and then extended along Epicurean lines;[10] as well as with a reference to two passages from Cicero which also emphasize the importance of this text by Xenophon, which Cicero had himself translated from Greek into Latin.

The first of the two passages from Cicero (*De officiis* II.24 and *De senectute* 17)[11] is worth mentioning briefly, since it addresses the connection between a credit system and societal morals, a topic to which Hildebrand devoted much time; from this connection the passage points in the direction of economics. Nothing keeps the state so much together, says Cicero, as trust, and this in turn presupposes both capacity and willingness to pay ('Nec enim ulla res vehementius rem publicam continet quam fides, quae esse nulla potest nisi erit necessaria solutio rerum creditarum', *De officiis* II.24). He reports that under his rule the frustration with credit fraud had increased more than ever before, to the point that it had become simply an expression of a passion for deception. Fraud had to be stopped and equality before the law had to be achieved; it is permissible neither to ignore the weak nor to envy the wealthy their possessions. Cicero cites Stoic tradition as the organizational basis for those things which people call useful, among which health and money are still counted, though they are occasionally omitted by philosophers. How people should look after their health is not relevant here. With regard to the economy, however, Cicero considers the household to be the real basis – he does not speak of '*oeconomia*' but instead of '*res familiaris*', which is contrasted with '*res publica*'. The '*res familiaris*' must provide for itself through honourable activity, it must be protected through care and parsimony, and in this way it will also grow. The passage in Cicero to which Hildebrand here refers is noteworthy for its particularly conservative understanding of economics, taking as its model the Roman institutions of credit which required close supervision because they represented a potential source of disruption for the life of the state. Cicero augments the reference to life in the household following the old customs by invoking the older Cato, who still ranked livestock breeding above agriculture as an honourable activity. Hildebrand cannot have been unaware that credit existed in the Roman era, and when he looked at the future development of the credit system as a later economic stage he must have linked this conception with a qualitative change which we will take up below.

In the 1845 speech Hildebrand set himself the task of gathering together the teachings of Xenophon and Aristotle from their scattered texts creating Xenophontic and Socratic economic systems which he then compared. This method assumes conclusions on the part of the two authors which does not correspond to the reality of their texts. I was unable to locate in any library the second part of the discussion on Aristotle, so it is fair to assume that it was either not written, or never published. It is named in bibliographies but is not cited in any of the related texts. Thus we have only Hildebrand's systematization of Xenophon, which attempts to argue Xenophon's consistency by attributing (not without reason, but not without some degree of arbitrariness) a Socratic influence to those passages from Xenophon that do not fit into (Hildebrand's reconstruction of) the system. Ancient authors certainly had their economic doctrines; however, these doctrines did not assume the character of 'systems' for reasons which are dealt with in other essays included here. Nonetheless, Hildebrand's attempt at reconstructing such a system is cleverly conceived and a challenge for those with an interest in Xenophon. What is interesting from the perspective of the history of economic thought, for example, are the details of the doctrine of goods (Hildebrand 1845, p. 10), the hypothesis that disdain for handwork is more Socratic than Xenophontic (ibid., p. 23), and the hypothesis that it was Socrates and not Aristotle who opposed slavery (ibid., p. 26).[12] Finally, even rudimentary attempts at the explanation of prices are identified with Xenophon (ibid., p. 30). There is, however, no space for further discussion here.

We have now acquired insight into the scientific perspective of the young Hildebrand. Toward the end of his scientific career, he summarized what he and others achieved:

> From the conflict of philosophical speculation which ignores all experience and the arbitrary and uncritical understanding of experience to which the politicians of the Restauration surrendered, the desire has gradually developed to achieve, through precise examination of real existing historical and present experience, an understanding of the true nature of the state and human society; an ambition that has inherited from the opponents of philosophy a sensitivity to the facts of experience, and from philosophy the keenness of contemplation ... Political economy has replaced the older Cameralism as a science which seeks understanding of the entire economic lives of peoples and its legal context, and which offers entirely new foundations both in the commercial, administrative and fiscal legislation of the disciplines of the state sciences which concern themselves with the influence of state power on economic culture.
>
> (Hildebrand 1872, my transl.)

Research into facts and awareness of the logic of development should be combined in the reconstruction of economic stages. Hildebrand thought an understanding of stages would have to communicate the conviction 'that the economic life of peoples is subject to a law-like development towards ever-higher cultures' (my transl.) and the notion from Lessing that 'education of the human race' ought to apply not only to religion and intellectual culture, but also to economic life (Hildebrand 1922, p. 357).

Hopes for progress, however, cannot be verified, as Karl Popper (1969 [1957]) demonstrated in his critique of Historicism, confirming an already common objection; Hildebrand, too, appears to want to communicate nothing more than the plausibility of progress as a guiding idea. Even this thought, in which Schmoller's work would culminate, was abandoned by the Younger German Historical School as the objectification of their scientific efforts led to the postulate of the exclusion of value judgments and, moreover, the experiences of the First World War led to a real pessimism about the chances of progress (Schefold 1996). The Younger German Historical School turned to the understanding and comparison of economic systems and styles, and thereby adopted the latest achievements of the humanities and cultural sciences. K. Bücher had already treated J. Burckhardt with respect, and Schmoller had cited Dilthey as an authority in the Humanities. The connection between the social sciences and the Humanities might have led to syntheses which have not yet been reached – perhaps not even attempted, if the National Socialists had not suppressed the Humanistic tradition and driven its best exponents into exile.

Hildebrand's theory of stages does not seek reference to cultural history, but instead to sociology. For him there may be unchanging laws of nature and an essential human nature; however, in economics he sees a higher development produced by human labour, created by the freedom of the human spirit (Kalveram 1933, p. 91). Following a learned reference to the ancient world and a critique of some of the newer stage theories, he explains the simple logic of a sequence moving from bartering, to money, and to the development of a system of credit – with a full awareness of the fact that credit could also be granted in an exchange economy and that the ancient world was familiar with institutions similar to banks. This construction cannot lay claim to universal-historical validity; it results from the application to the occidental world after the ancient era.

The forms in which goods are exchanged have 'wide-reaching effects on the entire social life of a people' and each establishes 'its own economic world with an independent organization and living conditions' (Hildebrand 1922, p. 335, my transl.). An example of an economy based largely on bartering is that of the early Medieval era with bondage. The monetary economy, which from the start presumes a sufficient surplus production of metals, would permit monetary compensation for labour, thus wage labour and capital. The state can raise greater sums in taxes, while capital places demands on its organization and its general jurisdiction (ibid., p. 349). However, there also occurs individualization and the dissolution of the bonds that unite the members of society.

Credit can save on coins and thus costs (ibid., p. 351); however, it can only develop when credit is given, not only to those who can lay claim to real security but also to those who can inspire trust that it will be used sensibly:

> There is not only credit for the person who has something but also for someone who is something. The moral character of people can also justify credit and be considered sufficient guarantee for the seller or the lender for the reimbursement of its worth. There can be sales relying on the future services of a person. If this is represented as personal, or rather moral credit and realized through bank or credit institutes like the modern saving and loans banks in Switzerland or the German advance cooperatives or credit cooperatives, then the monopoly of the capitalists, the gap between owners and non-owners, would come to an end. The moral value of people would attain the power of capital.
>
> (ibid., p. 354, my transl.).

Thus the banking industry will once again unite people with 'spiritual and moral bonds' and 'work toward the elimination of the proletariat'. It calls 'forth an economic organization of life which unites the advantages of both earlier epochs of economic development' (ibid., p. 355, my transl.). Consequently, this economic form could 'only develop when people are at a higher cultural stage' (ibid., p. 356, my transl.). And, in a longer footnote, Hildebrand attempts to prove, in opposition to Roscher, that at the very beginning credit which was not guaranteed by real security supported the founding of numerous factories, and that credit cooperatives were a mass phenomenon.

This theory of stages can be criticized in a number of ways. For instance, European economic development is employed here as an illustration, as if there were some necessary logic to this development. The theory can, however, be given additional support with further arguments: monetary exchange already required a more highly developed legal system than that found in a barter economy, to safeguard money against counterfeiting, for example. We could also cite the long, historical evolution of exchange, progressing from a conventional instrument to a developed law of exchanges. We could therefore follow the parallel development of economic institutions, secured first of all conventionally, and then later by the state.

Above all, consideration should be given to what the theory of stages was directed against: the Marxist conviction that only people who possess capital, who have inherited it and come from the capitalist class or who owe their wealth to 'original accumulation', which can in one way or another be traced back to a relationship of inequality, to robbery, to the enclosure of communal pasture lands, or the like, only such people can be considered capitalists. This antithesis, naturally, does not come out of thin air. And yet this description has little in common with our modern experience of quick changes of generations and people among the owners and the experience of business start-ups in young, dynamic national economies.

The thesis that credit is connected with higher morals should also be understood as a direct response to then-contemporary communist trends. The theory of stages can deny neither its political motivation nor the influence of French socialism (with its 'credit fantasies', Kalveram 1933, p. 93, my transl.). In contrast, in a manuscript that remained unpublished during his lifetime, the young Marx, the communist, wrote:

> The ... alienating nature of the credit system functions in the guise of the highest economic recognition ... in a two-fold fashion: 1) The opposition between capitalist and labourer ... becomes even greater because credit is given only to someone who already has it ... or because poor people see their entire existence confirmed or denied by some whim or decision of the wealthy, see themselves completely dependent on this random chance; 2) in that the mutual play-acting, dissimulation, and hypocrisy are carried to extremes, such that for the person without credit, in addition to the simple judgment that he is poor, he is also morally judged as untrustworthy, he

has received no recognition and is accordingly a social pariah, a bad person, and ... 3) because through this entirely *ideal* existence of money, the counterfeiting by a person can be undertaken on no other material than his very own person, he must obtain counterfeit coins and credit by deception, lying, etc. ... In *state credit* the state takes entirely the same position as the person above. ... The gambling with state money shows how the state has become a plaything for the merchants.

(Marx 1966, pp. 251ff., my transl.)

This text, too, was and is accurate to a certain extent. The modern theorist can attempt to take a step forward, first of all by attempting to assess the efficiency of credit allocation. Then it is less a question of the classification of borrowers as moral individuals than the assessment of the chances of making a profit with the project for which investment is being sought. Secondly, modern theorists take up Hildebrand's question without the requisite familiarity with his predecessors and, applying game theory, examine the conditions under which players in repeated games are interested in internalizing moral principles.[13]

In yet another sense, the moral dimension of our problem is revealed through consideration of the individual fates of our two protagonists and the movements connected with their names: on the one hand, Hildebrand's cheerfully optimistic, energetic entrepreneurialism which led to the establishment of savings banks; on the other hand, the painful existence of the London emigrant, who keeps the family above water by repeatedly borrowing money from his friend Friedrich Engels. While writing the notebook of excerpts, he was probably not aware of how much he himself would become an 'outsider'.

Hildebrand did not attempt to prove empirically whether his ideal typical stage development was also valid outside Europe; he had no information about Chinese paper money, for example. The ancient world was left out of the developmental order. Hildebrand wanted to classify it as a money economy – the economy in the Medieval era to a large extent relapsed to a barter economy – and in a collection of notes attempted to prove that the private and governmental credit transactions remained trapped in their beginnings (ibid., pp. 332ff.). 'The fact that the ancient world did not manage to develop lending is therefore no more an argument against the historical fact of the three forms of sales listed than the fact that some human tribes have not developed beyond the first of these forms' (ibid., pp. 334ff., my transl.). The problem did not go away, however, and in 1869 he formulated the hypothesis that because paper money did not exist in the ancient world, with the exception of money lent in return for securities, wealth could only be invested in slaves or in land and soil. Slaves were leased and commercially employed or put to work in mines, but most possibilities of use remained rooted in real estate. He therefore concluded:

While in modern states, capital assets and a capital aristocracy have developed in opposition to and in struggle with the landed aristocracy and often have worked toward a dismemberment and a mobilization of the land, in the ancient world the capital aristocracy and the landed aristocracy were one and the same. The landed princes were the sole capitalists and capital served them in the expansion of their rule over the land.

(Hildebrand 1869, p. 155, my transl.)

Many ideas can be attached to this hypothesis, for example concerning the loaning of ships in the ancient world, which Hildebrand does not mention here, or the specific character of slave labour and the very extent to which it spread during various phases of ancient development. Hildebrand's most significant service, and that of his generation, consists not in providing definitive answers to questions of economic history, but in reformulating the basic issues in such a way that for decades research was stimulated and would often generate an unexpected immediacy through repeatedly making comparisons with modern conditions.

Hildebrand's book *Die Nationalökonomie der Gegenwart und Zukunft* [Economics of the Present and Future][14], published seven years after List's book, reacted to Romantic and socialist critiques of the new industrial system. Logically constructed, it examined four stages up to Hildebrand's present. It is not immediately apparent that the book is based on Hildebrand's historical conception of a doctrine of stages: with previous Romantic authors like Adam Müller and Sismondi (although he unfortunately does not fully deal with the latter), Hildebrand shared a love, if restrained, of the social cohesion of the Medieval feudal era – or he at least recognized the problem that the differentiation of the money economy which he connected with the introduction of precious metals from the New World, did with the advance of economic progress lead to the isolation of individuals. The book begins with Adam Smith's system, which he views as an astonishingly masterful performance. Smith was the first to logically analyse how an increase in productivity, brought about by the division of labour in a market economy, is regulated by means of the formation of values and prices, and how the distribution of the growing number of products was managed according to certain laws – which Ricardo later modified and made more precise. Hildebrand considered this system brilliant if dated; his interest in historical relativity derived from the hope that he could obtain statements about current trends and the future through the analysis of developmental laws.

Adam Müller now appears to be a reactionary who believed he could reinvigorate the disappearing society of orders. List had the merit of understanding the modernity of the Smithian system, but to have qualified it in regard to developmental policy. Then comes the most thoroughgoing part, which comprises three-quarters of the entire book: the exploration of the socialist critique of the industrial system, which rightly includes social conflict, but which provides an exaggerated diagnosis and offers incorrect solutions. Hildebrand primarily deals with the French cooperative theorists and

German communists. In presenting the fate of the latter, Hildebrand's London experiences are obviously included. Passages from his letter quoted by Grünberg, cited above, are copied into the book virtually unchanged.[15] Here he now writes:

> The members of the same German fraternities that have produced so many advocates of contemporary conservative politics and German states-men are abroad transformed from patriotic enthusiasts into disseminators of social theory. [...] They were wedded to the principle that man was driven by ideas, and they recognised the diversity and variety of human qualities.
>
> (Hildebrand 1922, p. 103, my transl.)

Characteristically, they share a comparatively Platonic world view, and the organizational plans of some of the early German socialists actually included the notion that society should be headed by the three greatest philosophers as a ruling triumvirate.[16] This doctrine declares that 'in contrast to classical antiquity, it is not man who evolves into the citizen, but rather the citizen who evolves into man' (ibid., p. 103, my transl.), thereby negating state and nationalities. The high status accorded science reflects the fact that German communist clubs abroad were simultaneously educational organizations offering instruction in various scientific fields. Thus French authors wanted the rule of industry with equality for the workers, while the Germans wanted the liberation from industry and the abolition of factory labour.

Hildebrand saw Engels' *The Condition of the Working Class in England in 1844*, written after a stay in England from November 1842 to August 1844 and published in Leipzig in 1845, as a particular challenge. Since it was so resolutely factual, beginning with a description of the industrial revolution in England that Hildebrand endorsed, a large amount of factual material has to be advanced to demonstrate that workers did also benefit from industrial progress.

Hildebrand deals more quickly with Engel's essay 'Umrisse zu einer Kritik der Nationalökonomie' [Outlines of a Critique of Political Economy] (Engels 1844, pp. 499–524). He rejected out of hand Engels' attempt to derive the internal conceptual contradictions of the competitive system from alleged internal contradictions of value theory. Here he showed his firm roots in classical theory. Most importantly, he points out that the 'contradiction' cannot be resolved simply by abolishing private ownership:

> because even under the rule of the community of goods, the products of labour and the measurements of luxury goods which are to be distributed to individuals must be subject to calculation. As soon as complete anarchy no longer ruled there would have to be some fixed formula for the volume of the individual's labour contribution to the common good against the share of goods to be assigned to the individual.
>
> (Hildebrand 1922, pp. 136ff., my transl.)

As potential formulations for such allocation Hildebrand takes up the following: *Gleichviel Arbeit für gleichviel Lohn* [equal labour for equal wages] or *Jedem nach seiner Fähigkeit und jeder Fähigkeit nach ihren Werken* [from each according to his ability and to each ability according to its effect], or referring to J. Fröbel's statement from 1847: *Jedem Arbeit nach seinen Kräften und Güter nach seinen Bedürfnissen* [to each labour according to his powers and goods according to his needs]. It is evident that Hildebrand here anticipates Marx's later refinement in his 'Notes on the Gotha Programme' of the idea that goods should be distributed according to individual contribution into the famous principle: *From each according to his ability, to each according to his needs* (Marx and Engels 1966, vol. 3, p. 180, my transl.). It is clear to the unemotional Hildebrand that even phrases as exhilarating as those by Fröbel and Marx are not exempt from close examination of their precise substance, together with some kind of proof of how they would be satisfactorily implemented.

Since Hildebrand takes the moral core of the socialist critique seriously we may ask how he himself saw the solution. The second uncompleted volume would have contained the answer. But we can already find significant indications in the first volume. Opposing machine breakers (Luddites), Hildebrand advocated technical progress, which he considered to be connected with emancipatory social developments:

> The division of labour, the machines, and all the significant mechanical inventions of industry which have come about during the last 70 years of English history in an uninterrupted progression and which owe their existence to free competition – these all have had an initial impact which legitimates them as a necessary part of human cultural development, and which cannot be replaced by anything else in the world. They have neither caused nor increased the poverty of the lower classes of society; they have merely brought it to light. They have concentrated suffering and vice as well as wealth, cultivation and the moral and intellectual powers of men, and thus rendered the existing contrast a visible and undeniable fact. The constant rhythm of machinery has bent the workers to regular concentrated activity, to endurance and to conscientious use of time, raising their energy and willpower. They have driven the labourer from one branch of business to another and expanded his perspective through forcing him changing trades, lending him a certain flexibility in spirit and self-confidence. They have united in large associations hitherto isolated individuals pursuing the same trade and hence created in them for the first time a sense of self-awareness, social entitlement and a drive for perfection. Even all the recent communist and socialist endeavours, to the extent they have a base in the worker's world, are they anything but a fantastic expression of an awakened self-awareness on the part of the worker in modern industry?
>
> (Hildebrand 1922, pp. 184ff., my transl.)

The rhythm of the sentences in this long citation and the emotional invocation of historical tendency is reminiscent of the *Communist Manifesto*, which had appeared in February 1848:

> Wherever the bourgeoisie has risen to power, it has destroyed all feudal, patriarchal, and idyllic relationships. It has ruthlessly torn asunder the motley feudal ties that bound men to their 'natural superiors'; it has left no other bond betwixt man and man but crude self-interest and unfeeling 'cash payment'. It has drowned pious zeal, chivalrous enthusiasm, and humdrum sentimentalism in the chill waters of selfish calculation. It has degraded personal dignity to the level of exchange value; and in place of countless dearly-bought chartered freedoms, it has set up one solitary unscrupulous freedom – freedom of trade. In a word, it has replaced exploitation veiled in religious and political illusions by exploitation that is open, unashamed, direct, and brutal.
>
> (Marx and Engels 1963, p. 28)

I think it is as possible that Hildebrand was already familiar with the text of the *Communist Manifesto* and consciously alluded to it with the cadence of his sentences, as that the similarity of the formulation is based on a contemporary style of writing. At any rate, there are contrasting conclusions. According to Hildebrand, the growth of capital had not created the basic problem, but stated it more clearly and offered potential solutions. The condition of the workers had in particular improved through the expansion of their horizons and the creation of new institutions such as labour unions and cooperative societies, of which Hildebrand approved – though not without some reservations. However, he did not believe that all problems solved themselves, and anticipated much of later German social policy; Müller, List, and Roscher made no contribution of this kind. Hildebrand later supported the foundation of the 'Verein für Socialpolitik' – the German economic association mainly associated with the name of Schmoller.

Savings banks already existed and he mentioned them in his lectures,[17] reporting that in Bern there were two such banks for workers. These banks accumulated the savings of workers and made capital available to those running small businesses. Hildebrand even came out in favour of sometimes providing unsecured credit: 'There was also rather infrequently the provision of loans without security, based solely on a familiarity with the moral character of the borrower, so that even those who owned nothing could obtain capital' (cited in Franz 1928, p. 24, my transl.). Today the borrower's business plan would be examined, and loans sometimes made even if the risks were great and there was little or no security, so long as a higher rate interest could be paid. The modern creditor is still not relieved of the task of trying to get some sense of the person seeking a loan, for the entrepreneurial spirit is a personal characteristic, as Schumpeter has taught us. The dilemma Hildebrand was facing – how to help a worker who has no means – has become largely obsolete because of subsequent advances in social policy. The main purposes of such borrowing, like the collateralization of a home or further education, is dealt with through public assistance – which does not perhaps examine character thoroughly enough.

Technical progress saves labour. Hildebrand's answer to this was twofold. On the one hand he thought that:

> Machines increasingly free the working world from all mechanical and dehumanizing activities and lead the human being into a future in which for each individual, by facilitating the satisfaction of all physical needs, is afforded the prospect of a far greater degree of mental development. Once fully developed machines take the place of ancient slavery, and provide the basic conditions for the moral and intellectual perfection of all individualities.
>
> (Hildebrand 1922, pp. 186ff., my transl.)

On the other hand, he expected that in the future workers would leave factories in increasing numbers and find employment in other sectors. The modern reader will be reminded of Fourastié's *Le grand espoir du XXe siècle* (1989 [1949]), but it turns out that Hildebrand is thinking more of a return to agriculture than the migration to a new service sector. He values private ownership, which serves self-realization, and trade, which is the driving force of culture. Thus, he seeks to mediate between the individualist ideas of the Classicists and the universalist ideas of the Romantics. From this tension he establishes the necessity of social policy, which for him does not involve as much state initiative as might be supposed. His notion of the development of custom through the expansion of the credit system preserves at least one element of the eighteenth century inheritance: the hope that economic progress will further moral progress. 'What is united in the natural economy through external, sensual bonds, but is dissolved in the monetary economy, is united once again in the credit economy through intellectual and moral bonds' (ibid., p. 226, my transl.). A century and a half later we might consider some parts of this vision naïve and other parts of it brilliant. Hildebrand certainly did not understand clearly enough the functioning of the credit economy, since for him all speculation was immoral. If speculation increased in industrial England, a country of which he thought highly;

> this only proves that the moral power of people is more powerful than all theoretical principles and that, namely, in a country like Great Britain, where the state and the whole of public life is an ethical educational institute for the people, false theoretical principles destroy themselves.
>
> (ibid., p. 229, my transl.)

The 'unethical foundations of Smithian political economy' have not, as he thought, become 'impossible in the future'; instead, progress consists precisely in the integration of speculation within an institutional context, blocking fraudulent abuse and channelling the flood of information which promotes development.[18]

Although the second volume of Hildebrand's work was never published, we can still form an idea of the developmental tendencies Hildebrand saw at work, and determine to which he would have recommended support. Just as he aimed at a midpoint between individualism and universalism, he also sought a midpoint between the recognition of spontaneous tendencies or developmental laws and intentional attempts to influence historical development through political activity oriented to historical circumstance. He was a decisive advocate of economic freedom – and thus to that extent also of liberal economic policy. He thought, however, that this freedom only justified the 'prosperity of the people' so long 'as the moral energy within the people grows and public life as a whole fulfils conditions which are indispensable for the growth of the moral energy of the people as a whole' (Hildebrand 1863, repr. 1922, p. 301, my transl.).

Hildebrand has been the object of a great deal of criticism, and his texts are open to attack on many points. I have made an effort here to avoid nitpicking criticism,[19] and chosen instead to seek conciliatory formulations which might render his way of thinking accessible to us again – for example, when we confront the fact that Hildebrand's emphasis on morality leads to a call for extending the analysis of *homo oeconomicus* to an analysis of *homo sociologicus*. The historical method which he played a part in founding has also been subjected to general criticisms which do not specifically relate to Hildebrand's work. It has for example been objected that the logic of future developments is indeterminate, since each new discovery alters the basis of our activity. Naturally, one can still make educated guesses about future developments, based upon assumptions about future behaviour, and Hildebrand certainly viewed his confident expressions of hope in progress in this light. Yet another accusation against the Historical School is that its relativism merely reflected a lack of clear position, leaving its representatives prey to political deviations. Hildebrand certainly did not lack a point of view. It might be asked, however, whether he could convincingly explain his ideas, or could scientifically justify the manner in which he blended sociological and economic arguments; but that is an ongoing project, just as we still wrestle with the criteria that can be used to differentiate economic stages or systems from each other.

First and foremost, the Historical School itself remained active. While many modern economists dismiss the work of the Historical School without really having any acquaintance with it, it still presents a serious challenge across the whole of Europe. This can be shown in closing by introducing several English responses.

In his classic work, *The Scope and Method of Political Economy*, John Neville Keynes (1986, p. 9) differentiated two schools of political economy. The approach of the first he characterized as positive, abstract, and deductive, and that of the second as ethical, realistic, and inductive. He immediately takes back this sharp distinction in a conciliatory fashion, adding:

It should be distinctly understood that this sharp contrast is not to be found in the actual economic writings of the best economists of either school. In the method that they employ – when they are discussing the same problems – there is to a great deal substantial agreement.

(ibid.)

From this it follows that method has to depend upon the question; and this is actually a matter of course, although all too often forgotten in debate, and remains so today whenever a question is not clearly formulated.

Keynes pursues the method of the first school, beginning with Smith. From the immense wealth of phenomena, there are few basic facts which might form the basis of a deductive method, or as Mill expressed it, from which we can proceed on an *a priori* basis. This identification of the deductive approach with the starting point as a given *a priori* appears to me to have been an important distinguishing mark of the nineteenth century (ibid., p. 16). Modern representatives of pure theory will immediately identify their method as deductive, but will understand their premises as hypothetical and variable, and they will refer to the many models they employ as evidence of the flexibility of their assumptions. A real contrast exists here between mathematical economists of the late twentieth century and Neoclassicists of the late nineteenth century, to the extent that the latter – Böhm-Bawerk comes to mind – were actually convinced they had constructed their theories on the basis of eternal basic characteristics such as utility maximization, while the virtuosity of a Samuelson consists in repeatedly varying behavioural assumptions, starting out today from a Keynesian consumption function and tomorrow working with a life-cycle hypothesis. Looking a little deeper, however, we see that this difference is reduced when we consider that in the nineteenth century assumptions were also occasionally considered to be hypothetical, while on the other hand in the twentieth century many mathematical economists ultimately turn out to be Neoclassic in the old sense, to the extent that they admit to a belief in the dominance of private interest as an *a priori* truth, which then however is also assumed to be founded upon life experience. Experimental economists and institutionalists today, the Historical School of the past, both claimed by contrast that they are able to observe other forms of behaviour, or at least find them described in texts as ethically-based.

The revolt against the domination of the English Classical School was led in Germany by Roscher, Hildebrand and Knies. The movement, however, was not merely German but was also, Keynes added, composed of 'a rising school of economists in the United States, who expressly repudiate the view that the new movement is exclusively a German movement' (ibid., p. 21). In England, Richard Jones had previously established the historical viewpoint, which had recently been taken over from him by Cliffe Leslie, while Germany had in von Thünen an important representative of the abstract position. The Historical School's position was then given a more radical form by Schmoller in Germany and Ingram in Great Britain. They claimed that the deductive method had lost its force. They wanted a more activist economic policy, and thought that disciplines bordering upon economics were necessarily interdependent with it. Different perspectives on development, specifically, the comparison of 'European, Oriental and Savage States of Society' (ibid., p. 322) had been adopted. Here Keynes comes closest to the task of differentiating between the schools, starting with the questions they pose, but since he himself does not go into history and does not look toward the future, nor even enter into an anthropological comparison, his discussion remains dry and academic. Even from a methodological viewpoint he achieves little. The great methodological challenge in cultural comparisons, which those in Max Weber's generation who were familiar with economics were to take up, is not even perceived as a problem.

Ingram (1962) developed a much more lively polemic in a lecture delivered in 1878. It is printed in *Essays in Economic Method*, which gathers together lectures presented to Section F of the 'British Association for the Advancement of Science' between 1860 and 1913. Ingram was speaking at a time when some natural scientists were disputing the right of Section F, for statistics and economics, to exist within the British Association. Defending himself against this attack, Ingram turned to a European debate regarding the tasks which political economy might make its own:

> Dissatisfaction has risen to the dimensions of a European revolt ... The largest and most combined manifestation of the revolt has been in Germany, all whose ablest economic writers are in opposition to the methods and doctrines of the school of Ricardo.
>
> (ibid., p. 47)

But well-known scholars in Italy, Denmark, Belgium and England had also joined this movement; in France, it was not so clear, since they there traced their origins back to Comte. The key words are similar to those employed by Neville Keynes, even if variations in the explanations and assessments also arise. Ingram was certainly right to rely on Smith as a historian and a representative of the interdisciplinary approach, and to cite *Theory of Moral Sentiments* as evidence of a more comprehensive model in the writings of Adam Smith. On the other hand, it is false purism on the part of an author like Senior if he apologizes for asking questions about work and family life, thus entering the domain of sociology. The institutions of political economy had indeed been created – but there remained social questions and thus the duty to move into the territory of neighbouring disciplines. As for abstraction: Hildebrand states that it is necessary to examine the variety of motives in accumulating wealth; and with regard to deduction, he believed its capacity was exaggerated (he also equated it with *apriorism*). Induction was supposedly historical in character. There can be no understanding of circumstances without an awareness of their origins; however, developmental influences are too complex to allow future circumstances to be predicted. He revealed his fascination with the history of land ownership and the emergence of private ownership of land (he lists de Laveleye as the most important expert); he does not, however, believe in a return to common ownership, and backs away from socialist activities. Although he examined the methods to be employed by historical economics with regard to what they could achieve, he managed to provide neither a vivid comparative visual description of economic forms nor causal analyses of economic progressions. It must be concluded again, therefore, that the decisive step in methodological discussion was first taken out by the Younger Historical School.

Finally, there is Ashley, whose work forms a bridge between the claim of comprehensiveness on the part of the Historical School, and the more moderate conceptual formulation of economic history. Economic history here provides education and orientation: what is the origin of the economic and social forms with which we live, and which determine our existence?[20] Ashley laments that in Great Britain the Historical School did not receive sufficiently prompt attention because its beginning coincided with 'the time of Germany's humiliation, and I suppose the victories of 1870 did more to make us learn German than any spontaneous enlargement of interests' (Ashley 1962, p. 230). He also connects the adoption of Historical School tendencies with Cliffe Leslie, adding to that name that of Arnold Toynbee. What the Historical School could accomplish was naturally nowhere clearly outlined except in 'the Great Treatise of Gustav Schmoller' (ibid., p. 238). For Ashley, the Historical School was a means of limiting the claims made for Neoclassical Theory; he himself turned towards economic history.

As these examples demonstrate, the Historical School is a phenomenon whose spatial and chronological extension, and its thematic scope, are today generally unknown. Hildebrand's influence as one of its co-founders was great, but at some point this ended. Studying him, nevertheless, seems particularly rewarding for a variety of reasons. The questions and motives which led to the creation of the school, their visions, their methodological problems, their political and institutional successes and their limits can all be seen in his work. He was ultimately a liberal whose integrity, scientific thoroughness, and enterprise are worthy of respect.

### Wilhelm Roscher's 'Perspectives on the Economy from a Historical Standpoint'

Wilhelm Roscher was undoubtedly one of the foremost German economists of the nineteenth century. He enjoyed international renown as one of the primary figures in the older Historical School, the achievements of which are however seldom acknowledged today. Nonetheless, its influence remains evident in the work of Anglo-Saxon theorists like Alfred Marshall, who paid equal attention to the work of theoretical and historically-oriented economists. In 1897 he wrote:

> during the generation that is now passing away it has been made clear beyond doubt by many workers in many lands that the true inductive

study of economics is the search for and arrangement of facts with a view to discovering the ideas, some temporary and local, others universal and eternal, which underlie them; and that the true analytical study of economics is the search for ideas latent in the facts which have been thus brought together and arranged by the historian and the observer of contemporary life. Each study supplements the other: there is no rivalry or opposition between them.

(Marshall 1897, p. 133)

In his book *Grundriß zu Vorlesungen über die Staatswirtschaft. Nach geschichtlicher Methode* [Outline of Lectures on State Economy. According to the Historical Method] Roscher programmatically applied the historic-legal method of the Savigny School [Historical School of Law] to economics. He argued that economics was not a doctrine of enrichment, but instead a political science which had a necessary connection to neighbouring disciplines such as law and the cultural sciences. It learned from the contrasts which can be observed by historical comparison, particularly by the observation of older peoples whose process of development is already complete. It was such comparison that revealed the determination of economic institutions.[21]

The turn toward the historical method in economics for which Roscher is chiefly responsible, a path which shortly afterwards Knies and Hildebrand also followed, involved neither a confinement to the collection of facts, nor a rejection of the methods of classical economics. Although isolating abstractions (in modern terms: the construction of models) were eschewed, and Roscher had little use for the doctrine of value doctrine in particular, resort was constantly made to theoretical considerations, for instance in the evaluation of monetary questions or of foreign trade. Roscher's mastery of neighbouring disciplines was evident both in his economic work and alongside it. His early text on Thucydides is the work of a pure historian. His late *Politik: Geschichtliche Naturlehre der Monarchie, Aristokratie und Demokratie* [Politics: The Historical and Natural Theory of Monarchy, Aristocracy, and Democracy] (1908) revealed an encyclopaedic knowledge of political constitutions throughout European history, as well as the energies which new state forms unleashed and then suppressed.

Roscher had good judgment which he used prudently. He was in essence a liberal, influenced by the religious ideas and moral norms of the nineteenth century. His skill in representing economic thought and contexts was evident especially in shorter works, such as for example his monograph *Die volkswirtschaftlichen Ansichten Friedrichs des Grossen* [The Economic Views of Friedrich the Great] (1866). Here he expresses his deep admiration for Friedrich's governmental leadership, but identifies the limitations of this monarch, general and writer, particularly in the economic sphere.

The ambivalence of the Historical School between the establishment of norms and scientific objectivity, as well as the pluralism evident in their reliance upon diverse disciplines, was the source of some trouble in the 1950s for a post-war generation of economists who sought to separate themselves from the remaining adherents of the School. The great majority of German economists finally shook off the legacy around 1960 and turned toward the Anglo-Saxon theoretical tradition and Popperian methodology. Gottfried Eisermann's (1956) influential work *Die Grundlagen des Historismus in der deutschen Nationalökonomie* [The Foundations of Historicism in German Economics] provides a sceptical assessment of Roscher's attempt at historically-based theory-formation. It is however certainly no exaggeration to say that during the last third of the twentieth century the majority of economists did not share Eisermann's qualified acceptance, but rather rejected the School outright without any attempt to acquaint themselves with its works at first hand. Less and less differentiation was made between various representatives of the Historical School; but now this trend is being reversed, as a new generation takes up their texts and discovers much that is new and of interesting in them, beginning with the observation that the Historical School appears neither so one-dimensional nor so antagonistic to theory as was thought. When, for example, Roscher wrote about colonies, it became assumed that he must have been a colonialist, and in fact he was no enemy of colonization. But he was scholar enough not to ignore more problematic elements and, for example, he dealt with the wars against natives (Roscher and Jannasch 1885, p. 125). It is common knowledge that the Historical School has some roots in the German Romantic movement, but the critical distance which Roscher put between himself and his Romantic predecessors is little known (Roscher 1870).[22] It is therefore necessary to reassess the role of the Historical School with regard to its historical importance and the methods it actually employed.

The attacks made by Marx and his school represent a particular problem for the later reception of Roscher. Personal and political motives might explain why Marx belittled Roscher so mercilessly in a footnote to *Capital*. A liberalism that sided with the monarchy, even if a constitutional monarchy, was as repulsive to Marx as Roscher's religiosity or his unquestionably powerful position within academic circles at which Marx looked askance. Roscher enjoyed a recognition denied to Marx, although Marx, despite his errors, was intellectually and in historical importance far in advance of Roscher. There is also in the Marx-Engels correspondence consideration of how Roscher's influence could be reduced, for example through appropriate placement of reviews of Marx's *Capital*. The general approach is evident in the following passage, which concerns the economist Faucher and who was not of a rank equal to Roscher:

> Faucher is one of those 'travelling preachers' of political economy. The fellow has no place among the 'scholarly' German economists such as Roscher, Rau, Mohl, and others. It is doing him too great an honour even to mention him. And I have consequently never allowed him a role as a noun but only as a verb.
>
> (Marx and Engels 1983, p. 489)

Marx invented the verb 'fauchern' in *Capital* and as a rule only mentioned Roscher derisively in footnotes, refusing to discuss his work in the main text.

Marx towered above Roscher, but Roscher was a better judge of reality. His early *Betrachtungen über den Socialismus und Communismus* [Thoughts about Socialism and Communism] (1845), hence published before the *Communist Manifesto*, constitutes a brilliant analysis of the unavoidable functional deficiencies of communistic state bodies, Roscher being able to call upon the support of an unexpected wealth of historical analogies. However, he also describes the political processes which nourished communist hopes and indicated how, even if successful, they would lead to dictatorship.

In the first essay from *Ansichten der Volkswirtschaft aus dem geschichtlichen Standpunkte* (Roscher 1861b), 'Ueber das Verhältniß der Nationalökonomie zum klassichen Alterthume' [On the Relationship of the Political Economy to Classical Antiquity], Roscher works in the style of the Historical School. It is not a question of accumulating facts, but of creating a comprehensible theory. That the essay is more than a mere description of facts can be gathered from the generalizations (his 'inductive' theory construction) obtained from accurate observations, which might be completely wrong because they lack universal validity or because they contain specific internal contradictions. In the following I will direct attention to successful examples of logical theory construction, rather than find fault with weaker cases. These examples are illuminating so long as Roscher remains aware of the connection between abstraction and the object from which such abstraction was derived.

It was undoubtedly a central concern of the Historical School to create a parallel between the rise, prospering and decline of the ancient world and the course of history in Central Europe from the Medieval era to the Renaissance and up to the present. Roscher always referred to the time of Homer as the Greek Middle Ages, while we characteristically displace this into the dark centuries and consider the Middle Ages to be the period between the Mycenaean and the archaic epoch. Historical analogies do still occasionally arise today, but we do not treat them so unequivocally; and more importantly, we are no longer willing to draw such far-reaching conclusions as was Roscher.

The parallels that Roscher drew, for which there was of course precedent but which in his hands were elaborated with especial thoroughness, were initially quite obvious to him and his admirers. The Idealist educational tradition had taught them to see life in the ancient world as exemplary, to be admired for its achievements and to be abhorred for its calamities. Educated people were familiar from their youth with classical literary sources and no report on China, Japan, or India, no travel description of meeting with 'primitive' peoples, and no archaeological reconstruction was a match for Antiquity as a contemporary counterpart against which the progress or decline of technology and the conquest of nature, of economic institutions or societal morals, in science and culture could be observed. While ethnology as an academic discipline hardly existed – Japan was closed to Europeans, and China resisted European incursions – they had read the Greek and Roman poets, philosophers, historians and geographers. The development of the ancient world was before them, complete, like a wide arch; something had to be learned from it. Marx and the Socialists thought that with industrialism something new had entered the world, a prelude to a radically different future. Roscher believed he could see in the 'new' something that was quite old. There were not only abstract economic laws such as that regarding industrial location which might be modified as a result of institutional change, but under analogous circumstances analogous political and social trends developed. The Socialist undertaking constituted just such an example because – according to Roscher, at least – it had also existed in the ancient world.

To describe the transformation Roscher employs more organizational or holistic analogies whose unscientific nature was later rightly criticized by Max Weber. The stages of nature, labour, and capital which he elaborates in the first essay of *Perspectives*, are almost banal in its simplicity. Nevertheless, Roscher's explanation retains a suggestive power, which at the very least invites scholars to pose questions once more. Only then does it become plain how difficult it is to improve on his answers.

Roscher somewhat unoriginally identifies slavery, which he considers 'essentially wicked', as the 'most important difference between the old and new economy'. It presupposes a low level of need, for otherwise 'it would require stronger and more imaginative incentives for the labour of a people than the mere fear of the slaves; and these incentives are only possible under freedom' (ibid., p. 20, my transl.) He predicts an end before long to slavery in the South in the United States; here there is a certain political immediacy to his essay.

Roscher apparently overestimated the number of slaves and the importance of slavery for production in the ancient world. His successor in Leipzig, Karl Bücher, sparked a famous controversy about the developmental status of the Greek economy in the classical period when he expressed the opinion, contrary to that held by the historian Meyer, there were no factories nor manufacturing in the fifth and fourth centuries BC worthy of notice, the number of slaves was small, most citizens were themselves small farmers, and the comparison of the Attic empire with conditions in England or the Netherlands in the early mercantilist era was completely misleading. Modern historians of the ancient world, like Finley, align themselves much closer to Bücher's primitivism than to Meyer's modernism (Schefold 1988).

Roscher's essay is however remarkable for the variety of his observations on the slave economy, connecting the characteristics of slave labour with those of a type of economy and a culture supported by slavery. 'From the ineffectiveness of slavery and its lack of inventiveness' it follows that manufacture produces more for luxury, while slaves fulfil their needs with only the most basic goods. Gradually the emancipation of slaves occurs, some in Rome having their own capital (*peculium*). Roscher notes the differences between Athenian and Mercantilist economic policy. He deals with care for the poor, which is quite characteristic of the form of the economy, as well as finance and the monetary system. At the same time, he recognizes the particular individual importance of the liturgy system for Classical Athens. He describes the contrast between the simplicity of agriculture and advanced level of communications, particularly maritime communication. Lastly he considers the intellectual attitude to technology and its religious stamp. In sum: he examines the transformation of economic styles in the ancient world.

Roscher's title for the essay only suggests that Roscher might want to consider what the science of economics of his day had to say about the ancient world, a world which Smith only dealt with marginally and which Ricardo ignored. Roscher's achievement is that he refuses to stop at negative characterizations of the ancient world, pointing out which institutions were not or not yet developed, but instead goes beyond conventional ideas of progress (which ideas are, however, occasionally encountered in his texts). He seeks to establish the significance of institutions and values for the continued existence of the economic style of the ancient world, showing how the elements of the economic system are mutually determining: contrasts such as slavery and luxury production, and the relation between the preparedness of citizens to donate money and the level of cultural development. Links between socio-economic and political relations are also repeatedly sought. The older Historical School's idea of stages already pointed beyond the simple categorization of epochs. Roscher employed the triad nature – work – capital, and Hildebrand barter economy – money economy – credit economy. In this way, Roscher anticipated the idea of an interdependence between individual characteristics in economic styles or systems, as would be developed later in the twentieth century by Sombart, Spiethoff, and Eucken.

In the essay 'Ueber die Landwirtschaft der ältesten Deutschen' [On the Agriculture of the Oldest Germans], Roscher seeks to prove that the Germans had a very simple agricultural system and were unacquainted with the three-field crop rotation economy. Roscher usually works only from literary sources, for in his time archaeology was not sufficiently advanced to provide adequate complementary evidence on Western civilizations.

His essay 'Ein nationalökonomisches Hauptprincip der Forstwissenschaft' [A Primary Economic Principle of Forestry] summarizes the contemporary knowledge of forestry knowledge, attempting to show that forests are less intensively cultivated than fields and meadows. However, in comparison with Thünen, whom Roscher genuinely admired, there is here a want of clear theoretical insight.

'Ueber Industrie im Großen und Kleinen' [On Large and Small Industry] first of all lists the conventional advantages of the division of labour, but then primarily explores the social differentiations which follow in the wake of economic concentration. Roscher here describes guilds and the putting-out system of production, analyses their advantages over factory production, and expresses regret for the erosion of the small and medium-sized producers. He finally attempts an assessment of a modern 'shareholder-owned factory' which provides new openings for an 'intelligentsia without capital' which hitherto would have been destined for employment by state or church: this represented 'a new and weighty moment of popular freedom' (Roscher 1861b, p. 172, my transl.).

The next essay, 'Ueber die volkswirtschaftliche Bedeutung der Maschinenindustrie' [On the Economic Importance of the Machine Industry], is interesting for its treatment of what we call today the Law of Mass Production and Increasing Returns, the implementation of technical progress, and the discussion of technological unemployment. Roscher does not equal Babbage (Babbage 1992 [1832]) in his description of concrete technological developments and managerial organizational principles, but in comparison to the achievements of the Ricardian School he presents a quite significant discussion of the connection between mechanization, effective demand, and employment. He says, first of all, just like Ricardo:

> If the consumption of a good which has become a luxury increases at the same rate as the price has decreased, the exchange value .... of the national wealth remains unchanged; if it increases at a faster rate, the national assets grow not only in use value but also in exchange value.
>
> (Roscher 1861b, p. 194, my transl.)

In fact, the labour value of goods produced annually in a country remains constant when the level of employment is constant, even if the mass of produced goods increases with productivity improvements. The labour value of individual goods then falls in direct proportion to the growth in quantity. The increase in quantity, however, cannot be determined without index numbers, since economic sectors do not grow at the same pace. Ricardo (1981 [1951], Ch. 20) settles for the idea, therefore, that the 'value' which can be precisely determined with the aid of the labour theory of value can be contrasted with the vague increase in 'riches'. Roscher devotes more attention to the extension of demand, and recognizes that production, rendered cheap because of the growth of productivity, can lead to a 'geometrical' growth in quantity, if new groups of buyers are reached. It could be said that Roscher is here feeling his way toward the term elasticity of demand, but without formulating it in so many words. However, he seeks reasons for changes in demand more in the composition of purchasing groups than in individual purchasing behaviour, and is thus more under the influence of Classical rather than Neoclassical conceptions of demand.

The most interesting contribution of the chapter is his consideration of the possibility of compensation for redundancy resulting from the introduction of machinery into the workplace. The formulation of the problem derives from the following consideration: 'If cotton cloth sinks to half its earlier price due to the development [and use! BS] of machines, this frees for all consumers of these goods half of their usual expenditures' (Roscher 1861b, p. 200, my transl.).

And then, in a move which anticipates Marxian critiques of Say's Law, Roscher launches into an investigation of the circumstances in which either a decline or an increase in demand might be expected. He has already ascertained that the introduction of an expensive machine does not in itself endanger employment because the capital costs for the machine can be traced back to labour; thus each share of the production costs previously spent directly on labour and which now goes to the machine represents an indirect wage payment. He does not consider, however, whether non-neutral technical development might lead to distributional conflict. For Roscher it is not the development of capital intensity that is so significant but the use of the means which, following an increase in productivity can initially be saved if consumption levels remain steady: 'only through wanton destruction or the completely pointless hoarding of money saved would absolutely no new demand for labour arise from that' (ibid., p. 201, my transl.). What Roscher has to say about this can be translated into the language of multiplier analysis. He prefers, however, to argue by means of clear examples; it should be obvious that as a rule the money saved will be compensated by new expenditure, but he acknowledges that this outcome is not, as Say thought, a logical necessity.

Then he turns to the social effects of factory labour, women's labour, and child labour. He sees the burden of suffering in factories, the danger for social cohesion and for health, and thinks he can show that Engels' critique of the early factory system was exaggerated and the worst conditions must be attributed directly to the early and poorly-developed stages of the factory system. He develops an effective polemic against machine-breaking and finally comes out in favour of factory legislation enforced by inspectors.

The essay 'Zur Lehre von den Absatzkrisen' [On the Theory of Sales Crises] anticipates much that Marx says about economic crises, a topic for which in the third volume of *Capital* he is considered a pioneer. In the description of many circumstances Roscher even appears more straightforward and precise than Marx. He explicitly rejects Say's Law and then discusses an important cause of crises: changes in distribution lead to fluctuations in effective demand when the tendency toward consumption is dependent upon income. Then he takes up structural factors, changes in fashion, and speculation.

The clear differentiation between underconsumption and overproduction can be seen as a particular strength of Roscher's description. With a rare clarity he explains that a mere temporary extension of demand can be damaging. He explores psychological factors here and outlines barely familiar experiences of the effects of discoveries (i.e. new goldmines) of outbreaks of war and conclusions of peace treaties which, according to Roscher, do not of themselves necessarily lead to an improvement in the economic situation. A high level of economic debt can lead to the worsening of a crisis, as can be shown with clearly described multiplier effects, and Roscher even has examples for this from antiquity.

Finally, a significant part of the essay is devoted to a discussion of the contrast between the currency principle and the banking principle. Roscher, as an advocate of a theory of effective demand, sides with the Banking School and, specifically, views with scepticism Peel's suggestions on regulating the issue of bank notes. His argument amounts to endogenizing the money supply: 'In a word, the increase in bank notes is not the cause so much as the result of the increase in business transactions, as is the price increase which precedes or follows this increase' (Roscher 1861b, p. 357).

For a looming crisis Roscher recommends that monetary policy be carefully accommodating. He means, however, that in times of over-speculation little can be done to help: 'on the whole preventative state protection is really merely an illusion here' (ibid., p. 398, my transl.). Roscher's book concludes with the essay, 'Ueber den Luxus', whose theme itself betrays Roscher's roots in the older tradition of political economy, since the later neoclassicists increasingly sought, by use of the term 'utility', to move way from such judgmental differentiations in the field of consumption, towards an objective science which reached its first high point in Pareto's indifference curve analysis. Roscher is liberal enough not to mourn Medieval and early modern luxury laws, but he has moral problems with certain forms of luxury, and he is in the Classical tradition to the extent that he describes the dynamic of economic growth through the expansion of needs, the continual discovery of new luxuries by the upper classes, and the transformation of these luxury items into necessities when the lower strata, whose purchasing power was increasing, imitated the upper classes.

Roscher makes a link to Smith when he connects the transformation from the Medieval era to the Modern era with changes in the objects of luxury consumption. The rich lords of the Middle Ages could only display their luxury by maintaining large entourages and providing hospitality for thousands. 'When the nobleman later began to purchase expensive clothing, etc., rather than feeding so many servants, he thereby indirectly supported just as many people, indeed, perhaps many more; only these people were not *indebted* to him for anything' (ibid., p. 422).

Courtly and bourgeois luxury are both further characterized sociologically. The highest cultural stage is reached when people voluntarily renounce private luxury in favour of public luxury. It is a classical Greek ideal; ancient historical research has indeed shown that in Periclean Athens, and by comparison with other democracies, there was a marked predominance of public rather than private wealth.[23] So Roscher attempts here a periodization which has not however gained a large following.

Can luxury really be directed? A 'people in the throes of robust development' does not need the 'leaden strings' of luxury laws; Roscher suggests abstinence. He himself feels that in this regard the difference in cultural levels, which is his basic interest, has not yet been grasped. There remains the taxation of luxury, whose fiscal purpose is only achieved when moral purpose has failed. The essay thus ends on an open question. Roscher does not arrive at a conclusion, a further demonstration of the ambivalence of the Historical School.

### Hans von Mangoldt's: *Grundriß der Volkswirtschaftslehre*

Hans von Mangoldt's *Grundriß der Volkswirtschaftslehre* [Outlines of a Theory of National Economy] cannot be overlooked when considering the development of economics in the German language. In the half century between the publication of Ricardo's *Principles* and the Neoclassical revolution, a period that in the field of economics in England belonged almost entirely to the Classics, characteristic transitional forms were developing in Germany in which Gossen and others were anticipating the basic ideas of Neoclassical theory. Other authors like Rodbertus and in some respects Wagner who, together with his student Oppenheimer was still influential in the first third of the twentieth century, held fast to the basic Classical concepts for longer. They added socio-political ideas to them, while the theoretical rigor weakened in comparison to their English masters. Scholars followed several trends, among them Historicism. Even some of the best, like Roscher and Knies, backed away from a definitive commitment to one or another trend, on the one hand because their theoretical approach was eclectic, and on the other because they were considered leading representatives of the older Historical School. Erich Streissler (1990) referred to Carl Menger as a German economist who had provided an important impetus to the development of Austrian theory through the compression and clarification of neoclassical trains of thought which had already developed in German economics, not least of all because of the theoretical tradition which originated with Roscher.

Influence and recognition seldom go hand in hand with status as a theorist. From a modern point of view Gossen, who was not acknowledged at all by his contemporaries, is of primary importance. Mangoldt, who may in the mid-nineteenth century have received greater recognition with his *Grundriß* [Outlines] – though still far less than was his due – then certainly takes the second rank. His influence on Menger and Marshall was accordingly less than it might have been – if the appropriate edition of the *Grundriß* had been known to these authors, or even to Walras and Jevons, soon after its publication.

A clear differentiation must be made between *Grundriß* as it appeared in its original version in 1863 and Mangoldt's other books. First of all, the second 1871 edition of Mangoldt's *Grundriß der Volkswirtschaftslehre* which was revised by Friedrich Kleinwächter after the author's death, represents a source of confusion. After Mangoldt's early death, which perhaps prevented him from being recognized as a co-founder of the Neoclassical revolution, Kleinwächter published the *Grundriß* in his series 'Kaufmännische Unterrichtsstunden' [Lessons for the Businessman] in an honest attempt at popularization. The concessions to the public's level of understanding led him to 'set aside the mathematical and graphic depiction he [Mangoldt] had selected for the theory of prices' and also 'to some additions and changes so that only a few paragraphs could be included in their original form in the second edition' (Mangoldt 1871, p. VI, my transl.). Kleinwächter's simplification of the text was not simply an attempt to reach a wider public. Rather, he was himself extremely sceptical about whether graphic representations and mathematical formulas could facilitate 'the understanding of economic laws'. Mangoldt himself had also known that practical application of the mathematical formulas he had developed for setting prices was not possible for the time being, since the statistical foundation for the determination of supply and demand was still lacking. He also emphasized, not unreasonably in theory, that algebraic formulas should only be used where their parameters could be empirically determined. Thus the reception of precisely the best of the new ideas in *Grundriß* was greatly impeded.

At the same time, Mangoldt had decided to publish a more understandable and systematic version of his *Grundriß*, under the title *Volkswirthschaftslehre* [Economics] (1868). This book, which was practically complete at the time of his death, was posthumously published later that same year. It should not be confused with the second edition of *Grundriß*. Unfortunately, important authors – among them Böhm-Bawerk – cite only *Volkswirthschaftlehre*. [24]

Finally, Mangoldt's postdoctoral thesis, *Die Lehre vom Unternehmensgewinn* [The Theory of Enterprise Profit] (1855), must also be remembered. It was reprinted 111 years after its initial publication because it contains an excellent and much-praised discussion of the various reasons for the accrual of a surplus profit, so that with skilful entrepreneurship a profit beyond a normal profit could be made. Additionally, the text generalizes the classical term differential rent. Streissler believes that Mangoldt did not grasp the implications of declining marginal utility, and thus to that extent did not anticipate Menger, while on the other hand Menger did not understand Mangoldt's treatment of entrepreneurial risk, expressed in a concave utility function mirroring risk-aversion (Streissler 1990, p. 173).

The reader of *Grundriß* will come across many interesting thoughts which have received little attention in the literature, for example on transportation, enterprise types, the ethical problems of labour, commodities (*Warenkunde*) and banking, all of which refer to various sub-disciplines in economics, from management theory to business ethics to money, credit and business cycle theories. Still, every modern reader will immediately notice the canonical importance of the book when Mangoldt begins to deal with price theory, once he has classified goods according to needs and recognized that an increase in stock reduces the value of additional units. Mangoldt here comes close to the idea of an equilibrium of marginal utility. He deploys geometrical figures to represent supply curves, and explores various cost trends and their implications.

The attempt on the part of J. H. v. Thünen to devise a marginal productivity theory of distribution is then also applied by Mangoldt in an analysis of factor markets. He generalizes the term 'rent'. His credit theory forms the basis for crisis theory, and the divergence from what we would call market rate of interest and natural interest rate forms the starting point. Thus while *Grundriß* remains a conventionally structured book, its content is of major interest (Hennings 1980).

Mangoldt's work can serve equally well as both proof and critique of the notion of a Neoclassical revolution. The critique can assume, as we have just acknowledged in Mangoldt, that the fundamental ideas of Neoclassicism were already circulating before 1870. *Grundriß*, however, sets the old and new side by side. He thereby proves that in spite of everything the intentional break with tradition had yet to come. Smithian ideas of natural prices and the gravitation of market prices toward this natural price still play a central role, without the opposite, as with Marshall, being developed for a differentiation between short and long periods and the associated neoclassical equilibrium of the firm. The book has even almost conservative aspects, in comparison to which Jevons (1995 [1871]), simply by virtue of his formulations, appears to be a revolutionary. Without a doubt, Mangoldt's geometrical, algebraic, and numerical examinations of complements and substitutes stand out, as do his analysis of joint production and the effects connected with consumption. He greatly expanded the theory of international trade compared with Mill (Niehans 1990, pp. 128, 133). His discussions of the creation of expectations also include much that is interesting. Nevertheless, it cannot be maintained that Mangoldt systematically worked his way through a treatment of the interdependence of markets in the sense of a general equilibrium, a point on which he was criticized by Walras (Hennings 1980, p. 659). Moreover, there exists no real connection between exchange theory and distribution theory in his work. He can however certainly be counted among the pioneers of mathematical economics.[25]

## Karl Knies' *Das Geld* [Money]

Karl Knies' *Das Geld* [Money] is among the crowning achievements of German economics in the nineteenth century – written by one of the founders of the older Historical School. This work alone would be enough to disprove the accusation that the Historical School was untheoretical.

Karl Gustav Adolf Knies (1821–98) was born in Marburg, the son of a police official (Schefold 1987, p. 55). He grew up there in straightened circumstances. His studies in history, philosophy, and theology led to a doctorate in 1846, and the qualification to teach in a university in the fields of history and political science. Living as a lecturer in Marburg from 1846 to 1849, he got caught up in the political movements of 1848 and under the influence of Bruno Hildebrand – professor, colleague and older friend in Marburg – turned his attention to the social and economic problems of his time. The liberal revolutionary government in Kassel appointed him as a teacher at the Polytechnical School in Kassel, a position he was forced to give up when the political climate altered once more. Knies emigrated in 1852 to Switzerland, and that same year took a teaching position in Schaffhausen. In 1855, however, he was able to return to Germany. The University of Freiburg appointed him to a professorship in political science. The first edition of his methodological masterpiece, *Die politische Oekonomie vom Standpunkte der geschichtlichen Methode* [Political Economy from the Standpoint of the Historical Method], was then published in 1853.[26]

Although Protestant and not a native of Baden, he was elected to the parliament and assumed a leading function in the university and in educational reform. When it became clear that his ideas could not be implemented he was pleased to be able to move within the same state to the University of Heidelberg, where he remained until the end of his life. For the next thirty years, from 1865 to 1896, his seminar became one of the most important centres of economic studies in Germany. J.B. Clark and E.R.A. Seligman studied here; and so for a time did Wieser and Böhm-Bawerk – the latter made a presentation in Knies' seminar which already contained the essential elements of his later theory of interest[27] – and Max Weber became familiar with Knies' views, which he criticized when dealing with Knies' first main work (Weber 1982). On the occasion of his 75th birthday a commemorative publication was dedicated to him, to which Clark and Seligman contributed and which contained Böhm-Bawerk's famous essay *Zum Abschluss des Marx'schen Systems* [Karl Marx and the Close of his System] (Boenigk 1896).

In *Die Politische Oekonomie vom geschichtlichen Standpuncte* [Political Economy from a Historical Standpoint], Knies expresses a preference for inductive method, for historical relativity when assessing the validity of economic theory, and for taking account of the variety of human motives and interests. The economic life of societies cannot be based solely on self-interest. Justice could only be done to the variety of economic forms through discovering analogies with the development of different peoples and epochs.

He considered economic life to be embedded in culture and politics, determined by moral and legal frameworks, and like Hildebrand he believed in a connection between technical, economic, and moral progress.[28]

While the book received only a moderate initial response, it came to be read programmatically at the same time as Schmoller's 'Younger' Historical School was gaining acceptance. The most detailed obituary on Knies, published in the *Economic Journal* in 1899, celebrated the breakthrough that Knies achieved with his *Politische Oekonomie* of 1853: 'A generation has elapsed since its first appearance, in which the reputation of this book has steadily increased.' The author of this obituary made it clear that in later works Knies did not at all adhere to his own method, as Max Weber also later argued. In these works Knies spoke out in favour of a modernization of statistics. He wrote about railways, the effects of telegraphy, and finally wrote his second important work on *Geld und Credit* [Money and Credit], the first volume of which, *Das Geld. Darlegung der Grundlehren von dem Gelde* [Money. Outline of the Fundamental Doctrines concerning Money] (1931 [1885]) we will examine here.

In 1885 Henry Sidgwick commented on this work as follows:

> When Knies ... is discussing the natures and functions of capital, money and credit ... the lenders and borrowers, whose operations are contemplated, exhibit throughout the familiar features of the old economic man ... we find everywhere the old economic motives and the old method unhesitatingly applied. The proof of the pudding ... is in the eating; but our historical friends make no attempt to set before us the new economic

pudding which their large phrases seemed to promise. It is only the old pudding with a little more ethical sauce and a little more garnish of historical illustrations.

(cited in Kisch 1962, p. 432)

There is certainly a contrast between the important works of the older and those of the younger Knies, but it should not be exaggerated. If the older book still speaks, echoing the pathos of the revolutionary year 1848, of a 'self-love' of individuals which blends with altruism, even for the liberals of the time this did not imply an absolute contrast with self-interest. A characteristic passage is as follows:

> And if I, as indeed all contemporary German political economists, find it undeniably supported by historical experience that the pursuit of 'self-interested' economic goals harms the general good to this or that degree and extent, I likewise hold it on the basis of experience to be indisputable that the general good is fostered in diverse ways by private activity which is *characterized as self-interested*. Man, like all creatures in the animal kingdom, 'naturally' possesses an instinct for *self-preservation* and *well-being,* while his – individual – spirit too is born with the desire to assert itself, to perfect itself, to complete itself. This instinct and impulse working within the reasonable and thereby self-objectifying man appears as the *self-love* of the individual, which for its part is also sanctified by religion, which always seeks to make present the knowledge of other-worldly interests; Christianity elevates the latter to the same level as the notion of altruism which it commands. This concept of man's *self-love* involves no contradiction with love of family, kin and country.
>
> (Knies 1964 [1883], p. 236, my transl.)

Such considerations, which Schmoller sought to make concrete in his theory of institutions, move backstage in *Geld und Credit*. But traces can still be found, for example in his thoughts on the possibilities and the limitations of cooperatives in systems of finance and credit. And his method bears clear historical markings in the examples he uses in explaining the functions of money. These comments remain worth reading today, for in the explanation of money forms it is not merely a question of revealing how existing money circulates through the economic system, and in so doing influences economic activity and prices. Instead, the primary task consists in explaining why money forms exist. The statement 'If A, then B exists with necessity' has a different logical mode than the statement 'A has the property B'.

Knies did not consider monetary institutions to be simple inventions, nor did he embrace a rigorous historical determinism. Karl Marx, in his *Das Kapital* of 1867 (and before that in *Zur Kritik der politischen Ökonomie* [Critique of Political Economy]), had attempted to develop a theoretical language in which the theory of value could be derived from the structure of a commodity-producing society, and money forms from the relationships of production and exchange – presented therefore in their necessary existence. This was one of the theoretical influences that Knies, as an outspoken anti-socialist, sought to confront critically. Where Marx sought to develop an abstract logic – and it still has not been fully explained to what extent this logic is supposed to correspond to a historical progression (and if so, then to which one?) – Knies everywhere places money forms in historical context which accounts for their emergence. This text does not therefore have a purely illustrative nature, as Sidgwick claims; rather it provides an explanation for the origin of institutions.

In contrast to Marx, Knies's doctrine of money is not based on a doctrine of labour value but instead begins with exchange processes and factor payments. When the subject of money is raised in introductory lectures reference is sometimes made to prison camps where parcels from the Red Cross are made available. Prisoners have their preferences – one prefers chocolate, the other cake – so they trade, establishing habitual exchange relations and use, finally, cigarettes to measure value, as a means of exchange, and perhaps even as a means of payment.

In Knies, too, the exchange of goods has a primary position, but not exclusively. The book begins, logically, with the economics of individual households, in which the problem of distribution already exists. Originally, goods were directly allotted to family members and dependents. If the economic unit becomes larger and more complex, if there are servants in the household who can also assert legal claims, the allocation of real goods will still conflict with the idea of equal pay for equal work. Knies, having sketched the conditions of an early-Medieval manorial barter economy, proceeds as follows:

> Once in those manors the most immediate tasks have been met by its own production, so that individual labourers receive housing, clothing and food in proportion to their different respective efforts, then a problem arises if labourers have been granted the right to make related claims – and this can becomes very burdensome even to an unconstrained master with just intentions since it of necessity gives rise to serious conflicts. Differences in labour performed can only be reflected by allocating different living quarters and clothing, which are then very clearly visible and remain in being, while 'service and compensation' will correspond to each other only very roughly.
>
> (Knies 1931 [1985], p. 5, my transl.)

Money, therefore, is apparently required not only for the exchange of goods, but also for factor payments:

> Moreover, any future planned 'organization' of the economy which sought to do away not only with bartering but also with the use of money

would also encounter precisely this dilemma and in even greater proportion, after such great increase in *different* kinds of labour and goods...

(ibid., p. 6, my transl.)

Measurement of performance is identified in the first chapter as a central
problem of the socialist system. I will not here attempt to trace the historically
and logically based approach of Knies' book. Much appears obsolete and
superseded, especially in the area of value theory. Still, we find in this work a
wealth of suggestions whose contemporary and indirect effects can be seen in
the great influence which it exerted on Böhm-Bawerk, who often referred to the
book as a source. Böhm-Bawerk did not take up the relevant suggestion from
Knies that money as a good could neither be classed as a production good
nor consumer good – a division often presented as exhaustive. Von Mises
(Mises 1953, p. 79), in contrast, took into consideration Knies' suggestion of
introducing a special category of exchange means (alongside capital goods
and consumption items). Knies' explanations of capital theory are also of
interest at least to historians of theory. In his *Geschichte und Kritik der
Kapitalzins-Theorien* [History and Critique of Interest Theories], Böhm-Bawerk
later significantly expanded Knies' historical examination of the term capital.

Knies' work bears bullionist as well as nominalist characteristics. He
acknowledges the power of the state to expand the circulation of precious
metals (he came out in favour of a gold standard) through the circulation of
banknotes, and calls for state control of issuance. In so doing, he did not
envisage that paper money could be redeemed with gold, but he had on the
other hand already distanced himself in his value doctrine from Classical
ideas of gold and money value based on labour-value theory.

The historical circumstances surrounding Knies' work were unfortunate,
and the history of economic thought has not so far considered this historical
reception. Knies is not included among the great, international classics of
economics, but *Das Geld* stands out as an important peak among the books
of the Historical School, and German contributions toward monetary theory.

## Wilhelm Roscher's *Geschichte der National-Oekonomik in Deutschland* [the History of Economics in Germany]

Not every scholar is aware of how much scientific progress depends upon
critical self-reflection on its own history. In times of upheaval, this is true even
of the natural sciences, as the crises in mathematics and physics in the first third
of the twentieth century have shown. This is even truer of the humanities,
which not only observe human culture but also help give it shape, and, in
times of shifting lifestyles, always reinterpret it. Economics, with its approach
characteristically standing somewhere between the two, often believes that it
should only analyse the functioning of a given economic context – if history
of economic thought can be practiced at all from this perspective, then only
to chart the progression of discoveries in of new models for the analyses of

the system. A history of economic ideas of this type would perhaps hardly lay claim to being included among the classic works of economics. However, if the other position is taken, if – as in traditional humanities – economics explores historically evolving social, cultural, and political assumptions about economic action, as most of the important representatives of this subject have done to varying degrees, the history of theory then assumes a far more important task. It must relate the history of theory, in the narrower sense, to the broad context of intellectual and historical developments.

To provide an account of the history of progress in analytical methods in economics is what Joseph Schumpeter attempted in his *History of Economic Analysis* (1972), when he purposely placed the development of knowledge in the foreground of his account of modern theory; but in so doing he over-stepped his aim and made use of his broad historical knowledge. A contrast to that, for example, is Edgar Salin's *Politische Ökonomie. Geschichte der wirtschaftspolitischen Ideen von Platon bis zur Gegenwart* [Political Economy: History of Economic Ideas from Plato to the Present] (1967) – a work that seeks to interpret the political and sociological characteristics of these theories and in so doing differentiates between a 'pure' theory, which Salin calls 'rational', and an 'intuitive'[29] or 'visual' theory. An intuitive theory situates an economic system from the start in its historical and institutional context.[30]

Roscher's *Geschichte der National-Oekonomik in Deutschland* [History of Economics in Germany] has a prominence owed to a number of factors. Although there are older monographs in the history of economic thought, Roscher's came at a time when the concept of systematic history of economic ideas was still emerging. Ewald Schams (1932) has suggested dividing the literature of the history of economic thought from its beginnings to the present into three epochs: the 'primitive epoch of historiography' extends from the Physiocrats to Blanqui (1837), which Shams calls the 'bibliographic-pragmatic' epoch. The *early epoch*, stretching from Blanqui to Dühring (1871), includes authors who now had access to sufficient material and intellectual distance for their accounts, but who still could not bring a systematic and coherent approach to their material. The 'scientific' epoch of the history of economic thought began therefore with the works of Dühring, Roscher, and others, through whom the writing of economic history was in Germany made into a systematic discipline. The attempt to formalize the ideas of older authors in mathematical terminology not available to such authors, an approach not without its risks, is only a very recent development.

Although the beginning of the scientific epoch of history of economic thought is determined somewhat arbitrarily by Schams, it is clear that in the second half of the nineteenth century the history of thought began to assume more systematic form. Karl Marx also belongs here, with his *Theorien über den Mehrwert* [Theories of Surplus Value] (1968 [1863]), in which he rigorously evaluates the history of economic thought from the perspective of his own system, and by virtue of this one-sidedness achieves a rare consistency in analysis. He was however very unfair to contemporary German authors, especially Roscher. To represent his theory of the decline of Ricardianism and the emergence of 'vulgar economics' as a historical caesura, he ignored the fact that the roots of subjective value doctrine went back before Ricardo, and that some German economists were pioneers in its development.

Roscher's *Geschichte der National-Oekonomik in Deutschland* does not aspire to lofty standards in the systematic structuring of its material. The book is divided into three main sections: the theological-humanistic age, the police-Cameralistic age, and the scientific age of German economics. Within each chapter Roscher proceeds more or less chronologically. He distinguishes schools and tendencies from each other, a normal approach when dealing in terms of 'eras'. The monumental character of the work is not due merely to its sheer extent. Although the development of economics involved contributions from many European nations, there was in the German-language area a particular course of development which Roscher outlines. Many little-known details are presented without losing sight of the larger picture, and the focus on national development does not ultimately preclude a cosmopolitan standpoint.

The number of authors and works dealt with attests to Roscher's extremely wide reading. His ability to take up each individual strand of an argument and to classify each in its appropriate context is impressive; this presupposes extensive knowledge of the general historical, and specifically economic, developments and institutions around which debates take place. Today the book has become indispensable. Roscher perhaps seems more original in his shorter texts on the history of economic thought than he does here, but there can be no doubt this will be regarded as his central work for a long time to come.

Roscher, born in Hannover in 1817 and who taught at the University of Leipzig from 1848 until his death in 1894, is considered the primary founder of the Historical School, though the roots of the school can be found still farther back, before List, in Romanticism. His early texts on antiquity demonstrate his philological knowledge and provide an interesting insight into the relationship between economy and the state in the classical period of Greek antiquity (Roscher 1838, 1842b). His multivolume *Grundlagen der Nationalökonomik* [Foundations of Economics] was first published in 1854 and went into many editions, providing a foundation for the historical understanding of economics in Germany. Roscher also published critical interpretations of socialism and communism, together with accounts of colonial policies and the evolution of systems of government. Among his works on the history of economic thought his essays *Zur Geschichte der englischen Volkswirtschaftlehre* [On the History of English Economic Doctrine] (Roscher 1857) should be set alongside his *Geschichte der National-Oekonomik*.

Roscher seeks to describe the evolution of the economy rather than construct or derive an optimal organization. Such an account could provide a guide to the future. His conceptions of development were formed by a weak organic analogy according to which nations rise and fall. Nature, labour and capital dominate in a succession of stages until decline sets in. Institutions must be appropriate to the particular developmental stage attained. Roscher believes that the historical standpoint provides, if not the only, then at least a key to the understanding of economic policy. Hence only someone who understands, for example, why guilds were once useful could assess their abolition.

His historical perspective does not preclude his thinking in theoretical terms; and he bases it above all on Classical doctrine, if eclectically. When, for example, he takes up the wage fund theory, he criticizes classical theorists for adhering to the idea for far too long, since he recognizes the influence of (effective) demand on the level of employment. It is not easy to say to what extent there is a coherent idea behind his theoretical eclecticism, as he also takes up the arguments that Thünen made about marginal productivity:

> Only a very short-sighted or a very arrogant person, in any case someone who is completely ahistorical, will allow the history of a discipline to begin only where the systems emerge which are already quite similar to those that he himself has adopted.
>
> (Roscher 1924, p. 2, my transl.)

Roscher thus acknowledges, in his preface to *Geschichte der National-Oekonomik in Deutschland*, the relative nature of economic knowledge as well as of his own knowledge. His talent for characterizing the distinguishing features of a particular economic form in a few words quickly becomes clear to the reader: 'While today it is regarded as desirable to mobilize even landed property, in the Middle Ages one sought to immobilize capital by making its investment irrevocable, and labour by binding workers to the land' (ibid., p. 2).

Naturally for Roscher, who was a religious man, an examination of Humanism and the Reformation is not purely an academic task, to be described distantly and objectively. For him, Luther is 'the noblest, the greatest, the most German man' (ibid., p. 54, my transl.). However, he does not overlook the complexity of the questions of each era – whether he finds economic wisdom in the sayings of Erasmus' *Adagia*, this wondrous and spirited depiction of the ancient world, or whether he goes into the obscure details of fiscal systems, in order to arrive at an understanding of Cameralistic arguments.

And yet he does not get mired in details – even this compendium of German economic thought is surprisingly readable and leads the reader from the treatment of one author to the next. He cleverly connects assessment relating to the history of thought with commonsense suggestions for economics specialists, for example when he writes in a section on Jacob:

> Now from experience, affiliation with an important school system, whether as a simple pupil or even as its standard bearer, might be a splendid means of quickly arriving at some sort of validity. But afterwards this validity disappears just as quickly, and it disappears never to return. One's reputation is very much built by slash and burn!
>
> (ibid., p. 687, my transl.)

Or he warns in what was for his time a characteristic connection of history of philosophy and ethics 'against every steep path which leads from commercial freedom to freedom to gamble, thence to the freedom to go bankrupt and so finally to the freedom of the criminal' (ibid., p. 1045, my transl.).

One should not however be too distracted by such picturesque views and diversions. Roscher's strength rests, first of all, on the historical classification of economic conceptions which relate a particular system to economic development, and thereby anticipates the later development of notions of economic style. It is certainly more than simply situating ideas. Thanks to his talent for visual evocation, Roscher knows how to indicate which concepts are characteristic of nations, of epochs, and of schools of thought. The value and difficulty of producing syntheses in this manner is easily overlooked at a time in which the isolated discovery has become a model for all scientific activity.

When, however, readers turn to those parts of the text which deal with leading German theorists, they encounter real theoretical confrontations. Roscher considers that von Thünen belongs indisputably among those 'for whom mathematics is the organ through which they construct their inner world and thus rule the outer (Goethe)' (ibid., p. 896, my transl.).

There is a distancing in this, since Roscher had no right to consider himself one of them, nor did he do so. He discusses with some care Thünen's theory within the limits that his book allows. Certainly, he does not isolate Thünen's theoretical arguments in the way that a modern interpreter would. Where Thünen takes up the problem of the intensification of agriculture by making the increase in the productivity of the soil dependent upon the increase in an investment in labour and capital investment, he fails to make the necessary distinction between gross net product and marginal net product.[31] Instead, Roscher offers something else: a brief discourse on agricultural chemistry which is supposed to show just how far Thünen had already anticipated Liebig when discussing agricultural intensification through the use of dung. And he describes his own attempt to orient Thünen historically (Roscher 1924, p. 891).

He finally also justifies theoretically Thünen's suggestion that wages be increased:

> Socialism, in contrast to economics, teaches a community which goes beyond public spirit, which even – because it weakens the mainsprings of industry and thrift – is always on the whole exploitation of the national wealth, and as a result in no position, often does not even have the intention, to provide full compensation to those persons injured by their constraints. Even non-socialist, truly economic policy forces some reforms through, but only those which strengthen the mainsprings of industry and thrift, through which thus a surplus arises compared to the national wealth up to that point, from which injured parties can be fully compensated and yet the rest can still be raised up.
>
> (ibid., p. 893, my transl.)

Here he addresses the possibility of compensation as a criterion for the justification of intervention undertaken on the basis of welfare theory.

It should in conclusion be pointed out that Roscher possessed a remarkable overview of the 'latest developments' in his field, as demonstrated in his assessment of younger theorists like Schmoller, Wagner, or Menger. It is therefore the blending of encyclopaedic historical knowledge, great descriptive skill, and eclectically employed theory which lends this work its importance.

## Adolph Wagner's *Grundlegung* [Foundation]

Adolph Wagner is one of the most important, frequently-named yet seldom-read authors of German economics. Like his colleague Schmoller, he assumed a commanding position in the academic world. At the same time, he was involved in politics as a party leader and a representative. Schmoller and Wagner were both about the same age, came from southern Germany, but were taught at the University of Berlin and advocated Prussian supremacy in the Reich. The two men had common experiences and aspirations: the dissolution of the old liberal school, the formulation and influencing of social policy, moderate protection for agriculture and large industry. And yet 'by nature Schmoller was predominantly an investigator, while Wagner was primarily driven by his aspirations. Schmoller was essentially an empiricist, whereas Wagner was the absolute rationalist' (Tönnies 1918, p. 110, my transl.). While Schmoller was sought to start from facts, Wagner wanted to extend Classical theory, for example through systematic observation of self-interest, only one form of which was the drive toward acquisition.

Wagner was still barely forty when Wilhelm Roscher's *Geschichte der National-Oekonomik in Deutschland* [History of Economics in Germany], acknowledged his talent, describing him as one of the most thoroughly 'knowledgeable people in banking, paper currency, and finance', who later inclined to the Historical School. His interest in this regard involved more comparative than historical approach strictly speaking; but his truly historical character was evident in his 'preference for the historical critique of economic thought' (Roscher 1924, p. 1044, my transl.). Wagner's principal works, *Allgemeine oder theoretische Volkswirtschaftslehre* [General or Theoretical Economics] (1991 [1876]) and *Finanzwissenschaft* [Finance] (1883) were at that point still unpublished.

Schumpeter (1972 [1954], p. 851) also ascribed theoretical importance to Wagner's early work in the field of monetary theory: 'Always excepting the field of money, his originality or even his competence in analytic economics cannot be rated high. Yet his name will live much longer than will that of many inexpert analysts.' This last comment suggests that the author of *History of Economic Analysis* approved of the posthumous fame Wagner enjoyed in the history of ideas and of policy. Since Wagner stood between schools and maintained his individuality it is not easy to summarize his importance. There are several aspects to this, and we can begin here with method.

1. In his *Principles* Marshall paid respect to the German merging of historical, legal and economic studies: 'A splendid instance is to be found in Wagner's contribution to economics.' He said of the leaders of the Historical School:

> It would be difficult to overrate the value of the work which they and their fellow workers in other countries have done in tracing and explaining the history of economic habits and institutions. It is one of the great achievements of our age; and an important addition to our real wealth. It has done more than almost anything else to broaden our ideas, to increase our knowledge of ourselves, and to help us to understand the evolution of man's moral and social life...
>
> (Marshall 1960 [1949], p. 634)

Marshall, whose orientation towards Neo-classical theory was in part fostered by the study of German economists like Hermann, referred to Wagner when discussing the motivation of human action (ibid., p. 646). This was a compliment from one of the founders of Neo-classicism most strongly oriented to history and applied economic analysis, directed to a writer who, from afar, could be considered a leading theorist of the Historical School.

Nevertheless, Schumpeter was right when he said that behind such professions of esteem there was no essential theoretical affinity. Moreover, Marshall's and Wagner's methods, analytical foundations, and political conceptions were very different. There were, moreover, rifts in the pan-nationalist understanding between the two scholars. Political differences developed even before the First World War in the peaceful competition of conflicting scientific systems; the German critique of Classical economic theory connected the rejection of liberal principles with national sentiment against England. It could even be said that Historicism laid the foundations for the linkage of German chauvinism with National Socialism.

2. However, in the second half of the twentieth century the historical-institutional approach which Wagner had in particular developed acknowledged in the Anglo-Saxon world as a necessary and essential enrichment of neoclassical analysis. Musgrave and Peacock (1967) published a well-known collection of texts by authors from Germany, Italy, France, and other countries which compared continental public finance with the Anglo-Saxon tradition. In their introduction they write that after the Great Depression the theory of public economics was initially dominated by the problem of the effect of fiscal policy on income, employment, and prices. Subsequently interest returned to the older question about the criteria for when and why resources should be used publicly or privately. For Adam Smith, income was both the measure of individual capacity and of personal interest in general welfare. In the nineteenth century the idea of individual capacity was extended by the idea of personal sacrifice; on the other hand, it was assumed that the goal of state expenditure was the maximization of satisfaction.

Wagner is credited with the concept of dividing tax effects into fiscal and social welfare effects. The following basic concepts, prominent in the Classical inheritance, appear to be of particular importance: the state is a compulsory institution able to enforce the payment of taxes and the provision of services. While it can also operate commercially, the latter functions are best privatized. Fiscal theory is of interest where the state conducts business differently from the private sphere. It has alternative means of reward, for example by conferring rank or status, or security of employment. Since its revenues derive not from exchange but compulsion, profitability provides no standard of success. Consequently, the state has to serve the interests of the people – a characteristically general formulation which the Historic School felt able to fulfil. Frugality is not therefore an adequate principle for the administration of state services, and the Treasury should be monitored by the legislature according to its own political goals. The question of the appropriate level of taxation led Wagner to his law of increasing state activity, which is not limited to the central instances of the state since the needs of local government also increase in the course of cultural progress.

Among the goals of taxation is also the promotion of social policy through redistribution. Wagner does not question the impact of such intervention, but he devotes much time to a discussion of how desirable it may be. He also emphasizes the historical relativity of principles of taxation. As in the Aristotelian theory of just distribution, it is not the general framework but the concrete substance which is historically variable. For Wagner, it appears that the time has come for progressive taxation, the taxation of property, and the taxation of inheritances – postulates whose fulfilment required the establishment of clear principles of taxation which are today still discussed in relation to Wagner (Andel 1990, p. 271 and Neumark 1965).

3. Zimmerman (1967 [1953], p. 117) calls Wagner one of the fathers of modern theory of business cycles. Schumpeter (1972 [1954], p. 726) writes of Wagner's 'boundless enthusiasm for Tooke' because the importance of Wagner's work on the theory of money rests on his adoption and implementation of the Banking School position. His work is noted by Valentin F. Wagner in his *Geschichte der Kredittheorien* [History of the theories of Credit] (1966 [1937]), who emphasizes that Wagner's discussion of the socio-economic functions of credit belong to legal credit theory, in which political considerations retreat behind administrative matters, and economic theory gives way to classification. From a theoretical point of view, he offers the classic answer to the question of what the economic and functional importance of credit as a means of payment is. When is additional credit acceptable, and when does it become a cause for concern? (Wagner 1862) Credit, as such, represents purchasing power (whether as a means of circulation or not). In this way, credit becomes a potential factor in the disturbance of equilibrium. Wagner thus tends toward a theory of business cycles oriented to credit rather than money. He believes banks could certainly ease the process. The difference from the Currency School is that it considers the danger to come primarily from the influx of

additional purchasing power, while the Banking School is more concerned about a misdirection of the money capital saved. Thus credit is a contributory factor in the upswing, when speculative movements primarily affect commodity markets. This was not taken any further into the issue of how this affected the sphere of production.

Wagner's treatment of prepaid discount was particularly characteristic of someone influenced by Tooke. Prepaid discount arises when the entrepreneur has already sold the commodity against a bill which is to be discounted. If the bill is now discounted, the seller receives a bank note, so that here the money supply is oriented to commercial needs. Current parallels to this can be found in post-Keynesian theorists (Kaldor, Minsky) who do not deny a (chronologically-displaced) parallelism in the development of price level and money supply – as the monetarists postulate – but they consider the money supply to be the dependent, not the independent variable, and admit the influence of money policy on prices only via the indirect chain of interest – investments – volume of production. Wagner sought to unite the best ideas of the Currency and Banking Schools. Later, he developed more in the direction of the Currency School. There has been up the present no convincing synthesis of monetarist and monetary-post-Keynesian thinking on this matter.

4. Among questions of contemporary concern that Wagner took up was that of the connection between statistical observation and causal analysis. Wagner was an admirer of Quetelet. He may not have wanted to interpret statistically observed regularities as natural law, but he still chose to support theoretical statements with statistical investigations. Together with many of his contemporaries, he wondered whether crime rates, suicide rates and the like suggested a limitation of free will on the part of anonymous forces (Wagner 1864).[32] He also considered whether averages would have any meaning in the social sciences, as they did in physics where there were laws regarding, for example, the attraction or in creating the centre of gravity of various masses in the transmission of impulses. Cournot denied this. For people averages are not always meaningful. For instance, the average growth of young people is unambiguously regular, because every adolescent experiences a typical growth spurt – though not at the same age. While Wagner believed in the causal interpretation of statistical regularities, the critique involved the theoretical objection that scientific laws for social phenomena were specific, and could not generally make use of statistical methods based on the natural sciences, a criticism which joined itself to the emphasis on individuality typical of the Historical School.

5. Although early on Wagner leaned toward the ideas of liberal economic policy, he increasingly turned into a sceptical and socially engaged conservative observer of the capitalist economic form. Employing a formula Max Weber later adopted, he went so far as to call capitalism 'masterless slavery' (Hennis 1987, p. 182). Slavery refers here to the dependence of wage labourers, and masterless to the fact that the personal relationship between employer and employee can be ended at any moment and cannot be interpreted

according to the standards of an older, traditional ethic. What new ethical system should replace the old loyalties?

The working classes bore a heavy burden in the phase of rapid economic development following German Unification. It was a time of flight from the countryside, and the decline in craft industries was set against by the millions working in the industrial sector. Hard physical labour for more than ten hours a day was gruelling, and later its intensity increased when working hours began to be shortened. Proletarianization was therefore experienced as a burden and as deracination. However, it was accompanied by a slow increase in living standards and a breaking of old bonds which could have been experienced as constraints.

Wagner is among those who, their expression of social ideas marked by their nationality, saw a path into the future. They placed great trust in the state in the form of a constitutional monarchy, as guarantor not only of order and transition, but also of a positive arrangement of economic and social life: through regulatory policy including wealth redistribution, education, family and population. Wagner's programme included the establishment of public enterprises in particular sectors, among them the nationalization of the railway system. He sought to appropriate the reforming ideas of the Socialists and anchor them as 'state socialism' in the framework of a constitutional monarchy, more resolutely and profoundly than did the professorial socialists.

Wagner's texts and those of the Historical School often go beyond the limits of objective science, simply because they sought to understand the interdependence of economy and society and to influence them. The 'Socialists of the Chair' (*Kathedersozialisten*), who founded the 'Association for Social Policy' (*Verein für Socialpolitik*) with Wagner's cooperation, sought a greater social equality which could not be accomplished merely by monetary redistribution. Wagner was not only a political advisor, but also a representative in the Prussian parliament. Schumpeter reports that many *Kathedersozialisten* delivered lectures as if they were making speeches to political assemblies. 'Wagner shouted and stamped and shook his fists at imaginary opponents, at least before the lethargy of old age quieted him down' (Schumpeter 1972 [1954], p. 802).

In his fatal book on 'German Socialism' an aging Werner Sombart accommodated himself to National Socialism. It cast a shadow on his early achievements. It is true that in this text Sombart raised many issues that would be popular with modern readers, such as the question of how nature is to be protected from destruction by technical progress. He evidently had hopes of the more strictly conservative elements of National Socialism. Within the Party of course the opponents of conservatism triumphed. They not only pursued employment policy but also militarization, so that they might achieve the familiar goals of power politics with the most modern technical means and destructive weapons. Sombart was more humane, but he also employed expressions like the 'mongrelization' of the German race, which for him was a result of the mixing of peoples in large cities (Sombart 1934, p. 125, my transl.). While his *Die Juden und das Wirtschaftsleben* [Jews and Economic

Life] (1911) expressed admiration for the Jewish spirit, equality was now denied them 'without explanation' (Sombart 1934, p. 193, my transl.) – an outrageously ambivalent formulation.

The phrase 'German socialism' presents us with the difficult question of how it relates to older concepts and traditions. The terrible rise and the horrible end of the Third Reich seems to leave the term entirely compromised if we fail to make differentiations. But a more nuanced perspective presupposes first that we observe the historical relativity of legal terms, of for example civil law. There is nonetheless a human core which has endured through the ages, for centuries by turns understood, admired, or condemned, fairly or unfairly. Secondly, the openness of history has to be considered: the sense which we lend actions in hindsight is affected by the experience of the outcome of events which could also have turned out differently. The responsibility which we seek assumes the freedom to make decisions and just such openness. On the other hand, this would be a void if we could not recognize the causes and consequences of actions.

For the idea of a national socialism Sombart cites Plato, and for German socialism he invokes Goethe and Nietzsche. The discussion of totalitarianism has dealt with these associations, in a sometimes misleading manner. What all three have in common is that each of the three writers had, in their own way, experienced the triumph of oligarchy, revolution, and extreme nationalism; they therefore outlined at an abstract level ideas about cultured people living a communal life together – whether it was in a utopian concept, or a critique of a present thought inadequate. The connection that Sombart makes in naming predecessors of 'German socialism' is more disturbing: he selected those who had sought a practical scientific and social policy which connected to National Socialism. Sombart's reference to Adolph Wagner could be understood in this way.

Indeed, on the occasion of his hundredth birthday in 1935, Wagner was celebrated in *Schmoller's Jahrbuch* (Vleugels 1935) as a forerunner of National Socialism. However, as a forerunner he was seen as a contributor to precisely those aspects of National Socialism that cannot be simply dismissed: the welfare state which has become the general practice of industrialized nations since the Second World War, moderate protection of agriculture, and Christian-ethical principles which should also inform business practices.

The persistent concern, today again an issue, of how limits are to be drawn to increasing governmental intervention and bureaucracy was raised by Wagner himself, and has since been passionately debated. For example, Lorenz von Stein raised the objection that Wagner's state socialism could lose its relationship to moderation. He was concerned that Wagner allowed such latitude to arbitrary political intervention, ignoring critiques of the division of tasks between public and private volition. Wagner's anti-critique attributed a higher level of insight to the state. Even in *Grundlegung* the joint control of government organs (the government, the parliament) is at least mentioned; the debate remained and remains open.[33] What Wagner specifically called for, what he attempted to carry out, and what he achieved would require a small book.

The dead can no more defend themselves against false praise than against hostile critique. Even the contemporary literature emphasizes the distance between state socialism and National Socialism (Vleugels 1935, p. 138).[34] The view that Wagner was an early proponent of the welfare state has little bearing on the level of intervention today – his own social proposals have been superseded and large areas of infrastructure are today state owned – nor can it be seen as inherently National Socialist. His ideas were echoed in the policies of democratic states everywhere after the Second World War. In comparison to Keynesian employment policy during the depression, the National Socialist employment policies are to be condemned not for the goal of creating jobs but for the authoritarian methods of carrying this goal out; together with the aim of conquest which fuelled rearmament.

In 1940, an article appeared in the United States which attempted to trace a direct line which went from Wagner as a nationalistically-oriented economist to the doctrines of National Socialism, making many references to his chauvinism (Clark 1940). Wagner's admiration for and defence of Prussian and German power politics is laid out in this article. He advocated the annexation of Alsace-Lorraine and the integration of marginal populations like the Dutch. Wagner was also a leading member of the Christian Social Labour Party, founded in 1878 and led by Stöcker. The party made anti-Semitism into a political programme, and they were recognized by friends and enemies alike as instigators of anti-Semitic agitation. At the turn of the century, Wagner advocated colonial expansion and the end of British naval supremacy (ibid., p. 404).

Wagner's military nationalism is unwelcome today, but he was also criticized by contemporaries and considered a threat. Clark's article is entirely one-sided. Nationalism, colonialism, a predilection for wars of conquest and for annexation were not unique to the German empire. Anti-Semitism was also widespread, naturally with variations in form and goals.

It is quite correct that in the 1860s and 1870s, at the time of the unification of Germany and Italy, Wagner wrote in great depth about national questions. Clark's tendentious representation is perhaps understandable given the wartime atmosphere, but Wagner's *Die Entwicklung der europäischen Staatsterritorien und das Nationalitätsprinzip* (1867) [The Development of European Territorial States and the Principle of Nationality] argues, for all its patriotism and its promotion of the principle of nationality, that the right of nation-building belongs to *all* wherever the relationships between peoples allows for the sensible construction of national territories. Wagner's scientific nature led him to make a thorough statistical analysis of the mixing of populations in the lands between the Baltic Sea and the Balkans. He remarked that among the 22 nationalities and population groups which he registered, many were too small and lacking in distinction to be able to form a territorial state. He came to the conclusion, which naturally was strongly opposed to the later goals of the

League of Nations, that the domination of much of the area in question by Germany or Russia was unavoidable. If there were any doubt, however, then a decision should favour national independence. And, speaking of the Balkans, he wrote:

> With smaller population groups, an often strongly-developed national pride which frequently appears to be in inverse proportion to its internal justification will endanger such states all the more, because it has a strong tendency to treat the rights of other nationalities living in the territory in contempt. [...] Precisely here, where the federal principle would be justified, the somewhat stronger tribe often reveals itself to be invincibly domineering.
>
> (ibid., p. 11, my transl.)

He concluded from the mixture of population groups that: 'The domination of the Germans bringing culture,...like...the Russians is morally and politically justified by these relations' (ibid., p. 28, my transl.).

The diagnosis was appropriate – and still applies to parts of the Balkans today – but the therapy of spreading 'culture' through domination, reminiscent of the colonialist ideology of all large and many smaller powers ('The white man's burden'), contributed to a European problem which not even Versailles could solve, and which would later be modified by others into the disastrous doctrine of 'German living space in the East'.

While the text on the 'principle of nationality' contains hardly any economic considerations, the popular pamphlet 'Gegen England'[35] [Against England] does in fact begin with all the familiar historical statements which are supposed to justify the German position in the First World War, particularly in the series of wars between Germany and France reaching far back in history. Here the less obvious hostility to England – the 'tribal relatives' – is given an economic foundation. The text includes a general economic-historical treatment of industrialism combined with a characteristically 'mercantilistic' interpretation: English customs duties and the colonial realm create the market. Subsequently free trade allowed them to claim the resulting cost advantages. The German customs union was a challenge, even more so the German empire, whose colonial possessions were few but whose position in world trade was growing, until Germany reached second place behind Great Britain. These economic reasons explain what Wagner felt to be England's powerful enmity. He responded in kind, accusing it of a hypocrisy demonstrated particularly in its repression of a pauperized Ireland – '*Oderint dum metuant!*' – that justifies, in the editions published before 1914, the preparation for war and the related increases in taxation and armaments. Here we meet an eloquent Wagner, but entirely consumed by the conceptual world of rival great powers. But in that he was not alone.

He himself once risked, as he put it, a 'fantastic dream', when on 27 January 1900 he gave the Kaiser's birthday speech in the assembly hall of the Royal

University of Berlin. There he described the German Reich of the coming century as a potential

> crystallization of a new Central and Western European union of peoples and states, based not on violence, but on voluntary association in the self-interest of all, resting on economic connections and alliances, the core of the civilized world ... a revival of Carolingian thinking...
>
> (Wagner 1900, my transl.)

After state socialism, the welfare state and the nation, there remains one fundamental charge to explain: that of anti-Semitism. Jewish people were granted civil emancipation in the United States in 1776, in France in 1791,[36] in Great Britain in 1858, in the German Reich in 1871 – at approximately the same time as Austria-Hungary, Sweden, Switzerland, and Italy. Norway (1891) and Portugal (1910) lagged behind, while in Eastern Europe pogroms took place every decade – 1881/82 in Russia, for example. During this time of upheaval, in which some Jewish people quickly achieved enviable economic success and exerted political influence, there were many attempts – modest ones by Schmoller as well as Marshall and by Jews themselves – to define Judaism in various ways: as a religion, as a nationality, or based on their character, their ancestry, their morals. Similar attempts were made with many other groups. Here, however, it assumed a particular importance, because the categorical description could also result in restrictions on, as well as a questioning, of the rights of other ways of life, if not actual civic equality.

The court preacher Stöcker and the Christian Socialists, with whom Wagner linked himself politically, originally hoped to win the working classes over to a socialism that was Christian, patriotic, and loyal to the king. When electoral success eluded them in 1878, Stöcker turned to anti-Semitic language which, with the exception of verbal attacks against the Jewish press and financial speculation, basically called for the assimilation, and the administrative removal of Jewish teachers ('We have to remove the poisonous Jewish drops from our blood') – a line of political argument that would quickly gain support and also proved to be an embarrassment for Bismarck.[37]

And Wagner? Franz Oppenheimer wrote in his autobiography: 'the young people enthusiastically followed the powerful speaker Court Preacher Stöcker, who was at the time the first to express the new anti-Semitism. My dear friend Adolf Wagner also had a leading role in the movement ... arising from his anti-capitalist attitude; he feared Jewish capital more than Christian capital probably because he did not hope to find in the Jewish psyche the anchor for brotherly love, which he invoked to at least blunt the sharpest points of an economic development which he deplored of and against which he struggled. [....] But then the cultural level finally sank too low, he was probably so disgusted by the reverse of mammonism, the pure materialistic envy which continually spread, and in 1896 gave up his position in the movement' (cited in Heilmann 1980, pp. 98ff., my transl.).

Thus, Wagner's anti-Semitism was of a limited duration, and very different from other contemporary as well as later manifestations – he energetically opposed agitation for pogroms and anti-Jewish conflicts (ibid., pp. 74ff.). In a review, he argued:

> We rightly recognize in Austria, in Germany, the political, social, etc. importance of each nationality and should not be allowed to emphasize again what was once the biggest difference of all, that of the Jewish nationality among the peoples in the Indo-European world! ... A blind person cannot overlook the extraordinary hard-working characteristics of the Jewish race, but alongside this there are certainly some dubious sides to the character of the Jewish tribe.
>
> (Wagner 1880, p. 782, my transl.)

Wagner drew the conclusions which he outlined in the *Grundlegung*, raising objections to the free immigration and movement of Jews (Wagner 1896, p. 452, 491–93).

Many countries restrict immigration. It is therefore understandable that Wagner indignantly denied the accusation of 'anti-Jewish agitation' and 'Medieval intolerance' (Wagner 1880, my transl.). But he underestimated the danger of his distancing from Judaism. According to Oppenheimer's report, cited above, he finally sensed himself that the exclusion of the Jews, which bordered on the irrational, was developing into an evil and retreated.

After such a long digression, we are now going to examine the book which, for a thinker as profoundly systematic as Wagner, can actually be considered the *foundation* of his entire system. The second edition no longer contains a reference to Rau in the title, because the first edition was already

> in plan, execution, content and form entirely my work, and it was only a sense of reverence that inspired me to include Rau's name on the first general title of the book, since it at least developed from a plan to revise the work of the honoured, past master of German economics.
>
> (Wagner 1896, foreword to 2nd edn, p. VII, my transl.)

Wagner defines his perspective as one of 'social rights'; he is close to the 'sociopoliticals' – a reference to the *Kathedersozialisten* – especially since he also seeks to set the limits within which open competition could best functions, while wishing to delegate responsibility for everything outside of this to the state. Within this general framework, he seems to develop a system comprised primarily of institutions and legal principles. It is also a question of *theory*, however, and in fact not only because Wagner was more concerned to correct the Classical school than make a complete transition to historical thinking, to the exclusion of deduction – even Schmoller did not want this. It is rather that, founded upon a broader understanding of the motivations and the types of organizations which initiate and frame human interaction, he constructed a set of principles from descriptions of circumstances which we consider untheoretical in part because there is no attempt at formalization. Some examples will demonstrate this.

Just as for Aristotle, acquisition through exchange is for Wagner only one of a large number of options. Forms of distribution such as gift-giving and seizure, much discussed by modern ethnology, are among these. Recent literature[38] also shows that there are other forms of acquisition than the acquisition of factor incomes in the market process and that these can also be represented mathematically. Wagner presents differentiated forms of self-interest as well as social impulses which can lead to economic activity. Therefore, he not only contrasts use-value with exchange-value, but also with 'tax value' (determined, for example, by guilds or state institutions who set prices). With respect to use-value, he seeks to define subjective and objective factors; although this attempted synthesis of Classical and Neoclassical approaches is only attempted at the conceptual level.

Wagner refers to the 'difficulties of acquisitions', hence to Ricardo's 'difficulty of production', for an explanation of exchange value. In an attempt at a more precise determination of the difficulty of production, however, he finds himself unable to move beyond Marx's term 'socially necessary labour'. Since Ricardo had already introduced the time element into the analysis of exchange value and, to that extent had deviated from the labour theory of value, it is not dealt with in the early chapters of *Grundlegung*. Wagner repeatedly comes back to the theory of value and distribution. Special note should be made of his historically remarkable attempt, related to his conception of state socialism, to ascertain theoretically when shares of profits and yields represent 'an income of which the true purchaser is unfairly deprived' (Wagner 1896, p. 627), thus to determine in which particular cases accusations from the socialists (Lassalle) are partially correct. The Marxist doctrine of exploitation is rejected.

Many moments are decisive in the development of an economy: the personal and the national rooted in older historical conditions, a legal and a political, expressed in the state itself, along with natural circumstances. The distinctiveness of the state has emerged with in the early modern era with the creation of a large, unified market. Global economic integration is not equally advantageous for states at each stage of their development. He warns, however, against exaggerating List's perspective.

It is strange to us that Wagner speaks of business cycles first in connection with the dependence of individual economies upon 'external influences'. Cyclical explanations in the modern sense are rare in his works, since he does not aim to derive economic fluctuations from the macro-economic interdependence of investments, employment, and income. Instead, he lists a range of factors, from fluctuations in harvest yields as a result of the weather to fluctuations in demand triggered by distribution, which might influence production levels. The reader is forced to the conclusion that business cycles are neither predictable nor avoidable and from there comes the call for governmental compensation.

In other places, his classificatory thinking leads to distinctions which have assumed a new importance today. He differentiates between the costs for the individual enterprise and those for the economy as a whole – not because problems related to the claims on nature are important, but because different legal systems in different economies are encountered (his counterpoint here is ancient slavery), and the varied conventions arising from this differ in the way in which they enter into economic costs and burdens (ibid., pp. 112ff.). Today, such differences in historical rationality are well-known, above all thanks to Max Weber. Wagner was interested here in the most appropriate delineation of community tasks.

With the theory of distribution we approach the most difficult challenge the state socialists face. Given the way in which Wagner starts from a normative order, it becomes clear to us that he introduces a theory of needs because distribution has to secure a living. He begins, logically, with a kind of Maslovian pyramid which first of all demands a guarantee of the basic necessities for all individuals, and then allows for the setting of limits regarding inequality of income. With this he confronts the emergent marginal utility school which rejects the idea of basic needs arising out from social standards. Egalitarian postulates must conflict with the call for efficiency, and for that reason Wagner differentiated himself from the socialists by seeking a 'middle point' consisting of the reform of economic law and an efficient combination of private and communal enterprise.

His trust in a state which will find a fair compromise will not meet the demands of modern readers who seek criteria for justice and concrete details. If such readers are surprised by the historical digressions it has to be understood that these digressions are not only intended to broaden knowledge, but also to clarify that for some questions a decisive consensus was achieved only after lengthy struggle.

Which cultural needs, for example, justify an institution like slavery, and what kind of development justifies its supersession? Discussion of this, luckily for Germany, abstract question which goes beyond its own interest, is conceived as a kind of preamble to discussions of future claims – for example, whether teaching should be free or for creating a legitimate basis for progressive taxation. It is easier to come to terms with this when it is read less as an apology for ancient slavery than as an expression of satisfaction with the consensus on freedom which has finally been achieved. Wagner suggests that redistribution would not only be fair, but would also help in the avoidance of market crises. More important than redistribution, however, are productive uses of and increases in national income.

The structure of the economy should not be thought of only in mechanical terms. The word 'organism', although tolerated by Wagner, is only used metaphorically, in order to characterize the manner in which institutions co-operate. Alongside private and general economic structural forms, there is also the system of charitable organizations which, as a moral necessity, provide an important complement to the first two. When Wagner speaks here of the great importance attached to charity during transitional periods we should recall and admire how beneficial private religious foundations and organizations were in aiding the poor during this time.

This discussion of the interconnectedness of various distributory and guiding instances, which sounds very modern when referred to as a 'mixed economy' (Samuelson), is mainly based on a critical appreciation of competition. This is seen as a historically young institution. Wagner's critique of liberal optimism here is once again not based on a critique of the individual theoretical arguments from Classical theory about markets, production, prices, or demand. Instead, it is derived from information about functional weaknesses such as business fluctuations and monopolization, and following that reference to 'moral potential' compared with self-interest. Moral potential modifies self-interest, which is why economic activities are classified among ethical ones, for which individual responsibility exists. What Wagner has to say about natural inequality and inequality which has developed over time, about talent selection and the outlook in the 'struggle for existence', about the danger that those without any conscience rather than the more responsible will win out, and, finally, about the advantages and disadvantages of large businesses in comparison to small businesses, is of important historical interest and, in part, still worthy of consideration today.

Wagner then turns to an original and significant discussion of those communal needs which can be differentiated from individual needs. This is the origin of the term for public goods. They have in part the character of indivisibility of goods available to the public (i.e. the legal system which was cited first by Wagner).

Further examples of collective needs introduced in the *Grundlegung* reach from the infrastructure and education to claims of later generations in respect of the preservation of natural wealth. Wagner speaks of common needs, to the extent that these may also be partially satisfied through the private economy and the system of charitable organizations, but which for the most part have to be fulfilled by the general economic system. Free and forcibly-united communities nevertheless each have their own possibilities and limits. Wagner also sought to rigorously assess the potential of the system of charitable organizations without neglecting their moral impetus, and he acknowledges that 'free communal undertakings' could hardly survive without one.

Thus Wagner finally arrives at the definition of the legitimacy of the state's authority as an enforced grouping and the definition of its functions. Here we finally discover the famous 'law of increasing expansion of public or government activities', *the* Wagnerian law. It is formulated for 'advancing cultures' (although it is an open question whether, for example, it is always valid for the ancient world) and supported with various arguments (inductive and deductive); specifically, in part through the discovery of newer general needs, in part through the results of progress in the private economic sector. Overall, for Wagner it is not a question of a loss of autonomy, but of the manifestation of a growing civilization.

Here we shall stop, where Wagner connects economic considerations to the legal framework (in the second edition of the *Grundlegung*); because the question, unusual today, would take us beyond the scope of this essay. Many observations can also be found there, some of which still await theoretical elucidation, and which are of interest today from the point of view of the modern theory of institutions, property relations, or the economic understanding of law in general. Naturally, Wagner's examples are often dated, as is the desire itself to make a connection between economy and the law which corresponds entirely to an era in which political upheaval, the transformation of economic structures, and technical progress inspire and require a broad legislative effort. Labour and social legislation, competitive law and the organization of finance systems are examples.

Taking up this point, Hutter (1982) summarized Wagner's result: legal institutions and economic conditions are mutually reinforcing. Wagner's critique, that economic theory largely ignores this connection, remains correct. Freedom and ownership cannot be taken for granted but appear in changing, historically dependent forms, defined by laws – and evolving with them. The balance between state and private economy, in particular, alters.

Wagner's unique position, with his contributions to the theory of money and finance, and his characteristic understanding of state socialism, has been justifiably emphasized. His role as a mid-point between the Historical School and the inheritance of Classical economic theory still remains – in part – to be discovered.

## Wilhelm Launhardt's *Mathematische Begründung der Volkswirtschaftslehre* [the Mathematical Foundation of Economic Theory]

Nineteenth-century German economics was not so averse to theory, nor even so unmathematical, as is often claimed. Claus Kröncke, Joseph Lang, and Georg von Buquoy are among those who early on wrote essays employing mathematics. There is also in the work of Karl Heinrich Rau a perceptible effort to give theoretical considerations mathematical form, to the point of introducing supply and demand curves which he developed independently of A.A. Cournot.[39] The only widely known name from this group also happens to be the most important: Johann Heinrich von Thünen.

In particular, Thünen's wage formula inspired a discussion in which a range of economists participated and then offered mathematical formulations: Johann von Helferich, Etienne Laspeyres, Georg Friedrich Knapp, as well as Lujo Bretano. Shortly thereafter came Hermann Heinrich Gossen's (1987 [1854]) revolutionary work, as well as essays from Hans von Mangoldt (1995 [1863]), who exerted such influence on Marshall.[40] According to Wicksell, it was only the adherents of the Historical School who 'becoming ever more deeply engaged in historical research in special fields, wanted in the end to condemn almost all theory' (Wicksell 1954, pp. 30, fn. 1). In its more highly developed form, the Historical School sought unapologetically to produce theoretically informed material by seeking out the historically-determined character of economic 'laws'. Edgar Salin (1963) developed this in the case of spatial economics, reinterpreting Alfred Weber's 'rational' spatial economic theory in a comparative framework. Along with rational factors in the determination of location, he emphasized traditional factors. He pointed out the range of considerations in the choice of location, the dwindling importance of older theories given the possibilities of decentralization resulting from electricity and atomic power, and finally the tendency to adapt the infrastructure of existing locations rather than optimizing the location in particular places, as for example with railway rates. His attempt to embed theory in such 'perspectives' drew on Thünen, seeking to connect theory as closely as possible to economic, political and empirical perspectives. His retreat from pure theory might today be understood as directed against theory itself. However, he sought to establish a broader validity for theory through its adaptation to historical circumstances.

Launhardt's *Mathematische Begründung der Volkswirtschaftslehre* [The Mathematical Foundation of Economic Theory] stands apart from the historically-oriented German economics of its era. In the foreword he makes it unmistakably clear that his work is modelled on that of Walras and Jevons, and indeed in his attempt to integrate mathematics into economic theory this also involves the subjectivist orientation of the value doctrine. He met Cournot just before he completed his book, and he was not able to find a copy of Gossen's book – he was not even able to provide its correct date of publication. The thoroughness with which Launhardt pursued the mathematization of theory will impress any reader. He begins with a consideration of free competition. His scepticism, expressed in one passage regarding the unimpeded 'rule of free competition' (Launhardt 1993, p. 54) refers first of all to the exchange of two products between two people, an approach which disturbed even Edgeworth. His attempt to establish calculable results by starting with simplified assumptions and proceeding through functional procedures which were supposed to provide empirical investigations with useful working rules – such as, for example, how to measure the level of entrepreneurial profit – still reveals, however, a distant relationship to the practical orientation of German economics. Above all, his most important achievement, his contribution to spatial economic theory, which 'bears the stamp of an originality that is truly powerful and productive at the highest levels' (Schneider 1963, p. V, my transl.), belongs to a line of investigation which has been especially influential in Germany. Examples were supposed to clarify how he envisaged empirical application (Launhardt 1882, pp. 114–16).

Launhardt has been badly neglected by the history of economic thought. Wicksell may have occasionally cited him in his 1893 book *Über Wert, Kapital und Rente* [On Value Capital and Rent] (Wicksell 1954), but he almost exclusively dealt with weaknesses in Launhardt's treatment of isolated exchanges and failed to be fair to the originality of his ideas, specifically in the treatment of spatial economic theory. While Baumol and Goldfeld (1968) provide interesting excerpts from Launhardt's theory of optimal freight rates, their brief introduction offers only an incomplete appreciation. Beckmann and Sato (1975, pp. 235–44) also cite a section from Launhardt's theory regarding the shipment of goods. In the early 1960s a reprint of Launhardt's book with an introduction by Erich Schneider (1963, pp. III-VII) provided a fine and brief characterization of Launhardt's relationship to Walras and his other predecessors and contemporaries and, as already mentioned, draws attention to the chapter on the shipment of goods. However, both Launhardt's originality and his faults have been more precisely acknowledged only by Jürg Niehans (1987) in *The New Palgrave*, as well as in other publications. The account of the history of economic thought for which we are indebted to Jürg Niehans (1990) is remarkable for the extraordinary precision with which he determined which basic concepts and model constructions are essential from a modern perspective, and when and by what author they were initially formulated and/or later re-adopted. Launhardt's achievements are there dealt with in some detail.

It was Launhardt's misfortune that the synthetic formulations of the basic concepts of neoclassical theory had already been made by others. His own contribution lagged behind Jevons, Walras, or even Böhm-Bawerk, while his more expansive formalizations were simply too much for the time, and were therefore not at first understood. Lehr's (1885) review shows that Launhardt still had competent individual readers among his contemporaries in his own country. Lehr only wished to 'express favourable views about the work as a whole' (ibid., p. 165, my transl.), although he found individual results open to criticism since they would have been altered by the employment of a utility function different to the one used by Launhardt.

Many of his conclusions corresponded to the spirit of the age in Germany, for example when Launhardt at the end of his book spoke out in favour of state protection from economic concentration. On the whole, however, he expressed faith in progress (particularly in transport). He supported such judgments with his analytical results: thanks to an improved transport capacity local fluctuations in harvests could be evened out. He demonstrated that farmers in districts with lower population densities are better off with poor harvests, while those in districts with high population densities are better off with good harvests. His discussion of wages also echoes contemporary debate. His backward-sloping supply curve for labour is one of his few concepts which was immediately accepted and taken up by other authors. His discussion of interest rates fits in well in Böhm-Bawerk's discussion of time preference. Given that Böhm-Bawerk's much more carefully discussed formulated discussion of the problem of interest rates caused such a furore, it is somewhat odd that so little attention was devoted to Launhardt's solution of the problem.

The response that Launhardt got for his *Mathematische Begründung der Volkswirtschaftslehre* [The Mathematical Foundation of Economic Theory] fails to measure up to what we might reasonably anticipate today for a work which, while possibly not among the few books of the greatest importance, was still one of the classic works of economics. From obituaries and biographies it does not appear that Launhardt suffered from a lack of recognition. His academic career went brilliantly. He was elected rector of the Technical University in Hannover, received an honorary doctorate, and was appointed representative of his university as lifetime member in the Prussian Upper House. He published widely in the field of civil engineering and, stimulating person that he was, he supposedly also wrote poetry (Hoyer 1928).

'He also stood tall as a man. Despite all the success and honours, he remained essentially unpretentious, kind, and modest' (Troske 1918, my transl.). The modesty, confidence, and sympathy of this man is mirrored in his books, which were marked by a factual, plain style in which the most important statements were developed step by step, without too much consideration for readers less well-versed in the subject, but also without any artificial complication of the argument, a fault to which mathematicians occasionally succumb. His concise lines show that he approached the bitter ideological debates of his time with sober powers of judgment, but was not disinterested. As with other authors in the founding phase of neoclassical theory, readers are inspired with new ideas because the arguments, sometimes familiar, are developed clearly and placed in a context. Not only does he use terms other than the usual, he also sometimes develops different explanations.

## Max Weber's *Protestant Ethic* as an inquiry into economics

Fritz Neumarks's wonderful overview *Deutsche Ökonomen des frühen 20. Jahrhunderts* [German Economists of the Early Twentieth Century] (1989), written when he was almost 90, describes who was master, who was journeyman, and who was apprentice in economic theory in the early twentieth century. Of Max Weber, he writes:

> So far as the first is concerned, I intentionally set Max Weber aside since I still view him primarily as a sociologist, as he was when I got to know him in Munich in 1920 in lectures and seminars – the most important person by far that I came in contact with in my academic life, as a person and researcher to a large extent the exact opposite of his contemporary, Werner Sombart....
>
> (ibid., p. 128, my transl.)

Except for Gustav von Schmoller, 'the uncrowned king of his field', Neumark counts very few among the 'masters'. But this picture of Weber removes him from his disciplinary colleagues. These colleagues are now to be found in a run-down wing of the museum with 'Historical School' written above them; whereas Weber has a splendid new set of rooms where he is honoured and admired by sociologists and methodologists. Economists, on the other hand, seldom come this way.

Even Schumpeter (1991, p. 225) wrote in his obituary of Weber: 'Weber was a sociologist above all.' According to Schumpeter, Weber's interest was in the succession of historical types in their social-psychological entirety. He pointed out that he organized the *Grundriß der Sozialökonomie* [Handbook of Social Economics] and had made a major contribution to it with *Wirtschaft und Gesellschaft* [Economy and Society]. Apart from that he wrote some famous economic expert reports on agricultural conditions in the East, on the stock exchange and others. For Schumpeter, Weber's scientific-theoretical critique was important because it tore his contemporaries away from the casual and unreflective combination of the search for empirical and historical facts with the philosophical evaluation of normative political ideas. The Weberian critique of science doubtless assisted the consolidation of Schumpeter's own methodological position. But Schumpeter's praise also involves a demarcation. If he begins: 'He was the living among the shadows', if he speaks of the 'brilliance' which 'surrounds the figure of Max Weber', if he speaks of Weber's unlimited intellectual and moral courage, his sense of duty when he considers 'the faces that would be pulled by the routine political figures of today if this Lohengrin in his silvered moral armour suddenly appeared among them' (ibid., pp. 220ff.), Schumpeter also calls attention to the fact that there is no easily identifiable political or, more to the point, economic position associated with Weber; for example the free trade position of the Classics or – like Schumpeter himself – the promotion of entrepreneurialism. Thus this charismatic figure exerted, apart from his critical function, no lasting or marked effect on economics from either a theoretical or an economic point of view, an effect which would be appropriate to the historical grandeur of the man and his importance for the young science of sociology.

As a rule, economic textbooks treat Weber either with caution, or open ignorance. Contemporaries asked about the important German economists of the twentieth century would certainly only rarely mention his name, and most do not know that he held chairs of economics – that he was a trained lawyer, and not at all a professional sociologist. Weber was rarely referred to in my own economic education, so I must ask for leniency in the following essay. I have been undecided about whether I should attempt to deal with him here, but it seems to me that the existing tension between the two disciplines of economics and sociology has to be acknowledged.

In 1932, Karl Jaspers strongly emphasized Weber's refusal to commit himself to the sociological viewpoint:

> Officially, Max Weber was a political economist. He opposed the establishment of professorial chairs in sociology, not concealing the fact that sociology deals with a science that everywhere rests on the foundations of other sciences, requiring considerable individual research experience in these other individual sciences, and an extraordinary degree of critical ability.
>
> (Jaspers 1989, p. 98)

'Most of what goes by the name sociology is a fraud', he said in his Heidelberg valedictory address. This harsh judgment of the science with which Weber only half-heartedly wished to be associated has to be understood as of its time. However, we can clearly see that his works range over of almost all the human sciences, making technical classification a challenge. He also expects the reader to have considerable background knowledge – starting with his citations in various ancient and modern languages in the original; less obviously, but no less important, because his message is almost impossible to decipher without a deeply historical perspective.

Let us examine the problem of classifying the present text by turning first from content to method and then back to content. In order to read the *Protestant Ethic*, knowledge of the political history of England and the United States is required, as well as a knowledge of the history of economics and a familiarity with the great works of literature. The text explores theological questions in such depth that the theological tyro would be entirely in the dark were it not for the way that Weber, with his presentational skill, constantly helps the reader, although this can lead to such a tangled line of argument, complete with inserted asides, that it is exactly the unfamiliar basic ideas which are difficult to grasp, as the never-ending controversy surrounding the significance of the book demonstrates. At the core, apparently, a suggestion about historical causality is advanced – but what is the connection? And more to the point, causal in what sense?

When a historian visualizes a historical situation he has to separate the real event from those directions in which the actions, ways of thinking, and results could also have developed, so that one can obtain a causal notion of which events determined the actual outcome. The causal conjecture which is obtained in this manner is rarely capable of direct confirmation, however much an understanding of intentions might be of assistance. This conception of understanding is a leading characteristic of the human sciences, distinguishing them from the natural sciences in which hypotheses are accepted or rejected according to their survival of the test of falsification; an approach which is not here appropriate since the method of experimental repetition is inapplicable. It is a question, therefore, of discovering correspondences between actions and states of consciousness which we find in history. In this sense, Weber says that the life conduct which reformed Protestantism generated was 'adequate' to capitalist development.[41] The causal conjecture is therefore largely nullified; but not completely. Therein lies a difficulty which requires methodological elucidation.

A deeper understanding of historical contexts can be achieved by undertaking universal-historical comparisons of the kind Weber undertook in his sociology of religion. The historical possibilities which exist in the dissemination of particular ways of thinking and life forms are revealed by the historical reality in which it becomes apparent that particular forms of religious and cultural development correspond to economic and political realities. As in a modification of Spinoza's *determinatio est negatio*, Weber repeatedly asks whether it would have been possible for particular images to have also been conceived in other contexts. Thus, from the very beginning he expects the reader to know that Milton's idea of the human 'inner paradise' is foreign to medieval notions of paradise.

In Milton's epic, the Archangel Michael comforted Adam at the Fall: if the Christian virtues are supplemented by Christian love, then Adam will not be unwilling to leave the original paradise, since he carries within himself a more divine paradise.

> One feels at once that this powerful expression of the Puritan's serious attention to this world, his acceptance of his life in the world as a task, could not possibly have come from the pen of a medieval writer. But it is just as uncongenial to Lutheranism, as expressed for instance in Luther's and Paul Gerhardt's chorales.
>
> (Weber 1976, p. 88)

Weber calls this insight only an indefinite perception, in whose place a more intellectual formulation must be set in order to question the deeper reasons for the difference. To refer to 'national character' would not only be no explanation (a 'confession of ignorance'), but would also be historically inaccurate. Weber first of all works out precisely just the religious historical context. It is the power of religious movements which makes this difference, and which we today sense.

However, Weber does not view that Puritanical religious idea, which prescribes the particular way in which people must live their lives if they wish to enhance their chances of future salvation, to be a one-dimensional cause of capitalist development. A developmental process of this kind is in no respects intended by these agents, and hence by religious founders. Weber formulates it more modestly here:

> We are thus inquiring only to what extent certain characteristics features of this culture can be imputed to the influence of the Reformation. At the same time we must free ourselves from the idea that it is possible to deduce the Reformation, as a historically necessary result, from certain economic changes.
>
> (ibid., p. 90ff.)

He thereby rejects a materialist interpretation in which forms of consciousness derive from economic forces. (The question whether those economic forces can, moreover, be traced back to a dialectic of productive forces and relations of production, as postulated by Marxists, does not arise at all.) On the other hand, there is similarly just as little attempt forge an idealist chain of causality, tracing capitalism back to its spirit and this spirit back to some religious transformation:

On the contrary, we only wish to ascertain whether and to what extent religious forces have taken part in the qualitative formation and the quantitative expansion of that spirit over the world. Furthermore, what concrete aspects of our capitalistic culture can be traced to them...

(ibid., p. 83)[42]

The great multiplicity of interactions between economic, social, and political bonds and spiritual development would only allow for the observation of correspondences (Weber says here 'elective affinities') between religious and economic forms, which Weber emphasizes for his purposes with the term 'vocational ethics'. Having observed correspondences and their historical developments, he can proceed to impute modern forms of action and thought to their historical forerunners, and thus attempt to impute the emergence of economic forms to determining causes.

Before it is possible to attribute causes, there must be evidence of correspondences which, again, presuppose the consolidation of historical materials for the purpose of intellectual comparisons. The correspondences are based on an intellectual structuring of reality in abstract terms. The rigour and originality with which Weber constructs the terms he needs certainly makes a strong impression on every reader. He pursues a goal of consistently starting with the acting individual:

If I am now a sociologist (according to the terms of my employment), then primarily to bring to an end once and for all the racket which works in terms of collective concepts. In other words: even sociology can only be practiced by starting with the action of one, a few or many individuals, proceeding according to a quite strictly 'individualistic' method.

(letter from Max Weber to Robert Liefmann, dated 9 March 1920, cited in Jonas 1968, pp. 31–2, my transl.)

The postulate of starting from individual action reminds economists of the principle established in Schumpeter's methodological individualism. This is, however, also delimited by Weber by the associated rationality postulate, which represents a central problem for this text, and the *Protestant Ethic* in particular. Forms of rationality change, and the modern form is a developmental product; thus, seen theoretically, an explanandum, not the explanans. First, 'instrumentally rational action', analogous to Pareto's 'logical action', when related to the world of goods and when utility and profit maximization represent goals (objectives), formally corresponds in Weber precisely to the concept of rationality which modern neoclassical theory perceives as the *definiens* of its field of work. However, Weber asks how rationality *develops*. Affective (emotional) and traditional (customary) action, in Pareto 'non-logical action', are the opposite to instrumentally rational action.[43] In Weber's later writings the affinity between his concept of rationality and that of neoclassicism appear to emerge more clearly – although economic theory up to this point does not appear to be in a position to execute analytically[44] the differentiation of the concept of rationality which Max Weber has effected.[45]

Traditional action would, for example, be a farmer's investment in a form of farming that has been handed down, a farmer who – at the price of lost profit – wants to live as his father did. In an economic model this would involve a very unusual goal.

Ludwig von Mises (1960) criticized Weber and understood each chosen action as instrumentally rational, even those determined by tradition or ideology. Such a flattening of the concept of rationality would, however, leave historical sociology little to say if a differentiation of the kind made by Weber were not reintroduced into the new terminology, as representations of various 'goals'.

According to Weber, it is possible to understand individual action, to interpret it as reasonable, even when the concept of rationality concept employed is not the modern concept. With historical actions he therefore speaks of adequate causes if their meaning is understood; the action is accordingly 'sufficiently motivated' (Weber 1975, p. 127).

The importance of this necessary step toward abstraction for scientific discourse, the insufficiency of naïve description, can at least be suggestively explained by pointing out the contrast between the expression of a feeling and its replication by others. Weber chooses as an example the 'feeling of totality' experienced when wandering through an architecturally interesting city.

> In this case, the claim that 'knowledge' of this sort is subjective is equivalent to the claim that it is not 'valid'. It is not valid simply because it has not been analytically articulated. In consequence, 'mutual participation in the feelings of others' is withdrawn from the domain of demonstration and verification.
>
> (ibid., p. 180)

In fact even art historians employ ideal-typical concepts, such as the 'baroque language of forms' or 'Impressionism' – and it is very well documented in the case of the latter how this 'style' arose from the programmatic will of a group of artists, such that the 'meaning' of motives and affects can be reconstructed from identifiable individuals. As we have learned from Kant, there is however a more critical contrast to the precise natural sciences, since mathematics here provides a tool for the description of concrete processes, a tool that logically exists prior to and independently of them. By contrast, the concepts developed for the description of cultural phenomena cannot be a priori given terms, and pre-defined expressions can only be constructed in advance of a particular experience to a limited extent. In extreme cases, they are based on a direct relationship to the specific phenomena to which they refer ('Raphael's style'), so that the evocation of the artistically talented person through the 'apt word' in the description of the 'style' often ultimately achieves more than an attempt at 'conceptual' reconstruction. The cultural treasure trove represented by cultured language is not, therefore, replaceable by any scientific language. In the social sciences too, even in economics, it seems to me that this happens more often than we would like to acknowledge (e.g. in the attempt to hermeneutically understand the fact of the variety of economic styles in various countries and epochs).

In effect, Weber narrowed the scope of the discipline of 'science', even if not as much as 'neo-positivism' later did, and operated on the more solid ground of an explicit reliance on the action-orientation of subjects, which orientation would open the way to a sufficient objectification of his conceptual world. Subsequently he stumbled on a problem later well-known to neoclassical theory, despite the more general nature of his concept of rationality: that the assumption of utility maximization facilitated theoretical development, but did not guarantee its reality content. He clarified this by contrasting the outcome of action-orientations – which reveals an ultimate connection or, assuming consistency on the part of the subject, permits hypothetical conclusions, and so leads to deduction – and an inductive approach:

> In the final analysis, a so-called 'empirical' law is an empirically valid generalization the causal interpretation of which is problematic. A teleological scheme of rational action, on the other hand, is an interpretation the empirical *validity* of which is problematic. The two concepts are, therefore, from a logical point of view, polar opposites.
>
> (ibid., p. 191)

The structuring of reality by abstract concepts occurs by characterizing potential historical configurations in terms of a particular meaningful context. This context must be thought of via a pure form of abstraction; so Weber (1968) speaks, for example, of the types of rulership (charismatic, bureaucratic, etc.). These 'ideal types' thus correspond to an intellectually consistent and coherently constructed context of meaning conforming to a particular rationality (whose forms change historically), relative to which the historical succession of events can be explained by the superimposition of types, or through deviations at irrational moments (due to a different rationality). Weber even conceives of Puritanism in this sense of ideal types.

Weber's approach yields a characterization of the special features of Western development. Occidental capitalism, in comparison to ancient or oriental forms of capitalist economic organization (all of which are focused on a monetary surplus), has particular traits, among which Weber pointed out the separation of household and economic enterprises (facilitating business accounting) and free labour, because '[e]xact calculation – the basis of everything else – is only possible on the basis of free labour [therefore not, e.g. with serfdom or slavery]' (Weber 1976, p. 22). But free labour is not in itself sufficient to overcome a traditional orientation to work which seeks only to achieve subsistence. Only if wages are low will workers be forced to work an entire day – Weber elaborates this in the *Protestant Ethic* in respect of the difficulties encountered in introducing payment by piece.[46] In bourgeois enterprise capitalism the obverse to the development of rational labour organization is the 'emergence of the Western bourgeois class and of its peculiarities' (ibid., p. 24); its economic rationalism is apparent in the emergence of 'the ability and disposition of men to adopt certain types of practical rational conduct' (ibid., p. 26). The *Protestant Ethic* begins with the explanation of these last elements.

Weber thus approaches the goal of the objectification of historical analyses whose accounts might otherwise be tainted with emotion. For Weber, value-free means here above all a scientific stance which accepts the different forms of rationality as givens, hence as valid; only then does he trace their development, as we have already seen.

Commentators have, however, not been slow in pointing out again and again that Weber himself continually judges: choosing concepts, choosing questions, when drawing conclusions related to fateful developments. If for example the Puritan life form, rationality, has marked the 'spirit' of capitalist economic activity, then humans are involved in a causal connection which imposes upon them the fulfilment of vocational responsibilities without the certainty of salvation enjoyed by previous generations. And even more remote is the enchantment of lost worlds when human attention focused directly on the good life, despite existential difficulties, or on the aspiration of broadly-based personal development which rules out the possibilities of accumulation opened up by modern rationality: 'The Puritan *wanted* a vocation; we *have* to have one' (ibid., p. 181, trans. revised). For Weber, therefore, objectivity did not preclude proclaiming such matters, but he demanded of himself, as a scholar, the abjuration of evaluative discourse, the presentation of conclusions in prophetic or polemical form; instead he turned anew to the study of causes. According to his understanding of the situation, as evidenced by the very many historical and empirical works which he produced with an almost indescribable energy, there remained very little scope for Weber the politician:

> For Weber, the value freedom of science then does not mean that valuations should not be made in life, but just the reverse: The passion of valuing and willing is fundamental to the genuine objectivity of scholarly ability, illuminating and edifying such activity.
>
> (Jaspers 1989, p. 91)

Weber's stance imposed its own limitations, methodologically by the starting from the activity of individuals as the empirically reality and, as we saw, by scepticism when faced with given, sensed, totalities not open to intellectual appraisal, such as the 'spirit of the people'. According to Jaspers' account, the real renunciation however lay in accepting the findings. Weber can therefore also be understood in various ways: in his methodological rigour he is considered the founder of Neopositivist social science. Jaspers cited him as one of the philosophers who laid the foundations for Existentialism because of his failure to find a solution to, or even properly describe, the question that really concerned him: the degree to which human beings were actually defined by processes, which he understood as rationalization, as the development of capitalism, as demystification:[47]

> The human being born into the world of Homer and the Jewish prophets did not lose himself in Nietzsche. He has his last great figure, for the present, in Max Weber, a figure of our world, a world which is being transformed at such a frantic pace that the special features of the Weberian world have already passed away in such a short period, though the fundamental questions of human existence, the ability for knowledge, and the decisive tasks remain. We no longer have a great man who could bring us to our senses in this manner. He was the last great man.
>
> (Jaspers 1989, pp. 133ff.)

Weber's work as an economist also exists in the tension outlined here. For it was the conclusion of Weber's mature work that capitalism had to be understood as an element in a larger rationalization process which in its own time acquired certain additional distinctive characteristics.[48]

Among the achievements attributed to Weber are in particular the analysis of increasing bureaucratization, which for economists goes hand-in-hand with the concentration of business and the increasing division of labour, reaching beyond the political sphere (which naturally is of primary interest to Weber) into the private. The diagnosis of the development of middle classes, which interpose themselves between the propertied and the working classes, and whose position is based on their authority within a bureaucratic hierarchy, also belongs in this context. In his emphasis on the essential role of the entrepreneurial function for capitalistic production, Weber was a precursor for Schumpeter; charismatic leadership must also have its way at the top of bureaucratic organizational divisions. To that degree, Weber was viewed as a forerunner of the 'Managerial Revolution' thesis. A corollary to this is that he predicted the inefficiency of complete bureaucratization under a socialist economic system,[49] with the accompanying forms of clumsy administration and political repression which included the labour movement itself.

If this reading of Weber's work – as extending into the discipline of economics – is justifiable, his inclusion among the canon of classical works requires no further defence.

The *Protestant Ethic* challenges modern economists like few other works. Its finding can hardly be disputed: that a profession and a calling provides an axis for the modern conduct of life upon which the existence of individuals revolves to such an extent that incorporation into a vocational life could be perhaps the most important emancipatory demand. The question of whether the recent reduction in working hours, the orientation toward material consumption, and other factors are contributing to a transformation in values which might again undermine the work ethic has led to many important, current, socio-economic controversies (Beck 1986, Ch. VI). The challenge lies however not only in doing justice to the consequent economic and political relationships (Will work at home increase again? Are there new cooperative forms, even a dual sector?), but rather in whether economists will feel that they have anything to say. If they leave such territory primarily to sociologists, then this will also limit their relevance to areas which affect central disciplines like social policy and incomes policy.

They must also find Weber's historic approach off-putting, his explanations of what were for him pressing current concerns beginning far in the past. If he traces the roots of the nature of the modern professional back to the inner asceticism of Puritans, a historically-attuned generation nearly a century ago would have understood something that is still not natural and easy to understand: *De te fabula narratur.* It understood the inescapability of the form of life that capitalism determined, as 'fate'. Weber will not convince anyone today who believes that this view of the problem is behind us today, as many economists do. This much is clear: as mere historical reconstruction, Weber's *Protestant Ethic* is far too complicated to interest more than a few specialists. In these two essays, however, the charisma which those who encountered Weber felt is also in evidence – if not immediately, then through the discussion that echoed across the Atlantic.

An interesting spotlight was thrown on this from one of the most important studies that followed on from Weber: Tawney's *Religion and the Rise of Capitalism* (1972 [1926]). The foreword to the 1937 edition (ibid., pp. VI–XIII) raised objections and listed additions, as well as literature, which had come out since the first edition. Even the term 'capitalism' met with resistance: it was not understood why Weber had silently ignored economic factors which had facilitated the rise of the new economic form. Scholars sought to supplement it with descriptions of economic thought during the Renaissance or the later development of Catholicism. Tawney also made informative remarks about precursors (ibid., p. 282, note 1; p. 283, note 11). In the book itself, of course, Tawney was less discriminating and more critical of Weber, seeking a causal explanation for the rise of capitalism via religious factors which he then deemed inadequate (ibid., pp. 312ff.). In his review of the first edition, Salin (1928) said that Tawney had been just as unfair to Weber as the German historians once were. Salin attempted to construe the concepts of 'interpretive economics' [*verstehende Nationalökonomie*] and sociology as 'intuitive' or 'visual' theory [*anschauliche Theorie*].[50] Weber had intentionally examined only the one causal connection, 'Protestant Ethic' and 'the Spirit of Capitalism'. He had attempted to explain the connection of a particular denomination and a particular economic practice; he does not want to include all the various forms of expression and work, but rather the 'ideal type' Calvinism, or Puritanism. So, he not only rejected the view that the spirit of capitalism could only have emerged as a result of influences during the Reformation, but also the even greater mistake that capitalism, as an economic system, was evidence of the Reformation (Salin 1928, p. 619).

The theoretical reconstruction of particular, historically important causal connections with the aid of ideal-type constructions remains an important scientific task which – as with Weber – links various scientific disciplines and, in economics in particular, requires a combination of theory-construction, knowledge of economic historical facts, and the history of economic thought. With the increasing specialization of the individual sciences, scholars require courage to expose themselves to criticism from the specialists of other disciplines. If such criticism intimidates or even threatens to crush interdisciplinary research, then one can turn to model predecessors. Currently there is no shortage of attempts to understand economic history, to add depth to history with history of mentalities, and other comparable approaches. For the work of synthesis that is necessary Weber still sets a standard that is difficult to match.

To understand how Weber, his question so well-posed in the *Protestant Ethic*, could in any way be viewed as an economist, we now have to take a look at his generation.[51] Max Weber inherited the tension between theory and history from the Historical School; in part because it dominated economics in Germany while he was a student himself and the colleagues with whom he later dealt as a mature scientist came from the Historical School; in part because, despite some deviation, the themes with which he dealt corresponded to older ones.[52]

Schmoller thought he did his best work in linking economics and history, although his understanding of both is less theoretical than we are used to today. Among his elements which lent his approach unity were the psychology of the social subject, which created a link between social behaviour and economic interests; the intuition that perceives a unity of *Gestalt* in a society that and which recognizes connections between economic and social institutions; and finally the ethics which arise from the necessary compatibility of individual and societal norms, and in which Schmoller hoped to be able to distinguish the real advances of economic and social evolution in their higher development.[53]

Weber sought to escape the historicist elements in Schmoller's construction through his methodology.[54] He deepened the psychological element with his action theory, he transformed the naïve-intuitive element theoretically with the construction of ideal types, and he replaced the concept of progress with his principle of value-free analysis. For his own scientific goals, however, he remained imprisoned by the problem of interdisciplinarity. Nearly 50 years after his death Salin characterized his teacher, Weber, as follows:

> United in him were not only economics and its neighbouring disciplines; law and history, religion and art seemed to find a place here, too. However, he was not concerned with the unity that these still found in his person: instead of a lived unity ... he admitted only a multitude of 'inescapable' specialized sciences, connected ... by the unity of a 'causal connecting problem' and everything was held together only by the concept 'social economics'.
>
> (Salin 1967, p. 150, my transl.)

Nearly all of the elements of Salin's later view are included in the brief, provocative first version of his 1923 *Geschichte der Volkswirtschaftslehre* [History of Economics].

'Historical sociology' was also used to describe the subject matter under examination by the younger Historical School. The relationship to economics will become clearer after a brief discussion, here, of Weber's colleagues and descendants, among whom one stands out the most – better known in his time or in any case more popular than Weber, more fortunate in his production of compact descriptions, but who clearly stands behind Weber in depth of insight and posthumous fame: Werner Sombart. He used the expression 'interpretive economics' in order to characterize his theory of the history of the development of capitalism in the sense of Salin's 'intuitive' theory.

In his *Modern Capitalism*, at the price of a simplified hypothesis, Sombart risked constructing a general representation of the inner logic of capitalist development from the medieval era to the modern era. He coined a term for the economic system, which pointed in the direction of Eucken's term for system, but differed from this because the basic terms were not yet formed on the basis of the simple dichotomies of competencies in economic decisions. Eucken compared the coordination mechanisms, the budget and the market, to each other, with regard to production, consumption, or both. In the case of the market, he subdivided further based on potential market types which, according to a logical *a priori*, were formed before the intuitive experience. System researchers should interpret real systems as superimpositions of such model-like exemplary concepts, supported by concrete economic organization and the resulting competencies.

In contrast to this, Sombart's basic terms are closer to Weber's because the inner core of the system is supposed to be composed of the economic views governing at the moment. In working out forms of thought with isolating abstraction – therefore also focusing on ideal types – Sombart does not even approach Weber's discrimination, his astonishing ability to trace the ramifications and the counter-tendencies in the rationalization and secularization process. He was also not as scrupulous as Weber not to fall back on universalistic concepts as Othmar Spann employed them.

That monumental work, however, became an important success, well outside of Germany,[55] which has in the meantime faded, however. Today it is remembered that Sombart remained controversial and alone. He himself considered 'interpretive economics' to be a venture of no practical use, as a so-to-say aristocratic luxury of cognitive development, which could be compared to an empirically supported economic theory on the basis of its hypotheses and basic terms, which could be used instrumentally through its understanding of economic occurrences as a mechanistic system in principle, so long as the interactions were correctly understood. Anticipating Keynes, the business cycle and monetary theory of the 1920s began to assume just such an instrumental character. In contrast to the economic research institutes, which at least promised to provide useful prognoses for policy and business leaders – employing awkward meteorological analogies they advertised with 'business barometers' [most importantly the so-called Harvard Barometer] and similar things – Sombart's objective of representing the fate of modern people in the capitalist system against the backdrop of escaping medieval bonds was attributed no cultural, to say nothing of political, importance beyond a certain educational value.

In the early 1930s, Sombart made an attempt to cross over the boundaries of the scientific goals which he had set himself and to offer the National Socialists the concept of a 'German Socialism' anchored in the 'spirit of a people'. With the exception of some remarks correctly pointing in the direction of employment policy and some noteworthy considerations anticipating environmental policy, it is a weak, unpleasant work, as a result of the compromise with Nazi ideology. Nothing came of it since the party, in meantime intent on armaments and mechanization, rejected it.

A certain logic can be traced through Sombart's development (Brocke 1992), but that it did not have to take the direction it did can be demonstrated by the fact that works comparable to Sombart's 'interpretive economy' developed, in the hands of others (e.g. Alfred Weber and Rüstow), into a critique of totalitarianism. A personal distancing from materialism and the belief in progress, social conventions and power politics, which was felt to be dominating in the years before the First World War, was typical of the generation that comprised the youngest Historical School. Military defeat, political revolution, the humiliation of the Treaty of Versailles all created an atmosphere in which the voices of the critics of progress – which since the age of German Classicism had never been entirely silent and the most eerie of whom, those who had inherited Nietzsche's mantle as a questioner of morals, now droned out audibly – were finally heard. Since an alternative economic order also seemed to have become possible in the Soviet Union, the need arose to understand the cultural situation not only in itself but also in the context of the transformation of the economic order (Schefold 1992c).

Weber had basically already anticipated the model of the best of this development in 1905 in his *Protestant Ethic*. The geniality of his approach lies in the fact that, far superior to his successors in methodological strictness and conscientiousness, he does not seek an impossible understanding of the totality of modern economic forms and life forms, but instead considers only one – crucial, however – aspect, the historical roots of the rational definition of business life. An additional factor is that among the determinants he explored only the religious ones. And the result is still provocative today.

The correspondence thus found (between the turn from the certainty of salvation through a life led in obedience to God, which can only be understood theologically-historically, to the rational organization of business life) did not in fact provide an exhaustive explanation for the rise of capitalism, but it still reveals a causal nexus which in a materialist-thinking era (Weber himself and Tawney point out that the idea had been current decades earlier) must have appeared puzzling and difficult to understand (today we would say 'counter-intuitive'). He casts doubt, specifically, on the common conviction of the primacy of material factors, which is at the basis of Marxist historical thought and surprisingly many opponents of Marxism as well, and allows 'rational' capitalism to appear as a characteristically 'irrational' fate of modern humans by unveiling its religious roots. Although capitalism was still considered a powerful source of economic growth in the Classic economic sense and from then on as 'efficient' ('rational') in the neoclassical sense, the historical characterizations suggested by Weber pulled the rug out from under the notion of capitalism as a 'natural' system. If others hoped for another release of irrational forces, Weber found such a release possible and threatening. And the person who had discovered and publicized this strange scientific revelation now prepared to politically defend the acceptance of just this capitalism and to limit science, through his methodological critique, to the tasks of clean well-versed technical representatives.[56]

Thus, in carrying out his work, Weber treated economics as high ranking humanities, which boldly asked questions about the position of modern people in history and refused the arrogance of the belief in progress by naming the price of that progress while at the same time accepting it. In the decade after Weber's death, the strong response that met understanding economy (or historical sociology), crossing disciplinary borders, coincided with the rise of a new methodological understanding. In its turn toward theory, however, it could also refer to Weberian methodological foundations. 'Pure' theory was 'rational' in the sense of a sharpening of Weberian terms and making them formally precise.

It was and still must be recognized that the clearly evident inner contradictions of Max Weber's scientific persona were held together finally by his strong character, by his theories, and through the thoroughness of his conclusions. However, opponents who wanted to learn from him felt these contradictions quite strongly. We can find an example of this in the interpretation above by Edgar Salin, who as a student of Eberhard Gothein had also studied in Heidelberg with Alfred and Max Weber and, as a result of his closeness to the Stefan George Circle, brought in a different attitude. Agreeing with Weber, he emphasized that the comprehension of real life as rational and predictable was not exhaustive. It was fulfilled in the varied forms of human development, as they make communities and societies possible, it is improved through the acquisition of cultural inheritance, and it has its highest expression in art, and poetry in particular. Tension resulted from the various consequences for the understanding of art, science, and lifestyle. The George Circle sought to set its own life world in opposition to the rationality of modernity rather than conforming to it, as Weber called for.

In Heidelberg, the George Circle boasted important names. Among the achievements of the Circle can be reckoned that Norbert von Hellingrath rediscovered Hölderlin, that Gundolf translated Shakespeare into German, and that they sought a new understanding of Plato through interpreting the dialogue situation as an expression of a lively collaboration between the philosophical master, students, and opponents. Salin experienced this intertwining of art and science as a rebirth of the Goethian educational world; he even risked a comparison with fifth century Athens which he felt to be related, reflecting the circle's bright and serious discussions as well as its cultural production. It often appeared incomprehensible to the young Salin that Weber did not partake of the opportunity to improve his own life and instead opposed George because he thought the call for a non-rational imbued life world was an illusion (George said: 'Only by magic is life kept awake', George 1974, in the poem 'Man and Faun', p. 378) and the elitist character of George's movement was dangerous, to the extent, specifically, that tendencies toward political implementation of the aristocratic spiritual impulses were visible in political actions.[57]

Weber was also attacked from philosophical positions which were taken by members of the George Circle and which perhaps could best be described with a reference to Goethe's natural philosophy. The observer, who naturally had to be educated and made capable of seeing, revealed essential truths therefore through the comprehension of form, of *Gestalt*. For such sciences a continuum exists between the artistic understanding of truth and that which in usual language is deemed science. No evidence is required here to recognize the antithesis to Weber's methodological positions.[58]

Another form of opposition among the students arose against Weber, a nationalist and liberal, from the left. Here I will only cite Staudinger who had also studied in Heidelberg and who, until his emigration and assumption of a professorial position in New York after the Nazi of seizure of power, was an official of the empire, holding an important position in Prussia. Weber warned students that the guarantee of personal development lay in equality before the law, in the political electoral system, in the tendency toward equality of educational opportunities. Staudinger, however, did not believe Weber's 'ideal type' expression could be objectified: 'In my opinion, most people have very little free choice to live according to their own values. They are not only predestined by family and upbringing, but also economically forced to pursue the essentials for life or to starve' (Staudinger 1982, p. 8, my transl.).

It is clear here, too, the similarity of the diagnosis and the differently-conceived conclusion. Staudinger who had decided to join the 'radical-Marxist movement' confessed to Weber that he was struggling for the dictatorship of the proletariat. Weber, who did not hide his 'evil premonition' about the 'result of power usurpation', laughed as Staudinger said that this would free the workers from their dependence. The values that would develop would not be that of freedom but those of solidarity and conformity. While Staudinger busied himself preparing the way for the downfall of capitalism, Weber still wanted to grasp the various reasons and motives for the emergence of rational profit-seeking, to solve the puzzle of this development, 'and to draw conclusions from that about the chances of capitalist development' (ibid., pp. 10ff., my transl.). Because of limited discussions, it was often difficult for students and professors, working on joint tasks, to remain conscious of the fact that they both distinguished themselves when, despite opposing viewpoints, they cooperated scientifically and humanly. Weber's liberality enabled him to also join with the adversary but occasionally the tension led to an apparent rift.[59] For example, Weber came to Staudinger at the end of 1918, commissioned him with what he called a 'historic' mission to make clear to Ebert that without the immediate integration of the old imperial bureaucrats and officers, some of whom were treated with disdain, some of whom had been dismissed, the Weimar Republic was already endangered. The Allies had to be confronted with a strong nationalist feeling. Ebert said that Weber, with his historical experience, might be right, but the workers could not be inspired by the previous values. When Staudinger reported this to Weber, adding that international understanding was indispensable for the well-being of the nation-state, Weber flared up: the Weimar Republic would be destroyed within nine years and he never wanted to see Staudinger again (ibid., p. 21).

It was not detachment and distance from the world that made it possible for Weber to subject himself to a work ethic and to devote himself to science, but rather will, conviction, and awareness of necessity. It can be said of him, more than of others, that his impact was due to questions which he left behind and which led to such a rich literature of exegesis. The interpretation of the work is strongly influenced by the image of the person. In the shadow of the person and his work, for modern economists it is not an unimportant question whether they confront his legacy, which means in particular whether they want to carry on with his line of questioning, and those that arise from the 'interpretive economy', in a changed world in which capitalism has triumphed globally but has, for historical reasons, endured varying levels of success from country to country.

## Notes

1  The paper was drafted in 1998.
2  'Est enim non modo liberale paullum non numquam de suo iure decedere, sed interdum etiam fructuosum. Habenda autem ratio est rei familiaris, quam quidem dilabi sinere flagitiosum est, sed ita, ut illiberalitatis avaritiaeque absit suspicio' (Cicero, *De off.* II.18). 'For it is not only liberal to occasionally yield something to which one is entitled, but also has to be kept in mind, however, which to let decay would be shameful, but in such a way that no suspicion of a lack of generosity and of avarice arises' (my transl. – BS).
3  On the decline of the progress paradigm in the Youngest Historical School, cf. Schefold (1998c).
4  I thank Knut Borchardt for this comment.
5  Schapper was a proofreader for the *Neue Rheinische Zeitung* in 1848 and, later assumed various functions in the German workers' movement which brought him into frequent contact with Marx; most importantly, he would become a member of the Central Council of the First International.
6  'The same laws of rightfulness, which community followed, were followed in the endeavours and businesses of the citizens' (my transl.).
7  In his main work, Hildebrand later turned out to be a sceptic on the subject of cooperatives and a harsh critic of cooperative utopias.
8  'The thought which antiquity followed shall grow together with that which we used to follow' (my transl.).
9  'which concern morals and the State' (my transl.).
10  For the reference to Xenophon, cf. 'Xenophon's *Oikonomikos*: the beginnings of an economic science?' Chapter 1.

11 Cicero, *De officiis* II.24 (only partially cited in Hildebrand) and the same, *De senectute* 17.

12 Hildebrand refers here to Aristotle, *Politics* (Book I, section II.3. – 1253 b 20–23), where it says the lord and the slave are from nature the same, the differential between them is only convention (νόηῳ), thus unfair and a relationship based on violence (διόπερ οὐδὲ δίκαιον, βίαιον γάρ).

13 For an example with an explicit reference to the problem of credit: W. Güth, 'Do Banks Crowd in or out Business Ethics? – An Indirect Evolutionary Analysis', presentation given before the Theoretischer Ausschuss des Vereins für Socialpolitik [Theoretical Committee of the German Economic Association of today], 17 April 1998.

14 In what follows, the edition from Gehrig is cited (Hildebrand 1922).

15 Especially the passage cited above in § 27 (Hildebrand 1922, p. 102).

16 'W. Weitling', in ibid., pp. 107ff.

17 The lecture manuscripts were still available while G. Franz was writing his dissertation *Studien über Bruno Hildebrand* (1928); they appear to have been lost in the Second World War.

18 In a lecture Hildebrand spoke out in favour of limiting securities transactions by banks, under the impression that Crédit Mobilier had failed, and looked to the English deposit bank as a model (Franz 1928, pp. 24ff. comment).

19 Franz's dissertation offers numerous examples of this from the literature.

20 Cf. the lecture 'A Survey of the Past History and Present Position of Political Economy' (Ashley 1962) as well as the book *The Economic Organisation of England. An Outline History* (Ashley 1963 [1914]), which traces the emergence of the modern economy back into the Medieval era employing the central ideas of stage theory, though in so doing the ancient world is carefully left out.

21 Cf. the entry 'Roscher' (Bücher 1971 [1907], pp. 486–92).

22 Incidentally, for the viewpoints of the young Roscher, his review of Friedrich List's *Das Nationale System der politischen Oekonomie* (Roscher 1842a) is of particular interest. Smith is defended here against List, and the argument over protective tariffs given a liberal twist. On the other hand, the importance and originality of List does not go unnoticed.

23 Cf. on this 'Aristotle: the classic of ancient economic theory', Chapter 1.

24 I thank Bert Mosselmans, in Brussels, for this information

25 Cf. on this: Baloglou (1995).

26 In the following I refer to the revised edition (Knies 1964 [1883]).

27 Published by Yagi (1983). Cf. Schefold (1994e).

28 A standard work is Knies' (1892) contribution to the history of economic thought.

29 For the 'Intuitive Theory' of Salin, see Schefold (2004b).

30 First of all in Salin (1927).

31 Thünen's complex analysis was interpreted from a modern point of view by Recktenwald and Samuelson (1986). See also: Suntum (1988).

32 Cf. on this Porter (1986).

33 Cf. Heilmann (1980, pp. 123ff.) and Winkel (1977, p. 128).

34 Sharing Vleugels' (1935) inclination but weaker is the text by Heubner (1942).

35 First printing in *lllustrierte Zeitschrift überall für Armee und Marine* (Wagner 1912); cited here, after many revised editions, from the book *Gegen England* (Wagner 1914).

36 Rescinded in 1808 with the *Décret infâme* which was then repealed again by the Bourbons.

37 Cf. Berding (1988, esp. p. 96); see also Wawrzinek (1971 [1927], p. 417), Lazare (1894, pp. 241–45).

38 For example, cf. Holländer (1990), where the acquisition of public goods through cooperation is analytically compared to a market solution.

39 Cf. Theocharis (1961); as well as Homberg (1971). New evidence that Rau's supply and demand diagram was developed independently of Cournot can be found in Baloglou (1995).

40 Cf. Baloglou (1995) and Theocharis (1993).

41 Weber shows how the readiness to save and to accumulate came into being because holding on to possessions becomes as depraved as its opposite, 'the enjoyment of wealth with the consequences of idleness and the temptations of the flesh' represents a distraction from 'righteous life' (Weber 1976). In contrast, ancient philosophers sought a middle way, because both poverty and excessive wealth interfere with the enjoyment of the good life (cf. Schefold 1992a).

42 The general result of the development process does not correspond to the intentions of individuals. And yet Weber emphasizes the achievements of farsighted individuals when he depicts the dilemma of John Wesley, who recognized that the Methodist religion undermines itself because its ordered conduct of life leads to wealth, while the rich lose the desired connection to religion.

43 Cf. on this Eisermann (1989, ch. 3). 'Charismatic' authority also tends to be irrational, for example, when administration is connected neither through legality nor tradition – as far as arbitrariness can be spoken of in particular with 'administration' (Weber 1969, p. 9).

44 'Satisfaction of needs' and 'acquisition' are traditionally understood, from an economic perspective, as two different forms of rationality. The question, which in my opinion has yet to be satisfactorily answered, is how far the intended forms of behaviour could be described or even reasonably understood as two special cases of a single economic theory with a 'concept for rationality' when the meeting of needs involves a greater preference for leisure, a lower propensity to investment, and a stronger aversion to risk-taking.

45 Particularly in Weber (1995 [1927]).

46 Today we would speak of the lack of contractual incentives.

47 Tenbruck considers this question of 'demystification' in the *Protestant Ethic* to be absolutely central to Weber's work. According to the *Protestant Ethic*, life could be rationalized under very different ultimate viewpoints. 'Rationalism is after all a historical term, which cannot be made concrete terminologically.' For Tenbruck (1975, p. 667), therefore, the current development of the rationalization process is also disturbingly open.

48 Cf. on this Beetham (1987).

49 Cf. Hayek (1975 [1935], p. 34).

50 Cf. Salin (1927).

51 We could, of course, also take up supportive or critical economic questions, in the traditional sense, which are dealt with in the *Protestant Ethic* and which, on a first read, are obscured by the unusual theological material. A large number of problems in the history of economic thought are included. (Critical, e.g., on Weber's treatment of fair prices: Roover 1958). However, pursuing such uncontroversial individual 'economic' problems would obscure rather than illuminate the core question.

52 The tension between theory and history also applies to Weber's talent as a researcher, since he thought in theoretical terms and possessed stupendous historical knowledge. Alfred Heuss called Max Weber's book *The agrarian sociology of ancient civilizations [Die Agrarverhältnisse der Altertums]* the 'most original, keenest, and forceful presentation which the economic and social history of the ancient world had ever received.' And, he added an array of ancient scientific discoveries, which were found in Weber's text and later – mostly independently – rediscovered (Heuss 1965, p. 538, 549).

53 Cf. Schefold (1989b).

54 On Weber's association with the Historical School with a simultaneous critique of stage and progress conceptions cf. Hennis (1987, pp. 117ff., pp. 205ff.).

55 T. Parsons was not only in large part responsible for making Weber known in the Anglo-Saxon world through, among other things, his translation of the *Protestant Ethic* (Weber 1930), but before that he had also produced a summary of Sombart's work which is still readable and essay on Weber (Parsons 1928).

56 So just as the rationalization of economic life in the Protestant Ethic emerges as an unintended result of a development in religious thought, Science as a Vocation shows how the original philosophizing intellectuals, striving for religious truth, finally produced a rational science which forbids the biggest questions even to be asked (Weber 1989).

57 On ambivalences in Salin's text from the Heidelberg period and on the evidence, cf. Schefold (1992d).

58 Cf. on this the pamphlet from Erich von Kahler, which however was not approved by George, which already refers to Weber in the title Kahler (1920); Landmann (1923); Landmann (1960).

59 For example, Weber's understandable attacks on the almost 20-years-younger Schumpeter in their famous discussion as related by Somary.

# 5  Asian classics

## Asian classics in a Western collection of the history of economic thought

I here present revised translations of my introduction to the Chinese and the Japanese classics. Most of the introductions which I wrote to the *Klassiker der Nationalökonomie* were strictly focused on the texts and primarily provided a summary as a basis for an interpretation, preceded only by a brief description of the real economic background, of the life and work of the author and the state of the discussion to which his book was addressed. I feel that here the proportions must be reversed. Most of the sections below concern the context, while the summaries of the texts themselves are relatively short. I have chosen this exposition, since I feel that the knowledge of the context is necessary for most of the readers whom I have in mind: historians of economic thought who know the European tradition, but are interested to learn how one might go beyond it. If specialists find this inadequate, I can only express my hope that future interdisciplinary research between Sinologists, Japanologists and historians of economic thought will lead to accounts which will be both more complete, and more correct.

### China and the Chinese classic

Europeans noted a long time ago that China presented an economic system of its own, with a high degree of autarky. The sphere of influence of the system extended beyond the political borders of the empire, but the core of the Chinese world was relatively homogeneous internally; a characteristic economic psychology could be and was formed. Missionaries wrote about it in eighteenth century Europe, Max Weber dealt with it extensively in his sociology of religion (Weber 1920–3), Sinologists like Wilhelm (1930a) described it, and 'the spirit of Chinese capitalism' is an object of modern sociology and even management studies (Redding 1993).

Individualism is an outgrowth of modern occidental culture. Confucianism, the state religion of imperial China, demands conformity in a stratified society with changing elites, partly defined by merit (scholarship), partly by inherited social rank. The nobles serve the prince, the prince serves the people, and the people fulfil their duty in daily work. All venerate their parents and ancestors and take delight in the unity of their family. The state, in imperial China, is the family at large. The prince, like the father for his family, is supposed to be a model for his subjects and the more he impresses as a model, the less he needs to make use of punishment as a means of governing. The subject grows accustomed to following moral rules by habitually following rituals. Ideally, one is content with modest wealth, not daring to strive for a more passionate life, for riches and glory. Such is the measure of conduct. Politics and poetry, adapted to this measure, will beautify the good life and render depth to it. These aspects of what one might call popular Confucianism caused the European philosophers like Leibniz to praise Confucianism, despite its worldliness, as comparable with a Christian ethic.

Although Confucianism dominated for more than 2,000 years, up to the beginning of the twentieth century, there were powerful opposing trends, in particular legalism with its ideal of a strong central state, the authority of which was to be enforced by way of harsh punishment and recompense. Legalists believed that the opposition of the poor and the rich need not lead to internal strife, if the power of the state was consolidated and some material progress took place (Fu 1996). Daoism thought it wise to withhold learning from the manual labourers and not to generalize emancipation through education.

But neither Confucianism nor legalism prevented the persistence of opposing tendencies like a vital individualism, which showed and shows in the deliberate pursuit of personal interests. At the same time, the state represented, from early imperial times onwards, a considerable economic power (except in periods of disintegration). The surplus extracted was not only used for art and ornament and scholarship and for the defence of a very extended empire, but it also served material reproduction, with an extended system of state granaries, the building of roads and canals for communication, together with a network of ditches for irrigation, and the engagement of the state in mining, although not on a permanent basis. As we shall see, early on it was at least ideologically an aim to displace large private traders through bureaucratic redistribution. There was much growth in scientific knowledge, as Needham has shown in his comparative studies, and much technical progress (Ronan 1978–86); Elvin (1973) argued that we should even speak of a technological revolution which took place in the Chinese Middle Ages and which put her ahead of the West, until a gradual saturation from the fourteenth century onwards followed. It is well known that China has a complicated monetary history, with paper money circulating from the eleventh century onwards, and paper money was the main means of circulation during the time of the Mongol domination.

All this was necessarily accompanied by intense debates about economic questions.

Oikonomia in the ancient Greek tradition was the art of house-holding in the wider sense, which included family life and education as well as the art of managing and maintaining an estate, and 'political economy' was occasionally used to denote the management of the finances of the state, in particular the art of obtaining revenue, not only by means of taxation.[1] The economic sphere as a whole did not however exist as a clearly defined and separate entity. The Chinese did not consider economics as a separate discipline either, prior to the adoption of an equivalent term around the turn from the nineteenth to the twentieth century, but texts involving economic issues are to be found along the entire spectrum of written Chinese texts (Mende 2002, p. 53). Economic issues play an important role, especially in books giving advice to princes and, more generally, in historical writings, where individual questions such as taxation, agriculture or welfare are treated. The economic chapters of works of history, from the Han dynasty onward, contain economic chapters, which typically deal with demography, agriculture (including the production of cotton), land tenure, welfare and state granaries, taxation, transport, local taxes, monopolies, the control of markets and prices, and finally monetary matters (ibid., pp. 55–6). The text[2], also chosen for the series *Klassiker der Nationalökonomie*, however, is more distinctive: the debate on Salt and Iron of the year 81 BC. There is a French translation (Walter 1991 [1978]). It is not literal, but it renders the debate quite dramatic through apt selection, the introduction of chapter headings and the use of a very lively language. It brings out the personal conflict between the old, proud, energetic and domineering statesman and the group of modest but determined Confucian scholars, with their dedication to virtue and the values of the agrarian society. Then there is the older and more exact translation by Gale (1931 and 1934).

### China, as seen by early European economists

China has remained a *terra incognita* for most economists until recently, but what was known was used to debate some points of great importance.

Montesquieu, who favoured a constitutional monarchy according to the English model, interpreted despotism as the unification of the several powers of the state. Religion and morals are formed so that individual despots cannot change them: 'Les législateurs de la Chine … confondirent la religion, les lois, les moeurs et les manières: tout cela fut la morale, tout cela fut la vertu. Les préceptes qui regardaient ces quatre points furent ce que l'on appelle les rites … On passa toute sa jeunesse à les apprendre, toute sa vie à les pratiquer' (Montesquieu 1793, vol. 2, p. 95).[3] In spite of the power of tradition, dynasties change cyclically. They originate with military power and discipline, and they decay because of increasing luxury and corruption: 'Le palais devient l'ennemi de l'empire' (ibid., vol. 1, p. 173).[4] China is thus essentially a negative example: 'La Chine est donc un état despotique, dont le principe est la crainte' (ibid., vol. 1, p. 216).[5]

François Quesnay, the greatest economist who dealt with China at length, arrived at a more favourable judgement than Montesquieu on the basis of the reports of the missionaries, whom he attacked in his treatise 'Despotisme de la Chine' (1965 [1888], pp. 622ff.).[6] Quesnay describes the state, the economy, and the daily life of China, as if he had himself travelled in the country. He seeks parallels between myths from the earliest times in China and the chronology of the Old Testament. The old traditional institutions, with a clear social order and infrastructure, well-established agriculture and developed irrigation system, have combined to produce a degree of wealth which has led to a great increase of population (for it is not that population increases riches *pari passu* through its increase, but that the growth of population tends to overstep the limits set by the existing degree of wealth, ibid., p 579).

Instruments are simple, and artisans with their instruments look for clients in the streets – barbers with a chair on their backs – and even the most modest resources are used intensively, down to human faeces, which are bought and sold and end up as manure for the fields.

Quesnay is impressed by a religion in which the ruler is obliged to lead a model life, sacrifices in person for a good harvest, and to this end descends from his throne (ibid., p. 587). In the event of natural catastrophes the ruler blames himself and his deficient virtue, but he lays no blame on lower officials.

Quesnay reports extensively on Chinese science, the canon of the holy books, the intellectual tradition, printing, and the hierarchy in education where boys are beaten into the learning of characters and wisdom. Quesnay also reports on the examinations of the officials, and the surveillance of the merito-cratic apparatus of the bureaucracy by the emperor. He believes, contrary to Montesquieu, that failures are investigated and negligent officials punished in accordance with the law. The emperor is said to inspect the activity of the bureaucracy times and again in person, and to act in cases of irregularity with exemplary severity. Hence the powers of the emperor are extensive, but he remains subject to the law.

It is nonetheless clear that Quesnay, the economist and founder of Physioc-racy, was most impressed by the economic organization of China, based as it was on agriculture as the primary sector, in accordance with the intellectual world and institutions of the Chinese. This was the source of sustenance, it was here that the majority of the population was occupied, and it was also the source of taxation; all of which was in accordance with Quesnay's thinking. He had heard that there were also other taxes, but he wrote:

> On dit qu'il y a à la Chine, outre la contribution sur les terres, quelques impôts irréguliers, comme des droits de douane … Si ces allégations ont quelque réalité, cela marquerait qu'en ce point l'État ne serait suffisamment éclairé sur les véritables intérêts…
>
> (ibid., p. 634)[7]

He argues that a single tax on land would be for the best, and argues that this could be proved by calculation. Generally, China seemed to be the great confirmation of his intellectual system: not the historical accident of a favourable geographical position, but the stability of her order was the reason for the permanent existence of China.

The inspiration of China for eighteenth century European reformers was plain, and much remains in part to be discovered. Rainer Klump (2004) has pointed recently to a curious episode which also was commented upon in Europe: the foundation of a kingdom of Ponthiamas in the south of Vietnam by a rich powerful Chinese trader around 1700. This kingdom existed for about 70 years and became in the eyes of the French observer (Pierre Poivre) the model of a physiocratic state, on account of a just distribution of land and a liberal order. Klump cites other influences on Physiocracy by China. At the same time, the kingdom of Ponthiamas shows how offshoots, so to speak, could be formed on the borders of the Chinese realm, especially in periods of decline. Strong personalities, in particular rich merchants, could secede from the central state power and form subsidiary centres based on trade and agriculture.

There is less interest for China in English classical political economy. China is for Adam Smith one of the great examples of a culture that develops by itself, trading little with the outside world but achieving an impressive level of riches on the basis of inland navigation (Smith 1976 [1776], vol. 1, p. 35). For Smith, parallel examples are Egypt and India. At the same time, China is an example of how far the division of labour can be driven in a country even without foreign trade, if only it is large enough:

> But the great extent of the Chinese empire, the vast multitude of its inhabitants, the variety of climate, the consequent range of products in its different provinces, and the ease of internal waterborne communication, render the home market of that country of such an extent as to be sufficient for the support of very great manufactures, admitting very considerable subdivisions of labour.
>
> (ibid., vol. 2, p. 680)

Smith believes that the domestic market of China is, in itself, not much smaller than that of all the European states taken together, but he also speculates how China's trading power might increase if the Chinese decided to trade in their own ships. This was written at a time when China was relatively closed, compared to earlier periods of more active foreign trade. It is only recently that China has begun to reorient herself to the outside world.

Richard Jones was the first in England to argue for a historical approach in contrast to the abstract theory of classical political economy. He devoted one chapter of his book to the specificity of Asiatic forms of production (Jones 1964 [1831]). He gives especial weight to systems of irrigation. Among them, he is especially fascinated by those which exist on the borders of deserts, as in Persia and Xinjiang. Rain falls almost exclusively in the mountains, so that canals can facilitate fertility at the desert margins in artificial oases, but these channels often need to be underground so as to prevent losses by evaporation. A supreme authority like that of the emperor of China, or the Shah, or the Mogul, can regulate the allocation of land and the distribution of water. On the other hand, Jones points to a secondary foundation of central authority:

conquest and superimposition by alien people, like the nomadic Mongols. However, conquest will not always lead to such a superimposed form of rule. The Germans and the Afghans for instance, have not, unlike the Mongols, formed large realms or occupied them (the realm of Western Rome decayed after the migration of peoples); this is to be ascribed to different tribal traditions and to their origins in different ways of life. Explanations similar to those of Jones can be found in John Stuart Mill (1976 [1909, 1848]) when he writes of an 'Oriental Society', with however less detail than that of Jones.

Marx' concept of an 'Asiatic Mode of Production' represents a condensed form of such images of an oriental society. He published the core of this conception in his essay on 'The British Rule in India' (1984).[8]Wittfogel (1957) traced the development of this conception in Marx, extended it, and then turned the resulting conception against the totalitarian Marxism of the twentieth century. Among the elements necessary for the understanding of the oriental society Marx notes the sheer geographical fact of size as a precondition for the central authoritarian organization of public works, whereas in smaller-scale communities, such as in Flanders and in Italy, private enterprise and free cooperation is sufficient to organize the allocation and use of water (Marx 1984, p. 129). Marx also emphasizes that, while the rulers of Asia changed, they left unchanged the foundation of this mode of production – farming and domestic weaving in the villages. Marx was inclined to view the cohesiveness of the village as related to the existence of a primitive community. When he grew older he wondered whether Russian villages might become a basis for the socialization of the country as a whole, bypassing capitalist industrialization. But for him the Asiatic mode of production was not part of the sequence of modes of production that he attributed to Europe: from antiquity via feudalism, the capitalist mode of production to his postulated future communist social form. Wittfogel turned this theory around against Stalin and his successors, interpreting the centralization of decisions on production under the dictatorship of the proletariat as the basis of a more intense form of totalitarianism.

Forms of government and administration, in particular the administration of public works, thus play the principal role in the accounts given by some of the most famous authors in the history of economic thought who were not Sinologists, but nonetheless interested in China. Max Weber (who is mainly known as a sociologist, but held positions as an economist) was especially interested in the religious dimension of China, an interest to which we shall return. I should like to add here some remarks on the political dimension contributing to growth and decline, centralization and decentralization.

Other great empires of the past were conquered, or disintegrated and disappeared; China however re-emerged after sometimes prolonged periods of disintegration. The preservation of unity in a hostile world is only possible if the empire possesses sufficient cultural homogeneity to permit a unified administration to seem desirable, combined with sufficient diversity for the growth of an internal market, based on the growth of a division of labour leading to increased productivity. The empire cannot be too large; the relevant measure is not geographical distance as such, but rather speed of communication. The Roman Empire could be extended because the Mediterranean permitted swift communication and facilitated trade at costs which were low in comparison with overland communication – in China canals and rivers had this function. The empire also had to keep ahead of rival nations, and technical advantages in warfare usually presupposed a higher level of skill and understanding. But rival nations will learn from the empire. The German tribes thus learned from the Romans, and the Romans eventually had to share power with them. Similarly, the Mongols learned from the Chinese, and once they could combine their advantage in large masses of mounted troops with the use of iron weapons they were able to rule China.[9] Periods during which the empire came under outside pressure led to internal tensions (for defence requires the extraction of a greater surplus, and the population will seek local protection against tax collectors, strengthening centrifugal forces). The empire of the Han dynasty, roughly contemporaneous with the Roman Empire and in occasional contact with it, in its later stages suffered like the Roman Empire from the growth of latifundia. Here the failings of central organization permitted the growth of banditry and robbery which in turn made local protection more desirable, and during the third century AD the Roman Empire began to break up (Elvin 1973, pp. 35–41).

Only the eastern part of the Roman Empire survived, and here there were fewer latifundia. The dynasty of the Sui re-established the unity of the Chinese empire by force (581–617) and created the basis for the subsequent Tang dynasty (618–906). There is a chapter devoted to the economy in the Sui history, translated into French by Balazs. The emperor Wen is there praised for securing the borders through the establishment of military colonies to the north of the Great Wall (Balazs 1953, pp. 153ff.). He also reformed the compulsory labour system (improved controls were introduced to prevent fraud, e.g. by pretending to be older than one was), and the imperial household became noted for its parsimony. Taxes were reduced, but the granaries remained full (ibid., pp. 156ff.). Taxes were annulled for farmers in cases of calamities, canals were built, and there was an effort made to prevent public servants from lending monies belonging to the state and directing the profit into their own pockets.

This account presents a positive image of this regime by comparison with the negative treatment of the maladministration of the subsequent emperor Yang (605–617). It is true that there were extraordinary achievements. He also had irrigation canals built – in particular the imperial canal, more of which later – and he led a costly expedition against Korea. But it is now said that nearly one half of the compulsory labourers and soldiers died, that the tax revenue began to decline, although he did have magnificent ships built to celebrate the opening of the canal: 'De plus (l'empereur) fit construire des bateaux-dragons, des vaisseaux-phénix, des (bateaux ornés de) dragons jaunes, des navires rouges, des embarcations à étages (pontées), des barques jumelées de bambou' (ibid., pp. 160ff.).[10]

The crews towing the ships were dressed in brocade, using green silk ropes. The entire empire had to contribute to this. Requisitioning became necessary, and as the provisions dwindled, prices rose (ibid., p. 167). The dragon ship of the emperor is said to have been four stories high, and 80,000 sailors manned his fleet. The chronicler mentions these facts so that the reader might shudder at such prodigality, but the modern editor adds:

> On peut voir les choses d'un oeil tout différent: après tout, ce n'était peut-être ni folie, ni pur agreement, mais un acte éminemment politique que de vouloir conférer le prestige d'un voyage impériale ... à l'artère principale destinée à réunir pour toujours le Nord et le Sud, séparés depuis quatre siècles!
>
> (ibid., p. 226)[11]

In consequence, there was hunger, robbery, and revolts that were suppressed while the military ambitions of the emperor failed. But no-one dared to open the granaries; only the opening of the 'granary of perpetual abundance' by the revolutionary army of the new Tang dynasty brought relief to the people (ibid., p. 173).

The text, written in praise of the economic achievements of a dynasty, turns repeatedly to political events. This demonstrates that the economic condition of the population was a matter of serious concern, the population being continually subject to fluctuations in their diet due to adverse harvest conditions, natural calamities and the arbitrariness of civil and military undertakings, the basic conditions of agrarian life remaining unchanged in the long run. The contrasts between on the one hand the large structures of government and its irrigation system, with countless subordinate villages, and on the other never-ending political strife, creating a constant cycle of destruction and reconstruction, were for Marx the characteristic features of the Asiatic mode of production. But there were important secular changes which do not fit into this simplified picture.

### Economic institutions

We have to return to the beginning. Why did Chinese feudalism of the Zhou-period lead into a developmental path so different from that in Europe? During the Zhou period rulers endowed vassals with fiefs, land and population. Loyalty was highly-rated; vassals were obliged to participate in military campaigns and to appear at court, to pay contributions and to provide compulsory labour. Between the nobility and the mass of farmers, artisans and traders there was a middle stratum of scholars and officials. As central power decayed, the princes became independent, and their dominions expanded and turned into 'warring states', Confucian morals were invoked to strengthen the threatened feudal order. Private property and trade in land had grown, especially from the fourth century BC onwards (Elvin 1973, p. 24). The feudal and communal characteristics of the old economy separated, monetary circulation increased, and in the early Han empire free farmers dominated. The Confucian Mencius did not simply condemn rebellions occurring early on in the transition, but blamed them on the selfishness of princes. It seems that there was in this period some increase of slavery, but slavery never became a widespread institution in China (except in households).[12] Princes reacted in different ways to the emancipation of traders, some by interfering in trade, others (in the state Zheng) by granting trading rights.

It has been said that a more worldly orientation replaced a more secular art in this period, and that a certain individualism developed along with imperialism (Wilhelm 1960, p. 23). Roads were built. Two military innovations of the fourth century were the introduction of the crossbow and of mounted archers (Elvin 1973, p. 26). The power of domination rose. It is said of chancellor Zi Zhan, head of government in the second half of the sixth century BC in the state Cheng, that he accepted popular criticism and did not close schools, when it spread there, but Zi Zhan also sought to promote security and legality by the promulgation of new criminal laws.

The growth of legalism, an intellectual current which favoured government by means of formal rules, did not portend a movement towards a more liberal order, but instead strengthened the role of government. According to the book Shen Dao, the law should suppress the personal, while the prince should prevent strife among the people. The book deplores that sages are venerated, for this leads to conflict between princes and sages. A state pursuing the correct path will, by contrast, impose laws, terminate private discussions, appoint princes, and cease to venerate sages (Wilhelm 1960, p. 23). The attitude of the legalists is apparent in the *Debate on Salt and Iron*, where the imperial advisor is irritated by the moral advice of Confucian scholars, and does not hesitate to make this clear. The school of the logician Mo Di instead invoked the general love of mankind, human equality and self-restraint.

A well-known example of the irrigation system in the Zhengdu-basin dates from the late Zhou-period; it still exists and is shown to tourists. A river bend is dammed and the canals which lead from it are so arranged that sand and sediment tends to settle on the riverbed and not enter the canal system, the regulation of river turbulence tending to prevent this happening.

One of the distinguishing features of the Chinese administrative and economic system, administration by means of examined officials, had its origins in the Warring States period, the Confucians emphasizing the necessity of educating administrators (the imperial system of state examinations developed later, of course).

Another element of state economic administration, later discussed in the *Debate on Salt and Iron,* regards state trade.

> Since food shortages were common in most other societies in human history, food storage was, not surprisingly, an activity common to most civilisations ad cultures, even those characterised by hunting and

gathering. But in the Chinese case, grain storage became an important political concern in the early times and remained so for more than two millennia.

(Will and Bin Wong 1991, pp. 1ff.)

In the *Debate on Salt and Iron* the imperial minister advocates granaries administered by the state and shows some tolerance for large traders, whereas the Confucians looked to more modest local solutions.

It has been said that the Great or Imperial Canal linking the Yangtse, the Huai He and the Yellow River system played an integrative role similar to that which the Nile did in ancient Egypt, the task of supervision lending power to the responsible public officials. They rarely permitted the use of water for private mills (Wilhelm 1960, p. 45). The extension of the channel to Beijing was done much later by the Ming emperors (Elvin 1973, pp. 104ff.).

We cannot understand *The Debate on Salt and Iron* in historical perspective without some remarks on later developments. Whereas in Europe the Middle Ages represented a retreat from the achievements of the Roman Empire, the period of the Tang dynasty can be viewed as a point of cultural culmination. Great power was invested in the symbolism of imperial rule. The majesty of the emperor was articulated in a complex system of rites. From the economic point of view these were costly and brought no benefit. The veneration of the dead imposed a tax on the living, but also helped stabilize the social order. But one would have to create a very convoluted argument to justify the existence of such rites in terms of either the new political economy or materialism. Legal codes were likewise thought to exist to support customs and moral values. The death penalty was envisaged for beating one's parents, while there was a very modest punishment for beating anyone else. The state would intervene only in cases of grave violations of the public order; and otherwise acted only if there was a plaintiff.

And yet there was a medieval economic revolution (ibid.). During the Middle Ages the European centre moved northwards, clearing woods and using horse-drawn ploughs to turn heavy soils; by contrast, the Chinese economy shifted southwards, building dams and ditches to distribute water for rice production using different types of water pump. Small farmers lacked the means to promote such changes, which were done at the manorial level. Contemporaries were so struck by the results that they even wrote poems about agricultural techniques (ibid., p. 115, p. 125). Paved roads were built under the Song dynasty, locks were built on watercourses when Europeans still had to drag ships overland to bypass rapids. Most remarkable was a revolution in money and credit. Paper money appeared in AD 1024, first issued by private consortia, later developing into the primary circulating medium under the Mongol emperors, although it eventually went into decline, as we shall see below (ibid., p. 157). The greatest degree of open trading was reached under Mongol rule when foreigners like Marco Polo could rise to important state positions.

The Ming emperors were more ambivalent in their attitude with regard to foreign trade[13]. There was some private Chinese colonization, in particular in the Philippines, which was brought to an end by the Spaniards. But in general restrictions on foreign trade grew. The manorial system of the high Middle Ages did not develop into a feudal structure with vassalage. While undergoing some setbacks the centralized system of government prevailed, but the personal dependence of farmers gradually diminished as rents were transformed into monetary payments; absentee landlordism, with landlords resident in cities, developed in the late imperial period.

It has often been asked why China did not retain its technological lead over the West. For example, iron was produced in the high Middle Ages using coal, not charcoal, and Mongols using iron weapons, manufactured with techniques learned from China, reached Kiev. The familiar stories of the Chinese invention of the compass and of firearms could be retold. Elvin believes that late imperial China arrived at a 'high-level-equilibrium-trap': technology had been developed in all fields to a high degree of sophistication, but a higher level of productivity was extremely costly. Innovation did not seem not worthwhile while labour remained cheap and the population was plentiful. A foreign trade offensive might have broken this deadlock, but China had grown defensive as far as foreign relations were concerned.

This condition of economic stagnation dominated the images of early nineteenth century China formed by European observers who were no longer missionaries, but traders or their representatives. Davis, Governor of Hong Kong, provides a detailed picture recalling that of Quesnay: a vast country, with a cheerful and diligent population and marvellously dexterous artisans, with monumental bamboo waterwheels irrigating endless fields. Davis described family rituals, and also the work of a fairly efficient administration conforming to laws which sometimes seem strange to the European traveller. He also reported on the administration of the emperor, whose solemn ceremonies can occasionally be attended by a European guest.

The conflicts between East and West began to become apparent with differences over values and disputes about trading rights and court protocol. There were some initial skirmishes. Davis, as an educated British official, tried to respect Chinese cultural traditions, but when discussing for example Chinese medicine he found it difficult to see anything but superstition. He also believed himself to have a superior knowledge of political economy, observing that the current Chinese system of public grain storage was only the outcome of faulty economic understanding. The government builds stores at great expense and has them run by administrators who were often corrupt; if they had instead permitted private trade in grain an adequate and more regular annual supply could be achieved. Private traders are better able to smooth the fluctuations of grain prices (Davis 1847–1848, vol. 1, p. 214; vol. 3, p. 145).

This lengthy digression on Chinese economic history seems necessary if only to give an impressionistic view of how the themes discussed in the *Debate on Salt and Iron* can be seen within the general context of Chinese development. Profound changes were occurring, and yet there is a recurrence of ideas which could well be regarded as characteristic. In particular, and irrespective of arguments about detail, the continuity of Confucian thought – a state religion after all – during two millennia can hardly be disputed.

There is an important Confucian ideal that the ruler, like the mythical emperor Yu, does not need to issue orders; or at least, as described by Quesnay, the emperor need not appear to be busy with the administration of the state apparatus, but should instead be regarded as a strict supreme overseer of a society with a complex structure and a vigorous life of its own. It is said of Confucius:

> The master travelled to a province, for the administration of which Zilu had been responsible for three years. The pupil Zigong – who guided the carriage – wondered why Confucius, long before they arrived, repeatedly praised the effective administration by Zilu: 'Master, you have not yet seen Zilu administrating, and yet you have praised him thrice. May I hear of his excellence?' The master replied: 'I saw him administrating. When I entered his district, all fields were well ploughed and carefully weeded; all ditches and drains were in order. So I saw that he won the confidence of people by exactness and conscientiousness, for they were all scrupulous. Entering his city I saw that all walls and buildings were solid and durable, and that they were surrounded by trees. This shows that he is loyal and dependable and open hearted to-boot, for people are not interested in mere appearance. When I arrived in front of his office house, all was silent and empty, each servant got on with his work. This showed how he adjudicated trials with wisdom and intelligence, for his administration worked without disturbance. Hence it is clear that I did not say too much when I praised him thrice'.
>
> (Zotz 2000, pp. 88ff., my transl.)

On the other hand, the necessity of pragmatic and discretionary intervention in states and economy grew to be inevitable times and again. On the occasion of his seventieth birthday the stern Kangxi emperor, the second Manju (Quing)-ruler, summarized his government as follows:

> I am now seven decades old and I have been sitting on the throne for over fifty years. The world is more or less at peace, and there is order within the four seas. It is true that I have not achieved an improvement of our customs and I have not been able to guarantee that the families and the people have enough; though I have been active relentlessly ... and I have not permitted the least negligence to myself, day and night. ... If one is neglectful in a single matter, that will entail mischief for the world as a whole; if one is inattentive just once, that will entail sorrows for uncounted generations.
>
> (Wilhelm 1960, pp. 79ff., my transl.)

*Chinese economic thought*

Seeking to place the *Debate on Salt and Iron* in historical perspective we now turn to a broad survey of the history of Chinese economic thought. We are compelled to rely on one single secondary source, Jichuang Hu (1988), since so far as I know there is no other comprehensive modern book on the same subject, while only a few texts have been translated into Western European languages, mostly in the form of extracts. Hu wrote large parts of his work during the decade of the Cultural Revolution in a three-volume Chinese version, which he then shortened and translated into English before the end of Maoism. His historical interpretation is not free of the spirit of his time. His sympathies are more with legalism; he views Confucianism as a predominantly reactionary element. The reader can to some extent ignore these factors. More difficult for the economist is that Hu knows little about modern economic theory, and is therefore not really able to identify those elements in the old Chinese economic literature which anticipate modern ideas. Most of the other secondary texts which we use to supplement this work are even older, so that it could be said that in this section we attempt made more to designate a problem than to solve it. Finally, it is understandable that Hu wishes to emphasize the world historical significance of Chinese discoveries in the field of economic theory, and to demonstrate a Chinese priority for important ideas and institutions, or at least argue that Chinese developments paralleled those in the West. I feel he sometimes goes too far in this, but on other occasions he understates his case because he does not sufficiently differentiate between intellectual traditions.

I propose to anticipate one conclusion, arising from consideration of the material before me: the early beginnings of abstract economic theory in Aristotle and in antiquity, their later development in scholastic literature and in mercantilism, even more the achievements of the classical economic period – none of these really have a parallel in China, because of a failure to develop a theory of value. But on the other hand core economic institutions like state monopolies of trade or paper money have been the subject of discussion in China on the basis of a solid, sometimes only implicit understanding of the logic of economic processes. This happened earlier than in Europe – the *Debate on Salt and Iron* offers clear evidence for it.

There is a 1926 German Ph.D. thesis on the Economic Views of the Chinese Classics (Böhme 1926), which is still worth reading for the undogmatic way in which it seeks to isolate the particular properties of the economic forms and the economic thinking of the early Chinese. The author, Karl Böhme, explicitly dissociates himself from Huan-Chang Chen (1974 [1911]) and his history of economics in China, which is Confucian in character but ordered according to Western economic concepts. Böhme criticizes Chen for having transformed Confucius into a modern occidental political economist. Böhme refers to Chayanov (1999 [1923]) in his introduction, and to Chayanov's attempts to distinguish pre-capitalist forms of production. He concentrates on the first millennium before Christ, for in this:

occurs the splendid spiritual extension of Chinese culture, which is of influence down to today. The well-ordered state of vassals is transformed in this period under a central authority via the growth of individual vassal states to the centralised state of officials, as it existed up to present times. And, economically speaking, the form of economic governance originated in this time, which has been preserved in China with minor transformations.

(Böhme 1926, p. 5, my transl.)

As we indicated above, this transition is seen today as more complicated; there were important structural changes, and progress did exist.

Böhme's interpretation of the early period remains of interest. According to the old writings, and especially according to the book of rights from the Zhou period, agriculture was based on cooperation between families in clans and villages. An ideal is defined by the nine field economy, more accurately described by Mencius. One can imagine a square divided up into nine partial squares. Eight families work on the eight squares laying around the central square, each working for itself; the square in the middle, where there is also a common spring, contains a field, which the families will cultivate jointly for their joint tribute. The *Book of Rites* of Zhou also describes the division of labour, with an enumeration of nine major occupations, with fertilizing and irrigation regulated by authorities, cultivation subjected to systematic official inspection, various means of exchange being used (without coins provided by the state, however) and with the payment of tribute to the granaries of the government. The *Book of Rites* outlines the principles of good storage keeping on the part of the government, which will still be quoted by Miura Baien, as we shall see below:

> A country without a nine-year store of foodstuff shall be described as being in a state of deficiency, without a six-year store of foodstuff as being in a state of emergency, and without a three-year store it can no longer be called a country at all.

(Hu 1988, p. 14)

This sentence was hardly to be taken literally, but symbolically – the use of the holy figure 'nine' is sufficient indication of that. Grain could be kept in granaries for many years; their construction was sophisticated. To have a store for, say, six years probably never meant that six times the annual consumption of grain was stored, but rather the capacity to compensate for harvest deficiencies over such a period.[14]

Tributes are paid in kind; officials receive payments in kind from state granaries. Moreover, they and the nobility receive allotments of land which is cultivated by forced labour. The overseers are there 'to balance the general consumption of the people'. Foodstuffs are distributed in times of need, especially to persons living alone and without an income. It is also said that grains are to be distributed in spring and to be collected in the autumn, which probably means that seeds should be distributed to farmers in the spring and surpluses from the harvest collected in the autumn. Hu speaks of market regulation, the state controlling prices according to a moral judgement. High prices for luxury goods were interpreted as signs of moral decay – for without such decay, these goods would not be demanded in excess. The concrete prescriptions in the *Book of Rites* correspond to a mythical order discussed in other canonical writings like the *I Ging* (see Wilhelm 1924).

The subsequent Spring and Autumn period (772–476 BC) and the period of the Warring States (475–221 BC) were regarded as culturally fruitful, a golden period of Chinese history which is also important in respect of the origination of economic ideas. According to tradition, Guan Zhong, who lived through the beginning of this period and died in 645 BC, is said to have been the author of a collection *Guan Zi*, but important parts of the *Guan Zi* were added subsequently right down to the beginning of the Han empire (Rickett 1965, 1985, 1998). Only a few ideas can be attributed to Guan himself with some certainty; among others that he argued for a division of the people into classes: warriors, farmers, artisans and traders.[15] Professional employments were thought to be heritable and members of these professional groups were supposed to live close together, so that the advantages of specialization like the fortitude of warriors and the dexterity of artisans could also be inherited and improved. It could be said that this anticipates an insight into external effects of concentration, apparently then regarded as more important than problems resulting from the ensuing possibilities of collusion.

Shan Qi, a statesman of the spring and autumn period in the first half of the sixth century BC, developed a monetary theory whose elaboration used visual concepts, quite typical for an entire subsequent tradition:

> In antiquity, when natural disasters fell, a monetary measure would be taken to balance off the 'light' and 'heavy' coins in circulation for the relief of the people. If people were troubled by the 'light' coins, 'heavy' ones would be minted and put into circulation. This was to use the *mu*, or 'mother' coin (i.e. the newly issued 'heavy' big coin) as a new circulating unit of account to balance off the *zi*, or 'son' coin (i.e. the 'light', small coins already in circulation). In so doing, all the people would be satisfied.
>
> (Hu 1988, p. 25)

'Light' is the expression for a commodity (here a certain kind of coin) supplied in excess, which therefore has a low price and is exchanged against small amounts of another commodity, so that money is inflationary. 'Heavy' is a commodity in short supply, which is regarded as expensive. A coin minted with a high metal content can serve as an example. The heavier 'mother' coin is meant to be a counterweight to the 'light' son coin. This means that inflation should be countered by means of better money. Inflation could be caused by a bad harvest (the natural disaster in the quote). This visual conceptualization appears in refined form in the *Guan Zi,* and reappears in monetary writings of the Chinese time and again. Shan Qi used his argument against the king, cautioning that the property of the people should not be diminished through the use of old coinage when a new coinage was introduced by declaring the old coins illegal. It was instead suggested, using the image of a pair of scales, that the two kinds of coins be left to find an equilibrium; this may well mean that the market should be left to determine the exchange relation between them.

Fan Li, a rich merchant and later first minister in the state Yue in the fifth century BC, believed that harvest fluctuations depended on the stars. He advocated the accumulation of foodstuffs in good years, when the price of food was low. The prices of other goods moved anti-cyclically. That meant that storage would tend to smooth the price movements of food goods and the contrary price movements of other goods. It was not price control, as in the *Book of Rites*, that would stabilize prices, but the storage of surpluses.

The task of finding a balance was thought to be a cosmic principle; it is mentioned by Laotse in his *Tao Te King*. Daoism had become influential among hermits who sought to relate with nature and keep themselves apart from a mankind which had deviated from the right way. But Daoism also influenced Legalism, attempting to impose order by force, if necessary.

Some quotations from the literature may here be useful to illustrate the economic dimension of Confucianism. We can begin with the observation that Confucius rejected a withdrawal from life and the use of force: 'The master said and sighed "I cannot commune with birds and other animals. With whom shall I be together, if not with these people? If the world were in order, I would not have to try to change them"' (Confucius 1998, p. 121, my transl.).

The extent to which Confucius trusted the power of culture to form society is very striking: 'Confucius said "The songs elevate man, the rites provide him with stability, music renders him perfect"' (ibid., p. 47, my transl.). This will supposedly be understood only by those living according to the superior order: 'Confucius said "Who does not know his obligations to other men – how can he conform to their rites and manners? He who does not understand his obligations with regard to others – how can he understand music?"' (ibid., p. 15, my transl.).

There are passages touching on economic relations, like the following which may be compared with the Socratic and Aristotelian[16] maxim that the cobbler should think of making good sandals, and not of selling them: 'Confucius said "If you serve the ruler, mind in the first place to be conscientious in your work. Your wage is secondary"' (Confucius 1998, p. 105, my transl.). Another analogy between Confucian and Aristotelian economic thought may be seen in the fact that they both are critical not of barter, nor even of money as a means of exchange, but of trade – without thinking that it could be abolished completely – and that they have a high regard for the principle of reciprocity. Aristotle developed a complex logic of reciprocity, while

Confucius insisted on correct behaviour: 'Custom protects the regular communication of relationships. To yield to the other without meeting reciprocal action does not correspond to custom. Accepting something from others without acting in reciprocity does not correspond to custom' (Wilhelm 1930b, p. 345, my transl.).

We can conclude this series of quotations with the following, which relates activity in the material sphere to the higher order:

> The pupil Ziyou asked how one should behave with regard to one's parents. Confucius replied: 'When one talks today about one's duties towards one's parents, one thinks of their material support. But men also feed their dogs and horses. If one does not venerate one's parents – what difference then exists between care for parents and the elevation of dogs and horses?'.
>
> (Confucius 1998, p. 11, my transl.)

Hu recognizes the overwhelming influence of Confucius on Chinese history, but he regards him as an obstacle to development and as a pillar of the ruling class. Confucius was not opposed to production, but the noble was not to take part in it. He recognized that non-equal distribution leads to social unrest and that poverty was less pressing under conditions of equality. More people meant more riches, therefore more education. Confucius was against heavy taxes so that this process of development might not be hindered. The early Confucian idea of a 'great unity, according to which all work sincerely for each other', is interpreted by Hu (1988, p. 58) as an anticipation of a system with common property. He compares this utopia, evaluating it positively, with that of Plato. Plato's communism concerns only the guardian of the state, among whom also women and children are communal, whereas the Confucian ideal of the family is also to be retained in the context of the 'great unity'.

The Confucian Mencius (ca. 390 to ca. 305 BC) is regarded as a co-founder of the school of Confucius despite their separation by more than a century. Mencius emphasizes that only permanent private property leads to 'constancy of purpose'; he therefore advocates private property in actual life. He says that spiritual and manual labour must be separated, that manual workers provide food and that intellectual workers should be creative. He envisages taxation in terms of compulsory services, since fixed rents may ruin the farmers in bad years. He advocates the nine-fields system (which is taken literally by Hu and regarded as absurd – he also doubts that the *Book of Rites* by Zhou advocates the nine-fields system). Traders are people who observe price differences more quickly than others, who profiteer and who therefore should be taxed (ibid., pp. 64–74).

Mo Di (late fifth century BC) started from the general love of man and also claimed natural equality in real life (Zotz 2000, p. 95). By helping others one helps oneself and increases welfare; the useful is to be increased, not the superfluous ornament. This orientation towards material progress and the postulate of obedience made Mo Di's conception appear at the time of the Cultural Revolution to be a progressive historical alternative to Confucius (ibid., p. 98). Mo Di advocated compensation based on actual achievement; he therefore argues against the Confucian emphasis on inherited merit. He also argued for satisfaction of the needs of simple people, pursuing an ascetic life with his school. The Mohists also identified the difference between use and exchange value in stating: 'Shoes made as a means to buy are shoes no more' (Hu 1988, p. 80). Even this example reminds us of the Aristotelian saying that a shoe is produced in order to be worn, not for the sake of exchange. The far-reaching implications of the Aristotelian theory of chrematistic acquisition begin from this consideration (Schefold 1994a). The Mohists also have an idea of an appropriate price, at which clients want to buy and which presumes that all goods are sold. Such prices represent an equilibrium because of this dual determination (Hu 1988, pp. 80–1. I assume that this refers to market price in the short period). Instead of asking how in the long run market prices move towards an average which as in the West might then be regarded as 'just' or 'natural', in China the issue was how the state might guide market prices.

I have already mentioned the great significance of the collection of writings preserved under the name *Guan Zi*. The guidance of prices here plays an important role. The prime concern of a good guardian of the people is to let them produce, to fill the granaries and to maintain and sustain subjects (Böhme 1926, p. 32).

> To only collect, and not to distribute, renders people rebellious; the people unleash their force. To collect little where many are to be maintained leads to deceit among the people; not to collect and not to distribute will destroy the welfare of the people.
>
> (ibid., my transl.)

The self-interest of people is recognized: it is in human nature to look for profit, and a wise ruler will make use of this propensity. Even if some individuals are foolish, the ruler must listen to the masses. If they remain poor, they will become insubordinate and prove hard to rule; if some gain exorbitant wealth they cannot be ruled, for this renders them independent. The ruler therefore must see to it that a balance is created. The government will, if necessary, advance money for future harvests and grant a reduction in taxation. The *Guan Zi* proposes a monopoly of iron and salt (and of forests and rivers), and this will be discussed in the *Debate on Salt and Iron* (Hu 1988, pp. 108–15). The prince shall 'circulate the collected goods, maintain the roads leading from the borders to the markets, care for the lodgings along the roads for the merchants: this is what one calls making riches circulate' (Böhme 1926, p. 35, my transl.). Even the formula 'this is what one calls…' is characteristic; the economic texts assemble insights into economic policy, explain them, and distil them into sentences or sayings which facilitate the recollection of rules.

Böhme renders the theory of 'light' and 'heavy' as follows:

> Corn is not suitable as money, and not at all as a measure of value. The value of money is unstable; it is high if the harvest is bad, and low if the harvest is good. In good years, when corn is cheap, the farmer must sell his surplus at a loss. But if there is a bad year and the farmer has to buy corn for his own use, he will not be able to buy corn with the revenue gained in the good year, given that the price of corn has risen in the meantime. This gives rise to much misery, but can be counteracted through intelligent monetary policy on the part of the government. The government must issue a variety of coinage. If corn prices fall, the government must issue bad coins, in order to engender a rise of corn prices. Conversely, the government will withdraw bad coin from circulation and issue good coinage to depress corn prices and facilitate the buying of corn on the part of farmers.
>
> (ibid., my transl. Compare also what was said<br>above about Guan Zi)

Hu quotes such a variety of such proposals according to the characterization of goods as 'light' and 'heavy'. For instance: the state administers the provision of corn; by opening the granaries, corn is rendered 'light' and money 'heavy'. Hu writes: 'The 'light-heavy'-theory is somewhat like equilibrium analysis in modern economics. According to the modern theory, however, the process occurs spontaneously, while according to the *Guan Zi*, the equilibrium must be managed by the state' (Hu 1988, p. 127). The author of the *Guan Zi* advocates such state intervention for three reasons: for the advantage of the people, for the profit of the state, and for the evening-out of prices. The expression always remains visual: in good years, corn becomes so 'light', that the pigs eat it, in the bad ones so 'heavy', that one sees people dying of hunger in the streets (ibid.).

Goods always should be kept 'heavy' in international comparison to prevent their outflow. There are however arguments in *Guan Zi* in favour of the export of commodities such as salt, in exchange for obtaining gold; for this purpose they have to be 'light'.

The possibility not only of ironing out price fluctuations, but also keeping them constant by means of state trade is explicitly mentioned in *Guan Zi*, but rejected as an exaggeration:

> There are four seasons in a year and tax is paid four times. When the state decrees at each season that taxes be collected the 'lightness' or 'heaviness' of things may vary tenfold to a hundredfold. Hence it is unnecessary to stabilise the prices of things permanently, and that is why I say the balancing of prices is not reliable.
>
> (Guan Zi cited in Hu 1988, p. 139)

However, the hope is expressed that the state may in this way appropriate profits which are otherwise made by merchants, and that in this way the state will be able to reduce taxes ('the common people need pay no tax', ibid., p. 140). The monopoly of salt (the state controls the production of salt, and to some extent salt markets) and of iron are to be established for fiscal purposes. It is argued that salt and iron are indispensable to the population, so that such imposts cannot be evaded. The state can profit also from the forests, but taxation shall not here be too burdensome; for instance, the poor population should be able to obtain cheaply wood for coffins.

The state needs data to conduct such a programme. The prince needs to know how many farmers live in each village, which qualities of lands are available, how many women are working at the looms, and he must also know what land reserves exist to be endowed upon retired soldiers (ibid., pp. 148–50). Parsimony and redistribution are advocated, but the unequal distribution of wealth and income is an economic necessity; the princes must spend in order to employ the people. If more employment is necessary, one can for example prolong state mourning: 'To make a large and beautiful tomb would employ many poor people ... to make big coffins would require more carpenters and to increase in number the expensive clothing of the dead would engage more female hands' (ibid., p. 118, compare Rickett 1965, p. 319). If this is not enough: 'Additional outer decoration of the coffin and of the grave, more trees at the burial place, and more precious and valuable things as burial objects can be tried' (Hu 1988, p. 118). Is this not the same thought as in Keynes: 'Two pyramids, two masses for the dead, are twice as good as one; but not so two railways from London to York?' (1967 [1936], p. 131). Keynes argues without any proof that it might be possible to interpret the funeral rites of oriental societies as policies for increasing employment; here we see a confirmation of his insight. When I read this passage in Keynes for the first time years ago I thought it to be an example of the cynicism so often encountered among economists. But Plutarch tells us that Pericles also thought of the employment effect when he had the Parthenon built. However, the consideration of religious art as an ornament which can be multiplied at will is, to the best of my knowledge, not to be found among ancient Greeks.

The economic ideas of the *Guan Zi* reappeared in the history of Chinese economic thought in time and again, related to the use of monetary policy and that of grain storage. If the state imposes taxes money will become scarce, therefore 'heavy', goods become 'light' and the state is unable to buy grain for store. There are therefore two superimposed cycles (state expenditure and taxation on the one hand, the harvest on the other). The task is to take advantage of their interaction – one does not dare say to 'optimise' them, since utilities and disutilities of the most diverse actors have to be balanced.

The great opponents of the Confucians were the Legalists. The *Guan Zi* has been said to represent a middle way between the two (Binswanger 1997); W. Allyn Rickett (1965, 1985) classifies parts of *Guan Zi* as legalist. The philosopher Karl Jaspers famously compared the teaching of Confucius, of Socrates, of Jesus, and of Buddha, and pointed to the weakening of Confucianism in the centuries after the death of the master (Jaspers 1967 [1964]).

Confucius' ideas were handed down in a dogmatized form, the emphasis on humanism yielded to utilitarianism and his philosophical thought became formalized and resulted in enforced laws. Finally, the principle of saving face showed how superficial his philosophy had become in practice.

The legalists in the period of the Warring States, especially Shang Yang (around 390–338 BC), sought to control the population through their interests and guide them by laws. The populace shall not become too rich, and all shall work according to a system of rewards and punishments. Crimes are to be prosecuted through a system of group responsibility and denunciation. Ten neighbouring families have to guarantee jointly that none of their members violates the law. Agricultural production is the basis of warfare, and agriculturalists are better soldiers. Shang Yang therefore advocates a policy of high prices for agricultural products (Hu 1988, pp. 185–96). Han Fei (third century BC) derives the interests of people from their economic positions. They work for the sake of profits: 'Hence, a cartwright who makes carriages desires other people to become rich and noble, while a carpenter who makes coffins desires people to die even when young' (Hu 1988, p. 198). The Smithian insight, according to which we do not expect our meat and bread from butcher and baker as a result of their benevolence, but from their own interests, is here expressed most pointedly in the example of the coffin maker. Common interest is also assumed in the case of collaboration. The ruler should not believe himself able to perpetually and completely satisfy his people – the people remains insatiable. Han Fei gives an example which anticipates the Malthusian law (Zinn 1997) of the multiplication of population according to a geometric rate; people become 'too many' (Hu 1988, pp. 200–2).

The image of strong rule would be based on the legend of the Yellow Emperor; in 1973 the following text was found in a tomb of the Han dynasty:

> The ruler stands facing south. His ministers are sombre and reverential; none dare to hide [any secret] from him. The inferiors are obedient and dare not to hide [any secret] from their superiors. The myriad people live in peace and harmony, and are eager to serve their ruler. Possessing a vast territory, a teeming population, and a strong army, the ruler is matchless in the world.
>
> (Fu 1996, p. 131)

The early legalists at least regarded the teaching of virtues on the part of Confucianism as useless and even harmful. The ruler must use his power without regard, even it is may seem useful to him to feign love for his subjects. Books can be dangerous. The wise ruler claims the merits of his ministers for himself and lets them take responsibility for mistakes. The legalist's totalitarian art of rule had delayed consequences in university textbooks of the 1980s, where it is written: 'The burning of books and burying alive of Confucian scholars played positive roles in the consolidation of political unity' (ibid., p. 131).

### Salt and iron

The *Debate on Salt and Iron* by Huan Kuan of 81 BC (there is little we know about him and about the accuracy of his rendering of the event) represents a response on the part of Confucians (Confucianism having become a state religion under emperor Wu, who reigned from 140 to 87 BC) to Sang Hongyang (who lived from 152 to 80 BC) in the year 81 BC. In itself the debate is not without drama, for several times the scholars manage to find arguments which render the arrogant imperial counsellor speechless. There is an evident contrast between his own riches and the relative poverty of the scholars. The debate takes place in the presence of an emperor who, being 13 years old and the son of the last concubine of the preceding emperor Wu, remains silent. We should also know that there is enmity between the general Huo Guang, the most important personality in the government, and Sang Hongyang. A few months later, Sang Hongyang will be executed for his alleged participation in a conspiracy against the emperor. Less important is the first Minister Tian Qianqiu, who is also present (Loewe 1993, Mende 2002). What we know about the author and the history of the text is described in Mende (2002, pp. 57–60).

Sang Hongyang seems to have shown remarkable gifts for calculation in his early youth and was introduced to trading practices as to help his father, a merchant (Loewe 1974, p. 20). He says during the debate that he has had the honour of serving the imperial house for more than 60 years in various positions, and now as minister (he had begun at the age of 13). He states that he has received many favours and rewards from his monarch that he also has had to spend on carriages, horses, dresses, the maintenance of his family, servants, but that he has nonetheless gradually built a fortune. The scholars challenge this proud self-representation, and point to older times when it was not permitted to accumulate offices, nor use their proceeds for private enterprise (Walter 1991 [1978], pp. 119ff.). In fact, in the early Han period, merchants and even their descendents were not allowed to become officials. This prohibition was no longer observed after the middle of the second century BC, but the origins of Sang Hongyang may still have been a provocation to Confucians engaged in the debate (Mende 2002, p. 62). Sang Hongyang is a Confucian in the larger meaning of the term, according to Chen (1974 [1911], p. 557), but he clearly often takes a more legalist position and develops the economic ideas of the *Guan Zi*. In particular, it is a historical fact that he further developed the idea of evening-out price fluctuations and proposed a procedure for controlling prices at a national level, described as follows in the economic chapter of the history text *Han Shu*:

> Sang Hongyang, [at that time] ... (a subordinate of the ministry of agriculture) became acting chief of the ministry [in 110 BC] ... in control of salt and iron throughout the empire. [Sang] Hongyang considered that government offices ... wrangled in competition, and that merchandise for this reason [rose] by leaps and bounds, and that [furthermore], when

imperial poll taxes … were transported, at times they did not compensate for the cost of cartage. Then he proposed [the following:] that 'there be established in the ministry of agriculture as assistants several tens of men. [Let] them be divided into sections to have charge in provinces and fiefs, where from time to time in each [according to the need] there would be set up … (offices for equalization of prices through transportation); and offices for salt and/or iron. [Let] orders be given that in places far distant [from the capital], each in lieu of poll taxes deliver [for sale by local authorities] in other places load after load of its native products which in the past have been carted out of the locality for sale by travelling traders and resident merchants. In the imperial capital [as central office] establish the … (office for standardization of prices) to receive [paid up taxes from sale of goods, or merchandise in lieu thereof], transported cartload after cartload from all over the empire. Call upon the office of labour [subordinate to the ministry of agriculture] to manufacture carts and the several [kinds of] equipment. [Let] all [the above agencies] look for sustenance to the ministry of agriculture. [Allow] the several officers of the ministry to corner completely the money and merchandise of the empire. When prices are high, then they will sell; when prices are low, then they will buy. In this manner will rich traders and great merchants lose that by which they gained excessive profits. Then will [the people] return to the fundamental (that is, agricultural pursuits); and [prices of] merchandise of all sorts will have no chance [to rise] by leaps and bounds. By these means [prices of] all the merchandise of every kind throughout the empire will be restrained. [Let] the name [of the system] be the … (standardization of prices).' The Son of Heaven looked upon [the plan] as right, and gave his approval.

(Swann 1950, pp. 314–6)

This is how the state tried to supplant private trade, to appropriate its profits; it used the buying and selling of goods delivered as taxes for this purpose. There was moreover the goal of evening-out prices, which is clearly expressed in the above quotation. What is not clear is how it was thought that the contradiction between the aim of maintaining stable, low prices and the existence of taxation might be reconciled.

Sang Hongyang's interventionism is also evident in his insistence on state property in natural resources, of forests and waterways in particular. These monopolies were also used to extend infrastructure, to support private activities and simultaneously to improve the fiscal position of the state; by for example improving the imperial gardens.

Salt was mainly produced by private enterprise, according to Hu (1988, pp. 264–6); and it had soon been made subject to taxation. The large iron salt pans were provided by the state when the salt monopoly was instituted. Salt was then bought at fixed prices, and the state acted as wholesale dealer. The monopoly of iron – still more important – comprehended both production and sale (Hu 1988, p. 266) – the equipment of private ironforgers being confiscated and ironsmiths punished. State control of iron production began with the mines and ended only with the selling of finished implements. As a consequence the state also controlled the production of weapons. Mines and iron works were probably in remote areas where groups of a few hundred people worked, for a great deal of charcoal was needed – this was the limiting resource, since iron was transported, not wood or charcoal (Wagner 1993, pp. 257–9). Details of the administrative structure of the offices for salt and iron are known from bamboo documents which have been found (Vogel 2002, p. 81). The institution of the state monopoly of iron seems in part to have been a reaction to the concentration of power in the hands of princes and merchants who had had private control over the relevant resources and their exploitation in earlier centuries (ibid., p. 86). The history books report that the monopoly was repeatedly violated by rich entrepreneurs in the Han period. The state, on the other hand, used different forms of organization: wage labour, forced labour and even military production are mentioned in the sources (ibid., pp. 87–8).

The economist will ask why state activity was extended to such a degree, and may suppose that it was a response to an economic and fiscal crisis. Loewe (1974, pp. 17–36) demonstrates in fact that the position of China under the Han had been better 20 years earlier. The difficulties were not only economic, there were also political and strategic threats. The realm was under attack from the North. There were domestic tensions and palace intrigues – one group sought to eliminate another, by for instance accusing it of witchcraft (ibid., pp. 37–90). One can admire the determination and realism of the imperial counsellor, but the moral rigour of the Confucians needs to be interpreted as a response to arbitrary government in a dangerous period of crisis.

An economist would not be surprised that there was opposition to the recurring failures of state enterprise. The debate reports that essential goods had become more expensive, that farmers suffered from lack of salt and had in part returned to the use of wooden spades. The poor quality of commodities is deplored in the debate, sales are said to be badly organized, clients allegedly are urged to buy iron implements since otherwise those selling for the state cannot fulfil their quotas. Hu believes that more than a hundred thousand persons were employed in the iron monopoly. He would like to see this as a pioneering achievement of Chinese planning, but has to recognize that there was the criticism as well. He writes: 'These censures might tally with the objective facts, because they were unavoidable consequences of government-operated business under feudalism' (Hu 1988, p. 267). But under which system is state administration more efficient than 'under feudalism'? On the other hand, Sang Hongyang's mechanism to equalize prices favoured market relationships, insofar as deliveries in kind were to be sold on the market to a greater extent and not so frequently be brought to the capital. Moreover, the *Debate on Salt and Iron* cannot be interpreted as a discussion between a minister inclined to planning and an opposition favouring the market economy. The Confucians recall older forms of state economy in pre-monetary times.

Sang Hongyang is more liberal as far as foreign trade is concerned. He recognizes the advantages of a regional and international division of labour and shows no scruples in making use of them by trading; although the examples he presents necessarily concern luxury goods, for long distance trade in goods related to everyday needs was rendered impractical on account o the high transport costs involved.

The reader will regard the responses by scholars to Sang Hongyang's arguments on foreign policy as strange, indeed as incomprehensible. They pretend that the threat from the northern peoples is irrelevant, so long as one remains virtuous. The scholars probably wished simply to deal honestly (virtuously) with the tribes and to win their friendship with gifts. Loewe identified the conflict between the agrarian Chinese empire and the nomadic tribes as the rational kernel of the argument. Sang Hongyang argued in favour of strengthening the northern frontier through colonization. But these colonies were vulnerable to nomadic attacks, and only major expeditions could seriously menace the mounted nomads, who could easily withdraw when confronted by smaller defending units. And sending armies deep into the vast northern spaces was expensive (Loewe 1974, pp. 96–9).

The northern Hsiung-nu barbarians (commonly identified with the Huns) represented a recurring threat. The Ch'in, the dynasty preceding that of the Han, had already tried to occupy the north, but agriculture did not produce enough, the women were not able to spin and weave sufficient cloth for tents and clothing, the colonists were ruined and a rebellion followed. Hence the emperor Wen of the Han dynasty (179–159 BC) refused to follow the advice of his general and reinforce the north again; he preferred a passive form of defence, which may have been a model for what the Confucian scholars had to say in the debate (Elvin 1973, p. 27). All China would have been affected by the necessary increase in taxation. Davis, the representative of British imperialism in Hong Kong, thought however that the barbarian invasions called for a military response (although he had in mind later invasions). He felt that paying tribute to the Tartars dishonoured China and that such a policy, if followed by a dynasty, would eventually bring about its ruin (Davis 1847–48, vol. 3, p. 155).

It is not therefore so easy to determine who was right in the long run. The sympathy of the chronicler or author Huan Kuan is with the Confucians – Loewe (1974, p. 106) counts 11 occasions in the debate as a whole in which the representatives of the government fail to find a response. The monopolies – which were the immediate cause for concern – were abolished: that of alcoholic beverages at once, the salt and iron monopoly was to be suspended (44–41 BC), until it eventually was abandoned during a period when China had no central government, after the Han (ibid., p. 112). The question of whether money should be privately minted or issued by the state would recur for many centuries. Granaries existed up to the nineteenth century; and the granary system (which still provided occasional relief under the Manchu or Ch'ing) has been studied extensively.[17]

Kroll (1978–9, p. 16) emphasizes the limits of Sang Hongyang's realism: 'his world-view never severed its ties to the ancient Chinese model of a world in which the imitation of Heaven plays an outstanding role'. It can be shown that Sang Hongyang really did advocate redistribution from the rich to the poor, adhering to a universalist conception of balance that is, as indicated above, present in the canonical books.

But Sang Hongyang appeared as a modernizer to Confucians for whom every innovation had to be weighed against the old and the venerable. When for example indirect taxation via the price-equalization mechanism was praised because it reduced merchants' profits (to which Confucians especially objected), the scholars replied: 'In earlier times, one used to tax activities of the people which they knew, and not activities which they did not know' (K'uan 2002, p. 116, my transl.). The Confucians mean that taxes had earlier been paid in kind, from domestic agricultural and textile production which was tangible, whereas the scholars thought that the unpredictable new system of markets and payments in money caused farmers to sell too quickly, so that they might have the cash needed to pay the new taxes. And speculation on the part of traders is not eliminated, for if the government buys, prices rise, and traders who hold reserves can then sell at favourable terms. Sang Hongyang responds that it is not enough in a changing world to refer to a moral order; it is necessary to change the laws.

This contrast also shows in the discussion over monetary matters. Sang Hongyang believes that the issue of coins by the state was an essential reform; the scholars point to the fact that changes in monetary policy can be postulated, understood and anticipated by experienced merchants who profit from the withdrawal of better coins from circulation; the older system of barter was more transparent for everybody. Here we can see that Gresham's law was well understood even in the earliest times. During the European Middle Ages Oresmius understood clearly that merchants were better able to respond to changes in monetary policy than the general public.[18] This discussion (which could be interpreted to be about the unequal distribution of information) leads on to the question of whether policy can depend on a sufficient number of capable officials; Sang Hongyang tries to reassure his listeners, but the scholars voice doubts: 'Not one of the higher officials so far has asked to abolish the superfluous offices and to dismiss profiteers. Since this problem remained unsolved for such a long time the people focussed their hopes on the emperor' (K'uan 2002, p. 132, my transl.). But the emperor was still very young.

The debate as a whole reflects a number of oppositions (following Mende 2002, pp. 65–6):

Sang Hongyang starts from pragmatic considerations, his opponents from superior principles of humanity and justice; both claim that they want to reduce the plight of the people.

Sang Hongyang favours trade and industry (handicraft) and seeks the support of the state for the development of resources, while his opponents wish to see the primacy of agriculture reinforced.

Sang Hongyang believes in the necessity of military expansion and consolidation, in order to keep down China's rivals for the domination of Eastern
Asia. He wants secure borders and a market for Chinese surpluses. His
opponents favour a more passive foreign policy, since an active policy puts a
heavy burden on the people in terms of forced labour and taxation.

Sang Hongyang wants to have technically competent officials appointed,
while his opponents wish to select officials according to character and their
adherence to Confucian principles.

Sang Hongyang argues that the state monopolies tend to raise the general
standard of living, secure state revenues and reduce the excessive riches of a
few. His opponents reject an orientation to profit and utilitarian considerations as independent principles, but they also doubt the efficiency of the
monopolies. The expansion of the money economy is regarded as a threat to
the agricultural way of life.

Sang Hongyang points to the growth of cities and the abundance of luxury
goods as justifications for his policy, while his opponents see only repressive
government monopolies of power, economic inequality, corruption, bureaucratic
tendencies, and a resulting impoverishment of agricultural areas.

The debate remains open but moves in circles – in the 28th chapter Sang
Hongyang's secretary deplores the manner in which arguments are not dealt
with successively; to this the scholars make no response. Important arguments
are not made at once, but left until later. For example, only in the 15th chapter
is it shown, when discussing something unrelated, how the middle social
strata got into the difficulties noted earlier: rich families were able to withhold
taxes because the tax collectors were afraid of them, poor farmers abandoned
their villages because cultivation had ceased to be profitable, increasing pressure
on the middle stratum. Sang Hongyang observes that it is not enough just to
talk, one must also be able to act. The Confucians reply that if action had
been just they would not have had to express the concerns that they had
(K'uan 2002, p. 183).

### On some later developments

We return to Hu's *Concise History of Chinese Economic Thought* and add a few
observations on the progress of economic thought in China. It is consistent
with Elvin's description of a Chinese medieval economic revolution that Su
Shi (AD 1036–1101) proposed to leave the equalization of prices entirely to
free trade – he is said to have been the first to seek an alternative to the system
of grain storage run by the state. Su Shi also observed that time is important
for traders: he suggests than merchants increase their profit by delaying payment
when they buy, and bringing forward the timing of payments when they sell.

Most important were the monetary ideas connected with the introduction
of paper money and credit. The old vision that the quantity of money influenced the level of prices was refined. Shen Kuo (1031–1095) saw that money
might become scarce because of population growth, and that there was

inevitable wastage as coins were either lost or became worn, making an increase in the supply of coins necessary. He also thought that circulation should be favoured and hoarding discouraged, and he discussed the disadvantages of an outflow of coinage in favour of the foreign peoples in the north (Hu 1988, p. 391). Burns (1965 [1927], p. 293) is convinced that the purchasing power of copper money could not greatly deviate from their metallic value, since when the metallic value exceeded their face value they would be melted down, or they would conversely be counterfeited. The quantity theory only holds between these two somewhat indefinite limits, but which still provides an intermediate zone in which the state can gain from depreciation, price rises, the introduction of new coins and the withdrawal of old coinage.

The Chinese conception of 'light' and 'heavy' money now seemed to hover between a quantity of money and a metallist position; but it remained adequate for discussion of simple problems of monetary policy. Zhou Xingji in twelfth century China is said to have been the first explicit metallist. Hu (1988, p. 397) quotes the following sentence from him: 'The government issued big copper money with the par value of ten coins but with the intrinsic value of only three coins. Its par value will fall to three coins eventually.' Zhou Xingji also advocated paper money, which should be convertible into metal coin, provided a sufficient reserve was kept. Paper money had first been used in Sichuan – notes replaced the local circulation of heavy iron coins; and these notes were first issued by private persons around AD 1.000 (Hu 1988, pp. 400ff.).

The paper money of the merchants was issued on promise to pay in cash, and this is also how the issuing of state paper money began. The circulation of paper money became a national phenomenon in the twelfth century, and played a significant role under Mongol rule. Marco Polo observed it during his travels. His comparison of the emission of paper money with alchemy is reminiscent of the second part of Goethe's *Faust*, where the printing of paper money fulfils the earlier promise to make gold – and of course this use of paper money has inflationary consequences. Marco Polo also describes the production of the special paper used for the notes and their printing, and he states that nobody dared refuse them as means of payment (Lemke 1908, p. 268). Foreign caravans also accept this money, but they buy other commodities with it before leaving China. He continues with the observation that the troops of the imperial majesty are paid in this way; hence the Mongol emperor seems to be the richest monarch in the world (Lemke 1908, p. 269).

Marco Polo reported that old paper money could be exchanged against new paper at a charge of 3 per cent. This had in fact been regulated in 1287 in an ordinance translated and commented upon by Herbert Franke (1949). This decree fixed an exchange rate between old and new money in the proportion 5 : 1 and contained detailed prescriptions regarding the duty of the public to accept the money in various forms of business. The government held reserves of the precious metals, but prohibited private trade in gold or silver. Such trade was basically to be punished by confiscating the property of the trader combined with some corporal punishment; but the punishment for counterfeiting was death.

The reserve seemed to guarantee the value of the circulating paper, but the prohibition of private trade in metal made the reserve irrelevant. Officials educated in the Confucian tradition expressed their scepticism: 'When paper money was first printed, silver was taken as a basis. Nominal and real value stood in a fixed relationship; now, after more than twenty years, this relationship … has shifted and is ten times what it was' (ibid., p. 155, my transl.). And:

> Clearly, if one tries to fix a relation of value in the introduction of new paper money for the old, this is only an exchange of denominations. If neither gold nor silver are used as the primitive value relationship and if the military expenditures of the state are not again reduced, the new paper money will be just as valueless as the old after three or more years.
>
> (ibid., p. 116, my transl.)

Franke thought the main cause of inflation during the final years of the dynasty lay in state deficits. One can add that the state budget would not have shown such extreme deficits if the issue of paper money had been limited, and the trade in the precious metals freed.

Wang Yi (fourteenth century) proposed the private minting of gold and silver coin. This had been an expression of the sovereignty of trading cities like Florence and Venice in the West. Earlier, minting golden coins was a prerogative of the emperor of Constantinople; then there were also the golden coins of Frederick II. These gold coins were stable standards of value, relative to which the inflation of debased coins issued by local princes and other cities in Europe was evident. China later made a transition to the use of silver in the fifteenth and sixteenth century. Up to this period:

> the crucial role of the state in managing the supply of money in order to balance the exchange ratios between money and commodities and satisfy the needs of both producers and consumers remained beyond dispute. From early times Chinese political economists recognised that modest inflation stimulated production, while deflation caused hardship to primary producers. Therefore the proper role of the state was to issue money in sufficient quantities to insure stable, or gradually rising, prices.
>
> (Glahn 1996, p. 47)

### Concluding remarks on Chinese economic thought

The logic of Chinese economic discussions thus seems to have followed a course somewhat different from that of the West. The core of Western economic theory is the analysis of prices and incomes. The normal postulate of a uniform price was first the norm of the just price. There then followed the natural price, made up of the incomes which this price covered, and eventually there emerged the normal long-run price. The theory of distribution, accompanying the explanation of the natural price, revealed a conflict between classes which neoclassical theory tried to overcome by means of the theory of marginal productivity. The debate over usury played a decisive role in the origin of this theory or, rather, chain of theories, for the debate over usury led to the question of how incomes could be justified in ways other than by work.

The Chinese theories considered here recognized the state to be the central agent in the economy, whereas in European discussions of the just price and usury the state plays no central role. These differences exist, although Europe also had to account for the origins of agrarian society in the beginning, with some growth of handicraft and trade. Grain storage under the supervision of the state plays some part in the European tradition – the feudal lord is under some obligation to provide for his serfs, and there was discussion of village-based granaries or, in *ancien régime* France, state granaries. But European grain storage was mainly regulated by trade, and it was not the resulting price fluctuations which were denounced, but usury. Should we say that the Chinese were more reasonable, because they did not engage in hair-splitting scholastic discussions about usury? Or should we follow what a liberal modern economist might say in criticism of the early Chinese authors, for trying the wrong solution, state trading?

We could also consider the form of the theory, and see an advantage either in the deductive nature of the Western theory, or in the more immediate integration of abstract economic principles with social considerations in the East.

Perhaps we should not dwell too much on such simple dichotomies, and point again to some of the remarkable early insights of Chinese economic literature in the Han period. The quantity of money is seen to matter. At the same time, it is noted that traders have an advantage over the general public during a time of debasement since they are in a position to select good coins. The Confucians insist that excessive taxation will lower revenue. It has been observed that Chapters 6 and 36 of the *Debate on Salt and Iron* discuss scale economies of the concentration of production (Sang Hongyang's point of view) and the possibility of adapting goods to the wishes of clients in handicraft production (the Confucian point of view). It has also been shown, analysing early Chinese textbooks of calculation, that Sang Hongyang's system of the equalization of prices implied concrete problems of calculation at the level of the rule of proportion, or rule of three (Wagner 2001). A challenging task for the future might be to describe the programmatic rationality behind the economic policy expressed in the *Debate on Salt and Iron*.

One inevitably returns to the most pressing question: what has remained? There is the legacy of Confucianism, there is also that of legalism. Vogel (2002) analyses the continuing reception of the *Debate on Salt and Iron* in the People's Republic of China, listing seven recent editions (2002, p. 102). Mao identified with the legalists, and the *Debate on Salt and Iron* was re-interpreted in the light of the cultural revolution; essentially, the Confucian scholars were regarded as deceitful and Sang Hongyang as progressive. More varied interpretations followed later, and continue to be published. We do not expect the individual economic ideas of ancient authors to retain their relevance, but patterns of thought are more durable, and the classic texts of a culture continue to influence contemporary education. We can therefore have good reasons to be interested in the history of Chinese economic thought; and it also represents a large and fascinating part of a universal history of economic thought which is today slowly becoming better known.

### The Japanese author Miura Baien

My commentary to the Japanese classic *Kagen* by Miura Baien in the series *Klassiker der Nationalökonomie* was also an attempt to present the author and his work in a broad historical and cultural context.

### Japanese culture and the West

Every European observer is struck by the success of Japanese development – still the only major country outside the European tradition which has become an advanced economy. The Japanese ascent from an isolated island empire to world importance was essentially based on an extremely rapid transformation process occurring during the lifetime of one generation in the last third of the nineteenth century – the consequences of this would be a source of fascination throughout the twentieth century. The first visible surprise was Japan's military victory over Russia in 1905; the next, the success of Japan's exports after the First World War. There followed the menace of colonial expansion prior to and during the Second World War. Following another period of rapid growth, Japanese per capita income has now reached that of the Western countries. Cultural differences continue to be felt, however. The spread of Western technology and Western forms of civilization did not displace Japanese culture, but led to a unique synthesis. Some comments on cultural heritage might be of help here.

One of the most famous Japanese traditions is Zen Buddhism, with its exercises in meditation and self-control. They can be seen in Japanese monasteries, Japanese sports like archery, Japanese gardens and Japanese writing. Extreme patience, endurance and concentration are demanded from those who wish to participate in traditions radiating into social and even economic life, for Japanese businesses also depend on these virtues. The precision of Japanese work, of handicraft products, the spirit of community are often mentioned in this context. Similarly there is a synthesis in Japanese art, combining elements of an older style of painting, providing a creative basis for modern art. Wooden temples demand frequent renovation. Local celebrations are observed, and Japanese theatre performs traditional plays not – as seems now almost generally to be the case in the West – transfigured with modern forms of expression, but in which play, dance and recital follow defined artistic traditions. The beauty and cheer of Kabuki impresses, but the tragic majesty of Nô theatre is overwhelming (Zeami 1991 [1960]).

A different synthesis would have resulted if Japan had not been closed for 250 years prior to modernization. The West knew very little about the country in those days. Montesquieu, to whom news of China was so important as a contrast to European monarchies, reported only on Japanese forms of punishment and remarked that the closure of the country to the outside world could lead to a distorted form of development: 'Les Japonais ne commercent qu'avec deux nations, la Chinoise et la Hollandaise ... Toute nation qui se conduira sur les maximes Japonaises sera nécessairement trompée. C'est la concurrence qui met un prix juste aux marchandises...' (Montesquieu 1793, vol. 2, p. 132).[19]

Adolf Muschg, the Swiss writer, has described the 'isolated station in the harbour of the fishing village Nagasaki where the Dutch had their settlement ... The Japanese understood that they had first to adopt firearms' (Muschg 1995, p. 108, my transl.). What the Europeans learned 'did not spread beyond learned circles, whereas European know-how ... which seeped into Japan, covertly prepared the revolution' (ibid., p. 120).

Kurt Singer, a German economist of Jewish descent who was highly thought of by Keynes and was also a friend of the poet Stefan George, spent 'a hundred months' as a visitor and later emigre in Japan. He wrote a book (Singer 1973, 1996 [1991])[20] on Japanese characteristics which has been described as the best of its kind. The strangeness of Japan, felt by so many travellers since the sixteenth century, is reduced to a 'connection of meanings', which provide a rigorous 'formative unity' to cultural phenomena: the poems, the buildings, the pictures, the gardens (Singer 1996 [1991], p. 235, my transl.). 'Civilisation in the Far East centres round ceremony and etiquette conceived as a ritual ordering life both in human and non-human sphere' (Singer 1973, p. 111; 1996 [1991], p. 261). The Chinese *Book of Rites* (Li-ji) states: 'Music is the expression of harmony of heaven and earth. Ritual is the expression of the hierarchical order in heaven and earth' (Singer 1996, pp. 261ff., my transl.). Singer (1973, pp. 162–163; 1996 [1991], p. 321) concedes that Japanese rites are simpler and more spontaneous. But the severe style of rites, morals and the images of an honourable life became a national ethos as it extended from the nobility to the bourgeoisie during the Edo-period, and later. The 'polite society' has certainly persisted.

Conversely, Japan felt the difference of the West. Fukuzawa's (1971) autobiography expresses it very well; his life ran from his youth as a member of a poor samurai family under the old regime to the founding of Keio University, in which modern Western science was first systematically taught. Fukuzawa had been educated in the tradition of Confucianism, was well read in the Chinese and Japanese classics; but he learned Dutch and English, accompanied the first Japanese mission to the United States as an interpreter in 1860, also visited Europe in the same capacity and finally made a significant career as chancellor of the university which he had founded and as a writer of numerous works on economics, politics, history, and other matters of science and of daily life. He always sought a way of overcoming the traditional order, and how one might lead an independent way of life. Daily practice and education had to change immediately. When Fukuzawa first reached the United States he was astonished less by technology than by customs: that for example good manners dictated that women should have precedence, or that no special honours were conferred on the descendants of the founder of the state, George Washington. His readiness to accept what was new led to conflict with the Tokugawa government. He had for instance to translate the word 'competition' into Japanese and chose the Japanese character for 'strife'. The official for whom the translation was made took offence at the idea that 'strife' among merchants regulated prices not only in Western countries, but also in Japan. There was no strife in the empire! The word had to be left untranslated in the submitted text (ibid., p. 218–20).

Fukuzawa summarized as follows:

> with regard to national riches, military strength, and the greatest happiness for the greatest possible number of people, the East is to be ranked below the West. If these differences are due to national strength in the education of people, there necessarily must be a difference in the form of education of both. If one compares the Confucianism of the East with the civilisation of the Occident, one recognises that the orient lacks two points, physics in the material sphere and the idea of independence in the spiritual realm.
>
> (ibid., p. 248, my transl.)

Fukuzawa concluded that a mere opening-up of the country would not be enough; it was necessary to overcome the Confucian orientation in education, and his own private school, the later Keio university, was reorganized according to rational principles. But even in the Meiji period there were well-known scholars who cherished the idea of a renewed closure of Japan, desiring to preserve the existing order of life and, and in particular, to keep out technical innovations which threatened traditional handicraft (Sugiyama 1994, p. 1).

Fukuzawa today is generally considered to be the most important historical personality in the diffusion of Western economic thought in Japan. He advocated laissez-faire and free trade (Ikeo 2001). The pursuit of profit, traditionally considered negatively, was now interpreted as striving for the order of good behaviour (*li*), and he provided the English translation: 'fighting for profit is nothing but fighting for *li*' (Kumagai 1998, p. 30). He thus used Confucian concepts to displace Confucianism. He partly held Western culture in high regard for its own sake, but partly he also despised it. He deplored the colonization of India, and observed the beginning of the subjugation of China. He was afraid for Japan and while he first saw the adoption of Western culture as a means to strengthen Japan, he later saw it as a means of reaching beyond the islands to become a colonizer in turn.

Miura Baien[21] is a classical author of the Edo period. Various intellectual currents of his epoch come together in him: his Confucian notions of social life, his fundamental interest in philosophy (together with some interest in

Western natural science), his understanding of economic laws and the super-imposed norm of the preservation of a traditional social order. He belonged to the classical authors of the Edo period who influenced the Meiji reformers. Fukazawa testified:

> Baien was the teacher of my grandfather, and I, too, have always venerated him highly. He reached astonishing insights in questions of politics and economics, and also in astronomy, geography and other areas, which made him the leading scholar of Japan.
>
> (Komuro 2001, p. 98)

This section of the essay follows what I wrote as an introduction to the commentary volume for Miura Baien in the *Klassiker der Nationalökonomie* (Schefold 2001). I should like to thank my co-authors of that volume: Günther Distelrath and Josef Kreiner, Masamichi Komuro, Kiichiro Yagi and Hidetomi Tanaka, and Kurt Dopfer. What follows is an inadequate attempt to learn from them.

### The Japanese economy in the Edo period

Modern economic history attempts to assess the living standards even of pre-modern economies in quantitative terms. Maddison (1995) emphasizes that Asian countries made up the greater part of the world economy around 1820, with 69 per cent of the world's population and 57 per cent of the world's gross domestic product. These countries were fairly similar at that time, but the gross domestic product per head in Japan was 27 times that of Bangladesh in 1992. Maddison also stresses that China had more developed technology in the early and high Middle Ages than that of Europe. By the nineteenth century India had become a colony, China was reduced to a quasi-colony, while the Japanese created the pre-conditions for catching up. The following table for gross domestic product per head is based upon Maddison (ibid., pp. 194–206, p. 163) and my own calculations.

These figures, primitive as they are, show how the catching-up process in Japan led to equality with the West only very recently and that Japan was

*Table 5.1* Gross domestic product per head

| Year | Germany | USA | Japan | China | India |
| --- | --- | --- | --- | --- | --- |
| 1820 | 1,112 | 1,287 | 704 | 523 | 531 |
| 1870 | 1,913 | 2,457 | 741 | 523 | 558 |
| 1920 | 2,986 | 5,559 | 1,631 | n.a. | 629 |
| 1970 | 11,933 | 14,854 | 9,448 | 1,092 | 878 |
| 1994 | 19,097 | 22,569 | 19,505 | 3,098* | 1,348* |

Note: *1992. The values are expressed in 1990 Geary-Khamis-Dollars, which take account of differences in purchasing power.

already richer on average than China and India during the Edo period. The level of wealth of those early times can at least be compared quantitatively with that of African countries today. According to Maddison, Egypt reached the level of $700 per capita around 1960; Ethiopia, like Japan once an empire, fell to a level of $300 in 1992, having reached a level of $410 in 1972.

We now turn to the Edo period itself, to see the extent to which a foundation for later developments was laid. Japan had a greater population in the first half of the seventeenth century than each individual European country, and this population grew rapidly – only China under the Ming dynasty and the empire of the Moghul in India were larger. There had been peace since 1615. The country was more closely controlled and centralized than European states. The Shogun controlled directly about 25 per cent of the territory; the remainder was divided among about 250 princely vassals (daimyô). About four-fifths of the population remained occupied in agriculture, but subsidiary agricultural and handicraft activities increased, and about one-sixth of the population lived in cities of more than 3,000 inhabitants. Edo, the centre of Tokugawa rule, is said to have been the biggest metropolis of the world in those days.

Early on barter and deliveries in kind were important. Deliveries by farmers made it possible to pay the Samurai – who were for the most part no longer living on their own land – in rice. Warriors became officials, dependent on their prince, if they still had one. The rice delivered was sold to merchants in the cities, and the monetary economy grew. Not only merchants had wholesalers concentrated in Osaka, institutions such as bills of exchange, banks, and even futures markets developed. The daimyô, obliged to maintain residences both in their principalities and in Edo, tended to accumulate debts and occasionally even pawned future harvests. Goldsmith (1987, p. 133) has attempted to estimate the wealth of the early Tokugawa period. According to his estimates, gross domestic product per head was 15 grams of gold in Japan around 1616, around 7 grams in Moghul India in 1600, around 67 grams in England and Wales at this time, and 100 grams in the Netherlands around 1650. Goldsmith estimated that real per capita production doubled during the Edo period, with a somewhat higher rate of growth in the seventeenth than in the eighteenth and early nineteenth century.

The system of money and credit which developed had peculiar features. Gold, silver, and copper, later also iron, were used for coinage; rice also possessed some of the functions of money. There was no general trade in bonds and no insurance market, but there was paper money and money substitutes issued by the central government, by a single daimyô, and also by merchants.

Inflationary processes resulted from the debasement of the coinage, as in Europe, and an effort was made to relieve the pressure of higher expenditures by laws against luxury. The society was divided into the four classes of farmers, artisans, merchants and samurai; each was subject to traditions and pre-scriptions regarding their appropriate way of life, and these differences grew more pronounced as Japan closed her borders. The first Tokugawa ruler,

Ieyasu, at first tolerated Catholics, but he then shifted his preference to the Protestant Dutch, who traded without proselytizing; Christians were prosecuted after Ieyasu, and ultimately eradicated. Relations with China were also discontinued because Japan was reluctant to recognize Chinese supremacy, although some trade persisted. Nevertheless the education to which the samurai aspired remained marked by Chinese tradition. A degree of specialization in farming resulted, and the formation of small handicraft enterprises; a stratum of well-to-do artisans, farmers and officials developed in the countryside seeking social advancement. On the other hand, small farmers grew poorer, and had to find complementary work or sell their labour power to the rich, or in the city.

A noted mathematical economist, Michio Morishima, has in a successful book defended the thesis that Japanese successes were owed to a special ethos. He made the connection with Max Weber:

> a remarkably idiosyncratic ethos prevails in Japanese society, and as a result of these ethical feelings Japanese capitalism has to a considerable extent deviated from the typical free enterprise system. The question ... is why the possessors of this kind of non-Western attitude came to gain such control over the industrial techniques produced by the West.
>
> (Morishima 1984 [1982], p. 15)

Morishima's thesis was in short: Confucianism is, like Puritanism, rational in Max Weber's terms; but Puritanism wanted to control the world, while Confucianism adapts to it. The main virtues of Confucianism are benevolence, justice, etiquette, knowledge and trust. Society needs to be governed by a virtuous government, but a constitution and abstract social norms, defended by laws and punishment, are not as important as social models and the exercise of virtue by means of etiquette or ritual (Chinese: *li*, Japanese: *ri*). Hence dignified behaviour is cultivated; and there is shame in deviating from it. Within this context, Japanese Confucianism especially emphasizes military virtues and loyalty. This was based on the continuity of imperial rule, despite this being nominal, given that the Shogun had the real power. Dynasties in China ruled without such a division of authority and changed cyclically, because in exercising their power, they usually provoked revolts and regime changes after a few generations by the increase of expenditure and an exuberant life, increased taxes and weaker defence. Morishima calls Chinese Confucianism humanist, Japanese nationalist. The Chinese bureaucracy, with its literary education, found no way to adapt to modernization; the Japanese, oriented towards the military, were ready to appropriate new technologies.

This ideological pattern was maintained in Japan for centuries. Confucianism was the orthodoxy of government, the people tended to Buddhism, the imperial court to Shintoism. Morisihima interprets Shintoism as a transformation of Chinese Daoism. All three, Confucianism, Buddhism and Daoism, reached Japan almost simultaneously in the sixth century AD Daoism – more rooted in the countryside, more critical of government, closer to the people than Confucianism, with Shamanist traits – produced Shintoism. Morishima differs from prevailing opinion in regarding Shintoism as not simply autochthonous.

We cannot here go into the way in which Morishima delineates the different effects of these religious forces during the various epochs of Japanese society, especially during the Japanese Middle Ages. Morishima thinks it legitimate that the Japanese wished to imitate the West more in the technological realm than the spiritual after Japan was opened, so long as the spiritual element was more than militant nationalism. He identifies economic advantage using an argument reminiscent of Friedrich List (1989 [1841]): The comparative advantage of Japan in her trade with the Portuguese in the sixteenth century lay in the export of agricultural products and ores. By closing the country, the danger of an excessive specialization in the export of raw materials was closed off. The industries manufacturing weapons, ships together with similar enterprises of the late Tokugawa period could then become seedlings for Japanese industrialization, even if they were not very developed.[22]

Closure also created useful preconditions for the turnaround of the Meiji period in the sphere of education, for Confucianism at least fostered morals, generalizing the ideals of the samurai; it was nationalist and intellectual, and could be combined with bureaucratic efficiency. Hence there were not that many prejudices to be overcome in adopting Western science – less perhaps than had to be overcome by the Catholic Church, when it was challenged in Europe by the discoveries of Galilei.

Powelson goes even further than Morishima in attempting to represent the Edo period as one of a transformation, in which Japan herself created the essential preconditions for modernization. Powelson (1997 [1994]) discusses striking parallels between Japanese and European development since the Middle Ages. He affirms that the Japanese already had 'sophisticated banking and exchange practices, commercial law, and bureaucracies capable of handling advanced economic policy' (ibid., p. 2), when the American ships appeared on the horizon. The essential precondition of successful development is not the endowment of land, labour and capital, not even entrepreneurship, but trust and institutions to ensure the appropriate division of powers, therefore an equilibrium of forces between different interest groups. History is said to have shown that liberalism cannot be achieved through authoritarianism; it has to be anchored in history. The medieval system of agriculture in Japan did not simply mean feudal dispersal, but also a multiplicity of defined but stratified rights of lords, owners, and administrators. The coexistence of Shogun and emperor long preceded the Edo period. The farmers had in part the possibility of seeking greater protection from the government, in part also from powerful families, in seeking to better their lot, and sometimes they even collaborated with merchants. The revolts which occurred were not directed at the system itself as a form of class struggle, but represented attempts to improve living and working conditions. The guilds, formed early on in Japan, were not simply cartels to raise prices and an expression of imperfect competition, but also organs of self-organization. Self-organization was also visible in the complicated monetary history of Japan, where coinage issued by princes and by merchants coexisted, where bills of exchange and a spontaneous organization of traders developed. Lawmakers had to adopt these organizational principles, and a complex civil law already existed by 1868. Powelson suggests – but he does not provide quantitative proof – that a living standard similar to that in Europe was achieved already during the Edo period.

Powelson thus describes a developmental process, proceeding relentlessly according to the logic of economic processes and the formation of political institutions, which differs from the classical-liberal image of the necessary transformation of feudal into capitalist modes of production. He lays emphasis on the genesis of institutions – they are the cause for the characteristics of this particular path. He does not speak of the growing weight of bureaucracy. His vision of linear progress is in contrast with cyclical elements, such as the occasional retreat into barter and deliveries in kind which, in view of the Confucian tradition, were not regarded as bad in themselves. The rule of the Tokugawa was originally based on revenues from their own domains. When they tried to overcome their lack of financial resources through debasement they prompted a longing for a more orderly past; in the East a step backwards was more easily taken and appreciated than today, and in the West. Intellectual tradition, so important according to Morishima for the entirety of Japanese development – one might speak of the change of form of an economic style, using German terminology[23] – is not taken into account by Powelson at all. But the power of this tradition showed in the way that merchants (despite arbitrary rule, if debt relief was ordered in favour of the daimyô) oriented themselves towards the culture of the cities, patronized the arts and adopted the ideals of the nobility, including that of the code of honour.

Hence the evaluation of Japanese economic history remains controversial. Kurt Dopfer (1985), in one of his earlier publications, denies the thesis of a Japanese 'Sonderweg' in the Edo period by means of comparisons with other Asian countries and emphasizes List's argument of timely economic and political closure. But those late nineteenth century Western observers who faced Japan as a rival in world markets and as an ancient great power shortly after Japan had seemed so marginal, turned naturally to specific virtues to account for this rapid ascent.

One example is the chaos of currencies in Japan before the adoption of the gold standard in 1897, which Foxwell (1900) wrote about in *The Economic Journal*. In 1868 the Imperial government found itself confronted by the coexistence of depreciated Tokugawa coinage with a broad array of paper money issued by the daimyôs (the report speaks of no fewer than 1600 'varieties of Han-paper', ibid., p. 233). Most gold had disappeared, since in Japan gold was in 1855 worth only eight to nine times as much as silver; and so foreigners quickly bought up Japanese gold with silver and resold it abroad. Therefore in 1870 first a silver standard was tried, then a gold standard, then a bi-metallic standard until, after heavy losses, the gold standard was finally adopted in 1897.

Foxwell was 'impressed by a sense of Japanese *buoyancy* – that most characteristic virtue of the race. What other country in the history of the world has had thrust upon it such a chaos of revolution and such Herculean labour of reconstruction to be faced? And what other country would have achieved the end so quickly or so serenely … That curious combination of qualities should be noted by European observers, as capable of producing strange economic results in future years' (ibid., p. 245). A century later, the world is still astonished at economic conditions in Japan; and this was also one of the reasons a Japanese author was included in the series *Klassiker der Nationalökonomie*, helping to provide some insight into the roots of Japanese economic thought.

### Japanese economic thought in the Edo period

Foxwell names Jiuchi Soyeda as a figure central in the transition to the gold standard; and in 1893 Soyeda had also published the first account of the study of political economy in Japan in *The Economic Journal*, referring explicitly to the writings of the Edo period. He included a table of about a dozen authors who, active between the sixteenth and the mid-nineteenth century, wrote mainly on agricultural problems and the administration of the principalities. 'Most of this school favoured the equalization of property, especially of the land, and the problems which they discussed involved political and moral considerations. Some of these writers held views more or less akin to State Socialism' (Soyeda 1893, p. 334). Soyeda organizes these authors according to Western categories – into Cameralist, Physiocrat or socialist tendencies (ibid.). Even today we lack clear categories that are not in this way adopted from European conditions. The use of the term 'Physiocracy' would seem appropriate in the Japanese context to the extent that agricultural production is central to an order which is not simply traditional, but shaped by 'laissez-faire' principles. It would also seem appropriate insofar as there is criticism of the 'unproductive' nature of industry and trade. But the Confucian emphasis on agriculture has a rather different origin than that of the Physiocrats. The Physiocrats believed in a mechanical natural order. The use of the term 'Physiocracy' in the Japanese context is discussed in Distelrath and Kreiner (2001) and Henri Denis (1974 [1966]) provides a short account of the conception of order in 'Physiocratic' thought. I should prefer to read the Japanese texts of the Edo period as increasingly original and independent developments of a broader East Asian tradition.

The collection of Edo writings that Neil Skene Smith (1934) edited and introduced is still worth reading. His translations are drawn from the *Nihon Keizai Taiten* (ibid., p. 38). He selects: 'The monetary proposals of Hakuseki … during a period of inflation'; 'The monetary proposals of Sorai … during a time of deflation'. His last chapter, without mentioning the name of the author in the table of contents, concerns 'An elementary theory of value', therefore our *Kagen*, of which he says: 'The work outlined in this chapter was selected at random from the *Nihon Keizai Taiten*, vol. 17, solely on account of the title' (ibid., p. 80). As we shall see he chanced on important writings. He was interested in Baien not only because of his remarks regarding value and the quantity of money, but also because of his scientific versatility. He emphasizes how Baien was active practically in support of the poor, founding a credit cooperative aiming to lend money and goods in bad years and to borrow them in better. This is how Baien contributed on his own initiative to the solution of the problem central to *Kagen*.

In his comprehensive treatise on economic theory and the economic history of Japan in the Edo period Eijirô Honjô (1965) argues that economics and politics could not then be separated. Once the nobility and Buddhist priests no longer had a monopoly on knowledge many of the pamphlets which were written concerned monetary problems. What they had in common was unquestioning acceptance of the ruling order and the special position of the samurai, and the view that Chinese influence was of far greater importance than Western influence. Hence the high status accorded to agriculture. The production of rice was to remain the starting point of any economic considerations. Expenditures must match incomes, and thrift was praiseworthy – this was of greatest importance for the ruler, for if he was in financial difficulties he could not in case of emergency fulfil his duty of supporting his dependents. If he became indebted he had to put pressure on his peasants, and so his position deteriorated. Since Japan often experienced bad harvests and could not rely on imports from other countries the authors of the early Edo period emphasized the importance of maintaining a sufficient stock of provisions, and they saw that a readiness to maintain such stocks was endangered by the spread of a monetary economy, where there was an incentive to use surpluses for the acquisition of luxury goods. As the merchant class became more prominent other voices began to be heard. Access was gained, hesitantly at first, to some non-religious western texts and, towards the end of the eighteenth century a new Russian influence developed. There was a desire on the part of some to counteract the loss of precious metals to the Dutch traders in Nagasaki by stricter frontier controls, but others argued for a more active trade policy; they wanted, in effect, to purchase imports by selling exports.

Kumazawa Banzan (1619–1691) is an author who regarded agriculture as the foundation of production and embedded this view in conservative social criticism. As a youth he had been a poor samurai without a sword; then he found an occupation for some time as an administrator, and eventually became a wandering scholar. He was opposed to the luxury of the cities where goods seemed more highly estimated than those humans who, in the countryside, barely managed to scrape a living. He sought to trace agrarian poverty to the luxury of the cities, such luxury being a deduction from an agricultural surplus.

Clearing woodland was no solution, since that would only bring inferior land into cultivation.

The treasure of the people is grain. Gold, silver, copper and so forth are the servants of grain. ... The enlightened ruler stores grain plentifully for the people, and, since all buying and selling is performed with grain, the people enjoy abundance. ... It is difficult to transport large quantities of grain, and therefore, if grain is used [as a means of exchange], trade cannot easily be monopolised. So the price of goods is lowered and luxury does not increase. Samurai and farmers are prosperous, while artisans and merchants also have secure fortunes.

(Morris-Suzuki 1989, p. 17)

Ogyû Sorai (1666–1728) was close to the 'Physiocratic' ideas of Banzan. He studied the old Confucian sources. He was sceptical with regard to the *li* concept; the oldest Confucians did not have this concept, and later Confucian classics did not use it to describe a natural ideal, but rather the society shaped by the early kings and their etiquette. Sorai thus denied a universal order of society. He saw that the old order, which he venerated, was being subverted by the growth of a money economy. He therefore argued for a return to the countryside, but on another occasion he recommended an expansion of the money supply to counter an economic crisis (Komuro 2001, pp. 5–7).

Arai Hakuseki (1657–1725) was a consultant to the Shoguns Ienobu und Ietsugu. More an official than a scholar, he appeared readier to accept a monetary economy. He also confronted the problem of trade with the Dutch. He put forward the argument that Japan had lost a quarter of her gold and three-quarters of her silver in foreign trade; and so only the import of books and medicines should be allowed. It is therefore wrong to say that he argued like the mercantilists – rather, he argued like their opponents; his argument may be compared to that of Ernestine, who in 1530–1531 opposed the export of silver coins from the Duchy of Saxony and, in order to limit the loss of silver, proposed that imports of luxury goods be reduced – in his case by debasing of coinage, not by means of border controls.[24] Hakuseki also discussed the process of inflation, which was associated with the depreciation of 1695. But when in 1714 he proposed the introduction of a smaller quantity of better coins his reform failed because the older bad coinage continued in circulation. Sorai commented that while a lesser amount of gold and silver was circulating, the level of prices still remained high. This he attributed to a failure to observe the cities of exchange, and to the increased power of the merchants. Other cases that he identified were transport costs and customs duties, these latter increasing because of the rise of the cities, the pricing policies of the merchants and increased demand (these arguments were likewise discussed in the 'Münzstreit'). He maintained that precious metals could be replaced by bills and notes.

Kaiho Seiryô (1755–1817) was a wandering scholar interested in economic questions. He treated merchant capital and the profit orientation as natural phenomena. He proposed that 'All things in this world are commodities for exchange, and it is in the nature of the commodities that they should produce other commodities. There is no difference between fields that produce rice and money that produces interest' (Komuro 2001, p. 8, my transl.). And:

> Feudal lords are the rich who have commodities, called domains. They loan their domain as merchandise to those under their rule and earn interest from it. What they do is the same as the activity of the vassals who sell their knowledge and power to their lord, or that of porters of sedan-chairs who earn their food and liquor by providing service to other people.
>
> (ibid., my transl.)

It is striking how everything, which is interpreted in terms of moral categories by Confucianism, is here dissolved into market relationships. Seiryô recommended that the samurai imitate traders, which reminds one of Savary (1993 [1675]), who suggested that the nobility invest their capital in bourgeois undertakings. But this had already been advocated by Ishida Baigan (1685–1744), whose teaching has also be compared with that of Weberian Puritans (Morris-Suzuki 1989, p. 28). He regarded trading incomes to be of equally legitimacy to that of the samurai if based on fair dealing; and as with scholasticism, price fluctuations were permitted so long as the trader did not cheat.

Yamagata Bantô (1748–1821), the principal wholesale rice trader and financier in Osaka, emphasized the rational kernel of Confucianism, and therefore the possibility of understanding the order in nature and society. He also started from the productivity of agriculture, the total yield of which had to increase with the number of farmers. The surplus might however increase, if the outflow to city consumers could be reduced. He did nevertheless argue for long distance trade. The government should not interfere with price formation, for nothing in the world was as rational and efficient as the rice market (Komuro 2001, p. 10).

Satô Nobuhiro (1769–1850) adhered to the Confucian postulate of benevolent government, but called for a contribution to be made to the development of productive forces. He proposed a refined subdivision of the social classes; one ministry was to be allocated to each, charged with fostering development. He also proposed the establishment of state schools for all children. He compared Japan with a more powerful, nationalist England – whose stalwart inhabitants would colonize the East. The tension between state socialist and liberal ideas thus first became apparent, becoming more marked during the Meiji Period.

This literature is wide-ranging, and the extension of the money economy was approached in different ways. Tanaka Kyûgu (1662–1729) himself originated from the countryside, and he examined the influence of monetary policy on agriculture. He thought that monetary depreciation had relieved the lives of poor farmers to some extent, and this was obviously true where they were in debt; but he mainly thought in terms of a stimulation to demand through depreciation. The wish to bequeath something to one's children was an important motive in Japan. A money economy allowed families to accumulate small sums for this purpose, while progress and growth created free time, which could in turn be used to promote productivity.

From the perspective of the Confucian tradition these processes furthered personal autonomy and hence brought with them the danger of moral decay. But Motoori Norinaga (1730–1801), a noted scholar in the Japanese tradition, thought that, if the government did not act precipitously but reformed steadily and with moderation, the people would be in the best position to make their own arrangements. A notion of spontaneous control arising from the economic process began to gain acceptance. But this did not go as far as fully-fledged support for the idea of laissez-faire.[25] The government of the day remained intent on keeping farmers in a state of dependency. Their children were to be educated to believe that they could not abandon the plough, and the good farmer was one interested in rice, but not in the price of rice[26] – like Plato's shepherd, who was supposed to be interested in his sheep without any thought that he might eat or sell them. This was of course also a Confucian idea, as we saw above.

The merchant academy in Osaka, Kaitokudô, warrants special mention. This flourished in the eighteenth century and was closed at the end of the Tokugawa-government.[27] This academy has been described by Tetsuo Najita in an extensive monograph. It was open in principle to all, and was attended by future merchants. Yamagata Bantô, mentioned above, was a teacher there. In their attitude to society they were really quite similar to mercantilists. Up until this point aristocrat and great merchant had tended to regard each other as ignorant; now a critical science was to overcome class-prejudices. The arguments were far-reaching (from Confucian moral philosophy via a natural science, increasingly influenced by the West, to pure economic arguments). Here the high price of rice was defended because it induced traders to maintain reserves which could be used in hard times. This was in clear opposition to the older Confucian economic thinking that we have seen above. But Najita (1987) argued that Confucian philosophy was still important, since it clarified human relationships. He then added that it permitted economic phenomena to be understood without the mystifications of the past, which is a more doubtful claim (ibid., p. 277). But now we turn to Miura Baien himself, following this brief survey of some economic authors during the Edo period.

### Miura Baien

Miura Baien (1723–1789) lived through the middle section of the Edo period. Apart from some travelling, especially to Nagasaki where he showed interest in Western teaching, he remained in his home province of Bungo on the southern islands of Japan, as a doctor, as a teacher of philosophy and a landlord. His interests included education, economics, anatomy, astronomy, Christian religion, and Chinese poetry; such versatility and catholic interests were not uncommon among scholars of his time. He cannot be regarded as an isolated thinker because of his extensive reading and personal relations, through which he was also connected to the Kaitokudô academy in Osaka. Distelrath and Kreiner (2001, p. 49) report that he wrote poetry himself, and that this early intense interest led him to edit six volumes of poems, where he mainly collected Chinese poems of the time of the Han dynasty. He must therefore have penetrated deep into the spirit of the early Chinese empire, for poetry touches all aspects of life. *Gengo*, a philosophical text, is said to be his most significant work. Its title can be translated as *Deep Words* (Mercer 1991). Reference works describe his philosophy as Hegelian because of its dialectical character, but Mercer (1991, p. 492), his translator and interpreter, rejects this characterization as inadequate.

It is beyond my competence to discuss the philosophical thought of Baien here, nor is it appropriate. But it should perhaps be said that his knowledge of Western science was only indirect, mediated through Chinese renderings of what the missionaries had taught in China. He favoured for example a geocentric system: 'The true shape of heaven and earth is a single sphere of which the earth is the core' (Mercer 1991, pp. 69ff.). But some quotes may indicate the character of his thinking. In an earlier text, the *Genkiron*, he says: 'destiny is both the law by which we bring about those things that we are able to do, and the law by which it is impossible for us to do anything about those things beyond our power'. 'The naturally caused consists both of what we can and what we cannot do anything about' (ibid.). And in *Reply to Taga*:

> For it is not strange things that should arouse our curiosity, but everyday things like the falling stone. That is what Confucius means when he asks how we can expect to understand death when we do not understand life. People wonder what will happen to them when they die, yet they do not know how to conduct their present lives.
>
> (ibid., p. 155)

Baien describes how he suffered from doubt in his childhood and youth, and found inner certainty only towards his thirtieth year.

The result is in a peculiar tension between tradition and renewal: 'his philosophy is not, as is commonly said, to be judged as the prenatal stirring of the concepts of modern science, rather, it should be described as the highest culmination of late Confucian style natural philosophy' (Shimada in the Appendix to ibid., p. 196). Distelrath and Kreiner (2001, p. 60) emphasize the Daoist origins of Baien's thought. Similar continuities appear in his economic text.

Miura Baien is still venerated in his home village. His house has been preserved, his family has kept his books; a Baien village, endowed with a modern observatory, commemorates him, and his name is celebrated each spring.

### Kagen

My reading of *Kagen* is based on Distelrath's beautiful translation. Here we can observe the tension between the eastern tradition and the influences of modernity, which as we have seen were in part endogenous, and in part exogenous. Attempts have been made to make a systematic summary of his economic thought in modern terminology; although this has not in my view met with much success. Rather we should follow Baien's own argument – according to the translator, the windings of his thought are indicative of his 'holism'.

Proletarianization is the determining theme from which Baien starts. He who has lost his fortune – as becomes quickly apparent, Baien thinks mainly in terms of the loss of a farmstead – has to seek occupation as a wage labourer, as an agricultural labourer, working for daily wages or something similar. If, because of a bad harvest, many are touched by such a mishap, wages will fall because not all can find employment. To discuss what he recognizes is a complex problem, Baien turns to the oldest traditions, and quotes from the Shujing (Miura 2001, p. 151), one of the five canonical books put together from ancient texts at the time of the Han dynasty in China. The benevolent prince must promote the satisfaction of what we today call 'basic needs'. Water, fire, wood, metal, earth, and corn are mentioned as symbols which seem to indicate a very simple life. They are also enumerated in the *Li Gi* as the six stores which, it is said, may be used to understand the past and explore the present (Wilhelm 1930b, p. 74). And this is how Baien proceeds. He mentions something like an enlarged catalogue of basic needs, with examples, which indicate the basis of a higher culture permitting education and scholarship: 'Fortresses, bridges, houses, fences, ships, carriages, agricultural implements, cauldrons, iron tea kettles, swords, porcelain, tiles, the hundred kinds of instruments, kitchen implements, clothing, food' (Miura 2001, p. 150, my transl.). Manners in Japan, however, have remained simple, if comparison is made with China (literally: 'Han-dynasty'), and one can recognize that the six stores represent the greatest treasures (ibid., p. 151); the problem is not a lack of money.

It seems as if we are faced with an Aristotelian argument: the good life is not possible without an endowment sufficient for the attainment of intellectual development. Chrematistics, the acquisition of money for the sake of money, involves according to Aristotle an overstepping of this limit to natural riches. If money, introduced only to mediate exchange, is being accumulated for its own sake, then there can be no natural limit to accumulation. Baien also contrasts a given endowment of needs acquired both through natural exchange and through the use of money, suggesting that the latter gives rise to distorted development resulting from the transforming power of a monetary economy. But there are essential differences: Aristotle tries to convince citizens that they should dedicate themselves to the good life and remain within the confines of natural riches. Those who chase money for its own sake are socially different: they are foreigners. Their activity may be necessary, but it is not worthwhile to pursue it. Baien is looking for a solution in the context of a feudal order. He is looking for ways to evaluate goods that differ to those of Aristotle. As we shall see, he is at once more restrictive and more tolerant than Aristotle. More restrictive, because he must find a solution which encompasses all members of the society; he cannot, like Aristotle, leave foreigners to themselves and their own standards. His morals must provide guidance for princes, even for merchants. And this is why more tolerance will be required, for the money economy will be shown to follow a logic of its own. The foundation must be insistence on his own vision of the good, simple agrarian life, the 'real treasures' of life, as Dopfer (2001, p. 129) puts it.

But his society is not as simple as the feudal society of ancient China in which Confucius and his scholars lived – Japan was growing to become a modern economy, even in seclusion from the West. Hence *Kagen* is a political economy for feudal princes in a society of transition – this was emphasized by Komuro (2001, p. 76). For deviation from the simple agricultural life of Confucian times requires the complexity of complex administration; the central powers and those of the princes are at odds; urbanization involves new needs, not just luxuries, and social strata are becoming more differentiated. The wage labourer stands out especially as a new figure. In Aristotle he cut a poor figure, rather below the slave who at least had a secure position in the household. Baien now sees the precarious position of the wage labourer in the earliest phase of industrialization, and examines the economic constraints under which he and his family must live. This is why Yagi and Tanaka (2001) have compared Baien's theory of wages with that of Adam Smith.

This all unfolds gradually. The virtue of the prince, the availability of goods and the welfare of the people belong together – this has been evident from the earliest times (Miura 2001, p. 148). Customs have changed; people do not strive for the valuable goods which will satisfy their basic needs, but for luxury, which is quite useless. Baien here has his own way of formulating the paradox of value – and this is perhaps the justification for the later title of his work. The means to satisfy basic needs are 'available in sufficient degree and by no means difficult to attain' (ibid., p. 150, my transl.), while luxury goods are difficult to obtain. The goods usually confronted in the paradox of value, water and diamonds, fit easily into Baiens categories of true and false treasure. For him, too, the utility of true treasure is high, but it is not said why they are easy to attain. He means, perhaps, that they are, like the goods with well-defined costs of production in Ricardian economics, producible, whereas the luxury good, such as in his example of jade, is obviously scarce (cf. ibid.). Baien does not have appropriate concepts at his disposal and so does not develop his argument like a classical economist, who would consider either scarcity or producibility; instead, he immediately relates variations in the availability of money to society: 'Usually it is assumed that a society is poor, if money is scarce, and that there is welfare in the society, if there is much money. But this is not true...' (ibid., p. 151, my transl.). He shows that fundamental needs can also be satisfied in kind, without the intervention of money entirely, or at least with only small amounts of the circulating medium; to this extent a society without money can be 'rich'. He also intends to demonstrate that high prices, and inflation, do not indicate real wealth.

To this end he points first to the simple beginnings of the Japanese economy, when, beginning in the seventh century, modest amounts of coinage were brought into circulation. He discusses the advantages of the monetary metals, the relations between copper, silver, and gold, and he demonstrates how perfection of the monetary system with an adequate copper coinage leads to more plentiful goods, but also to a tendency to covet money rather than goods (ibid., p. 154).

This reversal leads to a weakening of the country, as he seeks to demonstrate in his famous example of the isolated island. He thinks of an island whose inhabitants produce autarchically, at first without wage labour and on the basis of barter. The subsequent introduction of coins facilitates only exchange without inducing greater production, and the price level rises, which he shows with figures proportionate to the number of circulating coins. This version of a quantity theory of money permeates the entire text. It seems nowhere complemented by metallist considerations, of the type for example that if there are too many coins circulating, the prices of goods will rise to in the same degree that the purchasing power of coined metal sinks, with the consequence that the production of coins and of metal will cease to be worthwhile. The argument is therefore close to that of the old Chinese Confucians, but elaborated with greater clarity and detail.

Here the metallist argument as developed in the Chinese Middle Ages and in European *Münzstreit* has no place, for Baien's argument takes an altogether different turn. At some point, increased circulation changes the character of production and society:

> the higher rises [the amount of money], the more the complications increase: The number of idlers … and therefore of those [unproductive] labourers who consume the goods raining down from heaven and earth will increase, because of the mass of money.
>
> (ibid., p. 155, my transl.)

One conclusion points to the quantity theory of money: 'If prices are low, money is expensive. If prices are high, money is cheap' (ibid., p. 156, my transl.). There is no explicit reference to the old terminology of 'light' and 'heavy' of the *Guan Zi*, but in substance this is the same argument. It would be interesting to examine more closely, as I cannot unfortunately do, whether the terms employed by Baien indicate a familiarity on his part with the old Chinese texts, or whether he came across these ideas through later summaries, whether he owned the corresponding books or had them at his disposal; or whether this is all coincidental. On the other hand – and this is Baien's original rendering again of the old view – the character of production changes with the extension of the monetary economy. The quality of goods is reduced because they are produced in greater amounts, more coarsely and with lesser skill, but they find 'broader fields of application' (ibid., my transl.). The abandonment of agriculture begins, and we see the beginnings of a proletariat.

Baien now is forced to transcend the confines of the older Chinese economics not only in form, by using less symbolic, more scientific expressions, but also in substance, for the genesis of an urban proletariat is a new phenomenon. The decisive idea seems to be this: a greater amount of money means, if monetary transactions and barter coexist, that there are relatively fewer direct exchanges. In particular, rent paid in kind is transformed into money rent. This transformation is harmful to small farmers, for they will have to sell their surplus immediately after the harvest, and are then induced to use the money not paid out as rent for the purchase of other goods, nothing being held back in store for hard years. The feudal lord will do the same: he will spend the money raised as rent on luxury goods and will neglect to keep back a reserve of rice and other goods with which he could supply his dependents in times of need, as is his moral duty. Baien is very clear on this problem of monetarization, but only in subsequent explanations.

We return therefore to the problem of who should maintain the granaries. Mention can be made of authors who discussed it in the West: Ortiz in the sixteenth century in Spain, or the German economist Carl, who wrote in French in the eighteenth century.[28] Both saw that either the state could maintain granaries, or that private traders should speculate in goods; but the latter was only possible if prices were allowed to fluctuate sufficiently to meet the costs of storage. The commitment of the state during the Han period in China to maintain granaries was only formal; it was supposed to be guaranteed by decrees and supported by a bureaucracy – Sang Hongyang was a minister in charge. Baien is closer to the older Confucian views which regarded storage keeping as a moral duty of feudal lords. In Japan such lords were still there in the Edo period, but the economy was much more modern than that of the Han dynasty.

Instead of first analysing the causal connection according to the mathematical and mechanical approach becoming common during the eighteenth century in Europe, and instead of proposing solutions only at the end of his treatment, Baien moves immediately to monetary policy. Author and reader are thus spared a dry and abstract argument which would have to be followed without any idea of whether it will ever be of any use. Baien asks which equilibrium between the monetary and natural economy is appropriate, using the image of a pair of scales: 'One calls this using one's power meaningfully' (Miura 2001, p. 157, my transl.).

The equilibrium of the scales is established by seeking, and supplying, the appropriate amount of money. He observes that foreign commodities sold in Nagasaki are cheap compared to Japanese commodities; he therefore surmises that there is less money in circulation abroad. He does not appreciate that the real exchange relations in foreign trade are not merely determined by the availability of the means of circulation. He probably has in mind only the comparison of prices expressed in silver.

Money facilitates the circulation of goods. Here he means transport costs; he quotes empress *Genmai* of the year 710 (ibid., p. 159). She said that compulsory labour gave much trouble to the populace of mountainous Japan; the people were now to be compensated by means of a circulating medium. This probably meant that, as long as rice was the means of exchange, great amounts of grain had to be moved back and forth to bring to market other goods like the products of artisanal labour. Money facilitates exchange. This very remarkable account of how money was consciously introduced reminds the reader of an insight by Marx. Only a spontaneous process, guided by no-one, could make a single good a general equivalent in the process of barter. But it was a socially conscious act to replace this general equivalent by (coined) money. It is a peculiarity of Japan, equally important for economic history and for the history of economic thought, that reports regarding the introduction of money have been preserved, presumably because rice retained monetary functions down to the end of the Edo period, and because repeated discussion was necessary concerning the borderline between barter and monetary exchange, and this required moving rice from wherever it happened to be.[29]

Baien explains the origin of markets with reference to a Chinese legend; a mythical hero is said to have introduced money in the same way that mythical heroes brought other arts.[30] Different kinds of money are useful according to different conditions of circulation and transport costs. Paper can also be used as money instead of metal. The specific problems of paper money (excess issue, counterfeiting) are not discussed here.

Money accumulates because of a failure to follow the old Chinese rule: to look for a high level of production and a low level of consumption. Here we have an explicit reference to the *Book of Rites* (*Li-ji*, ibid., pp. 162–3). Baien's Confucian scepticism regarding the need for money in a morally good society allows him to see how precious metals could easily be replaced by paper money. He then turns to the structure of the economy, based on the social structure of four classes and their tasks. They are shown to need each other, and are therefore obliged to serve the whole. The job of merchants is to: 'to bring the power of money to move goods to fruition' (ibid., p. 164, my transl.).

Only idlers are unnecessary. How could they exist in this more complex society? Baien's explanation starts from the historical origin of peace during the Edo period. Internal strife was terminated by means of peace-preserving institutions like the system of alternating residences for the princes (in Edo and in their home locations), a practice which is however costly (ibid., p. 165). Forms of superficial luxury spread. The money which indebted princes and poor farmers lack accumulates in the hands of merchants.

Of course, it would be more accurate to say that the wealth of merchants increases because of the increasing credit granted to princes, while coins circulate and are by no means hoarded, but lent out times and again. Since expenditure on the part of the princes has increased, the pressure of taxation on farmers increases in step. Those among them who cannot make ends meet must try to make a living as wage earners. Agriculture becomes neglected and fields lie fallow (ibid., p. 169). If the number of the rich accumulating money (more correctly: wealth) increases, the number of the poor also rises (ibid., p. 166). Baien thus seeks to explain something we had earlier missed: the description of the economic transformation caused by an increase of money (more correctly: the growth of the monetary economy).

Baien deepens this analysis in a Confucian spirit by interpreting the actions of the princes as the rationality of private (selfish) individuals, their duty by contrast being to calculate economically (benevolently), having the welfare of the community in mind.

There follows a quote from Mencius regarding a prince who fed wild geese with bran; the farmers would eat millet (ibid., p. 170). As the bran ran out, its price rose (the exchange rate of millet to bran fell), and the officials proposed feeding the geese on millet. The good prince turned against them, using the moral argument that millet should be reserved for human consumption. A prince who thinks in this way is prepared to accept an economic constraint: fewer geese and better fed subjects, less luxury and more stability.

Baien then draws a parallel between the raising of taxes and the debasement of coins as measures taken by the ruler in exploiting the people (ibid., p. 171). He explains his conception of policy for development: fostering the provision of goods, of agriculture and of handicraft, thriftiness in running the government's business, and moral improvement. It is not enough to limit the increasing circulation of money. His examples regarding the simplicity of life at the beginning of the Edo period highlight the economic growth *e contrario* which took place, which Baien interprets as decline because the older times provide the moral standard. The possibility of progress through raising agricultural productivity is neglected:

> If the number of people working in agriculture falls, fewer goods will be produced. But if there are fewer goods, the foundations of the state are weakened. Population in the countryside is diminished year after year; the number of city dwellers rises day per day.
>
> (ibid., p. 177, my transl.)

His description of pleasures in the city illustrates the urbanity of the Edo period. As long as agricultural production cannot be raised, the agricultural surplus is consumed, not stored. The Confucian principle, however, is familiar: 'If there are no provisions for nine years, deficiencies arise. If there are no provisions for six years, urgent needs arise. But if there are no provisions for three years, the state has ceased to exist' (ibid., p. 180, my transl.). This again is explicitly taken from the *Li-ji*, i.e. the Book of Rites.[31]

And Baien now also explains what he might have said earlier, had he followed the modern expositional logic of theoretical economics: he explains why adequate storage is not provided. For the advantages of storage keeping reveal themselves only late and indirectly, whereas he who sells his provisions makes a quick gain. If the money is invested, it yields interest. Whoever spends instead of investing has the immediate satisfaction of consumption. But he who becomes addicted to luxury will soon find that current revenues are inadequate. He begins to get into debt. Such a clear-cut economic step-by-step reasoning about time and the rate of interest is not often found in older texts. Nevertheless, Baien concludes lyrically in a more traditional vein: 'If many are in debt, the gods of money flee' (Miura 2001, p. 180, my transl.).

If indebtedness is reduced more provisions will be created. One might think of a cyclical movement around an equilibrium determined by preferences, but Baien has a moral effort in mind which has to start from the rulers, and which should change preferences and thus limit indebtedness. Economic incentives which might render storage-keeping profitable are not mentioned. Instead of increasing the allotments of rice, it is necessary on the contrary 'to reduce the payments to the [Samurai officials]. One has to see to it that farmers produce surpluses, that people return to agriculture, that handicraft prospers and that idlers are made to live on the work [of their hands], and one has to see to it that money does not flow away to other regions' (ibid., p. 184, my transl.). If no order is created the attempt to provide people with the necessary goods is 'like seeking fish without having knotted a net' (ibid., my transl.). This observation is central: Baien believes in the possibility of restoring the traditional social order so as to achieve a sustainable level of development on an agrarian basis, a foundation which is at present being undermined. This is an educational task requiring severity; the prince able to carry it out will not be loved by his people while the task is being done, but only afterwards, when he has been successful.

Then an explanation regarding wage labour is added. The abuse of the agricultural surplus for luxury consumption instead of building reserves means that farmers, endangered by years of bad harvests, abandon their fields and offer themselves as wage labourers: wages therefore fall in bad years and rise in good ones. The fluctuations of wages and prices could be moderated if greater stability allowed the farmers more certain tenure. Baien is confident that farmers will readily return to their lands and integrate into the village community, if conditions allow it. There is 'probably no one who would not wish to sit together every morning and evening with their old parents and in loving conversation with wife and children or visit a dear friend' (ibid., p. 189, my transl.). This is said by someone who spurned the attractions of city life for all of his life. Rising wages in subsidiary farming employments are to be welcomed because they indicate that the situation permits a return to agriculture, and that farmers will not sell the lands which they have temporarily neglected, but will return to work on them (ibid., p. 191).[32]

As a philosopher Baien liked to deal in opposites, and he also took delight in showing that economic phenomena could be looked at from different angles. The high wages are here, 'a cause of concern for the employers, but a cause to rejoice for the officials' (ibid., p. 191, my transl.). Or he says: 'From the point of view of the circulation of money, the most useful people are those who have much money; while from the point of view of production, they are similar to idlers' (ibid., my transl.).

And thus, in a dialectical manner, he eventually arrives at a description of the striving for money similar to Aristotle's examples of chrematistic acquisition; even the servants of religion, of knowledge, and of health adopt trading principles: 'The monks sell Buddha, the *miko* (the female servants of a Shinto shrine) sell the [Shintoist] goddesses, the scholars sell knowledge, the doctors sell medicines. Although it takes different forms in different cases, the behaviour of merchants becomes universal' (ibid., pp. 192ff., my transl.). Now 'it is not possible simply to abolish money' (ibid., p. 193, my transl.), but it is possible to introduce the reforms which have been described and to see to it that 'the people of the four classes find pleasure in their work' (ibid., my transl.).

Hence one cannot get on without the gold and silver obtained by especially hard labour. Baien takes up the argument mentioned earlier by Arai Hakuseki, according to which a large part of Japanese precious metals flowed abroad via Nagasaki. We miss here a consideration of how inflation was possible in Japan, given the belief in the quantity theory of money and the observed reduction in the quantities of the precious metals. (The explanation is probably that coins were debased and that substitutes for money were introduced, so that while the quantity of money increased, the quantity of precious metals was reduced.)

With respect to the outflow of precious metals, Baien discusses the world beyond Japan and the influences of Western science and Western religions. Two arguments, which are not made explicitly, seem to justify this excursus. On the one hand, the loss of precious metals expresses a weakness of Japan by comparison with the rest of the world, a weakness that requires examination. Baien points out, with the caution requisite under Tokugawa, rule that the challenges of Western science and power have to be taken seriously. The contrast allows him on the other hand to return once more to a critical overview of the cultural development of Japan and of the expansion of luxury and idleness. These considerations provide many rich insights into Japan, into images of Japan, Japanese knowledge of the foreign world, and Japan's consciousness of her own history. Paradoxically, the reader is impressed by the limits of what Baien knew about the outside world. It must have been painful for such a learned a scholar to accept laws that withheld precious information from him. And there is a degree of triumph in how much he made of the distorted news to which he did gain access.

Baien eventually returns to his vision of social and economic order. Rightfulness and honesty can spread only if a minimum living standard is reached, because people in misery can be overwhelmed by their weaknesses. Extravagance and lack of self-control lead on the other hand to the immizeration of the marginal strata (ibid., p. 210). But if a rational utilization of resources secures welfare, and if models of behaviour diffuse virtue, it is as easy to lead man as it is 'to let water flow down the valleys' (ibid., p. 211, my transl.). Baien's trust in the power of the patriarchal guidance of society is in part based on arguments capable of a liberal interpretation. He quotes from Mencius:

> If there is property in fields which is secure in the long term, there is permanence in the feeling and thinking of man. If property is not fixed

[in the long run], the feeling and thinking of man becomes insecure and volatile.

(ibid., p. 209, my transl.)

How critical he was not only with regard to modern developments, but also to those of his own time, can perhaps be inferred from the fact that he wished to revive the old Chinese rituals of etiquette, but himself doubted the effectiveness of his own words:

> If one tries to explain the significance of the ritual to a man who only knows the customs of today and who is only interested in the pursuit of [material gain], one will be laughed at as naïve and silly. And yet no state can long persist and peace in the world cannot be long preserved if there is not the institution of ritual.
>
> (ibid., p. 207, my transl.)

The insistence on ritual is surprising, since it seems to be commonly agreed that the rituals instituted in imperial China in accordance with Confucian thought were never practised in Japan (note by Distelrath as the German translator to Baien's text, ibid., p. 184). And yet Baien's insistence on the importance of ritual recurs several times in the text (cf. ibid., pp. 184, 207, 208, 209). I see two possible, not radically exclusive, explanations: Baien may have regarded his own suggestion as utopian. Its invocation was then an expression of criticism and doubt with regard to the prevailing order, and of the possibility of reforming it. Reforms could be tried, they might help, but, since they did not touch the substance of the matter, they would not lead to a permanent solution. Or he thought that simple equivalents of the Chinese rites could be found, perhaps in the form of the cultivation of existing etiquette and forms of politeness – an endeavour in which Japan is more successful than most others, and a view which could still be held with confidence and conviction by so penetrating an observer as Kurt Singer.

### Concluding remarks on the Japanese classics

All attempts at social development in the past, in the present, and presumably in the future as well move in contradictions, but we tend to see our own contradictions less clearly than those of the others. In a country with the then (and today) largest metropolis of the world, with rising trade and proto-industrial manufacturing, Baien makes use of Chinese wisdom which ran back two or three thousand years so that he might restore and reinforce a social structure, as if he were talking of a single village. Representing a prince who forces his nobles to discard their court attire and work in the fields as a model – this sounds like a totalitarian nightmare, even if his people eventually loved him like a father (cf. ibid., p. 186).

But the concrete measures actually proposed are much less radical. No class is to be lowered in its rank, luxury consumption only is rendered somewhat difficult; money is not abolished. Help is to be provided to the lowest, the farmers, by means of improved grain storage – the theme that we have seen discussed so often. The spirit is that of Confucian humanism, not of some twentieth-century totalitarianism, although essential aspects of the emergence of capitalism are being confronted.

Neil Skene Smith in 1934, who was the first to bring Miura Baien to the attention of Western economists, summarized the reforms in slightly more modern terms, at a time when interventionism was on the rise:

> Many of Baien's arguments are twisted by the common errors of the time, but his practical advice to dictators seems to reduce itself to this: Save goods when they are in excess of immediate needs, but do not save money excessively. Raise wages to encourage efficiency, tax the rich to discourage idleness, undertake public works and organise technical education to speed up the production of the Essentials. This advice certainly contains some of the fundamentals of the long-period economic plans for a modern community, though his 'abundance' is not linked up with any ideas on cost of production. Of course, he did not consider the effects of rapid invention and the coming of a machine industry...
>
> (quoted in Schefold 2001, p. 38)

Only an economic historian of the Edo period can assess the reforms envisaged by Baien in detail, given the contrast between his utopian frame of reference and specific suggestions, such as might be expected by an experienced landlord and physician of his region. The modern – at any rate the European – reader is inclined to take the lessons learned from the Confucian tradition too literally, while Baien here moves in a universe of discourse where many expressions have a simple significance and invoke ideas well-known among Baien's contemporary readers. Each had to seek appropriate forms of realization for himself, but there was also some common knowledge of what reform principles could mean in concrete terms.

And, as we see contradictions in others and are unconscious of our own inconsistencies, Western readers are astonished that Baien makes use of a two-thousand years old tradition of the history of economic thought, although the same is still done in the West. The most obvious example, which we have used repeatedly, is that of usury. In Nelson's (1969) phrase, the development of the usury debate was one of from 'tribal brotherhood to universal otherhood'. The continuity of the debate on usury from the oldest strata of scriptures in the Old Testament and ancient Greek notions to Christianity, the Roman Church, Catholicism and Protestantism to the nineteenth century is known. Usury reappeared in the twentieth century – Ezra Pound, the poet, dedicated some of his writings to this problem, and the idea of usury is still a live one in the Islamic countries. A closer analogy is perhaps found in the debate about the social market economy. Usury is an abstract idea, while a social market economy is closer to *Kagen*, insofar as it is a political programme for the realization a market economy's potential, aligning the system of remuneration according to efficiency and work with principles of redistribution whose justification derives from Christian traditions – those who founded the social market programme in the Federal Republic of Germany had recourse in part to Catholic social thought, even though some of the most influential persons among them were themselves Protestants (Schefold 1999b). Age-old notions of social justice thus reappeared in modern economic discourse, in forms recognizable only to the initiated. Whether it is for good or bad: hardly a law is passed in Germany without prior discussion reflecting this continuity. The move towards a universal history of economic thought may thus help us to understand each other internationally, without effacing differences.

### Ibn Khaldūn's socio-economic synthesis: rise and fall in economic development

For a historian of economic thought to discuss Ibn Khaldūn means to venture beyond the European-American horizon and deal with a much-admired Arab who, I am convinced, deserves a place among the most important economic thinkers who have ever lived. He is far more important than many secondary Classical writers of the nineteenth century who are granted admission into the canon by economists. Ibn Khaldūn does not of course stand in a direct line extending from the ancient world to our modern economics, and he can hardly be considered a forerunner of modern analytical economics. The methodical introduction to his world history, *al-Muqaddima*, which has been translated by Mathias Pätzold as *Buch der Beispiele* [33] [Book of Examples] (Khaldūn 1992), has been called a methodology for the humanities, sociology, and an exposition of economics. However I see in it primarily a connection between theory and history, a connection which was the aim of political science in nineteenth century Germany. I would even go so far as to say that Ibn Khaldūn's mixture of history and theory was not only a pioneering achievement, but it remains a model today. People in Islamic countries identify themselves with him, and he has shaped our historical view of the Arabs. [34]

Are there no other Arab texts which might be better choices as economic classics? In Ghaussy's *Das Wirtschaftsdenken im Islam* [Economic Thought in Islam] (1986), Ibn Khaldūn is mentioned only as a political scientist because Ghaussy defines the term 'economic thought' more narrowly than we do. He thus excludes Ibn Khaldūn, who views the economy merely as one of many historic forces and does not describe it separately, but instead simply shows the central role played in the rise and fall of nations by phenomena that we would classify as economic.

We do not possess economic treatises from the early Middle Ages. Statutes relating to markets, like those compiled by Leon the Wise (emperor of Byzantium, around 900 AD, Koder 1991), or the *Capitularium de villis* by

Charles the Great,[35] or parts of Justinian's *Corpus iuris* (Behrends, Knütel, Kupisch and Seiler 1999) are not scientific texts, but collections of laws, ordinances, and commentaries that represent economic institutions in themselves, from which the particular economic context and development can be ascertained. The material assumes economic experience, but no systematic thinking, and not even an overview of economic processes. We also find with Ibn Khaldūn very few categories which refer to the general context of economics. However, his description of the rise and decline of empires, which are founded by dynasties, includes the economic context in each phase. The explanations which he sketches out of the upturns and downturns of wealth and power also make it possible to identify something like long waves of economic development. These waves, however, are not like those which are caused by autonomous fluctuations of innovative capacity, as in the corresponding modern theory. Instead, prosperity and depression are dependent upon the fluctuations of economic activity and the demand resulting from the rise and decline of social and governmental systems. Although Ibn Khaldūn is famous for his blending of social, economic, and political factors and is on this point compared to Machiavelli and Montesquieu, he goes beyond them. He not only characterizes the typical behaviour of rulers in particular situations (as Machiavelli does in *Principe*) and not only relates forms of rule and forms of sustaining life to each other (as Montesquieu does in *Esprit des lois*), but he describes and explains entire cyclical processes. We could, therefore, practically speak of a dynamic model. It does not claim to explain wave-type developments everywhere, but is focused on the conditions of North Africa, found and shaped by the Arabs in the late Middle Ages. Ibn Khaldūn reveals, step by step, a certain logic of development, more through description than through analysis: what keeps each empire together and what causes their destruction, obtaining in this way a systematic understanding of a historical process where previously only a chaotic and confusing succession of dynastic wars and territorial battles had been perceived.

I am going to venture a step further. After the hope for stable growth and a more equitable distribution of wealth in the third quarter of the twentieth century, the last 25 years have been sobering: growth is still not constant, lasting unemployment is possible, the natural foundations of wealth are being closed off, and a shrinking population threatens the balance between generations. The economic assumptions, the political compromises and the condition of society, upon which the German social market economy was established, are dissolving, and a gradual decline of this economy has to be anticipated. Perhaps a new system is simultaneously forming which we cannot yet really perceive. While reading Ibn Khaldūn, it is sometimes possible to recognize striking parallels to such processes of decline in the contemporary world, and to wonder how far the forces of renewal can carry. Ibn Khaldūn's conviction of the cyclical return of the same has conservative implications for society. This accords with his conspicuous idealization of tribal solidarity among the nomads from whom, he says, the renewal of history starts; this renewal is connected with a frugal yet virtuous life.

Nevertheless, I am convinced that his economic thought has liberal elements. He is in favour of low taxes which he defends with religious laws, but above all with the stronger economic dynamic which they foster. He also lists preconditions for entrepreneurial activity, for instance legal security, sufficient independence from the state, an organized monetary system, and demand that increases with prosperity and which is cumulatively reinforced in its employment effects through investment. Even if he does not abstractly formulate the theory of economic growth and he does not explicitly employ terms like 'investment' or 'total social demand', they are implicit. He describes the regular return of upturns and downturns, and he traces chains of causes and effects, thus presenting the economic process as something that runs according to laws. This all awakens curiosity about the author, the circumstances of the composition of the work, and its repercussions.

There is a stark contrast between the claims to power of Islam, which in the first two hundred years after Mohammed very quickly created a religiously and politically connected world empire under the caliphs, and the present day in which all traces of the Ottoman empire and colonialism have not yet been eradicated and positive developments which might redress the balance have only been partially realized. When Napoleon marched into Egypt, the superiority of western technology and science was obvious. The internal decay of the Islamic-Arabic central power had begun much earlier and forms the basis of Ibn Khaldūn's historical consciousness. The empire of the first caliphs and the Umayyads ultimately stretched from Spain to India and central Asia. Under the dynasty of the Abbasids, which came later, centrifugal forces began to be felt. The Mongol storming of Baghdad in 1258 put an end to it. In the fourteenth century the second large empire of Mongols, led by Timur, threatened a splintered Arab world. Ibn Khaldūn was the only one who undertook to investigate this process of growth and decay theoretically (Khaldūn 1992, p. 6), and the reader is struck by the seriousness and depth of his questioning. Though he had broad knowledge, which included the ancient world and the Jews, the European Middle Ages and Asia, and all have their place in his world history, he obtained his hypotheses about the causes and effects of historical processes from the observation of North Africa and the area west of Egypt to the Atlantic coast (Maghreb) in particular.

Nomadic tribes who had moved north were forced out of Egypt in the eleventh century and gravitated to this place; the destruction of their political stability and the emergence of localized feuds inflicted damage which would be felt for centuries. The uncertainty caused the peasants to leave their land, most of it then turning into barren plains. Only in the immediate vicinity of the cities, under the protection of the dynasties, could peasants till their fields. But even this security had often to be bought with tribute to the nomads (Simon 1959, p. 17). On the one hand, North African Berber dynasties needed the immigrant Bedouin tribes in order to strengthen their power, and, on the other hand, they had to force them back from city areas in order to provide security for the surrounding agricultural population. Thus, the Bedouins were often allied with the dynasties and were partly the instigators of confrontations, partly allies in confrontations between the small empires of North Africa. There was a contrast between the wildness of the tribes and the city culture; there was, at the same time, however, also a mutual dependency, which Ibn Khaldūn sought to explain. Cultural differentiation in the cities was furthered by trade – when conditions permitted – with distant lands; Christian Europe was not excluded from trade relations. The oldest existing trade contract refers to trade between Tunis and Pisa, and was concluded in 1157.

In the thirteenth century, three empires emerged: the Hafsids in Tunis, the Abdalwadids in contemporary western Algeria, and the Marinids in Fez (Morocco). These three competing Berber dynasties remained in existence for several hundred years. The cities, the aristocracy, and the administration each supported the central power, despite the fiscal burden imposed by the ruling family and court, increased religious surveillance, and greater legal uncertainty. In these urban cultures, Jewish and Christian business people and immigrants played an important role. Among the immigrants were Andalusians fleeing the (partial) Christian reconquest of Spain.

To this group belongs Ibn Khaldūn (1332–1406), born in Tunis to a family which had once possessed influence through important offices in Andalusia. At 16 he endured the loss of his parents and a teacher during a plague epidemic, and later he experienced the loss of his family – his wife and five daughters – in a shipwreck on the journey from Tunis to Cairo (cf. Mahdi 1968, p. 56). With astonishing drive and steadiness, Ibn Khaldūn combined high scientific learning with a respectable yet simultaneously stressful and even dangerous governmental career as judge, official, and diplomat in the three courts of Maghreb. He also took a position in the court of Granada and had to negotiate with the Christian king of Castile. For three years he withdrew to the mountains with a nomadic Arabic tribe; there, at the age of 45, he wrote the greater part of *The Muqaddimah*. After several years in Tunis, he arrived in Cairo. The libraries of these centres were important for him in order to complete his historical work on *The Muqaddimah*, which at that point only represented an introduction. However, he was also in Cairo repeatedly entrusted with official duties, as academic teacher and high court judge, positions which he later lost through intrigue.

A well-known chapter of his autobiography describes a diplomatic mission in which he travelled on behalf of the Sultan in Egypt to Damascus, which was threatened by the Mongolian Timur. From Cairo, in the second half of his life, Ibn Khaldūn undertook far fewer trips than he had in the first half, from Maghreb. He was already 70 years old when he rode with the Egyptian sultan and his army to Damascus. While he was there, the Sultan and the his leaders fled the city and agreed to a truce with Timur; the Sultan then returned to Egypt. Timur asked about Ibn Khaldūn, who had remained behind in Damascus; he had himself lowered down the wall of the besieged city and went to the Mongolian camp. In January 1401, there are supposed to have been 35 meetings between Timur and Ibn Khaldūn. The content of the discussions and the related circumstances are briefly sketched since they throw light on the circumstances, even without a more detailed analysis of the unique forms of conduct (Fischel 1967), in which this extraordinarily educated person worked.

Ibn Khaldūn first of all made himself agreeable to the feared conqueror by presenting evidence, by reference to astrological predictions and historical comparisons, of why Timur was the greatest ruler since Adam. Following that, they had a dialogue about the relationship of rulers to their people, based on Ibn Khaldūn's theory of tribal solidarity from which the ruling power must develop.

During the negotiations Damascus was surrendered, but not the castle, which remained under siege. At the same time, Ibn Khaldūn wrote within a few days a report of approximately 250 pages about the geography, history, and politics of Maghreb. This was at the request of Timur, who was possibly considering extending his string of conquests there as well. The report was submitted, and Timur ordered that it be translated into Mongolian. When the castle was conquered and razed to the ground, Timur extorted large sums of money from the population through torture. He ordered the city to be plundered; it burned down and the mosque was destroyed. In his autobiography, where he describes this meeting, Ibn Khaldūn called this a terrible crime. However, he continued his discussions with Timur. In this uncertain situation, Ibn Khaldūn presented a copy of the Qur'an to Timur – who, in a quick gesture of deference, placed it on top of his head, – as well as a prayer rug, a book of poetry, and sweets, which the recipient then had distributed in the tent. Now Ibn Khaldūn was called on for advice and had the opportunity to recommend to the conqueror that he transfer the government officials and the educated people of Damascus into his service.

On another occasion, Timur saw the valuable mule which had been made available to Ibn Khaldūn as a sign of his dignity as high court judge. Timur wanted to buy it and Ibn Khaldūn offered it to him as a present. The animal was led away and Ibn Khaldūn never saw it again. However, Timur later gave him money for the mule through a messenger to Egypt. Ibn Khaldūn allowed himself to accept the money only after he had in turn asked the Sultan in Cairo for permission. Thus ended the meeting between the most educated person of the time and Timur, the founder of the second Mongolian empire, who would die in 1405 in a failed winter crusade against China – Goethe's poem refers to this – and on whose mausoleum in Samarkand the unique inscription was placed: 'If I were still alive, you would tremble before me.'[36]

I now want to provide a brief summary of selected passages from *The Muqaddimah*. Initially, Ibn Khaldūn wished to research 'how and why dynasties and civilization originate' (Khaldūn 1992, p. 34; 1958, p. 11), supported by his studies of the peoples of the Maghreb. He wanted to write a critical history, avoiding the creation of legends, which would become a new science based on questioning, and a step by step consideration of the aspects and conditions that form the essence of human culture (Khaldūn 1992, p. 44;

1958, p. 77). This had only been achieved fragmentarily by his predecessors, as in the explanatory profile:

> Royal authority exists through the army, the army through money, money through taxes on land, land taxes through cultivation, cultivation through justice, justice through the improvement of officials, the improvement of officials through the forthrightness of wazirs, and the whole thing in the first place through the ruler's personal supervision of his subjects' condition and his ability to educate them, so that he may rule them, and not they him.
> (Khaldūn 1958, pp. 80–1)

– thus the circle closes. The links which Ibn Khaldūn would uncover form an entire network by comparison. Above all, however, his theory is a dynamic one.

Long before Adam Smith, Ibn Khaldūn discussed the division of labour as something without which humans cannot survive. For Ibn Khaldūn, human beings are not only rational, since aggression is also a human characteristic, and humans cannot survive without authority.

There are various ways of living, by agriculture or raising livestock. Greater surpluses can be generated through settlement; however, in his eyes, nomadism is older. 'Bedouins are the basis of, and prior to, sedentary people...' (Khaldūn 1992, p. 69; 1958, p. 253). Because of their way of life nomads are more virtuous and more brave than people in the cities. Naturally, bloodlines must be more important for them, and thus a marked solidarity emerges among them ('*asabīya*). Solidarity allows leaders and leading families of tribes to take possession of a conquered city; it enables them, as rulers and dynasties, to rise and to expand their power. However, later generations which have become richer drift away from tribal solidarity under the influence of a luxurious life. The young dynasties, used to a simple life, levy only a few taxes, specifically those prescribed by the Qur'an. Later, financial demands proliferate. The dynasties which are still caught up in a nomadic existence do little to oppress their subjects, who work peacefully, while the refinement of the ruling class leads to increasing obligations, for example duties on trade goods. When the ruler withholds taxes, business declines, and property taxes and other taxes also decrease. Tyrannical conduct means for the subjects that their property is becoming endangered. Encroachments lead to emigration, desolation, and decline. At the same time, these damaging, occasional encroachments only slowly become perceptible in large cities, but unjust taxes are arbitrary, and arbitrariness is tyrannical. This circle closes when the degenerate dynasty is conquered and replaced by a new one which is still deeply rooted in its tribal life.

The encroachments which lead to declines assume different forms. Tax collectors and government officials might themselves be oppressed. Rulers also use violence by forcing sales at reduced prices, then taking the goods and reselling them at inflated prices. This intervention in the price structure, which still occurs and which modern representatives of liberal economic systems particularly denounce, also appears to Ibn Khaldūn (1951, p. 130; 1958, pp. 93–4) as particularly corrupt. Such interventions take place chiefly in foreign trade, when those in power in a province monopolize import trade, purchase at prices they have determined, and then sell to their subjects at higher prices. The unfair ruler, finally, will not only have to finance the purchase of luxuries, but will also require money to pay mercenaries. Then he will restrain the sullen members of the court with violence, revenge himself on those who have turned their back on him, and seize their goods.

In the middle years of the dynasty, rulers will first of all be rich when, after modest beginnings, all tax sources are tapped. At the high point of the upswing, the economic power of the ruler furthers welfare more than it endangers it. 'As we have stated, the dynasty is the greatest market, the mother and base of all trade … the substance of income and expenditures' (Khaldūn 1951, p. 136; 1958, p. 103).

It appears that a conception of the cycle of circulation of commodities as well as a Keynesian notion of the stimulation of markets through an increase in demand lie at the base of this idea.

One gets the impression that Ibn Khaldūn would have become a theoretician of a liberal economic order had he systematically characterized the economic circumstances of the boom, and called for adherence to the preconditions which lead to it. In this he was hindered not so much by a lack of insight into the economic context – although he, in fact, described it more vividly than he defined it – but by the conviction that the shift to decline and decadence could not be avoided for political and social reasons. Among the most damaging developments he lists the imposition of compulsory labour, which at the height of a dynasty's power leads to arbitrariness and decline. Acquisition and profits make up the value of the labour of a civilized people. Whosoever is forced to work gains no benefit from the fruits of his labour and becomes discouraged. Even more dangerous is to force trade on people. Ibn Khaldūn characterizes the advantages of a free economy with moderate, regulated state activity not so much by the positive description of the development of markets and the emergence of business people, as through the denunciation of arbitrary interventions in the exchange of goods and factors and, above all, of poor financial administration in respect of incomes and expenditures.

Ibn Khaldūn also gains new insights into the dynamic of market processes by comparing locations of different sizes, from large cities to small ones, even down to villages and tented communities. In each case income corresponds to living conditions. The judge in the larger city receives a higher income, but has also greater tasks. Ibn Khaldūn assures the reader that the beggar in Fez has it better than the beggar in Oran. He then provides a remarkable differentiation: in the large cities, the necessities – grains for example – are cheaper, while luxury items like fruit are more expensive. The reason for this is that in the city there are many who work in order to provide the necessities of life; and relatively few, but with great purchasing power, who pay for luxury items. In the large cities there are good craftsmen who, as a matter of course, are arrogant; they become demanding as a result of competition for their services.

Ibn Khaldūn adds to this that in the cities more (indirect) taxes are levied, and for this reason prices are also higher there. Poor populations have a difficult time when emigrating to cities, since they do not have enough money to settle down. Corresponding differences would exist between countries.

These observations, which Ibn Khaldūn employs very carefully, are not represented as simple facts. Instead, they are connected with economic explanations. Necessities are mass-produced. Here the prices fall to costs, and wages to a subsistence level; Ibn Khaldūn even seems to consider the economies of scale of production. Demand takes a different form in the case of the products of artisans, hence a better life becomes possible for them. The fiscal burden becomes yet another influence on the price level (Khaldūn 1992, p. 186; 1951, p. 170; 1958, pp. 276–9).

Prices change during the rise and fall of dynasties. During declines, land is cheaper and a large estate develops during the period when a dynasty is recovering its power. In his own time, Ibn Khaldūn saw the east rising and Maghreb in decline (Khaldūn 1992, p. 119; 1958, pp. 342–3). The wealth of the Christian populations seemed to be unimaginable (Khaldūn 1992, p. 189; 1958, p. 281). In the Maghreb, the areas on the border of the culture were under the influence of nomads, in contrast to the capital cities, about which he writes:

> The only reason is that the government is near them and pours its money into them, like the water (of a river) that makes green everything around it, and fertilizes the soil adjacent to it, while in the distance everything remains dry.
>
> (Khaldūn 1992, p. 202; 1958, p. 302)

It appears to him unavoidable that wealth eventually leads to a decline of customs. Consumption of luxury goods leads to mismanagement by the state, the consumption of luxury goods itself becomes a burden – even a good family line provides no protection – and finally leads to religious corruption (Khaldūn 1992, p. 193; 1958, p. 287). A new dynasty takes over in the wake of a war, it relocates the capital, and all the supporters of the previous dynasty have to be sent away 'where (the new dynasty) can be sure that it will not be secretly attacked by them' (Khaldūn 1951, p. 187; 1958, p. 299).

Economic reflections are strewn throughout the work. Ibn Khaldūn moves from acquisition to exchange and to value: 'Every man tries to get things; in this all men are alike. Thus, whatever is obtained by one is denied to the other, unless he gives something in exchange (for it)' (Khaldūn 1992, p. 209; 1958, p. 311).

The acquisition, which has become a possession, at first facilitates living; to the extent that it provides more than this, it becomes an asset. Useful acquisition he also calls profit. Labour enables acquisition. A theory of labour value is suggested which also takes into consideration indirect effects:

> Some crafts are partly associated with other (crafts). Carpentry and weaving, for instance, are associated with wood and yarn (and the

respective crafts needed for their production). However, in the two crafts (first mentioned), the labour (that goes into them) is more important, and its value greater.

(Khaldūn 1992, p. 211; 1958, p. 313)

In labour he sees, as Petty will later, the active moment in the determination of value because, he says, even wells dry up if they are not developed. Natural wealth is, in itself, like an 'unmilked udder' (Khaldūn 1992, p. 213; 1958, p. 314).

His evaluation of forms of acquisition is not however based solely on the criterion of quantity of labour. The oldest form is agriculture; it is closest to nature. Next follows manufacture, which has something to do with science, and then trade, which Ibn Khaldūn also calls natural, although it cannot be reduced simply to transportation because it exploits market fluctuations. It is legal because it does not take without giving.

Being a servant is not natural employment because this form of employment suggests a lack of manliness. A simultaneously trustworthy and entirely satisfactory servant does not exist, because with such talents a person would not become a servant. Whoever is neither efficient nor trustworthy will not be hired. The lord must therefore choose between the two characteristics, ability and trustworthiness. The Maghreb author advises choosing on the basis of ability, and recommends that the lord protect himself against disloyalty.

Ibn Khaldūn, who assumes that a decline follows a rise, also has no great faith in the idea that people can be improved. Above and below, good and bad require each other. The classes influence each other. Those below need those above to motivate them. Pride and arrogance are reproachable; in order to be able to rise, a person must be prepared to flatter. The arrogant person will hate those that do not show enough deference. In the phase of dynastic decline, the descendants of those who were earlier successful become too vain and thus endanger themselves. Some professions make it possible for a person to keep a certain distance from acquisition and its pressures, but this has its price. Priests and educators are valued, but they do not earn very much. Noble occupations, like medicine, the making of books, and music must be practiced in the intercourse with powerful people. The transmission of knowledge is also an urban phenomenon, and knowledge is accumulated in famous cities, like Baghdad, Córdoba, and, in Ibn Khaldūn's own time, Cairo. The development of knowledge thus remains in the hands of cities and is connected with the general cyclical law of rise and fall. The final chapter of *The Muqaddimah* provides an overview of the sciences and their transmission.

The representations of rise and fall in *The Muqaddimah* are so suggestive that it is possible to forget to question more closely what increases and decreases, and what constitutes a reference point. Just as it is ridiculous to say that a person moves at a speed of six mph forwards and one mph backwards, but is reasonable to say that the person is walking on the street at five mph and is moving, simultaneously, at a much higher speed on it around the earth's axis and around the sun, the simple determination that the processes of rise and fall overlap is scientifically unsatisfactory so long as there is not at least an approximate scale for this rise and fall. For example, the base from which an economy has grown has to be clearly identified, and the system which is said to be growing or declining must be named.

Ibn Khaldūn does not refer only to the economy. The rise is not to be equated with the creation of a free market economy, the fall not with its decay through interventionism. His primary reference point in societies is tribal solidarity among the nomads, supported by strict beliefs and religious laws. However, the other reference point is urban culture in the full bloom of arts, crafts, the sciences, and these grow in a thriving economy in an organized, non-repressive state. The cultural-economic highpoint is arrived at when the decay of social bonds has already begun. Not everything decays with tribal solidarity, rather there are cultural gains under conditions of relative freedom. These even accumulate. Despite losses, literature, the arts, and science do not start over from scratch when a new cycle commences, for there is cultural inheritance. Material production does not grow significantly in the long run; it oscillates between generations. Knowledge is accumulated, by contrast. However, a secular advance cannot generally be presupposed because it does not affect all areas and, in any case, the religious seriousness which marked, for Ibn Khaldūn, the era of Mohammed will not be achieved a second time. Therefore there are connected movements in the areas of society, economy, culture, and religion, though they will not all approach the peak together: the prevailing opinion regarding worldly things remains sceptical.

Yassine Essid (1995) has shown how, in Arabic science, notions of organization for states, cities and households developed, influenced by ancient Greek ideas, which were communicated above all by an Arabian translation of the neopythagorean, Bryson. He mentions an 'Octagon of Justice':

> The world is a garden, whose wall is the state – the state is a sovereign who is glorified by the Law – The Law is a government at whose head is the prince – The prince is a shepherd, supported by the army. The army is composed of auxiliaries maintained by money – Money is the means of subsistence supplied by the subjects – The subjects are slaves, who are subjugated by justice – Justice is the link by which the equilibrium of the world is maintained.
>
> (ibid., pp. 56–7)

We saw that Ibn Khaldūn, too, in *The Muqaddimah* refers to such notions of order which have been passed down through the generations. He is critical of his predecessors when he dualizes the systems and has society swing between the two poles of tribal life and urban culture. A range is possible because humans are not merely rational, but also creatures of will and instinct, and he understands how people are differentiated, not as individuals but as generations, and according to origins, moving back and forth from one state of affairs to another.

Baeck (1994, p. 115) therefore writes of Ibn Khaldūn: 'Up to a point he initiates the "Verstehende Methode" [*interpretative method*] with ideal-types and contrasting dichotomies, such as city-rural, civilised-Bedouin, tribal and impersonal solidarity.' Baeck also praises Ibn Khaldūn's economic insights – his originality in demography, for instance – and his being a critic of the cheating involved in the debasement of coinage. He even thinks that Ibn Khaldūn is searching for macroeconomic accounting. His conclusion with regard to Ibn Khaldūn as the discoverer of modern insights is as follows:

> As a conclusion we can state that Ibn Khaldūn formulated the advantages of the division of labour long before Adam Smith, that he invented a population cycle theory before Malthus and that in fiscal economy he formulated ideas which are comparable with those of supply side economics.
>
> (ibid., p. 117)

Indeed, there was even an attempt at characterizing Ibn Khaldūn's theory as essentially economic. Jean David C. Boulakia (1971) has identified a theory of production in Ibn Khaldūn's works and theories of value, money, and prices, therefore a theory of distribution and a theory of cycles. Optimal distribution, for example, is characterized as follows (and each statement is supported by a citation): when wages are too low, sales stagnate; if they are too high, prices rise. If profits are too low, sales people have to sell the stock and deplete assets; if profits are too high, stocks will be sold without, however – due to inflationary pressure – the possibility of replacing them. If taxes are too low, government cannot fulfil its duties; if they are too high, the entrepreneurial incentive will be lost (ibid., p. 1113, my summary). He breaks the cycle down into that of the population and that of the public finances, as we already know. The population grows with the differentiation of employment and the possibilities of earning a living in the city. The cumulative powers of growth come to bear, but a city that is too large cannot be supplied with enough food and a catastrophic shrinkage results. Boulakia is sketching a modern system here, using modern terms, but he actually manages to create the bigger picture with citations from Ibn Khaldūn's observations. These citations are taken from completely different places in *The Muqaddimah*, so that the resulting scheme can only be attributed to the interpreter, although the causal relations expressed therein were actually seen by Ibn Khaldūn. In a similar sense, but less thoroughly, Abdoul Soofi (1995) reconstructs Ibn Khaldūn's economics and emphasizes, in particular, the Malthusian-Keynesian aspect, as well as his ideas about inflation.

Today, Ibn Khaldūn is not only famous, but is almost in fashion. Whoever does an internet search on him is inundated with references. Institutions which carry out sociological research bear his name, an Islamic Banking and Finance Network claims that his theory of history is too materialistic, and other contributions celebrate him as the actual founder of economics, with influence in the Arabic and Ottoman world long before Adam Smith. A broad interest in Ibn Khaldūn's *The Muqaddimah* appears to have emerged only with the first printing in Egypt in 1857, and, in the same year, in Paris in a scientific edition (Khaldūn 1992, p. 24). It is noteworthy that the interest in Ibn Khaldūn awoke simultaneously in the colonized and the colonizing worlds.

Among the sciences, sociology also lays claim to Ibn Khaldūn (Kamil Ayad 1930). On the constitution of society, for example, Kamil Ayad writes that socialization is, following Ibn Khaldūn, less the result of rational and intentional consideration, and more one of consanguinity and habituation. Although the economy plays a major role, it is less a target set deliberately, but rather a natural prerequisite of human cohabitation (ibid., p. 168). Faith in Ibn Khaldūn is, in consequence, also interpreted as a social phenomenon (ibid., p. 173), and Kamil Ayad quotes Ibn Khaldūn: 'Humans avow themselves to the religion of their kings' (ibid., p. 183).

Ibn Khaldūn's socio-economic statements today help in the understanding of development theory.

> Ibn Khaldun's insights are strikingly modern: four decades of economic development in some 150 countries have made it clear that social cohesion based on a reliable socio-cultural consensus and the satisfaction of basic needs of the population is, in fact, the decisive factor of success. Other elements are the commitment of the ruling elites to the development and a framework of suitable macroeconomic conditions – both subject to a number of contemporary structural adjustment programs – and the cultural disposition and qualification of the human factor linked with educational traditions, practice-oriented curricula, and achievement-oriented values.
>
> (Weiß 1995, p. 30)

Ibn Khaldūn is then invoked to explain cumulative processes, and yet another aspect of *The Muqaddimah* is exposed, hitherto barely noticed but which today is having an effect, specifically regarding the environment. With increasing population density, pollution and illnesses in cities are also increasing, and, indeed, as Ibn Khaldūn observed, the more heavily settled the cities are, the greater the pollution and the number of illnesses are (ibid., p. 33).

The modern reader, however, will most easily identify with Ibn Khaldūn's critique of the tax burden, and his suggestion of the attendant dangers. He was aware that the rates above a certain limit were counterproductive: they made the economy decline and thus reduced tax revenue. Excessive taxation in his time already had had a long history in the Orient.[37]

In 'the process of creative destruction', as Schumpeter describes economic development, the idea of rise and fall is used positively: the declining old economy will be replaced by a creative new one. With this thought, it is possible to take comfort in face of the disappearance of older forms of production, like the traditional farm, and the destruction of medieval buildings to make place for modern office buildings. Ibn Khaldūn shows, however, that entire dynasties – and 'dynasty' often represents for him what we would call a state – disappear as well and are replaced by others. The accompanying destruction affects the existence of many. Ibn Khaldūn himself repeatedly managed, with cleverness, willpower, and diplomacy, to create new positions, and even when he faced Timur as representative of the loser, he came out well. However, his book is full of the dangers which threaten states and populations, and even in an optimistic time it is wise to bear these warnings in mind.

## Notes

1  Cf. 'Xenophon's *Oikonomikos*: the beginning of an economic science', Chapter 1.
2  This choice was first suggested to me by Cherng-Shin Ouyang, Taiwan, who had consulted with members of the Academy of Sciences in Beijing.
3  English translation: 'The legislator of China … confounded together their religion, laws, manners and customs; all these were morality, all these were virtue. The precepts relating to these four points were what they called rites … They spent their whole youth in learning them, their whole life in practice' (Montesquieu 1777, vol. 1, p. 400).
4  '[T]he palace was at variance with the empire' (ibid., p. 132).
5  'China is therefore a despotic state' (ibid., p. 164).
6  This is based on a collection of four essays, which appeared 1767 in the *Éphémérides*.
7  English translation in Maverick (1946, p. 259): 'It is said there in China, besides the tax on land, some irregular taxes, such as custom duties … If these allegations have foundation, it would indicate that on this point, the state is not sufficiently enlightened as to its true interests.'
8  In English in Marx (1979); first publ. in the *New York Daily Tribune*, no. 3804, June 25, 1853.
9  See Elvin (1973) for an analysis of the strategic and economic impact of technical change in China and for comparisons of China with other empires.
10  'Moreover, [the emperor] had dragon-ships built, phenix-boats, [ships decorated with] yellow dragons, red ships, ships several stories high, boats linked by bamboo.' (My transl.)
11  'One can see things from a different perspective. After all, it was perhaps neither folly nor pure pleasure, but an eminently political act to give the prestige of an imperial voyage … to the main artery destined to unite forever the North and the South which had been separated for four centuries.' (My transl.)
12  There were several forms of slavery in the Han period which we shall have to consider, such as debt slavery, the selling of children, the enslavement of prisoners of war. Slaves were also used in agriculture and handicraft, as overseers, warriors, servants and in particular as we have said in households; but since slaves seem not to have accounted for more than a few per cent of the population, one cannot really speak of a slaveholding society, see Wilbur (1943, pp. 240ff.).
13  Long distance trade already played a role at the time of the Han Empire, especially in its second half, extending via Persia and Arabia to Rome. The Roman Empire was the largest foreign buyer of Chinese silk, and according to Pliny Rome spent a great deal of gold on this trade. The Romans sought to circumvent Persia by maritime trading, while the Chinese strove to prevent the Xiongnu, their aggressive northern neighbours, from closing the Silk Road. There was diplomatic contact between Roman emperors (Marcus Aurelius) and emperors of the Han dynasty. A Cyrenian trader reached present-day Nanjing in the year AD 226, Chinese ships entered the Red Sea, and the trade in silk later continued between China and Constantinople (Shen 1996).

14  Cf. Will and Bin Wong (1991) for technical details and later practice of storage-keeping.

15  In regard to his life and the legends surrounding it, compare: Zenker (1941).

16  Cf. 'Aristotle: the classical thinker of ancient economic theory', Chapter 1.

17  Cf. Will and Bin Wong (1991).

18  Cf. 'Nicholas Oresme: monetary theory in the late medieval era', Chapter 2.

19  English translation in Montesquieu (1777, vol. 2, p. 9): 'The Japanese trade only with two nations, the Chinese and the Dutch…very nation that acts upon Japanese principles must necessarily be deceived; for it is competition which sets a just value on merchandises…'.

20  In the following, reference will be made to both the English (1973) and German (1996 [1991]) editions.

21  It is customary to call scholars of the Edo period by their individual names, Meiji and later authors by their family names. In the case of the scholars of the Edo period we let the family names (in this case: Miura) stand first, as is generally customary in Japan. The individual name is placed first (e.g. Michio) in the case of later authors, as Japanese do, when they publish in the West. Indications to the literature are given, using the family name, followed by the abbreviated individual name. The spelling of names here follows that of the sources which we quote.

22  Cf. Morishima (1984 [1982], p. 60).

23  See Schefold (1994d and 1995).

24  See 'Economy and money in the age of reformation', Chapter 2.

25  For these last few authors and their arguments see Komuro (2001, pp. 12–20). Honjô (1965, p. 97) presents a different emphasis, because Norinaga was one of those authors who wished to restrict the monetary economy.

26  Cf. Honjô (1965, pp. 101–3).

27  Najita (1987) and Distelrath and Kreiner (2001, p. 59) describe the relationship of Miura Baien with the Kaitokudô.

28  See Azpilcueta Navarro and Ortiz (1998), Carl (2000 [1722–1723]).

29  Distelrath provides more up-to-date information on the history of the introduction of coinage in Japan in the footnotes to his translation; see in particular Miura (2001, p. 153, note 29).

30  See Distelrath's notes (ibid., p. 160).

31  Cf. Wilhelm (1930b).

32  Cf. Yagi and Tanaka (2001).

33  At the same time Khaldūn (1951) was cited. English translation: Khaldūn (1958). In the following reference will be made to both, German and English translations.

34  In the much read book *A History of the Arab Peoples* by Hourani (1991), a description of the life and work of Ibn Khaldūn serves as an introduction to Arab history in general.

35  The economic ideas in the *Capitularium de villis* are dealt with in the history of economic theory in Blanqui (1860).

36  We must forego exhausting the wealth of connections of this meeting. Cf. Mommsen (1988, pp. 477–85).

37  Erwin Rosenthal, an excellent interpreter of Ibn Khaldūn's economics, cites a text of the tenth century to illustrate this: 'The taxes in Egypt are a heavy burden … the Copt may weave textiles of Shatâ only if they are stamped by the government, and he may sell them only to state traders. What is being sold is recorded by a government official, then the textiles are being rolled, then tied, then put in boxes, these are corded, and a duty is levied at each step. Again something is taken at the port, each box is marked and the boats are searched prior to departure' (Rosenthal 1932, p. 89, my transl.).

# Appendix

Table A.1 The series Klassiker der Nationalökonomie

| First publication (publication of reprint and commentary volume) | Author and work (bold: translated commentary by B. Schefold in the present edition) | Reproduction | Title of commentary volume: Vademecum... | Authors (pp.) |
|---|---|---|---|---|
| 369–354 BC 1734 (1998) | **XENOPHON, OIKONOMIKOS ODER XENOPHON VOM HAUS-WESEN** | Facsimile reprint of the bilingual edition of 1734 (published in Hamburg) | ... zu einem Klassiker der Haushaltsökonomie | B. Schefold, K. Schefold, S.T. Lowry, A. Schmitt (198 pp.) |
| 335–323 1879 (1992) | **ARISTOTELES, POLITIK** | Facsimile reprint of the edition published 1879 by Franz Susemihl in Leipzig | ... zu einem Klassiker des antiken Wirtschaftsdenkens | H. Flashar, O. Issing, S.T. Lowry, B. Schefold (180 pp.) |
| 81 BC 1501 (2002) | **HUAN KUAN, YANTIE LUN. DIE DEBATTE ÜBER SALZ UND EISEN** | Facsimile reprint of the edition of 1501 (Hongzhi) | ... zu dem Klassiker der chinesischen Wirtschaftsdebatten | E.v. Mende, B. Schefold, H.U. Vogel, partial translation of Kuan by S. Ludwig with annotations by E.v. Mende (195 pp.) |

| First publication (publication of reprint and commentary volume) | Author and work (bold: translated commentary by B. Schefold in the present edition) | Reproduction | Title of commentary volume: Vademecum… | Authors (pp.) |
| --- | --- | --- | --- | --- |
| 44 BC 1465 (2001) | **MARCUS TULLIUS CICERO, DE OFFICIIS** | Facsimile reprint of the Editio Princeps published in Mainz 1465 | *… zu einem Klassiker des römischen Denkens über Staat und Wirtschaft* | H. Kloft, W. Rüegg, B. Schefold, G. Vivenza (164 pp.) |
| 1356–77 1485 (1995) | **NICOLAUS ORESMIUS, TRACTATUS DE ORGINE ET NATURA, IURE & MUTATIONIBUS MONETARUM** | Facsimile reprint of an illuminated manuscript of 1485 | *… zu einem Klassiker der mittelalterlichen Geldlehre* | F. Avril, O. Langholm, D. Lindenlaub, B. Schefold, H. Tietmeyer, translation of Oresmius by E. Schorer, with notes by B. Schefold (220 pp.) |
| 1267–73 1496 (1991) | **THOMAS VON AQUIN, ÖKONOMIE, POLITIK UND ETHIK AUS 'SUMMA THEOLOGIAE'** | Facsimile reprint (extracts) of the edition printed by Anton Koberger in 1496 | *… zu einem Klassiker der Wirtschaftsethik* | P. Koslowski, N. Lobkowicz, H. C. Recktenwald, H. Thurn, E.A. Synan, A.F. Utz (86 pp.) |
| 1401 (2000) | **IBN KHALDUN, ÖKONOMIE AUS MUQADDIMA** | Facsimile reprint (partial) of the manuscript written in 1401/02 | *… zu dem Klassiker des arabischen Wirtschaftsdenkens* | H. Daiber, Y. Essid, A. Hottinger, B. Schefold, partial translation of Khaldun by A. Schimmel and M. Pätzold (184 pp.) |

| First publication (publication of reprint and commentary volume) | Author and work (bold: translated commentary by B. Schefold in the present edition) | Reproduction | Title of commentary volume: Vademecum… | Authors (pp.) |
|---|---|---|---|---|
| 1524 (1987) | **MARTIN LUTHER, VON KAUFFSHANDLUNG UND WUCHER** | Facsimile reprint of the first edition published by Hans Lufft at Wittemberg | … zu einem frühen Klassiker der ökonomischen Wissenschaft | H. Hesse, G. Müller (103 pp.) |
| 1530, 1530, 1548 (2000) | **DIE DREI FLUGSCHRIFTEN ÜBER DEN MÜNZSTREIT DER SÄCHSISCHEN ALBERTINER UND ERNESTINER** | Facsimile reprints of 'Gemeyne stimmen von der Muntz', 'Die Müntz Belangende. Antwort und bericht', 'Gemeine Stymmen Von der Müntze: Apologia … und vorantwortung' | … zu drei klassischen Schriften frühneuzeitlicher Münzpolitik | K.H. Kaufhold, M. North, C. Perrotta, B. Schefold (174 pp.) |
| 1556 + 1558 (1998) | **MARTIN DE AZPILCUETA, COMENTARIO RESOLUTORIO DE CAMBIOS; LUIS ORTIZ, MEMORIAL DEL CONTADOR LUIZ ORTIZ A FELIPE II** | Facsimile reprint of the first edition of Azpilcueta and facsimile of the manuscript copy of Ortiz | … zu zwei Klassikern des spanischen Wirtschaftsdenkens | M. Grice-Hutchinson, E. Lluch, B. Schefold, partial translation of Ortiz by A. Ixmeier (200 pp.) |
| 1605 (1999) | **LEONARDUS LESSIUS, ÖKONOMIE UND ETHIK AUS 'DE IUSTITIA ET IURE'** | Facsimile reprint of the first edition published in Leuven | … zu einem Klassiker der spätscholastischen Wirtschaftsanalyse | L. Baeck, B. Gordon, T.v. Houdt, B. Schefold (160 pp.) |

| First publication (publication of reprint and commentary volume) | Author and work (bold: translated commentary by B. Schefold in the present edition) | Reproduction | Title of commentary volume: Vademecum… | Authors (pp.) |
|---|---|---|---|---|
| 1613 (1994) | **ANTONIO SERRA, BREVE TRATTATO DELLE CAUSE, CHE POSSONO FAR ABBONDARE LI REGNI D'ORO & ARGENTO** | Facsimile reprint of the first edition published in Napoli | *… zu einem unbekannten Klassiker* | A. Heertje, C. Poni, R.R. Portioli, A. Roncaglia, B. Schefold (136 pp.) |
| 1651 (1990) | THOMAS HOBBES, LEVIATHAN | Facsimile reprint of the first edition published in London | *… zu einem Klassiker der Geistes- und Naturwissenschaft* | H.C. Recktenwald, J. Aubrey, H. Maier, L.S. Moss (79 pp.) |
| 1664 (1989) | THOMAS MUN, ENGLAND'S TREASURE BY FORRAIGN TRADE | Facsimile reprint of the first edition published in London | *… zu einem frühen Merkantilisten* | H.C. Recktenwald, F. Gehrels, C.P. Kindleberger (108 pp.) |
| 1668 (1990) | JOHANN JOACHIM BECHER, POLITISCHER DISCURS | Facsimile reprint of the first edition published in Frankfurt | *… zu einem universellen merkantilistischen Klassiker* | J. Klaus, J. Starbatty (120 pp.) |
| 1675 (1993) | **JACQUES SAVARY, LE PARFAIT NEGOCIANT** | Facsimile reprint of the first edition published in Paris | *… zu einem Klassiker der Handlungswissenschaft* | J.-F. Fitou, E. le Roy Ladurie, B. Schefold, D. Schneider (112 pp.) |
| 1684 (1997) | **PHILIPP WILHELM VON HÖRNIGK, OESTERREICH ÜBER ALLES, WANN ES NUR WILL.** | Facsimile reprint of the first edition | *… zu einem Klassiker absolutistischer Wirtschaftspolitik* | B. Schefold, H. Matis, M. Streissler, E.W. Streissler, K. Tribe (336 pp.) |

| First publication (publication of reprint and commentary volume) | Author and work (bold: translated commentary by B. Schefold in the present edition) | Reproduction | Title of commentary volume: Vademecum... | Authors (pp.) |
| --- | --- | --- | --- | --- |
| 1690 (1992) | **WILLIAM PETTY, POLITICAL ARITHMETICK** | Facsimile reprint of the first edition published in London | ... zu einem Klassiker der angewandten Nationalökonomie | T. Aspromourgos, A.W. Coats, D.P. O'Brien, B. Schefold (144 pp.) |
| 1692 (1993) | JOHN LOCKE, SOME CONSIDERATIONS OF THE CONSEQUENCES OF THE LOWERING OF INTEREST, AND RAISING THE VALUE OF MONEY | Facsimile reprint of the first edition published in London | ... zu einem Klassiker der merkantilistischen Geldtheorie | H.C. Binswanger, W. Eltis, B. Schefold, K.I. Vaughn (192 pp.) |
| 1697 (1996) | PIERRE DE BOISGUILBERT, LE DÉTAIL DE LA FRANCE. SOUS LE RÈGNE DE LOUIS XIV | Facsimile reprint of the edition published in Rouen | ... zu dem Kolumbus der Nationalökonomie | A. Heertje, G. Faccarello, P.D. Groenewegen, J. Hecht (312 pp.) |
| 1735–1737 (1999) | GEORGE BERKLEY, THE QUERIST | Facsimile reprint of the first edition published in three parts between 1735–1737 in Dublin | ... zu einem irischen Klassiker der politischen Ökonomie | A. Heertje, C.G. Caffentzis, S. Rashid, K.-H. Schmidt (184 pp.) |
| 1714 (1990) | BERNARD DE MANDEVILLE, THE FABLE OF THE BEES | Facsimile reprint of the first edition published in London | ... zu einem klassischen Literaten der Ökonomie und Ethik | H.C. Recktenwald, M. Perlman, F.B. Kaye and F.A.v. Hayek (138 pp.) |

| First publication (publication of reprint and commentary volume) | Author and work (bold: translated commentary by B. Schefold in the present edition) | Reproduction | Title of commentary volume: Vademecum... | Authors (pp.) |
|---|---|---|---|---|
| 1741 (2001) | JOHANN PETER SÜSSMILCH, DIE GÖTTLICHE ORDNUNG | Facsimile reprint of the first edition published in Berlin | ... zu dem deutschen Klassiker der Bevölkerungswissenschaft | H. Hax, H. Birg, E. Elsner, J. Hecht (215 pp.) |
| 1750 (1986) | FERDINANDO GALIANI, DELLA MONETA | Facsimile reprint of the first edition published in Napoli | ... zu einem frühen Klassiker der ökonomischen Wissenschaft | P. Dongili, L. Einaudi, E. Ganzoni (66 pp.) |
| 1752 (1987) | DAVID HUME, POLITICAL DISCOURSES | Facsimile reprint of the first edition published in Edinburgh | .... zu einem frühen Klassiker der ökonomischen Wissenschaft | A. Peacock, E. Topitsch (116 pp.) |
| 1755 (1987) | RICHARD CANTILLON, ESSAI SUR LA NATURE DU COMMERCE EN GÉNÉRAL | Facsimile reprint of the first edition published in London | .... ... zu einem frühen Klassiker der ökonomischen Wissenschaft | J. Niehans (52 pp.) |
| 1756 (1993) | J.H.G. VON JUSTI, GRUNDSÄTZE DER POLICEY-WISSENSCHAFT | Facsimile reprint of the first edition published in Göttingen | ... zu einem Klassiker des Kameralismus | H. Rieter, B. Schefold, K. Tribe, J. Wysocki (172 pp.) |
| 1759 (1986) | ADAM SMITH, THE THEORY OF MORAL SENTIMENTS | Facsimile reprint of the first edition published in London and Edinburgh | ... zu einem frühen Klassiker der ökonomischen Wissenschaft | H.C. Recktenwald (106 pp.) |

| First publication (publication of reprint and commentary volume) | Author and work (bold: translated commentary by B. Schefold in the present edition) | Reproduction | Title of commentary volume: Vademecum… | Authors (pp.) |
| --- | --- | --- | --- | --- |
| 1763 (2002) | VICTOR RIQUETTI MARQUIS DE MIRABEAU & FRANÇOIS QUESNAY, PHILOSOPHIE RURALE | Facsimile reprint of the first edition published in Amsterdam | … zu einem Klassiker der Physiokratie | A. Heertje, J. Cartelier, W.A. Eltis, P.D. Groenewegen, B. Schefold (152 pp.) |
| 1767/68 (1987) | FRANÇOIS QUESNAY, PHYSIOCRATIE | Facsimile reprint of the edition published in two parts in Paris | … zu einem frühen Klassiker der ökonomischen Wissenschaft | W. Leontief, H.C. Recktenwald (72 pp.) |
| 1767 (1993) | **JAMES STEUART, AN INQUIRY INTO THE PRINCIPLES OF POLITICAL OECONOMY** | Facsimile reprint of the first edition published in two volumes in London | … zu einer klassischen Synthese von Theorie, Geschichte und Politik | T.W. Hutchison, D.A. Redman, B. Schefold, A.S. Skinner, J. Starbatty (109 pp.) |
| 1769/70 (1990) | A.R. JACQUES TURGOT, RÉFLEXIONS SUR LA FORMATION ET LA DISTRIBUTION DES RICHESSES | Facsimile reprint of the first edition which appeared in the form of three successive articles in Paris | … zu einem Verfechter des aufgeklärten Individualismus | H.C. Recktenwald, C. Jessua, P.D. Groenewegen, A. Alcouffe, J. Frayssé (141 pp.) |
| 1771 (2000) | ISAAC DE PINTO, TRAITÉ DE LA CIRCULATION ET DU CRÉDIT | Facsimile reprint of the first edition published in Amsterdam | … zu einem niederländischen Pionier des Denkens über die Staatsverschuldung | A. Heertje, A.E. Murphy, I.J.A. Nijenhuis, K.-H. Schmidt (123 pp.) |

| First publication (publication of reprint and commentary volume) | Author and work (bold: translated commentary by B. Schefold in the present edition) | Reproduction | Title of commentary volume: Vademecum… | Authors (pp.) |
| --- | --- | --- | --- | --- |
| 1773–1789 (2001) | **MIURA BAIEN, KAGEN. VOM URSPRUNG DES WERTES** | Facsimile reprint of the manuscript (written between 1773 and 1789) | … zu einem japanischen Klassiker des ökonomischen Denkens | G. Distelrath, K. Dopfer, J. Kreiner, M. Komuro, B. Schefold, translation of Baien by G. Distelrath (232 pp.) |
| 1776 (1986) | ADAM SMITH, AN INQUIRY INTO THE NATURE AND CAUSES OF THE WEALTH OF NATIONS | Facsimile reprint of the first edition published in London | … zu einem Klassiker der Weltliteratur | H.C. Recktenwald (36 pp.) |
| 1798 (1986) | THOMAS ROBERT MALTHUS, AN ESSAY ON THE PRINCIPLE OF POPULATION | Facsimile reprint of the first edition published in London | … zu einem frühen Klassiker der ökonomischen Wissenschaft | J.P. Henderson, W.J. Samuels (38 pp.) |
| 1803 (1986) | JEAN-BAPTISTE SAY, TRAITÉ D'ÉCONOMIE POLITIQUE | Facsimile reprint of the first edition published in Paris | … zu einem frühen Klassiker der ökonomischen Wissenschaft | H.C. Recktenwald, W.J. Baumol (58 pp.) |
| 1815 (1996) | DIE 'CORN-LAW-PAMPHLETS' VON 1815 (TH. R. MALTHUS, E. WEST, R.TORRENS, D. RICARDO) | Facsimile reprints of five first editions published in London | … zu den Klassikern der Differentialrenten-Theorie | S. Hollander, L. Pasinetti, B. Schefold, M.S. Skourtos (164 pp.) |
| 1817 (1988) | DAVID RICARDO, ON THE PRINCIPLES OF POLITICAL ECONOMY AND TAXATION | Facsimile reprint of the first edition published in London | … zu einem frühen Klassiker der ökonomischen Wissenschaft | K.J. Arrow, M. Ricardo, H.C. Recktenwald (84 pp.) |

| First publication (publication of reprint and commentary volume) | Author and work (bold: translated commentary by B. Schefold in the present edition) | Reproduction | Title of commentary volume: Vademecum… | Authors (pp.) |
| --- | --- | --- | --- | --- |
| 1819 (1995) | JEAN CHARLES LEONARD SIMONDE DE SISMONDI, NOUVEAUX PRINCIPES D'ÉCONOMIE POLITIQUE | Facsimile reprint of the first edition published in Paris | … zu einem Klassiker der Sozialökonomie | B. Schefold, A. Alcouffe, G. Eisermann, P. Schiera (184 pp.) |
| 1820 (1989) | THOMAS ROBERT MALTHUS, PRINCIPLES OF POLITICAL ECONOMY | Facsimile reprint of the first edition published in London | … zu einem wegweisenden Klassiker der ökonomischen Wissenschaft | H.C. Recktenwald, J.M. Keynes, S. Rashid, J.P. Henderson, W.J. Samuels (100 pp.) |
| 1821 (1998) | CLAUDE-HENRI DE SAINT-SIMON, DU SYSTÈME INDUSTRIEL | Facsimile reprint of the first edition published in two parts in Paris | … zu einem Klassiker des utopischen Sozialismus | A. Heertje, L. Bergeron, P.D. Groenewegen, C. Jessua (123 pp.) |
| 1826 (1986) | JOHANN HEINRICH VON THÜNEN, DER ISOLIERTE STAAT | Facsimile reprint of the first edition published in Hamburg | … zu einem frühen Klassiker der ökonomischen Wissenschaft | H.C. Recktenwald, P.A. Samuelson (88 pp.) |
| 1832 (1987) | FRIEDRICH BENEDIKT WILHELM HERMANN, STAATSWIRTSCHAFTLICHE UNTERSUCHUNGEN | Facsimile reprint of the first edition published in Munich | … zu einem unterbewerteten Klassiker der ökonomischen Wissenschaft | H.C. Recktenwald (95 pp.) |
| 1832 (1992) | CHARLES BABBAGE, ON THE ECONOMY OF MACHINERY AND MANUFACTURES | Facsimile reprint of the first edition published in London | … zu einem Klassiker der Arbeitsteilung | H.M. Enzensberger, H. Hax, N. Rosenberg, B. Schefold, K. Steinbuch (192 pp.) |

| First publication (publication of reprint and commentary volume) | Author and work (bold: translated commentary by B. Schefold in the present edition) | Reproduction | Title of commentary volume: Vademecum… | Authors (pp.) |
|---|---|---|---|---|
| 1836 (2000) | NASSAU WILLIAM SENIOR, AN OUTLINE OF THE SCIENCE OF POLITICAL ECONOMY | Facsimile reprint of the first edition published in London | … zu einem Klassiker der Verteilungstheorie | H. Hax, S.F. Frowen, T.W. Hutchison, H.-M. Trautwein (95 pp.) |
| 1838 (1991) | ANTOINE AUGUSTIN COURNOT, RECHERCHES SUR LES PRINCIPES MATHÉMATIQUES DE LA THÉORIE DES RICHESSES | Facsimile reprint of the first edition published in Paris | … zu einem Klassiker der mathematischen Wirtschaftstheorie | A. Alcouffe, J. Fraysse, H.L. Moore, B. Schefold, W.G. Waffenschmidt (86 pp.) |
| 1841 (1989) | FRIEDRICH LIST, DAS NATIONALE SYSTEM DER POLITISCHEN OEKONOMIE | Facsimile reprint of the first edition published in Stuttgart and Tübingen | … zu einem schöpferischen Klassiker mit tragischem Schicksal | H.C. Recktenwald, K. Häuser, W. Lachmann, H. Scherf (152 pp.) |
| 1844 (1997) | THOMAS TOOKE, AN INQUIRY INTO THE CURRENCY PRINCIPLE | Facsimile reprint of the first edition published in London | … zu einem Klassiker der Banking School | A. Arnon, M. Pivetti, H. Rieter, B. Schefold (174 pp.) |
| 1848 (1988) | JOHN STUART MILL, PRINCIPLES OF POLITICAL ECONOMY | Facsimile reprint of the first edition published in two volumes in London | … zu einem frühen Klassiker der ökonomischen Wissenschaft | H.C. Recktenwald, G.J. Stigler (92 pp.) |

| First publication (publication of reprint and commentary volume) | Author and work (bold: translated commentary by B. Schefold in the present edition) | Reproduction | Title of commentary volume: Vademecum... | Authors (pp.) |
| --- | --- | --- | --- | --- |
| 1848 (1998) | **BRUNO HILDEBRAND, DIE NATIONALÖKONOMIE DER GEGENWART UND ZUKUNFT** | Facsimile reprint of the first edition published in Frankfurt | *... zu einem Klassiker der Stufenlehre* | G. Eisermann, V. Gioia, T. Pierenkemper, E. Rothschild, B. Schefold (288 pp.) |
| 1854 (1987) | HERMANN HEINRICH GOSSEN, ENTWICKELUNG DER GESETZE DES MENSCHLICHEN VERKEHRS | Facsimile reprint of the first edition published in Braunschweig | *... zu einem verkannten Klassiker der ökonomischen Wissenschaft* | W. Krelle, H.C. Recktenwald (72 pp.) |
| 1860 (1998) | LORENZ VON STEIN, LEHRBUCH DER FINANZWISSENSCHAFT | Facsimile reprint of the first edition published in Leipzig | *... zu einem Klassiker der Staatswissenschaft* | H. Hax, H. Grossekettler, M. Heilmann, S. Koslowski, T. Shibata (200 pp.) |
| 1861 (1994) | **WILHELM ROSCHER, ANSICHTEN DER VOLKSWIRTHSCHAFT AUS DEM GESCHICHTLICHEN STANDPUNKTE** | Facsimile reprint of the first edition published in Leipzig and Heidelberg | *... zu einem Klassiker der historischen Schule* | B. Schefold, E.W. Streissler, F. Baltzarek, K. Milford, P. Rosner (212 pp.) |
| 1863 (1995) | HANS V. MANGOLDT, GRUNDRISS DER VOLKSWIRTHSCHAFTSLEHRE | Facsimile reprint of the first edition published in Stuttgart | *... zu einem frühen Klassiker der Preistheorie* | B. Schefold, P.D. Groenewegen, K.H. Kaufhold, J. Schumann (120 pp.) |

| First publication (publication of reprint and commentary volume) | Author and work (bold: translated commentary by B. Schefold in the present edition) | Reproduction | Title of commentary volume: Vademecum... | Authors (pp.) |
| --- | --- | --- | --- | --- |
| 1867 (1988) | KARL MARX, DAS KAPITAL. ERSTER BAND | Facsimile reprint of the first edition published in Hamburg | ... zu einem revolutionären Klassiker der ökonomischen Wissenschaft | C.C.v. Weizsäcker, I. Fetscher, H.C. Recktenwald (135 pp.) |
| 1871 (1990) | CARL MENGER, GRUNDSÄTZE DER VOLKSWIRTHSCHAFTSLEHRE | Facsimile reprint of the first edition published in Wien | ... zu einem Klassiker der subjektiven Wertlehre und des Marginalismus | H.C. Recktenwald, F. A.v. Hayek, J.R. Hicks, I.M. Kirzner (102 pp.) |
| 1871 (1995) | WILLIAM STANLEY JEVONS, THE THEORY OF POLITICAL ECONOMY | Facsimile reprint of the first edition published in London and New York | ... zu einem Klassiker der Grenznutzenschule | B. Schefold, R.D. Collison Black, T. Negishi, I. Steedman (132 pp.) |
| 1873 (1996) | **CARL KNIES, DAS GELD** | Facsimile reprint of the first edition published in Berlin | ... zu einem deutschen Klassiker der Geldtheorie | B. Schefold, G. Eisermann, K. Häuser, K. Yagi (143 pp.) |
| 1873 (1996) | WALTER BAGEHOT, LOMBARD STREET | Facsimile reprint of the first edition published in London | ... zu einem Klassiker der Banktheorie und Geldpolitik | B. Schefold, M.A. King, D.P. O'Brien, H. Rieter (192 pp.) |
| 1874 (1992) | **WILHELM ROSCHER, GESCHICHTE DER NATIONAL-OEKONOMIK IN DEUTSCHLAND** | Facsimile reprint of the first edition published in Munich | ... zu einem Klassiker der deutschen Dogmengeschichte | B. Schefold, J.G. Backhaus, G. Eisermann, P.D. Groenewegen, F. Schinzinger (180 pp.) |

| First publication (publication of reprint and commentary volume) | Author and work (bold: translated commentary by B. Schefold in the present edition) | Reproduction | Title of commentary volume: Vademecum… | Authors (pp.) |
|---|---|---|---|---|
| 1874–1877 (1988) | LÉON WALRAS, ÉLÉMENTS D'ÉCONOMIE POLITIQUE PURE OU THÉORIE DE LA RICHESSE SOCIALE | Facsimile reprint of the first edition published in two parts in Lausanne, Paris and Basel | … zu einem zentralen Klassiker der ökonomischen Statik | H.C. Recktenwald, M. Blaug, D.A. Walker (112 pp.) |
| 1876 (1991) | **ADOLPH WAGNER, ALLGEMEINE ODER THEORETISCHE VOLKSWIRTHSCHAFTSLEHRE (GRUNDLEGUNG)** | Facsimile reprint of the first edition published in Leipzig and Heidelberg | … zu einem Klassiker der Finanzwissenschaft | K. Häuser, K.-D. Grüske, B. Schefold, R.K.v. Weizsäcker (120 pp.) |
| 1881 (1994) | FRANCIS YSIDRO EDGEWORTH, MATHEMATICAL PSYCHICS | Facsimile reprint of the first edition published in London | … zu einem Klassiker der Vertragstheorie | B. Schefold, K.J. Arrow, W. Hildenbrand, P. Newman (116 pp.) |
| 1884 (1999) | FRIEDRICH VON WIESER, ÜBER DEN URSPRUNG UND DIE HAUPTGESETZE DES WIRTSCHAFTLICHEN WERTHES | Facsimile reprint of the first edition published in Vienna | … zu einem Klassiker der österreichischen Schule | H. Hax, H.-H. Hoppe, H.D. Kurz, J.T. Salerno, R. Sturn, E.W. Streissler (160 pp.) |
| 1884 (1994) | EUGEN VON BÖHM-BAWERK, GESCHICHTE UND KRITIK DER KAPITALZINS-THEORIEEN | Facsimile reprint of the first edition published in Innsbruck | … zu einem Klassiker der Theoriegeschichte | P. Bernholz, M. Blaug, H.D. Kurz, B. Schefold (184 pp.) |

| First publication (publication of reprint and commentary volume) | Author and work (bold: translated commentary by B. Schefold in the present edition) | Reproduction | Title of commentary volume: Vademecum… | Authors (pp.) |
|---|---|---|---|---|
| 1885 (1994) | **WILHELM LAUNHARDT, MATHEMATISCHE BEGRÜNDUNG DER VOLKSWIRTHSCHAFTSLEHRE** | Facsimile reprint of the first edition published in Leipzig | … zu einem Klassiker der Raumwirtschaft | B. Schefold, E. Knobloch, J. Niehans, A. Hofmann, R.D. Theocharis (120 pp.) |
| 1889 (1991) | EUGEN VON BÖHM-BAWERK, POSITIVE THEORIE DES KAPITALES | Facsimile reprint of the first edition published in Innsbruck | … zu einem Klassiker der Kapitaltheorie | B. Belloc, F. Gehrels, C. Menger, B. Schefold (124 pp.) |
| 1889 (1993) | RUDOLF AUSPITZ & RICHARD LIEBEN, UNTERSUCHUNGEN ÜBER DIE THEORIE DES PREISES | Facsimile reprint of the first edition published in Leipzig | … zu einem Klassiker der Preistheorie | B. Schefold, H. Barkai, K.R. Leube, J. Niehans, S. Jäggi (120 pp.) |
| 1890 (1989) | ALFRED MARSHALL, PRINCIPLES OF ECONOMICS | Facsimile reprint of the first edition | … zu einem ethisch engagierten Klassiker | H.C. Recktenwald, F.H. Hahn, G.J. Stigler, J.K. Whitaker, D.E. Moggridge (117 pp.) |
| 1896 (1988) | KNUT WICKSELL, FINANZTHEORETISCHE UNTERSUCHUNGEN | Facsimile reprint of the first edition published in Jena | … zu einem weitsichtigen Klassiker | H.C. Recktenwald, R.A. Musgrave, P.A. Samuelson, B. Sandelin (82 pp.) |
| 1898 (1997) | KNUT WICKSELL, GELDZINS UND GÜTERPREISE | Facsimile reprint of the first edition published in Jena | … zu einem Klassiker der Preis- und Geldtheorie | B.A. Hansson, H.-J. Krupp. A. Leijonhufvud, B. Schefold (128 pp.) |

| First publication (publication of reprint and commentary volume) | Author and work (bold: translated commentary by B. Schefold in the present edition) | Reproduction | Title of commentary volume: Vademecum… | Authors (pp.) |
| --- | --- | --- | --- | --- |
| 1899 (1999) | JOHN BATES CLARK, THE DISTRIBUTION OF WEALTH | Facsimile reprint of the first edition published in New York and London | … zu einem amerikanischen Neoklassiker | K.-D. Grüske, J.F. Henry, H.D. Kurz, P.A. Samuelson (124 pp.) |
| 1899 (2000) | THORSTEIN B. VEBLEN, THE THEORY OF THE LEISURE CLASS | Facsimile reprint of the first edition published in New York | … zu einem Klassiker des institutionellen Denkens | K.-D. Grüske, K. Dopfer, W.J. Samuels, M.R. Tool (168 pp.) |
| 1900–1904 (1989) | GUSTAV SCHMOLLER, GRUNDRISS DER ALLGEMEINEN VOLKSWIRTSCHAFTSLEHRE | Facsimile reprint of the first edition published in two parts in Leipzig | … zu einem Klassiker der historischen Methode in der ökonomischen Wissenschaft | H.C. Recktenwald, J. Backhaus, B. Schefold, Y. Shionoya (127 pp.) |
| 1905 (1992) | **MAX WEBER, DIE PROTESTANTISCHE ETHIK UND DER 'GEIST' DES KAPITALISMUS** | Facsimile reprint of the first edition published in two parts in Tübingen | … zu einem Klassiker der Geschichte ökonomischer Rationalität | B. Schefold, K.H. Kaufhold, G. Roth, Y. Shionoya (144 pp.) |
| 1906 (1991) | IRVING FISHER, THE NATURE OF CAPITAL AND INCOME | Facsimile reprint of the first edition published in New York and London | … zu einem Klassiker der Nationalökonomie | P.A. Samuelson, J. Tobin, B. Schefold (95 pp.) |
| 1906 (1992) | VILFREDO PARETO, MANUALE DI ECONOMIA POLITICA | Facsimile reprint of the first edition published in Milano | … zu einem Klassiker der Ökonomie und Soziologie | B. Schefold, G. Eisermann, E. Malinvaud (248 pp.) |

| First publication (publication of reprint and commentary volume) | Author and work (bold: translated commentary by B. Schefold in the present edition) | Reproduction | Title of commentary volume: Vademecum… | Authors (pp.) |
| --- | --- | --- | --- | --- |
| 1907 (1994) | IRVING FISHER, THE RATE OF INTEREST | Facsimile reprint of the first edition published in New York | … zu einem Klassiker der Nationalökonomie | R. Dorfman, M. Neumann, C. Panico, P.A. Samuelson, B. Schefold (140 pp.) |
| 1908 (1991) | JOSEPH ALOIS SCHUMPETER, DAS WESEN UND DER HAUPTINHALT DER THEORE-TISCHEN NATIONALÖKONOMIE | Facsimile reprint of the first edition published in Leipzig | … zu einem genialen Klassiker der ökonomischen Wissenschaft | H. Hanusch, A. Heertje, Y. Shionoya (96 pp.) |
| 1910 (2000) | RUDOLF HILFERDING, DAS FINANZKAPITAL | Facsimile reprint of the first edition published in Vienna | … zu einem Klassiker der Beziehung zwischen Industrie- und Finanzkapital | E.J. Nell, B. Schefold, R.H. Schmidt, E.W. Streissler (134 pp.) |
| 1911 (1996) | FREDERICK WINSLOW TAYLOR, THE PRINCIPLES OF SCIENTIFIC MANAGEMENT | Facsimile reprint of the 'Special Edition printed for Confidential Circu-lation' published in New York | … zu einem Klassiker der wissenschaftlichen Betriebsführung | H. Hax, E. Gaugler, M. Lohmann, M. Tajima, D.A. Wren (127 pp.) |
| 1912 (1998) | ARTHUR CECIL PIGOU, WEALTH AND WELFARE | Facsimile reprint of the first edition published in London | … zu einem Klassiker der Wohlfahrtsökonomie | K.-D. Grüske, R.A. Musgrave, U. Raab, Y. Shionoya (127 pp.) |

| First publication (publication of reprint and commentary volume) | Author and work (bold: translated commentary by B. Schefold in the present edition) | Reproduction | Title of commentary volume: Vademecum… | Authors (pp.) |
|---|---|---|---|---|
| 1912 (1988) | JOSEPH ALOIS SCHUMPETER, THEORIE DER WIRTSCHAFTLICHEN ENTWICKLUNG | Facsimile reprint of the first edition published in Leipzig | … zu einem zukunftsträchtigen Klassiker der ökonomischen Wissenschaft | H.C. Recktenwald, F. M. Scherer, W.F. Stolper (115 pp.) |
| 1922 (1996) | LUDWIG VON MISES, DIE GEMEINWIRTSCHAFT | Facsimile reprint of the first edition published in Jena | … zu einem Klassiker liberalen Denkens | K.-D. Grüske, H.H. Hoppe, K.R. Leube, J. T. Salerno, C. Watrin (140 pp.) |
| 1922–1930 (2001) | J.H.CLAPHAM, A.C. PIGOU, L.C. ROBBINS, D.H. ROBERTSON, J.A. SCHUMPETER, G.F.SHOVE, P. SRAFFA, A.A. YOUNG, DIE SKALENERTRAGSDEBATTE IM 'ECONOMIC JOURNAL' 1922–1930 | Facsimile reprint of the first editions published in London | … zu der klassischen Debatte über Kosten, Wettbewerb und Entwicklung | K.J. Arrow, S. Blankenburg, G.C. Harcourt, B. Schefold, P.S. Labini (146 pp.) |
| 1923 (1999) | ALEXANDER W. CHAYANOV, DIE LEHRE VON DER BÄUERLICHEN WIRTSCHAFT | Facsimile reprint of the first edition published in Berlin | … zu einem russischen Klassiker der Agrarökonomie | B. Schefold, A.K. Bagchi, G.G. Bogomasow, N. Drosdowa, G. Schmitt, B. Streck, A.W. Chayanov (198 pp.) |
| 1924 (1995) | JOHN R. COMMONS, LEGAL FOUNDATIONS OF CAPITALISM | Facsimile reprint of the first edition published in New York | … zu einem Klassiker des amerikanischen Institutionalismus | J.E. Biddle, W.J. Samuels, B. Schefold, V. Vanberg (116 pp.) |

| First publication (publication of reprint and commentary volume) | Author and work (bold: translated commentary by B. Schefold in the present edition) | Reproduction | Title of commentary volume: Vademecum… | Authors (pp.) |
| --- | --- | --- | --- | --- |
| 1931 (1995) | FRIEDRICH AUGUST VON HAYEK, PREISE UND PRODUKTION | Facsimile reprint of the first edition published in Vienna | … zu einem Klassiker der Marktkoordination | B. Schefold, I.M. Kirzner, H.D. Kurz, K. R. Leube (148 pp) |
| 1934 (1993) | HEINRICH VON STACKELBERG, MARKTFORM UND GLEICHGEWICHT | Facsimile reprint of the first edition published in Vienna and Berlin | … zu einem Klassiker der Theorie der unvollkommenen Konkurrenz | W. Krelle, H. Möller, B. Schefold, F.M. Scherer (140 pp.) |
| 1936 (1989) | JOHN MAYNARD KEYNES, THE GENERAL THEORY OF EMPLOYMENT, INTEREST AND MONEY | Facsimile reprint of the first edition published in London | … zu einem bahnbrechenden Klassiker in seiner Zeit | H.C. Recktenwald, M. Friedman, D.E. Moggridge, D. Patinkin (160 pp.) |
| 1938 (1997) | JOHAN HENRIK ÅKERMAN, DAS PROBLEM DER SOZIALÖKONOMISCHEN SYNTHESE | Facsimile reprint of the first edition published in Lund | … zu einem Klassiker des skandinavischen Institutionalismus | B. Schefold, G. Eisermann, G.M. Hodgson, L. Mjøset (148 pp.) |
| 1939 (1997) | JOHN R. HICKS, VALUE AND CAPITAL | Facsimile reprint of the first edition published in Oxford | … zu dem Klassiker der Theorie des temporären Gleichgewichts | B. Schefold, K.J. Arrow, C. Bliss, S. Zamagni (112 pp.) |
| 1940 (2001) | AUGUST LÖSCH, DIE RÄUMLICHE ORDNUNG DER WIRTSCHAFT | Facsimile reprint of the first edition published in Jena | … zu einem Klassiker der Standorttheorie | A. Heertje, M.J. Beckmann, R.H. Funck, H. Giersch (104 pp.) |

| First publication (publication of reprint and commentary volume) | Author and work (bold: translated commentary by B. Schefold in the present edition) | Reproduction | Title of commentary volume: Vademecum… | Authors (pp.) |
|---|---|---|---|---|
| 1940 (2002) | LUDWIG VON MISES, NATIONALÖKONOMIE | Facsimile reprint of the first edition published in Geneva | … zu einem Klassiker der neuen österreichischen Schule | K.-D. Grüske, P.J. Boettke, E. Colombatto, K.R. Leube (132 pp.) |
| 1940 (1990) | WALTER EUCKEN, DIE GRUNDLAGEN DER NATIONALÖKONOMIE | Facsimile reprint of the first edition published in Jena | … zu einem Wegbereiter der modernen Theorie in Deutschland | G. Bombach, H.O. Lenel, O. Schlecht (103 pp.) |
| 1942 (2002) | WILHELM RÖPKE, DIE GESELLSCHAFTSKRISIS DER GEGENWART | Facsimile reprint of the first edition published in Erlenbach-Zurich | … zu einem Klassiker der Ordnungstheorie | F.A. Blankart, H.K. Peukert, B. Schefold, J. Starbatty (160 pp.) |
| 1944 (2001) | JOHN VON NEUMANN & OSKAR MORGENSTERN, THEORY OF GAMES AND ECONOMIC BEHAVIOR | Facsimile reprint of the first edition published in Princeton | … zu dem Klassiker der Spieltheorie | K.-D. Grüske, J.M. Buchanan, W. Güth, H. Kliemt, G. Schwödiauer, R. Selten (184 pp.) |
| 1947 (1997) | PAUL A. SAMUELSON, FOUNDATIONS OF ECONOMIC ANALYSIS | Facsimile reprint of the first edition published in Cambridge (Mass.) | … zu einem Klassiker der Gegenwart | B. Schefold, J. Niehans, P.A. Samuelson, C.C.v. Weizsäcker (128 pp.) |
| 1947 (1999) | ALFRED MÜLLER-ARMACK, WIRTSCHAFTSLENKUNG UND MARKTWIRTSCHAFT | Facsimile reprint of the first edition published in Hamburg | … zu einem Klassiker der Ordnungspolitik | A. Müller-Armack, B. Schefold, O. Schlecht, C. Watrin (160 pp.) |

# References

Akhtar, M.A. (1978) 'Sir James Steuart on Economic Growth', *Scottish Journal of Political Economy* 25/1: 57–74.

Andel, N. (1990) *Finanzwissenschaft*, 2, Tübingen: Mohr Siebeck.

Anderson, G.M. and Tollison, R.D. (1984) 'Sir James Steuart as the Apotheosis of Mercantilism and His Relation to Adam Smith', *Southern Economic Journal* 51/2: 456–468.

Andresen, C. (ed.) (1965) *Lexikon der alten Welt*, Zürich: Artemis.

von Aquin, T. (1991) *Summa theologiae*, Klassiker der Nationalökonomie, Düsseldorf: Verlag Wirtschaft und Finanzen.

Arena, R. (1988) 'Réflexions sur la théorie monétaire de Nicole Oresme' in Souffrin, P. and Segonds, A.P. (eds) *Nicolas Oresme: Tradition et innovation chez un intellectuel du XIVe siècle*, Paris: Les Belles Lettres.

Aristotle (1982 [1926]) *The 'Art' of Rhetoric*, with an English translation by J.H. Freese, Cambridge: Harvard UP.

Aristotle (1988) *The Politics*, ed. by S. Everson, Cambridge texts in the history of political thought, Cambridge: Cambridge University Press.

Aristotle (1990 [1926]) *The Nicomachean Ethics*, with an English transl. by H. Rackham, Cambridge (MA): Harvard University Press.

Ashley, W. (1962) 'A Survey of the Past History and Present Position of Political Economy', in R.L. Smyth (ed.) *Essays in Economic Method*, London: G. Duckworth.

Ashley, W. (1963 [1914]) *The Economic Organisation of England: An Outline History*, London: Longmans, Green.

Autorenkollektiv (1977) *Grundlinien des ökonomischen Denkens in Deutschland: Von den Anfängen bis zur Mitte des 19. Jahrhunderts*, Akad. D.Wiss. derD.D.R., Schriften des Zentralinst. f. Wirtschaftswiss., vol. 3, Berlin: Akademie-Verlag.

de Azpilcueta Navarro, M. (1556) 'Comentario resolutorio de Cambios', in M. de Azpilcueta Navarro, *Comentario resolutorio de usuras*, Salamanca: Portonarijs.

de Azpilcueta Navarro, M. (1965) '*Comentario resolutorio de Cambios*', Introducción y texto for A. Ullastres, J.M. Perez, L. Pereña Prendes, Madrid: Consejo Superior de Investigaciones Cientificas.

de Azpilcueta Navarro, M. (1978) 'Traduction du Comentario resolutorio de Cambios', French trans., in M. Gazier and B. Gazier, *Or et Monnaie Chez Martin de Azpilcueta*, Paris: Economica.

de Azpilcueta Navarro, M. and Ortiz, L. (1998) 'Comentario resulutorio de Cambios – Luis Ortiz', *Memorial del contador Luis Ortiz a Felipe II*, Klassiker der Nationalökonomie, Düsseldorf: Verlag Wirtschaft und Finanzen.

Baasch, E. (1927) 'Holländische Wirtschaftsgeschichte', in G. Brodnitz (ed.) *Handbuch der Wirtschaftsgeschichte*, Jena: G. Fischer.

Babbage, C. (1992 [1832]) *On the Economy of Machinery and Manufactures*, Klassiker der Nationalökonomie, Düsseldorf: Verlag Wirtschaft und Finanzen.

Babbitt, S.M. (1985) 'Oresme's 'Livre de Politiques' and the France of Charles V', *Trans Am Philos Soc* 75(1).

Badian, E. (1997) *Zöllner and Sünder: Unternehmer im Dienst der römischen Republik*, authorized trans., Darmstadt: Wissenschaftliche Buchgesellschaft.

Baeck, L. (1994) *The Mediterranean Tradition in Economic Thought*, London: Routledge.

Balazs, E. (1953) '*Le traité économique du "Souei-Chou": Études sur la Société et l'Économie de la Chine Médiévale*', Leiden: Brill.

Baloglou, C. (1994) Die geldtheoretischen Anschauung Platons, *Jahrbuch für Wirtschaftsgeschichte 1994/2*: 177–187.

Baloglou, C. (1995) *Die Vertreter der mathematischen Nationalökonomie in Deutschland zwischen 1838 und 1871*, Marburg: Metropolis.

Baloglou, C. (1998) 'Hellenistic Economic Thought', in S.T. Lowry, B. Gordon (eds) *Ancient and Medieval Economic Ideas and Concepts of Social Justice*, Leiden: Brill.

Baloglou, C. and Peukert, H. (1996) '*Review of a Xenophon edition*', off-print, Athens: Athena, 499–503.

Baloglou, C. and Schefold, B. (2005) 'Einleitung', in G. von Buquoy, *Die Theorie der Nationalwirthschaft*, ed. by B. Schefold, Historia Scientiarum (Wirtschaftswissenschaften), Hildesheim: Olms.

Bauer, C. (1954) 'Conrad Peutingers Gutachten zur Monopolfrage: Eine Untersuchung zur Wandlung der Wirtschaftsanschauungen im Zeitalter der Reformation', part 1 and 2, *Archiv für Reformationsgeschichte* 45/1: 1–42 and 45/2: 145–196.

Baumol, W.J. and Goldfeld, S.M. (eds) (1968) *Precursors in Mathematical Economics: An Anthology*, Series of reprints of Scarce Works on Political Economy, No. 19, London: The London School of Economics and Political Science (University of London).

Baurmann, M. (1996) *Der Markt der Tugend: Recht und Moral in der liberalen Gesellschaft: Eine soziologische Untersuchung*, Die Einheit der Gesellschaftswissenschaften, vol. 91, Tübingen: Mohr (Siebeck).

Becher, J.J. (1990 [1668]) *Politischer Discurs*, Klassiker der Nationalökonomie, Düsseldorf: Verlag Wirtschaft und Finanzen.

Beck, U. (1986) *Risikogesellschaft: Auf dem Weg in eine andere Moderne*, edition Suhrkamp, vol. 1365, NF vol. 365, Frankfurt a.M.: Suhrkamp.

Beckmann, M.J. and Sato, R. (eds) (1975) *Mathematische Wirtschaftstheorie*, Neue Wissenschaftliche Bibliothek 75, Köln: Kiepenheuer & Witsch.

Beetham, D. (1987) 'Weber, Max', in J. Eatwell, M. Milgate, P. Newman (eds) *The New Palgrave: A Dictionary of Economics*, vol. 4, London: The Macmillan Press Limited.

Behrends, O., Knütel, R., Kupisch, B. and Seiler, H.H. (1999) *Corpus iuris civilis: Die Institutionen*, text and transl., 2, Heidelberg: C.F. Müller.

Bellanger, P. (1856) 'Jacques Savary: Sa vie, ses ouvrages et son époque' in *Revue de l'Anjou et de Maine et Loire*, vol. 15, Angers: Cosnier et Lachè.

Benveniste, E. (1969) *Le vocabulaire des institutions indoeuropéennes*, 2 vol., Paris: Ed. de Minuit.

Berding, H. (1988) *Moderner Antisemitismus in Deutschland*, Frankfurt a.M.

Bernholz, P. (1992) 'The Discovery of the New World and the Development of the Purchasing Power Parity Theorem', in J.C. Pardo (ed.) *Economic Effects of the European Expansion, 1492–1824*, Stuttgart: Steiner.

Beutels, R. (1987) *Leonardus Lessius 1554–1623: Portret van een zuidnederlandse laat-scholastieke econoom. Een bio-bibliografisch essay*, Wommelgem: Den Gulden Engel.

Binswanger, H.C. (1985) *Geld und Magie*, Stuttgart: Weitbrecht.

Binswanger, H.C. (1997) 'Ordnungspolitische Ideen in der chinesischen Tradition', in *Neue Zürcher Zeitung* 30./31, August 1997.

Blanqui, A. (1860) *Histoire de l'économie politique en Europe*, 4, 2 vols, Paris: Guillaumin.

Bodin, J. (1945) 'La response de Jean Bodin aux paradoxes de Malestroit touchant l'encherrisement de toutes choses...', in A.E. Monroe (ed.) *Early Economic Thought: Selections from Economic Literature Prior to Adam Smith*, Cambridge (MA): Harvard University Press.

von Boenigk, O. (ed.) (1896) *Festgaben für Fünfundsiebzigsten Wiederkehr seines Geburtstages in dankbarer Verehrung dargebracht*, Berlin: Haering.

Bog, I. (1967) 'Geleitwort' in F. Blaich (ed.) *Die Reichsmonopolegesetzgebung im Zeitalter Karls V: Ihre ordnungspolitische Problematik, Schriften zum Vergleich von Wirtschaftsordnungen*, vol. 8, Stuttgart: G.Fischer.

Born, K.E. (1989) 'Jean Baptiste Colberte', in J. Starbatty (ed.) *Klassiker des ökonomischen Denkens*, Munich: C. H. Beck.

Boulakia, J.D.C. (1971) 'Ibn Khaldūn: A Fourteenth-Century Economist', *Journal of Political Economy* 79/5: 1105–1118.

Böhme, K. (1926) *Wirtschaftsanschauungen chinesischer Klassiker*, Hamburg: Ackermann und Wulff.

Brants, V. (1912) 'L'économie politique et sociale dans les écrits de L. Lessius (1554–1623)', *Revue d'Histoire Ecclesiastique* 13: 73–89 and 302–318.

Braudel, F. (1979) *Civilisation matérielle, économie et capitalisme, XVe-XVIIIe siècles*, Paris: Armand Colin.

Braudel, F. and La Bruce, E. (eds) (1970) *Histoire économique et sociale de la France, vol. 2: Des derniers temps de l'âge seigneurial aux préludes de l'âge industriel (1660–1789)*, Paris: Presses Universitaires de France.

Braudel, F.P. and Spooner, F. (1967) 'Prices in Europe from 1450–1750' in E.E. Rich, C.H. Wilson (eds) *The Cambridge Economic History of Europe*, vol. 4, Cambridge: Cambridge University Press.

Brauleke, H.-J. (1978) *Leben und Werk des Kameralisten Philipp Wilhelm von Hörnigk: Versuch einer Wissenschaflichen Biographie*, in the series Europäische Hochschulschriften, Series 3, Geschichte und ihre Hilfswissenschaften, vol. 108, Frankfurt a. M.: Lang.

Bridrey, E. (1906) *Nicole Oresme*, Paris: Giard et Brière.

von Brocke, B. (1992) 'Werner Sombart, 1863–1941: Capitalism – Socialism. His Life, Works and Influence Since (sic) Fifty Years', *Jahrbuch für Wirtschaftsgeschichte 1992/1*: 113–122.

Brockmeyer, N. (1987) *Antike Sklaverei*, 2, Darmstadt: Wissenschaftliche Buchgesellschaft.

Brodrick, J. (1934) *The Economic Morals of the Jesuits. An Answer to Dr. H. M. Robertson*, London: Oxford University Press/Humphrey Milford.

Brunner, O., Conze, E. and Koselleck, R. (eds) (1992) *Historisches Lexikon zur politisch-sozialen Sprache in Deutschland*, vol. 7, Stuttgart: Klett-Cotta.

Bruns, I. (1961) *Das literarische Porträt der Griechen im fünften und vierten Jahrhundert vor Christi Geburt*, Darmstadt: Wissenschaftliche Buchgesellschaft.

Burckhardt, J. (1944) *The Civilization of the Renaissance in Italy*, Oxford, New York: University Press.

Burckhardt, J. (2003) *Griechische Kulturgeschichte*, 1, Frankfurt a.M.: Insel Verlag.

Burkhardt, J. (1972) 'Wirtschaft', in *Geschichtliche Grundbegriffe: Historisches Lexikon zur politisch-sozialen Sprache in Deutschland*, vol. 7, Stuttgart: Klett-Cotta.

Burkhardt, J. (ed.) (1996) *Augsburger Handelshäuser im Wandel des historischen Urteils, Colloquia Augustana*, vol. 3, Berlin: Akademie Verlag.

Burns, A.R. (1965 [1927]) *Money and Monetary Policy in Early Times*, New York: Kelley.

Bücher, K. (1971 [1907]) 'Roscher', in *Allgemeine Deutsche Biographie*, vol. 53, Berlin: Duncker & Humblot.

Büchsenschütz, A.B. (1962 [1869]) *Besitz und Erwerb im griechischen Altertum*, Aalen: Scientia.

Bürgin, A. (1993) *Zur Soziogenese der Politischen Ökonomie: Wirtschaftsgeschichtliche und dogmenhistorische Betrachtungen*, Marburg: Metropolis.

Campanella, T. (1968) *Apologia di Galileo, a cura di Luigi Firpo*, Turin: Unione Typografica-Editrice.

Carl, E.L. (2000 [1722–1723]) *Traité de la richesse des princes et de leurs états et des moyens simples et naturels pour y parvenir*, with intr. and ed. by K. Kunze, B. Schefold, 3 vols, Hildesheim: Olms.

Chamberlain, C.H. (1939) 'Leonard Lessius', in G. Smith (ed.) *Jesuit Thinkers of the Renaissance: Essays Presented to John F. McCormick by his Students on the Occasion of the Sixty-fifth Anniversary of his Birth*, Milwaukee, WI: University Press.

Chamley, P. (1962) 'Sir James Steuart: inspirateur de la théorie générale de Lord Keynes?', *Revue d'économie politique*, 72: 303–313.

Chamley, P. (1963) 'Steuart et Keynes: Réflexions sur le commentaire de M. Lambert', *Revue d'économie politique*, 73: 105–109.

Chamley, P. (1965) *Documents relatifs à Sir James Steuart*, Paris: Dalloz.

Chayanov, A.V. (1999 [1923]) *Die Lehre von der bäuerlichen Wirtschaft*, Klassiker der Nationalökonomie, Düsseldorf: Verlag Wirtschaft und Finanzen.

Chen, H.-C. (1974 [1911]) *The economic Principles of Confucius and His School*, New York: Gordon Press.

Churchill, W.S. (1974 [1956]) *A History of the English-Speaking Peoples*, vol. 2, London.

Cicero (1932) *The Civil Law*, transl. by S.P. Scott, in 17 vols, Cincinnatti: The Central Trust Company.

Cicero (1953) *Paradoxa Stoicorum*, with introduction and notes by A.G. Lee, London: Macmillan.

Cicero (1960) *De Oratore*, with an English translation by H. Rackham, Cambridge: Cambridge University Press.

Cicero (1961a) *De Legibus*, with an English translation by C.W. Keyes, Cambridge: Cambridge University Press.

Cicero (1961b) *De officiis*, with an English translation by W. Miller, Cambridge (MA): Harvard University Press.

Cipolla, C.M. (1956) *Money, Prices and Civilization in the Mediterranean World: 5th to 17th Century*, Princeton: Princeton University Press.

Clark, E.A. (1940) 'Adolph Wagner: From National Economist to National Socialist', *Political Science Quarterly* 55/3: 378–411.

Clavero, B. (1996) *La Grâce de don. Anthropologie catholique de l'économie moderne*, préface de J. Le Goff, Paris: Michel.

Cohen, E.E. (1992) *Athenian Economy and Society: A Banking Perspective*, Princeton: Princeton University Press.

Collin, P. (1925) 'Le 'De iustitia et iure' de Léonard Lessius', *Bulletin d'Etudes & d'Informations de l'École Supérieur de commerce St. Ignace* 2/5–6: 245–263.

Columella, L.I.M. (1981–1983) *De re rustica. 12 Bücher über Landwirtschaft*, Latin-German, ed. and transl. by W. Richter, vols 1–3, Munich: Artemis.

Commons, J.R. (1995) *Legal Foundations of Capital*, Klassiker der Nationalökonomie, Düsseldorf: Verlag Wirtschaft und Finanzen.

Confucius (1998) *Gespräche (Lun-yu)*, transl. and ed. by R. Moritz, in the series Reclams Universal-Bibliothek 9656, Stuttgart: Reclam.

Conrad, J. (1878) 'Bruno Hildebrand [Obituary]', *Jahrbücher für Nationalökonomie und Statistik* 30: I–XVI.

Conrad, J. (ed.) (1910) *Handwörterbuch der Staatswissenschaften*, 3, vol. 6, Jena: Fischer.

Copernicus, N. (1965) *Treatise on coining money (De monetae cudendae ratione)*, transl., ed. and publ. by G.A. Moore, Chevy Chase, Md.: Country Dollar Press.

Copernicus, N. (1978) *Die Geldlehre des Nicolaus Copernicus*, transl., commentary, ed. by E. Sommerfeld, Vaduz, Liechstenstein: Topos.

Coulton, G.G. (1921) 'An Episode in Canon Law', *History* 6/22: 67–76.

Dante (1867) *The Divine Comedy*, vol. 3, transl. by H. Wadsworth Longfellow, Boston: Ticknor and Fields.

Davis, J.F. (1847–1848) *China und die Chinesen: Eine allgemeine Beschreibung von China und dessen Bewohnern*, transl. by. W. Drogulin from 2, 4 vols, Stuttgart: Expedition der Wochenbände.

Delachenal, R. (1927–1931) *Histoire de Charles V.*, 5 vols, Paris: Auguste Picard.

Demandt, A. (1995) *Antike Staatsformen: Eine vergleichende Verfassungsgeschichte der Alten Welt*, Berlin: Akademie Verlag.

Denis, H. (1974 [1966]) *Histoire de la pensée économique*, 4, Paris: Presses Universitaires de France.

Dessert, D. (1984) *Argent, pouvoir et société au Grande Siècle*, Paris: Fayard.

*Dictionnaire de Spiritualité, Ascétique et Mystique, Doctrine et Histoire* (1976) vol. IX: *Labydie-Lyonnet*, Paris: Beauchesne.

Diehl, K. (1941) *Die sozialrechtliche Richtung in der Nationalökonomie*, Jena: G. Fischer.

Distelrath, G. and Kreiner, J. (2001) 'Miura Baiens Naturphilosophie und Wirtschaftslehre', in B. Schefold (ed.) *Vademecum zu einem japanischen Klassiker des ökonomischen Denkens, Klassiker der Nationlaökonomie*, Düsseldorf: Verlag Wirtschaft und Finanzen.

Dopfer, K. (1985) 'Reconciling Economic Theory and Economic History: The Rise of Japan', *Journal of Economic Issues* 19/1: 21–73.

Dopfer, K. (2001) 'Baiens Ökonomie vom Überfluß der wahren Schätze. Auf den Spuren eines japanischen Klassikers', in Schefold, B. (ed.) *Vademecum zu einem japanischen Klassiker des ökonomischen Denkens*, Klassiker der Nationlaökonomie, Düsseldorf: Verlag Wirtschaft und Finanzen.

Dopsch, A. (1968) *Naturalwirtschaft und Geldwirtschaft in der Weltgeschichte*, Aalen: Scientia.

Dreitzel, H. (1987) 'Justis Beitrag zur Politisierung der deutschen Aufklärung', in H.E. Bödecker, U. Herrmann (eds) *Aufklärung als Politisierung – Politisierung der Aufklärung, Studien zum achtzehnten Jahrhundert*, vol. 8, Hamburg: Meiner.

Duby, G. (1981) *The Age of Cathedrals: Art and Society 980–1420*, transl. by E. Levieux, B. Thompson, Chicago: University of Chicago Press.

Dupuy, C. (1989) 'Introduction aux écrits de Nicolas Oresme', in C. Dupuy (ed.) *Traité des Monnaies et autres écrits monétaires du XIVe siècle*, textes réunis et introduits par C. Dupuy, Lyon: La Manufacture.

Dühring, E. (1900) *Kritische Geschichte der Nationalökonomie und des Socialismus von ihren Anfängen bis zur Gegenwart*, 4th rev. and significantly expanded edn, Leipzig: Naumann.

Dyck, A.R. (1996) *A Commentary on Cicero, De officiis*, Ann Arbor: University of Michigan Press.

Eckermann, J.P. (1971) *Conversations with Goethe*, transl. by J. Oxenford and ed. by J.K. Moorhead, London: Dent.

Edmonds, J.M. (ed.) (1953) *The Characters of Theophrastus*, Greek and English, London and Cambridge: Heinemann and Harvard.

Egner, E. (1985) *Verlust der alten Ökonomik*, Berlin: Duncker & Humblot.

Ehrenberg, R. (1896) *Das Zeitalter der Fugger: Geldkapital und Creditverkehr im 16. Jahrhundert*, 2 vols, Jena: G. Fischer.

Ehrenberg, R. (1925) *Die Fugger – Rothschild – Krupp*, 3, Jena: G. Fischer.

Ehrenberg, R. (1963) *Capital and finance in the age of the Renaissance: A study of the Fuggers and their connections*, transl. by H.M. Lucas, New York: Augustus M. Kelly.

Eisermann, G. (1956) *Die Grundlagen des Historismus in der deutschen Nationalökonomie*, Stuttgart: Enke.

Eisermann, G. (1989) *Max Weber und Vilfredo Pareto*, Tübingen: J.C.B. Mohr (Paul Siebeck).

Eltis, W. (1986) 'Sir James Steuart's Corporate State', in R.D.C. Black (ed.) *Ideas in Economics*, London: B & N Imports.

Elvin, M. (1973) *The Pattern of Chinese Past: A Social and Economic Interpretation*, Stanford: Stanford University Press.

*Enciclopedia Cattolica* (1951) vol. 7: *Inno-Mapp*, Florence: G. C. Sansoni.

Endemann, W. (1863) 'Die nationalökonomischen Grundsätze der canonistischen Lehre', *Jahrbücher für Nationalökonomie und Statistik* 1: 26–47.

Endemann, W. (1874) *Studien in der romanisch-kanonistischen Wirtschafts- und Rechtslehre bis gegen Ende des siebzehnten Jahrhunderts*, vol. 1, Berlin: Guttentag.

Endemann, W. (1883) *Studien in der romanisch-kanonistischen Wirtschafts- und Rechtslehre bis gegen Ende des siebzehnten Jahrhunderts*, vol. 2, Berlin: Guttentag.

Engelhardt, U. (1981) 'Zum Begriff der Glückseligkeit in der Kameralistischen Staatslehre des 18. Jahrhunderts (J. H. G. v. Justi)', *Zeitschrift für historische Forschung* 8: 37–128.

Engels, F. (1844) 'Deutsch-Französische Jahrbücher', in *Marx-Engels Werke (MEW)*, vol. 1, Paris.

Ermis, F. (2013) *A History of Ottoman Economic Thought: Developments before the 19th Century*, London: Routledge.

Essid, Y. (1995) *Islamic History and Civilization: A Ciritique of the origins of Islamic Economic Thought*, Leiden, NewYork, Köln: Brill.

Facius, F. (1959) *Wirtschaft und Staat: Die Entwicklung der staatlichen Wirtschaftsverwaltung in Deutschland vom 17. Jahrhundert bis 1945*, in the series Schiften des Bundesarchives, vol. 6, Boppard: Boldt.

Fanfani, A. (1933) *Le Origini dello spirito capitalistico in Italia*, Pubblicazioni della Università Cattolica del Sacro Cuore, Serie Terza: Scienze Sociali, vol. 12, Milano: Società editrice Vita e Pensiero.

Feilbogen, S. (1889) 'James Steuart and Adam Smith', *Zeitschrift für die gesammte Staatswissenschaft* 45: 218–260.

Finley, M.I. (1973) *The Ancient Economy*, London: Chatto and Windus.

Fischel, W.J. (1967) *Ibn Khaldūn in Egypt. His Public Functions and his Historical Research (1382–1406). A Study in Islamic Historiography*, Berkeley: University of California Press.

Fitzmaurice, E. (1899) 'Petty', in R.H.I. Palgrave (ed.) *Dictionary of Political Economy*, vol. 3, London.

Fourastié, J. (1989 [1949]) *Le grand espoir du XXe siècle, Édition définitive.* Paris: Gallimard.

Fournial, E. (1970) *Histoire monétaire de l'occident médiéval*, Paris: Nathan.

Foxwell, E. (1900) 'Report on the Adoption of the Gold Standard in Japan by C.M. Masayoshi', *Economic Journal* 10/38: 232–245.

Franke, H. (1949) *Geld und Wirtschaft in China unter der Mongolen-Herrschaft*, Leipzig: Harrassowitz.

Franz, G. (1928) *Studien über Bruno Hildebrand*, Marburg: Schröder.

Freis, H. (transl. and ed.) (1984) *Historische Inschriften zur römischen Kaiserzeit: Von Augustinus bis Constantin*, Darmstadt: Wissenschaftliche Buchgesellschaft.

Frensdorff, F. (1970 [1903]) *Über das Leben und die Schriften des Nationalökonomen J. H. G. von Justi*, Glashütten: Auvermann.

Fronsperger, L. (1564) *Von dem Lob deß Eigen Nutzen. Mit vil schönen Exempeln vnd Hostrien auß heyliger Göttlicher Schrifft zusammen gezogen / durch Leonhard Fronsperger an tag geben, Getruckt zu Franckfurt am Mayn 1564*, Frankfurt.

Fu, Z. (1996) *China's Legalists: The Earliest Totalitarians and Their Art of Ruling*, Armonk, New York: Sharpe.

Fukuzawa, Y. (1971) *Eine autobiographische Lebensschilderung*, transl. by G. Linzbichler, Tokyo: Die Japanisch-Deutsche Gesellschaft e.V.

Gadamer, H.G. (1986) *The Idea of the Good in Platonic-Aristotelian Philosophy*, transl. and with an introduction by P.C. Smith, Yale: Yale University Press.

Gautier-Dalche, J. (1988) 'Oresme et son temps', in P. Souffrin, A.Ph. Segonds (eds) *Nicolas Oresme : Tradition et innovation chez un intellectuel du XIVe siècle*, Paris: Les Belles Lettres.

George, S. (1974) *The works of Stefan George*, rendered into English by O. Marx and E. Morwitz, 2 revised and enlarged, Chapel Hill: The University of North Carolina Press.

Gerstenberg, H. (1930) 'Philipp Wilhelm v. Hörnigk', *Jahrbücher für Nationalökonomie und Statistik* 133: 813–871.

Ghaussy, A.G. (1986) *Das Wirtschaftsdenken im Islam: Von der orthodoxen Lehre bis zu den heutigen Ordnungsvorstellungen*, Bern: P. Haupt.

Giacchero, M. (ed.) (1971) *Edictum Diocletiani et Collegarum de pretiis rerum venalium*, vol. 1, Genova: Istituto di storia antica.

Gigon, O. (1979) *Sokrates. Sein Bild in Dichtung und Geschichte*, 2, expanded, Bern and Munich: Franke.

Glahn, R. (1996) *Fountain of Fortune: Money and Monetary Policy in China, 1000–1700*, Berkeley: University of California Press.

von Goethe, J.W. (1950) *Faust, Part I*, London: Penguin Classics.

von Goethe, J.W. (1976) *Gesammelte Werke*, ed. by E. Beutler, 3, vol. 24, Zürich: Artemis.

von Goethe, J.W. (1984) *Egmont*, 4th act, transl., with an introduction by C.E. Passage, New York: Frederick Ungar.

Goetz, B. (1953) *Italienische Gedichte, italienisch-deutsch, Nachdichtungen von Bruno Goetz*, Zürich: Manesse.

Goldsmith, R.W. (1987) *Premodern Financial Systems*, Cambridge: Cambridge University Press.

Gordon, B. (1975) *Economic Analysis before Adam Smith: Hesiod to Lessius*, London: Macmillan.

Gossen, H.H. (1987 [1854]) *Die Entwickelung der Gesetze des menschlichen Verkehrs*, Klassiker der Nationalökonomie, Düsseldorf: Verlag Wirtschaft und Finanzen.

Grice-Hutchinson, M. (1952) *The School of Salamanca: Readings in Spanish Monetary Theory 1544–1605*, Oxford: Clarendon.

Grice-Hutchinson, M. (1995) *Ensayos sobre el pensamiento económico en España*, Madrid: Alianza Editorial.

Grünberg, C. (1925) 'Bruno Hildebrand über den kommunistischen Arbeiterbildungsverein in London. Zugleich ein Betrag zu Hildebrands Biographie', in C. Grünberg (ed.) *Archiv für die Geschichte des Sozialismus und der Arbeiterbewegung*, vol. 11, Leipzig: C.L. Hirschfeld.

Hadfield, C. (1968) *The Canal Age*, London: Pan Books.

Hamilton, E.J. (1971) 'American Treasure and Andalusian Prices, 1503–1660. A Study in the Spanish Price Revolution', in P.H. Ramsay (ed.) *The Price Revolution in Sixteenth-Century England*, London: Methuen.

Hassinger, H. (1951) *Johann Joachim Becher 1635–1682: Ein Beitrag zur Geschichte des Merkantilismus*, publication of the Kommission für Neuere Geschichte Österreichs, vol. 38, Vienna: Holzhausens NFG.

Haupt, W. (1974) *Sächsische Münzekunde, Arbeits- und Forschungsberichte zur sächsischen Bodenkmalpflege*, Beiheft 10, Berlin: VEB Deutscher Verlag der Wissenschaften.

Hauser, H. (1925) 'Le "Parfait Négociant" de Jacques Savary', *Revue d'histoire économique et sociale* 7.

Hayek, F.A. (1975 [1935]) 'The Nature and the History of the Problem', in F.A. Hayek (ed.) *Collectivist Economic Planning*, Clifton: A. M. Kelley.

Heckscher, E.F. (1931) *Mercantilism*, London: Allen & Unwin.

Heilmann, M. (1980) *Adolph Wagner: Ein deutscher Nationalökonom im Urteil der Zeit*, Frankfurt a.M./New York.

Hennings, K.H. (1980) 'The Transition from Classical to Neoclassical Economic Theory: Hans von Mangoldt', *Kyklos* 33/4: 658–681.

Hennis, W. (1987) *Max Webers Fragestellung*, Tübingen: J.C.B.Mohr (Paul Siebeck).

Hesiod (1914) 'Works And Days', in *Hesiod, the Homeric Hymns and Homerica*, transl. by H.G. Evelyn-White, in the series Loeb Classics, Cambridge (MA): Harvard University Press.

Hesiod (2007) *Works and Days*, transl. by H.G. Evelyn-White, Charleston, South Carolina: Forgotten Books.

Heubner, P.L. (1942) 'Adolph Wagner: Einige Streiflichter', *Schmollers Jahrbuch* 66/6: 1–16.

Heuss, A. (1965) 'Max Webers Bedeutung für die Geschichte des griechisch-römischen Altertums', *Historische Zeitschrift* 201/3: 529–556.

434　*References*

Hildebrand, B. (1845) *Xenophontis et Aristotelis de oeconomia publica doctrinae. Particula I*, Marburgi: Typis Bayrhofferia Academicis.

Hildebrand, B. (1863) 'Die gegenwärtige Aufgabe der Wissenschaft der Nationalökonomie', *Jahrbücher für Nationalökonomie und Statistik* 1: 5–25 and 137–146.

Hildebrand, B. (1864) 'Naturalwirthschaft, Geldwirthschaft und Creditwirthschaft', *Jahrbücher für Nationalökonomie und Statistik* 2: 1–24.

Hildebrand, B. (1869) 'Die sociale Frage der Vertheilung des Grundeigenthums im klassischen Alterthum', *Jahrbücher für Nationalökonomie und Statistik* 12: 1–25 and 139–155.

Hildebrand, B. (1872) 'Die Verdienste der Universität Jena um die Fortbildung und das Studium der Staatswissenschaften [an academic speech delivered on 17 June 1871 in the assembly hall of the University of Jena]', *Jahrbücher für Nationalökonomie und Statistik* 18: 1–11.

Hildebrand, B. (1922) *Die Nationalökonomie der Gegenwart und Zukunft und andere gesammelte Schriften*, ed. and intr. by H. Gehrig, vol. 1, Jena: Fischer.

Hirsching, F.C.G. (ed.) (1796) *Historisch-Literarisches Handbuch berühmter und denkwürdiger Personen, welche im 18. Jahrhundere gestorben sind.*, vol. 3, 1st Dept. *Hartzheim–Hymnen*, Leipzig: Schwickert.

Hirschman, A.O. (1981) *Essays in Trespassing*, Cambridge: Cambridge University Press.

Hodgskin, T. (1969) *Labour Defended Against the Claims of Capital*, New York: A.M. Kelley.

Holländer, H. (1990) 'A Social Exchange Approach to Voluntary Cooperation', *American Economic Review* 80/5: 1157–1167.

Homberg, G. (1971) *Die Vertreter der mathematischen Nationalökonomie im deutschsprachigen Raum vor dem Erscheinen des Cournot'schen Werkes (1838)*, Freiburg i. Br.: Dissertationsdruck Johannes Krause.

Homer (1834) *The Iliad and Odyssey*, transl. by W. Sotheby, vol. 4, London.

Homer (1976) 'Hymn to Aphrodite', in N. Apostolos (ed.) *The Homeric Hymns*, Athanassakis, London: The Johns Hopkins University Press.

Homer (1990) *The Iliad*, transl. by R. Fagles, New York: Penguin Books.

Honjô, E. (1965) *Economic Theory and History in the Tokugawa-Period*, New York: Russell and Russell.

Horace (1988) *The Odes and Epodes*, with an English translation by C.E. Bennett, Cambridge: Harvard UP.

Hourani, A. (1991) *A History of the Arab Peoples*, London: Faber and Faber.

Hoyer, W. (1928) 'Nachruf [Obituary]', in *Deutsches Biographisches Jahrbuch*, ed. by Verbande der Deutschen Akadamien, vol. 2, 1917–1920, Stuttgart: Deutsche Verlags-Anstalt.

Höffner, J. (1941) *Wirtschaftsethik und Monopole im fünfzehnten und sechzehnten Jahrhundert*, Freiburger Staatswissenschaftliche Schriften, issue 2, Jena: G. Fischer.

von Hörnigk, P.W. (1708) *Oesterreich ueber alles / wann es nur will. Das ist Wohlmeynender Fuerschlag / Wie mittelst einer wohlbestellten Lands-Oeconomie die Kayserlichen Erb-Lande in kurtzem ueber alle anderen Staate von Europa zu Erheben / und mehr als einiger derselben / von denen anderen independent zu machen*, Regenspurg: Verlegts Joh. Zacharias Seidel.

von Hörnigk, P.W. (1997 [1684]) *Oesterreich über alles*, repr., Düsseldorf: Verlag Wirtschaft und Finanzen.

Hu, J. (1988) *A Concise History of Chinese Economic Thought*, in the series China Knowledge, Beijing: Foreign Language Press.

Hugonnard-Roche, H. (1988) 'Modalités et argumentation chez Nicole Oresme', in P. Souffrin, A.P. Segonds (eds) *Nicolas Oresme: Tradition et innovation chez un intellectuel du XIVe siècle, etudes receuillies*, Paris: Les Belles Lettres.

Hutchison, T. (1988) *Before Adam Smith: The Emergence of Political Economy. 1662–1776*, Oxford: Blackwell.

Hutter, M. (1982) 'Early Contributions to Law and Economics: Adolph Wagner's 'Grundlegung'', *Journal of Economic Issues* 16/1: 131–147.

Hünermann, F.J. (1939) *Die wirtschaftsethischen Predigten des hl. Bernhardin von Siena. Eine moralwissenschaftliche Studie*, Diss., Münster.

Ikeo, A. (2001) 'History of Japanese Economic Thought: The Present and the Future', *Annals of the Society for the History of Economic Thought* 39: 94–102.

Iklé, M. (1970) *Die Schweiz als internationaler Bank- und Finanzplatz*, Zürich: Orell Füssli.

Ilgner, C. (1904) *Die volkswirtschaftlichen Anschauungen Antonins von Florenz (1389–1459)*, Paderborn: Schöningh.

Ingram, K. (1962) 'The Present Position and Prospect of Political Economy', lecture 1878, printed in R.L. Smyth (ed.) *Essays in Economic Method*, London: G. Duckworth.

Instituto de España (ed.) (1970) *Memorial del contador Luiz Ortiz, Valladolid, 1. de Marzo 1558, Biblioteca Nacional – Ms. 6487*, Madrid: Instituto de Españam.

Jacobi, E. (1955) *Wechsel- und Scheckrecht*, Berlin: de Gruyter.

Jaspers, K. (1967 [1964]) *Die maßgebenden Menschen: Sokrates, Buddha, Konfuzius, Jesus*, Munich: Piper.

Jaspers, K. (1989) *On Max Weber*, ed., with introd. and notes by J. Dreijmanis, transl. from the German by R. Whelan, New York: Paragon House.

Jevons, W.S. (1995 [1871]) *The Theory of Political Economy*, Klassiker der Nationalökonomie, Düsseldorf: Verlag Wirtschaft und Finanzen.

Johnson, C. (1956) *The De Moneta of Nicholas Oresme and English Mint Documents*, London: Nelson and Sons.

Jonas, F. (1968) *Geschichte der Soziologie IV. Deutsche und Amerikanische Soziologie*, Rowohlts deutsche Enzyklopädie, vol. 308/309, Reinbek: Rowohlt.

Jones, R. (1964 [1831]) *An Essay on the Distribution of Wealth and on the Sources of Taxation*, New York: Kelley.

von Justi, J.H.G. (1756) *Grundsaetze der Policey-Wissenschaft in einem vernuenftigen, auf dem Endzweck der Policey gegruendeten, Zusammenhange und zum Gebrauch academischer Vorlesungen abgefasset*, Göttingen: van den Hoeck.

von Justi, J.H.G. (1782) *Grundsätze der Policey-Wissenschaft in einem Vernünftigen, auf den Endzweck der Policey gegründeten, Zusammenhange und zum Gebrauch Academischer Vorlesungen abgefasst*, 3 (corrected and expanded), Göttingen: Vandenhoek.

von Justi, J.H.G. (1970 [1764]) *Gesammelte politische und Finanz-Schriften über wichtige Gegenstände der Staatskunst, der Kriegswissenschaften und des Cameral- und Finanzwesens*, vol. 3, Aalen: Scientia.

von Justi, J.H.G. (1977 [1762]) *Ausführliche Abhandlung von denen Steuern und Abgaben*, Wiesbaden: Betriebswirtschaftlicher Verlag Dr. Th. Gabler.

von Justi, J.H.G. (1993 [1756]) *Grundsätze der Policey-Wissenschaft*, Klassiker der Nationalökonomie, Düsseldorf: Verlag Wirtschaft und Finanzen.

von Kahler, E. (1920) *Der Beruf der Wissenschaft*, Berlin: Georg Bondi.

Kaldor, N. (1983) *Grenzen der 'General Theory'*, ed. by B. Schefold, *1. Merton-Lesung an der J. W. Goethe Universität Frankfurt a. M.*, Berlin: Springer.

Kalveram, G. (1933) 'Die Theorien von den Wirtschaftsstufen', in K. Pribram (ed.) *Frankfurter Wirtschaftswissenschaftliche Studien*, in conjunction with Gerloff, W. and Löwe, A., issue 1, Leipzig: H. Buske.

Kamil Ayad, M. (1930) *Die Geschichts- und Gesellschaftslehre Ibn Khaldūns*, Stuttgart: Cotta.

Kasper, W. (ed.) (1997) 'Lessius (Leys), Leonardus', in *Lexikon für Theologie und Kirche*, 3, vol. 6: *Kirchengeschichte bix Maximianus*, Freiburg: Herder.

Kautz, J. (1970 [1860]) *Die geschichtliche Entwicklung der National-Oekonomik und Ihrer Literatur*, Glashütten: Auvermann.

Keynes, J.M. (1967 [1936]) *The General Theory of Employment, Interest and Money*, London: Macmillan.

Keynes, J.M. (1971 [1923]) *The Collected Writings of John Maynard Keynes*, vol. 4: *A Tract on Monetary Reform*, London: Macmillan.

Keynes, J.N. (1986) *The Scope and Method of Political Economy*, New York: A.M. Kelley.

Khaldūn, I. (1951) *Ausgewählte Abschnitte aus der muqaddima*, transl. from the Arabic by A. Schimmel, Tübingen: Mohr.

Khaldūn, I. (1958) *The Muqaddimah*, transl. from the Arabic by F. Rosenthal in 3 vols, New York: Bollingen Foundation.

Khaldūn, I. (1992) *Buch der Beispiele: Die Einführung al-Muqaddima*, translation, selection, preface and notes by M. Pätzold, Leipzig: Reclam.

Kirch, H.J. (1915) *Die Fugger und der Schmalkaldische Krieg*, Munich, Leipzig: Duncker & Humblot.

Kisch, H. (1962) 'Knies, Karl', in D.L. Sills (ed.) *International Encyclopedia of the Social Sciences*, New York: Macmillan.

Klotz, R. (ed.) (1855) *M.T. Ciceronis scripta quae manserunt omnia*, partis IV, vol. III, libri de officiis tres, Leipzig: Teubner.

Klotzsch, J.F. (1779) *Versuch einer chur-säschischen Münzgeschischte. Von den ältesten bis auf Jetzige Zeiten. 1. Theil*, Chemnitz: Stößel.

Klump, R. (2004) 'The Kingdom of Ponthiamas – A Physiocratic Model State in Indochina. A Note on the International Exchange of Economic Thought and of Concepts for Economic Reforms in the eighteenth Century', in I. Barens, V. Caspari, B. Schefold (eds) *Political Events and Economic Ideas*, Cheltenham: Elgar.

Knies, K. (1892) *Carl Friedrichs von Baden brieflicher Verkehr mit Mirabeau und Du Pont, bearbeitet und eingeleitet durch einen Betrag zur Vorgeschichte der ersten französischen Revolution und Physiokratie*, 2 vols, Heidelberg.

Knies, K. (1931 [1885]) *Geld und Credit. Erste Abtheilung: Das Geld. Darlegung der Grundlehren von dem Gelde, insbesondere der wirtschaftlichen und rechtgiltigen Functionen des Gelder, mit einer Erörterung über das Kapital und die Übertragung der Nutzungen*, 2 (improved and expanded), Leipzig: Buske.

Knies, K. (1964 [1883]) *Die politische Oekonomie vom geschichtlichen Standpuncte*, new and revised edn of '*Die politische Oekonomie vom Standpunkte der geschichtlichen Methode*' [1853], Osnabrück: Zeller.

Knittler, H. (1993) 'Die Donaumonarchie 1648–1848', in I. Mieck (ed.) *Handbuch der Europäischen Wirtschafts- und Sozialgeschichte*, vol. 4. Stuttgart: Klett-Cotta.

Knoll, A.M. (1933) *Der Zins in der Scholastik*, Innsbruck, etc.: Verlagsanstalt Tyrolia.

Kobayashi, N. (1967) 'James Steuart, Adam Smith and Friedrich List', in *Economic Series of the Science Council of Japan*, 40, Tokyo: The Science Council of Japan.

Koder, J. (1991) *Das Eparchenbuch Leons des Weisen*, introduction, editing, translation and index by J. Koder, Vienna: Österreichische Akademie der Wissenschaften.

Komuro, M. (2001) "Kagen' und die Entwicklung des ökonomischen Denkens in der Mitte der Edo-Periode', in B. Schefold (ed.) *Vademecum zu einem japanischen Klassiker des ökonomischen Denkens*, Klassiker der Nationalökonomie, Düsseldorf: Verlag Wirtschaft und Finanzen.

Kraus, J.X. (2000) *Die Stoa und ihr Einfluss auf die Nationalökonomie*, Marburg: Metropolis.

Kroll, Y.L. (1978–1979) 'Toward a Study of the Economic Views of Sang Hongyang', *Early China* 4: 11–18.

K'uan, H. (2002) 'Yantie lun: Die Debatte über Salz und Eisen', in B. Schefold (ed.) *Vademecum zu dem Klassiker der chinesischen Wirtschaftsdebatten*, transl. by S. Ludwig, annotated by E. von Mende, Klassiker der Nationalökonomie, Düsseldorf: Verlag Wirtschaft und Finanzen.

Kumagai, J. (1998) 'Enlightenment and Economic Thought in Meiji Japan: Yukichi Fukuzawa and Ukichi Taguchi', in S. Sugihara, T. Tanaka (eds) *Economic Thought and Modernization in Japan*, Cheltenham: Elgar.

Kunze, K. and Schefold, B. (2000) 'Einleitung', in E.L. Carl *Cours d'économie politique*, ed. by B. Schefold, 3 vols, Historia Scientiarum (Wirtschaftswissenschaften), Hildesheim: Olms.

Lambert, P. (1963) 'Steuart et Keynes: Bref commentaire sur l'étude de M. Chamley', *Revue d'économie politique* 73: 105–109.

Landmann, E. (1923) *Die Transcendanz des Erkennens*, Berlin: George Bondi.

Landmann, M. (1960) 'Um die Wissenschaft', *Castrvm Peregrini* 42: 65–90.

Landry, A. (1909) 'Notes critiques sur le "Nicole Oresme" de M. Bridrey', in *Le Moyen Age: Revue d'Histoire et de Philologie*, 2e série, tome XIII (tome XXII de la collection), Paris: H. Champion.

Langholm, O. (1992) *Economics in the Medieval Schools. Wealth, Exchange, Value, Money and Usury According to the Paris Theological tradition 1200–1350*, Leiden: Brill.

Lapidus, A. (1997) 'Metal, Money and the Prince: John Buridan and Nicholas Oresme after Thomas Aquinas', *History of Political Economy* 29/1: 21–53.

Larraz Lopez, D.J. (1943) *La epoca del mercantilismo en Castilia (1500–1700)*, Real Academia de Ciencias Morales y Politicas, Session de 5 de abril de 1943. Madrid: Diana.

Lauffer, S. (ed.) (1971) *Diokletians 'Preisedikt'*, Berlin: de Gruyter.

Launhardt, W. (1882) 'Die Bestimmung des zweckmäßigen Standortes einer gewerblichen Anlage', *Zeitschrift des Vereines deutscher Ingenieure* 26/3: 105–116.

Launhardt, W. (1993) *Mathematical Principles of Economics*, transl. by H. Schmidt, edited and with an introduction by J. Creedy, Hants: Edward Publishing Limited.

Lazare, B. (1894) *L'antisémitisme, son histoire et ses causes*, Paris.

Lehr, J. (1885) 'Launhardt, W…. Mathematische Begründung der Volkswirtschaftslehre' [Review], *Jahrbücher für Nationalökonomie* NF 11/2: 162–165.

Leitherer, E. (1961) *Geschichte der handels- and absatzwirtschaftlichen Literatur*, Köln and Opladen: Westdeutscher Verlag.

Lemke, H. (1908) *Die Reisen des Venezianers Marco Polo im 13. Jahrhundert*, Hamburg: Gutenberg.

de Lessines, A. (1864) 'De usuris', in *S. Thomae Aequinatis … opuscula, tam certa quam dubia*, vol. 2, Parma.

Lessius, L. (1605) *De iustitia et iure caeterisque virtutibus cardinalibus libri IV*, Lovanii: Johannes Masius.

Libanios (1980) *Briefe*, Greek-German, a selection edited, transl. and annotated by G. Fatouros, T. Krischer, Munich: Heimeran.

List, F. (1909) *The National System of Political Economy*, transl. 1885, London: Longmans, Green, and Co.

List, F. (1989 [1841]) *Das nationale System der politischen Oekonomie*, Klassiker der Nationalökonimie, Düsseldorf: Verlag Wirtschaft und Finanzen.

Lluch, E. (1996) *La Catalunya vençuda del segle XVIII: Foscors i clarors de la Il-lustració*, Barcelona: Edicions 62.

Loewe, M. (1974) *Crisis and Conflict in Han China 104 B.C. to A.D. 9*, London: Allen/Unwin.

Loewe, M. (ed.) (1993) *Early Chinese Texts: A Biographical Guide*, in the series Early China Special Monograph Series 2, Berkeley: The Society for the Study of Early China and The Institute of East Asian Studies, University of California.

Lotz, W. (ed.) (1893) *Die drei Flugschriften über den Münzstreit der sächsischen Albertiner und Ernestiner um 1530*, Leipzig: Duncker & Humblot.

Lough, J. (ed.) (1969) *The Encyclopédie of Diderot and d'Alembert: Selected Articles*, Cambridge: Cambridge University Press.

Love, J.R. (1990) *Antiquity and Capitalism: Max Weber and the Sociological Foundations of Roman Civilization*, London: Routledge.

Ludovici, C.G. (1932) *Grundriss eines vollständigen Kaufmanns-Systems*, 21768, Stuttgart: Poeschel.

Luther, M. (1962) 'Sermon on Trade and Usury', in J. Pelikan and H.T. Lehman (general eds) *Luther's Works*, vol. 45: *The Christian in Society II*, orig. trans. by C.M. Jacobs, slightly revised transl. by W.I. Brandt (ed.), Philadelphia: Fortress.

Luther, M. (1987 [1524]) *Von Kauffshandlung und Wucher*, Klassiker der Nationalökonomie, Düsseldorf: Verlag Wirtschaft und Finanzen.

Machiavelli, N. (1971) *Il Principe*, Nuova edizione a cura di Luigi Firpo, Torino: Einaudi.

Machiavelli, N. (1996) *The prince*, ed. by Q. Skinner, Cambridge: Cambridge University Press.

MacKendrick, P. (1989) *The Philosophical Books of Cicero*, London: Duckworth.

Maddison, A. (1995) *Monitoring the World Economy 1820–1992*, OECD.

Mahdi, M. (1968) 'Ibn Khaldūn', in D.L. Sills (ed.) *International Encyclopedia of the Social Sciences*, vol. 7, New York: Macmillan.

Maier, H. (1966) *Die ältere deutsche Staats- und Verwaltungslehre (Polizeiwissenschaft): Ein Beitrag zur Geschichte der politischen Wissenschaft in Deutschland*, Politica, Abhandlungen und Texte zur politischen Wissenschaft, vol. 13, Neuwied: Luchterhand.

Malynes, G. (1622) *Conseutudo vel Lex mercatoria or, The Ancient Law-Merchant*, London.

de Mandeville, B. (1990 [1714]) *The Fable of the Bees, or: Private Vices, Publick Benefits*, Klassiker der Nationalökonomie, Düsseldorf: Verlag Wirtschaft und Finanzen.

von Mangoldt, H. (1855) *Die Lehre vom Unternehmengewinn*, Leipzig: Teubner.

von Mangoldt, H. (1868) *Volkswirthschaftslehre*, Stuttgart: Verlag Julius Maier.

von Mangoldt, H. (1871) *Grundriß der Volkswirtschaftslehre*, 2, arranged after the author's death, rev. by F. Kleinwächter, in the series Kaufmännische Unterrichtsstunden, vol. 7, Stuttgart: Verlag Julius Maier.

von Mangoldt, H. (1995 [1863]) *Grundriß der Volkswirtschaftlehre*, Klassiker der Nationalökonomie, Düsseldorf: Verlag Wirtschaft und Finanzen.

Marperger, J.P. (1705) *Moscowitischer Kauffmann*, Lübeck: Böckmann. Reprinted (1976) Leipzig: Zentralantiquariat der Deutschen Demokratischen Republik.

Marshall, A. (1897) 'The Old Generation of Economists and the New', *Quarterly Journal of Economics* 11/2: 115–135.

Marshall, A. (1960 [1949]) *Principles of Economics*, 8, London: Macmillan.

Marx, K. (1863) *Theories of Surplus Value*, London: Progress Publisher.

Marx, K. (1887) *Capital, a critical analysis of capitalist production*, vol. 1, transl. from the 3rd German edn by S. Moore, E. Aveling, edited by F. Engels, London: Sonnenschein & Co.

Marx, K. (1909) *Capital*, vol. 1, transl. by S. Moore, E. Aveling, Chicago: Kerr & Co.

Marx, K. (1966) 'Aus den Exzerptheften: Die entfremdete und die unentfremdete Gesellschaft, Geld, Kredit und Menschlichkeit', in K. Marx, F. Engels, *Studienausgabe*, in 4 vols, ed. by I. Fetscher, vol. 2: *Politische Ökonomie*, Frankfurt a.M.: Fischer.

Marx, K. (1970) *Zur Kritik der politischen Ökonomie*, Berlin: Dietz.

Marx, K. (1974) 'Das Kapital', in K. Marx, F. Engels, *Werke*, vol. 23, Berlin: Dietz.

Marx, K. (1979) *Marx & Engels Collected Works*, vol. 12, London: Lawrence & Wishart.

Marx, K. (1983) *Marx & Engels Collected Works*, vol. 30, London: Lawrence & Wishart.

Marx, K. (1984) 'The British Rule in India', in *MEGA* I/12, Berlin: Akademie Verlag.

Marx, K. and Engels, F. (1963) *The Communist Manifesto*, ed. with an introduction, explanatory notes and appendices by D. Ryazanoff, New York: Russell & Russell.

Marx, K. and Engels, F. (1966) *Studienausgabe*, 4 vols, ed. by I. Fetscher, Frankfurt a. M.: Fischer.

Marx, K. and Engels, F. (1983) *Marx & Engels Collected Works*, vol. 42, London: Lawrence & Wishart.

Maverick, L.A. (1946) *China A Model For Europe*, vol. 2: *Despotism In China: A translation of Le Depostisme De La Chine by Francois Quesnay, Paris, 1767*, San Antonio: Paul Anderson Company.

McCulloch, J.R.M. (ed.) (1954) *Early English Tracts on Commerce*, Cambridge: Cambridge University Press.

von Mende, E. (2002) 'Einleitung zum 'Yantie lun', in B. Schefold (ed.) *Vademecum zu dem Klassiker der chinesischen Wirtschaftsdebatten*, Klassiker der Nationalökonmie, Düsseldorf: Verlag Wirtschaft und Finanzen.

Menger, C. (1976) *Principles of Economics*, transl. by J. Dingwall, and B.F. Hoselitz, with an introduction by F.A. Hayek, New York: New York University Press.

Menjot, D. (1988) 'La politique monétaire de Nicolas Oresme', in P. Souffrin, A.-P. Segonds (eds) *Nicolas Oresme: Tradition et innovation chez un intellectuel du XIVe siècle, etudes receuillies*, Paris: Les Belles Lettres.

Mercer, R. (1991) *Deep Words: Miura Baien's System of Natural Philosophy*, transl. and phil. commentary by R. Mercer, Leiden: Brill.

Meusnier, N. (1988) 'A propos de l'utilisation par Nicole Oresme d'une argumentation 'probabiliste'' in P. Souffrin, A.-P. Segonds (eds) *Nicolas Oresme: Tradition et innovation chez un intellectuel du XIVe siècle, etudes receuillies*, Paris: Les Belles Lettres.

Meuvret, J. (1971) *Études d'histoire économique, Cahiers des Annales*, vol. 32, Paris: Colin.

Meyer, C. (1986) 'Wie die Athener ihr Gemeinwesen finanzierten', in U. Schulz (ed.) *Mit dem Zehnten fing es an. Eine Kulturgeschichte der Steuer*, Munich: C.H. Beck.

Meyer-Abich, K.M. and Schefold, B. (1981) *Wie möchten wir in Zukunft leben? Die Sozialverträglichkeit von Energiesystemen*, Munich: C.H. Beck.

Michaud, J.F. (1969) *Biographie universelle ancienne et moderne*, vol. 38, Graz: Akademische Druck- und Verlagsanstalt.

Mill, J.S. (1976 [1909, 1848]) *Principles of Political Economy*, Fairfield: Kelley.

Millet, P. (1991) *Lending and Borrowing in Ancient Athen*, Cambridge: Cambridge University Press.

Minchinton, W.E. (ed.) (1969) *Mercantilism. System or Expediency?*, Lexington: Heath.

von Mises, L. (1953) *The Theory of Money and Credit*, enlarged with an essay on 'Monetary Reconstruction', transl. of the 2nd German edn (1923) by H.E. Bateson, London: Cape.

von Mises, L. (1960) 'Epistemological problems of economics' [Grundprobleme der Nationalökonomie], *The William Vilker Fund Series in the Humane Studies*, transl. by G. Reisman, Princeton, NJ: van Nostrand Comp.

Miura, B. (2001) 'Kagen: Vom Ursprung des Wertes', in B. Schefold (ed.) *Vademecum zu einem japanischen Klassiker des ökonomischen Denkens*, transl. into German by G. Distelrath, Klassiker der Nationalökonomie, Düsseldorf: Verlag Wirtschaft und Finanzen.

Molland, G. (1988) 'The Oresmian Style: Semi-Mathematical, Semi-Holistic', in P. Souffrin, A.-P. Segonds (eds) *Nicolas Oresme: Tradition et innovation chez un intellectuel du XIVe siècle, etudes receuillies*, Paris: Les Belles Lettres.

Mommsen, K. (1988) *Goethe und die arabische Welt*, Frankfurt a.M.: Insel Verlag.

Monroe, A.E. (1945) *Early Economic Thought: Selections from Economic Literature Prior to Adam Smith*, Cambridge: Harvard University Press.

de Montesquieu, C.-L. (1772) *Oeuvres de Montesquieu*, nouvelle édition, vol. 1 and 2, London: Nourse.

de Montesquieu, C.-L. (1777) *The complete works of M. de Montesquieu*, transl. from the French, 4 vols, Dublin.

de Montesquieu, C.-L.. (1793) *Oeuvres de Montesquieu*, nouvelle édition, 5 vols, Paris: J.J. Smits.

Morishima, M. (1984 [1982]) *Why has Japan Succeeded? Western Technology and the Japanese Ethos*, Cambridge: Cambridge University Press.

Morris-Suzuki, T. (1989) *A History of Japanese Economic Thought*, London: Routledge.

Moss, L.S. (1995) *Deception as a Theme in the History of Economics*, Mimeo.

Mratschek-Halfmann, S. (1993) *Divites et praepotentes. Reichtum und soziale Stellung in der Literatur der Principatszeit*, Stuttgart: Steiner.

Mun, T. (1954 [1664]) 'England's Treasure by Forraign Trade', in J.R. McCulloch (ed.) *Early English Tracts on Commerce*, Cambridge: Cambridge University Press.

Mun, T. (1989 [1664]) *England's Treasure by Forraign Trade: Or, The Ballance of our Forraign Trade is the Rule of our Treasure*, Klassiker der Nationalökonomie, Düsseldorf: Verlag Wirtschaft und Finanzen.

Muschg, A. (1995) *Die Insel, die Kolumbus nicht gefunden hat: Sieben Gesichter Japans*, Frankfurt a.M.: Suhrkamp.

Musgrave, R.A. and Peacock, A.T. (eds) (1967) *Classics in the Theory of Public Finance*, London: Macmillan.

Müller-Armack, A. (1944) *Genealogie der Wirtschaftsstile. Die geistesgeschichtlichen Ursprünge der Staats- und Wirtschaftsformen bis zum Ausgang des 18. Jahrhunderts*, 3, Stuttgart: Kohlhammer.

Müller-Armack, A. (1999 [1947]) *Wirtschaftslenkung and Marktwirtschaft*, Klassiker der Nationalökonomie, Düsseldorf: Verlag Wirtschaft und Finanzen.

Münzstreit (2000 [1530–1548]) *Die drei Flugschriften über den Münzstreit der sächsischen Albertiner und Ernestiner, Klassiker der Nationalökonomie*, Düsseldorf: Verlag Wirtschaft und Finanzen.

Myers, A.R. (1976) 'Europa im 14. Jahrhundert', *Propyläen Weltgeschichte*, vol. V, Frankfurt a.m.: Ullstein.

Najita, T. (1987) *Visions of Virtue in Tokugawa Japan*, The Kaitokudô Merchant Academy of Osaka, Chicago: University of Chicago Press.

Nelson, B. (1969) *The Idea of Usury. From Tribal Brotherhood to Universal Otherhood*, 2, Chicago: University of Chicago Press.

Nestle, W. (1922) *Die Sokratiker, in Auswahl übers. u. hrsg*, Jena: E. Diederichs.

Neumark, F. (1965) *Grundsätze der Besteuerung in Vergangenheit und Gegenwart*, Wiesbaden: Steiner.

Neumark, F. (1989) 'Deutsche Ökonomen des frühen 20. Jahrhunderts', in B. Schefold (ed.) *Studien zur Entwicklung der ökonomischen Theorie VII, Schriften des Vereins für Socialpolitik*, vol. 115, VII, Berlin: Duncker und Humblot.

Niehans, J. (1987) 'Launhardt, Carl Friedrich Wilhelm', in J. Eatwell, M. Milgate, P. Newman (eds) *The New Palgrave: A Dictionary of Economics*, vol. 3, London: Macmillan.

Niehans, J. (1990) *A History of Economic Theory: Classic Contributions, 1720–1980*, Baltimore: John Hopkins University Press.

Noonan, J.T. (1957) *The Scholastic Analysis of Usury*, Cambridge, MA: Harvard University Press.

Obert, M. (1992) *Die naturrechtliche 'politische Metaphyik' des Johann Heinreich Gottlob von Justi (1717–1771)*, Europäische Hochschulschriften, series 2, Rechtswissenschaft, vol. 1202, Frankfurt a.M.: Lang.

Oncken, A. (1922) *Geschichte der Nationalökonomie*, Leipzig: Hirschfeld.

Oresme, N. (1937) *Traktat über Geldabwertungen*, ed. and introduced by E. Schorer, Jena: G. Fischer.

Oresme, N. (1995) *Tractatus de natura, origine, iure & mutationibus monetarum*, approx. 1485, repr. in the series Klassiker der Nationalökonomie, Düsseldorf: Verlag Wirtschaft und Finanzen.

Parsons, T. (1928) '"Capitalism" in Recent German Literature: Sombart and Weber', *Journal of Political Economy* 36/6: 641–661.

Pecchio, G. (1971 [1840]) 'Geschichte der Staatswirthschaft in Italien', in A. . Blanqui (ed.) *Geschichte der politischen Ökonomie in Europa* [History of political economy in Europe], vol. 2, transl. by F.J. Buß, Glashütten: Auvermann.

Penndorf, B. (1925) *Die geschichtliche Entwicklung der Handelswissenschaften bis zum Ende des 19. Jahrhundert*, edition in honour of the seventieth birthday of Hofrat Professor Robert Stern, Berlin: Weiss.

Perotta, C. (1988) *Produzione e lavoro produttivo nel mercantilismo e nell' illuminismo*, Lecce: Galatina Congedo Editore.

Perotta, C. (1993) 'Earliest Spanish Mercantilism: the First Analysis of Underdevelopment', in L. Magnusson (ed.) *Mercantilist Economics*, Boston: Kluwer.

Perrot, J.C. (1992) 'Les dictionnaires de commerce au 18e siècle', *Une histoire intellectuelle d'économie politique*, 2, *Civilisations et sociétés*, vol. 85, Paris: Éd. de l'École des Hautes Études en Sciences Sociales.

Petrarch, F. (1966) *Il canzoniere*, Basiano: Bietti.

Petrarch, F. (n.d.) *The Canzoniere*, transl. by A.S. Kline, poem 82, available at: http://p etrarch.petersadlon.com/canzoniere.html?poem=84 (8 May 2015).

Petty, W. (1963 [1899]) *The Economic Writings of Sir William Petty*, edited by C.H. Hull, 2 vols, New York: Kelley.

Petty, W. (1992 [1690]) *Political Arithmetick*, Klassiker der Nationalökonomie, Düsseldorf: Verlag Wirtschaft und Finanzen.

Peukert, W. (1978) *Der atlantische Sklavenhandel von Dahomey 1740–1767*, Wiesbaden: Steiner.

Philodemos (1857) 'Über die Haushaltung', in *Philodem's Abhandlung über die Haushaltung und über den Hochmuth und Theophrast's Haushaltung und Charakterbilder*, Greek and German with critical and explanatory comments from J.A. Hartung, Leipzig: Wilhelm Engelmann.

Plato (2008) *The Republic*, ed. by G.R.F. Ferrari, transl. by T. Griffith, Cambridge: Cambridge University Press.

Plutarch (1841) *Plutarch's Lives*, transl. by J. Langborne and W. Langhorne, vol. 4, New York: Harper & Borthers.

Popescu, O. (1986) *Estudios en la historia del pensamiento economica Latinoamericano*, Bogota, Colombia: Plaza y Janes.

Popper, K.R. (1969 [1957]) *The Poverty of Historicism*, London: Routledge.

Porter, T.M. (1986) *The Rise of Statistical Thinking 1820–1900*, Princeton: Princeton University Press.

Posch, F. (1953) 'Philipp Wilhelm von Hörnigk. Werdejahre und österreich-steierische Beziehungen', *Mitteilungen des Instituts für Österreichische Geschichtsforschung* 61: 335–358.

Powelson, J.P. (1997 [1994]) *Centuries of Economic Endeavour. Parallel Paths in Japan and Europe and their Contrast with the Third World*, Ann Arbor: University of Michigan Press.

Priddat, B. (1991) *Der ethische Ton der Allokation. Elemente der aristotelischen Ethik und Politik in der deutschen Nationalökonomie der 19. Jahrhunderts*, Baden-Baden: Nomos.

Quesnay, F. (1965 [1888]) 'Despotisme de la Chine', in F. Quesnay, *Œuvres économique et philosophiques de Quesnay*, ed. by A. Oncke, Aalen: Scientia.

von Ranke, L. (1848) *The history of the popes, their church and state, and especially their conflicts in the sixteenth & seventeenth centuries*, transl. by E. Foster, vol. 2, London: Bohn.

von Ranke, L. (1933) *Deutsche Geschichte im Zeitalter der Reformation*, vol. 3, Meersburg und Leipzig: S.W. Hendel.

Rausse, H. (n.d.) [*La vida de*] *Lazarillo de Tormes* [anon. 1554], using the German transcription of the seventeenth century translation from Spanish, Stuttgart: Franckh (after 1908).

Recktenwald, H.C. (ed.) (1989) *Vademecum zu einem frühen Merkantilisten*, Klassiker der Nationalökonomie, Düsseldorf: Verlag Wirtschaft und Finanzen.

Recktenwald, H.C. and Samuelson, P.A. (1986) 'Über Thünens 'Der isolierte Staat'', in H.C. Recktenwald (ed.) *Vademecum zu einem frühen Klassiker der ökonomischen Wissenschaft*, Düsseldorf: Verlag Wirtschaft und Finanzen.

Redding, S.G. (1993) *The Spirit of Chinese Capitalism*, in the series De Gruyter Studies in Organization: International Management, Organization and policy Analysis 22, Berlin and New York: de Gruyter.

Reichert, K. (1985) *Fortuna oder die Beständigkeit des Wechsels*, Frankfurt a.M.: Suhrkamp.

Ricardo, D. (1981 [1951]) 'On the Principles of Political Economy and Taxation', in P. Sraffa (ed.) *The Works and Correspondence of David Ricardo*, vol. 1, Cambridge: Cambridge University Press.

Richarz, I. (1991) *Oikos, Haus und Haushalt. Ursprung und Geschichte der Hausökonomik*, with 43 illus., Göttingen: Vandenhoeck & Ruprecht.

Rickett, W.A. (1965) *The Kuan-tzu, A Repository of Early Chinese Thought, a translation and study of twelve chapters*, Hong Kong: Hong Kong University Press.

Rickett, W.A. (1985) *Guanzi: Political, Economic, and Philosophical Essays from Early China*, vol. 1, Princeton: Princeton University Press.

Rickett, W.A. (1998) *Guanzi: Political, Economic, and Philosophical Essays from Early China*, vol. 2, Princeton: Princeton University Press.

Romani, R. (1993) '"Storia dell'Economia Pubblica in Italia" by G. Pecchio', *European Journal of the History of Economic Thought* 1/1: 202–206.

Ronan, C.A. (1978–86) *The Shorter Science and Civilisation in China. An Abridgement of Joseph Needham's Original Text*, vols 1–3, Cambridge: Cambridge University Press.

Roncaglia, A. (1977) *Petty: La nascita dell' economia politica*, Milan: Etas Libri.

de Roover, R. (1951) 'Monopoly Theory Prior to Adam Smith: A Revision', *Quarterly Journal of Economics* 65/4: 492–524.

de Roover, R. (1955) 'Scholastic Economics: Survival and Lasting Influence from the Sixteenth Century to Adam Smith', *Quarterly Journal of Economics* 69/2: 161–190.

de Roover, R. (1958) 'The Concept of the Just Price: Theory and Economic Policy', *Journal of Economic History* 18/4: 418–434.

de Roover, R. (1969) *Leonardus Lessius as economist. De economische leerstellingen van de latere scholastiek* in de Zuidelijke Nederlanden, Meddelingen van de Koninklijke Vlaamse Academie voor Wetenschappen, Letteren en schone Kunsten van België, Klasse der Letteren, Jaargang XXXI, Nr.1, Brüssel: Paleis der Academiën.

Roscher, W. (1838) *De historicae doctrinae apud sophistas maiores vestigiis*, Goettingen: Dieterich.

Roscher, W. (1842a) 'Review of Friedrich List's "Das Nationale System der politischen Oekonomie, vol. 1: Der internationale Handel, die Handelspolitik und der deutsche Zollverein, 2nd edn"', in *Göttingische gelehrte Anzeigen unter der Aufsicht der Königl. Gesellschaft der Wissenschaften*, 25 July 1842, pp. 1201–1216.

Roscher, W. (1842b) *Lehre, Werk und Zeitalter des Thukydides*, Goettingen: Vandenhoeck und Ruprecht.

Roscher, W. (1845) 'Betrachtungen über den Socialismus und Communismus', *Zeitschrift für Geschichtswissenschaft* 3: 418–461 and 540–564; 4: 10–28.

Roscher, W. (1857) 'Zur Geschichte der englischen Volkswirtschaftlehre, nebst Nachträgen', in *Abhandlungen der philologisch-historischen Classe der Königlich-sächsischen Gesellschaft der Wissenschaften*, vol. 3, Leipzig: S. Hirzel.

Roscher, W. (1861a) 'Über die Blüte deutscher Nationalökonomik im Zeitalter der Reformation', in *Historisch philologische Berichte der K. sächsischen Gesellschaft*, 12 December 1861.

Roscher, W. (1861b) *Ansichten der Volkswirthschaft aus dem geschichtlichen Standpunkte*, Leipzig und Heidelberg: C. Winter.

Roscher, W. (1863) 'Ein grosser Nationalökonom des vierzehnten Jahrhunderts', *Zeitschrift für die gesammte Staatswissenschaft* 19: 305–318.

Roscher, W. (1866) 'Die volkswirtschaftlichen Ansichten Friedrichs der Grossen', in *Berichte über die Verhandlungen der Königl. Sächs. Gesellschaft der Wissenschaften zu Leipzig* 18: 1–55.

Roscher, W. (1870) 'Die romantische Schule der Nationalökonomik in Deutschland', *Zeitschrift für die gesammte Staatswissenschaft* 26/1: 57–105.

Roscher, W. (1908) *Politik: Geschichtliche Naturlehre der Monarchie, Aristokratie und Demokratie*, Stuttgart und Berlin: Cotta.

Roscher, W. (1924) *Geschichte der National-Oekonomic in Deutschland*, 2, Munich and Berlin: Oldenbourg.

Roscher, W. (1992 [1874]) *Geschichte der National-Oekonomik in Deutschland*, Klassiker der Nationalökonomie, Düsseldorf: Verlag Wirtschaft und Finanzen.

Roscher, W. and Jannasch, R. (1885) *Kolonien, Kolonialpolitik und Auswanderung*, 3, Leipzig: C. Winter.

Rosenthal, E. (1932) *Ibn Khaldūns Gedanken über den Staat: Ein Beitrag zur mittelalterlichen Staatslehre*, München: Oldenburg.

Rostovtzeff, M. (1972) *The Social and Economic History of the Hellenistic World*, vol. 3, 5, Oxford: Clarendon Press.

von Rotterdam, E. (1780) *ΜΩΡΙΑΣ ΕΓΚΩΜΙΟΝ, sive Stultitiae Laus. Des. Erasmi Rot. Declamatio, cum figuris …J. Holbenii Denuo typis madavit G.G. Beckerus*, Basle: J.J. Thurneysen.

von Rotterdam, E. (1989) *Praise of Folly*, transl. by R.M. Adams, New York: Norton & Company.

Sakellariou, M.B. (1989) *The Polis-State. Definition and Origin*, Athens: Research Centre for Greek and Roman Antiquity (National Hellenic Research Foundation).

Salin, E. (1923) *Geschichte der Volkswirtschaftslehre*, Berlin: J. Springer.

Salin, E. (1927) 'Hochkapitalismus: Ein Studie über Werner Sombart, die deutsche Volkswirtschaftslehre und das Wirtschaftssystem der Gegenwart', *Weltwirtschaftliches Archiv* 25/2: 314–344. Reprinted in E. Salin (1963) *Lynkeus. Gestalten und Probleme aus Wirtschaft und Politik*, Tübingen: J.C.B. Mohr (Paul Siebeck).

Salin, E. (1928) 'Tawney, R.H.: Religion and the Rise of Capitalism', *Zeitschrift für die gesammte Staatswissenschaft* 84/3: 617–619.

Salin, E. (1963) 'Standortverschiebungen der deutschen Wirtschaft im ersten Viertel des 20. Jahrhunderts', in E. Salin, *Lynkeus*, Tübingen: J.C.B. Mohr (Paul Siebeck).

Salin, E. (1967) *Politische Ökonomie: Geschichte der wirtschaftspolitischen Ideen von Platon bis zur Gegenwart*, 5, Tübingen: Mohr-Siebeck.

Samuelson, P.A. (1966) 'Dynamics, Statistics and the Stationary State', in J.E. Stiglitz (ed.) *The Collected Scientific Papers of P.A. Samuelson*, vol. 1, Cambridge: MIT Press.

Samuelson, P.A. (1977) 'Paradoxes of Schumpeter's Zero Interest Rate', in H. Nagatani and K. Crowley (eds) *The Collected Scientific Papers of P.A. Samuelson*, vol. 4, Cambridge: MIT Press.

Savary, J. (1675) *Le parfait négociant*, Paris: Billaine.

Savary, J. (1688) *Parères, ou Avis et conseils sur les plus importantes matières de commerce*, Paris.

Savary, J. (1697) *Le parfait négociant*, 4, Lyon.

Savary, J. (1993 [1675]) *Le parfait négociant*, Klassiker der Nationalökonomie, Düsseldorf: Verlag Wirtschaft und Finanzen.

Savary des Brulons, J. (1723) *Dictionnaire universel de commerce*, Paris.

Schams, E. (1932) 'Die Anfänge lehrgeschichtlicher Betrachtungweise in der Nationalökonomie', *Zeitschrift für Nationalökonomie* 3/1: 47–61.

Schefold, B. (ed.) (1972) *Floating, Realignment, Integration, 9. Gespräch der List-Gesellschaft*, Tübingen: Mohr.

Schefold, B. (1983) 'Laudatio für Lord Kaldor', in Fachbereich Wirschaftswissenschaften (ed.) *Verleihung der Ehrendoktorwürde an Nicholas Lord Kaldor am 23. Juni 1982 in der Aula der Universität*, Frankfurt a.M.: J.W. Goethe-Universität.

Schefold, B. (1987) 'Karl Knies', in J. Eatwell, M. Milgate, P. Newman (eds) *The New Palgrave: A Dictionary of Economics*, vol. 3, London and Basingstoke: Macmillan.

Schefold, B. (1988) 'Karl Bücher und der Historismus in der Deutschen Nationalökonomie', in N. Hammerstein (ed.) *Deutsche Geschichtswissenschaft um 1900*, Stuttgart: Steiner.

Schefold, B. (1989a) 'Platon und Aristoteles', in J. Starbatty (ed.) *Klassiker des ökonomischen Denkens*, vol. 1, Munich: Beck.

Schefold, B. (1989b) 'Normative Integration der Einzeldisciplinen in gesellschaftswissenschaftlichen Fragestellungen', in M. Bock, H. Homann, P. Schiera (eds) *Gustav Schmoller heute: Die Entwicklung der Sozialwissenschaften in Deutschland und Italien*, Berlin: Duncker & Humblot. Reprinted (1992) *Zeitschrift für Protosoziolgie 3, Lebenswelt und System* 1: 90–103.

Schefold, B. (1989c) 'Schmoller als Theoretiker', in. H. Recktenwald (ed.) *Vademecum zu einem Klassiker der historischen Methode in der ökonomischen Wissenschaft*, Klassiker der Nationalökonomie, Düsseldorf: Verlag Wirtschaft und Finanzen.

Schefold, B. (1991) 'Zur Neuausgabe von Böhm-Bawerks "Positive Theorie des Kapitals"', in B. Schefold (ed.) *Vademecum zu einem Klassiker der Kapitaltheorie, Klassiker der Nationalökonomie*, Düsseldorf: Verlag Wirtschaft und Finanzen.

Schefold, B. (1992a) 'Spiegelungen des antiken Wirtschaftsdenkens in der griechischen Dichtung', in B. Schefold (ed.) *Studien zur Entwicklung der ökonomischen Theorie XI, Die Darstellung der Wirtschaft und der Wirtschaftswissenschaften in der Belletristik, Schiften des Vereins für Socialpolitik*, NF 115/XI, Berlin: Duncker & Humblot.

Schefold, B. (ed.) (1992b) *Vademecum zu einem Klassiker der Theorie der Arbeitsteilung, Klassiker der Nationalökonomie*, Düsseldorf: Verlag Wirtschaft und Finanzen.

Schefold, B. (1992c) 'Nationalökonomie und Kulturwissenschaften – Das Konzept des Wirtschaftsstils', Meeting of the Thyssen Foundation, Deutsche Geisteswissenschaften in den zwanziger Jahren: Nationalökonomie – Rechtswissenschaft – Soziologie, 27–29 February.

Schefold, B. (1992d) 'Nationalökonomie als Geisteswissenschaft. Edgar Salins Konzept einer anschaulichen Theorie' [Gekürzte Fassung eines Festvortrages an der Universität Basel zur hundertsten Wiederkehr des Geburtstags von Edgar Salin am 10.2.1992], *List Forum für Wirtschafts- und Finanzpolitik* 18/4: 303–324.

Schefold, B. (1993) 'John Locke: Ein ökonomisch engagierter Philosoph', in B. Schefold (ed.) *Vademecum zu einem Klassiker der merkantilistischen Geldtheorie*, Klassiker der Nationalökonomie, Düsseldorf: Verlag Wirtschaft und Finanzen.

Schefold, B. (1994a) 'Platon und Aristoteles', in B. Schefold, *Wirtschaftsstile*, vol. 1, Frankfurt a.M.: Fischer Taschenbuch Verlag.

446    *References*

Schefold, B. (1994b) 'Spiegelungen des antiken Wirtschaftsdenkens', in B. Schefold, *Wirtschaftsstile. Studien zum Verhältnis von Ökonomie und Kultur*, vol. 1, Frankfurt a.M.: Fischer.

Schefold, B. (1994c) 'Antonio Serra: der Stifter der Wirtschaftslehre?', in B. Schefold (ed.) *Vademecum zu einem unbekannten Klassiker*, Klassiker der Nationalökonomie, Düsseldorf: Verlag Wirtschaft und Finanzen.

Schefold, B. (1994d) *Wirtschaftsstile*, vol. 1, Frankfurt a.M.: Fischer.

Schefold, B. (1994e) 'Eugen von Böhm-Bawerk: Entdeckungen und Irrtümer in der Geschichte der Zinstheorien', in B. Schefold (ed.) *Vademecum zu einem Klassiker der Theoriegeschichte*, Klassiker der Nationalökonomie, Düsseldorf: Verlag Wirtschaft und Finanzen.

Schefold, B. (1995) *Wirtschaftsstile*, vol. 2, Frankfurt a.M.: Fischer.

Schefold, B. (1996) 'The German Historical School and the Belief in Ethical Progress', in F.N. Brady (ed.) *Ethical Universals in International Business*, Berlin: Springer.

Schefold, B. (1997) 'Reflections of ancient economic thought in Greek poetry. Greek economic thought as a problem of historical dogma', in B.B. Price (ed.) *Ancient Economic Thought*, vol. 1, London and New York: Routledge.

Schefold, B. (1998a) 'Spontaneous Conformity in History', in H. Hagermann and H.D. Kurz (eds) *Political Economics in Retrospect: Essays in Memory of Adolphe Lowe*, Cheltenham: Edward Elgar.

Schefold, B. (1998b) 'The Relation between the Rate of Profit and the Rate of Interest: A Reassessment after the Publication of Marx's Manuscript of the Third Volume of "Das Kapital"', in R. Bellofiore (ed.) *Marxian Economics: A Reappraisal. Essays on Volume III of Capital*, vol. 1: *Method, Value and Money*, Basingstoke: Macmillan.

Schefold, B. (1998c) 'Der Nachklang der Historischen Schule in Deutschland', in K. Acham, K.W. Nörr and B. Schefold (eds) *Erkenntnisgewinne, Erkenntnisverluste. Kontinuitäten und Diskontinuitäten in den Wirtschafts-, Rechts- und Sozialwissenschaften zwischen den 20er und 50er Jahren*, Stuttgart: Steiner.

Schefold, B. (1999a) 'Antike Theoriebildungen', in W. Korff (ed.) *Handbuch der Wirtschaftsethik*, vol. 1, Gütersloh: Gütersloher Verlagshaus.

Schefold, B. (1999b) 'Vom Interventionsstaat zur Sozialen Marktwirtschaft: Der Weg Alfred Müller-Armacks', in B. Schefold (ed.) *Vademecum zu einem Klassiker der Ordnungspolitik*, Düsseldorf: Verlag Wirtschaft und Finanzen.

Schefold, B. (2001) 'Ein Leitbild für die Tokugawa-Zeit: Miura Baeins "Kagen"', in B. Schefold (ed.) *Vademecum zu einem japanischen Klassiker des ökonomischen Denkens*, Klassiker der Nationalökonomie, Düsseldorf: Verlag Wirtschaft und Finanzen.

Schefold, B. (2002) 'Reflections on the Past and Current State of the History of Economic Thought in Germany', *History of Political Economy* 34/Suppl 1: 125–136.

Schefold, B. (2004a) *Beiträge zur ökonomischen Dogmengeschichte: Ausgewählt und herausgegeben von Volker Caspari*, Stuttgart: Schäffer-Poeschel (Licensed edn Darmstadt: Wissenschaftliche Buchgesellschaft).

Schefold, B. (2004b) 'Edgar Salin and his concept of 'Anschauliche Theorie' ('Intuitive Theory') during the interwar period', *Annals of the Society for the History of Economic Thought* 46: 1–16.

Schefold, B. (2009) 'Einleitung', in K. Klock, *Tractatus juridico-politico-polemico-historicus De Aerario*, ed. by B. Schefold, vol. 1, Historia Scientiarum (Wirtschaftswissenschaften), Hildesheim: Olms.

Schefold, B. (2013) 'The Applicability of Modern Economics to Forms of Capitalism in Antiquity: some Theoretical Considerations and Textual Evidence', in A. Slawisch (ed.) *Handels- und Finanzgebaren in der Ägäis im 5. Jh. v. Chr* [Trade and Finance in the 5th c. BC Aegean World], BYZAS 18 Veröffentlichungen des Deutschen Archäologischen Instituts, Istanbul.

Schefold, B. (2014a) 'Economics without Political Economy: Is the Discipline Undergoing Another Revolution?', *Social Research* 81/3: 613–636.

Schefold, B. (2014b) 'Marx, Sombart, Weber and the Debate about the Genesis of Modern Capitalism', *Journal of Institutional Studies* 6/2: 8–24.

Schefold, B. (2016) *Great Economic Thinkers from the Antiquity to the Historical School: translations from the series Klassiker der Nationalökonomie*, London: Routledge.

Schiller, F. (1877) *History of the Revolt of the Netherlands*, 1, vol. 1, London: George Bell & Sons.

Schiller, F. (1880) *History of the Revolt of the Netherlands*, 2, London: George Bell & Sons.

Schiller, F. (2000) 'Was heißt und zu welchem Ende studiert man Universalgeschichte?' [Antrittsrede Jena 1789], in F. Schiller, *Werke und Briefe in zwölf Bänden*, vol. 6: *Historische Schriften und Erzählungen I*, ed. by O. Dann, Frankfurt a.M.: Deutscher Klassiker Verlag.

von Schmoller, G. (1860) 'Zur Geschichte der national-ökonomischen Ansichten in Deutschland während der Reformations-Periode', *Zeitschrift für die gesammte Staatswissenschaft* 16/3: 461–716.

von Schmoller, G. (1900–1904) *Grundriß der allgemeinen Volkswirtschaftslehre*, Leipzig: Duncker & Humblot.

Schneider, D. (1993) 'Jacques Savarys "Le parfait négociant"', in B. Schefold (ed.) *Vademecum zu einem Klassiker der Handlungswissenschaft*, Düsseldorf: Verlag Wirtschaft und Finanzen.

Schneider, E. (1963) 'Vorwort', in W. Launhardt, *Mathematische Begründung der Volkswirtschaftslehre*, repr. Aalen: Scientia.

Schneider, P. (1981) *Geschichte betriebswirtschaftlicher Theorie*, Munich: Oldenbourg.

Schöffler, H. (1936) *Die Reformation. Einführung in die Geistesgeschichte der deutschen Neuzeit*, Frankfurt a.M.: Klostermann.

Schulze, W. (1987) *Vom Gemeinnutz zum Eigennutz. Über den Normenwandel der Ständischen Gesellschaft der Frühen Neuzeit*, Schriften des Historischen Kollegs, Vorträge 13, München: Stiftung Historisches Kolleg.

Schumpeter, J.A. (1972 [1954]) *History of Economic Analysis*, London: Allen & Unwin.

Schumpeter, J.A. (1991) 'Max Weber's Work [1920]' in R. Swedberg (ed.) *The economics and sociology of capitalism*, transl. by G. Oakes, Princeton: Princeton University Press.

Sée, H. (1925) *L'évolution commerciale et industrielle de la France sous l'Ancien régime*, Bibliothèque internationale d'économie politique, Paris: Giard.

Sen, S.R. (1947) 'Sir James Steuart's General Theory of Employment, Interest and Money', *Economica* 14/53: 19–36.

Senior, N.W. (1920) 'Three Lectures on the Value of Money', in K. Diehl, P. Mombert (eds) *Ausgewählte Lesestücke zum Studium der Politischen Ökonomie*, vol. 1, 3, Karlsruhe: Braun.

Serra, A. (1613) *Breve trattato delle cause, che possono far abondare li regni d'oro, & argento*, Naples: Lazzaro Scorriggio.

Serra, A. (1994 [1613]) *Breve trattato delle cause, che possono far abbondare li regni d'oro, & argento*, Klassiker der Nationalökonomie, Düsseldorf: Verlag Wirtschaft und Finanzen.

Serra, A. (2011) *A Short Treatise on the Wealth and Poverty of Nations (1613)*, transl. by J. Hunt, ed. and intr. by S.A. Reinert, London: Anthem.

Seÿffert, R. (1956) 'Betriebswirtschaftslehre, Geschichte der ...', in H. Niklisch (ed.) *Handwörterbuch der Betriebswirtschaft*, vol. 1, 3, Stuttgart: Schäffer-Poeschel.

Seÿffert, R. (1957) *Über Begriff, Aufgaben und Entwicklung der Betriebswirtschaftslehre*, 4, Stuttgart: Poeschel.

Shen, F. (1996) *Cultural Flow between China and Outside World Throughout History*, Beijing: Foreign Language Press.

Simon, H. (1959) *Ibn Khaldūns Wissenschaft von der menschlichen Kultur*, Leipzig: Harrassowitz.

Simonde de Sismondi, J.C.L. (1839) *Précis de l'histoire des Français*, vol. 1, Paris: Treuttel.

Singer, K. (1973) *Mirror, Sword and Jewel: A study of Japanese characteristics*, London: Croom Helm.

Singer, K. (1996 [1991]) *Spiegel, Schwert und Edelstein: Strukturen des japanischen Lebens*, edited and transl. by W. Wilhelm, Frankfurt a.M.: Suhrkamp.

Skinner, A.S. (1962) 'Sir James Steuart: Economics and Politics', *Scottish Journal of Political Economy* 9: 17–37.

Skourtos, M. (1991) 'Corn Models in the Classical Tradition: P. Sraffa considered historically', *Cambridge Journal of Economics* 15/2: 215–228.

Smith, A. (1976 [1776]) *An Inquiry into the Nature and Causes of The Wealth of Nations*, Glasgow edn, Oxford: University Press.

Smith, B. (1990) *Aristotle, Menger, Mises: An Essay in the Metaphysics of Economics*, Vienna: Department of Economics, University of Vienna.

Smith, N.S. (1934) 'An Introduction to Some Japanese Economic Writings of the eighteenth century', *The Transactions of the Asiatic Society of Japan*, 2nd series, vol. 11: 47–54.

Sombart, W. (1911) *Die Juden und das Wirtschaftsleben*, Leipzig: Duncker & Humblot.

Sombart, W. (1934) *Deutscher Sozialismus*, Berlin: Buchholz & Weisswange.

Sombart, W. (1987) *Der Moderne Kapitalismus*, 2, Munich: Deutscher Taschenbuch Verlag.

Sommer, L. (1920) *Die öesterreichischen Kameralisten. In dogmengeschichtlicher Darstellung*, Wien: Konegan.

Sommer, L. (1967 [1920]) *Die österreichischen Kameralisten in dogmengeschichtlicher Darstellung*, Aalen: Scientia.

Soofi, A. (1995) 'Economics of Ibn Khaldūn Revisited', *History of Political Economy* 27/2: 387–404.

Sophocles (1912) *Antigone, transl. by F. Storr*, in the series Loeb Library Edition, Cambridge, MA: Harvard University Press.

Soyeda, J. (1893) 'The Study of Political Economy in Japan', *Economic Journal* 3/10: 334–339.

Speiser, A. (1925) *Klassische Stücke der Mathematik*, Zürich: Orell Füssli.

Spiegel, H.W. (1971) *The Growth of Economic Thought*, Durham: Duke University Press.

Spooner, F.C. (1972) *The International Economy and Monetary Movements in France, 1493–1725*, Cambridge: Cambridge University Press.

Spufford, P. (1988) *Money and its Use in Medieval Europe*, Cambridge: Cambridge University Press.

Sraffa, P. (1993 [1920]) 'Monetary inflation in Italy during and after the war', transl. by W.J. Harcourt and C. Sardoni, *Cambridge Journal of Economics* 17/1: 7–26.

Stadermann, H.-J. (1999) *Der Streit um gutes Geld in Vergangenheit und Gegenwart*, Tübingen: Mohr.

Stamm, V. (1982) *Ursprünge der Wirtschaftsgesellschaft: Geld, Arbeit und Zeit als Mittel von Herrschaft*, Frankfurt a.M.: Europäische Verlagsanstalt.

Staudinger, H. (1982) *Wirtschaftspolitik im Weimarer Staat. Lebenserinnerungen eines politischen Beamten im Reich und in Preußen 1889–1934*, ed. and intr. by H. Schulze, Bonn: Verlag Neue Gesellschaft.

Steuart, J. (1770) *An Inquiry into the Principles of Political Oeconomy*, Dublin.

Steuart, J. (1967 [1805]) *The Works, Political, Metaphysical & Chronological of Sir James Steuart*, in six vols, New York: Kelley Publishers.

Stieda, W. (1906) *Die Nationalökonomie als Universitätswissenschaft*, Abh. D. phil.-hist. KI. D. könig. Sächs. Ges. D. Wiss., Vol. 25, No. 2, Leipzig: Teubner.

Strasburger, H. (1972) 'Homer und die Geschichtsschreibung', in *Sitzungsberichte der Heidelberger Akademie der Wissenschaften*, Heidelberg: C. Winter.

Strasburger, H. (1976) 'Zum antiken Gesellschaftsideal', in *Abhandlungen der Heidelberger Akademie der Wissenschaften*, Heidelberg: C. Winter.

Streissler, E. (1990) 'Carl Menger, der deutsche Nationalökonom', in B. Schefold (ed.) *Studien zur Entwicklung der ökonomischen Theorie X*, Schriften der Vereins für Socialpolitik, NF Vol. 115/X, Berlin: Duncker & Humblot.

Strieder, J. (1935) *Zur Genesis des modernen Kapitalismus. Forschungen zur Enstehung der großen Bürgerlichen Kapitalvermögen am Ausgange des Mittelalters and zu Beginn der Neuzeit, zunächst in Augsburg*, 2, Munich: Duncker & Humblot.

Struik, D.J. (1967) *A concise History of Mathematics*, New York: Dover.

Sugiyama, C. (1994) *Origins of Economic Thought in Modern Japan*, London: Routledge.

van Sull, C. (1930) *Léonard de la Compagnie de Jésus (1554–1623)*, Museum Lessianum Publications, Section Théologique, No. 21, Louvain: Museum Lessianum.

van Suntum, U. (1988) 'Vindicating Thünen's Tombstone Formula √ap', *Jahrbücher für Nationalökonomie und Statistik* 204/5: 393–405.

Swann, N.L. (1950) *Food and Money in Ancient China. The Earliest Economic History of China to A.D. 25; Han Shu 24 with reated Texts, Han Shu 91 and Shih-Chi 129*, transl. and annotated by N.L. Swann, Princeton: Princeton University Press.

Tautscher, A. (1947) *Staatswirtschaftslehre des Kameralismus*, Bern: Francke.

Tawney, R.H. (1972 [1926]) *Religion and the Rise of Capitalism: A Historical Study*, Harmondsworth/Middlesex: Penguin Books.

Tenbruck, F.H. (1975) 'Das Werk Max Webers', *Kölner Zeitschrift für Soziologie und Sozialpsychologie* 27/4: 663–702.

Theocharis, R.D. (1961) *Early Developments in Mathematical Economics*, London: Macmillan.

Theocharis, R.D. (1993) *The Development of Mathematical Economics*, London: Macmillan.

Tortajada, R. (1992) 'La renaissance de la scolastique, la réforme et les théories du droit naturel', in A. Béraud and G. Faccarello (eds) *Nouvelle histoire de las pensée économique*, vol. 1: *Des scolastiques aux classiques*, Paris: Editions la découverte.

Toynbee, A. (1976) *Mankind and Mother Earth*, London: Granada.

Tönnies, F. (1918) 'Adolph Wagner', *Deutsche Rundschau* 44/4: 107–116.

Tribe, K. (1993) 'Polizei, Staat und die Staatswissenschaften bei J.H.G. von Justi', in B. Schefold (ed.) *Vadecum zu einem Klassiker des Kameralismus*, Klassiker der Nationalökonomie, Düsseldorf: Verlag Wirtschaft und Finanzen.

Troitsch, U. (1966) *Ansätze technologischen Denkens bei den Kameralisten des 17. und 18. Jahrhunderts*, Schriften zur Wirtschafts- und Sozialgeschichte, vol. 5, Berlin: Duncker & Humblot.

Troske, L. (1918) 'Nachruf [Obituary]', *Zentralblatt der Bauverwaltung*, 1 June 1918, 218–219.

Türks, P. (1951) *Das Gottesbild des Leonhard Lessius*, Diss., Munich.

Varro, M.T. (1996) *Gespräche über die Landwirtschaft*, Buch I. ed., trans., and annotated by D. Flach, Darmstadt: Wissenschaftliche Buchgesellschaft.

ter Vehn, A. (1929) 'Die Entwicklung der Bilanzauffassungen bis zum AHGB. Hat Savarys 'Parfait Négociant' und die Ordonnance de Commerce oder welche andere Tatsache die Entstehung der statischen Bilanzauffassung bewirkt?', *Zeitschrift für Betriebswirtschaft* 6: 161–169, 241–253, 329–345, 43–445.

Vickers, D. (1970) 'The Works, Political, Metaphysical, and Chronological of Sir James Steuart' [Review Article], *Journal of Economic Literature* 8/4: 1190–1195.

Vignolo, L. (1929) 'Le dictionnaire universel de commerce de Savary', *Annales de Bretagne* 38: 742–751.

Villar, P. (1984) *Gold und Geld in der Geschichte*, Munich: Beck.

Vivenza, G. (1999) 'Ancora sullo stoicismo di Adam Smith', *Studi Storici Luigi Simeoni* 49. Verona: Istituto per gli Studi Storici veronesi.

Vleugels, W. (1935) 'Adolph Wagner. Gedenkenworte zur hundertsten Wiederkehr des Geburtstages eines deutschen Sozialisten', *Schmollers Jahrbuch* 59/2: 129–141.

Vogel, H.U. (2002) 'Das 'Yantie lun': Ereignisse und Rezeption', in B. Schefold (ed.) *Vademecum zu dem Klassiker der chinesischen Wirtschaftsdebatten*, Klassiker der Nationalökonmie, Düsseldorf: Verlag Wirtschaft und Finanzen.

Wagner, A. (1862) *Die Geld- und Credittheorie der Peel'schen Bankacte*, Vienna: Braumüller.

Wagner, A. (1864) *Die Gesetzmäßigkeit in den scheinbar willkürlichen menschlichen Handlungen vom Standpunkt der Statistik*, Hamburg: Boyes.

Wagner, A. (1867) 'Die Entwicklung der europäischen Staatsterritorien und das Nationalitätsprinzip', *Preussische Jahrbücher* 20/1: 1–42.

Wagner, A. (1880) 'Dr. S. Neumann, die Fabel von der jüdischen Masseneinwanderung...', *Zeitschrift für die gesammte Staatswissenschaft* 36/4: 777–783.

Wagner, A. (1883) *Finanzwissenschaft, Lehr- und Handbuch der politischen Ökonomie*, Hauptabth. 4, 3, Leipzig: C. Winter.

Wagner, A. (1896) *Allgemeine und theoretische Volkswirtschaftslehre oder Sozialökonomik: Theoretische National-Ökonomie. Grundlegung und Ausführung*, 2, Berlin: Kroll's Buchdruckerei.

Wagner, A. (1900) *Vom Territorialstaat zur Weltmacht*, speech, Berlin.

Wagner, A. (1912) 'Gegen England', *Illustrierte Zeitschrift überall für Armee und Marine*, March issue.

Wagner, A. (1914) *Gegen England*, 6, Berlin: Boll & Pickardt.

Wagner, A. (1991 [1876]) *Allgemeine oder theoretische Volkswirthschaftslehre mit Benutzung von Rau's Grundsätzen der Volkswirthschaftslehre*, Teil 1: 'Grundlegung', Düsseldorf: Verlag Wirtschaft und Finanzen.

Wagner, D.B. (1993) *Iron and Steel in Ancient China*, Leiden: Brill.

Wagner, D.B. (2001) *The State and Iron Industry in Han China*, NIAS reports, no. 44, Copenhagen: NIAS Publ.

Wagner, V.F. (1966 [1937]) *Geschichte der Kredittheorien*, Aalen: Scientia.

Wallerstein, I. (1974) *The Modern World System*, vol. 1, New York: Academic Press.

Walter, G. (ed.) (1991 [1978]) 'Dispute sur le sel et le fer. Yantie lun', Presentation by Georges Walter, transl. from Chinese by Delphine Baudry-Weulersse, Jean Levi, Pierre Baudry, Paris: Seghers.

Wawrzinek, K. (1971 [1927]) 'Die Entstehung der deutschen Antisemitenpartein (1871–1900)', in *Encyclopaedia Judaica*, vol. 5, Jerusalem: Keter.

Weber, E. (1914) *Literaturgeschichte der Handelsbetriebslehre, Tübingen: Laupp'sche Buchhandlung* (Supplementary issue XLIX of the *Zeitschrift für die gesammte Staatswissenschaft*).

Weber, M. (1920–1923) *Gesammelte Aufsätze zur Religionssoziologie*, 3 vols, Tübingen: Mohr.

Weber, M. (1930) *The Protestant Ethic*, transl. by T. Parsons, London: Allen & Unwin.

Weber, M. (1968) *Economy and Society; an outline of interpretive sociology*, New York: Bedminster Press.

Weber, M. (1969) 'The three types of legitimate rule', transl. by H. Gerth, in A. Etzioni (ed.) *A Sociological Reader on Complex Organizations*, New York, NY: Holt, Rinehart and Winston.

Weber, M. (1975) 'Knies and the Problem of Irrationality', in M. Weber, *Roscher and Knies, The Logical Problems of Historical Economics*, New York: Free Press.

Weber, M. (1976) *The Protestant ethic and the spirit of capitalism*, transl. by T. Parsons, intr. by A. Giddens, 2, London: Allen & Unwin.

Weber, M. (1982) 'Knies und das Irrationalitätsproblem', in M. Weber, *Gesammelte Aufsätze zur Wissenschaftslehre*, 5th edition, newly examined, ed. by J. Winckelmann, Tübingen: Mohr.

Weber, M. (1989) 'Science as a vocation [1919]' in P. Lassman*et al.* (eds) *Science as a Vocation*, London: Unwin Hyman.

Weber, M. (1995 [1927]) *General Economic History* [Wirtschaftsgeschichte], intr. by I.J. Cohen, New Brunswick: Transaction Books.

van de Wee, H. (1963) *The Growth of the Antwerp Market and the European Economy (Fourteenth – Sixteenth Centuries)*, 3 vols, Den Hague: Martinus Nijhoff.

Weiß, D. (1995) 'Ibn Khaldūn on Economic Transformation', *International Journal for Middle-East Studies* 27/1: 29–37.

Wicksell, K. (1954) *Value Capital and Rent*, with a foreword by G.L.S. Shackle, transl. by S.H. Frowein, London: Allen & Unwin.

Wilbur, C.M. (1943) *Slavery in China During the Former Han-Dynasty 206 B.C. – A.D. 25*, Chicago: Field Museum of Nat. Hist.

Wilhelm, R. (1924) *I Ging: Das Buch der Wandlungen*, transl. from Chinese to German by R. Wilhelm, vol. 1 and 2, Düsseldorf: Diederichs.

Wilhelm, R. (1930a) *Chinesische Wirtschaftspsychologie*, Leipzig: Deutsche Wissenschaftliche Buchhandlung.

Wilhelm, R. (ed.) (1930b) *Li Gi: Das Buch der Sitte des älteren und jüngeren Dai. Aufzeichnungen über Kultur und Religion des alten China*, transl. from Chinese to German by R. Wilhelm, Jena: Diederichs.

Wilhelm, H. (1960) *Gesellschaft und Staat in China. Zur Geschichte eines Weltreiches*, Hamburg: Rowohlt.

Will, P.-É. and Bin Wong, R. (1991) *Nourish the People: The State Civilian Granary System in China, 1650–1850*, in the series Michigan monographs in Chinese studies, Ann Arbor, Michigan: University of Michigan, Center for Chinese Studies.

Winkel, H. (1977) *Die deutsche Nationalökonomie im 19. Jahrhundert*, Darmstadt: Wissenschaftliche Buchgesellschaft.

Wittfogel, K.A. (1957) *Oriental Despotism*, New Haven: Yale University Press.

Wolowski, M. (1864) *Traictie de la première invention de monnoies de Nicole Oresme. Textes français et latin*, Paris: Guillaumin.

Wolowski, M.L. (1920) 'L'or et L'argent', in K. Diehl*et al.* (eds) *Ausgewählte Lesestücke zum Studium der Politischen Ökonomie*, vol. 10, 2, Karlsruhe: Braun.

Wright, C.W. (ed.) (1961) *The Works of the Emperor Julian: Letters, Epigrams, Against the Galilaeans, Fragments*, transl. by W.C. Wright, vol. 3, Cambridge: Harvard University Press.

Xenophon (1968) 'Scripta', in E.C. Marchant (transl.) *Xenophon in Seven Volumes*, vol. 7, Cambridge: Harvard University Press.

Xenophon (1979) 'Memorabilia' and 'Oeconomicus', in E.C. Marchant (transl.) *Xenophon in Seven Volumes*, vol. 4, Cambridge: Harvard University Press.

Xenophon (1982) *Vorschläge zur Beschaffung von Geldmitteln oder über die Staatseinkünfte*, introduced, edited and transl. by E. Schütrumpf, Darmstadt: Wissenschaftliche Buchgesellschaft.

Xenophon (2002) *Minor Works*, transl. by J.S. Watson, Boston: Adamant Media Corporation.

Yagi, K. (1983) *Böhm-Bawerk's First Interest Theory*, Study Series, no. 3, March, Tokyo: Center for Historical Social Science Literature, Hitotsubashi University.

Yagi, K. and Tanaka, H. (2001) 'Baiens "Kagen" in der ökonomischen Dogmengeschichte des 17. und 18. Jahrhunderts in Europa und Japan', in B. Schefold (ed.) *Vademecum zu einem japanischen Klassiker der ökonomischen Denkens*, Klassiker der Nationalökonomie, Düsseldorf: Verlag Wirtschaft und Finanzen.

Youschkevitsch, A.P. (1988) 'La place de Nicole Oresme dans le développement des sciences mathématiques', in P. Souffrin, A.-P. Segonds (eds) *Nicolas Oresme. Tradition et innovation chez un intellectuel du XIVe siècle, etudes receuillies*, Paris: Les Belles Lettres.

Zeami (1991 [1960]) *La tradition secrète du nô, suivi de: Une journée de nô*, transl. and commentated by R. Sieffert, Gallimard: UNESCO.

Zenker, E.V. (1941) '*Kuan-tse: Das Leben und Wirken eines altchinesischen Staatsmannes*', Sitzungsberichte der Akad. d. Wissenschaften in Wien, Phil.-hist. Kl. Bd. 219, 5. Abhandlung, Wien und Leipzig: Hölder-Pichler-Temsky.

Ziegler, E. (1974) *Jacob Burkhardts Vorlesung über die Geschichte des Revolutionszeitalters in den Niederschriften seiner Zuhörer*, Basel, Stuttgart: Schwabe.

Zielenziger, K. (1966 [1914]) *Die alten deutschen Kameralisten: Ein Beitrag zur Geschichte der Nationalökonomie und zum Problem des Merkantilismus*, Beiträge zur Geschichte der Nationalökonomie, vol. 2, Frankfurt a.M.: Sauer & Auvermann.

Zimmerman, L.J. (1967 [1953]) *Geschichte der theoretischen Volkswirtschaftslehre*, 3, Köln: Bund-Verlag.

Zinn, K.G. (1997) 'Die politische Ökonomie im alten China – terra incognita der Theoriegeschichte der Wirtschaftswissenschaft', in *Alma Mater Aquensis*, vol. 32, Aachen: RWTH.

Zotz, V. (2000) *Konfuzius*, Reinbek: Rowohlt.

# Index

For Product Safety Concerns and Information please contact our EU
representative GPSR@taylorandfrancis.com
Taylor & Francis Verlag GmbH, Kaufingerstraße 24, 80331 München, Germany

www.ingramcontent.com/pod-product-compliance
Ingram Content Group UK Ltd.
Pitfield, Milton Keynes, MK11 3LW, UK
UKHW021024180425
457613UK00020B/1042